America's Master Dam Builder

America's Master Dam Builder

The Engineering Genius of Frank T. Crowe

Frank Crowe, circa 1935
Courtesy: John and Mary Crowe

Al M. Rocca

Renown Publishing
Redding, California

Library of Congress Cataloging*

Rocca, Al M.
America's master dam builder : the engineering genius of
Frank T. Crowe / Al M. Rocca
p. cm
Includes bibliographical references and index.
1. Crowe, Frank T., 1882-1946. 2. Civil engineers--United
States--Biography. 3. Dams--West (U.S.)--History.
4. Irrigation--West (U.S.)--History. I. Title.

TA140.C79 R63 2001 627'.8'092--dc21 [B] 2001046751 CIP

*Cataloging information from first printing, published by
University Press of America

Renown Publishing
ISBN 978-0-9643378-5-5

Dedication

This book is dedicated to John Crowe and the hundreds of hardworl
"construction stiffs" who helped build the dams and irrigation projects
American West.

Contents

Foreword

Frank Crowe was raised in the eastern United States and Canada, and went to the University of Maine. He had an opportunity to come west when still in college, and from then on was completely sold on the West.

He began working for the United States Bureau of Reclamation, but when they stopped actually doing the projects, instead putting them out for bid to the contractors, he resigned from what would have been a desk job in Denver. He began working for contractors who were actually doing the jobs. One of the principal companies he worked for then was Morrison-Knudsen of Boise, Idaho. Over the years, he worked as superintendent on many dams and irrigation projects, ending his career with the world famous Hoover and Shasta Dams.

Frank's son John died as a young boy, and in some way, I was able to take his place. I began working for Frank at 16 on Deadwood Dam and again on Hoover Dam. When I received my Civil Engineering degree in 1936 from the University of Idaho, Mary and I went to Parker Dam on the lower Colorado River where Frank was superintendent. This dam was constructed to take water out of the Colorado River through a canal to the Los Angeles area.

During the winter of 1937-38 specifications for the construction of Shasta Dam were issued by the Bureau of Reclamation. Immediately Frank was fired with enthusiasm for building this dam. We worked many hours on the concept. One day I said to Frank, "you know this cableway system will just not work spanning across the canyon where the dam is to be built. There has to be some other place in the middle." Frank said, "Let's build a mountain. Go for it, John. Go to work and see what you can come up with."

I built a plywood contour mockup of the area where Shasta Dam would be built. We eventually came up with the concept of a headtower up-river from the dam. This would control the various tail towers and the cables running to them. They moved on tracks and could be used in all phases of building the dam excavation, moving men, equipment, pouring concrete and moving forms.

Frank bid for Six Companies, Inc., but lost the bid by less than one-half of one per cent. Pacific Contractors, Inc., who won the contract, immediately hired him as superintendent. Incidentally, the headtower was placed within eleven feet of where we had planned it at Parker Dam.

Shasta Dam was completed ahead of schedule in spite of the difficulties of hiring during World War II. After World War II, Frank was offered the job of rebuilding the destruction in Germany under the Marshall Plan. He turned it down. He wanted to retire in Shasta County, do a little consulting work, and enjoy the five ranches he had purchased there.

It was not to be. He died in 1946 at the age of 63 of a heart attack. I was left with the sad task of administrator of his estate and of selling his ranches.

All of the many projects on which Frank worked as superintendent brought power, flood control, irrigation, clean water, and later recreation. It can truly be said Frank Crowe changed large parts of the West for the good of everyone.

John Crowe, Nephew of Frank Crowe

Preface

Ralph Waldo Emerson once wrote that "There is properly no History; only Biography." As a young boy growing up in Southern California, I had always enjoyed reading a good biography. For me it was the best way to learn history, and I never complained when my teachers read stories of famous Americans. As far as I understood, all history was comprised of the stories of countless individuals, their triumphs and their tragedies. As a graduate student, I appreciated the comments of Scottish essayist and historian Thomas Carlyle. He wrote, "Biography is by nature the most universally profitable, universally pleasant of all things." If history is the recorded interpretation of human interactions set in specific times and places, then biography offered an effective analytical tool. Yet, as I focused my studies in the history of the American West, I realized that few biographies existed about civil engineers; that group of hard working, dedicated individuals who, in a powerful way, domesticated and transformed the modern American West.

Elliot Paul, who wrote of his American West adventures in the early twentieth century said it best when he posed the following concern, "Romances have been written about railroading and mining and pioneer saloons. Why has there been so little about irrigation? The plan? The finagling? The speculations? The dams? The ditches? The men and women who dreamed them up and made them? I want to do justice to a few." This book you are about to read is an attempt to do justice to one man—Francis Trenholm Crowe, and his loyal army of laborers who helped transform the twentieth-century American West. It is a story about a young man who read and romanticized about life in the "wild and woolly West." For Crowe the most American part of America was the developing West, and he wanted to be a part of the experience. This is a story about rugged hardworking individuals laboring for a fledgling government agency, the United States Reclamation Service (later the Bureau of Reclamation) that struggled to answer the settlers' irrigation needs. This is a story of how one man rose to the top of the engineering world and supplied the drive and innovation that permitted the construction of large concrete dams, dams of unprecedented size, dams that would transform the American West.

This five-year project resulted as a natural follow-up to my work on Shasta Dam. As I interviewed dozens of ex-dam workers and their wives, it quickly became apparent that they felt great pride in belonging to an elite corps of experienced dam workers, who called themselves "construction stiffs." This army of hard working builders credited one man for organizing them and keeping the "army" together, Frank T. Crowe. His reputation as America's top dam builder, in their minds, was not only secure, but also obvious. All of the West's major construction companies looked to Crowe when considering bidding on large government dam building contracts, and if you wooed Crowe successfully, you got his "army." It was fascinating to see that Crowe's troops formed one giant construction family, a sub-culture with its own hierarchy and rules. A worker's entire family became part of Crowe's organization, initiating close personal friendships that lasted decades. Numbering in the thousands, Crowe's "army" followed their leader, doggedly, if not enthusiastically, from one government contract to another, relishing the thought that their work was rearranging the West's physical landscape in a powerfully bold and uncompromising manner.

At one level, this book looks at the engineering advances, from the crude horse-drawn wagon loaders used on the Lower Yellowstone Project to the advanced aerial cableway concrete delivery systems used on Hoover and Shasta Dams. The latter technique, perfected by Crowe, became the preferred engineering method for building most of the world's largest dams. How did these advances in irrigation engineering come about, and in what way did changing technology impact government irrigation plans? On the other hand, as a social historian, I wanted to investigate the working conditions, lifestyle and everyday experiences of construction workers laboring to build dams and canals. How did life in the government construction camps change over the decades as the Bureau of Reclamation expanded their projects? My research exposed, to a lesser degree, how the federal government's involvement in Western irrigation evolved over the years. What caused these changes and how did they affect the government involvement? At least one of the significant policy changes in the Reclamation Service and later the Bureau of Reclamation occurred as a key political event, the building of Hoover Dam, and is tied closely to Frank Crowe's participation. Lastly, I wanted to know if Frank Crowe deserved the accolades that his workers, competitors, and engineering colleagues appeared to be giving him. Did Crowe, a civil engineer, have a significant impact in the development of the American West?

The list of those who have contributed to this effort is long and to each I hold a special debt of gratitude. Frank Crowe's school records at the Governor Dummer academy were made available along with a history of the distinguished school. Matthew Pike supplied school photographs and yearbook drawings made by Crowe. Chet Rock of the engineering department at the University of Maine encouraged me to write this biography, sending information about Crowe's experience there, his relationship with Harold Boardman, Dean of Engineering in 1905, and with Frank Weymouth, a Maine alumni who fired young Crowe's imagination to go west. James Boardman supplied information and a photograph of Harold Boardman. Luella Dore of the MonDak Historical & Art Society sent information about the Lower Yellowstone Project and Montana, circa 1905. Carol Bowers, Assistant Archivist for the American Heritage Center at Laramie, Wyoming, eagerly forwarded copies of *The Dam Weekly* from the Robert V. Sass Collection. Sass, a close friend of Frank Crowe for many years, worked alongside him on a number of dams. Several archivists and reference librarians helped to search early twentieth-century records for information on Crowe, dams, irrigation projects and general lifestyles of the times. These persons include: Betsy Bernfield, Department of Commerce, Cheyenne, Wyoming; Joyce Sawczuk, Jackson Lake Historical Society, Jackson Hole, Wyoming; Phyllis Lyons, Idaho State Historical Society, Boise, Idaho; Martin Humphrey, Yakima Valley Museum, Yakima, Washington.

Rod Hunt, Records Manager of the Morrison-Knudsen Company, faxed issues of their company magazine *The Em Kayan* that included articles written by and about Frank Crowe. I want to give a special thanks to Angie Murray from the Montana Historical Society. She spent hours helping research a little known period of Frank Crowe's life that involved his work with a private contracting firm. Her youthful enthusiasm and excitement to find information is appreciated. I want to deeply thank the large number of reference and interlibrary loan technicians working at the major university libraries in Montana, Idaho, Wyoming, Washington, and Nevada. I particularly need to thank the staff at the University of California, Berkeley's Bancroft and Biological Science Libraries for making available bound copies of the United States Reclamation Service and the Bureau of Reclamation. Numerous county libraries, in the states mentioned above, sent microfilm copies of local newspapers that gave an almost day-to-day account of the dam building projects and Frank Crowe's participation.

I firmly believe that "a picture is worth a thousand words" and to the many people and organizations who contributed personal and professional photographs, I thank you. To this end, I want to mention Joan Howard of the Bureau of Reclamation National Archives in Denver, Colorado. Not only did she help locate government project histories, feature reports, and official memoranda, but also she later pulled project photographs and had them printed. Elizabeth Mudron, sister to ex-dam builder and author Marion Allen, shared photos of Parker Dam and gave insights into life in Boulder City. Albert Seamaster of the California Department of Water Resources is to be thanked for the photograph of Van Giesen Dam. Another debt is owed to Kelly Conner for filling my large request for Hoover Dam photographs. These photos are excellent and help tell the construction story of conquering Black Canyon. Additionally, I want to thank Brit Storey, Senior

Historian for the Bureau of Reclamation for his constant encouragement and recognition of this work. Dennis McBride, author of several books on Hoover Dam, provided his talents in a careful reading of the manuscript. It is with deep appreciation that I thank Brit Storey, Chet Rock, and Dennis McBride for their editorial reviews supporting the publication of this work.

Dozens of personal and telephone interviews were conducted in connection with this book and I want to thank each one of the ex-dam workers and family members who shared their stories. Of particular mention is Marion Allen, who worked for Frank Crowe, and who later wrote books on Hoover, Parker, and Shasta Dams.

On the family side, I want to first thank Frank Crowe's daughters Patricia Crowe-Lee, Elizabeth Crowe-Parry and their daughters, Diane and Linda, who consented to several personal and telephone interviews and who supplied family photographs and letters. Their recollections provided personal anecdotes of Frank Crowe the father and husband. A special thanks goes to John Holstein, the grandson of Catherine Crowe (Frank Crowe's sister). The poignant letters between Frank and Catherine that he supplied allow the reader to put Crowe's professional work in a human perspective and show the depth of his selfless, caring personality. Without the help and ongoing encouragement of John and Mary Crowe, this book would not have been written. John, Frank's nephew, and a talented and accomplished engineer in his own right, helped Frank Crowe design the extensive and innovative cableway system for Shasta Dam. Working alongside his famous uncle since the late 1920s, John enthusiastically supported my effort by explaining the engineering challenges on Deadwood, Hoover, Parker and Shasta Dams. His wife, Mary, continually found new sources of information for me to work with including photographs, letters, family stories and the Frank Crowe diary.

To my colleagues at Simpson College, I want to thank all those who have encouraged and sustained me professionally during the long research and writing stages. A sincere thanks is given to Carol Whitmer for her strong support of this effort and to Michael Borgaard, who shared my enthusiasm for dam building and Frank Crowe. Professor James Davies gave the manuscript a careful reading and I thank those students and readers who assisted in revisions.

Lastly, I wish to thank my family for putting up with this five-year project. I do not think there is a place within our house that has not, at one time or another, served as a repository for Frank Crowe material.

December 12, 2000

Chapter 1

The Early Years
1882-1905

Frank Crowe's grandfather Nathan Crowe, born in 1821, diligently worked years learning the woolen mill business. This enterprising English merchant hoped to share his knowledge and enthusiasm for textiles with his sons. While Nathan's first-born, George Crowe, disappointed his father by opting to become a railroad engineer, Nathan determined that his second son should follow in his footsteps. His next son John, born on Christmas day in 1845, grew up as the second oldest in a family with seven other brothers and sisters. His early childhood was spent in historic Huddisfield, England. Eager to exploit his talents in the woolen business, an energetic twenty-four old John Crowe, arrived in New York. He married Emma Wilkinson in Brooklyn, New York in 1880. Miss Wilkinson, born in 1857, had been raised near Hudson, New York. Looking for opportunities in the thriving woolen mill business, John moved his new bride to Sherbrook, Quebec, Canada. There in February of 1881, their first son was born, Joseph Wilkinson Hyde Crowe.[1]

Upon hearing of the need to build a woolen mill in the small nearby town of Trenholmville, John sold his home in Sherbrook and moved Emma and Joseph. John prospered using his knowledge of textile machinery and manufacturing to successfully establish a woolen mill. Emma gave birth to their second child on October 12 of 1882. The healthy, strapping young lad pleased John and Emma greatly and they named him Francis Albert Trenholm Crowe.[2]

In 1888, John looked for new investment opportunities in textiles. He sold his interests in the Trenholm mill, and then gambled everything on a venture opening in the Midwest. The family's move to Fairfield, Iowa proved troublesome for the Crowe family. After two years of little or no profit, John made the difficult decision to move the family back East. In Kezar Falls, Maine a large woolen mill was in need of a plant superintendent, and John's knowledge and experience helped him to acquire the position. Life settled momentarily for the Crowe family as Joseph and Frank grew tall and strong. During these formative years, Frank enjoyed the outdoors, hiking in the spring and summer, and "playing tag across the log jams of Maine's great Ossippe River."[3]

Never one to turn down new opportunities and challenges to set-up and run woolen mills, John accepted a job in Picton, New Jersey in 1892. The Crowe family remained here until 1899 when, once again, they moved. This time the Crowe's settled in Massachusetts, in a quaint community known as Byfield. It was here that a young and impressionable Frank Crowe completed his elementary school experience and entered high school.[4] Byfield, a small community of a few hundred persons did not have a common or public high school, but it did have the Dummer Academy. With a sterling reputation, Dummer Academy was the oldest school of its type (boarding school), having been established by Governor William Dummer in 1763.

The Dummer school had, by the time Frank Crowe enrolled in 1899, established a tradition for excellent academic training; alumni included: Rufus King, signer of the Constitution; Theophilus Parsons, drafted the Bill of Rights; and Samuel Osgood, first Postmaster General for George Washington. In fact, a visiting team of educators from nearby Harvard University filed the following report after touring the grounds, sitting in on classes, and discussing curriculum with the faculty:

> "...The Academy has more than a history and an exceptionally attractive site; it has at the present time an excellent and efficient staff of teachers, whose work challenges comparison with the best work done in the best schools of our country."[5]

As a seventeen-year-old, Frank Crowe and his parents walked the grounds of Dummer in the fall of 1899. They were quite shocked to see many of the buildings in a state of general disrepair. The Mansion House "was in lamentable condition, lacking in adequate sanitary facilities and proper heating."[6] Despite the apparent problems with the physical plant, John and Emma Crowe knew that Dummer Academy would provide their son with a solid educational foundation. Besides, the tuition fees were more than reasonable and the school was close to home, allowing Frank to commute by horse-drawn buggy to classes.

In 1899, five full-time professors and a number of part-time instructors offered 150 "recitations" (lesson or classes) a week, each professor averaging six classes a day. Frank Crowe was introduced to the usual classical languages of Latin and Greek, as well French and German. All students studied physics, chemistry, and mathematics. English was required every term, with a special emphasis on writing. Every boy needed to complete his daily theme writing assignment. Instructors consulted with students before and during the writing, and outstanding papers were published in the school newspaper, the *Dummer News*.

The first year at Dummer regimented Frank Crowe to a schedule where he spent 9:00 a.m. to 3:00 p.m. in classes. Latin and math consumed much of this time, along with English and science. Living only a few miles from the campus,

Frank Crowe (top row, right) at the Dummer Academy in 1905. (Dummer Academy)

the young student usually made it home by the supper hour. He was given a one hour lunch period. For boys housed on campus, life was strictly supervised. Supper hour lasted until 7:00 p.m.; from here they took part in a homework study session that usually went from 7:30 p.m. to 9:00 p.m. The bedtime hour of 9:30 p.m., being steadfastly adhered to, left on-campus students little time for leisure activities. Yet, Dummer Academy sponsored a number of team sports including: football, lacrosse, "ice polo," baseball, track, and newly invented basketball. Already over six feet in height, the young gangly Crowe would have made a fine addition to the basketball team; yet, no existing records can confirm his participation in sports. As most of the day-only students were needed to help with farm and home chores, most teams consisted of boarding students.

The academy challenged Crowe academically as he had never been challenged before. He quickly learned that many Dummer graduates went on to advance their education at Harvard, Boston University, and Columbia. Of particular interest to young Crowe was his awakening to the fact that he had a real talent in mathematics and science. Even before he graduated from the Dummer Academy in June of 1901, his parents had hoped that he would either go into the clergy or into medicine. Frank Crowe toyed with the idea of attending nearby Harvard University, where he would be assured of obtaining an excellent medical degree. However, tuition at the acclaimed institution proved to be astronomical, completely unreachable for the modest income of John and Emma Crowe. It was at this point that Frank's older brother, Joe, decided to attend the University of Maine in Orono where he planned to major in electrical engineering. During his senior year at Dummer, Frank learned from his brother about the college and its engineering programs, and it was then that he, reluctantly at first, decided to drop his dream of becoming a medical doctor.[7]

From its inception in 1868, Maine State College placed an academic preference for classical liberal arts education and engineering. By the time Frank Crowe entered the institution in 1901, now the University of Maine, the most popular concentrations of study included: Agriculture, Mechanical Engineering, Civil Engineering, Electrical Engineering, and Chemistry. The campus, originally a single two-storied building, the White Farm, had by 1901 mushroomed into an impressive array of three-storied brick and masonry structures. Most visible to newcomers was the Wingate Tower. Rising well above the other classroom and administrative buildings, the Wingate Tower bell chimed regularly for years. Arriving in late August of 1901, Crowe rode an electric car the short distance from nearby Orono to the university grounds. Making his way through Coburn, Fernald, and Holmes Hall's, he registered at the freshman dormitory where he discovered how Spartan life could be on a college campus. The 8x12-foot room included two single beds, husk mattresses, a table, a washstand, and two chairs. [8]

Not only were the dorm rooms austere, but classrooms too appeared bleak and barren. Venerable Wingate Hall, where the young enthusiastic Crowe attended some of his engineering classes, felt cold and drafty, as the gaps between the wooden flooring strips widened at times to 1/4 inch or more. Large rectangular windows, set effectively to gain maximum sun exposure on the southern side of the building, flooded the large classrooms with ample light and gave the impression of warmth on sunny winter days. Lamp-less large-wattage light bulbs hung randomly from overhead providing illumination for late afternoon and early evening classes. Students sat in beautifully carved pine seat-desks. Many rooms, where lectures dominated the teaching style, contained seat-desks with small 12x12-inch writing tops allowed students to take notes on appropriately sized paper. Crowe's chemistry classes in Fernald Hall took on a decidedly different look than formal Wingate Hall. The large 30 x 40-foot chemistry room sported long bench desks that accommodated four students each. These seven-foot benches proved uncomfortable as students were forced to sit straight, facing front with hands on lap. During extended demonstrations and in an attempt to relieve the tension of a one-position stance, students would twist sideways, placing their arms on the bench behind the adjacent student, causing a chain reaction from everyone else on the bench. These benches were located in the middle of the room, allowing group experiment tables in the rear of the room and a large demonstration table in the front of the class. Typically, chemistry professors delivered introductory lectures giving instructions for running the experiment of the day while the students eagerly listened from their bench seats. Immediately following this, the class moved to the experimentation tables, working with the same group of four assigned in the bench seating arrangement.

As the early snows of fall gently covered the grounds of the University of Maine in 1901, Frank Crowe began his first semester of professional preparation. Because of his fascination with the relatively new application of electricity and from the excitement shown by his brother Joe, he selected Electrical Engineering as his major. Classes proved difficult, challenging all of his math and science background gleaned from studies at the Dummer Academy. His schedule included: Chemistry, Chemistry lab, Declamations (speech), Mechanical Drawing, Rhetoric, German, Algebra II, Trigonometry, and Military Drill.[9] Frank Crowe's first year in the engineering program at the University of Maine revealed him as a hardworking intelligent student, bound for a successful career in the public or private sector.

By the turn of the century, fees and expenses at the University of Maine had jumped to approximately $120 a semester, of which the largest expense was room and board averaging around $45. Other expenses included books, drawing instruments, clothing, athletics, fuel and repairs, class expenses, travel, laundry/mending, military, and other items. Frank Crowe's parents worked diligently to help pay the expenses. Emma Crowe picked up several odd jobs including knitting and mending, saving most of these monies to help pay for her son's drawing instruments. John Crowe moonlighted during most of his son's tenure at college. He scraped together enough funds every year to "just get him by."[10]

Summer vacation offered Frank Crowe the opportunity to briefly visit his parents in Massachusetts and to earn money for next year's college expenses. Working at a variety of odd jobs, including train porter and dining room attendant, the ambitious Crowe saw much of the New England area. He was impressed with the way in which the landscape had been transformed; towns and cities everywhere linked with newly built bridges, roads, and tunnels. During this warm humid summer, young Frank Crowe, realizing his love for drawing and building, determined that he would become a builder. Upon registering for his sophomore year, he changed his major to Civil Engineering.[11]

Other forces worked on the University of Maine student to move him toward a career in construction. He had seen small dams throughout his childhood, including some in Maine, but now word spread throughout the engineering department that Congress had passed a bold new plan for domesticating the American West, the Reclamation Act. Irrigation enthusiast President Theodore Roosevelt signed the bill into law in June of 1902 arguing,

> Make the streams...of the arid regions useful by irrigation works
> for water storage.... The storage of floods in reservoirs at the
> headwaters of our rivers is but enlargement of our present policy
> of river control.... The government should construct and main-
> tain these reservoirs as it does other public works.

The highly energetic new President destroyed opposition to the bill by revealing
that massive irrigation programs were far too expensive for individual, or even
groups of states, to undertake. The federal government would need to fund and
build the dams, canals, and ditches with a promise from the states and the people
directly benefiting from the irrigation to pay back the government investment.
Roosevelt summarized his arguments when he said that large-scale irrigation construction was "properly a national function."[12]

In prior years, the Army Corps of Engineers, primarily occupied with
flood control in the east and the United States Geological Survey, focusing on
topographic map surveying, mineral exploration, and water supply, assumed that
civil engineering activities in the West lay in their realm. However, Western explorer and irrigation promoter, John Wesley Powell, convinced Congress in 1888
to authorize an "Irrigation Survey" of rivers, streams, and areas of irrigation potential. Powell's ideas influenced the chief hydrographer for the U. S. Geological
Survey, Frederick H. Newell, who came to realize that the West's enormous need
for irrigation works required a massive government involvement and its own gov-
ernmental agency and funding. Newell's opportunity for support rose greatly when
Theodore Roosevelt assumed the presidency after the assassination of William
McKinley. The idealistic aggressive Roosevelt, enthralled with Western romanti-
cism, looked to extend the government's influence in this country-sized area of
opportunity. Working through close advisors to the president, Newell sold Roosevelt
on the idea of a new irrigation-focused bureaucracy. The newly formed Reclamation Service, approved from within this act, drew most of its new human resources
from the Geological Survey. Newell became the department's first Chief Engineer.[13]

Although intensely interested over the creation of a Reclamation Service
to carry out the mandate of the new law, Crowe focused on his studies. Second
year course work focused on developing math skills; he studied, in separate courses,
Analytical and Descriptive Geometry, and for the first time, he was challenged
with Calculus. The first semester grades in these classes revealed a passing score,
but certainly not mastery level achievement. Knowing that success in the engineering field depended heavily on success in math, Crowe, once again buckled
down, and during his second semester, he earned outstanding marks in both Descriptive Geometry and in Calculus. Practical application of his math became
apparent in his Physics, Mechanical Drawing, Sanitary Science, Surveying, and

Fieldwork courses. Earning highest honors in his Mechanical Drawing class, it soon became clear, that Crowe, held a special talent for transforming mathematical equations and theoretical engineering ideas into high quality mechanical drawings. This gift would help earn him his first crack at an engineering job in the wild-and-woolly West, the next summer. This unique talent also set him apart from others in his field, earning a reputation for drawing accurate and clear field plans that allowed on-site engineers to move easily through construction phases.

This second year, Frank Crowe also took classes in French, Public Speaking, and again, Military Drill. He disliked public speaking, always preferring to communicate in small groups or on a one-on-one basis. In later years, even with all the national attention that came his way with the construction of Hoover, Parker and Shasta Dams, Crowe dreaded addressing large crowds. When speeches were required, he always made them short and to the point. For example, during a coast-to-coast NBC radio broadcast from Shasta Dam, he consistently gave one sentence, one-line answers to most of the questions put to him. A young Chet Huntley, interviewing Crowe on the progress of concrete pouring, worked hard to obtain extended explanations from the shy dam builder. Oftentimes, Crowe would refer news reporters to his foremen and shift leaders stating, "Those guys know where the action is."[14]

The junior year curriculum for engineers focused students on specific types of construction challenges and Crowe was happy to be applying the theoretical knowledge to practical construction problems. He enrolled in Railroad Engineering, Railroad Work, Highway Engineering, Mechanics, Hydraulics, Railroad Engineering II, and Highway Survey. Additionally, he continued his math studies with Calculus III and Advanced Algebra. Focusing his academic attention on the math and practical application courses, the aspiring engineer was somewhat taken back at the degree requirements of psychology and public finance. Courses in these areas competed for his study time, and sheer number of classes strained his abilities. Midway through the second semester he dropped both Advanced Algebra and Railroad Engineering II; his grades improved and he finished the year close to the top of his class.

Frank Crowe's talent for drawing did not escape from being recognized by his peers. Toward the end of his junior year, he was persuaded to draw pictures for the university's yearbook, "The Prism." In fact, after he submitted his first sketching, the yearbook committee selected him as lead artist, and etchings of his are seen throughout the 1904 yearbook.[15]

The engineering department introduced Crowe to the new Reclamation Service through its tradition of guest speakers (usually alumni) who came on campus to talk about their careers, suggesting job opportunities for upcoming graduates. It was at one of these times that Frank Crowe heard a "series of lectures on the plans for reclaiming vast regions of land."[16] The lecturer, Frank E. Weymouth, M. ASCE (Member, American Society of Civil Engineers), had graduated from the University of Maine in 1896 and was now actively employed by the newly formed United States Reclamation Service. He would play several key roles in helping Frank Crowe exploit opportunities with the Reclamation Service and later the Bureau of Reclamation.

With the creation of the United States Reclamation Service in 1902, Weymouth eagerly sought a responsible position. He asked Service Chief Engineer, Frederick H. Newell, for and received, in August of 1903, the challenge of organizing the effort to tame the Lower Yellowstone River in Montana and make its waters available for irrigation. His first assignment involved the preliminary investigation surveys of the entire Yellowstone Valley and planning for canal construction.[17] Shortly after this, Weymouth decided to visit his alumni institution and recruit talented engineering students.

Throughout most of January, 1904, Weymouth described in his University of Maine lectures how the fledging government department used the newly established "Reclamation Fund" to aggressively build canals, bridges, causeways, spillways, siphons, and dams; and they were using, for the first time, concrete on a large scale. Crowe was mesmerized as Weymouth described his work experience on the Lower Yellowstone River Project. To a young impressionable engineering student, here was the opportunity to help tame the West. Crowe admitted years later, as the man responsible for damming the mighty Colorado River, that Weymouth had given him the inspiration to build dams. He always reminded everyone that he had "been born at the right time and gone to the right college."[18] Friend and colleague, Marion Allen confided many years later "Frank knew the importance of the work he was doing, even from the earliest days with the Reclamation Service, and he knew that the settlement of the West depended on him harnessing the rivers."[19]

Toward the end of January, Weymouth in one of his lectures suggested that summer work experience would be available for any student that could afford to travel west to Montana. Immediately, Crowe became excited over the possibilities. Now for the first time, he would actually have the opportunity to put into actual practice the engineering talents that he had studied so hard to develop. On top of this, he would get to see the West and gain valuable work experience. Approaching Weymouth, Crowe questioned, "If I show up on your project this spring (after completion of classes), will you give me a job?"[20] Weymouth glanced up at the tall lanky young man, impressed with his initiative and assured Crowe that if he showed up at the job site there would be a position for him. The rest of the semester dragged as Crowe's thoughts wandered in a flurry of imaginative fantasies. Borrowing money from his father who had recently moved the family back to Quebec for a mill job, Crowe finished his coursework, packed lightly, and boarded the train for the great American West.[21]

The train whisked him through the Midwest, where Crowe had spent some of his youthful days in Iowa. How different the far West would be. Evenly spread small towns situated on level plains gave way to an incredible expanse of nothingness, no towns, no roads, no signs of civilization except for the occasional cattle ranch. Detraining at Glendive, Montana, Crowe boarded a wagon for the Reclamation camp nearby. Here in "Big Sky Country," the isolation appeared complete. He worked that summer on a survey party laying out the routes for a web of canals and waterways. In the brief period of several months Crowe "learned much about...the country...its rugged life, he could make camp, ride a bronco, and spin and throw a lariat (Will Roger's style)."[22]

The summer lingered and Crowe did not want to return to school. Yet, his desire to be an engineer overcame his passion for the outdoors and he finally rounded up his gear to return to the university. As he had sent most of his earnings home to his parents the nearly broke Crowe fortunately secured a temporary job as a cattle car drover, riding with the animal stock all the way to Chicago.[23] In this capacity, he earned his passage back to Bangor, Maine. His classmates were astonished to see the skinny boy return wiry and confident. Crowe proudly displayed a large buffalo skull to his friends; it was subsequently given a place of honor hanging above the fireplace of his Sigma Alpha Epsilon fraternity house. As he settled down into his classes, Crowe entertained friends showing off his newly acquired lariat talents. He would dare his classmates to run by "as fast as they could," while he tried to rope them. Longtime friends and fellow civil engineers recalled in Crowe's memoirs, "His interest in what he had seen [the West] showed in his every thought and action and he was extremely impatient to return to the west."

It was difficult for Crowe to concentrate and the last thing he wanted to do was to study more books. After a few early disappointments in grades, Crowe regrouped and finished the fall semester with good grades (86% cumulative average) in Structures, Design, Highway Field Work, Hydraulic Engineering, and Political Science.

In January of 1905, he registered for and passed the civil engineering examination at Bangor. Next, he enrolled in his last semester of coursework taking: Structures II, Design II, Hydraulic Engineering II, and Advanced Mechanics. It was during this semester that Crowe received an invitation from Frank Weymouth to join him again on the Lower Yellowstone—this time in a permanent capacity. The only catch was that the job offer carried with it a May 15 start date, and he would not finish classes until June. Without considering any other alternative, Crowe approached Harold Boardman, Dean of the Civil Engineering Department and arranged to take his senior exams early. Crowe liked the young Dean, and he took to heart Boardman's words, "Develop clear thinking, follow the golden rule, play square, don't worry, and make the most of your opportunities."[24] It was the last phrase that particularly stuck in Crowe's memory. The Dean, understanding the meaning of his own advice and having complete confidence in the aspiring young engineer, agreed to let the ambitious student test out before June. The exams, though difficult and challenging, proved no problem to the anxious Crowe; he passed with an average of 86%.[25] Crowe was indeed indebted to Professor Boardman for allowing him the opportunity to complete his studies early. In 1943 Crowe remembered Boardman by saying, "Whatever I've been able to accomplish since I was handed my diploma [received later], I attribute more than any other factor, to the inspiration supplied by my contacts with Professor Boardman who capped off his fine educational influence upon me by the practical and vital service of helping me get my first job."[26]

After completing the exams, Frank Crowe said good-bye to his teachers and friends at the university, and he briefly visited with his parents. His memoirs recall, "So, not waiting for commencement exercises or his diploma, he started west again—this time to stay and to begin a career which was to bring him fame as a great construction engineer and dam builder."[27]

Chapter 2

Go West Young Man
1906-1911

Heading west on the Northern Pacific Railroad, an eager Frank Crowe journeyed through the same countryside he had visited the summer before. Finally, he entered the Yellowstone territory (Dawson County) a landscape of endless sagebrush and short, sparse grass. Little did he know that, with his help, the Reclamation Service would eventually make it possible to irrigate 60,000 acres, most of it in eastern Montana, the remainder in North Dakota. From these newly irrigated fields, dedicated farmers would produce alfalfa, sugar beets, feed grains, and other forage crops. Yet, this northern region presented an incredibly harsh climate. Extremes abounded. Cold winters, hot summers, low annual precipitation and spring flash flooding were normal occurrences. The area usually received from 13 to 14 inches of rain per year, with most of that occurring between April and September. Snows often blanketed the gently rolling hills early in spring and caught the unexpected farmer or traveler unprepared. On numerous occasions before Crowe's arrival, disastrous early snowfalls buried people, animals, and crops, ruining farmsteads and cattle ranches. Thunderstorms quite literally dumped several inches of rain, along with pea-sized hail, in hours. Winter ice jams, allowed blocked water to rise up and flood low-lying fields. Brisk cool twenty-mile an hour eastern winds turned into fifty-mile an hour western gales in the fall and winter.

Before the Reclamation Service arrived on the scene, Montana already had a fifty-year history of private irrigation attempts. The Bitterroot Valley of western Montana had been irrigated before the mid-1800s, and the mountain valleys of the west, south, and central parts of the state were webbed with ditches carrying precious water supplies from small earth and rock dams. By the 1880s, the bustling community of Billings and the immediate fields around the area produced good crop yields thanks to the "Big Ditch" earth canal. Individual farmers and ranchers, associations of farmers and ranchers, or commercial investors hoping to cash in on selling the land and water rights to incoming families, financed these crude earth and rock irrigation structures. As one observer noted, "By around the turn of the century, just about everything easily irrigated was done."[1]

Since the passage of the Desert Land Act of 1877, the federal government continually encouraged private attempts at irrigation. When Congress approved the Carey Act of 1894, the states realized federal financial support in return for a promise to begin planning and building larger and more sophisticated water delivery systems. Western politicians soon learned however, that they could not undertake irrigation projects of the size needed without massive government spending, and they were impatient to attract more settlers. Ambitious Montana Senator Thomas H. Carter in 1889 spoke out, stating that with federal dollars:

> ...the lands of Montana [are] one-fifth good agricultural, three-fifths grazing land and one-fifth mountainous, and that by judicious husbanding of waters the three-fifths grazing land could be made good agricultural land, and that a part of the one-fifth mountainous could be raised to a high state of cultivation.[2]

During that same year western engineering pioneer John Wesley Powell, Director of the Geological Survey, reported to the Montana Constitutional Convention that one-third of the state could be irrigated, and all of the waters falling within the state's boundary could be saved, irrigated out, and used for successful agricultural purposes. Shortly after Powell's report the state's Society of Engineers offered its own projection for future irrigation possibilities. They claimed that twenty million acres, or about 21% of Montana's land could eventually be irrigated and made profitable. The engineers speculated that land values would soar, from $1 per acre to over $10 per acre. Calculating for average farm and ranch size, this would support a future population of one and one-half million people.[3]

Western federal and state legislators, and well-to-do farmers and ranchers, applied yearly pressure to Congress to take the lead in financing the development of arid lands west of the 98th Meridian. The 1902 Congress responded and passed the Newlands Reclamation Act. Program monies came from funds collected by the settlement of public land and would be reserved for future irrigation and reclamation projects. It was decided, according to this new act, that settlers on those constructed projects would repay the interest-free funds according to the cost incurred per acre. The new federal law stated that the United States Reclamation Service held responsibility for designing and supervising the construction of all sponsored projects. Settlers realizing benefits from the projects retained the rights to run any completed irrigation systems and pay for its maintenance.

The good news spread like wildfire throughout the western counties of Montana; shortly a group of irrigation-minded settlers, thirsty for more water and more profits, petitioned Congress and the Secretary of the Interior to begin an investigation of the potential for irrigating the Lower Yellowstone region from Glendive downstream to where the Yellowstone meets the Missouri River. Frederick

Haynes Newell, Director of the United States Reclamation Service, immediately ordered Engineer Frank Weymouth, already somewhat experienced with land surveys in the far West, to visit the Lower Yellowstone area and size up irrigation options. Weymouth had described to his 1904 audience of engineering students at the University of Maine how he first arrived on the scene in July of the year before and discovered a promising irrigation potential. He concluded that the Yellowstone River at this point provided ample water; he then suggested a full-scale land survey to determine if a gravity canal could service all the land in the Yellowstone Valley from Terry, Montana to the confluence of the Yellowstone and Missouri Rivers. Weymouth, given the approval to move ahead, remained in the area and began surveying in August of 1903. Crowe listened as the excited Weymouth pointed out that the "light fall of the Yellowstone River and the high elevation of the land above the river made it impracticable to cover any land above Glendive, so the surveys for a canal heading at Terry were abandoned and another survey was begun for a canal heading two miles above Glendive."[4] Weymouth's findings were analyzed, and it was found that the cost to develop the canal was prohibitive. Weymouth revised his estimate to show that if the canal were started at a point 18 miles downstream from Glendive substantial savings would be realized.

A visiting board of consulting engineers looked over the area in April of 1904 and agreed with Weymouth's findings.[5] The team included Reclamation Service Chief Engineer Arthur P. Davis, who would later come to recognize and appreciate Frank Crowe's engineering abilities. They recommended a detailed survey of the proposed canal route and they wanted to see plans and specifications for all aspects of the project. That first summer in the Lower Yellowstone had given Crowe experience surveying and preparing bids and estimates for this massive irrigation project. The latter skill would earn Frank Crowe recognition as one the world's best engineers.

The preliminary construction bid for the Montana irrigation project had been sent by Weymouth to the U. S. Reclamation Service western headquarters in Denver, Colorado and reviewed throughout the winter of 1904-1905. Official proposals, very close to Weymouth's original plan, appeared in April of 1905 and were sent out to private bid. In June, the bids were opened and contracts awarded at "very low prices" for the construction of the first four divisions of the main canal. At the same time, bids were awarded for a telephone line to run the entire length of the proposed canal. This telephone would allow field engineers to stay in communication with project chief Weymouth. The most challenging aspect of the project proved to be the building of a diversion dam to help store canal water. Intake Dam, as it was later named, would be the first of nineteen dams that Frank Crowe is credited with helping to build.[6]

The westbound train carrying Crowe pulled into Glendive, Montana, gateway to the Lower Yellowstone Valley. From here, he secured a ride on one of the many wagons headed northeast along the river to the diversion dam site camp, a distance of some eighteen miles. Since Crowe's visit last summer, the Reclamation Service had erected several buildings at the dam site and work continued stringing up additional wood plank housing for man and beast. A regular flow of sturdy flatbed wagons rolled into camp bringing much-needed foodstuffs and all of the building tools and materials. Crowe's wagon pulled into the Reclamation camp to drop off supplies and to check if the engineer in charge, N. C. Bebb, wanted them to carry anything on to the main headquarters at La Mesa Camp. Bebb, assigned to the project since February of 1904, greeted Crowe in his 36 x 24-foot sturdily constructed wooden-frame office building and told him that Weymouth could be found at La Mesa.[7]

After watering the horses and loading reports destined for Chief Weymouth's office, Crowe and his driver boarded their reliable well-greased wagon and continued the 16-mile journey farther down the Yellowstone River to La Mesa, field headquarters for the project. La Mesa boasted several large buildings and at least a half dozen smaller ones. The most impressive building, the main office, measured 60 x 21 feet and housed the work and records of the assistant engineers in charge of Divisions 2 and 3 of the project, as well as the main office of Frank Weymouth, overall project engineer. Two single story dormitories housed the survey crews and construction workers. It was structures like these dormitories, and sometimes field tents, that comprised Crowe's home for a number of years to come. He learned early that it was not an easy task finding cots long enough to fit his lanky 6' 3" frame. Weymouth's "Engineer's Cottage" at 29 x 25 feet surprised young Crowe, as the year before his boss had slept almost exclusively in tents and he figured that private residential structures for Reclamation personnel simply did not exist. Additionally, the camp consisted of an emergency bunkhouse, a store-house, a warehouse, a stable, an Engineer's House (for assistant engineers), and a mess hall.[8]

Frank Weymouth was indeed happy to see Frank Crowe. Weymouth knew that University of Maine civil engineering courses and requirements prepared students well for the challenges of construction in the untamed, isolated, and sometimes-dangerous West. For the first few days, the young engineer learned the everyday routine of camp life, meeting other engineers such as, H. F. Burkhart, and H. S. Morse. Morse ably directed work in Division 2, while Burkhart's responsibility lie farther downstream at Division 3. Through these men and other assistant engineers, Crowe quickly learned about the progress on the Lower Yellowstone Project since the summer of 1904.

Crowe, as required of newly arrived engineers, reviewed the government's plans for building the proposed canal, the laterals—smaller canals running perpendicular to the main canal—and the Lower Yellowstone Diversion Dam. The Reclamation Service's plan, as reported by Weymouth, started with an explanation:

The United States Reclamation Service camp at Sears Creek, Montana, 1905. (USBR)

The Yellowstone River from the point of diversion to its mouth has an average fall of 2.2 feet per mile and much of the land to be irrigated in this system lies in benches 90 feet above the river.

In order to reach these lands with a canal it will be necessary to raise the water in the river at the head gates by means of a diversion dam and then build the canal on as light a grade as if feasible.

Young Frank Crowe was assigned to one of the survey parties with the official title of Instrumentman.[9] These survey parties contained from three to eight men, with five the usual number. The teams would load up tripods, measuring rods, leveling devices, and theodolites in a wagon, packing them carefully for the rugged trip up and down the valley. The crews packed Government Issue tents, cots, blankets, and clothing. Food for several weeks also was loaded; dried meat, beans, breads, and canned goods provided the basics. Whenever they were given the opportunity, it was common for Service men to shoot and dress out a passing elk or deer. Of course, fishing in the Yellowstone River was excellent and provided an additional food source. Crowe's love for fishing, started here and continued through the years, is well known by family and friends.[10]

As the young engineer traversed the Yellowstone River Valley surveying and re-surveying the remainder of 1905, he reconciled the severe winter temperatures and burying snowfalls with the natural relatively untouched environment.

Ever the outdoorsman, Crowe thrived in this frontier atmosphere. Isolated groves of cottonwood, elder, and boxwood broke up vast stretches of plains grassland, with a clear, cool swift-running creek every few hundred yards. To be sure, there would be plenty of water to dam, divert, and distribute. Crowe, with an adventurous spirit, reveled in the thought that here was a land to explore and conquer. "Enjoy the land and enjoy life" was said to have been his philosophy these early years, for all that met the happy-looking instrumentman saw the spark of life within him. Elliot Paul, brother of Weymouth's assistant engineer Charles Paul, described meeting Crowe on the Lower Yellowstone and remembered that the tall ungainly new surveyman was "an indefatigable dancer who always asked for "Redwing" as a two-step."[11]

The word was out about the Yellowstone River Valley. Word of mouth, from state to state, explained how the United States Reclamation Service planned to irrigate the "whole darn valley." Now hundreds of families rushed in to purchase land at rates as low as $1.50 an acre. Minimum size parcels ran from 40 to 80 acres, with many people buying 160—a quarter section, or more. Letters from early settlers tell of their initial enthusiasm and optimism. One letter boasted, "In fertility the soil of this valley cannot be excelled. Other portions of our justly famed state may equal it in fertility of soil, but none, with the proper cultivation can be more productive than this valley, now only in the making."[12] Another resident compared Yellowstone with the Red River Valley in North Dakota. "The soil in the Yellowstone Valley is fully equal to that of the Red River Valley, and the drainage is much better. I think that owing to the soil and drainage the Yellowstone Valley is superior for the growth of all small grains."[13]

One newly arrived farmer described the valley in considerable detail. He suggested that, "To the eye the scenery along the Lower Yellowstone is most pleasing, with an abundance of treed and foliage in the tracts along the Yellowstone River, with the high bluffs on the east side and the stretch of level country extending from the timber to the foothills several miles away from the river, crossed occasionally by a running stream, ...Most of the people who came here a few years ago came with little or no money and have raised stock and ...are enthusiastic about the future of the country."[14]

All of the Reclamation Service field engineers and their crews became acquainted with these valley settlers and it was not uncommon to see farm families come out to watch the surveying, and later the main canal excavation. By the time Frank Crowe arrived in 1905, these farmers, ranchers, and hunters, many of them from the Midwest—particularly Nebraska and Iowa, were building homes and eagerly waiting for the irrigation work to begin.

Surveying continued throughout the summer and fall of that year, though as winter approached, Crowe moved into quarters at the newly completed La Mesa base camp. Located upstream a few miles from the headworks, La Mesa became the largest of several Service camps. His schedule, like everyone else, was 8:00

Young Frank Crowe as an Instrumentman on the Lower
Yellowstone Project, 1905-06. (Patricia Lee-Crowe)

a.m. to 12 p.m. with a one-hour lunch break and then back to work till 5:00 p.m.
The workweek included Saturday. The food served to all workers, according to
one eyewitness, was "badly out of balance and designed principally to discourage
men from going too often to the can, on the bosses' time." Workers below the
engineers level "who got the trots in a hot spell were fired." The breakfast meal,
served promptly at 7:00 a.m., routinely consisted of condensed milk over oatmeal,
"fried sow belly" and whatever potatoes and meat were left over from the last
night's dinner meal. Piping-hot coffee brewed quickly in large metal cans and
with few grounds, provided the waking workers with their only beverage. The
noon meal appeared to be a stew made of "meat the butchers could not dispose of
elsewhere." Unpeeled spuds, boiled whole, "stewed canned tomatoes of the cheaper
brands," and canned corn rounded out their lunch. On many days, cooks treated
the men to a dessert of fruit pie, tapioca, bread pudding, or stewed prunes. Dinner

looked similar to lunch with the exception that boiled beans accompanied the meat and there was no dessert.[15]

Miles from the nearest towns such as Glendive, most workers, Service employees included, lingered around the camps from 5:00 p.m. Saturday until work began again on Monday. A few tried to read local newspapers or dog-eared books passed from one worker to another. Others who disliked reading, or who could not read, gambled in the nearby stables, away from the ever-prying eyes of project foremen. Although discouraged officially, too many men lost their week's wages in ill-advised poker sessions lasting into the wee hours of the weekend nights. Cheating, always a possibility when the stakes soared, rarely occurred in the camps because "if a man was caught at it, he was beaten up and thrown out of camp without first aid." During the week, everyone worked hard, with contractors encouraging competition between crews. At times, incentives were offered such as special meal menus or a small money bonus. Usually, evenings ended early with exhausted workers resting in their bunks, smoking and talking until, one by one they dozed off.[16]

Crowe easily assimilated into the daily work camp routine and he felt the hot, sometimes muggy weather, turn quickly in October. Montana winters looked and felt much like his home in Maine, with temperatures ranging from 20s to -40s F°. Strong winds, from the west and north, drove the thermometer even lower on occasion, and made it extremely hazardous to move about outside. Oddly enough, settlers in the Lower Yellowstone Valley painted a somewhat different view of the climate. W. M. Post, a recent transplant from Dore, North Dakota stated, "I like the climate; it is healthful and pleasant. I think there is none better. The winters are not severe."[17] W. J. Sweeley agreed, "The climate could not be better, as a rule, [we have] later frosts here in the fall than they have there [Iowa]."[18] From inside Crowe's thin canvas-covered cabin, these observations appeared ludicrous as he watched the snow pile higher and higher. Movement outside was limited to a few days at a time and then only after adorning himself in three layers of thick under and outer garments. Roads, what few there were, disappeared by the middle of November and an eerie isolation dominated. Weymouth, keenly aware of the possible problems in trying to continue any kind of concerted construction effort, allowed contractors to release their men for the winter months, leaving only government engineers and instrumentmen—like Crowe, to brave the oncoming winter onslaught. Abandoning the outer camps, government workers retreated to the more established camps at La Mesa and Sidney. There they waited.

As the snows melted in the spring of 1906, Crowe returned to a full schedule of surveying and plotting the course of the proposed main canal. In addition, Weymouth assigned his young protégé to the headworks dam survey party where he helped determine the projected high water marks and record data to determine the precise location of the wood pilings, the dam crest, and the adjacent headworks structure—the device that would actually divert the river water into the canal.

Later, Crowe was reassigned to a surveying project under Assistant Engineer J. J. Kayes. Kayes organized several smaller teams, one under N. T. Olson, Max W. Wolff, and one under himself. The task of these well-equipped survey parties focused on re-surveying public lands starting from Division 4 northward to the end of the project.[19]

There was a wide discrepancy in the way Service contractors setup and maintained their work camps. Frequent visitors to many of these camps noticed discrimination against laborers from southern and eastern Europe. The immigrant men, known as "Bohunks," resided in separate sleeping quarters from their "white" or "American" counterparts. They received less in wages, earning $2.00 a day compared to $2.25 a day for "American" workers, "Bohunk" laborers paid 75¢ a day room and board fee, whether they used the facilities or not. These immigrant workers, many of them single, gambled everything by coming out West in the hopes of building a stake and for the sheer joy of adventure and exploration. Treated roughly by most construction contractors these "Bohunks" rarely lasted longer than six weeks on any one job. Ever wandering from one construction camp to another, they acquired a reputation that they could not be trusted.[20]

1906 proved to be a tough year for Weymouth and his chief construction engineer, Charles H. Paul. Plans called for private contractors to bid for project work. Blueprints and contract specifications were given to eager construction companies, they then submitted their bids. Once accepted, these contractors assumed that their projected profit margin would be safe. However, a nationwide financial dilemma brewed, beginning in 1906 and relentlessly moved toward a climax in 1907. Speculation in the stock market fueled an already obvious trend of spiraling prices and wages. In the West, nervous contractors watched as their material expenses climbed. At the Yellowstone Project, the price of cement, which had been $1.00 a barrel in 1905, soared uncontrollably to $1.60 in 1906. Wages went up as well, when contractors noticed workers leaving their jobs to secure positions with higher paying railroad companies. In particular, scores of men left to work on the Chicago & North Western Railroad that was extending a rail link west from the Missouri River to Rapid City, South Dakota. As one researcher noted, "Contractors locked into prices from 1905 agreements were placed under severe financial strain, and some were unable to survive the inflation."[21]

In his annual report to the Denver headquarters of the Reclamation Service, Weymouth discussed his financial difficulties explaining, "It became necessary to pay very high wages in order to obtain laborers of any kind, most of whom were very inefficient and of the 'hobo type', drifting from one piece of work to another and rarely remaining on one job for more than a few days at a time." On more than one occasion, reports came through noting that trouble broke out between the "Bohunks" and the "white workers" on the Lower Yellowstone. Elliot Paul described the time when he went to his brother, construction boss Charles Paul, to warn of a brewing situation at one of the outlying survey camps. The younger brother suggested that the "White men" were planning to "run the Bohunks out of the country." As his older brother mulled over the problem, Elliot added, "The same thing's getting started in some of the other camps." On top of this, wild rumors abounded that the newly formed Industrial Workers of the World (IWW) organization was made up of "anarchists" committed to disrupting government-sponsored projects across the nation. With all of this weighing on his mind Weymouth added to his report that, "The price of materials increased proportionately." In a more positive note, Weymouth claimed, "This section [Yellowstone Project] was not, however, as much handicapped by the hard times as some other parts of the country."[22]

One of the contractors Crowe met in 1906 was James Munn. It is believed that Munn, based out of Deadwood, South Dakota, had bid and won a small contract for lateral canal work on the Lower Yellowstone Project. This work included the construction of "siphons, sluiceways, and spillways." James Munn calculated early that the West needed brave, hearty, daring engineers to tame the drought-ridden region. He was ambitious; bidding low to get government jobs became his trademark. In 1906, he formed his own construction company, James Munn & Company. Munn was not shy about giving advice to foremen who worked for him. His logical, well thought out words made a strong impression on the inexperienced Crowe. In a later tribute to the pioneering Munn, construction executive Harry W. Morrison recalled that Munn became famous in engineering circles for stating, "A good foreman can get a lot of good work done with a lot of no-good so-and-so's, but a poor foreman can't get it done with a splendid bunch of workmen." Crowe learned to cherish Munn's terse and witty epigrams particularly one that went, "the price of true leadership is responsibility."[23]

Toward the latter half of 1906 and after careful consideration, the young engineer, uneasy about Service funding and eager to build, decided to leave the Reclamation Service and join up with Munn. In his words, Crowe explained, "I had tired of the transit and level." Just when Crowe left the Service, is not clear. It is doubtful that he would have left before the final surveying was completed, as he knew that Weymouth needed this data and he owed his start with the Service to his mentor. In fact, later in 1919, when once again, he was faced with the possibility of resigning, Crowe told Weymouth that, "I would not quit you under any circumstances if you needed me."[24] Additionally, since he would be leaving to work in actual construction, and very little construction work can be undertaken in the freezing snow-packed Montana winter, it might be assumed that Crowe remained in the Service until the spring or summer of 1907. A photograph taken on March 6, of 1907 shows a land survey party in action around Newlon, Montana and reveals the lanky tall Crowe standing next to his instrument. The survey party dressed in heavy clothing and wearing snowshoes, posed for this picture while staking property in Division 4 of the project.[25] However, at least two other accounts, one by Crowe himself, say that he linked up with Munn sometime in 1906.[26]

Whichever is the case, Crowe was not the only engineer to leave; in October of 1906 John Kerr, a division engineer left the project to work for a private construction company. This action was followed by George Colsom another division engineer, in early 1907, and C. J. Moody, engineer in charge of drafting. In fact, during the next few years numerous Service engineers throughout the West resigned.[27]

Newly installed (1907) Secretary of the Interior James R. Garfield may have had an impact on the flurry of Service resignations. According to sources at that time, President Theodore Roosevelt assigned him the dirty task of shaking up "that ponderous department." In a bold act of independence, the zealous Garfield issued eighteen yellow discharge slips to "incompetent" employees of his Land Office department. Most of these discharged government workers had been part of the "PD" (meaning per diem) club, a good-old-boy Washington tradition of providing government jobs, through congressional appointment, for political favors.[28]   Garfield's goal was to cut excessive government spending and to streamline responsibilities and functions. He would cut down on government-approved projects until the waste and graft had been eliminated. To this end, he also wooed Roosevelt to approve the removal of the Reclamation Service from the U. S. Geological Survey, where it had been since initiated in 1902, and establish it as a fully independent agency of the Department of the Interior. Garfield then convinced Frederick Newell, then Chief Engineer of the Service, to serve as the first Director of the Service.[29]

A third possibility exists where Crowe, while leaving to work for Munn, remained an active force-account contractor for the Service. This would allow him to contract with Weymouth separately for short-term work in-between Munn's jobs. This explanation is supported by the fact that his next major jobs, at Minidoka Pumping Plant and Arrowrock Dam were on a force-account or direct-work basis.[30] Crowe was no longer restricted to survey and mapping activities, as Munn placed him in a supervisory role of actual irrigation construction.[31]

Munn, a Scottish trained carpenter who immigrated to America with the hopes of become a private contractor, asked his new foremen to join him on a trip to Boise, Idaho, where Munn's "first big job," had already begun. The New York Canal, built years before to link the Boise River Diversion Dam and Deer Flat Reservoir (later renamed Lake Lowell), needed repair and enlargement, as did the dam itself. Crowe remembered this assignment as a "big dirt job enlarging the canal and a big concrete job lining it." In a memorial article to Munn written years later, Crowe describes how Munn, on his first trip to the new job site was introduced to Harry Morrison and Morris Knudsen, future big-time construction partners and Crowe's employer. Crowe remembered meeting Knudsen:

> We came up the ditch bank to the team gang which was
> being bossed by a big, husky guy, Munn pointed to him as he
> was directing some difficult plowing in the cemented gravel and

said to me, "You think you are a pretty good team man, don't you?" I said, "You know I am," and he said: "That guy is Morris Knudsen, and I'll tell you, he knows more about dirt moving than you and I both put together." That was my introduction to the elder partner of the contracting firm that was formed a few years later.

Continuing, Crowe recalled seeing Morrison that same day:

> We drove on up the ditch bank to the concreting opera-
> tions being bossed by a long, slim kid without a hat. Before we
> got close enough to him to meet him, he took off, hell bent, on a
> saddle horse. We learned he was running out of cement and had
> gone to build a fire under some skinners on the cement haul, so
> I didn't meet him that day. But I said to Munn, "What about the
> guy, is he any good?" and Munn said, "Well, that is some lad!
> He wants to line the whole damned ditch in one day. It will take
> several months but it won't hurt him to try, and one can't blame
> a boy for being ambitious. His name is Morrison—Harry
> Morrison."

Crowe began work on the Boise job and weeks later he finally met Morrison in a most interesting encounter.

> Munn called and asked me to drive up to the dam with
> him. He wanted to tell Harry that a flood was predicted for the
> little old Boise River. So we drove up to tent camp in the sage-
> brush under the ditch bank and met Morris and Mrs. Knudsen at
> the Commissary. Morris pointed to a lighted tent in the distance
> where Harry could be found. So I went to get Harry to come
> over and hear what Munn had to say. I rammed through the
> sagebrush and looked into the tent. It was lighted with a kero-
> sene lantern and beds were rolled out on the ground around the
> sidewalls. About a dozen husky young fellows were seated on
> the beds or on proverbial dynamite boxes, so handy in a con-
> struction camp. In the far corner sat a happy-looking boy with a
> guitar, singing one of the forty-nine verses of "Casey Jones"
> who manned the locomotive. I asked a boy near the door flap
> for Morrison. He said, "That's Morrison singing. Don't bother
> him, he has a four-bit bet up that he can sing popular songs for
> 30 minutes without stopping or repeating, and he only has two
> minutes more to win." Needless to say, he won. With the finish

of the songfest, Harry spent the night getting his equipment out of the riverbed.[32]

Crowe liked the Boise area, and although he did not know at the time, this area would become his "home" even though he would travel all over the West constructing dams. He learned that the original diversion of the Boise River had occurred long ago in 1864 when pioneering settlers and soldiers rerouted some of the water for use at Fort Boise and to supplement the needs of the new town. Private irrigation attempts proliferated in the early 1880s and continued until all the low-lying fields had been irrigated. With the coming of the Reclamation Service and federal intervention into the irrigation arena, Boise area residents and politicians convinced federal officials that additional large dams and canals were necessary in order to reach higher elevation farmlands. This area, away from the river looked like a desert wasteland, but Newell and others envisioned that it would become a productive framing region, with high expectations for becoming a world class dairy and seed-producing area.[33]

The Boise River Diversion Dam, located seven miles southeast of Boise was designed as a concrete and masonry weir (small dam) with a structural height of only 68 feet, although the crest extended 500 feet. It would take 26,000 cubic yards of concrete to complete the structure. An impressive direct overflow spillway could handle 40,000 cubic feet per second. Plans called for motor operated gates to divert a maximum 2,800 cubic feet of water per second to the carriage facility, the Main South Side Canal (formerly the New York Canal). However, Frank Crowe would not work directly on this dam. Instead, Munn's contract called for adding a section of a new canal, and increasing the nearby Indian Creek Channel. When completed the 4-inch thick concrete canal would measure 40 feet in maximum width and provide for a water depth of 8 feet.[34] For now, Frank Crowe's engineering future would be in canal building.

Starting in 1907, Munn assigned Crowe to supervise the construction of additional lateral canal work in Montana. New construction included work on the following irrigation components of the Lower Yellowstone Project: Crane and Sears Creek Aqueducts, and the Fox, Hay, and Four Mile Creek Siphons. As the financial panic of 1907 set in, more and more of the private contractors felt the money pinch of inflation and speculation. On top of this, weather conditions proved hazardous as blistering cold temperatures hung on through much of the spring. When the thermometers dropped, several moisture-laden storms dumped inches of water on the project area, making it difficult for construction operations. Weymouth in his annual report added that, "Delays were also caused by the fact that there were a few incompetent contractors who secured work."[35] It is not known if Weymouth was including Munn and Crowe in that group.

Frank Crowe wrote often to his parents, who remained back East. As his father John was gone much of the time securing contracts for his woolen business,

young Frank addressed most of his letters to his mother, whom he called "Mamma."
One such letter, dated April 20, 1908 has Crowe living in Ridgelawn, Montana,
part of Division 6 of the Lower Yellowstone Project. In the brief written note
Frank acknowledged a letter his mother wrote him describing a trip she expected
to take. He wished them a good journey and hoped his mother can make "Papa go
easy or he will get 'all in." Frank, in a gesture repeated many times in his career,
enclosed a check, in this case, $600—a very large sum of money for 1908.[36] This
gift represented a large portion of his earnings for the year.

For the remainder of 1907 and most of 1908, Crowe worked on and off
for Munn on whatever projects became available. Yet, the really big irrigation
projects, especially the building of large dams, were not in the immediate offering.
Frustrated over his brief venture into the world of private contracting engineering,
a somber Crowe buoyed when Weymouth announced in October of 1908 his impending transfer to the Minidoka Project of the Idaho Division.[37] Weymouth had
attended a regional conference for supervising engineers at Mitchell, Nebraska on
July 25, 1908 and came away optimistic about the future of the Service and excited about new proposed projects. Interior Secretary James Garfield declared
that he wanted to see "full information as to each new proposition submitted for
his consideration in order that he may act intelligently upon the feasibility of the
plan." Garfield explained that popular support must remain high if the Service is
to expand and prosper. To this end, the secretary suggested that all Service engineers develop "close relationships and mutual confidence with water users' associations" and that they remain neutral in local water rights controversies. He warned
engineers not to make statements that they will regret later or from which "wrong
impressions will arise." Also mentioned was the need for supervising engineers to
exercise "care and tact" in working with private contractors. Garfield acknowledged that while he had dealt with a number of complaints from Western contractors, he found none of them warranted; he declared that he believed that all contractors had been dealt with in a "legal and fair" manner. When the touchy issue of
the awarding of contracts came up, the Interior Secretary announced boldly:

> When the bids come in I want the local men [supervis-
> ing engineers] never to hesitate to throw out unduly low bids.
> There is nothing more distressing to the Department than to deal
> with a failing contractor [as had happened on the Lower
> Yellowstone Project]. The mere fact that it is the lowest bid
> gives the presumption that it ought to be accepted, but if any
> engineer knows that contractor has made a mistake or is not
> qualified or is not responsible or is negligent in the method of
> performing his work, that should be one of the prime conditions
> to be considered in making a recommendation for or against
> giving the contract to that contractor. I always want the word

responsibility to be given the fullest meaning that the law will allow it. It must be the responsible bidder in every sense. Much of our difficulty has been in dealing with men who were not responsible.[38]

With the renewed hope of strong support from the Washington office, Crowe agreed to quit his job with Munn and rejoin the Reclamation Service. Interestingly, Weymouth's second-in-command at Yellowstone, C. H. Paul, continued as construction engineer, finishing the main canal and laterals in January of 1909. From here, Paul, like Crowe, followed his boss to Idaho.[39] As Paul left the Yellowstone, water was released through the diversion dam and into the canal, irrigating 1,200 acres and even though more drains and laterals were added in the next two decades, the main components of the Lower Yellowstone Project stood completed.[40]

The upper Snake River area played a vital role in the early development of Idaho. Exploration and preliminary settlement, although sparse in the first six decades of the nineteenth century, rose significantly after the American Civil War. One of the earliest intrusions by white men into this area occurred when Captain Andrew Henry established a military post at the present site of St. Anthony in 1810. This lonely outpost was the first American owned and operated trading post west of the Rocky Mountains. Mormons moving into the area began sending missionaries as perspective farmers into southeastern Idaho around this time. These people helped to establish the towns of Rigby and Rexburg. Throughout the 1880s and 1890s, a slow but constant influx of families moved into and out of the region. Isolation, bitter cold, and the lack of a substantial irrigation network teamed to expel many of these homesteading hopefuls. While water flows were somewhat reliable for farmers owning land adjacent to the Snake River, others more distant from the main river or located near tributaries of the Snake River, found it difficult to acquire sufficient summer water for irrigation.

At the turn of the twentieth century, migration to Idaho and Wyoming increased significantly. Thousands of land-seeking families moved into and around the Snake River watershed. The Geological Survey conducted early investigations of irrigation possibilities in 1889 and 1890. These surveys provided the first examination of what would later be called the Minidoka Project. In 1895, under the authority of the State Engineer, additional surveys were included. At about the same time forward-looking private organizations also revealed an interest in developing irrigation for the Snake River Valley. At the time the federal Reclamation Act of 1902 became law the surveyed areas of the Snake River came under the jurisdiction of the new Reclamation Service. Federal engineers in that same year put together preliminary reports about the storage potentialities in the upper Snake River. On October 24, 1903, Idaho District Engineer, Douglas W. Ross, presented a report to the newly formed Reclamation Service's Chief Engineer, Frederick Haynes Newell, detailing the results of preliminary surveys and estimates for irrigating the Snake River Valley. In a subsequent letter dated December 1st, Ross informed Newell "owing to the efforts being made by promoters to establish rights to the use of the flow of Snake River for purposes other than irrigation, construction on the Minidoka project should be undertaken at once."[41] Realizing that southeastern Idaho and northwestern Wyoming held significant possibilities for extending irrigation, the Secretary of the Interior Ethan A. Hitchcock, federalized thousands of acres, withdrawing them from the public domain, in the proposed irrigation area of the Minidoka tract.[42]

On April 23, 1904, Secretary Hitchcock authorized the creation and development of the Minidoka Project. Initial plans called for two major dams to be constructed immediately. The first, Minidoka Dam, would be located in south central Idaho on the Snake River. The other dam, Jackson Lake Dam, located across the border in western Wyoming, would provide the headwater storage for the project. The Reclamation Service planned to build more dams between Minidoka and Jackson Lake later. Minidoka Dam, designed as a zoned earth-fill structure with a concrete-gravity powerhouse, was constructed between 1904 and 1906. When completed, the dam stood with a structural height of 86 feet, a maximum base width of 412 feet, and a crest length of over 4,400 feet, comprising a total volume of 257,300 cubic yards of fill. An interesting feature of the Minidoka Dam proved to be the five 10-foot diameter steel penstocks that delivered water to the powerhouse. The first power generated from the Minidoka plant occurred in 1909.[43]

The Minidoka Project centered on two counties in Idaho, Minidoka and Cassia. This area of the Lower Snake River Valley, about midway between the states eastern and western boundaries, had an estimated 120,000 irrigation acres in 1908. Surveying crews estimated the irrigation land extended up both sides of the river in an east and west direction for twenty miles, and north and south for about the same distance. It was calculated to use the Minidoka Rapids, six miles south of the town of Minidoka, as the point at which water diversion would take place. By the time Crowe arrived on the scene, an earth and rock filled dam had already been constructed.[44] The idea was now to begin work on two canals, one north and one south of the dam and roughly paralleling the Snake River in a westerly direction. On the north side, it was planned to extend the gravity canal eight miles to a system of laterals that would eventually irrigate 72,000 acres, past the town of Rupert and down to Heyburn. On the South side, water would flow by gravity to three planned pumping plants located miles downstream. Here the precious liquid would be lifted nearly 30 feet and dispersed through laterals to over 48,000 acres through the tiny towns of Delco, Springdale, reaching Burley, some 15 miles downstream. The main south side canal was designed to be 13 miles long with an initial flow capacity of 1,325 cubic feet per second.[45]

When Crowe arrived in at the Minidoka project office at Rupert workers were widening the south-side gravity canal with the hopes of bringing water to the planned pumping system. In addition, Crowe saw the crews excavating for the three pumping stations and preparing for placing the concrete foundations. Weymouth knew that cold weather did not deter Crowe from working, and he placed his hearty young engineer on the south side with orders to excavate and concrete as much as feasibly possible. Crowe energetically responded, directing the excavation of the No. 2 pumping plant foundation and eagerly overseeing the initial concrete placement. While others curtailed, or completely shut down, their operations in cold December, Crowe continued laboring all month. Relentlessly, the Maine engineer pushed the work rapidly along in January until a scowling ice storm and broken machinery forced a work delay and then, a temporary shutdown. Meanwhile, carloads of pumping machinery began to arrive on trains from Burley on January 19.[46]

Construction moved ahead on schedule and by April Crowe completed the station building at the No. 2 site. Next, Weymouth ordered the pumping machinery installed. The other two pumping plants neared completion, although it is not certain if Crowe helped at either of these sites. Weymouth, sure that crews would finish the pressure pipes that would carry the pumped water to the feeder canals soon, awarded contracts for some of the sub-laterals that would disburse water throughout the area. As the warm weather of summer approached, Weymouth's men installed the pumping machinery and completed the connection to the feeder canal. Excited farmers, near the pumping sites, were the first to receive irrigated water—on a rental basis—but, problems developed with the pumps and they were down for repairs off and on for weeks.[47]

Sometime in the early months of 1909, Frank Crowe, realizing that his responsibilities on the pumping plant were ending, decided to invest his name and money in a private contracting firm. His partner, Fred Lzicar, had convinced Crowe that the grading business was the way to make money. While Crowe remained in the Service as a contract-day engineer, making $3.50 per day working on the South Side Pumping Plant, Lzicar completed a few jobs.

Reclamation Service engineers, short on cash and manpower, concentrated on raising Minidoka Dam and decided to erect only a small, temporary timber dam at the Jackson Lake site. Plans called for this temporary structure to raise the level of the lake ten feet. Irrigation engineers estimated that this modest storage at Jackson Lake would satisfy the demands of local farmers for a few years. Plans were already being drawn up, however, for a permanent concrete structure that would provide greater storage. Charles B. Smith, Reclamation Engineer, surveyed the outlet of Jackson Lake in August of 1905 choosing a temporary dam site. Smith could see that the location of a permanent structure should be at a distance downstream from where the temporary dam would be erected. In this way, the timber dam could be used to control water moving into the construction site for the permanent dam. Smith's preliminary investigations were followed up in 1906 and plans were drawn for the temporary structure.[48]

This first Jackson Lake Dam and the subsequent permanent dams at this location have been considered some of the most difficult construction projects in the American West. While construction of the first dam proved difficult, the real problems arose from its remote location. John Markham, a Wyoming historian, related that the dam site at Moran, near Jackson Hole, proved excessively remote. He noted that most of the construction materials, such as: over 10,000 barrels of cement, 200 tons of reinforcing steel, 20 huge iron spillway gates, and several massive steam boilers—weighing 8 tons each and measuring 22 feet in length— arrived at the dam site after an agonizing horse and wagon trek across the Grand Tieton mountain range. Interestingly, the first Service Engineers identified an old outlaw trail, which served as a "construction highway" to the Moran dam site. These engineering pioneers learned quickly of the extreme temperature variations and challenging weather conditions of this Rocky Mountain area. Summer temperatures reached 100 degrees Fahrenheit[49], while winter lows dipped to 60 degrees below 0. Along with this, these first dam builders faced frequent and deadly blizzards, snowdrifts up to 15 feet deep, expansive treacherous marches, and deceivingly fast streams.[50]

This first Jackson Lake Dam constructed from local timber spanned 185 feet and was floated into place at the lake's natural outlet. Workers used stones obtained from nearby Signal Mountain to sink a makeshift wooden structure into the lakebed. As a final touch, Service Engineers installed 25 floodgates. Throughout the entire building phase from July 1905 to July 1909 all construction materials, food supplies, and clothing arrived over the outlaw trail, by 1906 now called the Ashton-Moran Road. Teamsters started this arduous 75-mile trip from Ashton where the Union Pacific had a railhead. According to one historian, "As a road it was better suited for outlaws than freight wagons. The weather and terrain made freighting on the road more difficult than the legendary twenty-mule team Borax hauls in Death Valley."[51]

This was an exciting time for Crowe. He had met and fallen in love with the sister of his close friend and co-worker, Robert (Bob) Sass. Marie Sass and Frank Crowe met earlier, possibly as early as 1906. Frank fell for Marie's fun loving and easy going personality. By June of 1909, Marie, still living at home in Helena, was attending nursing school and planning for her upcoming wedding to Frank, when she wrote a letter to Frank's mother, Emma on the 23rd. It offers one of the few glimpses into the kind of woman she was: "I was so pleased to have you write to me and wish to thank you for your kindly wishes, also for the flowers which came in pretty good condition considering the time they were on the road." She continued, "If they had all been dried up beyond recognition, they would be sweet to me because they expressed the kindly sentiments of Frank's mother. I know how much he loves you and I hope for his sake that you will learn to love me." Marie also wrote about her soon to be training as a nurse. She noted, "a little practicable knowledge of that kind would be very useful to me in the future."[52]

The first Jackson Lake Dam seen just before the center section failed in 1910. (USBR)

By the summer of 1909, engineers lowered the floodgates withholding thousands of acre-feet of water that were subsequently released to anxious farmers downstream. Unknown to local farmers and departing engineers was the fact that deep below the water the wooden crib had already begun to decay. Weymouth, planning to move ahead with a permanent dam at Jackson Lake, sent Crowe and his friend Bob Sass to search for a building site sitting on good foundational rock. Riding horses from Ashton over the Teton Mountains, the pair of happy-go-lucky partners mapped and wrote field reports of acceptable locations. After spending weeks in this Rocky Mountain wonderland, Crowe and Sass returned via Yellowstone Park and Helena, and filed their recommendations.[53]

While in Helena, Frank and Marie tried to plan their wedding day. A hitch was thrown into their plans when Weymouth asked Crowe to lead a party of Service engineers to the Jackson Lake site in August. He would not be sure how long the Service officials would take in their inspection. Writing his mother on August 25, Crowe explained his situation, "Well! I am back to Ida [Idaho] once more. Have just come in with my officials after showing them over the reservoir site and the wagon road location into the dam site. Everything seems very satisfactory to them. But I am glad they are through for it has been a pretty strenuous time for me. But I served them up the information as fast as they asked it." The letter provides some excellent insight into Crowe's travels in this area. He comments, "I start back across the mountains for Moran bright and early tomorrow morning then I will rush around and get my numerous crews lined up for a couple of weeks work then it is Me for Helena." Then in reference to the wedding Crowe announced, "I will go with a team through the park [Yellowstone] to Gardiner hence to Helena by train then after the big day [wedding] we will come back through the park. I will take a camping outfit along so we will have a great time." The usual confident and calm engineer admitted, "They say that knees get shaky at that time. Well! I risk my old bones."[54] Two days later Crowe writes another letter to his mother in which he describes a new business venture, "I would have some money to help you along soon, but I have been 'kinder pinched' this summer. Our grading outfit is not doing very good. I didn't realize that I was the business end of the firm so when Fred [Lzicar] got through with the job I got him in April he didn't land anything very good since then." Then in a fateful decision, he declares, "I am going to write him to sell out the whole outfit."[55]

On September 4 Crowe arrived in Livingston, Montana and wrote another letter, this one quite long, relating his adventures through Yellowstone Park in the three day, 120-mile journey. Crowe planned to leave the covered wagon and team in Livingston, take the Northern Pacific Railroad to Helena, and get married. He planned to bring his new wife back with him to Jackson Lake and he explained, "I hope we have better weather going back. If it is bad weather we will put up at the hotels, but the hotels are a[n] expensive way, $1.25 per meal." Frank told Emma that, "The Yellowstone Falls beat Niagara for being pretty. If the big dam goes in at Jackson's lake and if I am on it. We will have to figure some how for you to come out to see us and take in the park on the way in." Then he explained, "We won't decide on building the dam until I get this data worked up that I am getting this summer." To reassure his mother that his new wife will be properly cared for, Frank asked, "I suppose you are wondering how and where we are going to live. Well! I can handle all my work now from Moran (the building site for Jackson Lake Dam). I have an office cabin built like this. It is a dandy spot now." Realizing that Emma knew about the harsh winter conditions in the Rocky Mountains, he added, "I hope it don't close in to winter for a while yet. We will expect snow anytime now but it don't come on for keeps until about Oct. 15."[56] Frank Crowe arrived in Helena the next day, and on September 9, 1909, he married Marie Sass. The happy couple moved into their Jackson Lake home, Frank continued to plan and prepare all construction contingencies of the new dam.

Meanwhile, in the fall of 1909, it was noticed that the underlying cribwork of the Jackson dam continued to decay at an alarming rate. It is not certain whether Crowe reported this concern, or some other engineer. Desperately Service crews labored furiously to deposit several thousand cubic yards of loose rock, at the base of the structure in a fruitless attempt to shore up the structure. The submerged timbers continued to rot into the next year, destabilizing the foundation. An unusually large snow pack that winter resulted in a large swift input of water into the Jackson Lake reservoir swamping the dam. Disastrously, the middle portion of the dam gave way on July 5, 1910 just days before there were to be irrigation releases. Within a short period, a deluge of water, some 160 thousand-acre feet of Jackson Lake reserves gushed down the Snake River. Downstream bridges could not withstand the 10,000 cubic feet per second rush and several gave way.[57] One eyewitness to the collapse recalled, "The summer the old dam went out, I was working as a helper to the cook whose first name was Ed. On the morning the dam broke we heard a bid crash, ran to the door, and I saw about 75 feet of the dam go."[58]

Weymouth shocked by the news and under pressure to explain the failure and make repairs quickly, asked Crowe to checkout the damage, and file a complete report. He also wanted Crowe to get started on building a permanent dam. Weymouth and C. H. Paul agreed that it was time to give the energetic engineer an opportunity to start a major project from the earliest stages. An excited Crowe eagerly accepted his new assignment and asked to have Robert Sass, his good friend from the Yellowstone Project, accompany him as concrete foreman. It is interesting to note that in July, Crowe received his first national recognition by the Reclamation Service, a notation in their monthly publication the *Reclamation Record*. He is depicted as the head of the Snake River Storage Project, yet his designation, an Instrumentman, is the same rank he had when he resigned to work for Munn. Recognizing the need to update Crowe's rank to be commensurate with his new responsibilities, Weymouth rushed through a Service promotion, and by September he was an Assistant Engineer. By November, the fast rising Crowe made the rank of full Engineer.[59]

Acting with a rapidity and confidence that would be his trademark in years to come, Crowe organized the entire project. He knew if he acted quickly, he could complete a portion of the construction before the infamous Rocky Mountain winter set in. First, he urged Weymouth to give him wide-ranging powers and money to setup a warehouse and depot in Ashton—the end of the rail line and his gateway to materials and supplies. He hired locals, such as J. V. Allen and others, to widen and improve the Ashton to Moran road, and he immediately began erecting essential buildings at the dam site (Moran). These buildings included a hospital, office, commissary, warehouses, and shops. He also ordered houses built for himself (and Marie), and for the other foremen. According to one source, these homes were "sturdy houses, even if on the crude side. Each one had its own water system consisting of heavy wire, one end fastened to the house and the other end anchored to a heavy rock placed well out in Jackson Lake, with a small pulley on the wire and attached to a rope." The homeowner wanting water "simply snapped a water bucket to the pulley and let the bucket back up the wire—much easier than climbing up and down the hill."[60]

In a flurry of activity, the twenty-eight year old Crowe appeared everywhere on the job site and his drive revealed an amazing maturity, even veteran construction workers respected. He organized crews to string a phone line from

Ashton to Moran, and this was completed in early August. He sent word out in all directions that men were needed immediately for work. Eventually, Crowe supervised 400 men on all operations of the project, many of these new recruits were "Bohunks."[61] He hired a full-time doctor and nurse, who provided care for project men and local families alike.

The parsimonious Crowe hired G. E. Moore, as his chief clerk and J.P. Waite, as his fiscal agent. Their tedious, yet important job was to spend the allotted government funds very carefully, keeping track of every penny. Believing in promoting those who showed promise, Crowe elevated Joseph J. Markham, only twenty years old, but a hard worker with lots of grit, to be timekeeper, assistant superintendent. Anyone who muffed responsibilities would be reported to Markham and then to Crowe. Markham also was head purchasing agent, which meant he kept in close contact with Crowe at all times. The pressure would be on young Markham constantly to make sure that needed supplies such as hay for the horse teams, and grain and beef for the men, never ran out. From all over the country former construction colleagues, from the Lower Yellowstone, Minidoka, or from Munn's old organization, came to work under Crowe. Howard Wise, living in Phoenix, arrived to help with the accounting; Abe Johnson, an expert carpenter with a no nonsense reputation for getting results reported immediately after receiving a Crowe telegram; Harold Robey, an accomplished warehouseman and forwarding agent, came knowing that Crowe would want all building materials organized and readily available.

Second in command of the overall operation went to, good friend and now brother-in-law, Bob Sass. Sass also was placed in charge of bossing the concrete operations, once that phase of work began. Sass, now with a responsible position and a decent salary, decided—like Crowe—that it was time to get married. On December 10, 1910, with work in full swing at Jackson Lake, the harried Sass exchanged wedding vows with Libby Lzicar—the sister of Fred Lzicar, Crowe's old business partner. With only a few days off for the whirlwind honeymoon, Sass was back on the job.[62]

With everyone watching, from Interior Secretary Richard Ballinger and Reclamation Director Frederick Newell to the newly hired ditch digger, Crowe knew that this was an important turning point in his construction career. He was young and being tested, and he knew it. His future and that of his foremen and assistant superintendents—even his mentor Weymouth, was on the line. The news of the dam failure had reached newspapers across the country and the Reclamation Service's reputation was hanging in the balance. He wanted to do two things. He wanted to build the new permanent dam to high engineering standards and he wanted to build it quickly.

Crowe arrived at a strategy that would underlie all subsequent jobs of his and would become the foundation of his success. He would simultaneously sequence as many of the job operations as possible, thereby employing a maximum number of men to complete the maximum amount of work at any given time. This meant that he needed to review, which he no doubt did, with his team of foremen—especially Bob Sass, the entire planned sequence of work. How much of the job could be reorganized in complementary phases so that, like an assembly line, it would all come together in the shortest time possible? We already know that he rapidly organized his supply depot in Ashton and warehouse in Moran, while scores of men slaved against the onslaught of winter to grade the road between both locations. This assured him communication and supply. And to make sure that the maximum amount of material would be placed on each transiting wagon, the free thinking engineer used massive 14-foot Studebaker wagons, capable of hauling up to four tons of freight, to make daily runs between Ashton and Moran. Now, Crowe concentrated on purchasing, from Salt Lake City, a complete sawmill. Ingeniously, he had it "floated across the lake and set up on the west shore to provide 1.6 million board feet of lumber for the project." Meanwhile, he ordered a diversion channel dug and a cofferdam (temporary earth dam) piled so that the building site could be dewatered. This was completed by November. Immediately, Crowe pushed his excavation crews to hog out the riverbed and hit solid rock, which fortunately, he struck soon. As one area was scraped clean and the steam powered dirt shovels moved, Sass' concrete form crews moved in and framed. Weymouth was stunned by Crowe's success. He had ordered Norman Torrance, design engineer, to complete the engineering drawings; the frantic draftsman could barely keep up. Crowe was moving swiftly, and he was setting a new standard in large-scale construction methods.[63]

Appearing everywhere at once, Crowe performed with boundless energy. No one knew for sure, except Crowe, where he would go next. This hands-on vigilant policy won for Crowe a reputation for demanding an honest days labor from each worker. A chance meeting with the young engineer might reveal a mansuetude type demeanor, yet idleness and sloppy work were not tolerated. Warnings were rarely given, even though finding laborers proved difficult, and numerous men were fired. On the up side, his men discovered that good hard work was rewarded with additional jobs as the project progressed. The project came together just the way Crowe wanted and his orders, like medieval royal edicts, were followed to the letter. Of course, it would take more than Crowe's bountiful energy to accomplish his goals; he needed support, and support he received. It is clear that Crowe's management policy of "tough, but fair" struck deeply in his staff of foremen, assistant superintendents, and office personnel. What he expected from them is what they had to expect from the workers under them. Regular staff meetings ensured that foremen knew exactly what the short and long-term work objectives were.

With strong cold winds coming on, signaling dangerous winter weather ahead, Crowe stood unmoved. He wanted to not slow down or shut down the operations; to the contrary he launched into the concrete placing phase forthwith.

With the floodgates already ordered and on their way, Crowe and Sass hoped that the specifications for the gate sizes proved accurate, as their holding slots would already be set. In October, the Wyoming winter arrived, winds kicked up and temperatures dropped. Day after day, they continued to drop. Crowe, long on enthusiasm, but short on experience, tried any reasonable suggestion. Whether it was his idea or not, it is not known, but sometime that month large wooden sheds were erected over the concrete framing sections. Heat was brought in from coal-fired boilers, this allowed the cement to be mixed correctly with the gravel and sand mix. In what surely must have been a Western construction first, Crowe's men chipped chunks of frozen aggregate, carting them over snow-covered tracks to the mixing plant. The men, wearing surtouts, or close fitting heavy overcoats, did not complain and work continued. Sass remembered later that at one point the thermometer dipped to a chilly fifty degrees below and the coal supplies began to run low. Undaunted, Crowe discovered ample reserves at nearby Lava Creek and within days the boilers were back online, pressured to the limit. By mid-January of 1911, records showed 3134 cubic yards of concrete had been placed. It is doubtful if any other contemporary construction project, located in a similar climatic belt, was even open—much less operating at full speed.[64]

Working at such a frenzied pace and with the biting cold, one might expect that Crowe was taking unnecessary chances with men's lives. Yet, reported fatalities remained very low while non-serious injuries occurred frequently. Frostbite was common, but usually due to workers shedding gloves in order to work more effectively. One account asserts that a concrete worker was lost during a placement on the east end pier. His partner scurried out of the fast hardening concrete unable to help. Tales such as this need to be questioned seriously, as a decaying human body encased in concrete would cause significant weakness in the integrity of the concrete block. It is a well known fact in civil engineering circles, that concrete forms rarely exceeded five feet in height and that all construction engineers would halt the work to recover buried bodies. However, allegations abounded and stories of entombed concrete workers would plague the Reclamation Service (later the Bureau of Reclamation) and Crowe for years to come.

According to the highly suspicious accounts by eyewitness, and later novelist Elliot Paul, Crowe and his wife "Barbara" [Marie] formed a social coterie that included Paul, Sass, Norman Torrance and his wife, and others. Paul, in his book, *Desperate Scenery*, recounts how Frank and "Barbara" enjoyed having "the gang" over to their cabin twice a week. Amid coffee and candy the group relaxed to the sounds of popular songs played by Paul and "Doc." Far from being a stilted, or a cotillion type affair, the novelist claims "one by one the boys danced with Mrs. Crowe, in a space about six feet square." Paul, retelling this account some forty years later said, "Her [Marie] eyes would shine, her cheeks would glow."[65] To be sure, having any kind of a social life in remote Moran would be welcome by both men and women alike. Once the snows fell in earnest, around November, little or no outside contact was forthcoming for months.

Paul's account are verified, to some extent by an article published in *The Dam Weekly*, an "off the cuff" publication research and written by the dam workers themselves. In the first issue "reporters" described the October 31st "Halloween" party that Frank and Marie hosted. Meeting at their home the "Crowe's Nest," workers and their wives were entertained by Elliot Paul's piano playing, "apple-snapping, corn-popping, marshmallow toasting, and fudge-making." Marie is described as "charming." The Crowes ended the night's activities with the lights turned down low, and with guests gathered around their large fireplace, "weird and thrilling ghost stories were told." By midnight the happy group departed with "lighter hearts and clearer minds."[66]

By January of 1911, the twenty multi-ton head gates arrived by train in Ashton. Needing a miracle, Crowe called on Floyd Bous, his logging foremen, to "break" the road through. In a valiant effort, Bous proved up to the call. Despite imminent danger from blizzard and the resulting threat of being marooned in snow, Bous' men prevailed. Wasting no time in Ashton, he replenished his exhausted teams of horses, loaded the heavy gates, and returned to Moran, to a hearty round of applause and the grateful appreciation of Frank Crowe. As calculated, the head gates fit snugly into their preplanned frames; it was all coming together for the young engineer.[67]

Amazingly, by time the thaw began in Moran in the spring of 1911, Jackson Lake Dam stood nearly complete. Amid this achievement, Crowe received a telegram from Director of the Reclamation Service, Frederick Newell. Fully expecting it to applaud his success, Crowe reeled from its contents. It read: "Write and wire briefly the practicability of raising Jackson Lake Dam ten feet higher. Estimate roughly probable cost and increased storage up to one million acre feet." Unbelievably, the Service was actually considering raising the dam just as it was ready to start storing water. A miffed Crowe, in a rare episode of public emotion, fumed about Newell's notice. Particularly offensive was the fact that Crowe, and design engineer Torrance, had suggested a larger dam the previous July. If they had followed his advice, hundreds of thousands of federal dollars would have been saved. As it were, Crowe calmed and spent the next few months devising a cost saving plan to raise Jackson Lake.[68]

Early in 1911 Marie announced to her husband that she was pregnant; he was elated. However, the pregnancy did not go well, with Marie showing signs of high blood pressure and back aches. In October, while well along in the pregnancy, she developed kidney trouble suffering from uremia, a toxic condition of the blood due to the presence of waste products that are normally removed by the kidneys. Sadly, on October 17, 1911, she died; the fetus could not be saved. The cause of death was officially listed as Puerperal Eclampsia. She was 22 years old.[69]

Devastated by the death of his young bride and child, Crowe turned to his professional career to fill in the gap. He wanted to work now, more than ever, on bigger and bigger projects. Dams would be his preference, big dams, the biggest and most challenging that Man had ever seen. From now on, everything would focus on identifying and preparing for the construction on America's great dam projects. To be sure he was ambitious for this goal before Marie's death, after it Crowe was obsessed. Admittedly, later he would acknowledge that all of his previous training and experience was a preparation for the really huge quests of building Hoover and Shasta Dams. The first breakthrough step would come very soon after Marie's passing and Crowe anxiously leaped at the opportunity. The Reclamation Service had approved the construction of Arrowrock Dam, not far from Boise, Idaho and it was planned to be 350 feet tall, making it the world's tallest. Best of all, James Munn, had been hired to be construction superintendent.

Chapter 3

"I feel that I am simply marking time."

1912-1921

Crowe first visited the Arrowrock project in the spring of 1910 as field supervisor in charge of site investigations. He lazily cruised up and down the irregularly flowing Boise River from the Twin Springs area, some twelve miles upstream from the final selected site, to possible building locations just downstream from Arrowrock. Crowe reported that he had considerable difficulty in locating work crews for the investigation, having to pay an inflated rate of $3.00 per day, abnormally high for that kind of work. Interestingly, when labor became more plentiful in 1912, the wages dropped to $2.50 per day. Crowe's investigative drilling helped Weymouth and others determine that the Twin Springs site would not be acceptable. From there further research was done on the Arrowrock site; Crowe then, had a big part in helping determine the final location of what would become the world's tallest dam—for that time. Some of the major considerations in the final selection included; (a) being nearer to the base of supplies, in this case Boise, (b) possessing an appropriate geological foundation, at a reasonable depth, and (c) providing for a greater drainage area.[1]

When Crowe left the area and reported for work at Jackson Lake, Weymouth consolidated his drilling crews, placed J. F. Richardson in charge, and focused his efforts on the Arrowrock site. Richardson's men dug numerous test pits in and around the riverbed. In January of 1911, with Crowe busy at Jackson Lake, Reclamation Service Chief Engineer, A. P. Davis, Consulting Engineer, A. J. Wiley, Construction Engineer, C. H. Paul, and Project Supervising Engineer, Weymouth, toured the site and collaborated for several days over plans. Weymouth and Paul visited the site in 1910, probably with Crowe. Everyone was nervous; this was to be the biggest dam yet attempted and Davis, Weymouth, and company needed to be sure that they select the best possible site. Following the technical meetings and adventurous field trips around the area, it was decided to appoint Paul as construction engineer. Paul, in turn, with Weymouth's approval, nominated James Munn to be Superintendent of Construction. This meant that Munn would be in overall daily command of the actual construction and Paul would be responsible for the engineering aspects, making sure that Munn's work followed Reclamation Service specifications—as drawn up by the designing engineers. In effect, Munn would be hired, as Crowe would be, as a contract laborer, working for the Reclamation Service, but not as a Service engineer. Paul continued the investigation and discovered a problem that many dam building engineers face. The depth to bedrock does not always correspond to the narrowest abutment distance. Ideally, a short distance to bedrock would mean less foundational excavation and a narrow distance between abutment means a narrower dam, thus less concrete. In this case, the site with the least depth to bedrock was hundreds of feet upstream from where the canyon walls were the narrowest. In a compromise, Paul and Weymouth decided to move the site 150 feet upstream. Munn's engineering assessment of this decision stated, "this move, it was thought, would result in getting a smaller amount of masonry below water level even if it increased the quantity above, and would perhaps cheapen the cost and increase the stability of the structure."[2]

Beginning in April of 1911 and continuing through the next month, Professor W. O. Crosby, a Reclamation Service geologist consultant, and his team examined the proposed dam and reservoir site for stability. At the same time, Service personnel used diamond drills to extract borings. About ten miles away in an area of readily available lumber, carpenters erected a sawmill as workers used horses rigs to grade the future campsite. The decades old wagon road, leading east out of Boise to the Arrowrock area was widened and access cut in to the actual dam site. In the Boise office, engineering draftsmen completed working drawings and drew up detailed specifications. By June, horse-teams began laboriously hauling hundreds of board feet to the campsite, there they were unloaded, and immediately carpenters went to work framing. Weymouth wanted telephone communication to the site as soon as possible and toward the end of the month a line was up. Weymouth also worked out a deal with Bell Telephone to have the nearby lines that lie in the proposed reservoir, rerouted. Project Director Weymouth sensibly planned for a standard gauge rail line connection to transport the massive amounts of supplies needed to build a huge concrete dam. Quickly, he let out a bid for grading the first nine miles, along with contracts to provide ties and rails.[3]

Work continued methodically through the summer with sufficient rain to keep the roads from kicking up annoying dust clouds. Construction men from all over the West, most with previous work experience on dams or irrigation projects migrated into Boise and then out to the Arrowrock site. With workers spending most of their federal paychecks in town, business in Boise picked up and farmers and ranchers in the area anxiously followed the work progress. They understood clearly that with the completion of this great dam, their access to irrigated water increased business opportunities. Speculation on land in the proposed irrigated zones boomed.

With news spreading about the "world's tallest dam" engineering interest peaked nationwide. Envious engineers wanted to know everything they could about the plans and personnel given the responsibility of building the concrete monolith. Reclamation Service Director Frederick Newell, decided to hold the annual meeting of all supervising engineers at the Arrowrock site. During the week of September 11 through the 16th, the Service's engineers observed work progress, examined plans, and discussed construction strategies. During the last two days of the conference, the newly appointed Secretary of the Interior, Walter L. Fisher, visited the site and conferred with Weymouth and Paul. Unusually warm weather allowed Munn to push the work into November. Crowe, meanwhile, heeded a call from Munn to come and assist with the excavation and the preparation for concrete operations. He arrived sometime in July or early August. A third shift was started on the challenging and difficult job of excavating the diversion tunnel. Crowe, a strong believer in the use of air-compressed tools, engaged six heavy-duty drills in an effort to speed up the digging. At the same time, a large number of men worked on excavating the south side spillway.[4]

The engineering possibilities of air-compressed tools dated back to Crowe's studies at the University of Maine. Civil engineers were particularly impressed with the efforts of three major air-compression companies that pioneered the use of air tools in major construction methods. All three of these companies, Ingersoll-Rand, Chicago Pneumatic Tool, and Sullivan Machinery, boasted good reputations when Crowe started work on the Lower Yellowstone. Weymouth and Paul authorized the use of Ingersol-Sergeant drills to bore the blasting holes in the lava rock of the Minidoka diversion channel. Amazingly, heavy-duty hoses allowed the air compressed drills to operate at a distance of 800 feet from the actual drilling site. Again, Weymouth used air to operate the main concrete mixer, to supply the power for the cableway hoist engines, and to power a distribution system that pumped water to all parts of the work site and the construction camp. Air compression was becoming an important multi-faceted tool and Crowe would use it extensively on all of his jobs.[5]

Crowe returned to Jackson Lake to finish up and check his calculations on the estimate for the enlargement. He wrapped up Jackson Lake Dam and reported to Arrowrock. The rest of the winter of 1911 and into January of the next year, Crowe's challenging assignment focused on supervising the excavation of the main diversion tunnel and assisting the timber lining operation of the tunnel. The 487-foot tunnel had been devised as the most efficient means of diverting the Boise River. Records on flood rates of the Boise River confirmed a maximum of 14,000 cubic feet per second could swamp the construction site, bowling over any temporary earthen diversion banks. Service engineers originally planned on a concrete flume, chiefly because it was cheaper and quicker to build. However, problems with the foundation bedrock under the proposed flume led to "difficulties in carrying out that work." Trying to divert the flume from a straight shot one with deflections led to frustration "in design and to difficulties and uncertainties in computations for capacity." Paul and Munn decided to take another look at the tunnel concept.

This would be a gigantic tunnel, one of the largest and longest ever built by the Service up to that time. Designed to extend 30 feet in width and 25 feet high, just excavating the sheer rock abutment would be a major task. On top of this, newly drawn plans called for the monstrous tunnel, on the bottom and sides, to be lined with 9 inches of concrete. The top would be heavily timbered. The inflow and outflow portals, or openings—called bell mouths, were to be concreted as well. The bell housing portals, acting as giant funnels helped decrease the amount of water turbulence entering and exiting the tunnel. Once drilling and excavating began, Munn discovered that the hard granite rock was uniform through-out, except for a few lava rock pockets; this, hopefully, provided structural stability.

Crews excitedly began the drilling on August 22, 1911, from both tunnel ends. Tunnel surveying required constant checking, as mathematical computations needed to be precisely calculated for the excavated headings to meet exactly. Initially, one thrust heading 8 feet by 8 feet, was planned for the entire length. But, when foremen discovered that rock from above broke loose constantly, Crowe halted the drilling. A quick conference by Munn and Crowe resulted in a decision to widen each new heading with two parallel headings that would help absorb the constant jarring from the air-compressed drills. This technique appeared to be successful and the work resumed. The general procedure for drilling and blasting out the tunnel involved laying out a pattern of holes drilled from 4.5 feet deep to 6 feet then placing carefully measured explosives in each hole. The charges were then set off, first the center, then the sides and top. Ninety percent dynamite was used, the "quality varying to a slight degree, but an average of 50 to 60 pounds per round was used." Typically three to five feet of advance was made on each round. Munn employed two shifts on the outlet side and one shift on the inlet side of the tunnel. On November 4th, the headings met and by December, the entire tunnel had been roughed out.[6]

With the tunnel hogged out Crowe concentrated on helping Munn decide how to set up a unique system for excavating the dewatered riverbed and delivering the concrete. While cableways were certainly not new to construction work, or even dam building—as Weymouth had employed them on the Minidoka effort, Munn and Crowe, and eventually Weymouth, decided to invest a large sum of federal money to erect a cableway system on a huge, never before seen, scale. The $63,000 spent, while unprecedented, would allow young Crowe and his veteran boss, Munn, to realize speed and efficiency in building large dams. The cables themselves had been purchased from the Lidgerwood Company, one of America's few industrial firms, producing multi-strand 1" plus diameter size cable. The entire system included a well-planned setup of headtowers and tail towers, correspondingly connected with 1500 feet of cable. In this way the entire dam site would be covered. Excavation and concreting operations could be enhanced tremendously by not having to deal with clumsy hand loaders and primitive horse and truck usage. The cableways handled all transport. Materials and supplies, including men, could be transported from the top of Arrowrock canyon to the bottom and vice versa.

The three headtowers built on the northern slope, stood 60 feet high, while a corresponding tail tower, served as a convergence on the south side. The stationary towers later proved to be a problem as no lateral, or horizontal movement occurred and Crowe found that even with good planning, not all areas of the work site could be covered. Crowe answered this problem, ordering his men to move cableway #1, after its previous work-area had been completed to a new position further downstream. The #1 cableway was then designated #3. In later jobs, Crowe would solve this concern with a single headtower and movable tail towers. With a 1500-foot span and an operating height averaging 400 feet, Crowe and Munn's cableway operation easily represented the most grandiose and the most challenging concrete delivery system ever attempted in irrigation and dam construction. Each cable held a maximum of 12 tons of material—designed to handle newly configured 8-ton concrete placing buckets. This load could be hoisted at a speed of 300 feet per minute and travel along horizontally at 1200 feet per minute.[7]

With this giant play toy, Munn now needed to train and equip a crew of hardy intelligent workers, who would need to come together as a team. The operation was so big that cable operators on the top of the canyon could not hear, or sometimes see, their counterparts laboring on the bottom of the canyon. Crowe and Munn utilized a new Bell Telephone system and a backup bell system. Actually, Crowe wanted everyone working the cableway operation to be well versed in using hand signals, the bells, and telephone systems, so even though the phones worked well throughout the operation, he insisted that the bells be used as well. A designated number of short rings on the bell indicated a command to lift, steady, run, and set down loads. Crews constantly worked on their communication and practiced as teams until Crowe and Munn were satisfied with their efficiency rating. Both men realized that Weymouth and other Service officials would be watching to see if this new, large-scale technological approach reaped engineering benefits.

The task ahead proved formidable. Munn's excavation engineers had calculated the depth of the bedrock excavation would need to drop 60 to 80 feet and traverse the full 200 feet from canyon wall to canyon wall. Additionally, the huge dam would have a thickness of 240 feet at its base, measured up and downstream; all of this material was scheduled for removal. This amounted to over 230,000 cubic yards of material, not including stripping loose rocks from each side abutment. The entire operation, at least the full-scale excavation operation, needed to wait until the diversion tunnel stood completed and the riverbed sat dewatered. Using one of the cableways as a dragline, workers loaded loosened bedrock at the bottom of the canyon and employing steam shovels they placed the material (called muck) in skips (rectangular boxes attached to the cableway). Once loaded, cableway operators hoisted the rock and dumped it into a nearby crushing and sorting machine. This material could then be used as fill elsewhere during construction. Crowe, with approval from Munn, organized a three-shift operation; it would be around-the-clock excavating. This had been done sparingly before at Service projects sites, but Crowe would make this strategy another of his enduring trademarks. While the daytime and swing shifts worked all phases of the excavation process, Munn smartly, limited the graveyard shift to cleaning up, drilling, and preparing for early morning blasting.[8]

The sprawling impressive cableway system became a personal triumph for Munn and Crowe. Their operation increased the amount and speed at which large amounts of material could be excavated. Would it work equally well in placing concrete? Before they could find out, Weymouth asked his favorite young engineer to go back to Jackson Lake and make a detailed estimate of the cost and procedure (he already had completed a general proposal) for raising the dam there. He knew that if he did a good job putting together the specifications for the enlargement, he would stand a good chance of getting the top construction job there. The Service was looking to raise the dam at least 17 feet (based on Crowe's earlier estimate), which afforded 840,000-acre feet of additional irrigation water. Crowe spent the first two months of his new assignment at Moran. It is not known whether he moved in to his old cabin or not, or preferred to stay in Moran. He collaborated extensively with his friend and fellow Maine graduate, Frank Banks. Banks had completed design drawings of the enlargement, now Crowe would look them over, check available men and materials, and report to Weymouth with a schedule of construction.

In a letter dated February 20, 1912, Crowe explained to Weymouth that his findings were complete. Crowe, who later abhorred writing official letters and memoranda, at this stage in his career wrote in a professional and succinct style. The letter read:

> In compliance with your request I am transmitting herewith a complete schedule of procedure for the construction of the proposed enlarged Jackson Lake Dam as designed by Mr. F. A. Banks during January and February 1912, together with a complete estimate on unit costs for the features of construction required by the above-mentioned design.
>
> Very Truly Yours, F. T. Crowe, Engineer

What followed was an incredibly detailed account of the entire construction process. Assuming he would get the go ahead from Weymouth to move on construction in May, Crowe laid out an amazingly complicated month-by-month report of construction steps, for work through 1914. He calculated unit costs for each step of construction from materials used to the number of hours required to complete each phase. He estimated wages for every employee for 1912 and projected inflationary figures for 1914. Even the cost of fuel was delineated and he priced tools and supplies down to the dollar, while going as far as to estimate shipping costs! While Crowe asked Munn to help with the final compilation of figures, it was Crowe's bid and one of the most detailed ever produced by a Reclamation Service engineer up to that time. It proved that this young engineer felt completely confident in his ability to plan for and then construct a major irrigation public works project knowing that every possible item and contingency had been accounted for.[9]

Not content with his February 20th report, Crowe immediately followed-up with another letter to Weymouth on March 6 suggesting a complete organizational plan of labor. He cleverly listed "1 Engineer, Supt. of construction," at the top of the list, although there is no official record that he asked for the job. He then, again in much detail, listed various jobs, from assistant engineer to instrumentman, oiler, electrician and others. For some of the positions, Crowe did make recommendations, almost as if he was saying that the following people have been shown to be competent and would work well with him. He named F. W. Talbot for an assistant engineer, Leigh Cairns as an instrumentman, and A. C. Weise for the chief clerk. More in-depth reports found their way to the desk of Weymouth's Boise office and it became obvious that Crowe wanted the assignment.

In March, Crowe returned to Arrowrock where he discovered the work force had been reduced to 300 men due to the completion of the diversion tunnel. About half the flow of the Boise River now poured through the manmade cavity, the rest continued moving down the old river channel. Snow fell much of the month and Crowe busied himself checking on the installation of two headtowers and managing the layout of the cables themselves. Already planned, Crowe saw to the final details on his design for mucking diggers and for his concrete drop buckets. The mucking diggers would be attached to a dragline cableway; when lowered from above the giant claw gulped up yards of loosened rock. On command, cableway operators hoisted the load and deposited it elsewhere. Used in combination with the skips, mentioned earlier, excavation moved along ahead of schedule. Crowe learned from Munn that a new 70-ton steam shovel, scheduled to arrive that month, would be available for use in the spillway excavation area. Anyone visiting the operation at Arrowrock clearly saw that here was an operation of gigantic proportions, complete with sky-dangling cableways and monstrous sized digging machines. The aerial show began in May when both cableways were installed. Crowe's 2 1/2 yard digger, nicknamed the "orange-peel," bucket was put into operation on the dragline. Practice by the cableway team revealed that only a few days were needed to work out the kinks of the operating procedures.[10]

On into the summer, more and more men were hired back as the full excavation operations started up. Munn and Crowe reviewed safety rules and impressed on their foremen, including Crowe's friend Bob Sass, the need to make sure all new employees clearly understood and worked by these safety rules. However, on June 12, Thomas E. Murphy became one of the first fatalities. Novice lineman Murphy touched a "23,000-volt live wire, in a moment of inadvertence." The responsible foreman on that shift explained to Munn that Murphy had been moving unused lightning arrestors in the transformer house when, thinking the job done, he switched the current back on. With at least two other linemen present Murphy noticed a "wire that was crooked." He said, "Here is something we must fix" and without thinking, grabbed the live wire. The foreman immediately tried to administer artificial respiration by using the "Sylvester Method." The camp doctor, arriving on the scene shortly asked to transport Murphy to the camp hospital. There, for over two hours, the medical staff tried the "hypodermatic stimulation" method of respiration. The effort was to no avail and finally Murphy was pronounced dead.[11]

Recovering from this tragedy Munn pushed his men to continue the massive excavation job. By October, the cableway system was removing 35,000 cubic yards of muck a month, and with the assistance of steam shovels, riverbed excavation dropped 65 feet. Now Munn moved swiftly to erect a complete "sand cement" concrete mixing plant, and by the end of the month, he had crews running operation tests. On November 17, bedrock was struck and immediately Crowe inspected the outcropping for foundation suitability. He found very hard granite, "water worn and full of irregularities and small pot holes." Clearing away more of the base he discovered that despite these concerns, the foundation would anchor satisfactorily. His men cleaned out the remainder of muck and cut a key way, or v-shaped footing, into the bedrock. To finish off the year, an anxious Crowe drove his crews, partly due to the extremely favorable weather, to prepare for concrete placing. With everything in place on December 11, the first bucket of concrete was lowered into its awaiting form. The cableway appeared to work beautifully, swinging out over the huge canyon and gently easing down exactly as expected. Once in position, the bucket foreman pulled a lever and the freshly mixed concrete slopped downward into the form where awaiting men spread and tamped the material. The cableway system worked. Crowe could look back with great satisfaction for 1912 had afforded him the opportunity to be a major contributor to the construction of the world's tallest dam. The next year his success at Arrowrock would continue and there would be additional new construction experiences, and he would fall in love again.

Despite the five inches of snowfall and freezing cold temperatures of December, Arrowrock's cableway system functioned well placing over 20,000

An aerial view of concrete operations at Arrowrock Dam, July 1914. (USBR)

cubic yards of concrete. This was enough to cover the bedrock foundation to a depth of 20 feet. January of 1913 saw the thermometer drop to where Munn and Crowe realized that the safety of the operation was at risk. Still, whenever there was a break in the weather and temperatures climbed, construction moved ahead and 10,000 additional cubic yards of concrete were added to the dam. Once again, we see Crowe using every possible moment, every available man that would be willing to work, to keep construction going. Few engineers, on projects elsewhere in the nation facing similar climatic and construction challenges, continued to work during the deep winter months. February, with extreme cold, permitted almost no work. March proved little better. Crowe became impatient and ordered work anyway, which turned out to be the wrong decision. Concreting "was carried on at such times as weather permitted, but this work was handicapped and the expense of it was increased by continued cold weather." Thankfully, there were no serious accidents during this time, but Munn and Crowe agreed that concreting in these conditions could be hazardous and work was greatly cut back. The cold continued into early April, but warmed enough to increase production. By the middle of the month the first, or bottom section of the dam, stood completed with a total of 67,500 cubic yards of concrete placed, some 113 feet high. During this month, cableway #1 was moved into a downstream position. In the new location, the cableway could assist in the final excavation of the downstream portion of the dam.[12]

Through May, June and July excavation in the downstream section continued with excellent results. This area, where the dam's 52-inch and 60-inch outlet tubes would be located needed to be prepared for concreting as soon as possible. Luckily, bedrock conditions proved to be "extremely favorable as to topography, much more so than was expected from the diamond drill borings and the quality of the rock is all that could be desired." This meant that the time required for completing the excavation would not need to be extended, thus expediting concrete placing. A May 28 flood of the Boise River was easily corralled in the diversion tunnel "without taxing its capacity." With July, the hot weather arrived, along with a few bothersome thunderstorms, but by the middle of the month concreting started in earnest on the middle section of the dam. Crowe and Munn were pleased to see cableway crews work out all kinks in communication and delivery. Shift production amounts climbed and it became clear that, if used properly, cableways could deliver and place a huge amount of concrete. A new dam building era had arrived.[13]

Men now poured into the dam site looking for work. As the hot weather continued in August, Crowe asked for even more output from his crews and by the end of the month 35,000 more yards were added to the dam, making a total of 115,000 cubic yards. The dam was going up rapidly, so rapidly that Munn and Crowe had to be careful about letting the concreting run too far ahead of the other operations. The sand-cement plant worked furiously to keep up with Crowe's constant demand for more and more material. When it appeared that the aggregate material from the riverbed was running low, Munn ordered a new gravel pit opened nearby. A complete camp and plant needed to be erected there. Crowe had suspected that additional gravel would be needed and search crews had already selected alternative sites. Meanwhile, Munn prepared for concrete placing in the gigantic spillway located on the north bank of the river. The safety procedures were stressed during the intense building season but injuries at the dam continued. By the end of the summer, two deaths were attributed to injuries from work related activities. Four others died from sickness.[14]

In an unexplained action, Munn released Crowe from service on Arrowrock sometime late in October to work on the distribution canal works that would support the big dam. Over half of the concrete had been placed; rising up over one hundred feet already, the dam looked impressive, yet unfinished. Actually, Crowe was not needed any longer, as the cableway system ran smoothly. The carefully trained crew could now finish the relatively easy job of topping off the last portion of the dam. Since the width of concrete decreases rapidly the higher up the dam you go, the amount of concrete placed would decrease also. In any case, Crowe was reassigned to the Pioneer Drainage Works, west of Boise. Listed as "Construction Engineer," Crowe reported to the project manager G. H. Bliss. His work, though significantly, less dramatic than the Arrowrock high-rise dam, proved to be challenging and a key component of the Boise area irrigation goal. He supervised the surveying and excavating of miles of open canals and drains. This irrigation network would provide farmers living near the towns of Caldwell and Nampa, thousands of acres, with a reliable water supply. Many of them, though close to the Boise River, claimed no water rights and possessed no way of getting water without the federal government intervention. Crowe however, soon became disenchanted with the assignment.[15]

Despite the mediocrity of the new job, Frank Crowe announced plans to marry again. He had been seeing off and on, one of Boise's most eligible debutantes, Linnie Rosanna Korts. They had met during one of Frank's many visits into Boise from the Arrowrock job and now he was most anxious to wed again. The talented engineer, already over 30 years of age, had distanced himself from the deep memories of his first marriage and he wanted children. The wedding, on December 9, 1913, was a much talked about affair in the local area, simple, yet elegant. The church, described as "quaint," received a good-sized number of well-wishers and guests. At 3:00 p.m. the nervous bridegroom stood unattended while Linnie walked the long aisle. Linnie's gown proved stunning, a "chic traveling costume of bronze green broadcloth trimmed with fitch fur. Her attractive hat fashioned from cloth of gold dovarati with heavy lace, with a dull green velvet brim." Known as one of the "most beautiful brunettes" in Boise, Linnie must have stunned the gathered throng as she gracefully carried a full bouquet of roses. The excited bridegroom stood tall next to his bride, exchanged vows and rings, and hastily existed the church. Once outside, the happy couple said quick good-byes amid a rain of rice and rushed to the Boise train station, just in time to catch the 4:00 p.m. special to Portland. The honeymoon trip lasted a week.[16]

Upon their return to Boise, Idaho area, the Crowes moved into a small-

furnished bungalow. The Owyhee, Weiser, and Boise mountain ranges that provide a picturesque background to the extended Boise River lowlands surrounded
their new home, Caldwell, some twenty miles from Boise. Its unique geographic
location allows for only 11 inches of precipitation a year and a definite four-sea-
son climate. Surprisingly, summer temperatures climb over 75 degrees regularly
and winter temperatures average a livable 35 degrees. The newlyweds settled into
a comfortable predictable schedule with Frank journeying out to the drainage irrigation ditches during the daytime and Linnie organizing the household. The young
engineer's professional dreams were unrealized as of yet and he yearned for larger
more complicated tasks. His time at Caldwell allowed him to focus on developing
a solid close relationship with Linnie, one that would last the rest of his life. The
fruit of this new relationship became readily apparent early the next year when
Linnie announced she was pregnant.

Through the first part of 1914, Crowe dutifully carried out his duties
supervising the drainage layout, digging and compacting. He brought in two electric dragline excavators and extra men. Starting in March, Crowe organized three
8-hour shifts and put them to work on the construction of Mason Creek and Elijah
drains. Within weeks, news of his good progress was reaching engineers all over
the West. Crowe, once again, was proving himself a hard-driving competent engineer who brought new innovative strategies into play even in the most predictable
of construction assignments. By June, Crowe's crew encountered "softer material" and the operation of the excavators moved ahead considerably. Later that
month, one of the excavators, pressed into 24-hour service, broke down. The only
concrete placing that Crowe did at this time included small miscellaneous structures located on the banks of the drains and a "feeder" into the nearby Ridenbaugh
Canal. Finishing the Mason Creek and Elijah drains by the end of June, Crowe
jumped right into attacking the other components of the Pioneer District including, Wilson Creek and Purdum Gulch drains. With these drains well under way in
July, Crowe let Weymouth know that he wanted another assignment. As luck
would have it, word came through that the superintendent of construction on the
Jackson Lake enlargement, C. W. Farmer, was planning to resign due to poor health.
Weymouth knew that Crowe's abilities were being wasted on the Pioneer drains
and he recalled that Crowe had completed a detailed plan for completing the Jackson Lake enlargement. In fact, Farmer had only been given the job, in April,
because Crowe was still deeply involved in setting up the strategy for digging the
remaining ditches in the Pioneer District.[17]

An ecstatic Frank Crowe eagerly agreed to accept the new position when
Weymouth called him into his office. After explaining the situation to an anxious
Linnie, who was just getting into a comfortable marriage routine, Crowe wasted
no time in tying up loose ends at work. He and Linnie made the decision that it
would be better for Frank to go himself to Moran while Linnie remained behind.
For Frank, in many ways, this was a return home, and for Linnie, this was the first

Frank Crowe with a dredge bucket that he designed, June 1914. (USBR)

of many voluntary separations. Ironically, one of his first acts in his new assignment as Superintendent of Construction of Jackson Lake Dam was to write an in-depth report on the Pioneer Drainage Project for publication in the *Reclamation Record*, the journal of the Reclamation Service. Crowe's quality for being thorough is clearly seen. He provided a complete historical perspective and a discussion on ground water, and soil types before discussing his actual construction work. His concluding comments stated, "Excellent results are being secured both as to draining out of the water-logged lands and the costs and speed with which the work is going ahead." Crowe also noted that no additional private drains would be needed to properly irrigate the 34,000 acres and that a "conservative estimate of the cost based on the work already done indicates that the system will be completed for approximately $350,000." This was the amount originally designated in the Warren Act proposal.[18]

      Upon arriving in Moran, Crowe was briefed by foremen that excavation for the enlargement portion of the dam had reached bedrock. Crowe inspected the exposed outcropping and was dissatisfied with the hardness of the bedrock. He ordered excavation to continue an additional 15 feet. He immediately began hiring, putting out the word throughout the area. By the end of August, the workforce had doubled from 160 to over 300. To be clear, as to the hiring conditions, Crowe published a general order stating, "Eight hours shall constitute a day's work for laborers, workmen, and mechanics who may be employed by on behalf of the government of the United States." In the next paragraph he sternly warns that no contractor or sub-contractor can force an employee to work more than eight hours "except in case of extraordinary emergency." The penalty, he declared, for each and every violation of this federal regulation could be $1000 or six months in jail.[19]

Shortly after arriving in the area, Crowe met with Frank Banks, assigned to Jackson Lake as design engineer, to determine the location and kind of material to be used in building the upper cofferdam. This cofferdam would redirect water away from the dam site so that construction could begin on the upstream side of the existing dam. Originally, Banks had planned to use timber supported on short round piles, but Crowe remembered the rotting timbers of the earlier temporary Jackson Lake Dam and he recommended using dirt. Crowe's opinion won out. In September, Weymouth and his assistant A. J. Wiley visited the site to see how Crowe was settling in and to inspect Crowe's proposition for using hydraulics throughout the operation. Weymouth was becoming more and more convinced that Crowe understood the construction process and that his young protégé was on the cutting edge of new methods and strategies. Weymouth approved Crowe's mass hiring and upbeat schedule. A quick check found that everything was in order. Banks' designing and bookkeeping teamed with Crowe's hard-driving construction crews emerged as a winning combination. Crowe would supervise the actual work, at least temporarily, and Banks would carefully inspect the procedure and outcomes. Additionally, Banks wrote most of the field reports required by the Service; this suited Crowe fine, as his interest lay in directing the construction.

Receiving supplies and major construction components in a timely fashion proved to be an ongoing problem for Crowe. Recalling his experiences from the previous Jackson Lake job, he knew that an open road to the outside world could prove critical to his timetable. Two routes came into Moran, the first was the treacherous old Reclamation road from Ashton that Crowe helped to clear and improve back a few years earlier, and the other was the Teton Pass route. The latter came from Idaho and rose quickly, reaching mountain altitudes of over 8,000 feet. The long steep road challenged the hardiest of freighters, particularly from November on through April. Frustrated workers, due to poor road conditions months before, dumped six of the 14,000-pound boilers onto the trail; men came back later, improved the grading on the road and hauled the boilers on through to the town of Jackson, then north to Moran.

Sometime early that summer, Frank returned to Caldwell and brought his expecting wife back to Moran. The pregnancy had not gone well, and when Linnie gave birth to the baby boy in October, the newborn appeared weak. Frank Jr., died five days later. Frank Crowe had suffered the loss of his second child. Fortunately, Linnie recovered her health, although this would not be the last son they would lose.[20]

The operation at Jackson Lake though a complicated engineering task, due to the existing dam, required no unusual risk-taking and Crowe fully expected to finish the job without a fatality. In October unfortunately, W. E. Shippey, a concrete worker, collapsed for no apparent reason. When the Service physician pronounced him dead of a heart attack, everyone, including Crowe stood shocked. Ironically, the victim had informed Dr. Wise just days before that he expected to resign his job as soon the 15-day waiting period to receive government compensation had taken affect. Wise explained to an unhappy Crowe that Shippey, when first hired, was discovered to have heart problems and a "lame back." A government regulation required all prospective employees to undergo a physical examination, but often men with medical concerns were hired anyway, particularly when labor was in short supply.[21]

Although needed at Jackson Lake, Weymouth allowed Crowe to return to Linnie and his job on the Pioneer Drainage Project for the winter of 1914-1915. This allowed Frank to spend the holidays with his new bride and friends. Linnie was delighted to hear that Frank's appointment at Jackson Lake had earned him an increase in pay to $3300 a year, up $300. The following spring, as Crowe picked up the pace on completing the drainage work, he reported to the Reclamation Service that his men, using a technique formulated by him, had set new records in dragline excavation. This record was "so exceptionally high" that an article appeared in the *Reclamation Record*. In the article, Crowe stated,

> We are just completing the construction of approximately 50 miles of open drains, involving the excavation of approximately 2,000,000 cubic yards of earth. We have had an exceptional opportunity to organize one of the most efficient crews that I have ever seen on this class of work. Their March record, I believe, is a "world beater" for this size of machine. I would like to see their names in print, as they are a credit to the service.

What followed was a detailed list of the drains, men, and excavated amounts of earth that each crew had excavated. In that issue, Crowe's friend and mentor, Frank Weymouth was highlighted in a special biographical summary of his career.[22]

His mind engaged on thinking of ways to improve efficiency, Crowe, on the job in and around Caldwell, cleverly mounted two automobile engines on flatbed trucks. These portable powerhouses, when chassised properly, operated the sluice gates, allowing for testing and measurement. When Crowe was ordered to assume his duties back at Jackson Lake on April 3, 1915 he brought them with him. There they were reassembled to a slightly different configuration and operated as independent dinkey cars, transporting excavated muck to various sites. The relocation back to Jackson Lake was once again, without Linnie and while he enjoyed getting into the "muck" of dam building, he must have missed her greatly. Crowe threw himself into his work. Now the exciting part of the assignment came, concreting the corewall of the new enlargement. Commencing on April 12, dozens of men labored to work a systematic method of mixing and placing the thousands of yards of concrete needed to establish a strong corewall. By June 16, exhausted workers and a beaming Crowe stood over a resilient handsome concrete monolith. Cautiously, Crowe had mixing crews watch the exact composition of sand and gravel to cement. Remembering well the problems with the temporary dam and its resulting failure, he determined to blend the strongest possible mix.

The dam, designed to be a concrete gravity dam with embankment wings, posed an interesting problem for Crowe. The center of the dam would be solid concrete with the floodgates located directly above. On each wing, concrete corewalls buttressed huge embankments of hydraulic fill enveloping original earth fill. To keep operations going on all phases of the work, he needed to keep a close eye on the job sequences and efficiency. Whenever he saw an opportunity to redirect the way a job was done, he would talk to the crews, the foreman, and then sketch some ideas out. If the plan seemed doable, he would order his new device built and tried. At Jackson Lake, Crowe tried several new ideas. One involved the construction and use of a pipe that allowed the sifting and placement of different fine and coarse material. This he believed would help the compaction and therefore, ultimately the strength of the embankments. The device worked so well in one location, that others were built and used in the building of the temporary dikes. To help with the mucking, or removal of excavated material, Crowe decided to go with his Arrowrock design of an aerial cableway. This single, scaled-down model operated using a new 1/2 cubic yard bucket that mechanics built in the machine shop. Crowe enjoyed seeing his paper ideas come to real life; he personally supervised the machine shop personnel as they built the bucket.[23]

Interesting stories surrounding the men who built the dam still exist and one of the most colorful recollections comes from William Balderson. He remembered how Crowe and Banks allowed workers to take government horses on weekend fishing and camping trips. Likewise, Service canoes were placed at the disposal of off-duty workers, enabling them to troll Jackson Lake. Several existing photographs confirm Frank Crowe's love for fishing. For months, Crowe's fishing companion was a retired army colonel, A. E. Randall, who had come out from Washington D. C. for the expressed purpose of enjoying the great outdoors and catching prize-sized fish. Balderson remembered weekend treks up into the Teton Mountains, particularly Mt. Moran, where groups of off-duty dam workers explored the glaciers and mountain valleys. On another occasion, Balderson and a friend were canoeing on the lake when they came across a lone camper chopping wood along the shoreline. After beaching the canoe, Balderson talked with the

Frank Crowe (right) with his good friend and fellow Service
engineer, R. V. (Bob) Sass, at St. Ignatius Dam in Polson,
Montana, 1916. (Donna Sass-Holloway)

man, who appeared nervous and uneasy. Not thinking much about the incident,
Balderson and his partner returned to Moran. Days later, Crowe received a message from the Yellowstone Park rangers asking him to be on the alert for a lone
man responsible for robbing tourists over a period of a month. Unbelievably, the
desperado arrogantly asked his victims to take his picture after loading money and
jewels into his getaway bag. One of the photographs turned up and was sent to
Crowe. Everybody recognized the culprit as a drifter who had worked on the dam
for a time, then suddenly left. His canoe was found at the upper end of the lake
and he was apprehended later in Idaho.[24]

Marion Allen, later one of Crowe's veteran dam builders, was a young boy at Moran and he remembered Crowe well. Allen's father, J. V. Allen, moved back into the area when news was announced that Crowe would be expanding the workforce. The young Allen talked with Crowe on numerous occasions and he recalled running all around the construction camp, in and out of the government dormitories and mess hall. Allen was astonished to see "Chinese women" working the mess hall and he recalled "we would go by their cabins and they would always give us some little cards with pictures of dragons on them." On occasions, the women made ginger candy and gave it to the boys. Allen watched the construction of a freight barge, nicknamed the "Titanic." The ungainly boat, when completed, ran back and forth across Jackson Lake delivering logs to the lumber mill.[25]

On and off through the fall of 1915 Weymouth stopped in to see Crowe's progress. Usually his visits lasted several days, with Crowe giving Weymouth a full tour of the dam site; the pair also reviewed plans and specifications for the next phase of construction. In November, Crowe alerted Weymouth to the fact that he was going to erect another cableway to assist in the dredging of the river below the dam. Weymouth, convinced by Crowe and Munn at Arrowrock, that cableways could hasten the job, approved the added expenditure. Crowe wanted to get the new aerial system on-line before the cold weather set-in and before he left for Caldwell. Crowe headed for Caldwell, in mid-December, and a welcome reunion with Linnie. Traveling with him was a small entourage of workers, all reassigned to the Nampa Meridian Irrigation District, part of the Boise Irrigation Project. A. B. Gale and William Montgomery dredge runners, and A. Boris and Joe Oberstarzyk, dredge oilers, accompanying Crowe all were told that their reassignment was permanent, while Crowe was scheduled to return to Jackson Lake on April 1, 1916.[26]

Linnie was so glad to see her husband that shortly after he arrived home; she insisted that Frank take her to Moran upon his return. He agreed and after spending three months supervising the canal dredging around the towns of Nampa and Meridian, between Caldwell and Boise, he returned to Moran during the first week of April. Excellent weather prevailed and Crowe gradually increased the workforce from 50 men to over 200. Uppermost on his mind was preparations for concreting the center section of the dam, installing the floodgates, and completing the hydraulic fill on both embankments. As the upstream face of the dam was completed the water storage level rose and by July of 1916, over 400,000 acre-feet of water was already being withheld. Crowe's good luck held through the summer and dredging operations turned up excellent material that workers then re-deposited between the new and old abutments. Working conditions remained good, despite unannounced thundershowers and a freak temperature drop in August when the thermometer dipped to freezing on four separate occasions.[27]

Meanwhile Linnie tried to make the best out of a primitive living situation. The young engineer's bride, accustomed to the niceties of Boise, found little in the way of shopping or commercial activity in Moran. The readjustment proved difficult. Many couples did have get-togethers on the weekends, sometimes starting an evening's festivities with dinner at the local tourist lodge, the Teton Lodge. However, even the lodge, became unavailable when it burned down that summer. During the conflagration, Reclamation Service men voluntarily helped to douse the main blaze. They prevented nearby cabins from erupting in flames by throwing dirt on them. As hard as they worked, Crowe's men could not save the adjacent post office. This was a tragedy for that summer was expected to be a good tourist season, with the dam nearing completion and the reservoir filling.

Work on Jackson Lake moved toward closure in early August as Crowe's two-cableway system worked daily depositing fill on the embankments. All flood gates were being installed on the center dam section and the dike stood nearly completed. Crowe and Banks efficiently wrapped up construction work well ahead of schedule and they had kept spending within budget amounts. Obstacles, including geographical isolation and fluctuating labor supply, were overcome. Crowe's use of cableways had proven superior to other traditional methods. He was starting to get anxious for a new challenge toward the end of summer and he wondered where his next assignment would be. He didn't have long to wait, word came from Weymouth that "the big boss" wanted Banks to finish the Jackson Lake enlargement while Crowe would transfer to the Flathead Project in Montana.

The Flathead Project had been created to tap the numerous natural reservoirs located in and around the Flathead Indian Reservation. Most of the land was below Flathead Reservoir. Thousands of acres could be irrigated if outlet works with supporting canals, laterals, and conduits could be built. Eager to get a look at his next assignment, Crowe reported to St. Ignatius, Montana, August 8, 1916, where the project superintendent Ernest F. Tabor setup his regional headquarters. When his new boss told him that he would be construction engineer on the McDonald and Tabor Reservoirs Crowe withheld his excitement. As he inspected the site, he could quickly see that, once again, the engineering challenge looked minimal. No sooner had he reported to work than Tabor became upset that Crowe had reported without transfer orders. In a short terse letter to Weymouth, Tabor announced that there was no money in his budget to pay Crowe's salary, which at that time was $3300 a year. Weymouth came immediately to the defense of his protégé, writing back to Tabor on August 15 declaring, "The Secretary [of the Interior] approved an amendment to your organization providing for item 72a, Construction Engineer at $3300 per annum, under which Mr. Crowe should be carried." Now Tabor wanted to know the exact date so that payment would not overlap with Crowe's Jackson Lake payroll. To this end, Banks, back in Jackson Lake was brought into the controversy, as he had to supply payroll dates. Tabor even had to accept Crowe's automobile travel expenses from Jackson Lake to St. Ignatius. On August 21, in the midst of working out the transfer paperwork, Tabor became seriously ill with Peritonitis and died. Weymouth did not hesitate in appointing a replacement. The next day he shot a letter off to Crowe stating, "I have recommended to the Director and Chief Engineer [Arthur Powell Davis], and obtained his approval of your appointment to this position which I hope you will accept." Crowe could not believe it; he was being offered supervision over one of the biggest Reclamation Service projects in the West. The very same day he received Weymouth's offer, he wrote back, "I wish to thank you for the new assignment, and I assure you I will do everything in my power to carry on the work in an efficient and businesslike manner." Davis wrote to Crowe and Weymouth within a short time confirming that Secretary of the Interior, Franklin K. Lane, approved the promotion.[28]

Stunned, Crowe called in all construction engineers involved with the Flathead Project, conferred and tried to get a feel for the size and extent of the whole project. On the very day he took over, he issued an order to all contractors performing work for the Reclamation Service to have monthly work estimates completed and on his desk promptly by the last day of the month. His organizational abilities helped to make for an easy transition into the top job. He sent out a flurry of letters, memos, and notices to engineers, contractors, and local agencies letting everyone know that he was in charge and that he expected everyone to abide by government rules and conditions of employment. Nothing appeared too trivial; he even sent a special notice to all employees to clarify the payment policy for recognized holidays. In September, he compiled a complete organizational plan, listing positions and salaries, and all related project budget expenses. A large oversized flowchart, precisely placed top level and mid level engineers, with Crowe on top. The word came down that nothing would be approved without Crowe's signature.

Crowe struggled with his new role. He tried to learn to be diplomatic, as he knew a good administrator needed to be. In a letter to local farmers, he brought up the subject of missing survey stakes. Everyone knew that the farmers were pulling them up; some out of ignorance, others upset with government plans to take part of their lands for right-of-ways. He explained, "Destruction of the stakes delays the work and adds to the total construction cost which the farmers must ultimately pay." Then he pleaded, "It is urged that you take this matter up with the farmers and explain the situation to them. Your cooperation in this matter, for the good of the farmers as well as of the Service, is earnestly requested."[29]

He knew, once again, he was being tested. Tabor, regarded by many Service personnel to be an expert on canal location and construction, had impressively started the Flathead Project and successfully laid out the intricate plans. In fact, the *Reclamation Record*, the official journal of the Reclamation Service, described him as "an ideal project manager." "The varied and intricate problems of administration, engineering, construction, business, and law were successfully dealt with. The complaints and criticisms peculiar to such work were notably lacking," the account read. In dealing with the local Native American population Tabor was said to be "especially thoughtful and considerate, and he was always patient with their grievances whether real or imagined."[30] Crowe on the other hand, had limited experience in coordinating large spread out irrigation systems. Tabor had been called in all over the West as a consultant, at such places as Blackfeet, Milk River, Shoshone, and Sun River Irrigation Projects, whereas Crowe had only surveyed on one canal project and supervised in a limited capacity.[31]

The resilient young project director had barely settled into his new responsibilities when he received word from Service Director, A. P. Davis, that a national conference of project directors was to take place in Denver. All of the project managers from the entire West, including an excited Crowe gathered to hear Davis proclaim, "The principal object of the conference, as desired by the Secretary of the Interior, should be the discussion and determination of estimates for appropriation for the fiscal year 1918." "It was thought we would be very short of funds, so we wanted the advice of each individual in regard to any cuts we might have to make, but in compiling the estimates of work that is absolutely necessary and of probable funds, it was discovered that we are not going to be particularly handicapped in that respect during next year," Davis happily explained to the gathered group of project managers. Davis, always well respected by his men, added, "The greatest benefit I hope to obtain from this conference is a mutual acquaintance and exchange of ideas so as to get the best team work and strive for the same thing." The collected group of Western engineers heard Davis discuss administrative policy and shared leadership. "People have different minds, different points of view," said Davis, "and differences of opinions relative to the importance of things and regarding proper policies to be pursued." Davis continued by challenging his engineers, "we want your help and we expect suggestions, and at the same time, when a decision is arrived at, we want team work in carrying out the policy when it is arrived at." What followed were several days of intense formal presentations and exchanges. One of the formal papers presented was by J. L. Lytel, who would be Crowe's future colleague on the Yakima project. Lytel's paper entitled, "Concrete and Protection of Structures from Freezing" was on a subject that Western engineers were having to deal with during winter construction schedules, and a subject that Crowe would need help with for years to come.[32]

The Falthead Project, as Crowe soon learned, was a large project consisting of divisions: Jocko, Mission, Post, Pablo, and Polson all named after local towns. Over 200 miles of irrigation works were planned with the Little Bitterroot Diversion Dam scheduled for immediate construction. This would give a stable water supply to the entire western portion of the Flathead Project and help provide control of the Flathead River. It was calculated that 7300 acres could come under immediate irrigation with the dam.

1917 opened with the Crowe's happily installed in their government housing at the St. Ignatius engineering camp. In an effort to start work early, Crowe asked for and got additional appropriations in March to move ahead with all division work. Now would come the horrendous task of coordinating multiple divisions each with its own organizational plan. Crowe had never done anything like this before and it looked more like an administrative job than fieldwork. He constantly made the rounds of each division or spent time at locations where problems appeared. Almost every day it appeared he dealt with contractors. Contracts had to be bid out and he had to write up the government matching minimum bid. He then carefully traced the progress of each contractor, looking to make sure they completed the work correctly and within contract time. For Crowe, this became a crash course in mastering the bidding process and he would learn well, as later he became America's most successful construction bidder on large construction jobs. And so it went, day after day.

Writing a summary of the project history late that year he disclosed, "1917 has been the busiest in the history of the Flathead Project both from a construction and operation and maintenance standpoint." Crowe attributed this to the fact that the government made more money available and that the weather was "the driest in thirty years" and farmers were desperate for water. It is interesting to see in his report how many men he had brought with him from Jackson Lake. Leigh Cairns came and was placed in charge of the building of the Pablo Feeder Canal and for outletting the McDonald Reservoir. John McCabe, expert at mining operations, came only a few days after Crowe and helped with tunneling and excavation. Crowe's brother-in-law (from his first marriage), Bob Sass also appeared and he was put in charge of constructing the Camas "A" Canal. He was building a team, one that would follow him for years. The team, like their leader, probably felt a little let down. No large dams were planned for the project. Instead, his men would construct only small earthen fill diversion dams—basically, to funnel water into various canals.

Crowe had been promised a pay increase to match his new responsibilities and it came through in July. Weymouth recommended a $300 move up making his salary $3600, which A. P. Davis approved. Sass, to contrast salaries, made $160 per month or $1920 a year. The timekeeper earned $75 a month and a typical foreman made $5 a day. Crowe might have been happy about his salary increase, but he continued to become more and more disenchanted with his job. Letter writing increased in 1917 to the point where it was becoming a nuisance. One letter dated early in the year, asked all field personnel to inspect government animals to make sure they are all branded with the letter U.S.R.S. (United States Reclamation Service) and that no additional animals were to be purchased without Crowe's expressed approval. In another letter, Crowe wanted to know every employee who had access to any government keys. Field supervisors were ordered to supply a list of names and advise Crowe of any changes to the list. Stiff penalties would be paid if a key were lost. All new keys needed to be registered with Crowe. In March, he became preoccupied with the time keeping system. He wanted to make sure that no mistakes were made in tracking everyone's time and pay. In this long letter to "employees in charge," he gave precise instructions on how field reports should be written. He was clear in saying that no work would begin or continue until "procedures" were followed exactly.[33]

As the year progressed, he was making more non-engineering decisions than at anytime in his professional career. Much of the time, he simply passed on executive orders from Weymouth or Davis. Such was the case on March 15, 1917 when he notified the division leaders that "Beginning April 1, 1917, all employees taking meals in government messes will be charged for same at the rate of $2.00 per day, or 34 cents per single meal." Then he added, "There will be no charge for bunk-house accommodations." On this one day alone, he turned out three memorandums.

With America's entry into World War I in April Crowe received a barrage of correspondence concerning security and reporting. A major concern was finding sufficient manpower. As President Woodrow Wilson called for men to enlist, the Reclamation Service already stood shorthanded. Director Davis pleaded with Interior Secretary Lane and Wilson to give deferrals to men working on government projects in the West. Although it took some time to get this through, Davis did eventually get an agreement that any "essential personnel" would not be called for military duty. Crowe, late in April, checked the security of all government records at his disposal. He was also ordered to supervise the government's "Military and Naval Experience and Training" form. Washington wanted to know which men had "military and naval experience and training in different branches of the Army and Navy." Crowe told his division leaders, "We have been directed by the Director to furnish one of these [military experience forms] for all employees in the educational and non-educational grades, exempting those who are temporarily engaged." Crowe told his men that the "forms should be filled out with a typewriter, if there is one in camp." With war fever rising daily and the threat of mass desertion from their irrigation jobs, the Reclamation Service hurriedly raised the minimum wage to $3.00 a day.[34]

The degree of inaction for Crowe can be seen in his monthly project summaries to the Service. "Most of the camps have been closed down," wrote Crowe in the May summary. He goes on to report the weather conditions, give a brief update on runoff and provide estimates on when the spring plowing and seeding will take place. Even in terms of maintenance, he noted that little was to be done. Crowe learned, disappointingly, that from November through April little construction work was possible at this isolated Montana site.[35]

By June stern warnings from Weymouth via the Washington office urged Crowe to watch all expenditures and to recycle materials whenever possible. One of the first items that came up for consideration was cement saxs [sacks...Crowe used this term even in official communication]. Crowe, in all his precise calculations, even determined the number of empty cement sacks for any given month. His figures revealed 45,000 sacks could be reused. In June, he notified all employees that empty cement sacks were to be gathered up, counted, and returned to the project office for redistribution. In the spirit of competition, Crowe decided to keep a running count as to which division had returned the most sacks. With the war hysteria, engineering and construction occupied less and less of his time and he became swamped in a morass of paperwork. His correspondence exploded in a barrage of orders, suggestions, and helpful hints that Washington wanted him to pass on. There was a general feeling that the war could curtail all irrigation building for the duration. Some workers felt that better opportunities lie elsewhere. Again, Washington passed a pay increase, although they now began to charge for three meals a day, whether you ate them or not. The memoranda continued and it appeared they were becoming longer and longer in length.[36]

In March, Crowe sent a serious note to all employees warning them that the recent declaration by the United States Food Administration concerning conservation of foodstuffs would be strictly enforced. The federal decree had authority in all public and private eating establishments and thus Crowe was obliged to concur with the following program: Monday—all meals wheatless; Tuesday—breakfast meatless, dinner wheatless; Wednesday—all meals wheatless; Thursday—breakfast meatless, dinner wheatless; Friday—breakfast wheatless, supper meatless; Saturday—all meals porkless, dinner wheatless; Sunday—breakfast meatless, supper wheatless. He stressed the fact that, "Every Day—All meals wasteless." "Meatless" according to Crowe's note meant no use of cattle, sheep or hog meats, fresh or preserved. He also urged the men to conserve milk and sugar for "soldiers at the front need them all."[37]

As a follow-up, he sent down the line to all mess halls a list of thirteen wheat and sugar saving recipes approved nationally by the U. S. Food Administration. He requested that all mess hall chefs try the recipes immediately with the understanding that no all-wheat breads were allowed, stating "timekeepers and others in charge of messes will be held responsible for seeing that a mixed-flour bread and pastry are baked." He continued to lecture on the waste previously seen in pre-packed field lunches and that now he wanted fruit sent out put in small "jelly glasses" instead of the quart-sized jars where much fruit sat uneaten and spoiled. Finally, Crowe thanked his men for contributing to a winning war effort and requested that if any man should have a helpful suggestion for conserving food or other rationed supplies to please let him know.

All this war-preparation and hysteria made Frank Crowe nervous, especially with the news that Linnie was expecting again. The anxious couple was still recovering from the loss of Frank Jr. Frank continued to be plagued by the memory Marie's death and the child she was carrying. Linnie's pregnancy went well, with Frank watching her closely for signs of fatigue and illness. The big day arrived on May 15, 1918 when Linnie gave birth to a strong healthy boy. Linnie insisted that they name the round-face happy child, John, for Frank's father. As the first, few dangerous days passed and melted into weeks, then months, both Frank and Linnie breathed a tremendous sigh of relief. Still, ever vigilant, the couple carefully hovered over the little boy.[38]

1918 saw America deeply involved in the war effort with the resulting drain on personnel and money. The Reclamation Service, although important to the overall war effort soon realized that financial and human resources would be cut back or curtailed. Despite this, Crowe in his annual report summed up the year claiming that 1918 "has been a red letter year in the irrigation development of the Flathead Project." He had started the year being told that no new monies would be forthcoming. In fact, the only revenue reserves still held barely covered "the few odd construction jobs being finished and to maintain a small skeleton organization to hold over until a new appropriation should be made available." Finally, Davis was able to successfully lobby for additional funds and in May $375,000 became available. Crowe became nervous waiting for the money as the weather, once again, continued dry. As the months rolled on "thousands of acres of spring sown grain would not germinate without irrigation." However, without money the irrigation system could not be completed. In the meantime, Crowe organized a Flathead Irrigation Association consisting of concerned farmers, civic leaders, and Reclamation Service personnel. He was very successful in this endeavor securing many new memberships and preaching, "come early and avoid the rush" movement on the part of farmers in their demand for water. Crowe needed to reemphasize, "That although the ditches were completed for many thousands of acres the reservoirs were far from complete and that all possible advantage should be taken of storing the early spring run-off in the lands and lower the heavy demand for mid-summer water."[39]

During the year, Crowe himself finally had to apply for a war deferment and Weymouth, as Chief of Construction for the Western states was given the responsibility to draw up the papers for all of his top engineers. Crowe's actual deferment papers are interesting to analyze, they start out with Weymouth stating the authority given to him by Secretary of the Interior to defer critical personnel from military service. A brief, yet detailed, work biography follows beginning from 1904 and the Lower Yellowstone Project. Then Weymouth elaborated on Crowe's present responsibilities emphasizing the importance of the crops that the farmers were producing. He stated, "At present the project is in a position to supply water for approximately 80,000 acres and when the project is completed will furnish water for approximately 134,500 acres." He added, "That by reason of his [Crowe] special fitness for the work he is doing, food supplies which are produced in excess of the needs of the people of the vicinity and can be used for war purposes, he is necessary to the adequate and effective operation of such project and cannot be replaced by another man more than 45 years of age or a woman of adequate qualification with substantial material loss and detriment to the adequate and effective operation thereof."[40]

When money finally did become available, Crowe moved, despite what he called "very unreliable and inefficient" labor, to rapidly finish construction of the: South Pablo and Hubbard Dams, Tabor Reservoir tunnel and controlling works, as well as begin work on various siphons and feeder canals.[41] Additionally, he was able to complete the Little Bitter Root Reservoir and river channel. Crowe also formed a special board of trustees to formulate plans for 1919 and completion of the project. As the year closed he reported, "the general prosperity of the settlers who have their lands in good shape for irrigating and understand irrigation methods is excellent. However, those farmers are very few. The great majority are 'dry-farm' wheat growers and know very little about the value of irrigation or the kind of crops necessary to produce best results." This was difficult for Crowe to deal with, as he was such a strong believer in the agricultural benefits of year-round water supply. Why farmers would want to limit their land's potential to one low return crop did not make sense. He also referenced the sale of over 3,000 acres of local "Indian lands" at a price of $27 per acre. He closed his comments by offering, "The one greatest need on the project to make it a great success is real farmers. The land is here and to a greater extent each year, water is available, but farmers as a whole have not yet grasped the fact that the latter is essential to the maximum development of the former."[42]

The following year of 1919, proved critical for Crowe, resorting in a significant career change. Yet, the year appeared to start out routinely with the usual outpouring of notices to men working in each of the Flathead divisions. Already concerned about budget matters, he now demanded that government horses be grazed on certain pastures and that for each horse-day worked the division would be charged grazing fee of $.08. Realizing that he was not happy and becoming totally bogged down in clerical duties, he spent more and more time in the field. Yet, there too he was not really needed. Each division had its own construction superintendent and since the construction techniques and procedures for building canals and earthen ditches are straightforward, he was acting as an inspector more than anything else. The challenge was gone. He needed something more, and beginning in March and continuing he began to use more and more of his accumulated annual leave to get away from his duties. Several of these leaves were multi-day and a couple of them for an entire week. This was unprecedented for Crowe, who usually refused to leave a construction project in the middle of operations. There is a strong possibility that he was beginning to look for construction opportunities elsewhere. When he returned from the March sojourn he found himself again caught up in issuing memoranda. One such notice in April of 1919 discussed the trivial topic of whether or not signs should be posted along canals and headworks to notify "meddlesome farmers" of the rules and regulations covering federal property. He did not know whether it was a good idea or not, and so, he sought the advice of his water masters. Rarely, in construction matters would Crowe seek advice, but he appeared uncomfortable making administrative decisions that had nothing to do with project construction.[43]

Congress authorized money for completing the project in April and Crowe began the final phase of project planning. Pay increases came through and Weymouth, possibly sensing Crowe's unhappiness for the routine work, put through another $300 raise. Davis approved the increase and for a time it appeared their jittery project manager would be satisfied. However, money was not what Crowe wanted and Weymouth probably knew that. In fact, Weymouth himself was weighed down with clerical and administrative responsibilities for construction in all the Western states. He too yearned to be in the field. Weymouth notified Crowe of the pay raise and sent a letter indicating that the salary boost was "a small reward for your loyal and efficient services in the Reclamation Service." With 18 days of accumulated leave, Crowe began using more and more of them, a sign that he either needed rest and relaxation with Linnie or he needed time to look for work elsewhere. To show the seriousness of the situation, Crowe's figures for the number of leave days still available did not agree with the figures kept in the Denver regional office. A series of back and forth communication ended in August with the Denver office conceding that Crowe's figures were correct. He had kept precise notes and he wanted every possible day. Something was about to give.[44]

On September 15, Crowe used two more of the remaining days of leave and when he came back, he typed out two letters of resignation. One letter went to Davis in Washington. It was short and to the point, "I hereby tender my resignation as Engineer and Project Manager of the Flathead Project, of the U. S. Reclamation Service, to take effect as soon as it is convenient to appoint a successor to my place." The other letter was more revealing, "After much deliberation I have reached the conclusion that in view of the present status of the Reclamation Fund I had better seek employment elsewhere. I feel that I am simply marking time." Realizing his close friendship with Weymouth and the need to thank him, Crowe ended, "It has taken considerable effort to break away from your organization after so many years of the most pleasant associations and I assure you that the many boosts you have given have all been appreciated, and it is with much regret that I feel obliged to take this step."[45]

Weymouth must have been somewhat surprised for now he wrote back pleading with Crowe to reconsider and promising more money and bigger challenges. Saying no to your mentor must have been tough and Weymouth was persuasive. After weeks of torment, Crowe relented saying "In view of the possibility of securing additional funds for the Service, I will withdraw my resignation and await developments for a while." Then in a deeply personal touch Crowe confided, "I would not quit you under any circumstances if you needed me but under present conditions we are about on an O. & M. basis [organization and management]." Crowe lets the proverbial cat-out-of-the-bag when he added; "I have had two flattering unsolicited offers from very substantial firms at about double my present salary." In conclusion, Crowe revealed how anxious he was about the resignation when he chided, "This kind of stuff makes me as restless as an I.W.W

(Industrial Workers of the World, a labor union with strong socialist tendencies)."[46]

Thanksgiving and Christmas must have been tough on both Frank and Linnie for now their future, which looked so bright when they first married, was up in the air. As 1920 started, Crowe waited for word of a new assignment. Nothing came from Denver or Washington. Money was still tight and Davis, who was pressing as much as he could with Congress, felt frustrated. A post-war recession gripped the country and President Woodrow Wilson, who had suffered a cerebral hemorrhage, lay incapacitated in his White House bed. Advisors scurried in to fill the power vacuum but general confusion prevailed. Rumors spread that his wife was running most of the day-to-day affairs. Congress, still trying to understand and cope with the economic downturn, was in no mood to increase spending on a large scale. In fact, Congress was more interested in helping promote the 18th Amendment officially sanctioning Prohibition, which they ratified on January 29. None of the national news looked good. During the same month, Attorney General A. Mitchell Palmer began another round of mass arrests of suspected radicals and enemies of the state. A sense of paranoia surrounded the country with no clear visible leadership.

Crowe waited, paced the floor, and talked with Linnie a lot about their options. He again, began taking days off and he brooded while on the job. Required to attend a meeting of the Flathead Irrigation Project on January 3 in Ronan, Crowe spoke after a lengthy round of speeches and discussions on the history and future of the region. Feeling tired and depressed, the sullen engineer briefly talked about his recent trip to Washington D. C. and the construction accomplishments of his hard-working crews. Crowe told the crowd of several score that the Reclamation Service was doing everything it could to put pressure on Congress to provide the necessary monies to finish the irrigation project. Other speakers that day painted a bleak picture of future progress. One member D. A. Deilwo, described as a "prominent member of the association," challenged the audience when he said, "Do we want to complete this project, or let it hang over us?" Hinting at moving in a new direction, he added, "Shall we avail these means [local support] or wait for congress to act?" According to one source, Deilwo angrily "attacked the dilatory methods of congress." In an interesting turn of events, Crowe sat and listened as the crowd exchanged accusations on the pros and cons of finishing the project. Several farmers explained that they were perfectly happy with the incomplete status of the project because "as soon as the project is completed payment must begin [from water users]." Deilwo's answer to this challenge was terse and to the point, declaring, "this was the argument of the man who is unwilling to give his neighbor the opportunity that has been given him." On the meeting went with political arguments dividing farmers, business owners, government engineers and Flathead Indian representatives.[47]

Upon his return home to St. Ignatius, Linnie observed that her husband needed a change. Reaching what seemed to be the end of his patience, Crowe typed out another resignation letter on January 22, 1920. As before, one letter went to Weymouth and one to Davis. To Weymouth he admitted, "It is with much regret that I am forced to make this decision. I have chosen construction as my life work and I feel that I have gone backwards during the past 2 years, and the future of the Service looks very blue." He continued, "I want to thank you again for the consideration you have always given me in the many years I have worked under your direction." Crowe knew that he should tell his mentor what his plans were and so he disclosed, "I have secured a one-third interest in a contracting firm, which now has an $85,000 road contract in eastern Washington and a $35,000 railroad contract out of Eureka, Montana." It was clear that Crowe wanted immediate release from the Service to join these two operations. He also added, "I expect to bid on a number of large road jobs that are coming up in this state in the near future. I also hope to land a few consulting jobs on private irrigation projects around the state [Montana]." To Davis he simply stated, "I want to thank you for the many opportunities I have been given in the Service and I assure you that I will always be proud that I have been a member of this 'honest-to-God' organization." Weymouth knew Crowe would not reconsider a second time, but Davis, who was beginning to appreciate Crowe's value to the Service tried to change his mind. He did not immediately approve the resignation and on February 12 he wrote back offering hope by saying, "Oil and gas leasing bill just passed i[e]nsuring large increase for Reclamation construction coming year. At what salary would you reconsider your resignation and accept assignment on large construction work. Wire answer through Denver." Crowe, flattered that the Reclamation Service director thought so highly of him, but he quickly responded, "I have taken 3 large contract jobs so cannot reconsider my resignation at this time." It was over, and once again, the ambitious and forward-looking engineer, ventured out on his own. Before leaving, Weymouth asked him to remain a consultant, for $20 a day, on future projects; he agreed.[48]

News spread through Montana that a new road-building spree was about to begin in their state. Considered by Congress to be an area posing excellent economic development potential, money was finally being authorized to network the sprawling region. George Lautz, a Missoula based civil engineer and promoter of Montana, announced in January of 1920 that highway construction in the Northwest will be receiving the "enthusiastic support of congress." Lautz spent six weeks in Washington D. C. where he consulted on road survey work and preparing a report to look into a reclassification of salaries for government engineers. Even without federal money, road associations popped up all around Montana at this time. There were proposals for "state highways" stretching hundreds of miles east and west as well as spur roads connecting isolated valley communities. Given the priority of roads over water, Crowe could see that, for the near future at least, irrigation construction would take a back seat to road paving. Conceding the uncountable times Crowe had difficulty with the gravel and dirt roads connecting

St. Ignatius to Ronan, Polson, Ravalli[49] and most other places in his district, he could see that a bright future lie in bidding and securing road contracts.

Professional engineering memoirs mention that Crowe teamed up with a Missoula-based contracting firm of "Rich & Marcus" that now became "Rich, Marcus and Crowe." This is substantiated by Crowe's letter to Weymouth stating that he had bought into a "one-third interest in a contracting firm." Crowe's resignation, effective February 29, 1920 coincides with a new railroad job starting near Eureka, Montana—the $35,000 job mentioned in Crowe's letter to Weymouth. Records show that A. L Markhus, a contractor from Ronan, Montana arrived in Eureka on February 26, 1920 to begin construction of a new logging railroad for the Howe Lumber Mills. Markhus probably met Crowe during the Flathead Project, as Ronan is a small town located just north of Crowe's St. Ignatius Reclamation office and it is likely that Markhus was involved in some of the ditch and canal work for Crowe during this time. Markhus and his crew quickly assembled equipment, including a large pile driver, in order to start work on erecting a train trestle to cross over the existing railroad tracks of the Great Northern line. There is no mention of Crowe actually being on the location. A possibility exists that Rich was handling the eastern Washington road job while Markhus was in Montana on this project. Crowe's location is not certain, but he had no previous experience on railroad building, but much on road construction. Also, the eastern Washington job was valued at nearly three times the Montana contract, therefore it must have been much more extensive requiring Crowe and Rich to provide dual supervision. This makes sense when you realize that within one year Crowe would be working again for the Reclamation Service, and in eastern Washington.[50]

The Rich, Markhus, Crowe business venture worked well for road, railroad, and small irrigation projects, but the trio was too small and under-funded to bid on any of the really large federal irrigation projects. By the fall of 1920, Crowe realized that financially he could do quite well with the present business arrangement, but if he wanted to build dams, he needed to rejoin the Reclamation Service. The ambitious engineer stayed in contact with Weymouth and others in the Reclamation Service and was kept informed of future projects and pending congressional appropriations. After only six months of building roads, Francis Trenholm Crowe yearned for an opportunity to build another dam. He learned from his contacts in eastern Washington that the federal government was interested in building a large dam in the Yakima Valley. Weymouth verified that funds had just been made available and that construction would begin in the spring of 1921. If his upstart protégé would rejoin the Reclamation Service, Weymouth promised to give him the top job as superintendent of construction on the Yakima project. On hearing this, Crowe notified his partners that he wanted out; the fledgling business group quickly broke up.

Chapter 4

"I am here to go to work."
1921

J.L. Lytel, serving as manager of the Reclamation Service Tieton Dam project, recalled receiving hundreds of job applications by January 11, 1921. This was to be expected as newspapers in the eastern Washington area reported late in 1920 that the Reclamation Service "might soon open camps at Rimrock" (site of Tieton Dam). Lytel was amazed that curious job seekers from as far away as Seattle were phoning him and sending letters of inquiry. He knew that the U. S. Senate and incoming President Warren G. Harding would need to give a final approval for appropriations to build the dam. Lytel stated, "The matter of starting work at Rimrock on the Tieton d[D]am has not been decided yet. While the appropriation bill passed the House of Representatives, the Senate has not yet passed it, and the funds are therefore not yet available. No applications for employment will be received until it is definitely known when the work will start."[1] By mid-March Lytel traveled east to make a personal pitch for the Tieton Dam and the Yakima irrigation projects.

On March 13, readers in the Yakima, Washington area read that the Reclamation Service had announced that Frank T. Crowe had recently been appointed to "have charge of the construction of the Tieton Dam." In the article, Crowe was touted as "one of the most skillful and experienced engineers in the Reclamation Service." Frank Weymouth, now chief engineer for the Service, knew that previous attempts to start construction had ended in failure and construction men in the area were anxiously awaiting news of renewed activity. Weymouth assured readers that the Denver office of the Bureau was already moving ahead with plans to improve the road between Yakima and Rimrock.[2]

Yakima residents learned that Crowe served as first assistant under Weymouth on the Arrowrock job in Idaho and that he supervised the building of Jackson Lake Dam and "several dams on the Flathead project in Montana." Readers discovered that since Tieton Dam was expected to be a "difficult piece of hydraulic construction," the Reclamation Service sent its best hydraulic engineer, Frank T. Crowe. C. E. Crownover, a Reclamation engineer in the Yakima office explained that Crowe and Weymouth would be arriving in the area shortly to in-spect the existing Rimrock camp.[3]

The next day the Reclamation Service informed the public that Secretary of the Interior Albert Fall and a delegation of 50 to 60 Congressmen planned to visit irrigation projects in the West. Their intentions included collecting informa-tion, first-hand, on the widely scattered construction projects of dams, canals, and general irrigation works. The trip would cover "all irrigation states in the west, beginning in Wyoming and running through to the Pacific coast states and then south through Arizona and New Mexico, expenses of the trip would be paid by the various irrigation associations." The four-week trip included an intensive look at Tieton Dam and the Columbia River Basin projects.[4]

With the widespread excitement created by this resumption of work an-nouncement on Tieton Dam project and of Secretary Fall's visit, the *Yakima Morning Herald* newspaper requested census data on the current water and irrigation situa-tion for the Yakima Valley area. The paper proudly boasted, "The Yakima River and its tributaries supply 64 percent of the supply of water used for irrigation in the state of Washington and this water irrigated, during the crop season of 1919, a total of 337,293 acres."[5] The Naches River, of which the Tieton River is the main tributary, furnished water for irrigating almost 20,000 acres. It would be here, on the Tieton River, that the dam would be built, hopefully providing a substantial increase in irrigated acreage.

It was during all this publicity and excitement that an equally excited Frank Crowe arrived on the scene. Frank and Linnie arrived by car Tuesday March 22, a cool cloudy afternoon, and with his wife checked into a hotel room, Crowe reported to Crownover. Like an anxious young colt straining at the starting line, Crowe stated that he was anxious to start the work. With Weymouth, J. L. Savage, and other engineers heading out to meet with him and go over the technical engi-neering problems, the Yankee engineer from Maine quickly scanned topographic maps and reviewed government-building specifications. Late that day newspaper reporters caught up with Crowe. "I am here to go to work," he announced. Crowe made it clear that he wanted to see the existing camp facilities and the dam site as soon as possible. Asked about his priorities, he responded, "It will take some time to put the camp [at Rimrock] in shape to take care of the crew." He added, "but we are going to take as little time as possible to get things to moving." He explained that he and Crownover would make a complete survey of the Tieton Dam site and the Rimrock construction camp the next day and that he expected to bring in tal-ented engineers and dam builders from previous jobs. "I have heads of depart-ments moving here from all parts of the country, and they will soon begin arriv-ing," he said. In a rare testimony of detail, Crowe specified, "my master mechanic is coming here from Texas, my chief clerk from the Flathead project and several of the clerical force from the Denver office." Reporters asked him about the possi-bility of hiring local labor, to which Crowe replied, "I presume there are old employees here who are wanting to get on the job. It will take some time to get a line [telephone at Rimrock] up, but we will soon be ready to push things."[6]

The local Yakima paper introduced Crowe to the community with a brief article talking about his previous experience. The paper mentioned his dam building on the Flathead project and his work on towering Arrowrock Dam. The article said that Crowe "was assistant to Chief Engineer Weymouth in the construction of the Arrow Rock dam on the Boise project, acknowledged to be one of the finest structures the Reclamation Service has yet built." It was noted that Crowe had been out of the Reclamation Service for over a year while he engaged in private contracting with Missoula, Montana serving as his headquarters. In the article Crowe admitted, "I know nothing about the Rimrock dam except what I can get out of the blue prints. I am anxious to get up there and take a look at the job. I will be able then to form some definite ideas about the nature of the work. There will be a conference of Reclamation consulting engineers here about the middle of April to determine upon some of the construction problems. Mr. Weymouth told me to come up and look things over preparatory to taking part in that conference."[7] Crowe explained that Chief Engineer F.E. Weymouth of Denver, D.C. Henny of Portland, James Munn of the Denver office, C.E. Crownover and himself would make up the board that would discuss all the engineering problems raised in the construction at Rimrock and the decisions reached at that conference would layout the schedule and program for work.

Crowe spent the rest of the day getting himself and Linnie settled in the Commercial Hotel and in meetings with Crownover. Crowe revealed to Crownover that he was called in for the Tieton Dam project because of his background in hydraulic construction, which would be essential on the job. Specifications noted that a 115-foot trench needed to be cut into the bedrock, followed by the erection of a substantial concrete corewall. The corewall, with a still undetermined thickness, needed to rise up 220 feet above the riverbed making a total height of 330 feet. By early twentieth-century standards, this loomed as a formidable undertaking. He concluded by saying that the final dam would extent 1100 feet from side to side and be "built of earth heavily blanketed with rock."[8] Crownover then responded by providing information on the state of the Rimrock construction camp. Crowe was pleased to find out that the previously built camp buildings remained strong and livable. Crowe wanted to build the dam, not the camp. The impatient engineer remarked, "I dislike to go through the interval of making camp. The time it takes to construct a mess house, bunkhouses, machine shops and the like, in fact the whole process of getting ready gets on my nerves. I want to get busy on the job of construction." Upon hearing this news, Crownover assured Crowe that the Rimrock camp only needed a restocking of provisions and an overhauling of equipment.

In another newspaper interview that same day, Crowe talked about the contribution of Yakima farmers using irrigation (called "irrigationists") on the Flathead Project. He acknowledged them as pioneers and community builders, and the "most practical and progressive settlers there," who received their preliminary training in the Yakima Valley. Crowe explained that most early Flathead settlers were teachers, doctors, lawyers, preachers, and business men unfamiliar with agricultural work, knowing little about irrigation and the "handling of water in growing crops." In a final praise, he commented that in the last few years many experienced irrigators had come onto the Flathead project, with most of them coming from the Yakima Valley. "I want to say," said Mr. Crowe, "that Yakima farmers are pointing the way and leading the development of the Flathead project." When asked about his first impressions of Yakima, he noted that the area looked beautiful. Much to his surprise and delight Crowe saw green fields and many new and different flowers. An elated Crowe remarked, "Yakima valley is fully a month earlier that Montana in its crop season."[9]

A light rain began to fall as Frank and Linnie ate dinner at a Yakima restaurant. It had been a big day for Crowe, meeting community members and answering questions from townspeople about the construction process and when the hiring would begin. That evening Crowe learned that his arrival in Yakima provided a sad irony to another event that occurred that day. Fred R. Reed, a Yakima pioneer and former Idaho resident died. Reed, like Crowe, had been one of the original irrigation boosters in Idaho; he even served as Managing Director of Idaho's Reclamation Association. Crowe had heard of Reed's irrigation deeds as a resident of the Boise area, and he had learned that the irrigationist's career included a brief stint as America's Commissioner to the Panama Pacific Exposition.[10] The twenty-year resident of Idaho had left a strong legacy for irrigation development in the Yakima Valley. Everyone knew that Reed was enthusiastic about the future possibilities of irrigation expansion once Tieton Dam was built. On the day he died, Frank Crowe arrived in town.

Early the next morning Frank was surprised to hear that Crownover invited Linnie to join the expedition to the dam site. Crowe's boss explained that Mrs. Crownover would also be coming along for the thirty-mile trip to the Rimrock campsite. Linnie eagerly agreed to go. Rarely was she asked to accompany her husband on business trips such as these. As the foursome finished breakfast at the Commercial Hotel and walked to Crownover's car, they noticed the clouds gathering and darkening. The road headed north following the Naches River for eighteen miles then cut due west to follow the Tieton River. This heavily treed area, today part of the Snooualmie National Forest, reminded the Crowes of areas in Idaho; Linnie could see that the vegetation looked similar to that found near her home in Boise. What started out as a trace of rain in Yakima became a downpour as the pair of engineers and their wives reached the construction camp at Rimrock. Not to be deterred by the elements, Crowe insisted on inspecting every building, including the workers' dormitories. By noon, Crowe and Crownover joined their wives in the mess hall for lunch, soaking wet and caked with mud.

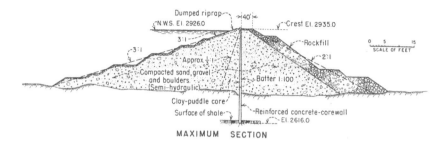

Section diagram of Tieton Dam. (USBR)

Despite the deluge, that continued all afternoon, a moderate southerly wind kept the temperature a comfortable 65 degrees. Linnie knew that her husband would not be happy unless he saw all the construction machinery. By late afternoon, Crowe decided to call it a day, and the party climbed back into the car for the slow trip back to Yakima.[11] Dodging recently formed potholes and swirling rivulets of running water Crownover drove carefully hoping to reach the paved Naches Road. Several potholes proved to be complete washouts and one of them caused damage to Crownover's transmission. Repeated attempts to move the car resulted in stripped gears and a frustrated and embarrassed Crownover was forced to take an umbrella and walk for help. Frank stayed with Linnie and Mrs. Crownover. By the time Crowe and the party reached Yakima, everyone was exhausted and hungry. Before dinner Crowe talked with a newspaper reporter about the visit to Rimrock. "It looks like a good job and it is one of the best camps I have ever seen in the Service," Crowe declared. Asked what would probably be the first construction work done he said, "We will finish driving the tunnel."[12] He went on to explain that a tunnel running through solid rock, used to channel the river around the construction site, would receive top priority. Without a dry riverbed, serious construction work could not start. Workers had practically completed the tunnel before the previous work closed down in 1917. Subsequent to the shutdown, Service engineers determined that the dam must be constructed several hundred feet below the first location, making it necessary to drive an additional 700 feet of tunnel heading.

In another unusual display of public detail Crowe told the reporter, "a crew will be put on the tunnel as the first construction work." He continued, "and following that we will begin digging the trench of bed rock to put in the corewall. Weather conditions were not very favorable at Rimrock while we were there, as it was raining, but I saw enough to realize that it is going to be a good job. The camp is one of the best I have ever seen during my experience in the Service. I thought we had a good camp at Arrowrock but this is a better one. With the camp in the condition it is we should soon be able to get things going." Crowe told the reporter that he was impressed with the size and condition of the cabins; he stated, "I was very glad that there are so many cabins in the camp, because it's easier to get along with the men if living conditions are of the best." He found the house built originally for C. H. Swigart, when he was construction engineer, very well located and ample for his use. Crowe saw that the hospital and mess hall had burned the previous summer, but he stated that all the other buildings could be utilized and work would begin without waiting for any camp construction.

Within two days, the impatient engineer hired a cook and instructed him to buy whatever supplies needed to feed a crew of twenty or thirty. The cook also received orders to move, post haste, to the Rimrock construction camp and prepare the kitchen and mess hall. At the same time, Crowe interviewed and hired several men with road building experience and sent them out to begin repairing the worn, pothole-ridden route to the camp. While conducting work interviews Crowe was meticulous in asking the same questions of each applicant. He wanted to know their previous construction work experience, if they had special experience in large-scale excavation or in concrete placing. At the end of the short interview, Crowe either hired the man or he explained that he was not in a position to hire a large crew yet—but to fill-out a contact memoranda, listing addresses and contact information. Many of the men not hired initially, would in time, join the payroll once the main operations started.

Continuing to feel public pressure to hire local unemployed men, Crowe announced that he expected to hire about 100 men, by the end of April, to begin work in the tunnel excavation. In the meantime smaller crews hired on repairing roads, machinery, and buildings at Rimrock. The construction camp needed to be fully operational, and able to house and feed a large crew of several hundred. He also announced that the wages paid to common laborers would be the same as the prevailing rate on other public works in the Yakima area. This translated to approximately four dollars a day. Crowe told all newly hired men that the payroll clerk would deduct a small amount from weekly paychecks to cover the cost of room and board, but not to exceed $1.40 a day. When asked about higher paying supervisory positions, Crowe replied that he had already engaged a few of his foremen and "master mechanics" as well as "some members of my clerical force." He knew the importance of considering local talent, so he promised to interview "several local applicants" as the need arose.[13]

With the first busy days behind him, Frank had the weekend to explore the town of Yakima with Linnie. They continued to take most of their meals at the Commercial Hotel Grill, where special discount prices teased room guests. The Public Market, a favorite for locals, provided Frank and Linnie their first look at Washington State grocery prices. They were pleasantly surprised to find fruits and vegetables, hard to get in Boise during the entire year, readily available in Yakima. Large sweet strawberries went for $.30 a box and leaf lettuce, advertised as crisp and tender, sold for $.20 a pound. A tour of Yakima revealed a surprisingly sophisticated business development. Large department stores, automobile dealerships and repair shops, full-line food stores, a variety of specialty outlets, and movie theaters all thrived. The most popular entertainment focus proved to be the Majestic Theatre. If Frank and Linnie wanted to relax and catch a movie the first Saturday night in Yakima, they would have paid $.25 apiece to see a "Big Double Header." Receiving top billing was "The Torrent" starring Eva Novack and Jack Perrins. The film offered the ultimate escape adventure fantasy—"just a man and a woman on a desert island. The conventions of society faded vaguely away. Then one day there were strange footprints on the sand—was it friend, or a foe?" Novack played a bored high society "flapper," while Perrins appeared as the perfect 1920s hero—a handsome adventurous aviator.[14]

With Easter approaching Linnie could see the Yakima stores preparing to push their spring merchandise. Kohl's Shoe Company declared in an advertisement, "We have the most beautiful Easter footwear ever shown. These include strap pumps, oxfords, colonials, and 'dame fashions.'" Not far away Grinspan's Clothing Store declared "We must have cash regardless—to pay our bills now due." They slashed prices on hats, shoes, and "men's furnishings." Shoes stores proliferated throughout the town and the largest, Walen's Big Shoe Shop, announced that their Easter specials included men's and boys' shoes for low prices starting at $6.65. On North Second Street, Yakima residents often completed their grocery shopping at Schwalbe's Groceteria. Here eager shoppers found mundane, but necessary items like white soap selling at a price of $1.00 for twenty large bars, or special occasional treats such as their famous five-pound cans of strained pure honey for $1.00. Potential customers could phone the store, three digit numbers (Schwalble's phone was 553) and check on current prices and stock availability. Yakima also boasted several medical and dental offices. Claiming to be the largest in town, Rogers Brothers dentists worked on their patients in their second story offices above Janeck's Drug Store. Claiming, "our work is painless, because we use—Anesthesia," the Rogers Brothers had been in business for over fifteen years. They advertised their longtime success on the fact that they "use: x-ray examinations in doubtful cases, extreme gentleness always, immediate service, and a written guarantee."[15]

At this same time, J. L. Lytel returned from his Washington trip to pitch for funding and consult with Reclamation officials. He told interested community members that Yakima residents should consider themselves lucky if the project received funds to move ahead with construction of Tieton Dam. After days of meetings with Reclamation Service Director A. P. Davis and the Secretary of the Interior, Lytel explained that he spent two days in Denver where he conferred with Weymouth, Chief Engineer for the Reclamation Service. Lytel discovered from

Davis and Weymouth that federal construction money was limited. In discussing the congressional appropriation bill he commented, "The sundry civil bill carried nice appropriations, but the trouble is that there is a lack of money in the reclamation fund." His understanding of the situation centered on the fact that Congress had authorized the spending of several millions for the full Yakima reclamation project, but the money was not available and the chances of it coming in during the current fiscal year appeared slim. He said, "The reclamation fund is made up of money coming back in re-payments on reclamation projects and from the leasing of coal and oil lands. Payments are slow from both these sources, and there is little money in the fund at this time for new construction. In my opinion, the only really big undertaking in the Reclamation Service for the coming year will be the construction at Rimrock, and Yakima is lucky in getting this recognition from the department." Lytel finished his point by disclosing, now more realized after talking with Reclamation officials, the depressed economic situation of eastern businesses and Mid-western farmers suffering from low-priced crops. Mining companies in the East and Midwest too, reeled from dropping activity; mining employment was sporadic, with men holding jobs for two or three weeks only. "Conditions are much better in the West and I am glad to get out here again. Work will be resumed at Rimrock and something like $600,000 will be spent there during the coming year. The storage water contract for the Wapato project [connected to Tieton] was worked out while Mr. Holt and I were in Washington and is now up to the president for signature. I think it was finally worked out to the satisfaction of all concerned," he summarized.[16]

Crowe now divided his time between checking the progress of the construction camp refurbishing at Rimrock and dealing with a flood of job applications. A meticulous head count revealed that over 200 men applied for work by March 25 and that number ballooned to 500 by the end of the week. Faced with a hiring decision, the veteran builder decided to give preference to former employees of Yakima Valley irrigation projects or men with dam building experience. Still, he knew there would not be enough work for even half the number of applicants, until full-scale operations began months later. Frustrated, and needing an escape from office pressures, Crowe delegated hiring responsibility to another engineer and turned his attention to the dam site. At Rimrock, he examined the water supply and the sewer system. He supervised the installation of a gravity flume that would supply water for a turbine generator. This generator supplied much of the early electrical and lighting power.

On March 30, 1921, Crowe's mentor, Weymouth arrived on the scene heading a small party of Reclamation Service engineers. Their purpose was to consult with Crowe, check his progress in establishing the camp, and plan for possible technical difficulties. Weymouth first conducted a full inspection of the site, escorted by Crowe, and then organized a multi-day conference, finalizing the construction sequence of operations.

Accompanying Weymouth were Crowe's ex-partner James Munn, back with the Reclamation Service as a consulting engineer, and J. L. Savage, another Crowe colleague from the earliest days and currently a top-notch design engineer. Joining Crowe and the three Denver engineers were consultant, D. C Henny from Portland, Lytel and Crownover. Savage immediately wanted to review the blueprints for the actual construction of the corewall and to check to see if Crowe thought modifications were needed. In these early days of large dam building, it was common to have original engineering plans re-drawn following field inspections that uncovered unfavorable bedrock conditions or errors in stream flow calculations.

For example, the location of Tieton Dam had already been changed from the original specifications, moving the dam 700 feet downstream when it was discovered that the dam could not be tied into bedrock properly. The strength of the foundation literally rested on the durability, and therefore the composition of the bedrock. This change in the location necessitated an extension of the tunnel driven to make the detour for the river during the time of construction and later to be used as the outlet for the reservoir. The team of engineers approved Crowe's new tunnel extension and his plan to begin that work first, using about 100 men. Munn and Weymouth looked carefully at the proposed plans for the all important inner corewall. The concrete corewall needed to be 115 feet deep, and excavators needed to shovel out a huge trench for this purpose. Crowe made it clear that this work rated his second highest priority, with preliminary digging to commence shortly. Weymouth wanted to know how Crowe planned to handle the huge task of moving the excavated muck (earth and rock). Crowe responded with a detailed plan for using hydraulic machinery to initiate an "around-the-clock" operation. Much of the muck would be "recycled" as top fill around the rising corewall. Savage, reviewing the corewall dimensions must have been awed by the sheer size of the proposed monolith. Rising 220 feet above ground level and stretching 930 along the crest line and with a toe thickness of 100 feet, this "inner dam," by itself would be one of the largest structures built by the Reclamation Service.[17]

Lytel, as the local Reclamation Service representative, with an eye and ear for local interest, brought up the topic of camp rebuilding. He had convinced Crowe to support his idea to have the hotel and Y.M.C.A. building in Rimrock, both destroyed in the 1920 fire, rebuilt as soon as possible. Lytel reasoned that curious "auto tourists" and Yakima citizens would want to make frequent visits to the dam during the period of construction. Crowe balked at first, fearing crowds might interfere with the work. Lytel insisted, and Crowe eventually conceded. After receiving approval on this point, Weymouth asked Crowe to go over his proposed time schedule for construction. Records revealed 40 men employed on the road crew and in "making the camp ready" for beginning construction. Weymouth and company looked impressed when Crowe disclosed that actual dam construction would commence within three weeks. Crowe went on to explain that obtaining personnel was not the problem, but rather acquisition of construction machinery, hauling trucks, and electrical supplies. Munn and Weymouth examined the large stack of worker applications and were impressed to hear of the hundreds of phone and letter applications made to Crowe, many included Reclamation Service veterans. Many of them expressly stated that they wanted to work on the big dam with "Mr. Crowe." Crowe told Weymouth that the wages for common labor had been tentatively fixed at $4 a day with $1.50 for board, with the provision that if board can be furnished for less the price will be cut.

At the conclusion of the conference visit on April 1 Weymouth announced, "Everything is ready for full steam ahead on the Tieton [D]dam at Rimrock. All plans have been worked out definitely as the result of our conference," said Weymouth. "Things were fairly well settled before we came but we went over the situation again and made some minor changes in details. The principle of them is the method of handling the material for the dam. We thought we would move it into place by hydraulics but owing to the nature of the material we have concluded to handle it with an electric shovel and load it in cars to be hauled to the fill. Once there it will be sluiced into place." Arriving back in Yakima at 10:00 p.m. Weymouth and Munn boarded their train for Denver. At the same time Crowe answered questions about the conference, "Things are moving." said Crowe, "I am going to Rimrock tomorrow to stay put. My furniture went up today and I am on the job. In about two weeks we can put on some men for actual construction work, first on the tunnel and next on the construction of the corewall and both jobs will be driven along at once. We will have at least 350 men when things get opened up. We tuned up the electric plant today and will turn on juice tomorrow."[18]

Crowe used this opportunity to describe the actual corewall construction process, which he termed as the "tunnel and stope" procedure. Using this method a shaft would first be driven down to the bedrock and a tunnel dug for a "convenient distance." Earth and rock would be "stoped out" (removed) and the concrete immediately placed for the corewall. Then the tunnel would be extended and the next section of the corewall would be completed. When quizzed on the subject of wages, he explained that the previously announced rate of $4.00 a day and $1.50 for board had been changed to $3.00 a day for (an eight hour shift) for "common labor," with additional charges of $.40 for each meal taken and $.15 a day for lodging. Crowe quickly added that this amounted to a significant decrease in daily wages; each worker's lodging included a complete "equipment of bed clothing."[19]

Within a week of Weymouth's return to Denver and Crowe's permanent move to the Rimrock construction camp, Arthur P. Davis, Reclamation Service director, announced to the world plans to build the "highest dam in the world." Making front-page news in the Yakima paper, townspeople read the article eagerly. Whether Weymouth, Munn, or Savage had discussed the announcement and future plans to build the Boulder Canyon Dam with him is not known.

Weymouth, as chief engineer, carried overall responsibility for the early investigations of site selection, while Savage drew up preliminary blueprints. The people of Yakima learned that this new dam would dwarf their soon to be Tieton Dam—rising, according to the report, to more than 500 or 600 feet within the canyon walls. Engineers were already floating down the turbulent Colorado River preparing to bore into the bedrock beneath. The sheer size of the resulting reservoir seemed enormous for the times. Compared to the projected size of Tieton Lake or reservoir, the lake that would form behind the Boulder Canyon Dam would be an ocean, estimates planned that the water would be backed up for 30 to 50 miles. They also learned that the world's tallest dam then in existence was the recently completed 348-foot Arrowrock Dam, built by Reclamation Service with the help of Frank Crowe. A listing of other high dams including: Shoshone Dam in Wyoming at 328 feet, Elephant Butte on the Rio Grande in New Mexico at 300 feet, and the Roosevelt Dam of the Salt River in Arizona at 290 feet, would be miniatures when positioned next to this newly proposed Colorado monolith. Davis explained that Congress had already appropriated $20,000 for the initial investigation and "local irrigators" contributed an additional $75,000. In an optimistic tone, Davis said that a site had been identified and preliminary borings taken. "While these are incomplete, bedrock has been located at a number of points and the outlook is favorable," Davis said.[20] The thirty-eight year old engineer, Frank Crowe continued to concentrate on the work at-hand even though the golden opportunity of a lifetime was already beginning hundreds of miles to the south. It would be years before Congress came through with the money to build the dam and years before the Reclamation Service would be authorized to move ahead with construction. For now, the ambitious builder needed to focus on the job at hand.

Frank helped Linnie move their belongings into the small, but comfortable, construction camp cabin. With sewer, running water, and electricity Linnie had it better than most in the camp that still awaited full amenities. She made it her concern to visit the other cabins, greeting newcomers, helping them settle into camp life. She constantly dealt with scores of visitors all searching for jobs. They wanted to know where her husband, "the big boss," could be found. The barrage of inquiries continued. He had only a small idea of the high unemployment situation. However, matters worsened. By April 20 with over 300 workers already employed on the camp construction and excavation Crowe complained about the situation. "This job is certainly well advertised," said Crowe. The steady tramp of up to fifteen job seekers, and their families, arrived on the scene daily. "The applicants are drifting in from all quarters of the northwest. Many of them walk in and others come in jitneys [a small bus or van type vehicle]." He added, "We will have no need for an employment agency but it keeps one man busy telling them there is no work at present for more men than we have employed."[21] Part of Crowe's frustration centered on the fact that with one crew digging in the main

tunnel and two crews in the cutoff tunnels there was no room to increase operations. Once the concrete placing commenced, he planned to hire more workers.

In an amazing display of energy, Crowe appeared everywhere on the job
site and soon earned the reputation for being a tough, but fair boss. He trusted his
foremen and supervisors, yet he wanted to see every aspect of the job. He even
supervised the rebuilding of the camp power plant as they increased its output
capacity from 200 to 1000 kilowatts. Wanting to take advantage of the good
weather, he rushed the installation of power lines so that heavy machinery could
be used. Almost daily, the conscientious engineer traveled back and forth to Yakima.
In town, he checked on the supply deliveries, and he sent telegrams to subcontractors and to the Reclamation Office in Denver. Weymouth wanted to be kept abreast
of Crowe's progress. In an effort to build camaraderie among the newly formed
construction crews, Crowe allowed a drilling contest between two contending
subcontracting firms as to "the efficiency of the jack drills they are seeking to
sell."[22]

Drilling indeed became the focus over the next week as Crowe reported
that his tunnel crews were struggling through some of the hardest rock layers
known. Andesite, as Crowe understood, is of volcanic origin, containing Horn-
blende and traces of other materials found in Basalt. Known as a tough material to
drill, miners nonetheless found that it "breaks out," or cracks and crumbles away
along expected lines of fracture. Once the tunnel miners put a few days behind
them, they were able to push ahead with five to fifteen feet of excavation a day.
Under the circumstances, Crowe considered this good progress. He reported that
the tunnel would serve to divert the Tieton River during construction and later,
would be the outlet for the reservoir. In this capacity, the tunnel had to be lined
with concrete and made structurally strong. Crowe enthusiastically commented at
this stage of the work that the tunnel would be "one of the finest outlets ever
constructed." He also revealed a strict timetable and the start of a swing shift—
and possibly a third, if needed. The no-nonsense engineer happily watched new
crews learn to work together, improving efficiency with each day. Some men quit
within days of signing on, most stayed and the labor turnover rate remained low.
This was good news to Crowe and the Reclamation Service, yet 1000 men still
waited for their opportunity to earn a spot. Crowe reminded prospective workers
that he was not anticipating any "material increase to the [work] force in the near
future."[23]

The first sign of inclement weather hit the Yakima area during this week,
alternating between "cold rain and snow storm." Crowe inspected the tunnel operation with a keen eye on eliminating standing water and identifying possible
mudslide zones. Foremen encouraged their men that everything possible was being done to keep the tunnel areas dry. By mid-week, the workers fought with a
whipping wind that turned bad conditions worse. Everything loose had to be tied
down. A safety announcement warned careless men of the serious consequences

inherent in strong windy conditions. Word spread that the "big boss" never gave a second chance to anyone breaking safety regulations. Workers scurried about locating loose sheets of wood and metal, always a problem during heavy winds, securing them in sheds and under tarps. Crowe refused to allow any let down in the tunnel work. This would become one of his trademarks and he would be criticized for his relentless efforts to complete large dams, such as Hoover Dam, despite inclement weather and/or unsafe working environments. Crowe defenders argued that correctly followed safety procedures minimized injuries, regardless of weather conditions. In this case, the tunnels remained dry and the excavation continued without serious medical injuries.

The Rimrock construction camp, by May, began to take on the look of any other Washington town, complete with steam heat, hot water, and garbage collection. "But so wonderful is the pressure from the central heating plant that the house[s] fairly leak steam," wrote an excited reporter. "There is an exhaust on each house—in the place where the hose faucet usually figures in the city home—and there is a constant and chorused sizzling from the various buildings except for the time between 9 p. m. and 5 a. m. when the steam is turned off at the central station." Alluding to the camp's hot water system the reporter declared, "This high temperature version of the Wild Cat [C]creek, which supplies the water for the camp, is a godsend to the reclamation housewife on wash day." It was true that Linnie had a separate "wash house" piped with running water, and her privately owned "electric boiler" and wringer. The small wood sided cottages were "sealed and stained and contain tiny but adequate kitchens, a living room, one or more bed rooms, and modern plumbing bathrooms."[24]

The home accommodations termed "cozy" by the reporter, remained open to married men exclusively, with limited opportunities even for them. Most single men lived in "Bunkville" a collection of bunkhouses and dormitories. Termed "clean and comfortable," the double deck bunkhouses provided some privacy in that they offered single rooms. The dormitory, affectionately termed the "bull pen" provided little privacy and was usually reserved for the newly hired single worker. As the worker "proved out" he could put his name on the list for a bunkhouse opening. Two large laundries allowed workers to wash their soiled and dirty clothes as often as they needed. Strings of hanging laundry became a common site around the bunkhouse.

Frank Crowe's role as field engineer in charge of construction now changed to include that of a city manager. This was his first job where a large number of residents, up to 1000 eventually, resided. Familiar with construction life from previous jobs, Rimrock presented him with new challenges foremost of which was sanitation. Crowe demanded that the camp be kept clean at all times. His orders expressly stated, "No open sewers, no uncovered garbage cans, no standing water to breed flies, or disease." He had a shipment of small black pigs brought in to the garbage disposal area, a short distance from the camp. The plan called for the little porkers to fatten up on the garbage, eventually ending up as "pork chops and sausage at the mess." Canned milk was the norm at the mess hall, but soon the J. H. Parmetier Ranch made a deal to supply five gallons of "cow's milk" every day. In total, the small village of 150 dwellings looked impressively stable to visitors by May of that year. The engineering staff, including Crowe and the clerical staff of Reclamation Service personnel lived on the overlooking hill. Workers with families and the single men lived in accommodations flanking the river and slightly upstream from the work. Few complained of any problems, for those hired knew that they were fortunate to have a home, a job, and three square meals a day.

One of the first items on Crowe's list of city manager duties included taking inventory of onsite government merchandise that had been stored from the original camp startup in 1917. Investigating the storage warehouse erected in 1917, Crowe discovered large quantities of old supplies. "Everything under the sun is there, from pipe couplings, to rat traps," the local newspaper reported. The report continued, " Dishes, blankets, coffee pots, sheets, even a little old printing press are stored upstairs, while one corner of the downstairs is a complete hardware shop." Crowe had everything cataloged and reconditioned for use. He also saw the need to provide proper medical and dental care. Though the original hospital had burned down years before, he ordered the construction of a new modern structure, one able to care for workers and their families. He made inquires into hiring a permanent physician and nurses. In addition, Crowe conceived of a plan to have a Yakima dentist "hold regular office hours at the camp on certain days." With an incomplete hospital and no resident physician, Crowe ordered one of his foremen to serve in an "advisory capacity." According to one report, this meant that he "describes the curative properties of the various pills, the men describe their symptoms and between them they match up the symptoms and the pills." Unbelievably, there were no reported cases of misdiagnosis! With Crowe's strict safety regulations in place and stiff penalties for violations, no serious accidents occurred in the first few months of operation.[25]

The government had planned for a recreation room and Crowe found money in his budget to bring in six billiard tables, stock a reading room and a card room, barber shop and a small movie theater. Films, usually low cost B-versions changed every two or three days. The recreation hall and shops came under the Reclamation Service's jurisdiction, and more directly, under Frank Crowe's control. One of his first decisions found the engineering "mayor" ruling on a request from "ex-soldiers" to set up a branch of the Y. M. C. A. at Rimrock. Advised by some to turn down this request, as it might lead to a host of other similar requests from civic groups, Crowe remembered his earlier discussions with Lytel. American Legion adjutant, Henry Connell described the interest that World War I veterans had for work on the dam and for development of the Rimrock community. Connell informed Frank Crowe of the sheer number of letters he received from "men in all parts of the country wanting a job on the dam." Many of them did not even know the name of the dam or the project, simply describing it as "the dam at the big rock." Sadly, many of these unemployed veterans along with numerous others continued to stream into Rimrock seeking jobs. Approving the request for the Y. M. C. A., Crowe next asked the local newspaper to, once again, let the people know that no jobs were available. The announcement failed and more men arrived. Many of these desperate job seekers walked the thirty plus miles from Yakima, arriving in Rimrock fatigued. Crowe noticed that a large number of them were quite old and in need of medical attention. "It seems a pity that they should make the effort in vain," he told a reporter.[26]

Even with an adequate recreation hall, Crowe knew that he needed to serve nutritious good tasting food to satisfy his hungry army of workers. He hired steward Roy Templeton, a veteran of camp cooking. Templeton's responsibilities included supervising the meal service for 300 to 500 men, with 100 to 150 per shift. Helping Templeton were fifteen cooks and assorted number of "flunkeys" [flunkies], all trained to work as a team in an efficient manner. Templeton's experience with federal dam projects included Bumping Lake Dam and Meadow Creek Irrigation Project. He enjoyed showing off his first-rate kitchen and the "modern" machinery in it. He was particularly proud of his new potato-peeling device. The round metal container sported a rough metal perforated whirling bottom into which the spuds were dropped. Water was added, and then the electric switch turned on. "The potatoes bob about very excitedly, losing a section of their jackets here and there till they come out skinless, save for a portion about the eyes—even this could be ground off, but it would be wasteful, so the spuds are quickly gone over by hand to remove the specks," a visitor to the kitchen noted.

Templeton's kitchen boasted a "huge range" and two electric soup kettles. His cooks used an electric griddle to make delicious hot cakes that were served at every breakfast. With a giant mixing machine Templeton brought together flour, eggs, sugar, and shortening to produce bread and assorted "concoctions." One large coffee pot held "gallons" of coffee; dam workers were known to love their coffee, whereas few consumed tea. After a meal, "flunkeys" cleaned the plates and loaded the dishes into large electric dishwashers. Templeton knew of Crowe's order to "keep everything as clean as possible." To this end, Templeton checked the cooking and eating areas regularly. Once in awhile, Crowe walked into the kitchen in unscheduled inspection checks. The sumptuous meals that Templeton served provided each worker with a "plentiful bounty," Crowe encouraged an "all you can eat policy." An average dinner [lunch] consisted of "a stew, a couple of kinds of meat, two or three vegetables, one or more varieties of pie, and a couple of kinds of cake." The cost for three meals remained at $1.20 per day, averaging out to $.40 a meal, "No restaurant in Yakima would set up such a menu at an average price of 40 cents per meal," one local visitor noted.[27]

Most of the foodstuffs arrived daily from the nearby town of Naches and

Yakima. Three trucks were "kept busy" delivering food and Templeton insisted that everything be boxed and clearly marked, as to its contents. "Eggs," the master cook declared, "must be on top." He went through several dozens cases of the precious cargo a day. Once delivered, the eggs and other temperature sensitive foods were stored in special "compartments in the cellar." If the canned goods, sometimes not individually labeled, were misplaced in the cellar, the workers ate "Irish stew." The veteran steward proved to be a wonder of ingenuity. Like Crowe, he made the best of material and circumstances. Once he had complaints about the coffee cooling off too quickly. He looked around the room and decided to have the carpenters install cupboards around the hot steam pipes that traversed the area. At night, he ordered the cooks to place all the coffee cups on or near the pipes. When checked in the morning, it was found that the "thick crockery" had absorbed the heat and did not "cool with uncomfortable promptness."

For those families that wanted home cooked meals, Crowe allowed a small grocery store and a butcher shop to open. Later he approved the running of a refrigeration and ice making plant. Residents, who could not afford their own refrigerator, could rent a small space for their perishables. Crowe guessed correctly that as the weeks wore on and men settled into their jobs, many of the workers would send for their wives and families. The home construction crews kept busy completing the family residences and Crowe started a waiting list based on seniority of hire. One of the first workers to bring his family out was Robert Calland. His wife, nervous about the crude dusty conditions, worried as she arrived with her small son and daughter. Calland assured her that in a short time a store would be in operation along with running water, electricity and sewer. She was happy to discover that the Reclamation Service had agreed to help build a small school. Calland, who worked in the engineering drafting room, worked hard to finish the interior and move their furniture in. Meanwhile, Crowe's assistant C. E. Crownover had a difficult time shortly after moving into his cottage. His wife received word that her sister, who lived back east, was serious ill and she left to be with her. Her husband found life difficult having to make his own meals. Day by day the dishes piled up. In frustration, he began taking all his meals at the mess. He was somewhat embarrassed when friends visited and discovered that, the well-organized conscientious engineer, had not a clean coffee cup or plate. Frank Crowe, on at least one occasion, floundered in the same boat with Crownover. Linnie left Rimrock for several days shortly after they arrived. She left with their son, John for "a brief sojourn" in Spokane. By May 1, they returned and Frank, once again, ate home cooked meals. Crowe enjoyed walking along the "boardwalk" (main street) holding his young son's hand. "The tall engineer and the short little son make a very loving couple going to the store or otherwise traveling along the board walk."[28]

Jack Ralston reserved the honor of being the longest resident. He and his wife had been part of the abortive 1917 construction attempt. Under government

Tieton Dam construction site. (USBR)

contract, he remained onsite serving as caretaker. Now with the renewed activity, Crowe hired Ralston as purchasing agent. It was Ralston, who had accompanied Crowe around the camp, when the lanky engineer first arrived. Others in the camp, mostly engineering and clerical staff were given preference in obtaining cottage space. Merritt Butler, a construction foreman, received one of the first available homes so that he could take care of his mother. Electrical engineer, Claude Gleason, with a "large family" also applied and secured a home early.

The tiny growing community of Rimrock soon became the object of regional attention. Crowe's estimates that Tieton Dam might exceed 350 feet provided much talk and excitement, as Arrowrock Dam—then the world's tallest, stood at 351 feet. If the bedrock turned out to be "soft" in critical areas then Crowe was fully prepared to sink the foundation deeper, creating a taller structure. By May, with dry warmer weather visitors and sightseers streamed into Rimrock. Sunday afternoons became the most popular time, and with some families, a regular event on the family social calendar. Again frustrated with having to deal with non-construction affairs, Crowe discussed the matter with Yakima city officials and it was decided that the government should begin a stage service. Running daily from late morning to late afternoon, visitors could spend two to three hours in the camp and make it home in time for dinner. It was also agreed that Crowe's road crew would continue to maintain the dirt road to Naches. While stopping short of banning outside cars and trucks, Crowe was relieved to see that traffic diminished considerably in his small town. Much of the success of the government-sponsored stage was the result of the low reasonable fares.

Many of the local visitors were not only interested in the construction progress, but also the opportunity to search for property. Word was out that once Tieton Dam was completed and the eight-mile lake filled, property on, or near the shoreline "will be at a premium." "Yakima loves its hills and turn out campers and cottagers by the thousands yearly with the coming of the warm weather," the local newspaper claimed. The assertion was that "once the nearby playground is completed, the population of the hills will grow amazingly." Rumors began to abound that with the addition of all this new water and resulting recreational possibilities, speculators would build the "finest variety of golf links." Others felt that mountain climbing with the region's "precipitous rocks and near-perpendicular mountain slopes" would attract those hardy adventurers looking for something more "strenuous." Still others began to look at the 100,000 plus acres downstream from the proposed reservoir with a renewed interest in future farming profits.

While on their visit to the dam site visitors could see small billboard-type signs describing the various construction phases and a conceptualization of how the completed dam would look. Some were surprised to learn that the corewall of concrete, the most striking and visually appealing component of any dam, would be hidden by "tons of earth." A twenty-five foot roadway was designed to crown the top of the dam. Spectators were impressed to see plans for the "most striking feature, from a scenic point of view, will be the spillway cut from the rock at one side which, when the lake is full, will make a waterfall of commanding proportions." This massive spillway would be able to handle over 30,000 feet per second, or "three times the greatest flood on record in the river."[29]

Crowe's chief assistant C. E. Crownover, head of the engineering department, in an interview tried to explain that visitors never fully understood or appreciated the hard work that goes into planning a project the size of Tieton Dam. "An earthen dam never brings any glory," he commented. He explained that the real engineering challenge, the corewall, is buried underground when the dam is finished, which, in this case, one hundred and twenty feet of the concrete wall rested under the riverbed. Crownover stated that one of the greatest tasks involved securing concrete pins in the foundation. These pins held the corewall firmly to the underlying bedrock.[30] In a dramatic interpretation of the process, a reporter explained, "The bed rock is reached by 'drifting' and 'stoping,' for the man-prepared concrete must be pinned to the primeval rock at each end as well as along the whole bottom." Crownover reminded the reporter that the concrete was mixed to exacting proportions and strongly reinforced all the way to the dam crest. In a paradoxical conclusion to his statements, Crownover wanted the public to know

Frank Crowe (left) with Arthur Powell Davis, director of the
Reclamation Service (center), and Secretary of the Interior,
Albert Fall, at Tieton Dam, spring 1921.
(John & Mary Crowe)

that "The way to build a dam is to build it absolutely water tight and, having done
that, to expect it to leak." He continued, "But unless the possible leak is provided
for, goodbye dam." In an effort to reassure Yakima residents about a possible
flood from a dam rupture, Crownover provided examples of Bumping Lake Dam,
which he claimed still had two leaks, but "it is none the less solid as a rock." One
way of guaranteeing strength Crownover added was to use a special mix of rock,
gravel, and sand on the "lower side of the dam to take care of water which by any
possible manner makes its way under the dam." He even explained why Tieton
Dam needed a concrete core of such large proportions. "Bumping [Dam] is a
rolled dam with no concrete core at all, while the others [dams in the West] have a

short concrete section below the surface. It was impossible to make a rolled dam at Rimrock because of the absence of clay," a reporter learned from the young engineer.

The *Yakima Morning Herald* gave front-page stories of the progress of Tieton Dam and the Rimrock camp. It provides an interesting look into the perception by the public. "There is no more interesting work at the dam than that of the diamond drills," one article claimed. When a fault was discovered in the bedrock of the original dam site, it was decided to relocate the dam hundreds of feet further downstream. This meant drilling out several hundred feet of additional material for the diversion tunnel. The equipment used were compressed air drills that were connected to an "air-compressing station" by "yards and yards" of reinforced metal coil hoses. Some people described the clattering of the drills as "like a thousand dentist's 'buzzing machines' all going at once." Crowe was interviewed about the drilling process and he admitted that the load on these drills was "unusually heavy" due, for the most part, on the extremely hard rock. He spent time reassuring the inquisitive reporters of Tieton Dam's safety features. With the river running through the diversion tunnels permanently, there would be little water pressure on the dam face. Crowe added that the installation of strong head gates at the tunnel portals assured total control.

In another interview, Crownover related how he planned to recommend that Crowe buy a new heavy-duty electric shovel. Attended by the "dinky," (large dump truck) it would have the big job of handling all the loose muck (rock, mud, sand) excavated from the tunnel and the riverbed. At a going rate of $45,000 each, Crownover exclaimed that it would be more economical in the long run than trying to use the older model steam shovels. "Wood is not a cheap fuel for this work, no matter how full the hillsides are of timber. For it has to be man handled at the going wage and once corded, does not give the best satisfaction. There is a constant waste of steam," it was explained. Crownover related how he heard of a "veteran steam shovel" at Naches City that had seen service on many regional government projects since 1909. Crownover was impressed to find out that the reliable machine had been in constant use for the twelve years, and sat idle during the interim period when the first Tieton Dam construction was halted. He understood that the shovel was still in good shape and he planned to use it at as a backup shovel. "That shovel owes the government," said Crownover. "It has paid for its cost and its keep."

One spectator to the goings-on at Tieton Dam in May of 1921 provided an interesting description of the work and the workers.

> There are about 300 men at work now at the camp
> and there are no prospects of an increased force for some
> time. The camp is so large and the work so varied that one
> looks about in wonder as to the whereabouts of the 300.

But they are scattered over the landscape, or underground
in busy little groups and when the whistle blows at the end
of the day's work they appear like ants from a hill, all moving towards the bunk houses to clean up for supper. And
the mess hall with its 300 diners leaves no doubt that Rimrock is a populous camp.[31]

As the work began to settle down into a routine, Crowe continued to
receive official reports and unofficial communications about the progress of future Hoover Dam. It was difficult for him to not think about the immense challenge that its projected 700-foot height would confront the construction engineer.
On May 15, 1921, Crowe learned that seven Western states had "united in asking
Congress to help them tame the unruly Colorado River and hitch it to the plow."
His boss, Arthur P. Davis agreed that the Reclamation Service would lead the
engineering investigation and compile a report for the states and Congress detailing the feasibility of building the major component of the plan—Boulder Canyon
Dam (Hoover Dam). Imperial Valley's new Congressman, Phil Swing supported
the measure for it would turn his district into an agricultural producer of immense
potential. He promised to introduce legislation supporting Davis's irrigation plans.
Swing knew he could count on the state districts where the new dam would have
an impact. "The plan is for these districts to finance the project by issuing bonds,
the various amounts being proportioned to benefits that shall accrue, this to be
determined by a federal commission." Crowe was skeptical of a "united state"
effort to raise the money necessary; he believed that only the federal government
had the resources to pay for the big dam. He had heard that rough estimates to
finance the project ran from $75 million to $100 million. The Yakima paper carried a short story on the progress of Davis and Swing along with a dramatic photograph of Boulder Canyon revealing the approximate location of the dam. For
many residents and for Crowe, the near-water level photo exposed near-vertical
canyon walls surrounded by a harsh naked desert. How could anyone confront
and overcome such enormous physical barriers? Crowe was determined to have a
look see.[32]

Yakima business owners disclosed more interest in taking full advantage
of the federal government's investment in Tieton Dam than in reading about a
colossal dam on the Colorado River. On May 20, the board of trustees of the
Yakima Commercial Club met to discuss the impact of Tieton Dam on their region. Members spoke out about the lack of plans for using the future stores of
water from Tieton; they recommended a series of canals to cover the region. Club
members finished their morning meeting and proceeded to visit Rimrock and so-
licit opinions from Reclamation Service personnel. Crowe was gone, his where-
abouts are uncertain, but it is entirely possible that he left temporarily on official
business, possibly surveying the Colorado dam site. A delegation of business

owners met with Crownover who assured them that "water will be made available by 1925." Crownover reviewed the Reclamation Service's plan to build a canal from below the dam, extending along the Yakima River. He told them that if Congress approves the funds, work could start in a year. O. C. Soots, secretary of the club tried to explain the urgency of the situation, "We must get busy and impress upon Congress that the dam without the canal isn't worth much and that unless the canal is ready at the completion of the dam, the water will lie idle." He continued, "If Congress refuses to grant sufficient appropriation to carry along both construction jobs simultaneously, it is up to the Yakima irrigation district to find a means to build the canal." Crownover and Soots discussed the figures for available water and possible number of acres that could be irrigated. Crownover had to explain that half of the water would go to the Tieton Project and the rest to the Yakima Irrigation District. Soots wanted assurances also that the Yakima share would be sufficient and guaranteed.[33]

Crowe could consider himself lucky to not have to deal with the persistent and aggressive businessmen, but many of them came away from their May visit with a new appreciation for the "immensity of the project." "They returned to Yakima convinced that Rimrock means a great deal to Yakima and that every citizen should become familiar with the work being done, preferably by making a trip to the dam," the local paper announced. While Frank Crowe tried to keep public visits to a minimum, and thus his involvement with politics, the local paper and his assistant Crownover urged everyone to see the dam. "We want the people of Yakima Valley to become interested in this work," Crownover said. "It is their job and they ought to know what it is, what it is for and what it means." Realizing that he might have over stretched his authority in Crowe's absence Crownover added, "I am not prepared to say just what will be done toward making it possible for visitors to the camp to see all there is to see. That is for Mr. Crowe to decide and it is very probable that a little later a guide will be provided to show visitors around." In way of summary, he claimed, "We certainly want people to be interested and realize that the best way to make them interested is to let them see what is doing."[34]

The local newspaper picked up Crownover's comments and reminded area residents of the "automobile stage" that operated every day, allowing visitors "four hours at the camp." Crownover, obviously enjoying his new found public spotlight revealed that while at the present time much of the work "is being done underground," within a few months "work on top of the earth will become heavier." He went on to say that within one year, concrete placing would be moving ahead full swing and it would be a great time to visit. However, he completed his interview by stating that all are welcome now, "I don't want to discourage anyone." The president of the Commercial Club, F. A. Duncan was impressed with Crownover, the camp, the construction, and the relationship that was developing between the Reclamation Service and the area. He reminded everyone that most of the federal payroll money given to the 349 Tieton Dam workers was spent in Yakima, adding measurably to the local profits. In promoting the project he said, "This work shows that the government has faith in Yakima and we mush have faith in ourselves and the valley. The dam will make possible the putting under cultivation of 70,000 more acres of Yakima land. This means a greatly increased wealth and population for the valley," he concluded. Duncan with an eye for public relations probed Crownover further about allowing a "motion picture news company" visit the site and make "pictures which will have distribution all over the nation." While it is not clear whether Crownover gave an approval to this or not, it placed him in an uncomfortable position of having to explain his comments to Crowe later.

Upon his return to Rimrock, Crowe had more to worry about than just the continuing flow of visitors and nervous business owners. He began getting pressure to cut wages, as he needed to hire more men, but necessary cash was not available. Fighting the move the best he knew how, by writing short memos to Weymouth in Denver, did little good. He would have to drop daily wages from $3.60 to $3.20 in order to hire more men. To add insult to injury, he consulted with Templeton about dropping the room and board fee, but his master cook held that food charges barely covered expenses as it was. On the positive side, Crowe was able to hire new workers. Henry Connell, assistant director of the regional Federal Employment Bureau reported in June that large numbers of men could now be hired at the dam. "Calls for workers increased by 70 per cent over the demand last week," he said. Most of the demand was for manual labor jobs starting at the new lower wage, but some jobs, such as "machine drill men" were also needed, and at a higher wage.[35] With fair weather forecast for an extended time and temperatures in the low 80s, Crowe was ready to attack the excavation with everything he could muster in men and machines.

Meanwhile, during the second week of June, a disastrous fire started in a privately owned clubhouse and quickly spread to an adjoining grocery store. A large number of hastily formed volunteers scrambled to halt the blaze. Crowe watched helplessly while his men threw buckets of water in an effort to extinguish the flames. Finally, with several hoses being brought to bear, the raging fire came under control, but not before both buildings were totaled. Crowe ordered the structures to be immediately rebuilt, and in an effort to help compensate the owners, he agreed to allow a "smoker." These amateur boxing events already popular in rural America at this time, always guaranteed a large attendance in construction camps. On the designated evening most of the single men and a good portion of the married ones as well, turned out "with great enthusiasm" to view the pugilists pound each other. After a series of minor "preliminaries" the crowd roared their approval as the "main event" fighters entered center ring. Scottie Clark, the so-called "fighting plumber," squared-off against "Sailor Hendrix" an ex-navy champion. Both Clark and Hendrix, workers on the dam and acquaintances, struggled the first few rounds to "get their fighting legs," as it had been some time since either man had stepped into the fighting ring. Hendrix showed signs of coming on after a few rounds, but "the 'plumber' knew a trick or two that the sailor champ had overlooked or forgotten and Hendrix was put to sleep." Even in victory, Clark staggered out of the ring, a sure sign that he would need some "consistent training to keep them [him] in form." The night proved so successful, both in terms of fund raising and moral boosting, that Crowe accepted the idea of setting up a regular schedule of smokers.[36]

With morale high and good weather forecast, Crowe wanted to move ahead as fast as possible with the excavation. To this end, he needed all of the heavy equipment planned for. Much of the new machinery came down from the Arrowrock project. Additionally, he supervised the overhauling of one of the old steam shovels and put it in operation around the clock. As was his style, Crowe wasted no time. His foremen trained new workers how to use the digging shovels and dingy system efficiently. "He [Crowe] has rigged up a steam shovel which is operating now in the tunnel, greatly facilitating the handling of the rock that is broken down by the shots [dynamite blasts]," reported a visitor in late June. Crowe, however, worried as a new problem cropped up, a rising Tieton River. Tunnel foremen reported a surging river spilling, at times, into the upper end of the tunnel. Crowe knew exactly what to do and he ordered men to continue building higher retaining banks. With emergency sump pumps standing by, Crowe waited for the water to recede. Meanwhile, Crowe would not allow a work slow down in the tunnels. Progress continued with tunnel miners reaching the 120-foot mark into the bedrock. Crowe and Crownover made ready to begin placing concrete. Unfortunately, another concern arose. The concrete mixing plant, located on the north side of the Tieton River, needed to be connected to the south side with a bridge. With high water still predominating, bridge construction had to be curtailed. Crowe planned to build a bridge once the water receded. Through this waiting period, he ordered the mixing plant finished and prepared.

Crowe now began going into Yakima on a regular basis to send telegrams to Weymouth in Denver and Reclamation officials at the Arrowrock site to send the promised heavy machinery. Weeks later the concrete mixers arrived in Naches by train along with a small locomotive and handling cars. Crowe's cableways arrived next. The heavy-duty system, designed for concrete delivery on Arrowrock, gave Crowe his most powerful tool. He hurried to Naches to coordinate the loading of the equipment on flatbed trucks for delivery to Rimrock. At the same time, the master engineer checked progress on renovating the power plant to generate 1000 kilowatts; it was critical that the electrical output be sufficient to run the new machinery.

Local newspaper reporters looked for Crowe whenever he arrived in Yakima. Though anxious to keep his mind focused on the pressing needs of the job and his men, Crowe appears to have been quite willing to grant interviews where he relayed progress on the dam. Reporters found him to give the facts straight and to report on all angles of construction and camp life. In late June, he told the *Yakima Herald* reporters that he had given priority to rebuilding the burned-out clubhouse so that his men could have another place to relax and socialize. Crowe allowed carpenters to remodel one of the older bunkhouses, removing the partitions to allow for " a pool table, counters, cigar stand, and other equipment." "The boy's can now drop around the 'Dinty Moore's' [the manager of the club-house] and spend a pleasant hour as they were wont to do before the fire," Crowe said. He also assured everyone that "on every part of the work the crews are making good progress." Crowe always aware of the health and safety responsi-bilities he bore revealed that there was no sickness and few accidents. He praised the work of camp physician Dr. C. H. Weir for his excellent hospital facilities and staff.[37]   On many of these short business trips into town, Crowe brought along V. G. Evans, chief clerk and C. J. Ralston, purchasing agent.

With Crowe busy between the Tieton construction and securing supplies from Naches and Yakima, his assistant Crownover began spending considerable time with Lytel, Project Manager for the Reclamation Service and in charge of the overall progress of irrigation in eastern Washington. Crownover now split his responsibility between Tieton and the work going on at nearby Keechelus Reser-voir. Crowe, concerned with his assistant's absent days, remained focused on his construction supervision. With Crownover away, Crowe welcomed Holland born David C. Henny of Portland, a consulting engineer for the Reclamation Service, to Yakima and drove him to Rimrock. Considered the Service's top consulting engi-neer on the Pacific Coast, Henny began a thorough check of Crowe's work progress, looking at everything from the use of equipment to excavation specifications to enforcement of safety regulations.[38]   The government's responsibility pervaded all phases of the work and the running of the camp, and Weymouth and Washing-ton officials wanted Tieton Dam—the only major Reclamation Service project currently underway—to proceed smoothly. Crowe complied eagerly, for he un-derstood that any major engineering problems, work related accidents, or material delays on the Tieton project could cause a Congressional investigation and there-fore, jeopardize future appropriations.

With the warm weather of July, Crowe laid off dozens of carpenters, as most of the necessary buildings stood completed. He hired more miners and gen-eral excavation laborers as he continued to push ahead with the bedrock tunnel mining. Few men complained of the work, since the overall employment outlook in the Yakima Valley was not good. At $3.20 a day for an honest day's work and a cool, damp underground environment to work in, morale remained high. Crowe kept muck removal quotas high. Crowe now had 315 men employed with respon-sibility for a monthly payroll totaling $32,905.[39]   The average pay per man equaled $105 a month, with the higher wages going to workers such as crane men and mechanics, some of whom received as much as $225. Over 150 of the workers, veterans of World War I, organized, in July, a post of the American Legion. Tom Granger, a county council official for the Legion, came to Rimrock and helped establish the new post.

Crowe hated distractions, and when a resurgence of the Ku Klux Klan made its appearance in Yakima he distanced himself from their meetings. He read that the "modern and up-to-date" Klan would soon have representatives in Yakima with plans to organize local chapters. "Residents are being given opportunities to join the clan and in that way help to 'preserve the supremacy of the white race,'" the newspaper reported. The article reported that C. B. Francis, a former *Yakima Herald* reporter then working in Chicago, noted how popular the movement was in that city. Seattle, "heart and headquarters" of the Klan's Northwest movement, too had "representatives" willing to sign-up potential new members. Crowe read that as close as Spokane "members of the colored clergy of the city are reported to be alarmed over the possibilities of the organization." Area residents complained when Yakima mails were flooded with Klan applications. With a vigilant eye he watched for Klan activity near Rimrock, but none materialized.[40]

Crowe worked closely with Crownover, now back at Tieton full-time, as the excavation continued. By the end of August, both engineers were satisfied that they had reached firm bedrock. At ninety-five feet below the river-grade, workers began to place concrete for the corewall foundation. Due to the unusual height of the dam, Crowe was pleased to have D. C. Henny as consulting engineer onsite to help in determining the condition of the bedrock. Crowe also drew ideas and approval from frequent visits by Weymouth and Davis. On August 21, the Service director and chief engineer "donned clothes and went down the shaft and into the drift to examine the formation and decided that conditions were favorable."[41] Weymouth next wanted to check preparations for supplying adequate steel reinforcement. Crowe, upon rolling out the oversized specification chart for the corewall, explained the bottom to top plan for metal rod placement. Pleased with the strength factor built into the corewall, Weymouth announced that reservoir clearing plans and bid announcements neared completion. Traditionally, dams built by the Reclamation Service were completed well ahead of the timber removal; in fact, separate funding approval for clearings usually ran months or years behind construction appropriations. With an estimated 34 million board feet of timber in the designated site, Crowe, and local job hopefuls knew that there would be plenty of employment for months to come.

The rest of the summer moved along uneventfully with corewall and abutment excavation. With the Tieton River at a low level, Crowe built a small truck bridge to bring the gravel to the newly completed mixing plant. All through August and September Crowe conferred with Lytel concerning progress. The latter was primarily concerned about the subsequent irrigation canal system that needed planning. Lytel and Crowe planned a 51-mile main canal, with over 150 miles of "distributing canals and laterals and 57 miles of small pipe lines." Crowe helped to plan the exact point at which the canal would take water from the Tieton River and deliver it to valleys down river, such as the Moxee Valley.[42]

During the month of September Linnie's mother visited for an extended time. Frank decided to take his mother-in-law and family to the Washington state fair, for he knew that his three-year old son, John, would have a great time. Accompanying them were V. G. Evans and his wife. Evans worked with Crowe at Rimrock and Linnie had made friends with his wife. It was an interesting time for Frank to leave the job in that the diversion tunnel was nearing completion and he always was present for the "holing through." With the concrete lining crews not far behind the tunnel excavators, Crowe announced that the diversion tunnel would be completed by October 15. This brought both joy and sadness to the workers and Yakima Valley residents. With the Tieton River completely rerouted, work on the concrete corewall could move ahead full speed. However, over one hundred men would be laid off and only a winter crew of approximately 150 workers would remain at Rimrock. Crowe did comment that he expected to hire many of the men back in the spring once the corewall operation was expanded. The only person in Rimrock relieved about the labor reductions was the community schoolteacher, who up until September was trying to conduct meaningful learning experiences with over 50 students in one room. County School Superintendent Mae Mark journeyed to Rimrock to see what could be done about the overcrowding. As the Crowe party headed toward Naches to pickup the main road to the state fair, they passed several flatbed trucks headed for the camp. These trucks carried the first of many thousands of cement sacks used for making the concrete.[43]

Frank had, many times, told Linnie that upon his retirement from dam building and service with the government he would like to raise cattle. At the fair he saw prize-winning Guernsey's, many of them from near Yakima. Two award winning firms, H. E. Angel & Son ranch and the Wallace & Fordyce farms, both brought the best of their outstanding herds. Crowe learned that proper breeding and state fair awards made for a profitable business. The highlight of the cattle competition was the showing of the Robert Nelson breeds. His animals, the Idaho champions, Washington state fair winners, and the Spokane Interstate fair "best of breed," pleased those looking to see the very best in Western cattle breeding.[44]

Frank arrived home on September 27 and began immediately to prepare for a regional meeting of all project chiefs. Representatives from Washington and the Denver office arrived for the weeklong talks. James Munn, Crowe's old partner and friend presided over the deliberations. Using the courtroom of the Yakima Federal Building, he first asked all managers and superintendents to give brief progress reports. This was followed by round table talks on the topic of how to streamline operations and minimize costs. Munn wanted to explore how to "unify the system of cost accounting." Crowe's report was made with the help of Evans and Lytel. Of all the projects currently funded, Tieton Dam was by far the largest and most challenging. It appeared that Crowe had arrived to a position of being

considered by the Reclamation Service as an authority on building dams; this reputation he would treasure and seek to expand in the years of construction challenges ahead.

Following this meeting Crowe was asked to speak to a Yakima business
group. A naturally shy individual, one accustomed to speaking to small groups of
men at one time, Crowe disliked these "opportunities." However, when he learned
that L. M. Holt, chief engineer of the Indian Irrigation Service would speak first
and that Munn would speak next, Crowe agreed. Munn had acquired a speaking
style in his new white collar role with the Reclamation Service and Crowe knew
that if he wanted to move up the Reclamation ladder, he would need to hone his
speaking skills. He spoke briefly, for only a few minutes, of the excellent progress
made and of his schedule for next year. When questions, from the floor, centered
on expected engineering challenges, he enthusiastically responded.[45] Lytel was
pleased with Crowe's performance for he sought to endear the efforts of the Reclamation Service to the public. Only a couple of days after the business owner's
luncheon, Lytel remarked, "One aim of the American Society of Engineers is to
make itself of use in community service." He continued, "In a general way and
acting for community benefit, members of the society will contribute their time
and experience to the solution of problems of vital interest within their scope."
Pressing his point home, Lytel affirmed, "We have voluntarily undertaken to investigate and report of the disposal of sewage in the streams here in the valley.
Tests of the water will be made at different points to determine the nature of the
supply, and the whole thing will be done at no cost to the community but as a
contribution by the society."[46] His comments were well taken by the people of
Yakima, and for Frank Crowe they were words to learn by.

With the onset of cold wet weather, work on Tieton Dam continued at a
rapid pace. During the remaining months of 1921 Crowe kept busy conferencing
with his foremen and encouraging the workers. Rain or no rain, weekdays or
weekends, he trudged around the dam site. No one questioned his persistence,
reliability or expertise. He rarely kept to a schedule, preferring to change his
inspection route and times, on a whim. Crowe even made regular trips down the
muddy pot-holed dirt road to Naches during this time to ensure it was passable.
Road crews earned their pay, for if the "big boss" found any substantial eroded
sections of the road, they heard about it. On occasion, Frank brought Linnie and
John along with him. After inspecting the road, he would drive the family into
Yakima for shopping and entertainment.[47]

Chapter 5

"No matter how bad the weather gets, the work at
Rimrock will not shut down."
1922-1925

The start of a new year brought unusually cold weather to the Yakima
Valley, with low temperatures dropping to below zero degrees on several occasions. On January 10, 1922, a record 4° F. below caused problems for both men
and machines. Crowe braved the bizarre arctic conditions, visiting each construction site, encouraging the workers, and looking for potential problems. By February, with the corewall within fifty feet of the surface, foremen reported that adjacent rock formations appeared to have changed from the hard rock strata to a
"loose formation of rock." Every time drilling or blasting occurred "cuttings"
crashed down onto the work area; worse, rockslides began to play havoc with the
concrete placing operations on the corewall. The ground near the surface was
simply not as strong as the geologic formations found near the bedrock and the
"frequent cave-ins were retarding work." Crowe, after a careful inspection, decided that it would be risky to continue drilling loose rock. He quickly came up
with a plan to "make an open cut" from above while allowing the miners to continue cautiously from below. Crowe pressed into service one of the old steam
shovels. He hired additional men and ordered them to dig the trench quickly, yet
cautiously. Crowe devised a sequence of operations to efficiently muck the loose
rock by using heavy-duty trams and dumping the material nearby. Using the same
trams he ordered a mixture of "silt and earth" to be brought in and dumped behind
the corewall to provide "a better backing for the dam." Despite the unusually
numbing temperatures, Crowe pressed his men to continue and within a few days,
crews reached the twenty-foot mark.

In spite of the problems with the weather and rock formations, workers
and their machines moved forward. He increased his work force to 215 men, as he
had done at Jackson Lake. Usually, the work pace slowed or stopped completely
for winter conditions; crews went home or reported on an irregular schedule. Not
Crowe, he assumed that the Rimrock construction camp could sustain the men and
their families through any harsh climatic conditions and he had been authorized to

"hire and fire" as needed. He gambled on a plan where additional crews would be hired in a construction sequence that was mostly dependent on successfully protecting men and machines from daunting climatic conditions. Protective coverings went up wherever needed and heavily padded work gloves became standard issue. It was always difficult for the impatient engineer to have outside interferences, such as weather and money, hold up a construction operation that he knew he could easily complete in half the time. Crowe compensated for these contingencies by planning construction sequences that optimized the endurance of men and reliability of machines. The mucking trams worked in synchronized harmony with the steam shovel, which together complemented the drilling of the miners below the surface. The result, the corewall excavation, was completed sooner than expected and the resulting imported "dam pack" proved stronger than the natural accumulation of nearby rock debris.

Lack of continued funding and ready cash flow hampered early Reclamation Service projects and discouraged engineers, workers, and expecting irrigation recipients alike. By February, Crowe had spent much of the $700,000 original appropriation for Tieton Dam. The new fiscal bill, just out of congressional committee, carried $950,000 for Tieton Dam. Crowe was visibly upset by this decision, as he had argued strongly for a minimum of $1,350,000 to carry the work on "as needed." "The work will have to be curtailed accordingly," Crowe told local sources. He informed his workers that unless Congress added additional funds later in the year, work on "the headgate and the spillway" would not occur this year. He continued, "It is a long road yet till we are free to handle this year's appropriation." This word was given to reassure residents that hiring would still move forward and that the Reclamation Service would continue to press its case with Congress. "The bill is reported out of the committee of the house favorably but it must pass the house then go to the senate committee where it will be threshed over again before it is reported out for passage in the senate," Crowe reminded local readers. Then he cautioned, "In my experience it will be the last days of the session before the bill becomes a law. In the meantime we are going on short rations [a work slowdown] but if the bill passes, after July 1 we can make fair progress."[1]

Cold weather continued into March with the Rimrock camp reporting a foot of snow on the ground. Crowe now used the company truck to make his regular visits into Yakima. On March 4, he explained to Yakima residents that he was already hiring more men in order to prepare for the expanded concrete operations on the corewall. His intentions included hiring three full crews for three full work shifts. This would become a Crowe trademark; no time would be wasted. He also mentioned that his excavation crews were preparing for an unprecedented "powder shot" using five tons of "TNT, the most powerful of all explosives." Crowe estimated that this single shot would "breakdown at least 10,000 tons of andesite, which is to be used as a fill for the lower toe of the dam." "This is the largest shot of TNT ever used in construction work in the Reclamation Service," Crowe proudly announced. Always desiring to try new methods and explore untouched ground, the excited engineer was anxious "to see just what it will do."[2] This "new" explosive was originally developed for use in World War I hand grenades. At the conclusion of the European conflict, surplus stores of TNT were turned over to the Reclamation Service. More powerful than dynamite or blasting powder, traditional explosives used in construction, Crowe became one of the first American engineers to use TNT.

At the dam site the buzz of usual activity was interrupted with everyone concerned about the coming big blast. A large shelf of rock needed to be taken down and Crowe directed his drilling crews as they made crosscuts and blasting holes. One hundred pound cartons of TNT were placed in each hole, for a total of 10,000 pounds. "If the charge was black powder or dynamite I would know just what was going to happen," said Crowe, "but, this is my first experience with a charge of TNT of this size. I do not know how far away one should stand, but I'm going to take no chances," he reassured his workers. "A Pathe photographer is coming up to see what happens and I hardly know what to do with him. I do not look for anything spectacular, but there will be something doing when the mine is sprung," he added. Crowe planned to use the broken rock for fill on the lower side of the dam. On the big day everyone, Linnie and the Pathe photographer included, stood well back as the ear deafening explosion was set off. Tons of debris shot into the air and were seen landing hundreds of yards distant. Carefully, inspection crews went in after the blast to check excavation. The entire shelf had quite literally "been blown away."

In another well coordinated sequence of jobs, Crowe immediately ordered his men to shovel the broken rock into trams for transport to the lower footing where "a layer of it will be spread over the bed of the stream." Crowe wanted to use the fill as a "filter for any leakage that might occur during construction or even after the dam is completed." More men were hired to help in this job of mucking and hauling, and 285 men appeared on the March payroll. Crowe now admitted that he was "rushing the corewall construction to avoid any delays by spring 'freshets' [early rains]" before high water comes again. With the river now at a season low, he knew there was no time to waste and the relentless engineer organized the attack. Crowe expanded the three shifts to include every day, with some workers allowed to put in overtime on other shifts. By March 18, 1922, the impressive concrete corewall reached the surface, spanning the entire distance across the open canyon. Urged on by this success, Crowe asked the local employment agency to send up able-bodied men. He needed muckers, tram drivers, and spreaders. He wanted to keep pace with the concrete crews adding to the height of the corewall daily. The job now would be to coordinate the earthen fill crews on both the upstream and downstream sides of the corewall. This proved difficult to do, as the tramcars did not work well with frost on the ground.[3]

The frosty mornings of March turned eventually to the warmer days of April and with each passing week Crowe increased the workforce. On April 6, 1922, he employed 500 men full time and with the corewall thirty-four feet above the surface, workers swarmed over its entire length. Crowe was excited and anticipating much progress. "We are ready for business and will soon be able to make a showing." He pressed into service all three steam shovels in addition to the newer equipment. "Two are at work excavating the loose gravel from the riverbed on the upper face of the corewall. About six feet of this will be removed and some silt, clay, and puddling material will be substituted as it will be more impervious to water," he commented. "The loose gravel of the riverbed is only about six feet deep," he continued. "Below that," he added, "is a strata of conglomerate rock and clay." Crowe used the third steam shovel to "ballast" the roadbed for a new railroad track. The 2.3 mile long route ran from the "borrow pits" to the dam. On the tracks, eight 16-ton locomotives pulled 75 mucking cars. Each car carried four yards of fill, and Crowe estimated that it would take two million yards to complete the filling in process. The master engineer pleased with the new electric shovel commented, "One man can handle this shovel with ease, and it is doing a giant's task on the job." His order for two new high pressure 200-horsepower pumps, used for "sluicing," or water packing the fill, elevated his expectations for fast, efficient dam construction. The sluicing operation formed the basis of creating the earthen-fill dam. Crews worked to bring the fill in on the railroad cars. After dumping the material, the plan called for strong-armed workers to sluice the collected muck into place using powerful, and dangerous, hydraulic hoses. In this way, the soft clay material would be placed on the upper side of the corewall and a fine-grained sandy material on the lower side "permitting any seepage to pass away readily."[4]

On April 12, Crowe tested the two newly installed hydraulic pumps. These mighty pumps worked at a tremendous pressure, about 100 pounds per square inch. At this rate, each pumping system could throw seven second feet of water. Used in the sluicing operation, Crowe and the hydraulic crews watched in disbelief as rocks over a foot in circumference flew about like pebbles. When the hoses were pointed skyward, they threw out a stream of water over a distance of a city block. Crowe explained the pumping and sluicing operation, "A pump will be installed in the pool immediately below the corewall which will pump a large amount of soft clayey material from the lower side of the corewall to the upper side of the corewall leaving a fine graded sandy material immediately against the downstream side of the corewall and a tight clayey puddle against the upstream side of the corewall. The volume of the embankment will be nearly 2,000,000 cubic yards," Crowe explained.[5]

In anticipation of a rising corewall, Crowe knew that he could not use the trestle way and trams for delivering the freshly poured concrete once the height reached forty feet. Above this height, he devised a plan to setup a cableway sys-

A cableway headtower at Tieton Dam with concrete bucket unloading into a shuttle. (USBR)

tem, much like he had pioneered at Arrowrock Dam to span the entire length of the dam. This was vintage Crowe, in his element and alive with the challenge of designing a network of cables that would reliably deliver the buckets of mixed concrete on a 24-hour basis, seven days a week. Again, as in Arrowrock, he oversaw the general design, the detailed drawings, and the erection of the network. To outsiders, it might appear that he was taking unnecessary time and expense to setup for the concrete placing. However, skeptics quickly changed their opinions after the new high wire system revealed impressive results. In the traditional trestle way, workers continually elevated the trestle tracks as the dam grew higher, a cumbersome and expensive task. With a properly installed cableway, only minor changes in cable orientation disrupted the schedule. The single setback in the erection of the cables occurred when a freak snowstorm hit Rimrock in mid-April dumping four inches of snow, curtailing progress.[6]

This was an incredibly busy and difficult time for Frank Crowe. In addition to the increasing building pace at Rimrock, Frank worried about his expecting wife. Linnie Crowe moved closer to her delivery date and Frank wanted to make sure that she have the right medical help. On April 15, he brought Linnie into St. Elizabeth's Hospital in Yakima. The next day, on a clear 70 degree Easter Sunday, Linnie delivered a beautiful healthy girl. Frank rushed in from the Tieton Dam site and spent the next day with Linnie. News spread quickly through the town of the new birth, yet reporters appeared more interested in news of any work speedup. Crowe did not disappoint the media; his "big steam shovels" continued to rip Tieton's river bottom while sluicing operations moved ahead on schedule. Returning to Rimrock to excited friends and co-workers, Frank told everyone that they had decided to name the child Patricia. Little John Crowe, who was staying with family friends in Rimrock, looked "overjoyed with his news of a new sister" and later "helped" Linnie take care of Patricia.[7]

Frank insisted that Linnie, stay in Yakima until she regained her strength. Frank Crowe, pushed to the maximum, now dealt with the busy work schedule, helping take care of his son, worrying about his wife and his daughter, and the shock of news from the Denver office that a major change in Reclamation Service organization was in the offing. He learned, along with everyone else in the Yakima area, through telegrams and newspaper articles that the Service was considering shutting down the Denver office completely. The argument centered on the fact that little, if any of the business now conducted in Denver could not be handled directly through the Washington D. C. central headquarters. In protest, Weymouth, then Chief Engineer, and Denver business firms sent scores of telegrams to fellow Service engineers, and irrigation and wateruser groups throughout the West. Weymouth hoped that a barrage of negative telegrams might change Washington's thinking. While there is no evidence that Crowe took sides on this issue, he certainly must have supported Weymouth's request. Crowe understood the advantages and disadvantages of having a Western regional office of the Reclamation Service. The Yakima wateruser groups however, viewed the Denver office as an unnecessary bureaucratic obstacle and a waste of precious reclamation funds. "Nothing being done at the Denver office that could not be done just as advantageously at the Washington [location], and keeping the Denver office open adds that much to the overhead which is prorated among the different projects," Yakima wateruser trustees explained. Floyd Foster, Secretary of the Tieton Waterusers complained, "Supplies are purchased through the Denver office now, but before the Denver office was established they were bought locally at points near the projects." As he spoke he held a copy of a recently received telegram from the Vulcan Iron Works Co., a Denver based supplier for the Reclamation Service. "If I should go out in Yakima and tell dealers that the Denver office was about to be abandoned I am sure they would join with us in commending the department on the move," Foster declared.[8]

While the debate over the proposed closing of the Denver office proceeded, Frank continued to visit Linnie and young Patricia in Yakima. Surrounded by engineers at Rimrock and by business owners in Yakima, Crowe had an earful of both sides of the issue. On April 26 he spent the entire day with the family, even though progress of the sluicing and mucking presented hourly challenges. "He was down to visit with his family, get better acquainted with his new daughter and make arrangements to move the family back to Rimrock next week," reported the Yakima newspaper. As usual, reporters cornered Crowe at every opportunity to ask about the dam. On one occasion, he described the current process for sluicing. "Earth and rock are being hauled from the barrow pits, dumped near the corewall and are being sluiced into place by the big hydraulics," Crowe remarked. He estimated that crews were moving about 3000 yards of fill per day, with the hope of increasing that number to 5000 yards daily once the new crews grooved their team work efforts. Crowe joked to one of the reporters, "I expected to see some of the mud I am stirring up in my glass of water at the hotel today, but was surprised to see that the water was clear." Becoming more serious, the tall engineer continued, "The big hydraulics are certainly churning up things in the Tieton, but the muddy water is creeping down the bank of the river opposite the P.P & L. company intake and the Yakima city water is not being contaminated." Feeling secure that the work on the dam was proceeding without a hitch he offered, "The job is moving now in all departments. We are through with preliminaries and are building a dam." Never content with the status quo he added, "I figure we must do 5000 yards daily to get done what is marked out for this season's work. This can be done when the crews are well broken in to the work they have to do."[9]

On May 2, Crowe welcomed D. C. Henny from the Portland Reclamation office and A. J. Wiley from Denver to Rimrock. There they met with Lytel and Crownover to conduct a survey of the progress and to look for possible engineering difficulties that might arise. The next day James Munn arrived to help with the inspection. After three days of intensive poking around the worksite and Rimrock, the committee met in Yakima and announced that Crowe was doing a good job. "Work at Rimrock is well under way," said Henny. "Our inspection was merely the usual survey," he claimed. Henny went on, "There were no problems to be solved or no new work to be planned. We found that Mr. Crowe was pushing

the work along lines already determined and was showing satisfactory results."
On another positive note Henny exclaimed, "It will be a matter of two weeks or so
before he [Crowe] gets going in full swing and then it will be worth your while to
see the progress that is being made." At the same time Crowe reasserted his claim
that he could push his men to move 5000 yards of backfill a day. Lytel jumped in
at this point and noted that Crowe's yardage totals had steadily increased and now
stood near 4500 yards. He added that the two steam shovels and one electric
shovel work in perfect harmony with men laboring two shifts on the steam shovels and three shifts on the electric model. Plans included running all three shovels
on three shift schedules. Munn reassured local residents that Crowe's work on
Tieton Dam represents the very best that the Reclamation Service has to offer and
that even though "Tieton Dam offers some very unique problems" they have "solved
them and that the structure will prove stable and trustworthy." Henny spoke directly to Yakima valley farmers stating that he kept a close watch on the development of the valley examining "production tonnage" and the "material prosperity
of the settlers."[10] When questioned on the plan to close the Denver office of the
Reclamation Service Munn replied, "It is by no means settled that the office is to
be abandoned and the forces taken to Washington." He informed everyone present
that the Denver office was fighting the move wholeheartedly and that U. S. senators from Wyoming, Colorado, and Arizona announced their determination to take
the struggle to the highest levels in Washington. He also supplied figures to show
that the Denver cost for managing the Tieton project was only $874.90 for the
current fiscal year, considerably lower than some farmers and local business owners had suggested.

After Munn and Henny departed for their home offices, it became increasingly clear to Crowe that he and his chief assistant Crownover disagreed on
several important engineering procedures. Details of their differences are difficult
to ferret out, as Crowe and Crownover did not discuss the problem fully with the
visiting team of Reclamation inspectors or with the press, when the final break
was reported on May 18. "Mr. Crowe and I could not agree about important
engineering problems in connection with the construction of the dam," Crownover
explained to local reporters. In defense of his position he noted, "I was not disposed to yield my judgment and have been let out by Mr. Crowe." At this point
Crownover realized that it was time to "let the cat out of the bag" by disclosing
that "the differences between us have been hanging fire for six months past, but
they came to a head last week, ending in my dismissal." He insisted that Munn
and Henny were not privy to the problem during their visit and that as far as he
knew, Crowe had not brought it up with anyone earlier either. This is difficult to
believe, as Crowe already had earned a reputation for doing things by the book
and Reclamation instructions to supervisory personnel were clear, serious disagree-
ments must be reported to senior officials. While existing government records are
not complete for this construction project, it is likely that Crowe, considering his

Sluicing operations are well underway at Tieton Dam, June 24, 1922. (USBR)

past close relationship with Munn and Weymouth, probably informed both of them a problem existed.

In his typical low-key posture, Crowe responded to the whole situation by exclaiming quite bluntly, "Let Mr. Crownover do the talking." He knew that Crownover was a "local boy" and that this matter needed to be treated as gently as possible. Crownover, who had fourteen years in with the Reclamation Service, first came to Yakima Valley to survey the Tieton canal construction. He immediately recognized the natural beauty of the area and determined to remain there. Crownover was well regarded by locals, having purchased a thirty-acre orchard near Yakima that he successfully worked.[11]

The dry weather and rising temperatures of June allowed Crowe to get back to concentrating on completing Tieton Dam. He asked paymaster E. V. Evans to put out another call for workers. Crowe wanted another 30 to 40 common laborers to help with the sluicing and mucking. He agreed to request a pay raise for common labor; he asked for and received a move from $3.00 a day to $3.20. With these added men, Crowe could now count just over 500 total workers, making Tieton Dam one of the nation's largest construction jobs. J. C. Gawler, fiscal agent for the job, reported to Crowe that May's payroll dished out $42,395, with room and board deductions amounting to $15,950.[12] During the early part of this month, Crownover moved from his Rimrock residence to his ranch in the Naches Heights district. Crowe had allowed his ex-assistant and his wife to remain in Rimrock until living arrangements could be made. However, Crownover did not have a residential structure on the ranch, so he moved into a temporary tent house on the property while his home was constructed. As the days moved along, Crowe appeared relieved that the potentially dangerous situation with Crownover ended with no apparent backlash from Yakima Valley residents.

On June 16 the *Yakima Morning Herald* headlines read "Will Rush Work on Rimrock Dam—Construction Engineer Declares Force Will Be Increased in Order to Have Corewall Advanced by Start of Winter." The construction engineer referred to was of course, Frank Crowe. Here he was again, to his chagrin, in the headlines. The beleaguered dam builder, speaking in front of a large crowd of local Rotarians and nervous about possible public questions concerning the Crownover affair, laid out his plans for summer construction. He reported a record 5000 cubic yards of backfill had been placed up against the rising corewall and that his 518 men were actively engaged in the work. Always looking to push his men and the work along, Crowe announced that he wanted to again, hire more men—to total 560. He also declared that he intended to keep his men "going at top speed" as long as work can be continued through the summer. His men knew that their "big boss" wanted to see the crews break May's record of 110,000 cubic yards.

With the dam standing now at 75 feet above the bed of the river on the lower end and 55 feet on the upper end, Crowe coached foremen in the art of sluicing the silt and finer particles against the corewall. Within days, Crowe watched husky laborers pulverize deposited layers of muck with high-powered pressure hoses. In defense of the work speedup Crowe reminded the Rotarians that winter rains of recent years had pummeled the valley racking substantial damage in all Yakima Valley communities. "He is guarding against a winter freshet [early down-pour] and wants the dam to hold any runoff that may come in December or in the midwinter," explained a reporter in the audience. Crowe reviewed that any significant flood could endanger the dam and the workers, as they were in a critical stage of packing debris against the corewall. This debris must be placed and packed in such a way as to afford maximum holding power against oncoming water.

To this end, Crowe wanted to move the construction quickly, but also efficiently, ahead. As usual, the biggest problem involved the coordination of men and machines in such a way that, within the narrow confines of the working canyon, they worked in unison. The problem of logistics may have been one of the areas that he and Crownover disagreed on. Crowe had pioneered the idea of mass sequencing of workingmen and machines and always looked for ways to improve and adapt the system to individual construction jobs. He would always take a long look at original work plans, and then revise them to increase the use of men and machines. Such considerations as efficiency of the workforce and given materials, always a concern of the Reclamation Service construction engineers, challenged standardized practices. Individual site problems and complexities needed customized answers and applications. While it is not known as to Crownover's exact objections to Crowe's work speedup plans, it appears the timing of this announcement is more than coincidental.

At the same speaking engagement, Crowe described how he planned to change the original blueprints for construction of the upper end of the corewall. At its base, deep in the bedrock, the corewall was five feet in thickness, slowly tapering inward and finishing at a two-foot thickness. Crowe, desiring to ensure strength throughout, revealed that he would now increase the thickness substantially. This may have been another area of discussion between Crownover and himself. Rarely, in Reclamation Service construction history, are major redesigns approved with work so far advanced. Knowing that approval for this change needed to come from both the Denver and Washington offices, this confirms Crowe's standing as an expert in dam design and construction.

Reminding Yakima residents once again of the enormity of the project, Crowe proudly proclaimed that Tieton would be the world's tallest earth dam. He described the huge corewall as the anchor "tying into bedrock from side to side of the canyon and extending to the crest of the dam." Crowe elaborated on the sluicing operation, stating that "great care" must be taken in the settling of the material against the upstream side. He described how tremendous pressures could be expected from the rising water of the future reservoir upon the sluiced material and the corewall. Impressed with his knowledge of dam construction, reassured of Tieton's durability, and excited by an early completion date, Yakima residents left the meeting pleased with what they heard.[13]

July's work moved ahead unimpeded with more men and machines engaged. Crowe's typical work schedule saw him rise early, probably around 6:00 a.m., and report to his office where he would confer with a number of assistants and foremen. Next, he headed for various parts of the work site, wanting to be on the job when the day shift started. He felt completely at ease moving among the workers and the work. Frequently, he would question workers about their responsibilities and their technique, offering alternative suggestions. Crowe rarely engaged his men in conversation about non-work related topics. Only with foremen or long-time associates did he allow himself to joke and discuss "other matters."[14] Crowe knew that he needed to set an example for his men and that he was constantly being watched. He amazed even the sturdiest of workers, as he briskly walked, for hours, from job to job checking progress.

Crowe's only break from the job, and for Linnie and the kids, included their regular visits into Yakima and a day at the county July 4th celebration. Touted as a "must see" affair, just about everyone in Rimrock attended. Frank enjoyed these brief sojourns away from the daily pressure at Rimrock. For Linnie, it provided an equally needed break from the rough living conditions of Rimrock and constant attention to household chores. An interesting and tragic event disrupted the Crowe's visit to Yakima's Hippodrome Park where a visiting circus had planned a series of performances for the Fourth of July festivities. An erroneous report quickly circulated that a local boy had been attacked and killed by a circus "cowboy." Word quickly spread of the beating and an unruly crowd of "at least one hundred people" descended on the main circus tent shouting "Mob him," and "Lynch him." Local residents needed to be restrained from shredding the swaying big top by security guards and local police. In this, they failed and considerable damage was inflicted to the flapping canvas and to furniture inside. By late afternoon, when most of the Rimrock families arrived, the crowd in attendance swelled to 10,000. Luckily, cooler heads prevailed when the facts came out. It was discovered later that the boy in question was alive and well, having only received a "blow to his nose" for stealing a look at the "Wild West show".[15]

Another interesting event transpired later in July when Rimrock residents petitioned to have their voting registration and voting location at the town of Naches instead of the more remote Cowiche. Naches was on the main road to Yakima and "more convenient" for the dam workers. County Prosecutor Sidney Livesey listened to the request and quickly ruled against Rimrock. Livesey declared that Rimrock, a recently constructed town, was not established when the voting precinct boundaries were reestablished two years prior, thus their area was under the existing Cowiche precinct, and could not be changed until after the next election. The attorney did note that if the town remained intact after construction and housed the legal requirement of 300 residents or more then they could petition for precinct status. Livesey sited several recent cases that the state attorney general reviewed along similar lines as the Rimrock case, and in every circumstance, the current law was upheld. For dam workers, such as Frank Crowe and colleagues, this was another in a long line of adjustments that needed to be made in dealing with life in construction camps. It is not known if Crowe voted in local, state, and national elections during the early part of his career, but it is certainly well documented that he did vote and actively engage in at least one major national election later in 1932.[16]

Late in July the Yakima chapter of the American Society of Engineers and their families visited Rimrock to inspect the government camp and to see progress on "the big dam." L. T. Jessup, chapter president, and L. F. Fairbrook, secretary, led the entourage of 30 cars into the busy Rimrock camp. Crowe arranged for a complete tour of the work that included lunch in the camp cafeteria. On such visits, it was not unusual for Linnie to help by "being available" to assist with the wives and children of visiting engineers. Crowe learned that many of the engineers had not only brought their families, but several guests as well. O. C. Soots, secretary of the Commercial Club in Yakima decided to tag along also; he arrived with his wife and guests in time for lunch. Crowe welcomed the visiting party and provided them with an informative tour. One engineer described the outing as "carefree and fun."[17]

Tragedy struck Frank and Linnie in August with the loss of their only son, John. The bubbly five year old complained of stomach pain on August 8 upon which Frank and Linnie drove their son promptly into St. Elizabeth's hospital in Yakima. Early examinations revealed some sort of intestinal infection. Doctors worked to pump the boy's stomach and identify any poison and by August 12, it appeared that young John was improving. The next day John's condition suddenly turned serious for no apparent reason. Working furiously, doctors were unable to prevent his death later that day. Subsequently, hospital officials announced that the boy had died from intestinal poisoning due to eating unripe fruit. The pain of this loss must have been unbearable; for Linnie this was her second child and for Frank, his third. Solemnly, they made the funeral arrangements in Yakima, remaining there for several days. The funeral at St. Michael's Episcopal Church was attended by scores of Rimrock friends of the family, and several from Yakima. The Reverend F. J. Mynard officiated in a touching eulogy that highlighted the brief life of John Crowe. Mynard reminded those present of John's playful enthusiasm around the workers at Rimrock, "He was the idol of the government camp."[18]

Within days of the funeral, Davis and Weymouth arrived for another inspection. Their planned visit could not be canceled at the last minute. J. L. Lytel knowing of Crowe's recent loss offered to pickup the Service officials. Lytel would drive them to Yakima and Rimrock. Both men offered Crowe their condolences, and not wanting to infringe on their trusted colleague in his hour of grief, only briefly toured the dam before returning to Yakima. Davis, who had not been in the area for at least a year, remarked that he was pleased with the construction progress. In a conference in town he was quoted as saying, "Construction under the direction of F. T. Crowe is making excellent progress." Adding detail to his comments he continued, "I was pleased to note in the material used for the backfill a large number of big rocks. These will give stability to the dam." And in an effort to reassure local residents as to the safety of the dam he concluded, "I consider the corewall type tying into bedrock the safest type of dam we could construct. It would be impossible to handle big rock[s] in such work under any other method than the one in use, but here they are a help rather than a hindrance."[19]

After reviewing, in detail, how the corewall was constructed Davis went on to note that the Reclamation Service would not ask for additional funds to be employed in the Yakima Valley until the completion of Tieton Dam. "It would be useless to speculate what to do next on the Yakima project till the Tieton Dam is completed," he said. "There will be no money available for any big construction till that work is done, but after that I think we can safely say that some one or the other of the highline units will be taken up for construction," Davis concluded. In defense of Crowe's "hurry-up" construction schedule, Davis stated, "The Service needs the Rimrock Dam now and this work will be pushed to completion. Not only will the new highline projects need this water but the other projects are taking more water year by year as they complete their department." To make his point, Davis reiterated, "The first thing is to complete the big dam and we are bending our efforts on that job now."[20]

In a surprise ending to the meeting, Weymouth publicly disclosed that the "controversy between F. T. Crowe, chief engineer at Rimrock, and C. E. Crownover, his first assistant, had been decided in favor of Crowe. Crownover had tendered his resignation," Weymouth stated. Later the disgruntled Crownover sent a report to the Washington headquarters of the Service. In response, Director of the Reclamation, Davis sent D. C. Henny and A. J. Wiley, consulting engineers to make an investigation of the situation. Weymouth, not wanting to stir up additional bad memories of the unfortunate episode simply concluded his comments by saying that on the basis of Henny and Wiley's report the Washington office "sustained" Crowe's position. Why this information had been withheld from the public until now was not readily apparent. It is also not clear whether Crownover attempted to bypass Weymouth, knowing of his close relationship with Crowe, and have Davis rule on the matter.

Davis and Weymouth, before leaving to return to their respective offices in Washington D. C. and Denver, gave Crowe approval to bid out for the clearing of the Tieton reservoir area. The heavily timbered tracts, five in all, ran from gently rolling hills to severely steep slopes. Crowe advertised the bidding on August 24, stating a deadline for submission by contractors. He estimated 100 acres lay within the designated reservoir zone, and he somewhat confused prospective bidders by declaring, "The clearing is either to be complete or only as concerns large growth, at the option of the engineer in charge." What is not clear is how should contractors bid, to clear everything including underbrush, or just "large growth"? Crowe did give a deadline, September 11 to complete the bidding and added that the job "in general is to be done in accordance with the rules of the United States Forestry Service." Wanting leverage in dealing with possible contractors, Crowe allowed proposals on one or more of the tracts. The price, he declared, is "to be on a per acre basis for each of the five tracts."[21]

The hot days of August melted away into a brisk cool September as Frank and Linnie tried to put the memory of John's recent death behind them. Linnie, in addition to her home chores and the need to care for Patricia, continued to help Frank with his social responsibilities. Visitors from all over the state of Washington and the Pacific Northwest, hearing news of the "big dam" continually flowed through the Rimrock camp. Whenever local or state officials visited, Frank and Linnie made the effort to escort them, answer questions, and arrange for mess hall meal tickets. The Washington state fair, with its prize winning Guernsey cattle, once again, lured Crowe into considering a short vacation, but work kept him tied to Rimrock in 1922. While record crowds of over 25,000 daily clogged the demonstration buildings and packed the exhibition grandstand, Crowe continued to

A 16-ton locomotive is hoisted by Crowe's cableway at Tieton Dam. Crowe is standing, back to camera, in the middle of track with white shirt. (USBR)

push his men. He did read that local Guernsey breeders, once again, came away with top honors, even in the junior and senior divisions. Besides his work on the dam, he worked with the county school committee to organize a playground committee and he answered technical questions about the recent muddying of the Tieton and Naches Rivers. He had warned farmers and Yakima residents that the muddy waters could be expected as long as the river levels remained low in the fall. Through all of this, Crowe also continued to deal with Service engineers. In October, Munn and Savage spent several days observing the sluicing operations. They left applauding Crowe's pace and quality of work.

No sooner had Munn and Savage left, when Crowe was notified that a film crew would be coming to Rimrock. Instructions from Denver clearly stated that he should cooperate and meet their needs. The railroad advertising film, a joint venture by the Northern Pacific, Great Northern and Burlington Railroads, would hopefully, lure thousands of new settlers to the Yakima Valley. At least corporate officials and financial backers hoped it would. Filmmakers Frank Arver, W. R. Mills and C. Phillips of St. Paul, Minnesota arrived in Rimrock full of enthusiasm to film the "big dam." Crowe was impressed with their genuine curiosity

about the technical aspects of dam building. They wanted to "shoot" every possible angle and capture each and every job sequence. Fascinated with Crowe's
innovative use of the cableway and concrete drop buckets, the eager cameramen
filmed "the big buckets used to convey the earth and rock to the dump above the
dam." After leaving Crowe and Rimrock, the film crew spent days "shooting"
orchards, irrigation works, and some of the prize winning cattle.[22]

That same month Crowe's impressive cableway system received head-
line coverage. Now in full operation, the 1200-foot span of steel, hanging from
opposing high towers, caught the attention and imagination of visitors and workers alike. Buckets, skips, or specially rigged platforms, hung securely from the
cable, moved along at a rapid rate of 300 feet per minute. Not only did Crowe use
this cableway to deliver concrete and to remove muck, but also on occasion, he
would allow guests to ride the skip and get a birds-eye view of the dam site. Such
was the case with Spanish-American War veterans, who decided to have their
annual picnic and celebration at Rimrock. Crowe invited them, women and kids
too, to go for an exhilarating five-minute high wire ride. Crowe's cableway head
foreman was Ben Rementeria, himself a veteran of the 1898 war. The visiting
veterans were surprised to discover that Rementeria had served on Spanish Admiral Cervera's warship. They also learned that he and several other Spaniards,
disgruntled with the war, moved to America and settled in Idaho, where "the sheep
industry was then practically in the hands of the Spanish herders." The cableway
boss revealed how he met Crowe near Boise and that he had been in his employ for
a long time, serving on various construction jobs.[23]

Crowe joined the veterans on the cableway and seeing their interest in
Rementeria recalled a story from Arrowrock Dam where crews of Spaniards, all
ex-sailors, were employed on the cable with a "Dane" who had never experienced
heights. The Spaniards told Crowe that the Dane would be "no good" and that
they did not want him. But, one day the cable jammed and a "bunch of them were
left in midair, it was the Dane who crawled up over the apparatus at great peril and
made the necessary adjustment," Crowe explained. "After that," Crowe concluded,
"they said he was 'all right.'" Later Crowe recalled another story about Rementeria,
praising him for his dedication to the job and his great singing ability. Crowe
remembered that on a previous dam job, a worker had been killed and it was his
responsibility to notify the next of kin. Crowe invited the man's widow to a benefit performance of the workers, where the Spaniard was given top billing. The
widow perked up upon hearing Rementeria's warm wholehearted interpretation of
several contemporary ballads. Crowe remembered, "His singing was the hit of the
evening."

Crowe must have been in an unusually talkative mood during the veterans' visit, for he began telling his visitors that anyone with a "mile long name" has
to find a "namesake." He joked about an episode that occurred while working on
Jackson Lake Dam. Two "Bohunk," workers with unpronounceable names and

with little English language background, christened their boss "Pat Crowe." They liked the name so well that one of them decided to take on the name himself. The other worker took the name Bob Sass, Crowe's longtime friend and assistant at Jackson Lake. Both Crowe and Sass, the real ones that is, were shocked when introducing themselves to the workers at a job site later.[24]

Crowe's fast pace schedule for sluicing and packing debris against the corewall realized 23 feet of vertical progress in October. With the dam designed like a pyramid, that is, the thickness footage decreased as worked continued upward resulting in less work. This fact spurred the driving engineer to announce on November 1, 1922, "no matter how bad the weather gets, the work at Rimrock will not shut down." He did expect to cut back to about 300 men. With these workers, Crowe planned to move "140,000 cubic yards of rock from the face of the spillway" and to move it "to the face of the lower part of the dam." He explained that if the weather becomes too cold to sluice, then the men would engage in "rock work." In addition, he notified the clearing contractor that he expected reservoir crews to work through the winter, unless heavy snowfall should temporarily stop work. Crowe mapped out the entire work schedule for months ahead, taking into consideration weather concerns. He planned to complete the dam in early 1924.[25]

The temperatures dropped steadily during November, but the accelerated work pace continued. On a regular basis, Crowe consulted with his foremen and assistants to make sure that all safety regulations were being met. He had learned, under Weymouth, that the Service placed the safety of the workers first. Up to this point, there had been no fatalities and only a few minor injuries. On November 9, Thomas Smith, a 42-year-old unskilled worker, became the first fatal statistic. He was on night shift riding the work trains carrying excavated earth to the fill site when, for no apparent reason, fell from his comfortable position. Smith was immediately crushed to death between the moving cars. Crowe asked to see his employment card so that he could notify his next of kin. Amazingly, no relatives were listed, and fellow workers told Crowe that he never spoke of family or friends. Regardless, Crowe insisted on proper funeral services at Yakima's Shaw & Sons' Funeral Home. He asked project clerk V. T. Evans to make the arrangements.

Late in November, Crowe presented an "illustrated lecture" to the Washington State Irrigation Institute held that year in Yakima. Reclamation engineers and bureaucrats from around the state were anxious to hear Crowe describe the construction progress and estimate the benefits of Tieton's projected impound of irrigation water. On the second day of the conference, Crowe escorted the excited group of 75 waterusers to Rimrock where they were served an "excellent meal," toured the dam and were shown a film of progress from the first year of construction. The Washington visitors were especially impressed with "the electrically driven shovel, with the corewall construction, and with the method of puddling the earth and silt against the corewall."

On Thanksgiving Day a "chinook" struck the Yakima Valley area dumping inches of rain in a short time. Rumors spread through Yakima that this was the worst downpour in recent years and fear spread that incomplete Tieton Dam might not hold the water back from quickly rising Tieton River. Several Yakima farmers and businessmen made repeated telephone calls to the construction office at Rimrock only to find that no one answered. J. L. Lytel tried to reassure residents that everything was all right and that the dam was in no danger. He reminded townspeople that Crowe had given the crew a two-day Thanksgiving holiday, and he called the report of a dam failure "an absurdity on its face." The situation turned even more serious when telephone service to Rimrock was completely cut. With the Tieton road washed out in several places, Crowe ordered special overtime crews to start repairs. Two days later with the holiday over and the rain subsiding, everything quickly returned to normal.

The rest of 1922 and the early part of 1923 moved along as expected for the relentless engineer. With the work crews reduced in size, the operation slowed somewhat, yet Crowe maintained three shifts for part of the time. Interestingly, Crowe's cableway system held up well in the freezing or below freezing temperatures. Workers regularly greased the heavy well-worn cables and trolley car wheels. The men continued to remove rock from the site of the spillway to the lower toe of the dam even with two inches of snow covering the dam.

The white blanket of snow piled deeper and isolation for Rimrock families increased, and with it loneliness. In early February of 1923, the entire community of Rimrock was not shocked to discover that Pearl Lydecker, wife of Tieton Dam worker, Charles Lydecker, sought a divorce on the grounds that, "life in construction camp made me irritable and nervous." Pearl told the superior court that her husband had "forced her" to live in dam construction camps for ten years and that she could not take it any longer.[26]

Early in March Crowe announced that "as soon as the frost is out of the ground" he would rehire most of the men he had laid off for the winter. "There is still quite a bit of frost on the ground," Crowe said. Explaining his wintertime slowdown and the need for warmer weather, he continued, "and the weather is freezing cold at nights. Earth for the fill cannot be moved under such conditions as it will not pack, and the water supply for sluicing is cut off on account of the cold." As soon as a thaw came Crowe expected to increase the workforce to an all-time high of 600, with "full crews in every department." Responding to concerns about the unusually high rainfall and possible threat of floods, Crowe concluded that the corewall at 100 feet above the "sill at the intake of the tunnel [diversion]" would carry off 10,000-second feet of water. He confidently declared, "We are past all danger from that source."[27]

On March 12, Crowe left Rimrock for a three-week inspection trip of western dam construction. His orders, from Weymouth, included visiting the Hetch-Hetchy Dam in California. Linnie remained behind to take care of young Patricia. Though not identified by name, it was reported that one of the California dams he would visit was quite similar to Tieton's construction design, though "considerably smaller." No sooner had he left the Yakima area than a huge, destructive wind descended on the valley. The sixty m.p.h. "gale" literally thrashed every town and farmstead in the area for a day and a half. Electricity was down everywhere and residents resorted to old dust covered oil lamps to see their way about. Telephone service halted abruptly, with poles "blown over and wires to the city [Yakima] were broken." Rimrock did not escape the hurricane type weather and all work ceased. Workers rushed immediately to their homes. Desperate residents struggled against all odds to save precious belongings and buildings. In Yakima "three men were kept busy holding down the roof of the Moose Hall on North First Street." The Barnett family arrived home to see their new barn's roof gone. They located it later, some two hundreds yards away. Incredibly, even brick buildings could not escape the onslaught. A commercial building on East Yakima Avenue, sitting squarely in the path of the onrushing wind, shook noticeably and loosened bricks, one of which fell two stories, "missing a man by only a few inches." Other stories of destruction spread rapidly. A truck loaded with hops was completely turned over, scattering its precious contents "far and wide." An automobile owned by A. E. Smith, of Naches, "ran away from him with the wind as its motive power." Smith, who had left his car parked on the side of the road, was talking to another resident about the storm when "it started to go down the road." Thinking quickly, and much to the amusement and shock of observers, Smith "chased after it and grabbed the steering wheel just in time to prevent an accident." At the work site, J. E. Moore, acting superintendent with Crowe away, reported that "tumble weeds passed me by like I was standing still" as he was driving into Yakima to report a complete work shutdown.[28]

When Crowe returned to Rimrock on March 30, 1923, he was glad to see that damage from the fierce windstorm repaired. After he quickly unpacked and checked in with his assistants, Crowe drove into Yakima to report his return to Lytel. As he drove into town, with Linnie by his side, he could see public utility crews still erecting power and telephone poles. Crowe told Lytel that he wanted to fill the work crews with qualified men as soon as possible. To this end, Crowe had stopped by to see the Service labor agent in Seattle during his recent trip asking for help in recruiting dam workers. Single men, in particular, formed a somewhat undependable work group. They came and went at all times. Upon returning to camp, he was approached by H. G. Cowling, his warehouse foreman, saying that he wanted to resign. Cowling, a Rimrock employee for several years, gave no reason publicly for the resignation except that he wanted to go to "southern California." Cowling had been on the job when Crowe first arrived, with the responsibility of stocking and organizing the warehouse when it was at Naches.

It seemed that if it was not one thing, it was another. In April, with the ranks of workers swelling, Crowe became bombarded with problems. The additional number of workers put strains on the mess hall capabilities, available bunkhouse space, and medical facilities; even recreation equipment was now inadequate. Many of the new recruits needed to be watched carefully during their on-the-job training. These "green," sometimes-anxious new employees would disregard safety rules in order to short cut the work and impress foremen with the quickness of their work. In the middle of this, Linnie became ill and was rushed immediately to St. Elizabeth's Hospital in Yakima. Frank, while realizing that his camp medical facilities could handle construction accidents, was not well equipped to run tests and diagnose general internal disorders. While it is not known what Linnie was suffering from, she did spend over a week away from her family. Frank, as often as he could, drove into town with Patricia to visit and encourage Linnie.[29]

With Linnie back home, Frank once again concentrated on the sluicing operations and the continuing effort to finish the corewall. Through May and June Crowe's team of veteran foremen honed the skills of the crews. The three shifts of workers learned to labor as a "well oiled machine," with ending crews leaving tools and machines in good operating order, cleaned, and ready to go for the next group. Within the shift teams themselves, Crowe paid particular attention to the logistics of coordinating hundreds of men within the confines of limited space. Each worker had to know his place in the overall sequence of jobs and act accordingly so as not to hinder, or temporarily halt, another crews' operation. Crowe insisted that his foremen make it perfectly clear that any man not working, as part of that team, would be immediately fired.

Meanwhile, the *Yakima Morning Herald* reported on June 10 that the San Diego chapter of the American Society of Engineers had made a special request asking the Yakima area engineers to support their call on Congress to build Boulder Dam. The message from San Diego stated that "this dam will irrigate additional land in the Imperial Valley," and it called for a resolution to be passed and sent on to Congress. Lytel, as president of the local chapter, was away on business at the time so Charles E. Hewitt, head of the executive committee presided over the brief meeting to discuss the request. A. B. Collins, chairman of the resolutions committee, reported that while the matter was discussed, no action was taken. The same day, Frank and Linnie who had driven into Yakima to shop the day before were approached by reporters. He did not comment on the resolution or his feelings about the building of Boulder Dam, for he knew it was wise not to become involved in political controversy. The questions shifted to work progress on Tieton, to which Crowe quickly countered, "We're just moving mud."[30]

In the middle of June a bombshell news report that Arthur P. Davis, director of the Reclamation Service, had announced his "retirement," dominated camp gossip at Rimrock. Davis, longtime supporter of dam building in the West, had strong ties to Crowe going back to the Yellowstone project in 1905. While Crowe understood the depth of Davis's problems with newly installed Secretary of the Interior Hubert Work, most dam workers and area residents were not sure as to why Davis, who was in apparently good health would suddenly resign. The new

Interior secretary, called to replace former scandal ridden chief Albert Fall, promised to place the Service on a sound financial foundation. Work had accused Davis of mismanagement of the Reclamation Service funds and pronounced him responsible for the continued "wasteful, inefficient, patronizing record of the Service." Work acting quickly and assertively, called for a complete reorganization, and designated a new name for the Service, the Bureau of Reclamation. Another Davis, D. W., former governor of Idaho was appointed to take over A. P. Davis' important position. Instead of using the title of director, D. W. Davis was appointed as Commissioner of the Bureau of Reclamation. Local business owners reacted favorably to the appointment, as Idaho's governor Davis had promoted irrigation development. It is not known what Frank Crowe's immediate reaction was to the announcement, although he must have thought it curious that D. W. Davis was not a trained engineer. While he had nurtured a good working relationship with A. P. Davis, he also knew of the new commissioner; Crowe having worked on numerous projects in Idaho.[31]

Within days of the Davis retirement announcement, Crowe was saddened by the loss of another worker. Twenty-eight year old Forrest Williams was instantly killed when his head was severed between two large gears on the electric shovel. Williams was working the graveyard shift when the terrible accident occurred. Apparently, the young oiler moved too close to the grinding gears, the mechanism grabbing a portion of his clothing. He had convinced Crowe back in 1921 to give him the opportunity to be in charge of maintenance of the big shovel and he had proven himself cautious and knowledgeable of machinery. Crowe was shocked as he viewed the grisly scene at six o'clock that morning. News spread quickly around the camp. Charlie Williams, the victims brother and longtime associate of Crowe, began the sad task of notifying the other six brothers and sisters as well as other family members. When it was learned that the dead man was to be married in August, only a month and a half away, Crowe took it upon himself to drive into Yakima and break the sad news to her. Williams' sweetheart "at first refused to believe" that her fiancé had been killed. Crowe also made it his responsibility to deliver the mangled corpse to the county morgue. He knew that Forrest Williams' death resulted from carelessness, and even though the death count was now up to three since starting work, the distraught engineer made it clear to all workers that safety must be their first concern.[32]

No sooner had Crowe driven back to Rimrock than he discovered that the Davis "retirement" was actually a dismissal. He also learned that the 50,000 strong American Engineering Society, of which Crowe was a member, officially protested the firing. The society filed with the Interior Department a lengthy note stating that Davis had given years of dedicated service and that "a thorough investigation and explanation will be demanded." Representatives for the engineers went on to say, "This procedure is looked upon with grave concern by all engineers and technical men." They sternly warned, "because such summary action as discharging an eminently successful employee after 35 years of service, without a hearing or adequate explanation will undermine the morale of all agencies of the government." Meanwhile, Work, in his haste, had unwisely taken the liberty to rename the traditional Service journal, *Reclamation Record*, the *New Reclamation Era* "in a clear attempt 'to denote the birth of a new regime in Government regulation.'" [33]

Caught in a major controversy, Secretary of the Interior Hubert Work, riding President Harding's train in Helena, Montana realized that he needed to explain his actions. On June 29, he disclosed that he had, for several reasons, accepted A. P. Davis' "resignation." First, a major reorganization would be necessary in the Reclamation Service. "I have Mr. Davis' resignation," Work declared. Without hesitating the Interior secretary continued, "We don't need two engineers in charge of the Reclamation Service." He was suggesting that Davis, as Director of the Service and Frank Weymouth, as Chief Engineer, performed the same duties. This was technically incorrect. Davis was located in the national headquarters in Washington where he supervised all aspects of the Reclamation Service, formulating budget requirements, providing technical information to the Interior secretary and Congress, and politically pushing irrigation funding. He reported directly to the Interior secretary, while Weymouth, who was in Denver, supervised dam and irrigation works construction in the West. Work, pulling no punches firmly added, "In the future the service head will be known as the Chief of the Bureau of Reclamation and will be qualified first to aid the farmers rather than supervise engineering works on the projects." Realizing now that the proverbial "cat was out of the bag" the strong-willed secretary exposed his reorganization plan. "D. W. Davis, former governor of Idaho, is such a man and I have appointed him as bureau chief; have abolished the office of Director and placed F. E. Weymouth, former chief of the service, in the position of chief of engineer of the bureau." Work provided federal financial figures to show that the government was losing money on irrigation projects and that someone was needed to manage the finances and recover the indebted money from farmers. "The government has expended, on the reclamation projects of the country, $135,000,000; has received only $15,000,000 from the farmers in return and there is $3,000,000 now due the government, which the farmers cannot pay," reported a local Yakima newspaper. In his concluding remarks Work again defended his reorganization by claiming, "Mr. Davis of Idaho will help the homesteaders to become successful farmers and pay off their debts." When asked about the letters of objection pouring in from engineer and waterpower interests and organizations, Work said that he would not give them his attention until after returning from Alaska. Realizing the political aspects of the situation he wisely added, "I will balance them [protest letters] in one hand against the recommendations received from those who regarded the reorganization of the reclamation service as a step in advance of the old system."[34]

Local engineers, at their monthly meeting in Yakima on July 1, conducted round table talks on the history of engineering achievements and on the recent developments in Washington D. C. No mention is made as to whether Crowe was one of the fifteen in attendance, yet it is safe to assume that he, like many others who had known A. P. Davis, remained concerned about Work's remarks and the direction he wanted to take the new Bureau of Reclamation. The possibility arose that new construction jobs would move ahead much more slowly under the new regime. Provisions would need to be made whereby farmers were held account-able for their portion of the federal construction tab. This approach added an intricate new layer of roadblocks that needed to be satisfied before Congress would appropriate new monies. At least this is how it appeared to engineers and prospec-tive waterusers. On face value, it was difficult to argue with Work, and many in Congress, who pressed for financial responsibility on the part of those receiving the benefits from the myriad of irrigation projects funded and built with federal money. On the other hand, if the government wanted more people to settle in the West, was it not the federal government's responsibility to provide an environ-ment where, at least in part, potential farmers homesteaded where ample water supplies existed? Crowe knew all too well both sides of the controversy, for he had now spent twenty years in the West building dams and irrigation systems. While no correspondence exists between Crowe and his mentor, Weymouth, on the subject of Davis' "resignation," it is quite possible that the reappointed Chief Engineer had kept Crowe informed from the beginning of the controversy. It is easy to see where sympathies lie: A. P. Davis was Weymouth's mentor, and Weymouth was Crowe's mentor.

Under an unexpected assault from across the country, federal officials struggled to grapple with the thorny problem. The president and Work, on their way to Alaska via railroad were unavailable for further comment. The new Bu-reau of Reclamation as a "fair assessment" of Work's opinion released the follow-ing statement:

> In the evolution of the reclamation service, the engi-neering problems are being subordinated to the business policy of making a commercial success of the farms embraced in re-claimed areas. The engineering problems are such that they can be handled by the chief engineer of the service. The crying need of reclamation is to devise means whereby the individual farmers can make reasonable profits. Under present conditions, their earnings are inadequate. They cannot pay even the water charges. Drastic steps must be taken if the overhead is to be cut down and the great commercial problem of making their farms pay solved. The [people of the] west believes the farming of those reclaimed lands is economically sound. Under proper di-rection the farmers' deficits can be changed into profits.[35]

Taking the opportunity to expound on their new choice of leading the Bureau officials declared:

> Governor Davis, the new commissioner, is believed to be the type of man who can accomplish that purpose. His long association with farmers' problems on reclamation projects and the fact that he has been the president for several years of the Western States Reclamation Association fit him for the task of solving the business problems of the reclamation farmer.

Moreover, in explaining the new position of Weymouth and the role of engineering in the new Bureau, it was said:

> In that connection it is pointed out that Governor Davis would delegate all engineering matters to F. E. Weymouth, the chief engineer of the service, who has the confidence of all water users. Secretary Work, however, recognized the value of the services of the dismissed director and tendered him employment at $20 a day to act as consulting engineer of the service. This Mr. Davis [A. P. Davis] declined.

With the above statement, it quickly became evident that Davis had not voluntarily resigned, but had actually been dismissed. Surprisingly, Bureau officials admitted:

> In addition to the principle involved in making the change, there is also the matter of Mr. Davis' personality. He had served under several secretaries and had come to regard the job as his own. He was in many cases arbitrary and frequently insisted on having [it] [h]is own way. At times he insisted on following his judgment rather than that of the secretary of the interior. This led to serious trouble between him and Secretaries Lane and Fall. He is that type of capable man who refuses to play the game and who makes teamwork impossible.

An editorial comment from an engineering publication regarding the dismissal, appeared at the same time as the above Bureau release stating:

> Mr. Davis will be able now to enter a consulting practice which has long awaited him at a compensation much greater than he has heretofore enjoyed, taking with him the respect of his professional associates to compensate him somewhat for this

reflection of the ungratefulness of republics.[36]

The sides were drawn, and the controversy though over for A. P. Davis, would continue for years to come. Crowe himself would soon come face to face with the changes of the new Bureau of Reclamation policies, forcing a life-changing decision.

President Harding and Secretary of the Interior Work returned from their Alaska trip by the end of July and the chief executive was spending some time in San Francisco when he was struck with bronchial pneumonia on July 30. Described as "fighting for his life" by the five physicians attending him at the Palace Hotel, Harding briefly recovered. Crowe, on the same day, visited Yakima and reported an all-time high of 677 men fully engaged in the work. While everyone in Yakima and Rimrock, and indeed across the country waited to see if the president would pull through, Frank Weymouth and James Munn decided to visit Tieton Dam. Crowe's mentor, Weymouth and his former partner, Munn were with him when it was announced, on August 2 that Harding had succumbed to "a stroke of apoplexy." As Crowe, Munn, Weymouth, and the entire nation mourned the loss of Harding, they also discussed the tumultuous changes taking place with the Bureau and wondered if the new president Calvin Coolidge would dismiss Secretary Work or back his new ideas for reorganization.

Work after initial consultations with Coolidge issued an official response to the American Society of Civil Engineers, and all of its members were notified— including Crowe, of his statement. Work claimed that the change was part of a "natural development" of Reclamation priorities. Whereas in the past, engineering and construction was highest on the list, now top priority would go to settling "the problems of water users and the collection of the original cost of the projects as contemplated by law." In a fighting mood, secretary Work issued a warning, "unless conditions which have obtained hitherto are improved many reclamation projects will be abandoned entirely by settlers." While this statement might, at first glance, appear to confuse the reader, Work believed the logic of it all. Wanting to clear the air and set the record straight that construction projects were not coming to a grinding halt, he commented, "This does not mean a diminished construction program, but rather an increased and accelerated construction, because with the money returned to the government under efficient business management there will be freed a fund to continue construction that otherwise will be retarded." The problem was deeper than simply making the water users pay off their federal debts, as the entire farming industry, in an economic depression since the end of World War I, had amassed enormous debts in terms of property, machinery, seed, and other agricultural equipment. The majority of farmers were operating on borrowed money and the federal government was low on the list of creditors to be paid.

In an effort to not alienate the engineers, Work reasoned that nothing had really changed and the importance of their work on the nation's growth was a vital as ever.

> To handle the engineering work, the engineering force of the service remains with the same chief engineer at its head who has been engaged in the work for many years. There is no thought of minimizing the importance of reclamation engineering. It was my purpose to retain Director A. P. Davis in the reclamation service as consulting engineer, he at first consenting, but subsequently declining the appointment.[37]

Not wanting to become preoccupied with the politics developing in Washington, Crowe remained focused on completing Tieton Dam. By September a record 656 men were employed and, as usual, he planned the use of full crews until the cold weather forced a reduction in construction. With her husband hard at work overseeing the large crew, Linnie spent several days in Yakima. It was a local tradition for women to visit the clothing and shoe shops at this time of year to view the new fall styles and fabrics. In 1923, satin crepes, twills, plaids, and other fabrics were popular items at local stores such as Ditter Bros. and Lemon's. Holding special 8:00 am store opening hours for customers wanting the latest fashion in coats and wraps, many local businesses took out quarter and half page ads. One read, "Coats and wraps for 1923 are garments of beauty and luxury. Taken from the standpoint of embellishment, embroideries, braids and buttons follow fur as trimming." Smith's furniture, wanting to capitalize on the clothing sale, had its own special display with "up to date furniture." Not to be outdone, a Yakima appliance store selling the newest model washing machines advertised, "This is your cue to act at once. Free yourself of laundry drudgery by buying today."[38] Frank found time to break away for a day and join Linnie in Yakima as she continued to shop and socialize.

In October, Crowe was asked by Weymouth to visit the Flathead project in Montana, where he inspected a dam under construction. Upon returning to Rimrock, Crowe discovered that two Japanese engineers, T. Shirakihara and C. Nakamma, representing their government and private Japanese construction companies had arrived, wanting a tour of the dam site and an opportunity to talk shop with Crowe. Viewing the rising corewall Shirakihara marveled "American engineering is a revelation." Shirakihara noted that in Japan the use of large concrete dams would be needed to fully tap the hydroelectric sources that existed on the Japanese home islands. He looked into every phase of construction.

Before leaving Shirakihara commented on the differences between the U.S. and Japan and their use of engineering material and personnel, "America has wonderfully skilled workmen. In Japan, only the highly educated engineers and foremen are able to operate machinery and here I see common laborers in charge of the most complex machines without direct supervision. Very few Japanese understand machinery. Because of this, construction work in Japan takes a much longer time to reach completion"[39]

The visiting engineers went on to explain that the cost of construction in Japan is "very cheap" due to the low wages paid to common laborers. In Japan, workmen only received about 90 cents for nine hours work and in the U.S. men received $3.50 to $4.00 for eight-hour shifts. The machinery costs were expensive as almost all of it was imported, making the overall cost of the new Uzanto dam on the island of Formosa in Japan twice the cost of Tieton Dam. Crowe was surprised to hear from Shirakihara, after eating a hearty meal in the Rimrock mess hall, that "laborers in Japan lived mostly on rice," and that American construction camp food was better than most Japanese restaurants. Crowe became irritated when local newspapermen cornered the Asian engineers into making a statement about the recent political problems that California was having with Japanese farmers. In response to their probing Shirakihara remarked that he had "found Americans friendly and kind and was sorry that the Japanese land holders on the Pacific coast were having troubles with American farmers." Then he added, "There is much to be said for arguments presented on both sides of the position." Crowe after learning that the foreign engineers were most interested in the construction of tall concrete arched dams recommended that they visit Arrowrock Dam where they could see the results of Crowe's expert use of the extensive cableway system in a canyon setting. Shirakihara, most anxious to absorb all he could, told Crowe that he would also like to see "as much as possible" in the way of irrigation and dam projects before returning to Japan, and that he would rely on Crowe to advise him of the sites to visit.

In November, a special advisory committee of the Department of the Interior wrestled with the continuing problem of reorganizing the new Bureau of Reclamation. Their preliminary findings on government investment in Western projects had revealed "although apparently bankrupt so far as there is probability of repayment of investment or of adequate returns to the average farmer, the projects have invariably paid substantial dividends in national wealth." The report went on to cite the wide range of returns coming in from Western farmers who agreed to help pay back the government investment in completing irrigation projects. Secretary Work took another opportunity with the issuing of these committee findings to reaffirm his belief that the "executive offices" of the new Bureau of Reclamation should reside in Washington D.C. and that Denver would remain the construction and engineering headquarters of the Bureau.[40]

Crowe, still dissatisfied about the handling of the A. P. Davis forced resignation, struggled to not get involved. All of his communication to Weymouth centered on the engineering status at Tieton, and not on politics. One of his contacts with Weymouth focused on the request by the Rimrock teachers to hire additional help. With Rimrock growing there were too many children for two teachers to handle so the school board agreed to contribute $50 a month for hiring one new teacher, and they wanted the Bureau to come up with the balance. Several women in Rimrock had normal (teacher) training and they applied to help with the primary grades. Through November, Crowe kept focused as he slowly downsized the Tieton Dam operation. He had to juggle his strong desire to finish the dam as soon as possible with the fact that winter rainy conditions would become a safety factor with large crews working. By Christmas, with construction settling into a winter schedule, Crowe was able to take his family to a special holiday concert in Yakima, where legendary bandleader John Phillip Sousa gave two rousing performances at the Capitol Theater.[41]

With a new year, Crowe was anxious to complete the dam. He announced in March of 1924 that work crews would be reinstated to full strength. By the 12th of that month, "the season of work at Rimrock was opened yesterday at 8 am with an explosion of 14 tons of TNT for completion of the embankment of the dam according to word received from F.T. Crowe," announced the Yakima newspaper. Crowe asked that additional men be sent to help in the sluicing and finishing the embankment concreting. He also wanted work to begin on the tall spillway and on the overflow pipes, emergency gates and machinery. Crowe was pleased to see that funding for completing the dam had been fully approved and that the Bureau was delighted to see that Tieton Dam would be finished ahead of schedule. Yakima townspeople, worried once again about dirt laden water ruining their system were assured by Crowe, "As long as the Naches river is high the Tieton dam furnishes very little of the water that gets into the city system. By the time of low water in the fall the fill at the dam will have been completed."[42]

In full swing by April of 1924, Crowe had dozens of large crews working on four major projects: sluicing and completing the earthen fill, concreting the spillway, finishing the corewall, and grouting. The master engineer always considered the grouting operation to be of vital importance and one that must be approached meticulously. The difficult job consisted of driving diamond drills at different angles from the gate chamber in the tunnel into the rock and of driving cement under hydraulic pressure into holes and in the crevices of the rock to shut off any possibility of a leak that might cause trouble later. Crowe realized that even though the mineral structure around Tieton was andesite, the hardest known volcanic rock, it is porous and the grouting needed to take place anywhere inspectors found signs of weakness. At this time, large shipments of machinery for controlling the release of storage water began to arrive. Carloads of 72-inch reinforced steel pipe sections needed to be joined by electric welders once placed in the final position. Crowe worked closely with pipe contractor, Coast Culvert & Flume Company of Portland, inspecting sections as they arrived.[43]

Another Washington D. C. bombshell was dropped on April 17 when newly appointed Elwood Mead announced another complete reorganization of the Bureau. With all the controversy surrounding the firing of A. P. Davis and the hiring of D. W. Davis, the Coolidge administration decided to take another look at the Bureau. With the hiring of Mead, who had been trained as a civil engineer and had been involved in many Bureau projects, veteran engineers like Crowe were satisfied. They were also pleased to see that D. W. Davis was reassigned to a new position, director of finance, where he would have little influence on engineering aspects of construction projects. Mead, understanding the reality of engineering and Western politics, decided to keep the Denver office open and he even agreed to expand its responsibilities and increase its workforce. Mead wanted Weymouth to stay on as chief engineer at the Denver office. Weymouth was pleased to hear this and even more pleased when Mead mentioned that with a new round of congressionally approved irrigation projects, an assistant chief engineer might be needed. Weymouth, without hesitating, knew just the man for this important new position.

Chapter 6

"I feel like a bull in a china shop."
1925-1927

Frank Crowe's successful challenge of coordinating the over 500 men and scores of large machines at Tieton Dam confirmed Frank Weymouth's opinion that Crowe would be the most qualified engineer to serve with him at the Bureau of Reclamation Western regional headquarters in Denver. By the summer of 1924 as Crowe's industrious crews capped the corewall, placed the last concrete in the spillway, and installed the large drum gates at Tieton Dam, Weymouth already had his protégé talked into accepting the new position. Crowe wanted to know exactly what the new job entailed, and Weymouth revealed that a flood of new construction endeavors were being planned and approved by Congress and that he needed someone to oversee construction of all new Bureau of Reclamation projects. The job title would be General Superintendent of Construction for the Bureau of Reclamation, in charge of all projects in the seventeen Western states.[1] In addition, when Weymouth was gone from Denver, whether in Washington D. C. talking with the commissioner of the Bureau or the Secretary of the Interior, or meeting with congressional members, Crowe would be in complete charge of the Denver office. Reclamation memoirs of Crowe state, "Thus it was that he became one of the top-ranking men of the bureau, having acquired an enviable reputation for organizing ability and ingenious and rapid prosecution of construction work."[2] To add to the excitement, his wife Linnie announced that she was expecting another child. An elated Frank Crowe eagerly looked to the future.

With the approaching winter of 1924, Crowe busied himself with the finishing touches on Tieton Dam and with arranging for his move to Denver. He knew that Linnie and Patricia would enjoy the amenities of a large city, where shopping and schools were well established. Eager to move in before Christmas, Frank made a couple of trips to Denver in search of housing. Linnie, well along in her pregnancy, remained in Rimrock with Patricia. Finally, with considerable snow on the ground during the early part of December, the Crowes settled into their new home in the mile high city. Just a few days into the new year Linnie delivered a healthy baby girl, that Frank and Linnie named Elizabeth.[3]

The expectation of working directly with his mentor Weymouth, energized the ambitious Crowe and he reported to work ready to tackle the Bureau's most difficult engineering challenges. Within weeks however, Crowe began to realize that his new opportunity centered on a 9 a.m. to 5 p.m. clerical routine. He was writing a continual flood of letters and official memoranda, something he hated to do, to project superintendents and Reclamation officials. By January 25, 1925, with only a few weeks of experience at his new administrative job, Crowe was waist-deep in paperwork. With the Bureau of Reclamation considering a large concrete dam for the Guernsey, Wyoming area, he needed to coordinate the final plans, specifications, and subcontract bidding process.[4] He was constantly inundated with requests, from small and large construction companies interested in building Bureau proposed dams and irrigation projects, to see various government building specifications. His job included keeping a running list of all interested private companies and to notify and update Bureau Commissioner Elwood Mead in Washington of each project's specifications, bidding process, and construction status. One such letter he wrote on January 29, 1925; it read, "It is kindly requested that a copy of the Guernsey Dam specifications be sent, when issued, to Dooling Brothers, 306 Bank Building, Denver, Colo."[5]

A major portion of his workload was spent reviewing field reports filed by the numerous project officials. He had spent many years writing these kinds of reports beginning with the Bureau's Flathead project in Montana and he knew how important they were. Yet, these reports appeared so routine, so mundane. His curiosity improved however with the rapidly increasing communication about Guernsey Dam. With Weymouth gone on a fact-finding trip, Crowe, in January, wrote A. J. Wiley, a consulting engineer at Boise, Idaho:

> You will recall that the board completed its discussion shortly before you had to take the train, and that the text of a short report was hurriedly written, after the designs, specifications and estimates were reviewed, it was thought advisable to prepare a detailed report. It is hoped that the report will be satisfactory to you, and if not, you should advise this office promptly.
> Very truly yours, F. T. Crowe Acting Chief Engineer[6]

As February progressed, Crowe, who had helped put together the final official Bureau cost estimates for Guernsey Dam, saw a deluge of requests for information from construction companies wanting to subcontract part of the work or to supply materials. He also yearned to be in the field again, supervising the construction of this large concrete-core spillway dam.

Sitting anxiously behind his huge oak desk in the Denver office, Crowe became both frustrated and excited. On one hand, he knew that Linnie, Patricia, and Elizabeth deserved the stable and comfortable lifestyle that Denver could offer. Yet, he wanted to be out there building dams. As he sat and reviewed dozens of Bureau blueprints for new large Western dams, he understood that this was a once in a lifetime construction opportunity. Within two decades most, if not all, of America's large concrete dams would be built and his window of opportunity would be gone. Actually, he had been led to believe that as general superintendent, he would be visiting all new dam sites and have final word on construction techniques and procedures. Yet, as fate would have it, the Bureau of Reclamation in the spring of 1925 initiated another major shakeup in the way they did business. President Calvin Coolidge decided, after consulting with Interior Secretary Hubert Work and Bureau Director of finance D. W. Davis, that the government would no longer build dams directly. Rather, they would allow private companies to bid, and risk, the money to construct federal dam and irrigation projects. In this manner, the Bureau would no longer be financially at-risk with construction hazards.[7] In fact, they could monetarily penalize private companies that did not hold up their end of the contract. In this new setup, the Bureau would only be on hand at the project sites to ensure quality control, serving as inspectors.

In the Denver office, Chief Engineer Weymouth and Superintendent of Construction Crowe reeled from the announcement. While much discussion on the subject of Bureau involvement in project construction had gone on around the country, both men were shocked by the decision. Weymouth immediately made plans to go to the Washington office of the Bureau and discuss the matter with his superior, Reclamation Commissioner Mead. Newly hired Mead, under pressure from a determined Secretary of the Interior, Hubert Work, could do little but go along with the restructuring. A nervous and anxious Crowe waited in Denver for some word on how this important reshuffling of Bureau methods for doing business would affect him.

Meanwhile, on March 10, 1925 Reclamation officials in Mitchell, Nebraska opened the bids for the building of Bureau's newest large irrigation structure, Guernsey Dam. The results were sent to Crowe at the Denver office. Crowe, becoming daily more disappointed in his desk-bound duties, read the cover letter accompanying the bid results and discovered that only one bid had actually been received. This note helped to force Crowe into a career changing decision; it read:

> The total amount of the bid being $61,748 lower then
> the Engineer's Estimate which was prepared in the Denver of-
> fice. It is probable that your office has full information relative
> to the financial standing of the Utah Construction Company, and
> their ability to complete the contract, if it is awarded to them at
> the price specified in their proposal.[8]

Crowe immediately passed on the bid information to Weymouth, who was visiting in the Washington D. C. Bureau headquarters. Meanwhile Crowe checked the Denver office files for information on the successful bidders, Utah Construction. It appeared that this Ogden, Utah based construction firm was eager to get involved in government irrigation projects. Their particular interest was in building concrete dams and canals. After waiting days for a reply from his mentor and boss, Crowe shot off a Western Union telegram asking, "Please advise status of Guernsey Dam contract. Acting Chief Engineer, Crowe"[9] In a quick response, Assistant Bureau Commissioner P. W. Dent wired Crowe that the Secretary of the Interior and President Coolidge were "investigating and making findings regarding feasibility of new project from which approximately half million of Guernsey expenditures must be recouped."[10] Crowe also learned that Utah Construction had deposited $45,000 as a performance bond, guaranteeing their commitment.

As the days wore on, no word was received from Weymouth and it was unclear whether the Bureau was moving forward with an official announcement on Guernsey Dam. Crowe now acted as a communication middleman between the Washington office and Utah Construction. Utah president W. H. Wattis, naturally worried about the status of his bid and contract, talked frequently with Crowe, who continued to serve, in Weymouth's absence, as acting chief engineer. These initial contacts proved to open the door for a new employment opportunity and a new career direction. Construction contractor H. J. Woodman of Ft. Collins, Colorado, contacted Crowe at this time. Woodman complained about the bidding process, and he wanted a postponement of the award and an investigation. Crowe learned that Woodman had also contacted Congressman Robert C. Simmons of Nebraska specifying his complaints. Crowe quickly sent off a telegram to the field office in Mitchell, Nebraska to ascertain if Woodman had ever visited the Guernsey site or the Mitchell office. On March 26, Ray Walter, serving as a consulting engineer for Weymouth, consulted with Crowe then wrote to Commissioner Meade summarizing Woodman's complaints:

> (a) He does not believe the minor officials of the Bureau of Reclamation are trying to carryout the plans of the Secretary in connection with contract versus Government force work.
>
> (b) He implies that the engineers of the Bureau have purposely written the specification in such manner as to discourage competitive bidding and to cause high bids. This alleged to have been done to make the engineer's estimate on Government force construction seem reasonable.
>
> (c) He infers that the failure to receive more bids was because the specifications were "veiled with mystery," and he claims to know two prominent Colorado contractors who, like his own firm, were greatly interested in the work until they read the specifications.

(d) He states that the cost of construct work for the government is increased above what it would cost an ordinary business organization due to the specification requirements.

(e) He cites in part one clause of the General Conditions of the specifications, which is believed to constitute the principal basis for his criticism, as follows, "The right is reserved to reject all proposals, and/or to accept one part of a proposal and reject the other."

Walter, in defense of Bureau of Reclamation action, countered Woodman's accusations with the following:

> Referring to the criticism mentioned in (a), it will be obvious to your office and we hope to the office of the Secretary that the minor officials of the Bureau could not possibly circumvent the Secretary's plans for constructing such work as the Guernsey Dam, even if there was any such desire. The specifications were prepared in the Engineering section under the direction of the Designing Engineer and were reviewed by the Project Superintendent, the General Superintendent of Construction [Crowe] and Consulting Engineer A. J. Wiley before receiving my approval. The specifications were then forwarded to the Commissioner's office for review and approval before printing. Under this procedure, the responsibility for the Guernsey Dam specifications certainly does not rest with minor officials of the Bureau.

Walter, intent in addressing as many of Woodman's accusations, continued,

> Referring to the criterion mentioned in (b), Mr. Woodman evidently did not know at the time he wrote his letter that the bid of the Utah Construction Company was nearly $62,000 less than the engineer's estimate. The fact that the only bid received was substantially lower than the engineer's estimate does not bear out Mr. Woodman's idea that the specifications were purposely written in such a way as to result in higher bids than the engineer's estimate.
> Referring to the criterion mentioned in (c), it is the opinion of this office that the reluctance of contractors to bid on the Guernsey dam was due to the hazard connected with the work rather that to the fact that the specifications were "veiled in mystery" as alleged by Mr. Woodman. The contractors, who took enough

in the proposed work to visit the site and to discuss the work with the project engineers and the engineers of this office, did not disclose by their questions any hesitancy to bid on the work on account of the wording of the specifications. However, several of them did indicate that they considered the work hazardous. The specific hazards mentioned by different contractors included particularly the following"

(a) The uncertainty in regard to the amount of seepage, which will be encountered in the excavation of the diversion tunnel.

(b) The difficulty of excavating the deep tunnels in the bed of the river.

(c) The danger of losing a part of the dam from floods in the spring of 1926.

Walter goes on hitting every point mentioned in Woodman's criticism and then recommends:

It is hoped that the criticisms on the part of Mr. Woodman will not be permitted to delay the awarding a contract to the Utah Construction Company. There is every reason to expedite the award as the contractor must complete the tunnel and build a large part of the dam before the spring floods next year, otherwise practically the whole construction season during 1926 will be lost. It is therefore, very important, both from the standpoint of the Government and of the Utah Construction Company, that the contract be executed at an early date.[11]

Dent followed two days later with a reply that instructed Walter and Crowe to not take any action, as Meade wanted to postpone a decision until his return to Washington on the 20th. Crowe and Walter became discouraged during this interim period. Crowe disliked the paperwork and the problems associated with supervising at this level. Had Walter not been in the Denver office at the time, it would have been Crowe's responsibility to write all of the extensive memorandums to Washington, Woodman, Mitchell field office, and to Utah Construction. H. W. Wattis worried as each day passed that his low bid was in jeopardy. Finally, on April 7 he fired off a letter to Walter in which he responded to Woodman's concerns. He retorted, "We have carefully studied this letter and are forcibly reminded of a somewhat trite quotation, that his letter contains "some things that are true and some things that are to the point, but the things that are true are not to the point and the things that are to the point are not true." Wattis goes on to state that Woodman, in his accusations, assumes that "all engineers are dishonest and looking for a chance to get the better of the contractor." He finished his letter with a supporting statement that Utah Construction "stands ready to furnish" any documents and papers that might help solve the situation.[12]   Crowe knew that Wattis and his company had followed the bidding rules completely, for he had been responsible for most of the communication. Now the situation rested in the hands of Commissioner Meade.

Through the rest of April, Mead and Secretary of the Interior Hubert Work waited for an opportunity to discuss the Guernsey matter with President Coolidge. On May 1, Meade telegrammed Walter in Denver that the president had approved the Guernsey contract for Utah Construction. He further notified a somewhat shocked Walter that he wanted him to assume Weymouth's job as chief engineer in Denver.[13]

It appears that both Crowe and Weymouth disagreed with the new Bureau of Reclamation directive to bid dam and irrigation projects in their entirety to private companies. This would mean that both men would be relegated to desk bound duties, acting more as administrators than builders. Crowe's memoirs state, "He was always happiest in the open spaces on the front line of a tough construction job, and the limitations of an executive office were most irksome to him." At one point during his brief Denver experience he was heard to say, "Do you know what I feel like sitting at this desk shuffling papers? I feel like a bull in a china shop." The two men most likely discussed the issue many times during the difficult months of March, April, and May. The Woodman affair only heightened the problems that Crowe's future, if he remained with the Bureau of Reclamation, would become less and less involved with field construction engineering and more and more embroiled in legal litigation. So too must have been the reaction of Weymouth who had, by May 1 notified Washington that he wanted out. Weymouth would stay on in an official capacity until October, but his protégé Crowe resigned officially on June 1, 1925.[14]

Crowe's resignation came promptly due to an offer of private employment from Harry Morrison, co-founder of the Morrison & Knudsen Construction Company. Morrison, who himself had started out in western construction in the Reclamation Service had by 1908 formed a partnership with Morris Knudsen. Struggling with limited capital until 1924, the fledgling company began to challenge the already established Utah Construction Company. It was at this point that Morrison contacted E. O. Wattis, Director of Utah Construction and older brother to co-founder W. H. Wattis, and secured a subcontract to supply the labor for the Guernsey Dam job. In looking around to select the most qualified construction superintendent, Morrison quickly focused on Denver and Frank Crowe.[15]   The pair hit it off and after consulting with Linnie; the bright ambitious Crowe accepted the position of Superintendent of Construction of Guernsey Dam for Morrison & Knudsen. On hearing the news, Wattis was elated, for he knew that Crowe possessed the skills necessary to make large scale dam building profitable.

F. F. Smith, a Bureau of Reclamation engineer and a colleague of Crowe, won the appointment as the government representative attached to the new Guernsey Dam project. Under the new construction plan, devised by Interior Secretary Work, the on-site Reclamation engineer would be responsible for acquiring all necessary material and machinery to be used by the private construction firm; for example, in the case of Guernsey Dam, Utah Construction. Smith would further be charged with verifying the quality of the work done by the Utah Construction Company and that all specifications had been met. Nervous about the enormity of the proposed project and a bit unsure of exactly what to do, Smith made several trips to the remote eastern Wyoming building site to move preparations along. Already in May, Smith noticed, "quite a large number of men are arriving in Guernsey" hoping to get on the payroll early. He was careful about making public announcements when equipment would arrive or when Utah Construction would show up and start hiring. The rest of the month Smith had his surveyors run final mapping coordinates and he organized a crew of Reclamation engineers to assist him.[16]

On May 21, 1925, the Bureau of Reclamation announced that its Superintendent of Construction, Frank T. Crowe had suddenly resigned his position and would shortly "go with the Utah Construction Company and will be on the Guernsey job." Since his official resignation did not take effect until June 1, Crowe remained in Denver where he reviewed the Guernsey Dam specifications, pored over topographic maps of the work site, and kept up communication with the Wattis brothers of Utah Construction and with field engineer Smith. Crowe had insisted that he be given full command over the building operations in return for which he promised to build the dam ahead of schedule and up to or surpassing government specifications. Wattis, excited over the prospect of completing the $1.2 million contract with a substantial profit, quickly reassigned the previously designated construction chief and placed Crowe in command. [17]

Linnie, seeing the excitement in her husband's face, must have hid much of her concern about returning to construction camp living. Frank's Denver job offered security, high salary, national recognition, and full amenities for raising a family. Yet, here they were again packing their belongings and preparing to move. What lay ahead, no one in the Crowe family knew for sure, but Frank had told Linnie, on numerous occasions, that the greatest dam building era was about to begin and that he did not want to be watching from the sidelines. He knew that his reputation was already established and that his Reclamation colleagues considered him an authority on dam construction; Arrowrock and Tieton Dam had won him that honor. In this position, he could now offer his valuable services to the highest bidder, and as long as the government continued to make a financial commitment to building dams then business would remain good.

The "bull" was officially released from the "China shop" on June 1, however the great dam builder was too excited. With special permission from Washington, Crowe left Denver on May 31, arriving in the little town of Guernsey late

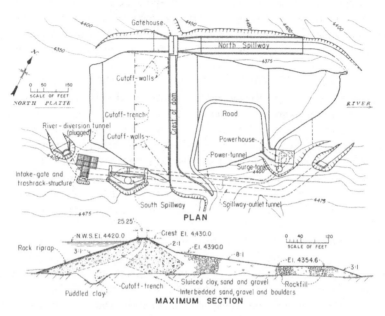

Plan for Guernsey Dam. (USBR)

in the afternoon. He promised Linnie that he would look for a home to lease or
rent immediately upon arriving. Crowe had asked Reclamation engineer Smith to
purchase and gather lumber and other building materials in order to hasten the
erection of a construction camp, always Crowe's first concern. When he stepped
off the train in Guernsey, Smith told him that Utah Construction foreman Charlie
Williams was hard at work with a crew of carpenters putting up company town
homes and a company office. Crowe had worked with this talented hardworking
carpenter and he knew that Williams could design and build anything out of wood
and that he had the respect of veteran construction workers. These qualities Crowe
admired. He was not disappointed; after checking into a Guernsey hotel, he met
Williams and saw some of the carpenter's work. The energetic woodworker informed Crowe that his crew would finish the company office and mess hall in a
few days, and that the water mains were already being laid through the camp
streets from the huge water tank installed at one end of the rising community.[18]

    Meanwhile, Crowe met Al Paisley, railroad construction foreman, in
charge of laying a spur line from the main Casper to Cheyenne track. Crowe was
quite pleased to hear that Paisley had hired scores of men and that blasting and line
grading were well under way. Crowe saw a huge steam shovel in operation on the
railroad grading. He ordered Paisley to use it in a three-shift operation. Everyone

soon learned that the bright young ex-Reclamation engineer meant to build this dam as fast as possible. No one was surprised when later that week they learned that Crowe had ordered another steam shovel and that it was to arrive soon to help grading from the west end of the spur.

Crowe not only moved quickly on the railroad connection but in his typical "I can be everywhere at once" motto, he surveyed and visited every component of the job site in the first few days. One of his first acts was to hire all the local labor he could. If they could run jackhammers, they were placed on the payroll immediately, such as Guernsey residents Martin Vaughn and Roman Dapra. Of course, no one told them that Crowe had just instituted a full night shift and all-new hires would start there; but at least it was an opportunity to make some regular wages. Crowe pored over government specifications in preparation of the general blasting and excavating. He checked on the availability of water, electricity, and he coordinated all his actions with Smith; he wanted the government engineer to know, well ahead of time, the material and supply needs of his ambitious schedule. Within days, everyone in and around Guernsey was talking about Frank T. Crowe. He would be the boss, and the boss was fair, but he wanted results. Nothing less would be tolerated.

Incredibly, within his first few whirlwind days at Guernsey, Crowe found time to look for a home for Linnie, Pat, and Elizabeth. On someone's recommendation, he looked over the William Wright residence, recently left vacant by another family. Wright, a longtime resident of the area, had died sometime earlier and the home had been leased in the interim. Crowe could see that the roomy furnished cottage would provide his family some source of comfort while they awaited their company home at the dam site to be completed. Day after day, Crowe made the two-mile bumpy jaunt from his Guernsey leased home to the construction camp.

Word spread quickly in eastern Wyoming that jobs were available at the Guernsey site. Crowe wanted men and he wanted them now. In one week, over one hundred new workers had signed their contracts and were taking meals in the just finished mess hall. Nels Christensen, a contractor from Utah and a brother of the vice-president of Utah Construction Company arrived the first week to check out progress and meet Crowe. Christensen was impressed to see that Crowe had taken command in such a forthright manner, organizing every detail. The Utah man was also happy to see that Crowe was giving a hiring preference, for skilled and unskilled labor, to any local Guernsey men. In this way, the nearby towns and local merchants could count on receiving some of the "trickle down" effects of new money infusion.[19]

By June 12, Crowe was completing his second week and true to his form, he had doubled his work force and moved the building of the company town ahead of schedule. Known by the locals as "the city of the Platte," (referring to the Platte River) the company town and dam site soon became engulfed in a flurry of activity. The *Guernsey Gazette*, the area's only newspaper reported on the action:

> The city on the Platte continues to grow. Today, 200
> men are at work and the construction camp at the dam presents
> a busy scene. Everywhere you look you will see new buildings,
> steam shovels, grading outfits and construction work in one form
> or another.
>
> Eleven bunkhouses are about completed and the force
> moved into their new quarters Tuesday night. The bunkhouses
> are large and roomy and contain 12 beds each, with a small wash-
> room. Each house will have running water, and electric lights.
> A shower bath house is to be erected with a laundry in connec-
> tion for the workmen. Present plans call for 20 bunkhouses.
>
> Besides the bunkhouses there will be a number of cot-
> tages built for the men with families and foremen.[20]

Carpentry foreman Williams continued to handle Crowe and Smith's pressure to get the building up as fast as possible. Williams' men worked on the huge
multi-winged mess hall and the adjacent kitchen. He had to build a modern ice
plant and cooler system for meat and cheese storage. In the side of an adjacent
hill, he built a large room for vegetable storage. Meanwhile, his men labored on
the 44 x 70-foot warehouse, located near the crest of the proposed dam. Other
buildings needed were a 24 x 112-foot machine shop, a 24 x 72-foot pool hall, a
voltage transformer station, and a truck and car repair garage. Along with all the
activity, Crowe pushed the installation of water lines and electricity. His goal was
to make the construction camp as self-reliant as possible. When asked if he expected any problems, Crowe responded that everything was moving along without a hitch. Reporters asked him how he planned on dealing with the unusually
steep slopes of the railroad grade route, and he commented that he had ordered a
"hogger that could put a Shay [digging machine] engine up a tree."[21] Crowe told
the reporter that many of his key men on the Guernsey job were veterans from
Yakima; the same men who helped Crowe build Tieton Dam.

Located on the banks of the North Platte River, the historic town of Guernsey had once thrived as a mining town and a stopover on the Oregon Trail. New
arrivals in town were all told the story of Register Cliff, where scores of Western
bound pioneers, some as early as 1847, carved their names. The town and the dam
site were surrounded by hills covered with juniper and pine, grass and sage. Pink-
walled sandstone cliffs abound providing an awe-inspiring landscape, particularly
at sunset. The Bureau of Reclamation had chosen this site for a dam due to the
narrow funneling of the North Platte River at this location and the need for reliable
irrigation by area farmers and cattle ranchers. With annual average temperatures
at 43 degrees and January averages at 25 degrees, the climate offered nothing

already encountered in previous jobs. He was told that the area could expect 24 inches of snow, but the average rainfall was only eight inches.[22]

In reviewing the government specifications for building, Crowe learned that Guernsey Dam would be a sluiced, gravel and rock filled structure, much like Tieton Dam. The approximately 150-foot tall and 500-foot wide dam would serve as a unit of the North Platte Irrigation Project. Crowe read that plans called for diversion of the river through an elongated tunnel on the south bank. Interestingly, the diversion tunnel would later be used in connection with the two 14 x 14-foot automatic spillway gates to help regulate lake levels and downstream flow. The upper end of the diversion tunnel would in itself be utilized as a huge settling chamber for the silt-ridden water before its movement into the power generating system. All of this presented a good challenge to the veteran dam builder, another opportunity to extend his knowledge and experience. The specifications clearly told him that the work was to begin within 30 days of the final award of contract and that all construction work was to be completed by June 20, 1927. This gave him two years to build Guernsey Dam.

Taking a few days off, Crowe slipped off to Denver where he told Linnie that he had secured good housing in the town of Guernsey. Frank informed her that he was only leasing the bungalow and that a company home would soon be constructed. On June 17, 1925, with a somewhat apprehensive wife and two very young daughters, Frank Crowe drove from Denver to their new life in Guernsey. Linnie, although she possessed unflinching confidence in her talented husband, must have wondered what lay ahead.

After a short couple of days off, Crowe was back on the job at Guernsey supervising the initial digging on the large diversion tunnel. He insisted on using a "big steam shovel" to start the extensive digging operation. Nearby, dozens of dump trucks waited, ready to relocate the excavated debris. At the same time, he checked on the nearly finished railway line to the dam site. When completed, all needed supplies and materials could then be brought directly to the warehouse. Crowe congratulated carpenter foreman Charlie Williams as forty buildings now stood completed, with a dozen more soon to be finished. Again, as at Tieton Dam, the construction camp of Rimrock rose quickly to resemble a town in its own right; so did the Guernsey construction camp. In size, Guernsey would rival Rimrock, housing approximately 500 workers and their families. For the times, this company town could boast wonderful amenities including running water, sewers, electric lights, and graded streets.[23]

Crowe was primarily interested in building dams and not tunnels. He knew that the 900-foot long and 30-foot diameter diversion tunnel at Guernsey would provide another opportunity to gain valuable engineering experience to serve him well when the really big dams came along. He knew that the Bureau of Reclamation was already putting together preliminary plans for huge concrete arched dams that utilized massive diversion tunnels, such as the one destined for

Boulder Canyon, Nevada. On June 22, 1925, Crowe ordered the work to begin on the west portal of the tunnel. As usual, the real challenge of the tunnel would be to excavate accurately within a designated time period, several months, and then have it concrete lined. Once the forms were removed and the concrete cured, the tunnel would accept all of the North Platte River, allowing Crowe's men to dewater the dam site. Later, the tunnel would serve as one of two spillways.

If things were not hectic enough, Crowe received word that Secretary of the Interior Hubert Work and Commissioner of the Bureau of the Reclamation Elwood Mead were arriving in the area. An important meeting was being called for June 23 in Cheyenne where "prominent citizens of the state" and other Reclamation officials would be able to hear Work's and Mead's vision for the future of government involvement in irrigation projects. Nervous Wyoming politicians, worried farmers, and an assortment of Reclamation project supervisors attended the landmark meeting, knowing that their futures were inextricably tied to federal support. Crowe, no longer a government employee and untrusting of Secretary Work, remained on the job at Guernsey, although he knew that Reclamation policy was directly linked to his future dam building opportunities. He kept informed of the meeting as the local Guernsey newspaper carried the proceedings as a major news item. Meade opened with some general comments that set the tone for the meeting by stating:

> Future population depends on this [Wyoming] being
> made an agricultural state. Mines will be worked out, forests
> cut off but the irrigated farm will endure. The kind of people
> who live on these farms and the kind of agriculture they will
> follow will determine the character of the state's civilization and
> its material prosperity.[24]

Meade went on to reassure the Wyoming audience that three additional irrigation projects were in the planning stages with the Reclamation, but "when they will be built depend quite largely on the results of the settlement and agricultural development on the older works." This was a direct reference to the Reclamation's concern about lack of payback from farmers and the states on completed government projects. Meade's comments were only a prelude to the much harder hitting words of Interior Secretary Work that would be read by Crowe weeks later.

At Guernsey, Crowe tried to keep his concentration on the job. This was a critical time as new men and machines were arriving every day. He watched as the machine shop was completed as well as the main power plant, comprising "two 250 horsepower motors with another motor pumping water for the camp." He now had seven small train locomotives hauling cars to and from the work site, and three large steam shovels digging around the clock. In addition, Williams finished the new wing of the mess hall, which was now able to feed 400 workers at a time. Crowe authorized a local resident, Charlie Cliff, to open a large pool hall in a corner of the building.[25]

Crowe also opened work on the east portal of the diversion tunnel using one of the new steam shovels and three "dinky dump cars" to haul away the excavated material. Meanwhile, crews made progress on the west portal as good dry weather prevailed. Large yield dynamite charges were set at both ends of the tunnel and thunderous explosions echoed all over nearby canyons. One old-timer, Charles Ragan, commented, "the blasting is even causing the rattlesnakes to leave the can[y]on." In early July, a worker on the diversion tunnel was seriously injured when a rock fell from a loaded dump car. He was struck in the lower part of the back while he was bending over some equipment. Workers who assisted the man first reported that it was a critical injury, but the camp doctor, after examining the patient told Crowe that he would live.[26] A concerned Crowe, who placed great pride in his dubious safety record, urged his foremen to discuss safety regulations with the workers. Meanwhile, he prepared for a visit from one of his new bosses, Utah Construction director E. O. Wattis, who was due to arrive within a couple of days.

An unexpected Rocky Mountain cloudburst erupted in late July and quickly threatened to become Crowe's first major problem at Guernsey. Centered over the nearby town of Hartville, the summer downpour was of "mean proportions" and within hours, the North Platte River had reached flood state. Crowe's newly erected bridge across the river soon became jammed with onrushing debris. He quickly set a small force of workers to task dislodging the branches, trunks, and assorted debris from the bridge piers. They heroically remained on the job all night. At one point, Crowe himself, worried about the possible disaster, worked with his men and at a critical stage ordered heavily clogged channels to be blasted away. Crowe was especially worried about the west portal where digging already was well below the level of the river. If the turbulent Platte River spilled into this area, he would lose valuable days dewatering the site. Immediately, he called for sump pumps to be placed into the area. Meanwhile, he and his men beefed up the embankment leading from the river into the portal, and then they waited and watched. At one point, some water seeped into the portal but crews quickly pumped the area dry. With daylight, the river level lowered considerably and the digging in the diversion tunnel resumed.[27]

Shortly after the flooding incident, Guernsey residents read an editorial concerning the recent Bureau of Reclamation reorganization controversy and the future of dam building and irrigation projects in the American West. Columnist John Dickinson Sherman, in an attempt to inform the general public as to the current status of the abrupt and dramatic changes taking place in the Bureau of Reclamation wrote an extensive defense of Secretary Work's reorganization plan in a full page editorial. He explained that the "sixty-ninth Congress" would no longer allow an unrestrained use of federal money for Reclamation projects and that ways would need to be found to recoup already spent funds. "The plain truth is that the Coolidge administration has inherited an unfortunate situation which has been broadly described as 'Our Reclamation Problem.' The problem is of national importance and has many complications and ramifications that call for prompt action by Congress." Sherman asserted that the new plan called for the Bureau of Reclamation to secure the funds and bid out the various irrigation jobs. Then it would be the states' responsibility to find competent and "hardworking" farmers to settle the land, "advise them and advance the money for machinery to equip their farms." The editorial noted that Work had made two comprehensive trips throughout the seventeen Western states in an attempt to "reclaim reclamation." Sherman, claiming that Secretary Work was "a practical irrigationist" had formed a "fact-finding committee" to advise him on steps to make the Reclamation more financially responsible.[28]

In light of this news, Crowe's decision to leave the Reclamation was a timely one. Sherman confirmed Crowe's fears that the Bureau of Reclamation was now focusing more on the financial and bookkeeping aspect of irrigation development and less on the engineering construction challenges. Future construction projects would not proceed with government funding unless the states began taking an active role in helping farmers become successfully established and encouraging settlers to pay back their irrigation loans and advances. Sherman continued his lengthy expose by quoting from a recent speech by Secretary Work:

> Changes are needed in the settlement clauses of the reclamation act if development is to go on in the Rocky Mountain States. Federal reclamation has not produced the desired agricultural results. It has not given the industrious, experienced settler the kind of an opportunity he should have. It has given too wide a range to land speculation. It has bred the menace of tenancy. Instead of the settlers on these projects having a sense of gratitude to the government, disappointment and bitterness prevail. We ought not to go on with a policy that creates these results. The question is: What can we wisely and safely undertake to improve these conditions?[29]

To press his point home, Work provided some hard-hitting financial figures on lost funds:

> There has already been spent for construction on the four projects of this state [Montana] $16,000,000. Of that, only $628,000 has been repaid. On four important divisions not one dollar of construction costs has been returned. It has cost to operate these projects $2,876,500. Of this only $926,300 has been collected. All the money that has been received would not

repay the government what it has expended in operation and maintenance. An irrigation work that is not worth enough to pay its operation should not be continued...

It is of vital moment to the future of federal reclamation that we first reclaim reclamation, that to restore lost confidence in its government representatives, re-establish the enthusiasm brought on to projects by settlers, and discredit those who live by farming the farmers. I am not willing to let federal reclamation continue to ride recklessly to its own ruin without an effort to save it to those who by their courage and industry have earned the right to home ownership.

In direct reference to previous Secretaries of the Interior and Commissioners of the Reclamation, Work declared, "It is our purpose to build Reclamation from the ground up. From the farmer to the government, rather than from the government to the dam and the dam to the desert."

The Reclamation bureau is not now being conducted in the interests of individuals but for the best interests of those who live on the land and whom we hope may eventually own it. It is the human element involved in reclamation that should be our first concern; to protect the interests of those already on the land and prepare for those we shall invite to come.[30]

The message was unmistakably clear, reclamation projects would only continue as long as the states took a more active and responsible role in helping the federal government earn back its invested construction funds. To engineer Crowe, this all seemed a replay of the controversy over A. P. Davis and his handling of the Reclamation Service. His mind was now clearly made-up, he wanted nothing to do with the political or financial concerns of the new Bureau of Reclamation; he would remain focused on identifying, bidding, and building the most challenging irrigation projects that would come along—big dams. Guernsey was another dam, not large, but challenging due to its large diversion tunnel and complexity of coordinating a large work force.

Just days after reading Secretary Work's detailed account of the new direction for the Bureau of Reclamation, Crowe was startled and dismayed when the project's first fatality occurred. The worker, a young newly transplanted Englishmen was killed when a rockslide from the face of the cliff came crashing down, smashing him and another miner. A protective cover over their part of the tunnel saved several nearby workers. Crowe rushed into the tunnel when notified. He immediately asked the tunnel foreman about the safety precautions. Crowe then, quickly realized that he himself had checked this section of the tunnel only the day

Heavy-duty shovel easily lifts and dumps large blasted "muck" at
Guernsey Dam. Frank Crowe is standing in the middle of the track.
(USBR)

before. Even though it was agreed by everyone that the heavy rainfall the night
before contributed to ground weakness, Crowe felt a heavy burden of guilt. Upon
additional inspection, it was discovered that much dirt had moved during the night
and that "the dirt was washed away and the ground softened to make possible the
slide."[31]

     More and more townspeople visited the dam site and Crowe began to
worry about their safety as well as that of his workers. On one hand he wanted to
let the public see the goings on but some of the equipment was downright dangerous, and it seemed that many Guernsey residents wanted to see the heavy machinery. One of the most dangerous new items to arrive was the Ingersol-Rand drill-
sharpening machine. In less than a minute the huge air stamp could completely
"dress a drill" in perfect shape. The ground within a few yards of the sharpener
quaked from the powerful lunges as the working hammer came slamming down.
Townspeople were amazed to know that the machine sharpened more than 500
drills each day. Between this and the gigantic steam shovels, Crowe soon restricted visitors to specific viewing areas where much of the work could be seen

with complete safety. Crowe explained the safety problems to Ray Shinn, a construction consultant for Morrison & Knudsen Construction Company. Shinn was impressed to see that the bright engineer was "taking all necessary and reasonable safety precautions," as his company and Utah Construction could be held liable for any violations. The local newspaper, shortly after the Petch accident, praised Crowe and his crews for undertaking a "big dangerous job," especially in their handling of "TNT and dynamite." Calling them "true soldiers of their country" the article added that the workers have the "thrill that their conquests build wealth and happiness, not destroy it."[32]

As a further precaution on safety worries and as a means to publicly show concern, two Utah Construction officials made a tour of the nearby Wheatland General Hospital (Guernsey did not have a hospital). The officials looked the medical facility over thoroughly, asking questions about the "arrangements for the care of their men." Local residents were indeed impressed by such concern, as construction companies of earlier years had earned a bad reputation for not providing prompt or appropriate medical care for their workers. Even the employees of the Wheatland Hospital declared that the "Utah Construction officials and work superintendent [Crowe] are to be congratulated on working for a company that has found by experience that the best possible care for their men is the best possible policy."[33]

With the coming of August, Crowe hired more men and pushed work in the diversion tunnel. By end of the first week of the month, his men had reached 122 feet in general underground excavation. Then miners drilled 150 blasting holes, the powder monkeys moved in and packed 700 pounds of dynamite. The resulting blast, heard for miles around, removed tons of rock that was slowing the drilling process. Crowe was pleased with the results and with the report of no casualties. Now his men began driving a drift (side tunnel) to the center of the already started power tunnel. [34] From this entrance, Crowe expected tunneling to continue from both directions. This technique of opening up as many drilling faces as possible was a Crowe trademark. The idea was to utilize the maximum number of men and machines on the same tunnel. He already knew that this strategy, if coordinated properly, would be the key to future large diversion tunnel operations, such as Boulder Dam.

At the same time, Crowe had men start to dig from the top of the cliff straight down into an area close to the center of the diversion tunnel. This cutting, when completed, was known as a glory hole. The 34-foot diameter excavation would act as a spillway from the dam. When the water pressure reached a high point, the water would be forced from the tunnel up the glory hole and through an open channel into the river below. This feature, although drawn into several previous Reclamation projects, had not been practically utilized at this time in government construction projects. So again, Crowe was setting another precedent and he paid close attention to the construction details as his crews excavated and began concrete lining. The main spillway, located on the north bank, was planned to be 52 feet by 52 feet and would dump the North Platte River overflow into the river below the dam after funneling through a huge gate. The huge steel gate, 50 feet by 50 feet would be the largest in the world, weighing just over one million pounds.[35]

With the north bank construction started Crowe now needed to move around considerably, first checking the main diversion tunnel and power tunnel progress, then walking over the bridge to the north spillway excavation. From here, he checked the machine shop, electric shop, concrete mixing operations, etc. With the installing of the air and water lines across the river, he ordered the jack-hammer crews to start "pounding away on the trenches for cutoff walls and rail-road grade along the north side." He also constantly checked the crushing, screen-ing, and mixing plant operations while on the north side, where gravel pits were being opened. It was during this time that men down at the river saw a horse floating by. In an effort to save the animal, mining men roped the frightened horse and gently pulled it to the south bank. Crowe was notified and after a check for branding marks or owner identification on the harness, the shocked superinten-dent decided to place an ad in upstream newspapers.[36]

As had happened at Tieton Dam, the Bureau of Reclamation received word from foreign countries concerning the latest irrigation projects and the types of dam designs being built. Countries such as Japan were greatly interested in learning about irrigation construction advances; so it was not uncommon for Com-missioner Meade to have several requests per year to allow these foreign engi-neers to visit American construction sites and observe the techniques in action. One of the leading Japanese civil engineers at that time was K. Ishizawa, who was employed by the Sonyo Chuo Hydro Electric Company. He was most interested in developing strategies for designing effective hydroelectric plants that were com-pact, yet productive. He arrived during the evening of August 27 and was imme-diately impressed with Crowe's knowledge of dam construction and power plant design. Ishizawa wanted to see the diversion tunnel and power tunnel drawings, then check on the building progress. He was amazed to learn that Crowe's three-shift operation with over 500 men and scores of machines worked together effi-ciently. The Japanese engineer, without the use of an interpreter asked extensive questions and took copious notes. It is interesting that Crowe himself probably did not realize the extent to which other countries would use his construction de-signs and strategies.[37]

By October over half of the diversion tunnel had been successfully exca-vated and Charlie Williams busied his carpentry crews readying the concrete lin-ing forms. Crowe, who believed strongly in building miniature models, helped construct a model of the forms. One of his management and planning strategies involved using these models during foremen meetings, for consultation with visit-ing engineers and company officials, and on occasion, to explain the construction phases to inquisitive visitors. By the 9th of the month the east portal was four feet below the level of the river with "considerable water seeping through continually." On investigation, Crowe and his tunnel foreman discovered that despite the possible problem the leaks might create, "a freak condition is that it drains out again." Crowe surmised that the water "runs into a large underground opening."[38] Tunnel crews reported that they were now digging through large quantities of high-grade iron ore and that the water leakage might be connected to this discovery.

In the last week of October, with cold weather approaching, a watchful and anxious Crowe reported that there was less than 200 feet of heading of the diversion tunnel to finish, with work "going ahead rapidly on the removal of the footing or lower portion." He forcefully stated that the concrete lining would commence in the first week of November, as he wanted this operation well underway before the end of the year. Crowe noted that all phases of the operation were ahead of schedule and that he planned to keep it that way. On the north side of the river, he revealed that forty-one feet of a 96-foot cut of that spillway had been completed; he used the fill taken from here to add to the "fill proper," or the earth packed dam itself. In addition to all this work, Crowe announced that another new operation, the cut-off wall, would start. The trench for the wall would help anchor the earthen debris to the river bottom and the canyon walls. Eventually, a 64-foot high concrete wall, erected within the trench would serve as the foundation for the entire dam. Crowe explained that all this work needed to proceed quickly in order to accommodate the expected spring floods. With the diversion tunnel completed and the north abutment spillway cut, work on the dam itself could move along without any threats of floods.[39]

A quiet, yet widespread celebration occurred on the night of November 6 as word spread that the diversion tunnel had been holed through. Using "giant powder," tunnel crews blew out the last earthen barrier and "let through the daylight." When measured, the tunnel extended 1081 feet long, blasted out of the solid rock and now claimed the title as the world's longest and largest manmade irrigation related tunnel. Crowe immediately ordered two of the large steam shovels from the tunnels to help in mucking out the remainder of the footing material. Already the west end had been blasted and loose material sat ready to be picked up and removed. Construction foremen were called together for a quick briefing on the next major step, lining the tunnel with concrete. Crowe understood that erection of the wooden forms for framing the concrete within the tunnel needed to be coordinated in a non-stop sequence and without hindering the concrete crews who would be working just a step behind. Across the river, the final touches on the $25,000 concrete mixing plant were being completed, with Crowe supervising the stringing of the cables that would transport "vats" of mixed concrete to the tunnel entrance. He was pleased that work was "a little ahead of schedule," whereas, at this time last month he had worried that excavation was falling behind. [40]

I. L. Figueroa, Mexico's Secretary of Agriculture, visited Guernsey during the same week as the diversion tunnel was being holed through. Figueroa explained that his "mission" was to study "methods of irrigation and economic problems of reclamation." Crowe met several times with Figueroa discussing, in particular, the excavation techniques and construction sequence. Crowe was impressed with the engineering knowledge of Figueroa and he wondered if Figueroa had an opportunity to meet Weymouth, his mentor, who was now working with Mexican irrigation officials. Crowe left it to government engineer F. F. Smith to escort the foreign visitor around the dam site and to nearby farms. Smith noted that Figueroa had an excellent command of the English language and that the only real problem in communication occurred when discussing measurement, the Mexican government using a "different system."[41]

It appeared that the number of visitors to the dam site increased rapidly throughout the months of November and December, and Crowe needed to give more and more of his time to talk with them. In early December, high-ranking board members from the Burlington Northern Railroad, sixteen officials in all, arrived on location wanting a complete tour. Smith and Crowe were both obliged to give the grand tour of the dam site, again with Crowe providing construction details, when asked. Representatives from the Utah Cement Company and Standard Oil Company were on hand as well.[42] Fortunately for the time-pressed Crowe, the visiting dignitaries decided to leave after a brief stay and head for Casper. He realized that his situation was really no different than before, where as an employee of the Reclamation Service he needed to give freely of his time with visitors. Now as an employee of Morrison-Knudsen sub-contracting to Utah Construction he was responsible for maintaining their reputations as honest and accommodating construction companies. His professional responsibility of meeting and hosting public visits became acute whenever it conflicted with the beginning of a critical new phase of the work or when a major problem developed unexpectedly. Such was the case at this time. He desperately wanted to start on the diversion tunnel concrete lining operations, just as the Burlington group arrived.

Within days of the Burlington group departure, Crowe gave orders to go ahead with the concrete lining. The operation proved interesting, another custom application of cables, dinkeys, tracks, and forms. Once the concrete had been brought to the south side of the river, waiting dinkey cars received the newly mixed concrete. The dinkeys were then hauled into the diversion tunnel on specially designed narrow gauge tracks. Charlie Williams' lining forms contained an elevator to hoist the dinkeys up close to the top of the form. From here, the concrete was emptied and gravity pulled the mix down the sides of the form. Once in place concrete tampers packed the fresh concrete mix tightly. The form itself, designed by Crowe and Williams, sat on a track. After the concrete had set, the form could be lowered enough to break off contact, allowing the entire form to be pushed on the track to a new position in the tunnel. Here the procedure of placing and packing concrete began anew. With several of these forms working at the same time, and from both ends of the tunnel, Crowe was able to move the work along quickly.[43]

Temperatures dropped significantly to below freezing as Christmas day approached. Crowe insisted that there be no let down in the lining operation, even though his foremen reminded him of the difficulty of mixing concrete in low temperatures and the strain it put on both men and machines. Men struggled to deal with the cold and even though foremen constantly enforced the safety rules, accidents occurred. On Monday December 21, Wilbur Vaughn a young diversion tunnel worker was injured when a loose rock fell from the roof of the tunnel. Not far away and on the same day another man was hurt as a broken air hose whipped around and hit him. Both men were at first reported to be in serious condition, but recovered quickly. Crowe was clearly responsible. He spread the word that extra precautions needed to be taken in cold weather and he notified the local newspaper, which had reported the injuries that "every precaution is being taken for the safety of the men."[44]

Despite the precautions and Crowe's insistence that work move ahead on schedule, bitter cold along with a deep snowfall in early January of 1926 began to impede construction. The main problem involved snow covering the dinkey tracks and roadways. Crews found it impossible to keep the roads leading in and out of the work site open. Chains on tires provided only some advantage, yet trucks skidded and slid everywhere. Dinkeys needed special covering, for the volume of snow falling in such short time periods was seriously affecting the concrete mixture proportions—too much water. Tarps were then pressed into service to cover the freshly mixed concrete on its journey from mixing plant to placing. With the onset of winter Crowe had dropped to two crews, he now changed his mind and decided to go back to three shifts, yet allowing each shift to work more slowly. William's carpentry crews dressed in layers of thick clothing and wearing clumsy heavy gloves worked to finish five more concrete lining forms for use in the west portal on the tunnel. Compensating for the weather-driven work slowdown, Crowe increased the number of forms and moved to three shifts. He now initiated concrete placing from both ends of the diversion tunnel.

As January wore on, the snow piled higher and higher. Crowe and Smith, along with local residents, expressed concern that an early thaw in February would result in a catastrophic flood in the vulnerable Guernsey Dam site. Local rainfall and water flow rates revealed that in February of 1911, a record 2,000-second feet of flow swept through the area. Crowe felt confident, although locals probably remained skeptical, that the work site could be secured dry.[45] H. J. Lawler, Superintendent of Construction for the Utah Construction Company, made the difficult trip from Boise to see Crowe and check on progress during the middle of the month. No sooner had he left, secure that Crowe was handling the weather effects on the work, than a Spanish engineer showed up at Guernsey. Jose Nunez Casquete,

a reclamation expert in his country, wanted to talk with Crowe about the construction of large dams. He was particularly interested in Crowe's use of cableways
and the coordination of job sequences over extended time. He spent several days
touring the snow-covered site, taking notes and asking detailed questions. Casquete
revealed that his government was about to embark on a "gigantic reclamation
program," and that Spain had made the commitment to irrigate thousands of acres.[46]

By February, the concrete lining operations became routine and progress
moved ahead as planned. At one point, Crowe placed an ad in the local newspaper
for additional men. With the initiation of a third shift, foremen found themselves
short men on the other two shifts. Inclement weather kept most job hopefuls from
reporting to work. Crowe, nevertheless, raised the concrete mixing and placing
quota to two hundred yards each day. Workers around the dam site began making
bets as to whether the concrete lining of the diversion tunnel would be completed
by the first of March. Those men who previously did not know Crowe, or his
reputation, bet against the odds, while Crowe veterans knew better than to bet
against the master dam builder. Several prized boxes of cigars, put up by one
skeptic as a bet against finishing on time, were quickly covered by eager old pros
from Tieton Dam who had seen their boss pull off one engineering miracle after
another. With hundreds of feet to go, it would be another determined test of men
and machines against the elements.

Meanwhile, Crowe unleashed a surprise weapon in his challenge to muck
out the deep trench of the main clay and concrete corewall—a slack line cableway.
With this he would be able to quadruple the rate at which his men could haul out
the collected muck. With a respite from the heavy snowfall, he ordered a steam
shovel crew to again work on the north spillway. Work proceeded as if it was mid-
summer, with a full-blown construction schedule. All over the northern West,
most heavy construction had either been suspended or, at least, cut back. Crowe,
however, continued to use all available men and machines on his job. Regular
meetings with his foremen allowed Crowe to carefully review the next anticipated
procedures and work sequences. He asked them to watch carefully for possible
safety problems.[47]

No sooner had the work increase been implemented than a fatal accident
occurred. S. V. Sinsabl, a carpenter at the dam, was "badly crushed" when the
elevator used in hoisting the concrete to the top of the forms in the tunnel came
down on him. Ironically, Sinsabl had helped build the elevator, and he was well
aware of the danger of lingering beneath the device. The doomed carpenter was
described as an energetic worker and when Charlie Williams had asked him to get
a crosscut saw, he gambled, instead of going around the elevator; he cut across its
path. The elevator operator saw Sinsabl, applied the brakes, but not before the
huge load had slammed into him squarely. He sustained massive head injuries and
many broken ribs. Crowe had him rushed to nearby Scottsbluff Hospital, but he
died the next day. Observers to the grisly scene admitted to Crowe that the acci-

dent was completely an error in judgment and that if the elevator had been stopped a fraction of a second sooner, Sinsabl would have been untouched. Crowe had the usual sad responsibility of notifying the next of kin, in this case, Sinsabl's wife, who lived in Casper.[48]

Undaunted, and convinced that his operation was safe if the rules were followed, the shaken master engineer urged his men to continue the progress made. Local papers reported that there was "a wonderful stride in the work." Their reference alluded to the fact that only 170 feet of the 1070-foot long diversion tunnel still needed concrete, along with 800 feet of the floor. Crowe's immediate boss, Harry Morrison, arrived at this time from Boise to check on progress and to provide assurance that the company had complete confidence in his methods. Crowe enjoyed this visit from Morrison, for Crowe was expecting to develop a long-term relationship with the ambitiously run construction company. They had already talked about bidding and building the great Boulder Dam project, as soon as it would come up for bid. Morrison had big plans for Crowe; he knew that this bright hard-driving engineer could propel the Morrison-Knudsen Company to the top of Western construction companies. Crowe knew that Guernsey Dam was another test, a test to see if he could pull off the same kind of engineering miracles that he had as a government employee.

It is interesting to note that the extreme cold encountered at the Guernsey Dam site was not a local or regional oddity. Newspapers were reporting uncommonly low temperatures all over the country. Dramatic pictures showed a completely frozen Niagara Falls forming as one paper put it "the most dazzling beauties of nature."[49] Thousands of curious locals came out to see a dry Niagara Falls. In Palm Beach, Florida lower than normal temperatures teamed with torrential downpours of rain to make it one of the worst winters on record. At one point, the heavy record-breaking rain fell unabated in sheets for a twelve-hour period and the cold temperatures continued for weeks.

Notwithstanding the bitter cold, Crowe's construction troops plied ahead with their work. By February 26, the concrete lining was nearly completed, the last form being placed at the outlet portal. Crowe now made plans to cut from the river channel to the diversion tunnel, allowing the Platte River to run through the 30-foot tube. He designed a plan to throw up a 35-foot high embankment on the west end of the fill, diverting the river water to the diversion tunnel entrance. As the work on the diversion tunnel neared completion, Crowe let go several scores of workers. Excitement increased as Crowe veterans reminded everyone about previously made work progress bets.

Frank Crowe did not make friends easily, but when he did, it was for a lifetime. One such friend, Anthony "Si" Bous, who was now working at Guernsey Dam, had started with Crowe at the Jackson Lake Dam, a decade previously. Frank and Linnie made regular visits to the Bous' house and vice versa. Usually, the couples had dinner and played cards, talked about work, and wondered where the

Guernsey Dam nearing completion. (USBR)

next big job might be. On the job, Frank and Si maintained a professional relationship, as Crowe did not want anyone to think that he was showing favoritism.
The wives of the two dam builders had also drawn close. Linnie and Mrs. Bous
regularly planned luncheons at their homes, where the wives of other close friends
shared crafts and conversation. It appeared that Crowe appreciated and cherished
his special friendships. Whether he spent time with family, or friends, it must have
been difficult to completely ignore his construction responsibilities. In effect, he
was on-call 24 hours a day, seven days a week. He made it clear to foremen that if
any problems should occur while he was at home, that he should be notified immediately. This constant pressure would, in time, begin to take a physical toll on
the seemingly tireless engineer.[50]

True to his word, Crowe finished the diversion tunnel by March. He
waited on diverting the full river flow through the tunnel until Smith and his Bureau inspectors had gone over the lining, checking for setting problems, cracks,
and weak joints. Meanwhile, in a gesture of openness to the Guernsey residents,
Crowe offered spectators a boat ride through the diversion tunnel to see the big
tube up close. Crowe gave a final report on the diversion tunnel to his superiors at
Utah Construction stating, the "work on the tunnel has been very successful."
Concreting appeared uniform throughout the 1000-foot run and no support timbering was necessary. Close inspection revealed no leakage from pressured-sealed
seams joining each concrete section.[51]

With the North Platte River completely diverted Crowe focused his men and machines on constructing Guernsey Dam. He realized that he needed to raise the dam to a height of fifty feet or more to hold back the expected onrush of water when upstream Pathfinder Dam released its bounty for irrigation. Within one week of diverting the river, Crowe using all four steam shovels and five small locomotives, each pulling numerous dinkeys, transferred tons of muck from the north spillway area and deposited the material at a point in front of the expected concrete corewall. Later Crowe acquired three smaller gauge trains and expanded the operation even more. With incredible speed, Williams' carpenters and other work crews erected a new trestle across the now dry riverbed where most of the muck was being dumped. Crowe had foremen coordinate the exact travel and dumping time of each train and dinkey, thereby maximizing access time on the one-track trestle.[52]

Once the fifty-foot mark had been reached in piling up fill in the riverbed, the threat of flood past and Crowe next ordered his crews to complete the grade cut on the spillway on the north side of the dam. In an effort to take advantage of the good building weather in April and May Crowe asked Williams to build another trestle across the river. This second high train bridge would allow workers to double their rate of depositing fill for the dam proper. With no expected floods materializing and with an upswing in hiring new or returning workers, Crowe was able to make quick progress in raising the dam. In later years, fellow engineers would look back on Crowe's successful career and point to his ability to reach and sustain high levels of production throughout each construction assignment—despite the high risk to men and machines. Much of this success can be attributed to his constant concern to maintain or improve each job responsibility and shift quotas.

By June, with the dam rising quickly, and dry warm weather in command, hundreds of tourists began visiting the site. Some of the locals were making weekly trips, usually on Sunday, to view the renewed activity. New dormitories, workers' homes, warehouses, restaurants, and a myriad of other buildings gave the work site the appearance of a sprawling new town. Visitors gazed in awe as they viewed the spectacle of hundreds of men working huge noisy and smoking machinery relentlessly digging, transporting, and depositing debris in the earthen dams temporarily guiding the river to the diversion tunnel. They also saw men assembling wooden forms, preparing to place more concrete in the ever-growing corewall, while still other crews deposited sluiced debris in the earthen dam just downstream from the corewall. Amazed they learned that upon completion of the corewall still more fill material would be brought in to join the core with the two earth dams, one above and one below the core, to form a huge permanent structure.[53]

With the work schedule well under way and most of the "bugs" of coordinating the fill process worked out, Crowe decided that it was time to follow through on a promise he had made to Linnie. He had always wanted a new car and he admired good machinery; in fact, for years friends had debated with him on the mechanical reliability of various makes of automobiles. Linnie had also made it quite plain to him that they needed a trustworthy car, one that could accommodate the entire family. Crowe also felt that Linnie deserved a new vehicle, as she had fully supported his desire to return to the field and give up his desk job in Denver. After looking around at various car agencies, he decided on a new "Buick coach," which he purchased from the nearby Torrington agency. As new cars were expensive and rather rare, particularly Buicks, Frank and Linnie became celebrities, of sorts, for a few weeks as Guernsey residents and dam workers admired the shiny new automobile.[54]

It was during this time that Crowe was collaborating with Harry Morrison and the Wattis brothers to bid for the Guernsey Dam powerhouse. With men and machines already committed to the job site the Utah Construction Company possessed an advantage over any other interested bidder. Utah's bid, calculated by Crowe, proved to be the lowest. At $163,000, Crowe's bid was half the estimate of the next bidder. For Crowe this was another engineering feather in his cap. He was earning a national reputation for being the best at estimating the lowest on heavy construction projects. This would prove to be a most valuable ability, as the company that employed Crowe could be assured of continued awarding of contracts. Of course, Crowe would be able to command higher salaries, selection of job sites, and participation in company incentive programs.

At this time, Bureau engineers redesigned the power output of the Guernsey power plant. Originally capable of 3,000 horsepower using two adjacent units, the engineers planned a second power tunnel delivering twice as much water and thereby increasing the turbine potential to two more units. It was understood that Utah Construction, to prevent a possible conflict of interest charge, would complete only the original plans and place two generators on-line.

During the hot days of July Crowe and Smith journeyed to Omaha, Nebraska for a few days to observe and inspect the huge spillway gate as it was being assembled. Already touted as the "world's largest steel gate," Crowe and Smith understood that the gate would be holding back tremendous amounts of water, and it would need to sustain high water pressures. The Omaha Steel Works constructed the giant 320-ton steel gate with only the finest materials and under close engineering scrutiny. The massive gate was to be fully assembled in Omaha; hence Crowe and Smith's visit, and would then be installed, by Crowe, at the dam site. He needed to learn as much about the gate as possible, for Crowe clearly understood that blueprint drawings could not reveal the construction and installation realities that he would face. Once assembled, it was decided that the massive structure could successfully be disassembled in Omaha, and then reassembled at Guernsey without jeopardizing quality and safety. Plans were then made to ship the metal monolith on August 4, with Crowe expecting to install the gate sometime later in October.[55]

Back at Guernsey work proceeded smoothly with hundreds of employed men helping in the main job of packing in the earthen fill around the corewall. The dinkey dump cars ran 24 hours a day delivering excavated muck directly over the dam. At a signal, the train of heavily filled cars stopped over their projected dumpsite, then workers pulled on the door levers allowing the earthen fill to fall down around the corewall. Next workers rushed in to the newly dumped fill and, using a power water hose, packed in, or washed in the earth gravel mix. This procedure now went on day after day in a routine that Crowe knew all to well. He constantly encouraged his foremen to remind their men not to let down their vigilance for safety concerns just because the work sequence had become regular and predictable. On the contrary, camp flyers reminded the men to stay alert, look for potential hazards and report them to foremen at once.

Crowe now spent considerable time in contemplating the construction sequence and possible problems in erecting the large power plant. At 72 feet long by 50 feet wide by 65 feet high the concrete structure needed over 250,000 pounds of reinforcing steel and more than 4,000 yards of concrete, to say nothing of the 27,500 yards of excavation that would be needed before starting the foundation. Crowe looked carefully at how jobs were finishing up on Guernsey Dam with the idea that men could move easily from that job to the power plant without employment interruption. This Crowe trademark was another reason why his workers remained loyal to him over the years; they could always be assured of a job without long idle work periods.[56]

On September 26, 1926, the local newspaper announced that Guernsey Dam, at least the huge mountain of earth forming the dam proper, had been completed. Crowe estimated that the fill equaled 326,000 cubic yards. His men, about 460 by this time, were now dressing down the slopes on either side of the dam and placing 21,000 yards of riprap (large rocks) on the upstream side.[57] Additionally, Crowe now ordered work on capping the structure with a concrete roadway and a bridge across the open spillway on the north bank. The paper reported that despite its finished look, the project still would take about a year to complete with many men engaged in finishing the spillways, installing the spillway gate, and in constructing the power plant. Crowe told the local newspaper that he and Linnie would take a few days off and drive to Denver. It was somewhat a tradition by locals, during the summer months, to make one or two shopping trips to the "big city."[58]

With no major injuries reported during the entire summer of 1926, Crowe and his foremen won praise from Utah Construction and Bureau of Reclamation officials, and from the wives of local dam workers. In early November, an unusual accident did occur, and when it was reported in the *Guernsey Gazette*, it both concerned and astonished readers.

Fate plays us peculiar turns at times and what the mor-

row holds for us is unknown. Last Friday evening Mr. Meadows, a workman at the dam, who had been working the past
several months on the south spillway on the most dangerous
part of the job, was lying on his cot in his bunkhouse reading the
evening paper when a rock from a heavy blast in the south spillway came through the roof of the bunk house and struck Mr.
Meadows on the leg, breaking both bones in the limb, and laying him up for several months. He had propped himself up in
bed and had changed his position only a moment before or the
rock would have struck him in the head and killed him.

During the past several months Meadows had been
working on the south spillway and gave but little heed to the
blasting while on the works, when heavy rocks would fall all
about him; it was dangerous but he survived only to have a rock
thrown clear out of range and strike him as he lay reading in his
bunk house. He was quartering in No. 8 bunkhouse, which is
considered well out of range of the works.[59]

Meadows was taken to a nearby hospital where doctors labored, with some difficulty, to set his bones. For days, the incident was the talk of town in and around
Guernsey Dam, and workers in the No. 8 bunkhouse shuddered, and scattered,
each time a blasting charge was set off on the south spillway.

No sooner had the Meadows' story played out at Guernsey than a serious,
fatal accident came to pass. Bert W. Fisher, carpenter at the dam, and well known
by most workers, including Crowe and his immediate boss Charlie Williams, fell
50 feet down the north counter-weight well. The well, located near the huge spillway gate was still under construction when Fisher slipped and plunged downward. He repeatedly struck steel spikes that protruded from the sides, fracturing
his jaw and other bones. He landed on the solid concrete bottom, on his feet, with
such force that the bones of his legs were forcibly driven through his shoes! Fisher
in an effort to remove concrete forms from the well wall was prying loose a board
which gave way unexpectedly, then the heavy board fell onto the supporting scaf-
fold and smashed the plank on which the worker was standing. Word spread
quickly of Fisher's accident and scores of off-duty workers wanted to see him in
the hospital. He died later that evening. Crowe, as superintendent, stood squarely
responsible for the entire work site. He immediately informed the victim's wife.
Crowe learned that Fisher planned on working for only two more weeks. The 28-
year-old dam worker had saved his salary from the previous 18 months so that he
could take over the running of his father's ranch in Chadron, Nebraska. Fisher's
wife and young son had just left for Chadron the previous night, only to be called
back with the sad news. Unbelievably, rescuers had found Fisher conscious and
heard him exclaim, "Boys, I believe my back is broken," before lapsing into un-
consciousness.[60]

Pressing on, Crowe watched as the 200 ton spillway gate was assembled. By the end of November, he had devised a special cableway and hoist system to gently raise then lower the gate into its permanent location on the spillway crest. Crowe enjoyed the challenge of quickly, and under pressure, having to devise new engineering techniques; this again would be another of his famous traits. Construction situations always change on the job site and only those engineers who could adapt and use existing materials would be able to move the job forward without costly time delays. Crowe, completely confident in cableway theory, was always looking for new opportunities to expand and implement the theory into practical use. Specifications were clearly drawn up and cableway testing religiously recorded to serve him later on other jobs. He was particularly interested in the stresses placed on the cableways and he searched for ways to increase the load weight that could be placed on existing interlaced cables. In this regard, he worked with his cableway and gate foremen to maximize the cables capability.[61]

As 1926 ended and the cold weather set in, Crowe once again reduced his work force. He limited the work to the spillway, gate, and glory hole construction. A devastating blizzard struck the Midwest around Christmas shutting down the entire job site. Already at sub-zero temperatures, the mercury plunged still further and Crowe worried about accidents and the inability of men to work in this freezing environment. Yet, he ordered work to continue. At twenty degrees below zero the wind kicked up and the wind chill factor made it unsafe to venture out of doors. On top of this, tall snowdrifts piled up all over the Guernsey area making road travel impossible. Snowstorm related deaths mounted as the days progressed and even the railroads were forced to cancel train schedules. In a rare situation for Crowe, all work was halted when he attempted unsuccessfully to thaw frozen water lines by building bonfires. The effort backfired when burning embers, caught up in the escalating wind, found their way to the nearby supply warehouse, which was destroyed by flames in a matter of minutes. Once the fire was extinguished, Crowe ordered a general shut down, using only skeleton crews to maintain critical water and electric supplies.[62]

One of those ordered to stay on the job was Crowe's colleague and friend Si Bous. Bous (brother to Floyd Bous) attempted to move one of the large steam shovels into a safe location under cover, when an apparently frozen steam pipe on the oversized shovel burst, spraying him with scalding hot steam. A worried Frank Crowe was notified and joined his injured friend at the infirmary. While Bous' injury was extremely painful, he was not seriously hurt; had it been so, it would have proved impossible to transfer him to the hospital in Torrington. All over the dam site and the town of Guernsey abandoned cars littered the streets, while nervous workers and town residents huddled around fireplaces and wood stoves. Those men still on work locations reported in with frozen fingers and hands; one worker's face was so frozen that he reportedly could not work his mouth open for hours.

On again and off again bitter cold temperatures slowed Crowe's progress through the first two months of 1927, however, by March he was ready to get moving again. Early in the month, his men set a 30-foot diameter concrete plug into the entry of the diversion tunnel and the reservoir began to fill. Most of the lower lying areas of the expected lakebed had already been cleared; these men worked under a separate contract and were not affiliated with Crowe or Utah Construction. The plug was set in place in such a way as to allow it to be moved, or opened later. Thus, the diversion tunnel could serve as an emergency spillway, and even as a water intake for future power-turbine expansion.[63]

March saw a flurry of activity at Guernsey as men rushed to finish the spillway sluicing, installing the newly fabricated steel gates on the north spillway, and concreting downstream abutment canyon walls. Si Bous, recovered from his painful steam burns, now led welding crews in fastening the steel gates into their permanent seating location. Crowe enjoyed watching his husky good-natured friend on the job, for Bous demanded a good day's work for a good day's pay— something Crowe believed in strongly. Their relationship had grown even stronger here at Guernsey as they spent more and more time socializing. Not that Crowe was known as an extrovert looking for social entertainment. Quite the contrary, however, their wives had developed a close personal relationship and it was they who arranged evening dinners and visits. On a regular basis through this period, Linnie and Mrs. Bous drove to nearby towns, including Cheyenne for shopping and social club visits. In late March Linnie fell sick. Frank drove her to Wheatland Hospital where she remained for over a week. On this occasion, Frank, with a good deal of help from Mrs. Bous, watched and cared for Patricia and Elizabeth.[64]

Workers began departing Guernsey as their current job responsibilities finished up. Crowe said goodbye to his carpenter ace Charlie Williams toward the end of April. Williams had been brought to the site by Crowe and had faithfully completed all carpentry assignments. Now with only finishing work left, Williams was free to leave. With his wife and friend Floyd Currier, a fellow carpenter at the dam site, Williams decided to take an extended vacation before seeking another work assignment. Crowe informed Williams it would be months before the next big job, with a possibility for a contract somewhere in northern California. On hearing this, Williams made plans to route his short vacation from Guernsey, Wyoming down to New Mexico and up through California and Oregon to his home in Yakima, Washington.[65] It is interesting to note that many of Crowe's famed construction army, despite their constant moving from job to job, built houses in certain areas and called this home. For Williams, Yakima was home, as he had helped Crowe build Tieton Dam and on seeing the beauty of the area decided to make this his permanent residence. Crowe, and from Linnie's standpoint as well, still considered Boise their home. This was especially true as Crowe was now part of the Boise based Morrison & Knudsen Construction Company. "Woody" Williams, the tough and construction-talented son of Charlie Williams remained with

Crowe for a couple of more months before he left with his wife for Oregon. Crowe had become much impressed with the building savvy of this young man and he planned to groom him for tough assignments in years to come. Crowe was particularly pleased in Woody's desire to hone his abilities in tunneling techniques.

The Crowe army dispersed all over the West. Some men, anxious for immediate work, engaged in short term jobs in Southern California while others simply moved back to their "home towns," worked until Crowe would wire them again. All of them told Crowe where they would be and for how long. If any changes came up, the workers notified the Morrison & Knudsen headquarters in Boise. To many of them, Crowe would have them wire him direct, either at Guernsey or later at his home in Boise. Talk of a new job in California proved exciting to those men exiting Guernsey, still carrying with them the memories of the bitter cold of a few months before. As the work neared completion, Crowe himself took off time to be with his family and to visit Harry Morrison in Boise. Linnie wanted one more trip to Denver before leaving Wyoming and Frank decided to make it a family vacation, staying in the big city for several days.[66]

In the final weeks before finishing Guernsey Dam, Secretary of the Interior Hubert Work and Bureau Commissioner Elwood Mead arrived for a final inspection. Several members from Congress and officials from Burlington Northern Railroad accompanied them. Work, who understood that Crowe felt lukewarm about him, praised the work at Guernsey stating that he was "highly pleased" and that Guernsey would be "one of the strongest dams ever built by the Reclamation Service."[67] Comments such as these, however received by Crowe himself, boosted his reputation within construction circles around the nation. It provided a tremendous advantage for future bidding prospects on Western dams for Morrison & Knudsen.

Guernsey Dam was officially completed during the first week of August and Crowe left the area with his family on August 3, 1927. Their destination was Boise, Idaho, and home. As a closing praise to Crowe and his men for a job well done, the people of Guernsey gave small presents and tokens of their appreciation. The local paper summarized the town's feeling with the following epitaph:

> With the completion of the dam brings a greater development for Wyoming industrially and agriculturally. Already a high voltage transmission line is planned to span the state, with many towns to be given power. More water is available for reclaiming our arid lands.
>
> To Guernsey it meant cheap power for our mines and increased production, municipal lighting and power for all kinds of industrial purposes, ice harvesting by the Burlington during the winter months, the creation of a place that will develop into the greatest summer playground in all western Nebraska and eastern Wyoming.[68]

Chapter 7

"I have never become 'desk broke' in all these years."
1927-1930

The Bear River flows out of the Sierra Nevada foothills eventually spilling its water into the Pacific bound Sacramento River. For years, local farmers in Placer and Nevada Counties in northern California complained that they were not realizing their full crop potential due to an unreliable year round water source. Water engineers for the Nevada Irrigation District, to which both Nevada and Placer Counties belonged, surmised that the construction of a high diversion dam, rather than extension of a canal upstream to a low diversion dam site, was "...economically desirable, due to the flat profile of the river for several miles above the dam site and the deeply indented slopes on either side."[1] Local residents also hoped that a high dam could induce Pacific Gas & Electric Company to develop hydroelectric power, making the generated electricity available in amounts that would meet their agricultural and home demands, and at an inexpensive rate.

A huge controversy erupted in the spring of 1927 as pressure from Yuba County landowners sought to bring the county into the Nevada Irrigation District, and thus be part of the new irrigation plans. Rumors of a financial rip-off spread quickly and proponents of the Yuba merger called for a public meeting inviting "Land Owners, Voters, and Interested Citizens." At the April 9th meeting, A. L. Wisker of the Nevada Irrigation District declared:

> ...A public demand for enlightenment on the affairs of Nevada Irrigation District, A. L. Wisker will address the meeting and will discuss the contract with Pacific Electric and Development Company, together with all pertinent matters connected with financing the construction of all works necessary for the irrigation of 275,000 acres of land in Placer, Nevada, and Yuba [C] counties.[2]

The landmark mass meeting satisfied the concerns of most local landowners and plans moved ahead for construction. The next month, May, engineers with the Nevada Irrigation District used power diamond drills to check the bedrock, taking dozens of samples. It was confirmed that the proposed site consisted of a massive black slate ledge on both sides of the river and extending downward—a natural foundation for a concrete dam. Local newspapers now began covering developments of the project, as expectations ran high for available water and cheaper electric rates. In their excitement, newspapers and local residents argued over a name for the dam. At one time or another during the later months of 1927 and thereafter, the proposed dam was referred to as: Van Giesen, an early settler of the area; Coombie, another well established local family; and Bear River Dam.

Frank Crowe first saw the plans for Van Giesen Dam while he was finishing up Guernsey Dam. He carried the plans with him on a site visit in August of 1927, shortly after bids had been let. This was one of Crowe's first official business trips to California and he marveled at the natural beauty of the Sierra Nevada foothills.[3]

Returning to Boise in late August, Crowe began the arduous task of compiling the figures for an official bid. By now, Harry Morrison had complete confidence in Crowe's estimating for materials and man-hours needed to complete the task. Van Giesen appealed to the dam builder, despite its small size, because it had been designed as a variable radius solid concrete overflow arch. This would provide him another challenge in designing concrete holding forms and the concrete delivery system. Additionally, the foundation rock and vertical canyon walls were found to be similar in structural composition to what he expected to find in Nevada's Black Canyon. Both the foundation and abutments would require contraction joints and grouting, another job sequence he expected to encounter later. Crowe's final bid was rushed down to the Nevada Irrigation District headquarters arriving just before the deadline date of September 28, 1927. When opened the next day, Nevada Irrigation Engineer Fred H. Tibbetts, announced that Crowe's bid (Morrison-Knudsen) proved to be the lowest out of ten total bids. The winning overall figure of $154,270 ranked $20,091 below the nearest competitor and $42,295 lower than Tibbetts' original bid estimate for the irrigation district.[4]

The eventual dam, some 12 miles by road from Auburn, California was designed to stand 90 feet above the foundation level, running a crest length of 800 feet. Crowe, intrigued over the unusual structural design, read the blueprints with great interest. He noted that the "normal stream flow will be confined to the depressed section in the center, where the back face is nearly vertical, and will fall well clear of the toe of the dam into a pool in the solid water-worn streambed rock." The abutments of the dam would need a thicker base than at the center and stress levels varied greatly from center to side, all the way up. Crowe knew that the structure would have to be strong as no floodgate appeared on the plans. In the unlikely event the Bear River swelled to more than 25,000 cubic feet per second, it would "present a Niagara-like spectacle as it sweeps over the crest and into the canyon below."[5]   The plans called for him to consider a maximum compression of 460 pounds per square inch in the concrete. He decided to attack this concern by inserting contraction joints at 44-foot intervals, filling the joints with grout after most of the concrete had been placed.

After inspecting the dam site in September of 1927, the observant engineer noted that the Bear River streambed covered a diabase rock strata, a hard water-worn structure that provided an excellent foundation bed. However, out at the canyon-sides preliminary core samples revealed that excavation to a maximum depth of 25 feet would be needed to hit hard, unweathered rock. In terms of removal, this meant about 10,000 cubic yards of unwanted rock would need to be carried away. With excavation equipment on-site the ever-anxious Crowe ordered foundation digging to begin on October 8, 1927.[6]

It is amazing to note the speed with which Crowe could harness men and machines to start a new job. Even the local residents of Grass Valley and Auburn noted how "The Morrison-Knutson [sic] Construction Company, who have charge of building the Nevada Irrigation District Dam at Coombie Crossing are rushing all preliminary work for the construction of the dam which is to be finished by May 1st."[7]   The bunkhouses, able to accommodate several hundred men, were erected within weeks and drillers bored scores of initial blasting holes at the proposed base of the foundation. Crowe demanded good communication and transportation; these were part of his key to successful dam building within contract time and under contract price. He had heavy equipment grade a wide road from the dam site to the county paved road near Meadow Vista School. Crowe's orders stated clearly that as soon as the road was in, he wanted "all heavy material" rushed to the site before the expected heavy rains arrived. Meanwhile, Crowe worked with Pacific Gas & Electric Company engineers to ensure that the promised electric power substation would be completed within the allotted time. It would be critical to have maximum electric power from the beginning in order to operate much of his equipment; he expected to use a "large amount of juice."

Linnie and the children did not accompany Frank to the Van Giesen Dam site at first. They remained in Boise, where they had purchased a small, yet comfortable home. Crowe, for a few nights at least, stayed at one of the many fine hotels in historic Auburn. The well-staffed Hotel Auburn and its attached coffee shop remained a favorite among locals and particularly appealed to those who wanted comfortable housing and good food. Their Saturday night special midnight dinner consisted of Chicken a la King, Au Gratin potatoes, celery salad, tea biscuits, and coffee, all for only fifty cents. If you suffered from "tired nerves," a customer could order a hot cup of Ovaltine for twenty cents extra. In catering to the needs of single men and their need for entertainment, Auburn boasted Hansen's Pastime Pool Hall, where "snooker pool" prevailed. Hansen stocked ice cream, candies, cigars and "tobaccoes [sic] of all kinds." It is interesting to note the emphasis that this California town placed on automobiles. Unlike the other Western locations Crowe lived, cars were numerous and in demand. New and used Ford, Studebaker, Buick, and Chevrolet advertisements appeared in large numbers. A 1923 Ford one-ton truck was listed at $150, while a 1926 Dodge Deluxe sedan sported an $825 price tag. Other not so familiar makes and models also were available such as: Hupmobile, Star Six Coupe, Jordan Brougham, Essex Coach, Stephen's Roadster, and Erskine Sport Coupe.[8]

Work proceeded on schedule in the warm California autumn. The diversion of the Bear River offered Crowe a unique opportunity to test a theory. He noticed that foundation bedrock formed a jagged wall roughly parallel with the riverbanks. The hard surfaced outcropping ran from an area within the proposed foundation site upstream several yards. It would be a relatively easy procedure to extend this natural wall up and down stream with hard packed gravel forming an extended crib. Crowe immediately put his best men working on this project and by November, they were ready to throw a gravel dike across the north side of the mid-river crib, channeling the water to the south side. This proved to be an easy and efficient method for quickly turning a river, and he was soon ready to finish excavating the north-side foundation area and he prepared to place concrete.[9]

One reason for Crowe's low bid resulted from the proximity of good quality gravel for the concrete mix. All he had to do was setup a slack-line bucket system that conveyed the sand and gravel to the concrete sorting screens and storage bunkers. When riverbed foremen notified him that gravel deposits lacked depth, Crowe surveyed sites downstream. He found an excellent deposit containing a wide variety of gravel and sand sizes. Within days, his capable men worked on constructing a rail track along the winding river from the new deposit to the sorting bunkers. He brought in a new Insley 1/2-yard dragline to load the cars and from here to the conclusion of concrete placing, the gravel and sand arrived in a non-stop flow. Episodes such as this made Crowe a respected authority in developing and using innovative building approaches. He reacted quickly to new construction problems, whether they are in transportation, supplies, excavation, or concrete placing. The transition to a new aggregate source was so smooth in the Van Giesen scenario that outsiders might believe the shift of gravel source sites had been planned.

Wanting to place concrete as soon as possible Crowe planned to use the gravel and sand shortly after its deposit in the storage bunkers. The screened material, wet from the river, proved a problem to the concrete mixing plant operators. To correctly calculate the water needs of a four-sack mix of cement, the amount of water in the sand and gravel had to be carefully controlled. All of the early batches had excess water. The alternative was to construct bigger holding bunkers and wait for the sand and gravel to dry completely or to custom mix each concrete batch allowing for varying wetness. Crowe, never one to settle for limited alternatives, devised a special two-compartment loading car, one side for the gravel and the other for the sand. Crowe ordered the bottom of the gravel container cutout and he instructed that a fine steel screen be inserted, allowing for full water drainage by the time the car reached the storage bunker. On the sand side, workers installed an adjustable lip, over which all excess water from the sand skimmed off when the wet sand was loaded to the brim.[10]

With the installation of a 28-cubic foot concrete mixer and the completion of the mixing plant, Crowe was ready, as 1928 dawned, to raise the dam. Using his already tested method of placement, Crowe had the freshly mixed concrete poured directly into his specially designed one-yard bottom gate cars. The steel cars ran on a small gauge train approximately 1000 feet along an ascending track to the dam. There, operators hoisted the freshly mixed concrete into the air, using Crowe's custom engineered cableway. Carefully, the valuable loads swung out over the construction site to the form blocks, where concrete form crews released the bottom swing gate, dumping the concrete. Crowe planned for two movable headtowers running parallel on either side of the river. With this layout, all parts of the curved dam could be reached. According to one engineer visiting the dam site, Crowe's cableway design and function "proved extremely satisfactory, as the concrete is placed in the forms with no separation of ingredients."[11]

Weather wise, January and February surprised Crowe and his men. Naturally conditioned to contend with freezing cold mountain temperatures and whistling fast winds, northern California basked in a moderate climate. Even nighttime low temperatures held moderate compared to previous jobs in Montana, Wyoming, and Idaho. Crowe ordered work to continue seven days a week. By February, all the newly hired men, in a reliable routine by now, helped Crowe press forward with his promise of placing 200 cubic yards of concrete a day. Observers noted that the "construction plant has proved to be reliable," with Crowe deserving much of the credit. He made daily rounds of the numerous jobs searching for potential problems and encouraging foremen and workers alike. Down in the pit of the foundation, Crowe inspected the five-foot high by 12 to 16-foot long wood panel concrete forms. To reduce moisture absorption through the wood, he asked the form supervisor to line the panels with sheet metal, improving results. The precisely constructed wooden forms sat anchored in place with two rows of bolts, one at the top and the other at the bottom. Van Giesen's relatively small dimensions allowed the crafty engineer to use only one line of panel forms across the width of the dam. After the concrete set in the form, specially trained crews raised the forms with "chain blocks" so that the top row of bolts in the completed lift became the bottom row for the next pour.[12]

As the concreting began, Crowe spent considerable time working closely with the concrete mixing plant foreman to ensure a proper mix. Three considerations occupied Crowe's concerns throughout the concrete placing operation: water tightness, workability, and a minimum strength of 1500 pounds at a 28-day test mark. The sand used from the Bear River revealed a fineness modulus, or variation in grading of 2.0 to 3.5 while the gravel averaged between 6.8 and 8.0. With this extreme size variation and the pronounced wetness of the sand and gravel, Crowe noticed that cement portions ranged from 3.6 to 4.4, sacks per batch. He was pleased to discover that the overall figures revealed a four-sack cement average mixture, just as he had planned. Early tests proved the workability of the mix good and measured maximum strengths of 3000 pounds per square inch and 1500 pounds per square inch minimum at the 28-day test. These equaled or exceeded the strength requirements of state engineering plans. As it turned out there appeared a wide variation in the gravel denseness and water content of the sand. When the sand is not well graded or lacking in density, its water content is greater and the concrete reaches the minimum strength. A lack of fine particles, within the sand, helped to account for the density reduction. Worried about keeping a uniformity of concrete strength, Crowe initiated 7 and 28-day tests for strength and visual screen analysis, three times a week.

While on the job at Van Giesen Frank Crowe did not work in conjunction with Bureau of Reclamation engineering inspectors, but rather with engineers from the Nevada Irrigation District. Fred H. Tibbetts, chief engineer, and Raymond Matthew, assistant chief engineer, remained on-site throughout the project construction, impressed with the efficiency of Crowe and his crews. Even State Engineer Edward Hyatt, who with his assistant W. A. Perkins visited the job site several times, marveled at the construction standards, set by Crowe. Hyatt was particularly pleased with the speed and efficiency in completing the foundation excavation and grouting, a difficult operation in most early stages of dam construction. State engineering geologist, S. A. Tibbetts, brought in to look at the bedrock foundation could see that Crowe's men had prepared the bottom surface of the riverbed to receive a large number of concrete placing forms, thus allowing for maximum effort.[13]

On into March of 1928 the concrete placing continued with Crowe's cableway system serving without flaw. The only problem occurred on March 25 when a flash flood, uncommon in the area, came crashing down the Bear River. The deluge came through with such force that the onrushing water rose to within a few feet of overtopping the 80 percent completed dam. Crowe had cleverly planned for such a contingency. He purposely left three flood openings at the base of the dam. These sections were to be the last concreted, sometime in April. Luckily, the openings proved sufficient to drain the accumulated floodwaters. Within days the remaining water funneled sheepishly through a single flume and work resumed at full speed.

Fortunately for Crowe the dam successfully held back the brief floodwaters, as everyone in the area became immediately alarmed upon hearing the news that a southern California dam, St. Francis, had broken suddenly on March 13. Located in the Santa Clara Valley, some 40 miles north of Los Angeles, the dam "went out" around one o'clock in the morning catching residents downstream asleep, taking 450 lives and wiping out farm homes. Property damage ran into the

millions. St. Francis Dam had only recently been completed and was under the
city of Los Angeles ownership. Immediately the victims blamed the city and the
contractor for faulty construction and authorities initiated an extensive investigation.[14]

Charlie Williams, by now one of Crowe's top supervisors, served as a
construction superintendent. This meant that his responsibility included each and
every phase of the work, not just carpentry. Williams took advantage of this new
opportunity to groom his son "Woody" for a supervisory position. The younger
Williams, who later would distinguish himself and gain national attention with
Crowe at Boulder Dam, proved to be a quick learner and soon appeared everywhere on the job site. Crowe liked Woody's tough physical conditioning and his
eye for improving construction productivity and for efficiently dealing with problems using available supplies. Since every job presented a unique series of construction challenges, it was critical to have reliable, competent, and fast thinking
men working for him.

The combination of Crowe's efficient cableway operation, the mild winter and spring weather, and the skill of the hardworking construction crews, combined to finish Van Giesen Dam in early May of 1928, well ahead of the projected
schedule. Frank packed up his belongings and with Linnie and the children, who
had been visiting for a few weeks, headed for his home in Boise. On May 12 at
the dedication ceremony a gathering of state engineering officials, P G & E representatives, and Nevada Irrigation District personnel talked about the fine construction operation and the benefits of Van Giesen. Hebert M. Cooper, Manager
of the Drum Division of P G & E summarized the feelings of most local residents
when he said:

> In my boyhood I saw Nevada County pass out of the
> rich mining days that made it famous. I can remember the old
> placer workings and the large hydraulic mines. Many of them I
> saw closed down and abandoned. As I saw them go I often
> wondered what would be the future of Nevada County. Like
> others, I dreamed of orchards and farms taking the place of the
> mines, but I never could see how it could be done until the pro-
> posal came to organize this great irrigation district...We rejoice
> with you today in the completion of this dam and hope to go
> forward with the District in the fullest cooperation, to the end of
> our contract and yours. As a son of Nevada County and a resi-
> dent of Placer County, I personally share with you the happiness
> of this day.

State Engineer Edward Hyatt remarked next that Van Giesen was constructed in a most efficient and desirable manner. He made mention to the fact that

the dam was extremely well built and had no chance of bursting. Hyatt wanted to allay the fears of any that day who still feared a St. Francis Dam type disaster. In a final tribute to Crowe, Hyatt told the nervous spectators that Van Giesen Dam is completely safe and that no one should question its structural integrity.[15]

Upon his return to Boise, Crowe served in an advisory capacity to Harry Morrison previewing prospective dam and irrigation bids. Considerable time was spent in discussing the upcoming Boulder Dam project on the Colorado River. Crowe had seen, first hand, the preliminary drawings for the proposed concrete superstructure and constantly talked to Morrison about "being in a position to bid for the greatest job of all-time."[16] While it is not known for sure how many on-site visits Crowe made to the Las Vegas area in 1929-30, he must have made several trips in hopes of gathering bidding reference information. Meanwhile, numerous smaller reclamation jobs, being considered by the Bureau of Reclamation, needed his attention. One of these projects, Deadwood Dam, was not far from Boise and looked particularly attractive to Crowe.

Early in 1929, Crowe busied himself checking out the environment and access to the proposed Deadwood Dam. He learned that the proposed dam would assist in storing waters from the Payette watershed to supplement the flow at Black Canyon Dam at Emmet. The remote dam site, located 65 miles from Cascade, Idaho, the nearest railroad point, required the construction of eight miles of road to connect the upper end of the basin with the Forest Service highway leading to Cascade. The area was hilly, heavily timbered, and primitive, just the kind of job Crowe yearned for. He understood that if they won the bid to build this dam the government would need to build an access road immediately, and depending on the time required to do this the building schedule on the dam itself would be held-up. In thinking ahead, the Bureau had already contributed $5000 toward improving the Forest Service road and was making plans to bid out the road-cutting job early. Additionally, Crowe could see from several vantage points overlooking the site that the Deadwood Basin was thickly timbered with lodge pole pine making the job of clearing more difficult.[17]

The Bureau of Reclamation officially announced, in early February of 1929 that plans for building Deadwood Dam had been completed. The Denver office declared a bidding period extending from April 15, with the opening of bids set for June 15. Crowe on inspecting the Deadwood Dam plans at the Morrison & Knudsen offices in Boise rejoiced; the specifications called for a 160-foot high solid concrete arch structure, exactly what Crowe excelled in building. Besides, it would be an excellent opportunity to, once again, hone his skills for the upcoming Boulder Dam project putting him in a position of continuing to have recent experience in construction of high concrete dams.[18]

As Crowe and Morrison, in conjunction with Utah Construction worked diligently to put together a competitive bid, news came in early May that the Bureau might be forced to abandon the Deadwood Dam project. The source of the problem arose when a number of local residents reported that their placer mining claims would be flooded if the proposed reservoir was completed. The hopeful miners banded together in seeking legal counsel and through their lawyers sought $600,000 as compensation for lost land and possible revenue. The complaint and the proposal for settlement was directed to Bureau Commissioner Elwood Mead, who having dealt with this concern on numerous occasions, immediately ordered "a halt of proceedings until the rights of the alleged owners are looked into." Meade made it perfectly clear that the government would abandon the project before it would pay any such amount.[19]

Within a couple of weeks, a court date of June 3 was set for the claimants to present their case against the Bureau. Meanwhile, word spread that the collective group of miners, known as the "Lee Bunch group" considered settling for much less money than initially urged by their legal counsel. As the days moved on, Meade, with a determined sense of not giving in, gave no signal that the government was willing to pay anything. Both parties, however, went into court willing to move their positions. The miners realizing that they could lose their opportunity to get some cash quickly lowered their settlement figure. From his side, Meade agreed to pay $15,000 for the combined claims. Meade was actually quite relieved with this outcome, as the Bureau saw great value in building Deadwood Dam at the proposed site. A relocation of the dam to another building site might easily consume the $15,000 and more in new surveys and engineering sampling, plans, and preparations. Within days of the settlement hearing, Meade, once again, opened bids.[20]

Meade worried about the delay in bidding and he further contacted the Denver office of the Bureau, who had drafted the completed set of plans for Deadwood, wanting to know "if the plans, as approved a month ago, are still satisfactory to the chief engineer at Denver." As everyone waited anxiously for the reply from the Bureau office, Crowe already knew that the plans were still good. As he had thoroughly checked out the situation, there were only so many variables that could impact the general approach of building the dam. He meticulously covered each contingency. A month delay would have some impact, but all the other variables remained the same. Crowe throughout the rest of May waited anxiously for the bidding blueprints from the Denver office so that he could put together the actual bid.

Meade announced on June 14 that the specifications were now available from the Denver office to any construction company interested in bidding the Deadwood Dam job. Harry Morrison had already notified the Bureau of his intent to bid and so they received one of the first sets of specifications. Meade wrote that all bids would be opened on July 16, giving only four weeks for Crowe to put together the complete bid. The bid would only include the cost for labor, as the government paid for all materials. There would be separate bids on road construction and reservoir clearing.[21]

Morrison and Crowe worked closely with the Utah Construction's Wattis brothers on estimating the bid and E. O. Wattis, nervous about the remoteness of Deadwood, wanted to check more closely, access and travel time to the dam site. It is not clear whether Crowe agreed with this concern or not, but the veteran engineer sent "auto trucks and trailer[s] into Deadwood Basin heavily loaded with gravel to get an idea of the cost of transportation before placing their bid on construction."[22]

The Denver office had decided to allow companies to bid for both the dam construction and the reservoir clearing at the same time, so that two schedules, or bidding areas were approved. Wattis and Morrison, with Crowe leading the way, eagerly submitted their bid at the traditional last minute. This was to allow for any sudden changes in personnel needs, price fluctuations in materials, or a reconsideration of the profit margin needed. When the time arrived, the Denver office had received four bids. The outcome was not even close. The Bureau estimated $641,400 for the construction of the dam and Crowe came through with $673,400, a difference of only $32,000, or five percent. Crowe's expertise here proved obvious, as the other companies were much higher: Strange, Maguire & Tripp, $803,400; Ward Engineering Company, $803,200; and Fuglee Construction Company, $1,094,100.

Interestingly enough, all bids on the reservoir clearing were rejected, with the invitation to rebid within 30 days. Notwithstanding this rejection, the Bureau wanting to move ahead with dam construction, urged Morrison & Knudsen and the Utah Construction Company to proceed. An elated Crowe immediately made plans to begin moving heavy equipment to the dam site. Road building equipment was on-site, along with Crowe on July 23, and with the help of Charlie Williams, a camp was started four days later. Named superintendent of construction for the job, Crowe wanted the access roads in as soon as possible; everything else depended on this. Especially since he was getting a month later start than expected and with the understanding that the Deadwood area was known for its cold bitter winter temperatures and heavy snowfalls, and with memories of Guernsey still lingering, Crowe wanted to get set up promptly. Wasting no time, his crews busily graded access roads by the 29th.[23]

Crowe, preoccupied with getting construction going on the Deadwood site did not become involved in the rebid. The clearing rebid called for 31 schedules or components and only two companies sent in bids to cover all the work, Utah Construction, without the benefit of Crowe's help, and the ambitious firm of Halmber & Norman Construction. This time Utah Construction was not the low bid; in fact, they were $43,000 more than the Halmber & Norman bid. Utah's total estimated bid came in at $200,000. The Bureau decided to allow Utah Construction to clear schedule #1, a site close to the camp, while the balance of the clearing schedule was lost to the competitors. Utah lost another bid when they again bid without Crowe's help on the Flow Line Road project, near the dam site. Their bid

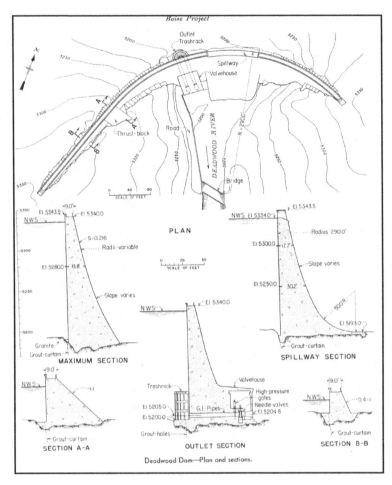

Plan for Deadwood Dam. (USBR)

of $24,700 ballooned to over twice the estimated Bureau estimate; officials quickly
rejected the figure, postponing the job.[24]

    Crowe's chief carpentry supervisor, Charlie Williams drove his crews to
start the engineer's camp as well as the contractor's camp. Here at Deadwood, as
would be true in other large construction sites, the engineering camp or government camp and the contractor's camp were little towns in themselves, many times
separated by some distance. The Deadwood engineering camp consisted of a large

log-cabin type office, garage and laboratory combined, one five-room log cabin for assistant engineers, three three-room log cabins with garages, and three one-room frame cabins connected by garage space. Water system and sewers were provided. The camp lie just above the expected high water line about 300 yards from the east end of the dam. The contractor's camp, warehouse and shops sat near the government camp but below the flow line. Cabin and dormitory space would be needed for 300 men. However, work in erecting these small, but stout dwellings went slow at first, much to the chagrin of Crowe, as Williams could not find men "skilled enough with an ax to do good log work."[25]

Once camp had been set up and operations began, Crowe discovered that the gravel and sand composition near the dam site was unsatisfactory. J. L. Savage, government engineer from Denver met with Morrison and Crowe, and they determined that coarser deposits "farther up the basin was less decomposed." Always flexible, Crowe's foremen made plans to use this source of aggregate for the concrete mix. On top of this, Crowe continued to worry about keeping supplies coming to the dam site. Once the winter weather came, the area could be blanketed in several feet of snow. It was decided to subcontract to a local trucking outfit, Knowles Brothers, to haul supplies and keep the road open until the heavy snow fall halted activity. Another subcontract went to Cascade Investment Company to move the gravel from the pits to the mixing plant. Crowe, with Morrison, met with foremen from these companies and briefed them on coordinating efforts.[26]

Using a large steam shovel, Crowe ordered an assault on the geologically solid bedrock in the foundation riverbed. The hard driving engineer realized that he had only three months, if he was lucky, of moderate weather in which to excavate and prepare for concreting. After that time, work would be shut down. He brought in special "gas-driven cars" and Mack trucks for hauling muck out of the riverbed. Five portable air compressors with drills operated by experienced dam workers chipped away on the bedrock. Simultaneous with this, Crowe began organizing the aggregate separation plant and the concrete mixing plant. A powerful and noisy jaw crusher pulverized oversized gravel. Crowe designed a 22-foot screen to separate the debris into five desired gravel sizes. From this stockpile, the aggregate would be delivered to the mixing plant by use of a continuously operating conveyor belt. Williams and Crowe planned for a sturdy trestle to support the belt the necessary distance. The mixing plant would be small, only a 2-yard mixer. Nearby was the 20 x 80-foot cement storage shed, considered ample by Crowe who would not authorize the use of any cement stored for more than ninety days.[27]

In anticipation of placing the concrete Crowe looked seriously at using his famous cableway system. After considerable deliberation, he decided on a 5-ton cableway with a span of 600 feet. Supporting the cables would be two steel towers, one 125 feet high and the other 25 feet higher. Using a 150-kilowatt diesel driven generator Crowe planned to power the cableway, mixer, and conveyor.

Headtower used for building Deadwood Dam.
(USBR)

While all this was going on, Williams' crews erected an on-site sawmill with the task of cutting 800 mill feet of lumber for building the trestle, small bridges, and concrete forms. His men began making shiplap one and a half inches thick and faced with steel sheets for use as concrete forms.

It was during September that Crowe learned how the Russian government had hired A. P. Davis, his former boss, as an irrigation consultant. Davis, who had been unceremoniously dumped by Interior Secretary Work in 1925, had spent the intervening years offering his engineering skills to Mexico and other foreign countries. Now, the Soviets wanted the talented engineer to supervise the gigantic $250,000,000 desert irrigation project in Russian Turkestan, where the government expected to raise massive amounts of cotton. While the price of Davis's fees for the consulting work were not disclosed, Crowe could assume that, like himself, the potential for high earnings remained obvious.[28]

More than usual, Crowe pushed everyone to his limit. After hearing from locals how bad the snow pack could be he pushed Morrison to authorize more money and men on the job. The eight mile long construction road was graded and in good condition. Progress had been made in excavating the canyon abutments, even though a special inspection was needed by Bureau engineers to check for decomposition of rock material in the area. J. L. Savage, Chief Designing Engineer, S. O. Harper, General Superintendent of Construction, and A. J. Wiley, Consulting Engineer spent time during September and October with Crowe in checking the natural joints in the abutment rock cliffs. It was critical to have excavated all decomposed rock or weak joints before preparing for concrete placement. Savage reported that, "while much rock has been removed from this abutment near the downstream face below elevation 5475 [feet], the joints are still open and the shape of the abutment still departs widely from radial lines." Realizing that the work season for 1929 was ending, Savage charged Crowe with the task of "more excavation near the downstream face will be required both to secure a more impermeable and a better shaped foundation." The poor rock condition of the right abutment did not hold for the left side, as Savage found that "the left abutment generally appears to be much better rock though two soft struts were encountered near the foot of the slope."[29]

On-site problems can always be expected and at Deadwood the master dam builder confronted a river diversion that looked insoluble. The original plan for handling the diversion of water from the Deadwood River called for Crowe to install outlet conduits to handle the expected river runoff. The conduits could be moved from one side of the riverbed to the other allowing dry access to one side at a time. When the opening bids were delayed due to litigation over property rights, thus affecting the entire work schedule, Crowe asked permission to divert the river by use of a tunnel in the right abutment. With this modification, Crowe's men would attain access to the entire riverbed area, allowing them to work a larger area and place more concrete. However, after Savage and others discovered the weakness in the abutment rock, they declined to approve Crowe's request. Now, Crowe needed to think quickly of an acceptable alternative or lose valuable weeks to inaction. He decided on erecting a dirt and gravel cofferdam at the center of the riverbed channel enabling him to turn the river down the east side while the west side was stripped and the foundation placed. Still problems persisted, but so did Crowe. When new excavation uncovered a "pocket" in the foot of the slope on the east side where large amounts of water would collect, Crowe decided to build a 8 x 24-foot flume to quickly channel water away. Within weeks, the completed diversion scheme, though hastily conceived, worked well. This allowed crews to complete excavation on the west bank.

Due to the rough isolated living conditions of the Deadwood Dam site and the snow-caused shortened work year, most workers did not bring their families with them. However, Linnie and the children lived in a tent for the first summer. Patricia recalled being "raised in a large tin tub." "The trees were beautiful and it was a lot of fun," she added. That fall Frank moved the family back to their home in Boise where Linnie cared for Patricia and Bettee.[30] Frank remained on the job site, except for rare occasions when he journeyed the rough 65 miles to Cascade. The tiny town, itself somewhat isolated, sat 50 miles north of Boise and served as a gateway to the Payeete and Salmon River wilderness areas. As any

Deadwood Dam nearing completion in late 1930.
(USBR)

small Western town of the late 1920s, Cascade struggled to support a variety of independent businesses including restaurants, clothing stores, and markets. The Casino Cafe, a local favorite, served everything from waffles to steaks, all day long. The Cascade Hotel served as headquarters for most visitors just arriving in the area, and was probably frequented by Crowe on several occasions as he inspected and prepared bid estimates for the Deadwood Dam job. It is interesting to note that most, if not all, advertisements in the local newspaper, the *Cascade News*, use the hotel as a point of location reference. Mrs. E. Wallaert, who operated a dry cleaning and laundering shop, advertised "excellent service," at XL Dry Cleaning, north of Cascade Hotel. The same references appeared for Miss Cooper's Beauty Shop and for independent contractor Harry Mitchell. Mitchell, a cement and brick-work specialist lived at the hotel and ran his business from there. Telephone numbers, for those fortunate enough to own a phone, consisted of three numbers and a letter, such as #34J2 for Wallaert's dry cleaning establishment.[31]

Remembering the cold-related obstacles of trying to continue construction through the Guernsey, Wyoming job, the Maine born engineer realized that the Deadwood location with extremely high snowfall expectations, regular ongoing below freezing temperatures, and complete isolation from the nearest train depot, combined to force a halt to activity. Just trying to keep the Cascade to Deadwood road open would require a huge investment in time and money. Accordingly, Crowe ordered a complete shut down on December 18. He and the rest of his men headed for home. Only two men remained behind at the dam site, C. B. Gunk, assistant to the Bureau engineer and Frank Baker, general utility man. Their responsibility included watching over the work site until next spring. Their isolation was complete because once heavy snowfall began, travel was dangerous and ill advised. Arriving back in Boise, Crowe reported to Morrison that progress at Deadwood, despite the late start and the current winter work break, looked promising and close to schedule.

The day after Christmas, Crowe penned an interesting letter to his sister Catherine that described the Deadwood Dam job, the rough climatic conditions of the area, and his winter departure from the site. It reads, "Rec'd yours of 7th on Xmas Eve when I 'crushed' in from the Deadwood Dam, 67 miles from the nearest R.R. point Cascade, Idaho. We were snowed in from the 9th until we walked out for Xmas and closed the job down for the winter." In describing the project Crowe states, "This is a concrete dam about 160 feet high located in the mountains at elev. 5400 ft. We have to go over three mountain passes 7000 feet high to get to it so it is a short season job. We expect to start walking back about April 1st." He goes on to describe the road conditions as not passable until around the middle of June. "It was some job pushing 82 men over that trail," Crowe relates to Catherine. "Most of them had never 'crushed' [walked long distance in the snow] before. And believe me "crushing" is some different from hiking on bare ground. We slept in shacks we had placed along the route."

The long letter, four pages in length, goes on to describe social life at the Deadwood camp as a "blank," with the hope of finishing the dam "about Dec. 1st '30." In reference to Patricia and Elizabeth, Crowe said, "Our two little kiddies are growing fast. Pat is doing fine in school and Bet is in kindergarten. We don't like my present work 'cause I am away from home most of the time." Interestingly, he next laments over his immediate career prospects stating, "But I don't know how to beat it just now. You see I have never become 'desk broke' in all these years I have lived and worked out in the open with only a few hours office work each day."[32]

Crowe did not return to the Deadwood site until late in March of 1930. Typical heavy snowfall completely buried the Cascade to Deadwood road. Crowe, from his temporary headquarters in Cascade, ordered a large caterpillar tractor to begin plowing the route. Frank's nephew John Crowe, 16 years old and still in high school, joined his uncle in the attempt to clear the Cascade Road. The younger Crowe, who would himself go on to become an engineer and join his uncle at Hoover, Parker, and Shasta Dams, remembered the Deadwood road clearing operation as "one of the most difficult jobs ever encountered."[33] At first, daily progress measured in yards, frustrated the older Crowe and his desire to get to the campsite and setup spring construction operations. After one week, the "big cat" had broken through to Warm Lake Summit, a few miles from the dam site, and the crew reported to Crowe that by April the route would be open. Crowe wanted to "get the road in shape so that the 'cat' with bob-sled trailers can do hauling of supplies and men."[34]

Snowmelt was slow and mid-April arrived revealing only seventy men at work on Deadwood Dam. The Cascade Road, in constant need of plowing and grading proved inadequate for Crowe's timetable. Crowe, and reservoir clearing superintendent De Long, contracted to have an airplane fly daily from Cascade to the dam site delivering men and small supplies. According to one eyewitness, the small plane carried "many hundreds of pounds of freight and 24 men for the clearing operation" in one week. On one day in April, the aircraft flew nine trips, averaging 40 to 60 minutes each.[35]

With the arrival of warmer weather in May, Crowe set work crews to grade the Cascade Road and to prepare the Deadwood site for concrete mixing and placing. Heavy-duty caterpillar tractors went back and forth over the winding, though wide, dirt route. By June, Crowe contracted with a local trucking company, Knowles Brothers, to engage their fleet of five "big Coleman trucks" to haul freight to the dam. He estimated that each truck could carry twelve and a half tons of material. To satisfy anticipated concrete mixing demands, Crowe wanted the trucks to run two trips a day, carrying cement and other supplies. Cleverly, the trucking operation setup a "big vertical gas tank" near the Cascade train depot so that the trucks could be fueled day or night.[36]

With forms ready by early June, workers began placing concrete in the foundation. Here the dam's cross-section spanned sixty feet. Crowe expanded his construction crew to approximately four hundred men, most of them hired from the southwestern region of Idaho. With an estimated daily payroll of $2,000, regional business owners rejoiced when Crowe initiated large scale hiring. As the first concrete flowed into place, Crowe welcomed Bureau engineer R. J. Newell to the Deadwood site. Crowe had worked with Newell on several occasions before and was pleased that the well-educated and highly respected Newell would be on-site as the resident Bureau engineer. Newell's job entailed inspecting all phases of the construction work, making sure that government specifications and requirements were met according to the awarded contract.[37]

As the concrete operation began in earnest, a regular flow of government engineers from field offices and the West and from the Denver headquarters visited Deadwood to watch Crowe's cableway system in action. Included in that group was Frank Banks, with whom Crowe had worked at Jackson Lake Dam. Banks, then construction engineer on the Owyhee Project in Oregon, toured the dam site with his old college classmate. Banks wanted to review Crowe's plan for placing large amounts of concrete in a short time, realizing that weather conditions permitted only five months of active work. Following the Frank Banks visit, a contingent of foreign engineers arrived. The four engineers, one of them a woman, became so impressed with the smooth sequence of operations that they returned twice later in June to check on progress.[38]

In a state of high anticipation, construction work moved along at a frenzied pace. Crowe hoped to complete Deadwood Dam by the Thanksgiving holiday. So as not to wait until the last minute to move out heavy equipment that was no longer needed, Crowe ordered the Knowles Brothers, the subcontracting trucking firm, to begin hauling most of the excavation machinery to Cascade. From there, the heavy loads would travel by train to the Morrison & Knudsen or Utah Construction headquarters. On November 7, the last of the concrete had been placed and the cleanup of the job began. By the 24th, despite "serious interruptions due to heavy snowfall," Crowe and the last of his crew left Deadwood and returned to their homes. At Deadwood, for 18 months the site of intense construction activity, only a single Bureau engineer, Don Keyes, remained with his family. His job would be to serve as observer and caretaker through the coming winter.[39] His presence was specially needed, as "it was necessary to protect the control works in the gate house from freezing." Newell and Crowe decided to "experiment with wood stoves at Deadwood," it would be Keyes' job to keep the stoves going.[40]

When asked by local residents about the difficulty of construction in erecting Deadwood Dam, Newell stated flatly, "It is somewhat of a feat for the contractors to have completed so big a concrete dam in five months." He reminded those listening that "the dam is 170 feet high and about 700 feet across the top" and that the area was remote and inaccessible.[41] Whereas most irrigation projects began seasonal construction in March or early April, the Deadwood site prevented serious large-scale work until June. Even with these severe restrictions, Crowe used proven methods, particularly the cableway system, to complete the assignment ahead of schedule and under the contract bid. Harry Morrison and the Wattis Brothers, once again impressed with the abilities of the ambitious Crowe, came away from the Deadwood project with the feeling that their man could build anything anywhere. They would pay serious attention to the quickly rising dam builder when he would recommend strongly that the two construction companies aggressively plan for building America's largest and greatest dam. Ironically, Black Canyon, the name of the Bureau project under which Deadwood Dam had been built, would once again preoccupy Crowe's thoughts and vocabulary, for Bureau engineers were now proposing to build a huge Colorado River dam in a remote and inaccessible canyon in southern Nevada with the same name.

Chapter 8

"I was wild to build this dam."
Hoover Dam, 1931

Early twentieth-century settlers lured to the southern California desert area of Imperial Valley believed an agricultural oasis was in the making. Beginning in 1901, crude earthen ditches carried precious water from the easterly Colorado River to the valley (actually a below-sea-level salt sink). Results were instantaneous and dramatic—crops flourished in the newly moist black earth, and word spread. Thousands of land-seeking families, over 7,000 by 1904, poured into this "irrigation wonderland." Speculators reasoned that another, larger canal, would significantly increase water supplies. With this understanding, the decision was made to bleed additional water from the main Colorado artery.

With the completion of this second Colorado canal the future looked rosy indeed as the additional life-giving water flowed into the area. However, early strong rains in 1905 proved to be a harbinger of disaster. Grappling to resist the dangerously high rising diversion, emergency volunteers attempted to stack rock and sand cofferdams. One attempt after another proved unworthy to restrain the growing deluge:

> During the anxious period between the development of the dangerous break and its closure, those engaged in battling with the river believed more than once that they were engaged in a forlorn hope; but they held on grimly to the task set before them. Almost at the instant that the channel was confined to any promising degree, the swift currents began burrowing and undercutting the obstruction of man's making. It is said that piles 70 feet in length were dislodged and swept away as fast as they could be driven into the waterbed. Indeed, any narrowing of the channel by the placing of an obstruction merely increased the velocity of the flow and intensified the stream's erosive strength so that it cut enormous gaps in the space of only a few hours.[1]

On the water came, pertinacious settlers finally gave up, evacuating much of the valley, as millions of cubic feet of water scourged the topsoil for miles around. Off and on for more than one year, the floods ravaged the entire Imperial Valley, destroying 40,000 acres, many farms and homes, and some people. Man's penchant for tinkering with nature had failed. The Imperial Valley appeared ruined.

News of the Imperial Valley flood spread throughout the nation. Frank Crowe, working on the Yellowstone irrigation project felt the effects of the unseasonable rainfall as northern gully-washers cleaned thousand of acres in Wyoming and Montana. He was aware that Arthur Powell Davis, then an engineer for the Reclamation Service, had surveyed the Colorado River system and conceived a comprehensive proposal to contain, develop, and exploit the Colorado River water. Davis wore himself out trying to convince non-believers that the Imperial Valley, lying below sea level, could be hit with disastrous floods year after year. The only reasonable solution was to build a massive concrete high dam to contain the mighty "Big Red" once and for all. "Two seasons of maximum discharge would flood the valley and destroy 10,000 farms and practically all of the development in the valley," he warned. Explaining the engineering aspect of the problem he noted, "the valley could not be drained, because it is below sea level. The slow process of evaporation would be necessary to restore the valley even after the river had been controlled, and for purposes of the present generation the valley would be annihilated," he concluded. To press his point home Davis stressed, "Unless flood control through storage is provided, this catastrophe is inevitable— the only doubt being when it will occur."[2]

As the years went on Davis and the Bureau saw their bold construction plan vigorously attacked. All of the states with land touched by the Colorado River, or its tributaries, Arizona, California, Nevada, Utah, Colorado, New Mexico, and Wyoming fought legal battles to protect their rights to water access and use. Arizona and several other states asked federal mediators to work out an accord. In 1921, a special investigative committee formed with representatives from each of the concerned states, Reclamation engineers, and headed by Secretary of Commerce Herbert Hoover. These new "water commissioners" worked through their differences and special interests, finally arriving at a compromise. The resulting political agreement, the Colorado River Compact, was approved on November 24, 1922. The representatives all signed this path finding agreement, yet Arizona's legislature refused. A clause in the contract stated implementation of the contract would require six of the seven states; Arizona's objection was circumvented.[3]

The Colorado River Compact argued for a high-dam to control the uneven flow of the river and an All-American Canal. Political action was now called for and Congressman Phil Swing and Senator Hiram Johnson of California drafted the 1923 Boulder Canyon Project Act after receiving a preliminary report from Reclamation Service Director Arthur Powell Davis and Chief Engineer Frank Weymouth. Davis and Weymouth calculated that two canyons, Boulder and Black, were deep enough to accommodate a high dam. Only twenty miles separated the canyons, located 10-15 miles east of Las Vegas. Weymouth greatly concerned about the potential disaster from a breech in a high dam of this size wanted assurances that the bedrock material passed strict hardness and permeability tests. Their decision pointed to Boulder Canyon's granite bedrock as superior to the volcanic composition of Black Canyon. The resulting report formed the basis of the first Boulder Canyon Project Act recommendations.

However, additional expeditions sponsored by the Bureau of Reclamation that involved extensive deep drilling of the bedrock discovered unstable jointing and faulting in Boulder Canyon. Black Canyon contained less silt and debris in the riverbed and the canyon walls, less wide than Boulder, would save concrete. Additionally, the resulting reservoir would be larger and a large supply of sand and gravel lie only a short distance away.[4] The new report, specifying site D in Black Canyon as the prime building location, passed from project engineer Walker Young's drafting table to the desk of Secretary of the Interior Ray Wilbur and finally to the offices of Representative Swing and Senator Johnson in Congress. Despite continued efforts by Arizona Senators Henry Ashurst and Ralph Cameron to kill the bill, Congress passed the Boulder Canyon Project Act and President Calvin Coolidge, finishing his term, signed the act a week later. Arizona continued the fight, this time resorting to legal actions in the various federal courts, but to no avail. On June 25, 1929, a final $165 million version of the act was passed through Congress and reached the desk of newly installed President Herbert Hoover. The chief executive, trained as an engineer, enthusiastically signed the bill into law, a satisfying finish to a proposal he had encouraged as Secretary of Commerce.

Immediately after receiving word that Congress and the President supported the Boulder Canyon Project, Bureau of Reclamation engineers began the difficult task of designing a massive concrete structure to meet the designated site. Ideas for the actual design had flowed into the Denver headquarters of the Bureau for years. Arthur Powell Davis, nephew of explorer John Wesley Powell, in 1902 initiated the first designs of the dam. These drawings were brief sketches he made while surveying the country. As an engineer and later Director of the Reclamation Service, he refined the early plans continuously through the period 1910-1920. Although he had left the government in 1923, many of his original suggestions made the final drawings. In the following years, the new Director of the Reclamation, Elwood Mead, approved additional plans. The design work became an ongoing task of modification and definition. With Weymouth's resignation, Raymond F. Walter, held the position of chief engineer while John L. Savage, as chief design engineer, carried much of the final design authority. Scores of other design engineers worked laboriously on thousands of fine detail carpentry, plumbing, electrical, and concrete form drawings. Frank Crowe, on several occasions working with the Bureau earlier, had contributed his thoughts. As early as 1921 Crowe, while driving through the Jackson Lake area, told J. V. Allen, a local rancher who had worked on Jackson Lake Dam with Crowe, that he was "going to build Boulder Dam."[5] Allen told Crowe that he was going to move his family to California, whereby Crowe indicated that there would be job opportunities once Congress appropriated the money. Later, Crowe floated down the Colorado River with Harry Morrison on at least two occasions to "get a feel for what to build." As General Superintendent of Construction of the Denver Office in 1924-25, Frank Crowe supervised all construction activities in seventeen western states. In this capacity, he spent long hours reviewing the eight original proposed sites for Boulder Dam. When the short list of acceptable locations was cut to two he consulted with Savage and convinced the latter to raise the dam height from an original estimate of 400-500 feet to 726 feet. This would clearly be the highest dam in the world, and it would dramatically rise between two, nearly vertical canyon walls.

The daring engineers, including Frank Crowe, drill core teams, and topographic survey crews had done their job. Through blistering summer heat waves, over desert terrain that proved unforgiving to those ill prepared, and on an equally unforgiving swirling Colorado River these modern day pioneers had prepared the way for the construction of America's greatest dam. As the Bureau of Reclamation readied its final plans, Mead, with the new title of Commissioner of Reclamation, reminded everyone of the courageous effort displayed in planning the dam:

> The survey of the dam site and reservoir was of unprecedented magnitude and difficulty. It involved coping with a river which, in the highest floods, rushed through the canyon with the speed of a railway train; of taking topography in more than 100 miles of canyon where precipitous cliffs, 1,000 feet high and of indescribable ruggedness had to be scaled. Three lives were lost in this hazardous undertaking. Every phase of the work involved great danger, but the dimensions of the possible dam and reservoir had to be known. Then there had to be a topographic map.[6]

Looking back after the completion of Boulder Dam [later named Hoover Dam], Crowe remembered his fixation to be the one selected to build America's biggest dam "I was wild to build this dam," Crowe declared. "I had spent my life in the river bottoms, and Boulder meant a wonderful climax—the biggest dam ever built by anyone anywhere." [7] From his earliest days with the Bureau, he recalled hearing talk of damming the Colorado River. Frank Weymouth had mentioned it several times during Crowe's experiences on the Yellowstone Project. A. P. Davis, Director of Reclamation in 1919 asked Frank Crowe to make a rough estimate of the dam—cost and materials— for him that year. And, here it was the golden opportunity described by one observer in March of 1931 as "the largest single engineering feat ever attempted in the U. S."[8]

Frank Crowe knew that for all his enthusiasm and optimism he would still need to place himself in a position with a construction company that could successfully bid the job. He began in 1928 to coax Harry Morrison and Morris Knudsen to seriously think about preparing for the bid. The result would be the creation of one of America's most successful business organizations—Six Companies, Incorporated.

The Six Companies affiliation took root in 1922 from the relationship between the Utah Construction Co. and Morrison-Knudsen. Utah Construction had established itself as one of the great railroad construction firms of the West. E.O. and W.H. Wattis, brothers and sons of a second-generation Englishman who had joined the California Gold Rush and then settled in Utah, founded it. They eagerly sought railroad work with the Great Northern, Canadian Pacific, and the Colorado Midland railroad companies. Their engineering experience grew modestly along with their incomes, until the great Panic of 1893 dashed their pocketbooks and their hopes. The younger brother, W. H. Wattis, struggled to maintain the business; while E. 0. Wattis went into sheep ranching. In 1900, the brothers, having saved some money for investment, decided to give construction a try. They formed the Utah Construction Co., utilizing capital supplied by Mormon bankers and investors. Quickly establishing themselves as a quality organization, the brothers garnered much of the Union Pacific's construction work in the far West. By 1910 other western contractors were arguing, "You can't do business with the U.P. unless you work through Utah."[9]

In order to derail the Utah monopoly train, Harry Morrison and his partner Morris Knudsen, working from a Boise, Idaho, base, underbid Utah on a variety of construction jobs. The Wattis brothers, sensing the new competition, asked Morrison to discuss the matter. The pair met in Ogden, Utah, and E. O. Wattis, wishing to share the opportunities, offered to cut Morrison in on Utah's ongoing contracts, if he—Morrison—would bid jobs higher. "They took me in," Morrison stated, "on the theory that when the competition gets tough and you can't beat 'em, then join 'em."[10]

Frank Crowe played a pivotal role in coaxing the two rising construction companies to build western dams. He had worked on and off with Morrison and Knudsen for several years and Crowe was ready to devote his full energies to being a site construction engineer. He knew that big profits could be made if he could find a construction firm willing to take on new government dam building contracts. Crowe, after all, was in a position as General Superintendent of Construction for the U.S. Bureau of Reclamation to know that dozens of large dam projects were being planned. He knew the Bureau's bidding process, and best of all; he knew how to bid low. With his technological secret weapon, the cableway excavating and delivery system, he could cut traditional construction costs tremendously. Morrison and the Wattis brothers knew all of this about Crowe; he could be their ticket to construction success.

With Crowe's enthusiasm, and assurances of sizable profits, the new partnership of Utah Construction and Morrison-Knudsen ventured into the world of constructing large dams. From 1925 through 1931, the Utah company and Morrison-Knudsen tackled the building of Wyoming's Guernsey Dam and Idaho's Deadwood Dam. Both jobs proved highly successful. The United States Bureau of Reclamation was pleased with the quality of construction; the Wattis', Morrison, and Knudsen were pleased with the profits and Frank Crowe was pleased with the challenges and experiences these two mid-sized dams provided. Now he was ready for something even bigger.

W. H. Wattis was also pleased with these early successes and he ventured, "We're the logical people to build it [Hoover Dam]." He added, "We've had the most experience." Wattis' optimism came partly from the understanding that he would have the considerable engineering talents of his general superintendent, Henry J. Lawler, at his disposal. Lawler, with an accumulated construction experience of over thirty years had built Hetch Hetchy Project and Wattis boasted that the combination of "Frank and Hank," he used to say, "will build that dam." E.O. Wattis agreed. At seventy-six the elder Wattis was physically fading; yet he was as mentally alert as ever. He wanted to "get moving" on the Hoover project as soon as possible, without consulting other construction companies or engineers. "Money's no problem," he kept saying. "We can raise what we need on the ranch."[11] His reference to the ranch meant that he had acquired a handsome reserve asset in his sheep and cattle ranch. Much of the previous construction profit had been put back into buying additional ranch land and stock. Both brothers realized that bankers and investors saw the land and stock as outstanding collateral, whereas construction investment alone was risky. By 1928, Utah Construction reigned as one of the largest ranch operators in the West, securing over 25,000 cattle, 30,000 sheep, and 250,000 acres. Annual earnings were approaching $1 million.

E.O. Wattis became concerned when Crowe and Morrison pointed out that Hoover Dam would cost at least $40 million and possibly as much as $50 million. The elder brother listened to their arguments then retorted, "If we can't do the job alone," he swore, "to hell with it." Morrison, alert to the danger of losing Utah's support assured Wattis that a thorough search for additional partners would include a top priority of finding "our kind" of construction men. Morrison, years later recalled that Wattis had the same remark every time he suggested additional partners, "Yes, yes, H. W. [Morrison]. But is he all right? Is he our kind?"[12]

Frank Crowe spent several months in 1929 meticulously calculating and considering the amount of working capital it would take to start the dam. Morrison reviewed Crowe's figures and together they arrived at a $5 million price tag. The Wattis brothers, surveying all available assets decided they could put up $1 million, and Morrison had already envisioned a $500,000 contribution—just about everything he had. Now the eager team collaborated on how to raise the additional funds, some $3,500,000.

Harry Morrison, always impressed with self-made men, took the initiative and approached up-and-coming construction leader, Charles A. Shea. Shea, a second-generation Irishman, grew up in the Portland, Oregon area. Trained as a plumber, by his father, he displayed tenacity to do quality work and perseverance to get jobs completed. Eventually, he went into a partnership with his father and he soon assumed leadership. Through the 1920s, the younger Shea became "one of the best-known tunnel and sewer men on the West Coast, laying the water supply lines for San Francisco, Oakland, Berkeley, and the East Bay area. In 1930 Charlie Shea was forty-seven, a pugnacious bantam, with flashing blue eyes, a corrosive tongue, and a mind of his own."[13]

Shea's early enthusiasm to join the group soon became tempered with the reality of having to scrape up his share of the working capital. A brief accounting of his liquid assets pooled $500,000; he offered this amount to Morrison, who eagerly accepted—three companies now stood together. Shortly after discussing his willingness to join Utah and Morrison-Knudsen (M-K), Shea called Harry Morrison to suggest another partner. Morrison listened intently as Charlie described the assets and abilities of the Pacific Bridge Company, a cooperative construction partner of Shea. Pacific Bridge worked alongside Shea on projects throughout northern California. W. Gorrill Swigert, former president of Pacific Bridge and a grandnephew of its founders, described their relationship with Shea as one of mutual respect. They divided the work as evenly as they could, giving specific jobs to the company that could best complete the task. "In all the years that we worked with Charlie Shea, we never had a written contract," stated Mr. Swigert, a slight, rather quiet man. "We'd divide up a job just by listing the things that had to be done, then we'd go down the list with a pencil, circling those Pacific Bridge would handle and putting an 'x' in front of the ones Shea was responsible for."[14]

Pacific Bridge, with assets equal to those of Shea, promised to contribute $500,000; now Morrison knew that the project was close to achieving the necessary capital. The good news of Pacific Bridge's involvement temporarily derailed when E.O. Wattis informed Morrison that his younger brother W. H. had been diagnosed with cancer of the hip. When doctors revealed that his cancer was in an advanced stage W.H. Wattis considered pulling out of the growing partnership with Morrison and the other companies. Morrison visited Wattis in the hospital and encouraged him to stay with the group. A couple of nerve-testing weeks intervened with Harry Morrison and Frank Crowe considering their options. Luckily, W.H. called Morrison, reassuring him that Utah Construction would continue to support the venture. It became clear to Wattis that Hoover Dam would be his greatest success, if he could only live long enough to realize it.

Morrison, on a trip to San Francisco, was urged by a construction associate to contact a highly successful local building contractor, Felix Kahn. From the outset of their meeting, both men appreciated the far-reaching vision required for large-scale projects. Kahn, an engineer trained at the University of Michigan, had considerable experience in steel, having worked for the Truscon Steel Company of Pittsburgh. Transplanted to San Francisco by his company, Kahn met Alan MacDonald, a mechanical and electrical engineer. They hit it off immediately and decided to go into business for themselves in 1911. They concentrated on bidding for large office buildings, hotels (the Mark Hopkins was built by them), and industrial plants. Through the 1920s, MacDonald and Kahn established a solid reputation building over $75 million in construction work.

Surprised, Morrison discovered that Kahn and MacDonald themselves considered bidding Hoover Dam. When they found out that Utah Construction had gone in with Morrison's company Kahn convinced MacDonald to "throw in with them." The Wattis brothers had no complaints about Kahn, as they recalled an earlier co-venture when Kahn and MacDonald subcontracted work for Utah Construction to everyone's satisfaction. Kahn and MacDonald when notified were overjoyed at the prospect of the project; they pooled together $1 million as their share of the capital outlay. Years later Kahn remembered his decision to join with Morrison and the Wattis brothers, "that made me one of the family right away."[15]

As 1930 progressed, Frank Crowe talked constantly with Harry Morrison suggesting this company and that company as possible candidates. They were getting close to the needed $5 million in capital commitments. Both men also realized that other large construction companies, many of them established eastern firms with enormous capital potential were beginning to consider the Boulder Dam Project. It was in the fall of that same year that W.H. Wattis received a call indicating an interest to join the venture from veteran contractor W. A. Bechtel. Bechtel had "come up the hard way"— working as an Illinois farm boy, laborer, and foreman in railroad construction gangs, and superintendent for an Oakland contractor. Following Morrison's line, Bechtel fought to elbow his way into some of Utah's railroad contracts. Wattis later reluctantly admitted, "We might as well ask him in as to have him bitin' our feet."[16] Bechtel explained to Wattis that he had been down to Cuba to collaborate with another contractor and the discussion about the Colorado dam came up. This contractor, Henry Kaiser, was completing a $20 million highway contract for the government of Cuba. Kaiser had heard about the upcoming bid for Hoover Dam and he talked with Bechtel about forming a company to bid the dam. Bechtel, known affectionately to many as "Dad," remarked in a subsequent interview about this meeting with Kaiser that he tried to warn Kaiser about rushing into any agreements stating, "Henry, it sounds a little ambitious." Henry Kaiser became so excited about the prospect of building the "biggest dam" that he persuaded Warren Brothers Construction Company of Massachusetts to follow his lead. Wattis was amazed that Kaiser, Bechtel, and Warren Bros. wanted in the group, and he was even more amazed when they agreed to put up $1,500,000 as a unit.

Henry Kaiser was born into a shoemaking family. His father, Frank John Kaiser, wanted young Henry work as an apprentice, but Henry cared little for shoes. Instead he became fascinated with photography, eventually taking over a small photographic business. Moving to Florida, he opened several photo shops. He married Bessie Fosburgh, whose lumberman father was well-to-do. Kaiser, however, neither waited for nor expected any of Mr. Fosburgh's money. Tiring of just doing photography sales and service Kaiser decided to try hardware. Spokane, Washington was his destination. Kaiser applied for a job at a large hardware company called McGowan Bros. and remembered, "hounding one man so steadily that he nearly threw me out." Henry's first exposure to heavy construction came later in Spokane when he changed jobs to go to work with the Hawkeye Sand & Gravel Company. At twenty-six, he found himself selling aggregate to construction firms. On a trip to Vancouver he decided to gamble on opening his own paving business. With borrowed money Kaiser bought some "secondhand wheelbarrows, concrete mixers, and a couple of teams." With these he successfully bid his first job—a $250,000 paving contract. Kaiser next moved to Victoria, then to Seattle, then to California. "We paved 1,000 miles of highway in British Columbia, California, and Washington," says its founder. "And, besides that, we built fifteen sand-and-gravel plants."[17]   Crowe and Morrison were, of course, both overjoyed with this latest news. Morrison had heard of Kaiser's success in securing road-paving contracts and he knew Bechtel's pipeline jobs had gone well. In fact, Bechtel and Kaiser had known each other since 1921 when Bechtel driving through northern California came across Kaiser laying a road between Red Bluff and Redding. Bechtel was impressed with Kaiser's organization skills in coordinating men and materials. Months after their chance meeting, Bechtel invited Kaiser to join him in a variety of western construction projects. Crowe especially was pleased with Kaiser's participation; he knew the secret of success in construction involved using men and machines in the most cost-effective manner. Yes, Henry Kaiser would, indeed, help the other investors see that Frank Crowe's expert use of men and machines would be the key to making a profit on Hoover Dam.[18]

The United States Bureau of Reclamation formally called for bids on Hoover Dam in December of 1930, warning any interested parties that they must assure the Bureau that they had secured the necessary bonds and guarantees. They further announced that the bids would be opened in the Denver office of the Bureau of Reclamation on March 4, 1931. Frank Crowe, ecstatic over the official announcement quickly met with Morrison to plan out a strategy for organizing the all-important bid. Morrison reminded Crowe that all of the construction firms must be in on the bid, even though everyone agreed that Frank Crowe was the best qualified to decide the final figure. After a series of long distance phone calls to Kaiser, Bechtel, Wattis, and the others, Morrison called for a meeting of company representatives. Meanwhile, Crowe visited Black Canyon on December 17 where he took additional notes on the proposed construction site. He also walked over the area where Boulder City [construction camp] would soon be built. Leaving

Las Vegas, Crowe returned to Linnie and the kids in time for Christmas. It was difficult for Linnie to get Frank away from his official reports and his bidding notes. It was just after Christmas when Frank learned that Morrison had arranged for a Six Companies meeting in the middle of February of 1931, so Crowe decided to visit the dam site one more time. He arrived on February 9 and remained for two days.[19] He consulted with other visiting engineers, many of them from the Bureau.

On a cold February morning, the group of profit-minded construction men who made up Six Companies nervously gathered in a large room at the Engineers Club in San Francisco. Each member company: Utah Construction; Morrison-Knudsen; J. F. Shea; Pacific Bridge; MacDonald & Kahn; and Bechtel, Kaiser, & Warren Bros. was represented by their leading officers, consulting engineers, and lawyers. Frank Crowe, representing his company, Morrison & Knudsen, walked into the club that morning accompanying Harry Morrison; Crowe carried with him an encyclopedia sized document—his bid for Hoover Dam.

Frank Crowe had prepared construction bids before, many times before. However, the Hoover Dam bid was like nothing he had ever attempted. The Bureau of Reclamation plans (over 100 sets of plans had been sent out to prospective bidding organizations) required sub bids on 119 separate phases of the job. Each job phase had to be calculated in overall relationship to the other. The two critical bids focused on placing over 3,400,000 cubic yards of concrete in treacherous Black Canyon and in excavating tunnels of 1,563,000 cubic yards of rock. The meticulous engineer had detailed these difficult tasks and the others, calculating down to the man-hours required to complete each task. This challenge had taken him hundreds of man-hours over many months, indeed, he had been planning for this bid since 1925, when he quit the Bureau. He was prepared now to describe his bid, in detail, to the gathering of illustrious construction colleagues.

The Wattis brothers presented a bid prepared by veteran construction planner J. Q. Barlow, Utah's chief engineer. Kahn offered his own bid calculated by Engineer Chad Calhoun. It was agreed that the three bids would be read, discussed, and then compromised. This usually meant that a midway figure would eventually be arrived at. Crowe's bid was the lowest at $40 million. The others came in surprisingly close, one at $40,700,000, and the other "in the middle."[20] With these figures in mind the group calculated that a peak cash outlay would not exceed $3,200,000 thereby confirming their initial figure of $5 million for up front cash. The surety companies later accepted this figure for insurance purposes, but added that Six Companies must be ready to bring an additional $3 million should trouble develop in building the dam. The discussions now centered on organization, selecting a name, and electing officers. Continental Construction and Western Construction received attention as prospective names, but neither could get a majority vote. Kahn threw out an idea. He suggested the group be called Six Companies, Incorporated. Without much discussion, everyone agreed to the name.

The new Six Companies officials decided that W. H. Wattis, though incapacitated with cancer, would serve as President, "Dad" Bechtel became First Vice President and E. O. Wattis became Second Vice-President. Shea agreed to the role of company Secretary, and Kahn began his duties as Treasurer.

The officials happily returned home promising to keep in touch and to meet again a few days before the bid opening to decide the exact final bid and profit margin. All of them agreed not to discuss any of the proceedings on the fear that an information leak would be disastrous. Back in Boise, Crowe worked diligently to construct a detailed scale model of the dam, complete with "movable parts for demonstrating crucial operations."[21] He planned to use the model in his final discussions with Six Company officials, hoping to convince them that his low bid was realistic. Frank headed back to San Francisco on the train—accompanied by Harry Morrison and the Hoover Dam model. The Six Companies directors, impressed with Crowe's model, decided to place casters under it and it was rolled in and out of their San Francisco conference room many times. W. H. Wattis slowly succumbing in nearby Saint Francis Hospital was still alert, and several meetings were held in his hospital room—they even wheeled Crowe's model in when visual explanations were needed.

On March 2, 1931, the Six Companies leadership team met for the last time in Wattis' hospital room. As agreed, no one had discussed the final figures, neither the planned actual construction expense nor the margin of required profit. In a short time, all of them agreed that a twenty-five percent profit was needed. Saying good-bye to W. H., the entourage packed their bags and headed for Denver, Colorado. They all secured rooms at the Cosmopolitan Hotel in the downtown area and waited anxiously. Morrison met continually with Crowe, who was busy putting the finishing touches on the final bid. The night of March 3 was one of the longest in Frank Crowe's life. He knew it was a critical turning point and he was not about to lose this opportunity. Everything he had worked for, all the studying, all the dam building experience of previous years, all of it was on the line. He worked well into the night adjusting bid prices on some of the 119 individual bid items. Emotionally drained and physically exhausted he finally said good night to Morrison. The final bid figure was sealed in the official envelope— it read $48, 890,000.[22] Would it be low enough?

March 4, 1931 began early for Frank Crowe. Too excited to sleep, he was up early thumbing through some 300 sheets of calculations. It seemed too much for a single man to comprehend; over a hundred jobs many of them occurring at the same time; thousands of man-hours toiling in the extreme temperatures of the Nevada desert. What if he had missed something? Was there a way to cut anymore from the bid? Was the profit margin too great? Would another anxious job-hungry upstart construction-company underbid him? After a quick breakfast in the hotel's restaurant the collected group of Six Companies officials headed off to the Bureau of Reclamation headquarters. An outward confidence shown on many of those cold faces; yet, inside these hard-working industrialists harbored the more numbing realization that this was the biggest gamble of their professional lives.

The Bureau expecting a large number of bidders, newspaper reporters, and curious onlookers decided to conduct the bid opening in an abandoned store directly below the main offices. Frank Crowe and associates entered the cold poorly lit chamber around 9:30 am. The Six Companies bid was handed to Bureau of Reclamation Chief Engineer Raymond Walter, who was already holding several other envelopes. Crowe could see many of the West's best construction men scattered about, all anxiously waiting for the big moment. By 9:45 am the room was jammed and "swarming with contractors, insurance brokers, machinery and materials agents, newspaper reporters, and other interested onlookers."[23] Walter, known for his punctuality, moved to the front of the room and placed the sealed envelopes on the table; a quick count by those lucky enough to be in the front rows of chairs totaled five. As the bids were opened it was found that only three of the bids were legitimate: Arundel Corportation, $53.9 million; Woods Brothers Corporation at $58.6 million; and Six Companies at $48,890,955.[24]

In a rare show of emotion, Frank Crowe jumped up from his seat in the back of the room and began congratulating Morrison and the other Six Companies officials. It was a decisively low bid. No mistake about it. Arundel was $5,009,045 too high. And, what was even more satisfying to Frank was the fact that Walter then disclosed to everyone that the Six Companies bid was only $24,000 more than the estimated low bid by the Bureau of Reclamation engineers. What an achievement! Never in the history of Western construction bidding had there been such a precise bid. Incredibly, this represented less than 0.05 % difference in bids for a $49 million job. .

The group of exuberant businessmen, Crowe included, briefly celebrated then discussed what to do next. Frank notified Linnie, telling her that he would be staying on one more day in Denver then come home for a few days before moving on to Las Vegas. He knew that there were no facilities built for her and the kids yet, but that as that became available, he would bring her out. The rest of March 4, the ecstatic engineer went through a list of key engineers and foremen that he wanted on the project. He had already contacted most of them beforehand to check on their availability; some were available now, others would follow as current job commitments were completed. The next day, starting at 8:00 am Crowe fired off a series of notifying telegrams. The first one went to Charles Holden in Clarkston, Washington. He wanted "Charlie" to supervise the building of the single men's' dormitory. Crowe's message in the telegram was brief and to the point, "OK for a job at Hoover Dam." When Holden hesitated, Charles Williams, Crowe's overall superintendent of carpentry sent a telegram on March 13 stating, "Come at once."[25] The pressure was on and Frank needed the dormitories built. Meanwhile, Six Companies announced to the media that veteran dam builder Frank

T. Crowe would be the General Superintendent for the construction of Hoover Dam. Upon questioning, Crowe announced that 3,000 men would be employed, with 1,000 on each of three shifts. Within days, newspapers all over the country reported the happy news of possible employment. Crowe's dam working veterans shouted for joy over the prospect of a job as big as Hoover Dam. They knew it would take years to build, years of dependable regular paychecks. Thousands of jobless men, many of them had never even seen a big dam, read the optimistic newspaper accounts of hiring, and wondered if their future lay in the forbidding desert of southern Nevada.

Not long after the bidding, Felix Kahn took some of the wives and friends of the Six Companies men on an excursion into Black Canyon, which at the dam site was like a vast box with nearly vertical sides. The water was swift, icy spray flew over the small launch, and between the sheer walls rising six hundred feet on either side the sky was a narrow slot of blue. In this beautiful, yet dangerous setting Kahn turned to his wife, a shy and gentle person, and shouted above the roar of the swirling river: "Think of it, we're going 150 feet this way [pointing into the river] and 750 feet that way [pointing up]." Mrs. Kahn clinging to him for support responded, "Felix, I don't know whether to call you courageous—or crazy."[26]

Meanwhile, in San Francisco ailing Six Companies executive William Wattis perked up noticeably when told that their bid won out. Taking a break from his ongoing cancer treatment, the white-haired, blue-eyed construction executive asked for a cigar, put on his bathrobe and agreed to meet with reporters. Not wanting to look too surprised or overwhelmed by the challenges that lie ahead in building Hoover Dam, the clever Wattis lectured confidently to the awaiting newspaper people, "Now this dam is just a dam but it's a damn big dam. Otherwise it's no different than others we've thrown up in a dozen places." He admitted that the job "involves a lot of money—more money than any one contractor has a right to have." When asked about recovering, leaving the hospital and joining the Hoover job the feisty Wattis explained, "I don't know when I'll get out of here. I think I am improving but don't worry, I'll be on this job."[27]

Linnie waited anxiously for her husband to arrive at the Boise train station. Frank had enjoyed the train ride home from Denver; snow blanketed much of the winter landscape, its serene surrealistic appearance helped the dam builder relax and sleep. A cold, crisp—almost sharp, wind slapped Frank in the face as he detrained and embraced his wife. Pat, only a month away from her ninth birthday, realized that her father was about to do something that would make him famous—she was already seeing his name in the local area newspapers. Six year old Bettee, overwhelmed with all the friends and relatives who visited in the next few days, stayed close to her daddy; often sitting happily on his lap. The brief interlude at home ended all too soon for Frank, Linnie, and the kids. Everyone wanted more time. Frank explained to the family that he would try to write often and that he would bring them out to the dam site as soon as "everything settled down" and a house was built.[28]

Reluctantly, Linnie drove her husband through the cold Boise snow to the depot. She must have wished she could be at his side in Nevada to help Frank handle, what was sure to be, tremendous pressure. The dying hopes of the frustrated Hoover administration, the expected plentiful profits of Six Company officials, and the desperate sheer survival needs of thousands of unemployed workers, rested squarely on Frank Crowe's shoulders. Picking up a copy of the *Los Angeles Examiner*, Crowe could not believe the degree of instant notoriety he now possessed. "Frank T. Crowe," the article started, "of Boise, Idaho is to be the General Goethals of Boulder Dam. As Goethals was the dynamite force that kept his organization driving ahead during tropic heat and jungles to complete the Panama Canal, so Crowe will be the mainspring of the machine that will build the world's greatest dam," the paper claimed. Referred to as "an important cog in the United States Bureau of Reclamation" the article asked Frank Weymouth, Crowe's mentor, what he thought of Crowe's ability. "Best construction man I've ever known," said Weymouth, without hesitation. In a powerful statement, the article argued that it was Crowe's forceful and convincing personality and experience that "brought six construction firms, including his own Morrison-Knudsen Company of Boise, together into the 'Six Companies.'" It was also noted that "several of the companies" would not proceed with the risky bid unless Crowe was named superintendent of construction. "At 48 years of age, Crowe will undertake a job that makes all his tremendous quarter century of struggle with the elements in building concrete dams seem like child's play." In closing the article predicted, "When it is done, Crowe will have built the biggest dam in the world, one probably tremendously bigger than any other that ever will be built. It is a safe prediction that like Goethals, he will retire from active field work." On both accounts, the predictions would be wrong.[29]

The train ride from Boise to Las Vegas provided Frank Crowe a brief physical rest, but, as he gazed out the club car windows Frank wondered what facilities would he find in Las Vegas, and at the dam site. The Bureau had given him an official report—a synopsis of their preliminary highway, railroad, and power connections. Crowe knew all too well that communication and transportation played major roles in the success of any construction project, but they became critical when building a dam of such great size. He worried too, as the Colorado and New Mexico landscape flew by, about the living accommodations and service buildings that needed to be built immediately. Crowe understood that he would share responsibility with the Bureau for laying out and building a new desert community that would house the labor force and the main services. The town, already designed, was named Boulder City in honor of the project. Saco Rienk DeBoer, a well-known city planner in Denver sketched the first drawings of Boulder City months before the project had gone to bid. He made an initial visit on July 17 of

Black Canyon looking downstream from the entrance of the canyon, 1920. (USBR)

1930. Returning to his office, DeBoer worked on preliminary drawings. On visiting the area a second time, October 3-9, 1930, DeBoer and government engineers chose a promising site some twenty miles east of Las Vegas at the edge of Eldorado Valley.[30] The gently sloping rise extended for miles then fell off toward the east and the Colorado River ten miles distant. From here, the terrain was too rugged for establishing a sizable settlement.

DeBoer's original Boulder plans included two huge concentric circles of development. The smaller center circle contained the restricted commercial center along with municipal buildings and permanent home residences. The larger outer area, where Six Companies buildings were placed including machine shops, storage areas, and rock laboratories. This original plan called for a beautiful lush 18-hole golf course with a greenbelt forest forming a division between the two inhabited zones. Each residential block formed mini-circles composed of dozens of wedge-shaped building lots.[31]

DeBoer's plan was quickly revised by government architects after Bureau Chief Walter and others recognized that the plan, grandiose beyond all practical standards, would not work in the desert site selected. The new proposal focused the community in a fan-shaped design with the Bureau of Reclamation headquarters standing on the highest ground at the radial point of the fan. Residential blocks would be rectangular instead of circular. Street-names represented the seven states touched by the Colorado River: Arizona, California, Colorado, New Mexico, Nevada, Utah, and Wyoming. Three major municipal parks planned for the downtown area were named for Spanish explorers of the American Southwest: Coronado, Escalante and Cardenas Plazas.[32]

Railroads and highways were another major concern for Crowe. He had seen during visits to the area in late 1930 that Union Pacific Railroad laborers, mostly Mexicans, struggled to lay a branch line from Bracken Junction, near Las Vegas, to the Boulder City site. Crowe had read about the well-attended Silver Spike Ceremony, here on September 17 of 1930, 10,000 spectators including politicians, engineering officials and Las Vegas citizens braved the repressive heat to watch Secretary of the Interior Ray Wilbur who tapped-in a silver spike starting construction. In his speech that day, Wilbur referred to the project as Boulder Canyon Project, but he made it clear that he wanted the dam to be named Hoover, after his boss, President Herbert Hoover.[33]

Crowe learned that the railhead to Boulder City, completed in January of 1931, would be extended an additional ten miles to the rim of Black Canyon. He was most anxious about the progress of this work, as railroad delivered supplies were a vital link in his overall scheme. The Lewis Construction Company, based in Southern California, initiated work on a 10.5 mile spur track from Boulder City to Black Canyon rim. From here, Crowe would order the final rail connection, a tricky descent to the water's edge. While the vertical drop is a few hundred feet, it would take twenty-six miles of slow even descent to reach the dam site. He was pleased to read in his summary report that seven parallel tracks, laid at the terminal in Boulder City, would be operating when he arrived. A constant flow of material could be unloaded without blocking other incoming trains.[34]

Crowe eagerly read on, for he wanted to know road building progress, another important key to success. He recalled his earlier overland treks from Las Vegas to the future Boulder City. The "road" was little more than "two tracks through the desert." "When one set of tracks grew too soft to follow, cars simply moved over a few feet and forged a new trail."[35] Timed trips by car out of Las Vegas prevented motorist from being caught in a sudden drenching downpour. More than once, the "Boulder Road" formed a mushy channel collecting the fast falling rain—each line track creating a miniature gushing river. Unfortunate motorists had the unpleasant choice of remaining in their stalled vehicles or abandoning their cars and trudging, rain-soaked back to Las Vegas.

The Bureau of Reclamation understood the importance of having an all-weather road in place, from Boulder City to the dam site, for Frank Crowe and his army of dam builders. Luckily, Interior Secretary Wilbur planned for this and bid the gravel-base oil-surfaced road in January of 1931. General Construction Company of Seattle, Washington won the right to the job, but decided to sub contract most of the work to R. G. LeTourneau, Incorporated of Stockton, California. Crowe, keeping abreast of this activity from his office in Boise, had been impressed with the speed and efficiency of LeTourneau's operation. They were on-site and working within four days and shortly thereafter, heavy equipment arrived allowing for a full assault on the excavation of 107,000 cubic yards of common material and 228,000 cubic yards of rock.[36] LeTourneau personally directed the backbreaking work, determined to complete the twenty-two foot wide road ahead of schedule. He knew that Frank Crowe was coming and Frank Crowe needed this highway. LeTourneau used all available equipment including Caterpillar tractors, Bucyrus-Erie 50-B shovels, scrapers, "LeTourneau Chariots," huge air compressors, five giant Atlas-Imperial diesel engines, and "one especially-constructed 40-ton trailer for moving equipment."[37]

Meanwhile, construction crews labored feverishly to grade and pave a road from Boulder City to the canyon rim. Already at the rim, federal survey crews conducted investigations looking for the best approaches to the riverbed. One possible road, located two miles downstream on the Nevada side, appeared to offer a reasonable grade to the diversion tunnel outlets. On the same side of the river, government forces recognized a natural approach two miles upstream near Hemenway Wash—a wide-open area that soon was overrun with newly arrived job seekers. Both roads into the canyon would need to be cut into solid black volcanic rock by Crowe and his men (as per contract), an almost impossible job. Yet, without river access men and machines would be useless.

By the time he stepped off the train in Las Vegas Frank Crowe, like a general preparing for a major battle, had planned his strategy. The enemy, notorious Black Canyon, arrayed an impressive list of natural obstacles. Each of these obstacles, to be overcome, required a unique tactical plan of attack. His responsibility was to plan, bring together, and use effectively his army of men and machines so that every obstacle was overcome in the most efficient sequence of operations. He knew it would take the best in heavy equipment: tractors, dump trucks, shovels, jackhammers, drills, and concrete buckets. And what about his army? Who would serve in Frank Crowe's army? He knew he could count on the hundreds of "construction stiffs" that had faithfully followed him from one dam building job to another, some like Red McCabe, J. V. Allen, Bob Sass, and Floyd Bous traced their relationship with Crowe back over many years. These men and scores of others would serve as his officer corps; dedicated foremen who were expected to meet their deadlines and quotas issued by Crowe. All of these men believed in Frank Crowe's work ethic, "work them hard, but work them fair."[38]

Crowe heard, mostly through newspaper accounts, that many unemployed men were anxiously awaiting the start of hiring; after all, this was the Great Depression. However, he was shocked to see that they numbered in the thousands already. You could not escape their presence. These newly arrived job-hungry migrants loitered in and around the Union Pacific Depot; the park in front of the depot resembled a "hobo jungle."[39] John Cahlan remembers, "If you haven't lived through it, you can't imagine what would happen to a little railroad community of 5,000 people having about a good 10,000 to 20,000 people dumped on it all at one time." He continues, "Believe me, it was terrible! They [city officials] didn't know what to do. I mean, nobody knew what to do, because they were here, and some of them could get jobs on the dam, and some of them couldn't."[40] Thomas Wilson moved to Las Vegas at about this time and he recalls, "It took us all day to get to Vegas. We got to Las Vegas in the late afternoon—maybe 4:30—and came down the street, and I was sitting behind the driver. And I asked, 'Is there going to be a parade or something?' He said, 'Why do you ask?' I said, 'Well, the streets are just black with people standing on the sidewalk—all these crowds.' He said, 'Oh, those are men waiting for jobs on the dam.'"[41]

Frank Crowe hailed a taxicab that drove him slowly through the migrant-choked streets of Las Vegas to the Six Companies temporary headquarters in the Clark Building. During the first days and weeks of Crowe's relocation in Las Vegas, he learned about the diversity of these unemployed anxious men and their backgrounds. John Gieck was "rough necking down in Long Beach and Culver City" before coming to Boulder Canyon. "If you got $3 a day, you were lucky— if you worked at all," recalled Gieck. In search of steady employment the young worker heard about the construction opportunities, so he made the decision to give Nevada a try. With his used automobile in questionable condition, he borrowed some money and left. Upon arrival in the area, Gieck found out that there was no employment office yet, so he visited the job site anyway. Given the opportunity, he tried to convince a number of foremen that he was a good worker. Down at the dam site he found out how uncomfortable working conditions were for the workers, with the heat being nearly intolerable. Gieck was able to get the attention of Charlie Williams, an assistant superintendent and shortly after this meeting he acquired a carpentry job.

Musicians, such as Tommy Nelson, enjoyed their careers, but watched their earnings plummet as the Depression deepened. He tried moving around the country to see if employment in bands was more fruitful somewhere else, but he learned that the bad economic times had hit everywhere and people were not spending what little money they had on a lot of entertainment. Finally, he decided to give Boulder (Hoover Dam) a chance and he joined the thousands of other unemployed men flooding into Las Vegas. Wilfred Voss, like many of the harried men flooding into Las Vegas, did so to avoid going on relief. Voss in his day-to-day search for a job ran into men from numerous walks of life, some of them had been in high paying jobs before the Depression brokeout. Some of the unemployed had served successfully as store managers and bank presidents. Fleeing desperate economic situations in the Midwest, people such as Harry Hall headed to Nevada with only a small savings and the money from his last paycheck. Luckily, he owned a new Chevrolet sedan, and he was in a position to move quickly. Either by

Officials on the job at Hoover Dam. Left to right: Charles Shea,
director of construction for Six Companies; Felix Kahn, treasurer
for Six Companies; Walker Young, construction engineer for the
Bureau of Reclamation; "Woody" Williams, assistant general
superintendent; John C. Page, office engineer for the Bureau of
Reclamation; Frank Crowe, general superintendent. (USBR)

reading the local Oklahoma newspapers, listening to the radio, or hearing stories
through casual conversation, Hall discovered that Hoover Dam was one of the few
places you could get a job. Like so many others, Hall moved into the area on the
blind faith that he could land a position.[42]

Some of these hardy job seekers came from the East Coast. One such
bright-eyed ambitious youngster, Milton Mudron, came from New Jersey. Having been trained as a carpenter by his father, he looked forward to a challenging
construction career. That is when he and some friends heard about the initiation of
work at Hoover Dam. To the young carpenter, Hoover Dam meant the West and to
him the West always meant wild adventure. He couldn't wait to get started. When
his friends backed out of the adventure, Mudron packed up his well-worn automobile, counted only $60 in his wallet, and headed for Boulder City. Arriving in May
of 1931, Mudron ignored federal reservation signs warning trespassers to keep out
and continued to drive until he spotted some carpenters. Approaching a man who
appeared to be in charge he said, "I am a carpenter and I need a job." Within
minutes of demonstrating his skills, the usually shy and introverted Mudron had

won himself a job.[43] Crowe enjoyed hearing stories such as the one mentioned above, for he wanted men who displayed confidence in their abilities and who had a strong desire to learn dam building methods and techniques.

To say that Crowe confronted tremendous challenges in starting Hoover Dam is an understatement--his concerns appeared insurmountable. Not least of which involved his relationship with Six Companies officials. The Wattis Brothers, Morrison, and Shea demanded that Frank be selected as General Superintendent. But, what did that mean? Would he have uncontested control—the final word on all construction decisions? Each of the Six Companies leaders felt they could themselves run the operation. Charlie Shea remembered later "our first hot argument was over the organization chart. Kaiser thought the job should be run like an army, with a general in supreme charge. That idea got nowhere because no one, least of all Henry himself, wanted to be a private."[44] The battle of the egos was on; and they all wanted "a piece of the action." Sensing that compromise was the only answer, Felix Kahn, suggested a functioning Board of Directors with each member given a title and position.

Frank Crowe felt uneasy with a Board of Directors breathing down his neck, watching his every move and questioning the operation. Sure enough, it did not take long for the parade of Six Companies officials to begin. Kahn appeared one day and gave Crowe ideas on how to handle a problem a certain way; a week later Kaiser would insist that it be done another way. Bechtel kept asking about the schedule. This top-down pressure began to take its toll on Crowe, his temper shortened as he struggled with the construction and the other myriad of problems confronting him. Charlie Shea could see that Frank was about ready to break and so he tried to act as a buffer between Crowe and Six Companies officials. Shea worried that Crowe might walk off the job unless given the freedom to make all construction decisions. Felix Kahn, seeing a worsening situation, observed, "A Board of Directors can establish policy, but it can't build a dam."[45]

Finally, after three nerve-raking months, the Board relinquished its construction control and assigned them to an executive committee of four, who alone could deal with Crowe. Charlie Shea, who had the best relationship with Crowe, became Director in charge of field construction. Felix Kahn looked after money, legal affairs, feeding and housing; Steve Bechtel, "Dad's" second son, assumed the duties required for purchasing, administration, and transportation; and Henry Kaiser was made Chairman of the Board of Directors, in recognition of his ability to bring together all the varying viewpoints represented in Six Companies.

Frank Crowe breathed a huge sigh of relief when Shea notified him of the decision. His first tough obstacle, the diversion tunnels, was getting underway and he wanted to settle the Six Companies matter first. He felt entirely comfortable with the new arrangement. Actually, Crowe enjoyed Shea's regular visits and helpful suggestions. As for the rest of the Six Companies officials, there were fewer reasons for them to "make the uncomfortable sleeper jump from San Francisco, to endure the hot, spine-jarring 200-mile drive from Mojave station across the desert to Boulder City." The intervals between the Directors' meetings at the dam and the Palace Hotel lengthened. Black Canyon, in the desert summer heat, was an inferno. Kaiser, on one of his visits, gave Crowe a bad scare by keeling over from heat exhaustion. Kahn, too, had a narrow escape there from the heat. Alone among the partners Charlie Shea stayed on the job; "the river had laid upon him the same fierce hold it had laid upon Crowe."[46]

Even though Crowe now worked directly with Shea, he visited with Kahn, Kaiser, Morrison and the others often. He gained a special knowledge of these construction pioneers. Frank came to know each of them, their professional and personal side, as the months and years moved on. In terms of construction philosophy, Crowe remembered that, "Kaiser and Morrison always thought of a job in terms of draglines and steam shovels. Kahn figured in terms of money and an organization chart. But, Charlie Shea always thought in terms of men. He was the kind of man who'd ask you the time not because he wanted to know but to see what kind of watch you carried." Crowe learned that, "they were just about as different as any men could be. Charlie Shea hated to write letters. If he wrote one a week, he thought he was talking too much. But, Morrison on the other hand thought nothing of dictating a hundred letters in a morning. Morrison never drank, never smoked, never gambled; he was a puritan. Charlie Shea didn't drink either, but he was crazy about gambling. I use [d] to meet him and Felix at the station when they came up from San Francisco and drive them across the desert to the dam. All the way—five hours—they'd shoot craps on the floor of the Lincoln."[47] Crowe recalled an incident on a trip with Kahn:

"One day I was driving them down Montgomery Street in San Francisco. Kahn spotted 'Dad' Bechtel headed for the bank. 'Drive over,' he said; 'this is going to cost "Dad" some money!' I pulled alongside the curb and Felix shouted,' "Dad," I'm matching you a double eagle.' 'Dad' didn't even say good morning. He just gave Felix a disapproving look, dug into his vest pocket for a coin, and slapped it on the car window. He took his hand off and said to Felix 'you lose' and walked off without another word. They were a great bunch to work for because they stuck together. Charlie and Felix used to say to each other, to settle an argument, 'Right or wrong, you're right, you son of a bitch.' They really felt that way toward each other."[48]

The first weeks in Las Vegas, Crowe met often with chief carpenter, Charlie Williams. Williams, a longtime Crowe associate, was Frank's right hand man, especially during the first organizing months. Carpentry was his trade and he was good at it. The husky overweight six-foot foreman commanded respect from all who worked for him. He covered his receding hairline with a short-rimmed hat and by the time work started at Hoover Dam he was forced to wear horn-rimmed eyeglasses. With his suspenders drawn tight, Williams constantly walked the job site encouraging his men to observe all safety rules. The "Wizard with Wood" Williams welcomed Charles Holden who finally arrived from Washington State and put him in charge of overseeing each step of the Six Companies River Camp dormitory and mess hall construction. Crowe and Charlie Williams carefully selected the river camp location where the Colorado River enters Boulder Canyon, two miles north of the dam site in Black Canyon. This area, known as Cape Horn, sported slopes of 45 degrees instead of the near 90 degree slopes farther into the canyon. Here, amid the rubble of rocks and boulders, some 150 feet above the river level Holden erected four two-story dormitories, a mess hall, and other small office buildings. Access to the roadway and rail-bed, 50 feet below, was gained by using several wooden staircases anchored into the rock hillside. Six Companies planned on housing up to 500 single men in these quarters. Married men, until Boulder City was completed, lived in Ragtown or McKeeversville. Living in the bottom of treacherous rock canyon with tall steep walls provided the worker-residents with unusual first impressions. During the day the sun would be visible for only a few hours and at night, if the sky was clear, a vertical slot of bright crisp stars shown as though in an observatory dome looking through the telescope opening.

Throughout the month of April and into May, the men of River Camp assaulted the lower Nevada side canyon walls relentlessly, struggling to lengthen the railroad bed and access road. Crowe, impatient to have full access to the dam site, drove down through Ragtown, a temporary settlement camp, and into the River Camp area almost daily to check progress. He was greatly disturbed to hear of a blasting accident on May 8 that seriously injured newly hired miner P. L. Lezie and companion Herman Schmitto. Crowe sent notices to all shift foremen to review safety procedures before scheduled detonations. Explosion related accidents were not the only disasters he and his men feared. With loose rock everywhere, unexpected avalanches could happen at any time. On May 18, four road-bed workers could not escape the thunderous crash of a 150-foot shelf of debris. The collapse buried all four men. Reacting quickly, nearby companions dug furiously and rescued two. Rescue efforts continued well into the night before the crushed bodies of the last two men were unearthed.[49]

Rising two digit temperatures of May turned ominously into three digit degree readings as June progressed. While the machines in the canyon remained oblivious to the newly arrived hot days of summer, Crowe and his foremen noticed men beginning to slow and wither. Rock surfaces soon absorbed the searing heat requiring heavy gloves to be worn by cursing rock mucking miners. The canyon effectively cutoff all air circulation, stifling workers who stripped to the waist and gasped continuously for relief. When the wind did come, it felt more like an oven door opening than a refreshing breeze. Men struggled on. Many of them, physically unfit for this daily grueling battle with searing summer heat bravely continued to work until overwhelmed and prostrated from incredibly high body temperatures. Helen Holmes, a resident of Ragtown, recalled the 1931 "summer temperatures went terrifically high." Almost daily, "the ambulance would go up so many times with the people." She lamented, "That siren—oh, it scared you 'cause you wondered if it might be your husband." Her husband Neil Holmes worked as a pipe fitter beginning his shift in the relative cool of 4:00 a.m. and continuing until noon. He remembered, "For a month during the summer, 30 days, the thermometer never went below 100 [degrees], day or night. It was from that on up to 138 [degrees]." On July 24, he and his crew needed to complete an emergency pipe repair to a damaged compressor plant. He worked diligently, although the direct sun began to sap his energy; he began to feel lightheaded. Incredibly, he finished the job walked slowly to the transport truck and sat dazed as the truck bounced him toward home in Ragtown. Helen could tell that something was wrong as soon as she saw her husband, he "just didn't feel well." Neil refused to eat dinner, preferring to retire early. He lay in bed perspiring from head to toes. Helen could tell that her husband was extremely weak and suffered from heat prostration. Leaving her husband momentarily, she hustled down to Murl Emery's store, purchased some ice and returning, gently patted and dabbed his over-heated body. The next day Neil convinced Helen to drive him into Las Vegas for a medical checkup. The doctor suggested that Neil take some time off work and try to stay out of the heat. Word had spread that the nearby peak of Black Mountain, elevation 5043 feet, provided soothing relief, and a number of miners already were encamped at high elevations. Off they drove to the relative cool temperatures of Black Mountain where he recovered for "about two weeks before he was even able to do anything at all."[50]

Dr. Clare Woodbury, physician assigned to treat prostration cases at the small Las Vegas hospital was amazed how little most of the workers knew about the effects of heat during strenuous work. As July and August temperatures soared, ambulances and automobiles raced into Las Vegas carrying "unconscious and in-continent" men, women, and children. Most victims were dam workers. Woodbury recalled, "We had no electric thermometer then, but with an ordinary thermometer their rectal temperature went up to 112 degrees." He continued, "We had half dozen bathtubs filled with cold water and ice floating in it." After an hour or so of a cool-down treatment the patient's temperature was taken again, if their body temperatures had come down to normal levels, "then we gave them the intrave-nous fluids they needed." This treatment became standard procedure for the rest of the blazing summer of 1931 and Woodbury gladly stated, "After that they all recovered."[51]

Personal accounts of the devastating heat wave and its affects on the men and families at Hoover Dam began to circulate nationwide. One worker wrote, "But the men, when they came in from the job, were so exhausted from the heat it was impossible for them to eat a substantial meal." He recalled, "Practically no one works in anything other than a pair of trousers and shoes." In the dining hall, hundreds of these half naked sun baked workers sat "with rivulets of sweat running down their faces and backs." There was no relief anywhere near the dam site. Ragtown, Boulder City, and Las Vegas baked and the number of air-conditioned buildings in the area was quite low. On the job or off, day or night made no comfort difference.[52]

Bureau engineer Walker Young, in charge of inspecting and directing construction progress, and Frank Crowe knew that they could not hide inside air-cooled rooms for four months while their army of workers toiled in the sun-blasted bowels of Black Canyon. In fact, both men continued to expose themselves to the same heat conditions by making daily inspection trips all over the job site, encouraging workers and foremen alike. Young had thermometers placed at strategic locations up and down the canyon, and on occasion checked the readings himself. He said, "I had temperatures taken myself that I'm positive were correct." One time, Young watched a crew nailing forms for the sedimentary tank. The skeletal framework rose high enough to cast a substantial shadow and Young decided to take advantage of the man-made shade. With thermometer in hand, he sat there observing the crew. After a few minutes Young glanced down at the glass thermometer to shockingly discover, "It made a temperature of 140 degrees." The job foreman soon joined Young, explaining that he dared not push his men in the heat. The foreman explained how he watched his men closely in the mid-day heat, any that showed signs of weakening or staggering were allowed to sit for fifteen minutes in the shade. Young noticed, "After they'd got accustomed a little bit to the heat, then they'd go to work again." Unbelievably, Young reasserted, "I know it was 140 degrees."[53] Crowe, raised in high latitudes of Maine and acclimated to the moderately cool summers of Montana, Wyoming, Washington, and Idaho, found himself suffering miserably in the energy-drenching blast furnace of the Nevada desert.

To their discredit, neither Young nor Crowe hired a doctor to be on duty at the canyon floor or at the River Camp during the early months of summer. Distraught "stiffs" felt helpless in the face of increasing heat associated medical problems. Mess hall employee Victor Castle remembered, "While I was [at the River Camp] two men were brought in who had passed out completely. One, a commissary clerk, collapsed in his tent after he finished work and had convulsions." Not knowing what else to do Castle hurriedly fetched "buckets of ice water" and threw them on the victim. Not only were there no medical staff to consult but also no training or information had been given the workers in how to deal with injuries.[54] For Frank Crowe, the devastating effects of the desert heat proved to be one element he had not foreseen thoroughly. As if the engineering obstacles were not enough, Frank Crowe, worried that his precise planning and organizational skills would not be enough to deal with the soaring temperatures, lack of housing, and the appalling human misery becoming more evident day by day.

Chapter 9

"We are six months ahead of schedule on the work now and we can afford to refuse concessions."
Hoover Dam, 1931

One of the most critical construction challenges Frank Crowe faced in 1931 involved excavating four cavernous Colorado River diversion tunnels. Each proposed tunnel would extend over 3500 feet through the solid rock walls of Black Canyon.[1] The plans called for Crowe to hew fifty-six foot diameter openings; workers would then work into place a concrete lining three feet thick. The completed tunnels would create a complete diversion of the Colorado River allowing "stiffs" to completely dewater the riverbed foundation area. Once dry, workers would excavate for the concrete foundation. Crowe wanted to get started as soon as possible; the government contract penalized Six Companies $3000 a day after Oct. 1, 1933 if the tunnels sat unfinished.

Work began, in May, on tunnels Nos. 3 and 4 (Arizona side) with the booming sounds of numerous explosions and the roar of machinery and grinding gears of struggling dump trucks. Frank Crowe placed two of his most trusted veterans in command of the tunnel operations. Floyd Huntington, whose name was "known to every miner in the far west," started working mines in 1902 at age fifteen. He told Crowe that he had run away from home, somewhere in Washington, and headed to California to look for work. The King Midas Mines, near Redding, afforded Huntington his indoctrination into the dark, damp world of underground mining. From Northern California, he migrated from mine to mine gleaning experience and learning new techniques; he soon became "at home underground as on the surface." Huntington's tenacity and ability to learn quickly earned him an improved job status from low paying mucker to foreman by the time he reached twenty-two. After a brief military stint during World War I he secured a job, mining silver in Jerome, Arizona. The wandering young man then journeyed to Seattle where he worked as tunnel superintendent on the Skagit irrigation and dam project. Between 1923-1930 Huntington's increasing expertise in tunneling landed him lucrative contract offers.[2] When he learned of the challenging tunnel opportunities on Hoover Dam, Huntington, now recognized as a world authority, offered Six Companies his services. Upon meeting Huntington, Crowe immediately realized that here was a hard-driving determined construction stiff who had "pulled himself up by his own boot straps"—much as he had. Their ensuing relationship revealed a mutual respect that lasted throughout the project. Crowe gave Huntington responsibility for completing tunnels #1 and #2 on the Nevada side.

On the other side of the river Crowe relied on the proven skills of his long-time associate Bernard "Woody" Williams, son of carpentry boss Charlie Williams. Two years of college studies was plenty for the sturdy broad-chested Williams. His desire to "get to work" landed him a job on Rimrock Dam, where he met Crowe. He followed Frank to the Guernsey Dam construction where his vibrant six-foot frame, quick intelligence, and steadfast reliability won him a shot as graveyard foreman. Later he served as concrete foreman on Tieton Dam and general foreman at Deadwood Dam. At 29 years of age, Williams, hitting his peak, was Crowe's first choice as assistant superintendent of the entire project and tunnel superintendent.

Bureau of Reclamation engineers, working with scale models and incredibly complicated mathematical formulas, determined the upper and lower portal locations and the angels of drilling. Survey crews, approached the portals by river barges and marked the openings. Tex Nunley, a rodman on one of the crews remembered, "I painted a cross right in the center on the face [of the canyon wall]. We took a 50-foot tape and went around, painted a line all around."[3]   Crowe and Bureau engineers had worked out a plan where two adits, small access tunnels, would be driven into the canyon walls at locations midway between the upper and lower portals. These two 10 x 8-foot excavations, dug perpendicular to the main tunnel lines would, once completed, be widened to create two additional faces to be excavated. Thus, the four tunnels, each with an upper and lower portal, allowed access to eight excavation faces; the adit midway approaches added eight more faces, for a total of sixteen, where crews could work simultaneously.

In preparation for tunneling, Crowe, on several occasions in March and April, employed veteran river captain Murl Emery to take him, A. H. "Gus" Ayers (chief engineer for Six Companies), "Woody" Williams, Huntington, and Bureau engineer Walker Young down river to the tunnel sites.[4] The group arrived quickly at consensus that access to the river bottom would take top priority. To begin with, Crowe decided to build and launch a flotilla of construction barges that would deliver men and machines anywhere along riverbanks. Like the World War II D-Day invasion, "General" Crowe ordered Williams to secure beachheads at the adit and portal entries. Blasting the canyon walls and depositing excavated muck (rock debris) along the river extended the beachheads. The amphibious assault originated from the Hemenway Wash, a broad gentle descending slope some two miles upstream. Trucks from Boulder City traversed a rough bumpy road to the Wash laden with eager workers, explosives, and drilling machinery. The first expedition steered for a spot on the Arizona bank, near the center of the dam site, where fallen

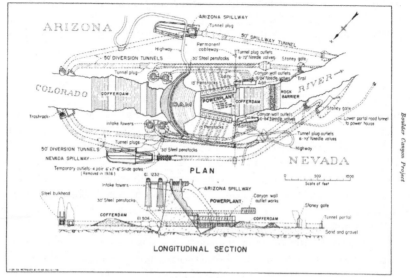

Hoover Dam and Powerplant.

Plan for Hoover Dam and powerplant. (USBR)

canyon debris had formed an alluvial-type fan. The mining marines struggled ashore, quickly mooring the barge and unloading air compressors, a portable black-smith shop and drills. Like Spanish conquistadors centuries before them, these twentieth century soldiers established their base camp and prepared to engage their enemy.

Watching this initial landing with great interest, Frank Crowe called a meeting of foremen and tunnel superintendents. Amid piles of tunnel blueprints and engineer schematic drawings the master dam builder felt completely at home, reviewing the proposed tunneling sequence of operations. The timetable was de-manding and unforgiving; nothing could be left to chance—even the most danger-ous unknown, floods, needed consideration. He made it clear that every man was expected to do his part, to keep the men and machines moving, or lose his job. The attack was ordered to begin on the morning of May 12, 1931. The eager troops probed the huge wall of rock with Ingersoll-Rand Type N-75 drifter drills while on the flanks Type S-49 "Jackhammers" clattered away. At the end of the first day, the offensive appeared a failure; hardly a dent had been made. Sweaty, dirty con-struction stiffs, however, did not retreat. Crowe sensing that nothing less that an all-out attack would be successful defiantly ordered an around-the-clock drilling barrage: Men and machines now relentlessly pushed ahead in three shifts of eight hours each. Day after day the battle continued. Crowe landed additional troops who shoveled the collected muck into dumping cars. A hastily built track carried the accumulated debris to water's edge where it was dumped, again enlarging the beachhead. A specially trained team of engineers, working with the precision and skill of a Navy SEAL team, erected a cable suspension bridge across the Colorado allowing access to the Nevada canyon wall.[5] A two-front war was now declared. With no shoreline to work, Crowe and Huntington planned a series of initial blast excavations to create a temporary shelf. Before each blast, nervous workers momentarily retreated on their barges to a safe distance. After the smoke cleared and the rubble settled, the barges once again moved into their moorings and anxious warriors waded ashore to check the enemy's damage. Williams, eager to begin actual tunneling, won approval from Crowe to commence digging the 10 x 8-foot adits that would provide access to the main tunnels' midline sections. The Arizona adit needed to extend 850 feet, the Nevada side 630 feet. This direct penetration into the canyon walls, like one armor-piercing arrow, proved to Crowe and his army that the enemy was fallible—the canyon would succumb. With every ten to twenty-foot penetration, Bureau geological engineering scouts probed the cavern searching for changing rock compositions and for potentially dangerous faults. None were found. The men pressed on.

Steve Chubbs, a "grunt," or new hire in Crowe's tunnel army, was employed as an electrician's helper, stringing wires to the loaded headings. He recalled the drillers would come into the tunnel first and drill loading holes for the dynamite. Then they would string the firing wires out to a detonator. The electrician then used rods to shove the primers back into their holes, some ten feet. Now the grunt and electrician backed off a discrete distance, usually to a nearby side adit, and "set the shot." Blasting accidents occurred frequently, especially at first, with most of the problems coming with anxious men tapping the priming load too sharply. The mercury fulminate material used in the priming operation left no room for error. On one occasion, the operator of an electric shovel hit a hidden primer and the resulting explosion killed one worker standing nearby.[6]

All through May and most of June the invading miners kept up the assault using two diesel powered air compressors. Crowe toured the tunnels almost daily and at all hours, encouraging his men and promising them electrical power soon.[7] Already, he had authorized the construction of a compressor plant near the Arizona adit and another close to the lower portals on the Nevada side. Frank waited impatiently for Southern Sierra Power Company and the Nevada-California Power Company, winners of the government bid, to bring power to Boulder City and the dam site, to complete the connection. The powerful transmission line originated 200 miles away at Victorville and San Bernardino, California. Field crews of 50 to 80 men labored continuously to string line at the rate of 1 to 1 1/2 miles a day. Chief Bureau engineer Walker Young pushed officials at Southern Sierras to hire more crews. They did and at one time had crews working a 125-

A blast is scaling down the canyon walls. Despite precautions, injuries to workers continued. (USBR)

mile stretch. The substation nearing completion on the canyon rim would furnish a .73-mile, 2,300-volt line into the canyon while a 6.83-mile, 33,000-volt wood-pole line ran back to Boulder City. Crowe was pleased when on June 25 a switch was flipped and electric current now became available to all construction sites.

  With full electric power now available Williams and Huntington prepared to implement the government's plan for large-scale tunnel excavation. Since this would be the largest, most challenging tunnel excavation ever attempted they conferred often with Crowe and Walker Young on properly coordinating drilling steps. Nothing in the construction world then existed that could hog out a 56-foot diameter tunnel. Crowe however, knew Bureau geologists reported that Black Canyon rock could easily be drilled and when loaded (drilled or exploded) breaks evenly into pieces conveniently handled by mechanical shovels. He was further advised that no faults or large seams had yet been encountered and that need for timber support would be unlikely.[8] His army of subterranean soldiers would first cut 12 x 12-foot headings, chip out the flanking wings, excavate the main 30-foot bench, and finally remove the invert. Drilling the top heading moved along at a good pace using a rig that supported men and equipment. Thirty-two holes, each about ten feet deep, were drilled resulting in shattered rock. The muck was removed, the rig moved up, and another 8-10-foot penetration began. Crews working in the adits alternated from one tunnel heading to the other so that drilling and mucking crews worked continuously. The month of June saw 410 feet of top heading removed; in July, with operations moving to full throttle, 1,045 feet of Black Canyon rock were excavated and carried away.

Crowe wanted results and he continually checked and rechecked progress in each tunnel. He not only checked his foremen, but he felt completely comfortable interacting with all of the workers. Sometimes, newly hired men did not know what "The Old Man" looked like and on one occasion this proved disastrous. Crowe, dressed in everyday work clothes, toured one of the tunnels and soon came across a worker just standing around. "Well, what are you waiting for?" Crowe barked. The worker, unaware who the man was, casually replied, "Ah, I'm just waiting for 3:30 [when the shift ended] and payday." Crowe, drawing up to his full height glared at the man and quickly retorted, "Well, I can't help you on 3:30, but I sure as hell can help you on payday—go get it!" The worker turned in his time card and never worked on the dam again.[9]

Living conditions in 1931 became another top priority for Crowe and Bureau engineer Young. The contract demanded that 80 percent of the working force be housed in the government sponsored community of Boulder City. The Bureau of Reclamation and Six Companies planned to erect the new desert community between March and November. However, President Hoover ordered Young and Crowe to move at all possible speed to hire workers and begin construction. Caught between this presidential order and their extensive planning, which called for completion of living facilities before work commenced, Crowe and Young had little choice. Already, thousands of job-seeking men and their families occupied unhealthy temporary camps, with dozens more arriving daily. One of the first, McKeeversville, sprung up just north of where Boulder City would be located. Michael McKeever, a government cook, at the temporary engineering camp on the Hemenway Wash, helped spread the word of construction activity to the unemployed in Las Vegas and by March of 1931 hundreds moved to McKeeversville to be near the job site. Bob Parker remembered the beginning of McKeeversville and its development. He recalled how his father set up tents in the area and soon others followed. The usual procedure was for families to sleep in tents while makeshift housing was being constructed from wood scraps. Parker, like most early residents lived in tents, using them as the core of a new home. Within a short time, tent-based structures sprang up all over the area. Residents hauled in their water and used primitive toilet facilities.[10]

Hobart Blair, a longtime resident of McKeeversville, worked hard to make life in the settlement more liveable. Living in the community for three years, Blair erected two tent-like structures that consisted of short wood walls with canvas over the top. He was able to put in wood strip floors, making the home bearable. Trying to get by with a wife and one son, Blair used gas lanterns and cooked meals

Make-shift housing was common in many areas surrounding the Hoover
Dam job site; this family is part of "Ragtown." (USBR)

on a small kerosene stove. He would lower the tent flaps during high winds to
keep the flame in the stove from blowing out. Finding and keeping access to
water proved to be a major problem. His family was forced to haul all of their
water for the first year, but later a pipe brought water to a single location among
the campsites. Crowe had authorized his workers to take home scrap, used or
damaged lumber and Bob Parker, like many others, obliged the boss. With a supply of scrap lumber obtained from the Six Companies warehouse he was able to
build a small garage. For heat, Parker used a small wood stove, which he fed
sparingly from a variety of scrap kindling that he collected. His method for personal cleanliness was cleverly worked out. Securely fastening a barrel to the top
of his newly completed garage, Parker filled it with water. Then he let the sun
warm the water. The warm water ran through a small pipe, while the flow of water
was controlled from ground level. His homemade shower system proved more
than adequate.[11]

    Meanwhile, migrant job hunters overflowed McKeeversville spilling down
to the foot of Hemenway Wash on the shoreline of the Colorado River. Here,

boatman Murl Emery operated his dock and general store. With the combination of nearby water and a store to buy groceries, Emery's location soon captured much attention. By June, over 500 people called this secluded oasis home. Early arrivals preferred to call this new community Williamsville after U. S. Marshall Claude Williams, himself a tent resident. Others, including visitors from Las Vegas dubbed the sprawling assortment of tent homes, Ragtown.[12] In the blistering summertime heat, energy-sapped inhabitants cursed their intolerable environment preferring to call their "town"—Hell's Hole.

Who would have authority in running this town and who was responsible for the thousands of jobseekers flooding the area? Was it Frank Crowe's responsibility, or should the Bureau of Reclamation be held accountable? On previous jobs, from Tieton Dam to Deadwood Dam, he had successfully housed and fed his family of "stiffs." Most, physically and mentally toughened by years of construction camp life, acclimated well to the rigors—or they got out of the business. The relentless heat, a climatic factor that the tireless engineer had never really faced before, mercilessly drained everybody, everyday. Something had to be done, and done quickly. Deaths related directly to heat prostration continued through June and rose alarmingly when thermometer readings exceeded a sizzling 110 degrees daily. Ray Hapland fell first on June 26. The next day Pat Shannon collapsed as workers stood by in shock. Another man, Mike Madzia, in apparent good health when reporting to work on the 28th, complained of a lack of water, staggered to find shade, then crumpled. An emergency meeting between Crowe, Young, Ayers, and other construction superintendents resolved little. The plain fact revealed unbearable heat everywhere on the dam site: in the tunnels, on the rock cliffs, or in the river bottom. River water, unpalatable due to the heavy sediment content, flowed temptingly close. Rules expressly forbade workers, while on duty, from bathing or soaking in the 60-degree temperature water. Many however, stripped off their shirts, soaked them in the Colorado River, and wore them as wet bandannas. Drinking water was available, but its cloudy residue and lukewarm temperature made it less than appealing.

Ironically, the first death in July had nothing to do with the oppressive heat. Joe Rolland, a Six Companies worker, and Martin Puluski, a visitor, fell into the swirling turbulence of the Colorado River on the 5th and drowned. Three days later Robert Core, an electrician working exposed to the unyielding rays of burning sunlight, sweated profusely for hours before succumbing. Again, medical help was too little, too late. Now, beginning around July 10, heat fatalities became an almost daily occurrence: A. E. Meridith; July 11, Joe Lyons; Earl Parker, July 13; John Swenson, July 15. After a few days respite with slightly lower temperatures a worker, A. A. McClurg, wilted and died. Following him came Tom Noonal a day later, Joe Ganz on the 24th and Lew Starnes on the 26th. The medical situation appeared out of control, with Crowe and Young helpless, or unable, to end the job related deaths.

The "town" of Williamsville became home to over a thousand job seekers and their families. (USBR)

A major labor problem began to crystallize as the long blistering summer continued. Rumors abounded that Industrial Workers of the World (IWW) organizers had arrived in the area, were setting up headquarters in Las Vegas, and preparing for some action. As a general news item, workers knew that the near-defunct radical organization was orchestrating a nation-wide comeback as the Great Depression worsened. With national attention drawn to Hoover Dam and President Hoover's insistence that "work begin immediately," Crowe correctly surmised that the IWW, whose members were derisively referred to by the American public as "Wobblies," eyed his project as a golden opportunity to regain strength. Clark County Sheriffs arrested IWW ringleader Frank Anderson on July 10, and two of his assistants, C. E. Setzer and Louis Gracey on July 11. The charge, vagrancy, was dropped after the defendants' lawyer, T. Alonzo Wells, effectively challenged the arresting officer.[13]

Confident with the acquittal, Anderson and his core of agitators, some of them worked on the dam, continuously bad-mouthed Six Companies and Crowe for unsafe working conditions, tainted food and drinking water, and primitive, unhealthy toilet facilities. Another assertion soon spread that the intense desire for Six Companies, and therefore Crowe, to avoid paying monetary penalties for falling behind in the work schedule, caused the conglomerate to order a work speedup. The assumption inferred that safety concerns became secondary, or were "neglected to save all important money."[14] While the beleaguered Crowe attempted to address these legitimate concerns, the increasing summer heat exacted its toll on the workers' physical condition and patience. The Wobblies looked for, and found, an incident that touched-off a confrontation between Crowe and his army of stiffs.

Hand muckers, responsible for scooping up the rock debris after tunnel explosions and loading the rubble onto trucks, were notified that their wages would be cut. At $5 a day the muckers reeled from the thought of reduced wages to only $4 a day. Crowe instructed his foremen to tell the crews that they would be assigned other work, newly arrived Conway tunnel shovels would replace them.[15] Several Wobblies among the muckers seized the moment; they vehemently argued that the pay cut foreshadowed additional strong-arm actions by money-hungry Six Companies officials. The workers called for an action meeting in the River Camp Mess Hall where several hundred frustrated and anxious men agreed to present a list of demands to Crowe and Six Companies. The River Camp workers explained their strategy and plans to over six hundred equally anxious and frustrated construction stiffs in the Boulder City Mess Hall. A general shutdown resolution, effective with the graveyard shift, passed with little opposition. Meanwhile, through the night a select committee representing all three shifts labored to write a declaration of grievances.

Swing shift foremen notified Crowe of the impending strike. He promptly informed Charlie Shea and other Six Companies' bosses. They agreed that no action would be taken until hearing workers' demands. That night Crowe asserted, to a local newspaper reporter, that this affair "was largely a result of IWW agitation." Crowe sternly retorted he "would be glad to get rid of such." Striking workers reacted swiftly to Crowe's assertion of IWW involvement by declaring "we wish to make it plain that the strike has nothing to do with the IWWs or the United Mine Workers. It is a matter distinctly among the workmen on the project, we're not Wobblies and don't want to be classed as such."[16] Although well ahead of schedule Frank Crowe worried about the demoralizing impact a strike could have, particularly if it turned violent. While he valued his relationship with his men—not just his long time associates who now served as foremen and assistant superintendents, but any hard-working newly hired construction stiff, Crowe wanted, more than anything else, to finish the dam. Alternately, he blamed the IWW for radicalizing the situation, then himself for not anticipating and preventing the crisis. Obsessed with meeting Bureau deadlines that prevented financial penalties for Six Companies, and worried over highly technical construction details, an aggravated Crowe nervously waited.

The next morning, strike leader, Red Williams handed Crowe a long list of workers' demands. They included eliminating the pay cut and boosting wages for tunnel workers, cleaning up the facilities at the river camp, and providing clean drinking water. The strikers also wanted the mess hall daily meal charges lowered to $1.50, and to have their travel time, to and from the dam site, count as part of their eight-hour shift. Lastly, they asked that the tunnel portals be equipped with dressing rooms so they could change out of their wet and grimy clothes, that a safety miner be on duty during all shifts, and that Six Companies obey Nevada and Arizona mining safety laws.[17]

Crowe immediately sent a telegram to Six Companies headquarters in San Francisco. In the interim, he analyzed the complaints then announced that the recent wage cut was due to the transfer of men from inside the tunnel, where wages were higher, to outside the tunnel. He added that the new shovels provided a more efficient way to clear out the debris muck and that no wage cuts had occurred. At the same time, Crowe, sensitive about safety issues, reassured the public by referring to Six Companies July accident reports; the records revealed no job fatalities or injuries. Government figures did show various cases of non-job related deaths. After this press release both sides waited: Frank Crowe could explain his view of the situation but he knew that Shea, Morrison, Wattis, Bechtel, and the others held the power and responsibility of reacting to the workers' demands.

Unbeknownst to the strikers Crowe had alerted Walker Young, Chief Bureau Engineer on the project, that federal intervention might be needed. In fact, Young after notifying his superiors in Denver and Washington, D.C., asked the Commander of Fort Douglas, Utah, to prepare his troops for possible riot control should federal property be endangered. Meanwhile, Crowe received his orders from Shea and Bechtel. He was to announce to the strikers that none of the demands would be honored and that the entire Boulder Canyon Project would be closed down indefinitely. The men would be given their earned pay and notices of dismissal. Crowe looked at strike spokesman Red Williams and firmly declared that new crews would be hired within a short time. Shell-shocked Williams and his strike committee compatriots sullenly exited Crowe's office. Outside the still uncompleted administration building news-hungry reporters learned from the stern direct-speaking Crowe why Six Companies refused to negotiate "We are six months ahead of schedule on the work now and we can afford to refuse concessions which would cost $2,000 daily." W. H. Wattis still seriously ill in San Francisco made plain the Six Companies decision "They're not going to tell us what to do. They will have to work under our conditions or not at all."[18]

Word spread quickly throughout Boulder City, the River Camp, Ragtown, and Las Vegas that Six Companies meant business. The proverbial ball was squarely in the strikers' court. After a heated debate, almost all of the workers voted to leave the area and head for Las Vegas; they hoped rehiring could begin in a few days. Some two hundred strike-hardened workers including Wobblies defied

Crowe's orders and occupied the River Camp dormitories. The next morning as the hungry strikers searched for breakfast in the nearby mess hall, Six Companies trucks roared into the camp. Dozens of armed strikebreakers began rounding up the strikers. Most of the trucks were loaded when a federal marshal drove up and ordered the release of the strikers, claiming that Six Companies had no authority to arrest anyone on a federal reservation.[19] The strike continued the next day until Assistant U.S. Attorney George Montrose accompanied by Walker Young and federal marshals confronted the workers explaining that the U.S. Government now sided with Six Companies and demanded the strikers exit federal property. After a few minutes of hesitation the workers realizing their tenuous position acquiesced, they boarded trucks that drove them to Railroad Pass, between Boulder City and Las Vegas—at the federal reservation border.

Almost all of the dismissed workers ended up in Las Vegas biding their time, waiting for Crowe to begin the rehiring. Many women and children unsure of the situation and tied to their homes [tents], remained in Ragtown. Murl Emery, unofficial "mayor" of Ragtown and owner of the town's only store, remembered, "All working men were fenced out of the area. A big fence, with guards, about halfway between Boulder City and Railroad Pass. All of the workingmen were sent outside, and their families were left down at Ragtown. So I had all these women and kids—no men down there—to feed." Everyone pitched in to share what little reserves were left. As already noted, Crowe did order Six Companies trucks to deliver food to the Ragtown residents and Emery did his best to distribute the supplies equitably.

However, desperate times usually breed insecurity and trouble was bound to break out. Muckers, blamed for starting the strike, suffered both verbal and physical abuse. Bob Parker, while in Las Vegas during this time, watched the town erupt. Fremont Street was the site of battles between muckers and truck drivers, both sides did not need much in the way of provocation to start the action. The Las Vegas police force, strained to its capacity with disruptions daily, struggled to "cool off" tempers. With men at the limit of their financial resources and overheated with the weather and the issues, city gambling house bosses hired extra private security forces. The Pioneer Club, and many others in downtown Las Vegas, armed their security men with the idea that the police would not be able to arrive in time. The casino money cages were prime targets, and extra security was placed in these locations. The situation teetered on the edge of a riot, "It would have gotten out of hand, but it didn't amount to much. It was mostly a drunken brawl. Things settled down pretty well after the police got all the drunks off the street."[20]

Confronted with a swarm of laid-off dam workers and newly arrived migrants, entrepreneurs in Las Vegas prospered with an assortment of enterprises. The center of town appeared to form around the courthouse park where "a solid lineup of gambling houses and drinking joints" lured the unwary. Close by was the "Skidway" or "Block 16," a square block in size where the "flotsam and jet-sam are herded together for the purpose of satisfying the sex appetites of the men who are building the Hoover Dam." Men of all ages, by the score, risked venereal disease by visiting these establishments on a regular basis. "Entertainment houses" were not restricted to Block 16 and two of the more popular sex hotels, the Blue Heaven and the Ye Bull Pen Inn, thrived out on Boulder City Highway. Low on money, or completely broke, hundreds of job seeking families squatted temporary sleeping spots on the lawns in front of the courthouse and the train depot. With nighttime summer temperatures cooling little, at least one squatter observed that "it was so hot all night, we woke up the next morning more exhausted than we were the night before."[21]

Rehiring began on August 13 with Crowe's order to give preference to "old worthy workers" and to blackball any Wobblies or other strike leaders. With the strike ending and work resuming, Frank Crowe breathed a little easier and once again turned his attention to conquering Black Canyon. He summed up his feelings about the incident and his optimism for moving ahead in a letter dated August 22, 1931, to his mother, "Your welcome letter rec'd. So you saw in the paper that we had a strike. It wasn't much we just canned a bunch of bums. We now have 1695 men on the payroll."[22]

Young and Crowe now agreed to give top priority to completing new, more comfortable housing in Boulder City. In this way, they could evacuate the "Hell-Hole Hothouses" known as the River Camp dormitories. It was also de-cided to move swiftly in constructing simple bedroom cottages for married couples now suffering in Ragtown shanties and other tent camps. By accomplishing this, the off-duty workers could recuperate from exhausting and debilitating 8-hour shifts, and family members would have some semblance of a normal lifestyle. Amazingly, the daytime temperatures dropped 10 to 15 degrees when moving out of Black Canyon to the top of the Wash where the new community sprouted.

Despite the slightly lower temperatures acclimating continued to prove difficult for new arrivals. One man, working as a waiter in the dining room for Lewis Construction Company (a subcontractor), worked his first eight-hour shift beginning at 12:30 p.m.; then was told to get some rest and report back at 5:30 a.m. for another eight-hour shift. He was paid two dollars a shift, plus three meals included. He found the food to be good but his accommodation was a small tent that he shared with three others. The tent "is utterly unprotected by any shade, mercilessly exposed to the sun and without any doubled roof." He found sleeping "simply impossible," preferring to layout under the stars. With only a drop of a few degrees during the night, he admitted, "I did not sleep, I dozed, for I was tired but with a temperature which never dropped below 130 during the night sleep was out of the question." The newcomer summarized his feelings by declaring, "By morning, I felt burned to a crisp." Shortly after this, he quit his job.[23]

Crowe next acknowledged the rapid progress that Charlie Williams, Charles

Holden, and the rest of the carpentry crew made in the summer. The large single men's dormitories, each rising two stories, formed an H-shape. Typical rooms measured 7 x 10 feet and had access to an inside hallway and to a well-constructed verandah that ran the full length of the dormitory. Many workers enjoyed spending their evenings on the verandah playing cards, trading work stories, and in the summer, sleeping there. Rent was $15 a month, deducted from their paycheck.[24] William D. McCullough an unemployed recent arrival to Boulder City watched as the dormitories were being constructed. He spotted a heavyset worker who appeared to be giving orders. Desperate for any kind of a job McCullough approached the man, Charlie Williams, and bravely asked him for work. "What can you do, Lad?" Williams asked. Not quite sure how to answer and not wanting to narrow his opportunities the 25 year old man responded, "Oh, I'll do anything." Wiping his sweaty forehead, Charlie Williams took a deep breath and surveyed the building. After a few seconds that seemed like hours to the anxious migrant, Williams pointed and said, "See that old guy over there holdin' his teeth in?" He continued, "Go over and talk to him." McCullough could not believe his ears; his boldness had now given him a job opportunity. With renewed confidence, McCullough approached the man and found out that his name was Kissel, one of Williams' daytime foremen. Kissel, upon hearing that Williams had sent him, said, "Well, just go ahead and go to work." McCullough did not hesitate. He reported to the carpentry shop and began building trusses. Eventually McCullough rented one of the rooms he helped to build. "They had great big showers for 15 to 20 people at a time," he remembered. "Each man had his own room, his own single bed and Simmons mattress—very good, and they changed the linen there whenever you wanted it."[25]

Another newly hired worker, Denzle Pease, lived in the dormitories for months and he recalled the rooms being quite plain and void of color. Despite the small room dimensions and spartan interior Pease believed that the quality steel-framed beds with good mattresses made the accommodations more than adequate. Frank Crowe realized that these dormitories needed to have some form of air conditioning or the men would not be much better off than their previous residences at the sweltering River Camp. However, dorm residents disagreed on the effectiveness of the air conditioning and their comfort. Pease recalled, "they had a semblance of air conditioning, but it wasn't enough to take care of the heat and make the room comfortable during the hot weather." Bruce Eaton argued that any worker living in the dorm "had a decided advantage." He claimed, "They had a cool place to sleep."[26]

A variety of cottage homes sprang up south of Wyoming Street. Married couples, depending on the size of their families and needs, could waitlist for a 2, 3, 5, and 6 room home. Charlie Williams and crew mass produced the houses with precut studs and designed rafters. Usually two carpenters worked on each house. They were given 12 hours to complete the framing for each house. Mary Eaton grateful to have decent housing still found shortcomings in these quickly built homes. Her complaints included the rough pine flooring, which left slivers in unprotected feet. Knowing this parents needed to be careful not to let children walk or run around the house barefoot.[27] Most residents in these homes completed the finishing work themselves. This could involve painting, wallpapering and other small jobs.

The overall square footage of these compact homes hovered under 1000 square feet. Typically, there was a small living room, kitchen, bath and one or two bedrooms. In some cases, family members converted the living room into an extra bedroom. With the oppressive heat, residents cleverly utilized wet burlap, hung over the opening of windows, to cool their homes. The idea was to locate a fan near the windows, draw the air through the burlap, thus cooling the nearby air. These makeshift swamp coolers, according to a number of residents, worked quite well. With the situation reversed in the winter, the families searched for a reliable heat source and most used small kerosene stoves.[28]

Though, small in size and modest in appearance, the Six Companies' homes surpassed, by far, the crude makeshift quarters that most workers were forced to live in. Few of them complained when officials set the rental rates: $15-19 a month for one and two room cottages, $30-$35 a month for the larger three and four room homes. Built in neat rows, visitors, and even Boulder City residents, sometimes found it difficult to differentiate between the identical little houses. "Every house was exactly alike," explained resident Rose Lawson. "You couldn't tell your own house." Lawson humorously recalled that it was a standing joke about how exhausted workers staggered home in the dark from swing shift and, on occasion, mistakenly went to sleep in the wrong house. She said, "I do know of cases where people got up in the morning and found a man sleeping on their couch. But, they'd just wake him and ask him what he was doing."[29]

The U. S. Bureau of Reclamation moved ahead, in the fall, to build dwellings for its battalion of engineers and inspectors. Their responsibility would be to oversee the work of Crowe's construction army, making sure that the specifications of all blueprints, drawings, and schematics were satisfied. Interior Secretary Wilbur instructed Walker Young to build these homes as "substantial structures." Taking a tip from the Spanish and Mexican period of settlement, Young's architects opted to use brick and stucco exterior; the high insulation values protected inhabitants from extreme heat and cold. Young wanted the homes, strung out along Denver, Colorado, Park, and Utah streets, to be completed by Christmas. Crews worked quickly to lay foundations and erect walls, a little too quickly. Young recalled, "In excavation for the foundation [of the government houses], we ran into a type of a clay there which had swelling characteristics." Later that winter residents noted the rain-soaked clay began to swell raising the houses "sufficiently to put zigzag cracks in the joints of the brick." Within months workers had to "go back and correct that."[30]

Just behind the government houses on Denver Street, three hilltops commanded panoramic vistas of rising Boulder City. On the highest hill, a two million gallon water-distribution tank neared completion. Immediately to the west, carpenters and electricians put the finishing layers of stucco on the two-story Six Companies Executive Lodge. This impressive looking mini-hotel became home to visiting Six Company officials: Morrison, Shea, Bechtel, and Kaiser used the facilities regularly. A few hundred yards to the west, and a little lower than the lodge, sat an excellent home building site. Frank Crowe had noticed it back in March and he had already described the site and its potential to Linnie. His contract allowed him to lease the lot and home for a small fee. Six Companies architects designed a roomy high-ceiling Spanish hacienda, a home that would compensate Linnie and the kids for having to live in a remote desert construction camp.

With the coming of winter, work continued in Black Canyon, and around Boulder City. The construction stiffs settled into a routine of work, honing their construction skills and collecting their bi-monthly paychecks. With the national Depression deepening, the workers and their families felt fortunate to have steady employment. There was something else too. Workers began to feel a sense of pride and accomplishment; what they were doing here in the bleak Nevada desert would somehow help the country. Claude Rader, a worker living at the River Camp, wrote a wonderfully descriptive poem entitled "Us Old Boys on Boulder Dam." Read in its entirety, the poem reveals much about the men who had come to build the big dam.

There are thousands we know that knock it,
And holler, that they are cheap
But to us, it brings no worry
Not a moment's loss of sleep,
For, we've been here, since it started
We're used to all the slam
And we're stickin' to the finish
Us old boys on Boulder Dam

And the fallin' rocks can't scare us
Nor the scorchin' rays of the sun
We've rode the rods and brakebeams
Ragged and on the bum
And they gave us jobs and fed us
When we needed it you bet
And we all are truly thankful
With no feelin' of regret
So we're stickin' till the finish

There's me and Ike and Sam
And we're gettin' fat and stakie
Us old boys on Boulder Dam.

Abe Lincoln freed the negroes,
And old Nero he burned Rome
But the Big Six helped depression
When they gave the stiff a home
In a nice bunk house there sleepin'
There workin' every day.
The hungry look has vanished
For they get three squares a day
You'll find tall Lou from Kal-a-ma-zoo.
And Slim from Alabam
Mixed in with all the rest of us
Old boys on Boulder Dam.

"Oh" that bacon and for breakfast
With those new morn eggs I'll say
You get down at river camp
Sure we get 'em ever' day,
And ice-cream, cake and puddin'
Pork-chops at two-bits a pound
Fresh milk from contented cows
And hot-cakes a golden brown
Fresh meat cooked fit to eat
Bread and butter, jam
Flunkies dressed in snowy white.
For us old boys on Boulder Dam.

And the rain may come a pourin'
With sleet and flaky snow.
But we'll dam the Colorado
Says our Super "Hurry Up" Crowe
And us stiffs, is goin' to help him
'Till she's solid and complete
While they pay us honest wages
With a place to sleep and eat
And down here in Black Canyon
You'll find us ever' day
Where the silvery Colorado
Slowly winds its way

Contended and all happy
As a peaceful rovin' lamb
And we're stickin' to the finish
Us old boys on Boulder Dam.[31]

As 1931 ended, Six Companies officials, called for a summary evaluation of their financial standing on the dam construction. They were happily surprised. Their accountants informed them, before the year was out, that they were in the clear. In drawing up the draft bid, "they [Frank Crowe] had cut the price on concrete and other items to the bone while inflating the excavation items." A reasonable price for excavation work would have been between $5 and $6 a cubic-yard; Six Companies bid at $8.50. Engineers called this an unbalanced bid. Kaiser and the others wanted to "throw a big part of their costs and over-all profits into an early phase of the job. Up to the halfway mark the government paid out on 90 per cent of the bid price as the work was completed." Since the tunnel excavation would be finished early in 1932, Kaiser's team of investors was able to acquire $6 million in profits before Frank Crowe and his men started to place concrete. "In other words, they got back all their working capital plus $1 million of clear profit within the first year."[32]

On Christmas afternoon Crowe stood impatiently at the Las Vegas rail depot, awaiting the arrival of Linnie, Pat, and Bettee. The time had come for the family to be reunited once again. At first, Linnie did not recognize her husband; he was much thinner. The scorching hot summer of 1931 and the daily around-the-clock stress of supervising construction teamed to trim him twenty-seven pounds. Nevertheless, she was happy to be with him again. It was with high expectations that Linnie stared out the window of their Buick sedan as they approached Boulder City. What would the town be like? Was this another frontier construction camp? Were all the rumors true about the extremes of temperature? Where would they live? After a brief stop at the administration building where Linnie met Walker Young and other government officials, Crowe drove his family to their temporary quarters in the Six Companies Executive Lodge. As they unpacked, he pointed across to the adjacent hilltop where crews placed the last ceramic tiles on the roof of their new Spanish-style residence. "There's our new home," he happily announced.[33]

Chapter 10

"We had 5,000 men jammed in a 4,000-foot canyon. The problem,
which was a problem in materials flow, was to set up the right
sequence of jobs so they wouldn't kill each other off."
Hoover Dam, 1932

The new year saw a renewed flurry of visits from Six Companies officials. M. H. Knudsen, Harry Morrison's partner and an associate member of Six
Companies Inc., motored from Boise to the Boulder site on January 2, 1932.
Knudsen, accompanied by his wife and four friends, spent the morning touring the
site and talking with public relations counsel, Norman Gallison. Crowe and Linnie
met the Knudsen party and entertained them at a specially prepared luncheon.
These visits never lasted long, Knudsen left for home early in the evening. Three
days later Charlie Shea appeared with Henry J. Kaiser and his wife. At the same
time newspapers proudly announced that doctors at the new Boulder City hospital, still under construction, delivered one of the first Boulder City babies just
hours before Shea and Kaiser arrived. Young dam worker, Kermit Williams, relieved that his wife had delivered normally, became ecstatic when he saw doctors
hold up the 7-pound husky boy—a future dam worker.[1]

Kaiser and Shea, although delighted about visiting the new hospital were
more concerned about their upcoming court battle with the state of Nevada on
working conditions in the tunnels. The pair of nervous Six Companies executives
met with Crowe and walked through a few of the dank tunnels, talking with foremen and taking notes. They left the dam site the next day, returned to San Francisco, and prepared for the trial. Federal judges listened intently as Gray Mashburn,
Nevada's Attorney General, explained the existing mining laws that prohibited
gasoline powered vehicles, namely trucks, from operating in tunnels. Emotionally, he added that the carbon monoxide fumes exhausted into the tunnel atmosphere was extremely hazardous to workers. Six Companies countered by asking
for a federal injunction against Nevada, preventing state intervention on the grounds
that Boulder Dam is located on federal property, therefore, outside Nevada's jurisdiction. They claimed that, if enacted, Six Companies would stand to lose up to
two million dollars in government penalties, as tunnel construction would be significantly delayed. Mashburn did not hesitate to respond to these charges stating

that the federal government did not have exclusive jurisdiction. At one point in the court debate Six Companies lawyers referred to Crowe and Shea's estimation that electric trucks, the only other possible alternative were "excessively expensive and inefficient." The contractors' counsel further argued that muck brought out of the tunnels in electric trucks would, by necessity, need to be transferred to the more powerful gasoline trucks for the long steep haul to the dump site. Kaiser and Shea, through their attorneys, offered evidence of adequate ventilation in all tunnel work areas. Mashburn refused to accept this statement. He claimed that injected air into the tunnels did not remove dangerous carbon monoxide and that the poisonous gases would become even more dangerous the deeper the tunnels extended. The three federal judges, Curtis Wilbur of California, William P. Sawtelle of Arizona, and Frank H. Norcross of Nevada continued to listen as Kaiser's lawyers offered to post bond covering insurance claims "pending settlement of the action." The judges then ordered a fifty-day fact-finding period, allowing both sides to submit evidence.[2]

Crowe was jubilant over the court announcement; fifty days would allow him to complete most of the tunnel work. He counseled closely with his tunnel superintendents and assistants to pump, what they believed to be, adequate supplies of air into the tunnel work areas, hold down unnecessary use of trucks, and push on as rapidly with the excavation as possible. In the digging of the side tunnels, adits, and the top heading Crowe had ordered Roots Blowers. These heavy-duty 18-inch pipes pumped eight thousand cubic feet per minute of fresh air into the tunnels. When driving the main bench headings this fresh air was drawn in through the 10 x 8-foot adits, and pushed into the top headings, which discharged this fresh air into the enlarged tunnels using special pressure fans, which varied in capacity from 35,000 to 120,000 cubic feet per minute. Additionally engineers discovered that 1 to 2 feet per second of fresh air was being forced naturally due to the temperature differences between the atmosphere outside the tunnel and the warmth of the material inside. According to at least one nationally recognized source this fresh air introduced into the top headings and then into the main tunnels "accelerated the natural air currents and maintained a cool, clean, and pleasant working condition for the muckers." Muckers surprisingly recalled that after tremendous blasts within the tunnels the fresh air system worked so efficiently that they could return for the chipping, mucking, and general cleanup within a few minutes. As one observer noted, "natural convection took the powder smoke to the vaulted roof and allowed men and equipment to move in under it." While it is not clear whether regular onsite testing of the air quality of the tunnels took place from the very earliest digging, it is reported that by March of 1932 that all the tunnels involving truck operations did have regular pollution checks. "The degree of viation (pollution), particularly with relation to carbon-monoxide gas, was insignificant in comparison to that of vehicular tunnels, particularly where these have a definite sag such as in the Holland Tunnel," reported one source.[3]

On the other hand, a number of workers discredited Six Companies' contention that air quality was not dangerous to their health. Tunnel worker Harry Hall noted that Crowe did not understand just how bad the exhaust fumes were in the tunnels. He claimed that the oxygen levels dropped to sixteen percent in some of the tunnels, and that nervous workers carried canaries with them to the job and judged the relative carbon monoxide levels. "When the canary looked like he was about gone, you'd better get out of there because there was less than enough oxygen to exist on," Hall stated. Other tunnel workers like Curley Francis, who drove one of the tunnel trucks, remembered that the gas problem was "real bad at times." "We usually could tell by looking at the lights in the tunnel. If they had a big blue ring around them, we would know the gas was getting pretty rough in there," Francis stated.[4]

While both sides could argue the degree to which the problem existed generally throughout the tunnel system, it was plain to see that on certain occasions, in certain tunnels, there were serious gas-related incidents. Carpenter John Gieck was sent down to the tunnel on April 1, 1932. He remembered reporting to work with seventeen men in his crew and after completing the night shift only three remained on the job. "All the rest was taken out sick," he reported. On another day, Colorado River boatman Murl Emery witnessed "a major catastrophe," as he put it, when he was asked to help remove gassed workers from one of the tunnels. "They were hauling men out of those tunnels like cordwood. They had been gassed," Emery recalled. He directly accuses Crowe of lying when he stated, "And that diehard Frank Crowe in the courthouse swore that to the best of his knowledge, there never had been men gassed underground working."[5]

Frank Crowe tired of the constant media attention given to working-condition related litigation problems. He wanted his men to have some diversionary entertainment other than the typical drinking and gambling in nearby Las Vegas. On January 10, he, Walker Young, and Boulder City's new government manager, stern-looking Sims Ely, approved a "smoker," complete with boxing and wrestling exhibitions. Organizer Frank Moran, himself an ex-heavyweight boxing contender, agreed to take on the talented current boxing contender Jack Johnson. Moran also won Crowe's approval to invite "home talent," selecting several "husky" dam workers to show off their pugilistic skills. For days prior to the event, anxious and excited dam workers engaged in "macho hype" on and off duty, freely soliciting opinions about the physical strength, toughness, and reputation of the boxing card.[6] Opinions were voiced and bets were made. Crowe encouraged events such as smokers for he could see, first hand, the resulting camaraderie that ensued and how it helped to break up the day to day routine of hard physical work.

Within a couple of days of the smoker announcement Moran busied himself searching the ranks of construction stiff workers for some of the "home grown talent" he had advertised. As he moved about the work site he, and everyone else, noticed that the afternoon winds gained in intensity daily. The January 12 gale force winds slashed through Boulder City, causing thousands of dollars of damage. Crowe felt helpless as the 50-mph gusts spirited away anything not tied down. He ordered a temporary work shutdown, allowing his men to check on the safety of their families. Ragtown residents, still using camp stoves, found it impossible to build fires and were forced to go without hot food all day. Two of the dormitories and numerous offices had their half-finished roofs torn away within minutes; even ceramic tile blew off newly completed government buildings. Frank Crowe's home, nearing completion on "Crowe Hill," suffered considerable damage. The not yet finished roof was torn apart, like billowing sections of temporary canvas in ship's sails, and carried hundreds of yards distant. Crowe rushed to the unfinished residence, securing wood sheathing, rolls of roofing felt, and plywood siding. Hardest hit were families living in tents or partial tent structures. Those unfortunate enough to have an open entry way facing the oncoming blast of air, lost their homes within minutes as their homes filled like so many inflated basketballs, ripping securing stakes from the ground or shredding rope tie-downs. Desert sand, caught up in the terrific wind gusts, pelted the faces and bodies of unprotected residents. Few ventured from their homes; those without homes sat patiently in the relative safety of their enclosed automobiles. Wednesday morning was strangely quiet as families scoured the immediate vicinity of their homes looking for lost personal items and checking damage. A local newspaper reported, "Sand littered practically every home and office in Boulder City. For hours a steady flow of it had whirled through the air with such force that it found its way into even tightly closed rooms."[7] Remarkably, no one was injured. For Felix Kahn and Charlie Shea the windstorm hit just as they approached Boulder City by airplane. Terrified by the prospect of having to land through the gale force gusts, their pilot circled the airfield at a safe altitude for over half an hour. With fuel low and the Las Vegas airport also experiencing high winds, the pilot daringly maneuvered the bouncing aircraft down in what must have been an exciting, if not horrific, landing.

Crowe was anxious to have Linnie and the kids move into their new home as soon as possible. As the new year started off, the family made daily side trips down the long driveway leading from the lodge, around the hillside and up their narrow driveway to their nearly finished tiled-roof house. He had promised Linnie a "real showplace," and it was: the largest, most expensive residence in Boulder City. Crowe cared nothing for the ostentatious appearance, inside and out, for he was just as at home living in the confining crude construction camp cabins of decades before. Nevertheless, he wanted his family to live in a beautiful home.

Viewed from just about any location in Boulder City the Crowe residence appeared huge, but actually the long rectangular-shaped home was quite narrow—around 20 feet. The overall square footage, not counting patios, totaled

1,500 feet. While the partially underground one-car garage, located forty feet from the main entrance, served Frank Crowe's needs well, Linnie preferred to drive the family's Buick up alongside the house. Workers graded the hilltop sufficiently to pave a twenty-foot blacktop driveway that circumnavigated the entire house. Bordered by a two-foot high masonry fence capped with red brick, the driveway provided a weed-free area for Pat and Bettee to ride bikes, skate, or toss a ball. In an effort to keep the intense summer heat out of his new home, Crowe insisted that the walls be double studded with dead air space in-between. The insulation factor was quite high and Linnie found the indoor temperatures, even on the hottest days, to be somewhat comfortable.[8] The eight-pane heavy glass entry door faces northwest and is recessed underneath a traditional Spanish mission-style front patio. The large square Mediterranean floor rough-hewn tile runs the full length, over thirty feet, of the porch. The main living area, 16 x 20 feet, appeared narrow and confining when filled with the Crowe's heavy furniture. However, cathedral ceilings in all the rooms, rising fifteen feet on the sides and cresting at eighteen feet, helped to make it more spacious. Crowe employed the same Spanish architect who had designed the Bureau of Reclamation Administration Building and government dormitories to build his home using a Spanish motif wherever possible. Accordingly, a highly ornate Spanish-Moroccan archway greeted visitors in the living room and provided entrance into the dining area. A massive built-in stucco fireplace graced the eastern wall and rose majestically to the heavy timber planked ceiling. Beautiful wide-stripped pine floors added to the elegance of each room. The master bedroom came complete with an attached bathroom, a real luxury for 1932. Pat and Bettee shared another bathroom, but each had their own closet. Frank Crowe enjoyed his new home and found it a peaceful hideaway from the tremendous decision-making pressures he faced every day.

The next day after the disastrous windstorm, Crowe had his crews back on the job. Down in the tunnels, the ever-pressing Crowe ordered Williams and Huntington to pickup the digging pace; he wanted to take advantage of the cold clear weather, and he wanted to finish before high temperatures returned. Crowe knew that the tunnel crews would respond to his request; the men responded and competition between tunnel crews increased. One veteran tunnel-miner and concrete finisher, Marion Allen, remembered the competition as major concern for workers. He noted that most of the on the job talk related to a crews standing in terms of progress measured against another crew. Many times crew foremen encouraged the competition, as they needed to make regular quotas of work gains.[9]

The rest of January, tunnel bosses drove their crews to outperform previous records. Beginning at midnight on January 19 Williams and Huntington reported to Crowe that rapid progress was being made. Sure enough after twenty four hours the combined crew excavation totaled 256 feet—more than 16,000 cubic yards of rock. Crowe was elated. He called a special meeting where he congratulated Williams, Huntington and their individual tunnel superintendents, T. C. Hargroves—his tunnel crew had recorded the greatest advance—Leigh Cairns, Paul Guinn, Tom Regan, and Jack Lamey. Frank Crowe reported to Six Companies and the media that:

> Since January 1 progress has been made at the rate of 217 feet per day, or an average of 27 feet per day in each of the eight headings [tunnels], 4,351 feet having been driven since the first of the year. The total length of all four diversion-tunnels is 15,892 feet. Of this distance 10,699 feet have been driven, leaving 5,193 feet yet to be excavated. 285,000 cubic yards of muck have been excavated from the diversion tunnels since January 1, or an average of 14,200 cubic yards per day.[10]

Crowe went on to report that Six Companies approved his recommendation to purchase twenty-three more trucks to speed up muck removal. These new vehicles, larger in carrying capacity than the present fleet, could carry fourteen cubic yards each.

Crowe's announcement elated Kaiser and the rest of the Six Companies officials, but most residents of Boulder City gave more attention to Chief of Police Bodell's dumping of hundreds of gallons of confiscated liquor. The accumulated stash of booze, previously used as evidence in earlier trials, was ceremoniously carried from the police building, driven to the outskirts of town and poured out into the desert sand. Crowe was more worried with the news that a nervous Depression-conscious Congress was concerned about its financial commitment to the Boulder Canyon Project and was considering cuts in appropriation. Interior Secretary Wilbur, in Washington, began a vigorous fight stating, "We are obliged to push work at the dam as fast as possible for simple economic reasons. The sooner it can be finished, the sooner we begin to draw interest on our investment." Bureau of Reclamation Commissioner Elwood Mead added that work was now progressing at record speed (citing Crowe's tunnel excavation figure), "Work at the dam is six months ahead of schedule and our appropriations must be made on that basis unless we wish to run into entirely unnecessary complications."[11] Mead added that 3,370 workers currently collected paychecks, with the promise of additional employment if funding continued.

For his part, Crowe knew another strong incentive for Congress to keep the money coming, tangible progress. Within days of the Wilbur and Mead announcement, he told the local papers that diversion tunnel No. 2 was "holed through." Crowe gave much of the credit to his two tunnel assistant superintendents Tom Regan and Jack Lamey. Regan's crew had cut through 2,134 feet of solid rock from the lower portal. Lamey's men worked the other heading and excavated 1,416 feet from the upper portal. Crowe added that tunnels No. 3 and 4

An inspection party standing in front of the outlet portal of Diversion Tunnel No. 2. Left to right: Sims Ely, Boulder City manager; Walker Young, Bureau engineer; Henry Kaiser, Six Companies; Ray Wilbur, Secretary of the Interior; Warren Bechtel, Six Companies; W. L. Honnald, Metropolitan Water District; Stephen Bechtel, Six Companies; W. P. Whitsett, Metropolitan Water District; Frank Crowe, superintendent at Hoover Dam. (USBR)

were within 500 feet and would be "holed" by February 10, tunnel No. 1 sometime in early March. He disclosed that a new device, a "drilling and trimming jumbo" had enabled his work crews to set a world record shattering pace in excavating the tunnels. With this came the announcement that Crowe planned to start lining the tunnels with concrete as early as February 20.[12]

Crowe smartly kept up a barrage of correspondence with Bureau engineer Young in an attempt to speed tunnel construction. Many of the requests involved changing the agreed upon specifications and Crowe knew that Walker Young, in most cases, would need to contact the Denver office before giving approval. On May 18, Crowe informed Young of a modified plan to excavate the inclined spillway tunnels. After reviewing his suggestion, Young approved the change. On another occasion in June, Crowe wrote an extensive letter to Young requesting permission to use a new method for curing the diversion tunnel concrete. Up to this point, all curing involved a water process. Crowe wanted to use the Hunt Process, still in experimental stages, which allowed for a quicker set. Young listened to Crowe's rationale, then wrote Chief Engineer Ray Walter in Denver for a decision. Young explained, having checked around the country where the Hunt Process had been used, good results were obtained. He recommended that Walter approve the use. Crowe, who nicknamed all Bureau engineers, "The Great Delayers," always submitted his requests well ahead of time in order to allow the bureaucracy to do its work. Bureau engineers, knowing Crowe's obsession with pushing men and machines to their limit, called him "Hurry-up Crowe."[13]

Much of the tunnel success can be attributed to the ingenuity of tunnel superintendent Williams. With the understanding that "necessity is the mother of invention," Williams pondered how to get the most out of his men and machines. In earlier conversations, Williams and Crowe brainstormed ideas and came to the simple conclusion of excavating several tunnel faces at once. In addition, Crowe decided to engage three shifts for a twenty-four hour assault. Now Crowe challenged Williams to come up with a way to utilize more men on each tunnel surface. Traditionally, a drilling crew went to work first standing side-by-side sinking blasting holes. Next, the blasting crew came in and set the charges, again standing side-by-side. For tunnels taller than 10 feet, this meant setting up scaffolding to reach the higher elevations. All this setup and takedown claimed precious time. Williams wondered if he could duplicate the work on ground level and two additional higher levels. Each working platform would have all necessary equipment allowing simultaneous drilling and setting of blasting charges. In essence the work time would be cut significantly, with workers attacking the entire fifty-six foot tunnel at all times. Williams further planned to put the entire platform, nicknamed "jumbo," on a heavy-duty truck frame, giving the jumbo quick maneuverability. An exhilarated Crowe, understanding the impact of this innovation, gave his carpentry chief permission to immediately build a prototype.

Williams wasted no time. He put mechanics like Neil Holmes to work hammering a huge three-tiered wooden platform onto a reliable International model truck. Holmes recalled, "I had to go in and pipe it up and put manifolds on so that the miners would have air and water. So whenever they moved, the air and water moved right with them." The air was used to power the twenty-six pneumatic powered drills, while the water kept dust particles from flying everywhere. "They [Williams and Crowe] found out that [the jumbo] worked all right, so then they built four new machines,"[14] Holmes added. Williams, nervous about reported problems with constant vibration working the jumbo's nails loose, ordered the new machines to be constructed of steel.

Once in action, tunnel assistant superintendents, foremen, and workers experimented with their "new toys." Their aim was to achieve maximum use of the equipment. Joe Kine, tunnel worker, recalled jumbo operation. "They'd back that up against the wall and drill out all the holes, then move it over and drill out another set of holes." Once all drilling was completed Kine remembered, "Then we'd all jump in there, [air] blow out the holes, load them with dynamite, and shoot." He noted that everyone helped with the dynamite loading: "There was no such thing as a powderman. Everybody was a powderman." Marion Allen worked as a "nipper" on one of the drilling jumbos. As the drilling commenced, Allen stood on the covered lower level ready to hand steel-shafted drilling sections to allow deeper penetration of the rock. He recalled, "It was a good safe place too. If something caved in, it might get the ones above you, but not you." He received five dollars a day as a nipper, and he "was constantly trying to get on one of those [drilling jumbo] machines. They paid $5.60 a day. That $.60 was important money." Steve Chubbs, hired as an electrician's helper, strung wires to the loaded dynamite heading at each hole. Nicknamed a "grunt," Chubbs stood by as the drilling jumbos were withdrawn to a safe distance and the holes were loaded with explosives. His crew would then "bring the primer wires out and tie them to a bigger wire. They had great big long sticks, and they'd shove the primer back with that." Chubbs assisted the electrician, holding a flashlight, in twisting the wires together. The main detonation wire was then run back down the tunnel, usually to a side adit where the shot was set and discharged. Numerous explosion accidents occurred when eager powder monkeys tapped the delicate primers, made of mercury fulminate, too hard.[15]

With drilling and blasting proceeding at a good pace in the tunnels, Walker Young informed Crowe that a new rash of liquor violations permeated Boulder City. Young wanted Crowe to cooperate in strongly enforcing the federal regulation of no alcoholic beverages anywhere in the government reservation area. In a span of only four days reservation officers, such as F. S. Lane, apprehended eight men for violating the liquor ban. One of the men was found in possession of twenty-one pints of hard liquor. Young, anxious to stop the recent rash of liquor violations, decided to make an example of this alleged criminal. He moved quickly, having him arraigned before U. S. Commissioner W. J. Flowers; he was bound over to the federal court and held with a $2000 bond requirement. Young immediately added extra men to the reservation police force. These new rangers patrolled every road entering Boulder City and checked all incoming cars.[16]

Meanwhile, Crowe refused to rest. Every day, at all hours of the day, he watched the progress everywhere. He became most concerned whenever he saw men working at a task in which they had no idea of what they were doing; he would blast his foremen for not keeping crews busy on work they understood. One night while touring the riverbed, he spotted a group of men apparently digging in a deep hole. Crowe stepped over to the edge and shouted down to the men, "What are you men doing down there?" After a moment, one of the confused workers shouted back, "We don't know." "Well, where is your foreman?" Crowe snapped. The dazed men, finally realizing that they were talking to the big boss replied, "He went off someplace." Crowe thought for a moment, took off his tie, jumped down into the hole, picked up a shovel and began digging alongside the other men. Within minutes the foreman returned and without taking more than a glancing look called down to the men, "How is it going?" Whereupon, Crowe stood up, making himself plainly visible to the foreman and calmly asked, "What the hell are we doing down here?"[17]

On February 10, a deluge of floodwaters from the Virgin River in Utah poured into the Colorado River some fifty miles above the dam site. Crowe received word that bridges upstream snapped and came apart under the tremendous onrush of water. One observer, at the Bunkerville Bridge location, watched as the flood "came roaring down in great waves, bearing on the crests a vast amount of drift wood which it used as battering rams against every obstacle." The bridge resisted the increasing pressure momentarily, but slowly gave way as more and more spans broke. Nervous, yet undaunted, Crowe spent hour after hour down on the banks of the quickly rising river. Bundled in a jacket and an overcoat he ordered his regular tunnel crews to fill sandbags and to stand ready. The most critical location to be protected was the upper portal openings. If water poured into the tunnels now, the resulting quagmire of mud would halt excavation and preparations for concrete lining operations for days. As usual, Crowe refused to leave the supervision of this emergency to his able-bodied lieutenants, preferring to brave the forty-degree nighttime temperatures with his workers and direct operations. Within a few hours it became clear that the flood waters would rise no higher than five feet above normal levels, and Crowe sent his men back into the tunnels to continue their shifts. He then drove home to grab a few hours sleep before starting his inspection rounds the next day. Episodes such as this became routine for Crowe, yet so much was at stake that he could not let his guard down even for a moment.[18]

At about this same time Crowe met with Walker Young and other Bureau officials to discuss the ongoing housing shortage. Young, anxious to have families vacate the unsightly tent cities of Ragtown and Williamsville, wanted Six Companies to begin constructing 250 additional homes in Boulder City. The Bureau, through city manager Sims Ely, issued orders months before for "the vacation of all temporary structures, but as yet many families have been unable to find permanent quarters, so fast have operations on the dam moved forward, demanding the employment of additional men." Rolling out a recently completed street map of Boulder City Crowe and Charlie Williams, watched as Young and his engineers pointed to flat desert land lying south of the present development. Young agreed to authorize the New Mexico Construction Company to begin work on the necessary sewers and new street paving. Crowe advised Williams to begin the new task as soon as Charlie Shea was informed and additional carpentry crews could be hired. With hundreds of jobless men milling about the busy streets of Las Vegas, Williams knew that acquiring more workers posed no problem. Young was pleased with Crowe's helpful attitude about starting the work immediately, for he knew that his superiors, particularly members of the Hoover administration, wanted the Boulder Project to go well and have its beneficial aura shine favorably on them. Young was also under pressure to beautify the already existing landscape in Boulder City and he called on Wilbur Weed, a landscape engineer, to give a lecture, "illustrated by lantern slides," to interested homeowners. Young, hoping to generate a renewed enthusiasm for home and yard upkeep, offered a $25 prize to the best-looking house and yard.[19]

A week later Frank Crowe called a special night meeting of his entire force of sixty foremen. He wanted to review general safety regulations and the enforcement policy as well as discuss preparations for handling emergency situations, such as the recent flood. The tragic death of shovel mechanic Jason Talbert in the No. 2 diversion tunnel was reported in the Las Vegas newspaper days before and raised some eyebrows. Accident or not, the wary engineer knew that he was being watched for safety violations. Crowe started the evening by thanking everyone for their conscientious hard work and their enthusiasm for wanting to move the work along. He introduced W. T. Brockman, Director of Safety, J. J. Rosedale, consulting safety engineer, and C. J. Seymour, resident safety engineer. Following their brief recap of safety rules, the three safety engineers held an "open discussion, several problems arising on the job [recently] were brought up and threshed out."[20] Crowe wanted everyone in a supervisory position to be fully aware that he would not tolerate any slack in conforming to safety regulations. The disastrous situation of the previous summer, with so many deaths and injuries, could not be repeated. His reputation, as well as the reputation of Six Companies, and for that matter, the federal government was on the line.

Not long after this, Crowe's daughter Pat complained of a tremendous pain in the lower abdomen. Linnie drove her to a Los Angeles hospital for testing and treatment. Frank Crowe was kept informed and on March 14, after hearing that Pat needed an operation for appendicitis, traveled over the desert to be with his family. The procedure went well and Crowe remained with his daughter for a couple of days before returning to the dam site.[21]

Part of Frank Crowe's official duties included attending myriad special lunches to show support for community activities. Boulder City, by April of 1932, had organized an active American Legion branch, and George Malone, a national committeeman planned to visit the sprouting new town. Local members scheduled a welcoming meeting for Malone. Along with Crowe, Bureau personnel including Walker Young, Office Engineer John Page, and Engineer Ralph Lowry attended.[22] These social events became routine for Crowe after 1931, as more and more national and international attention focused on the construction of Hoover Dam. Crowe was never comfortable wearing a suit and tie, yet Linnie insisted that he "look the part" of an engineering executive. She made sure that a freshly laundered and pressed white shirt was ready for her husband to wear each morning. On many occasions, particularly when it was warm or he was working outside most of the day, he would abandon the tie before noon and roll-up his long-sleeved shirt.[23]

For her part, Linnie too was launched into a leading social position. Married to one of the most important and powerful men living in Boulder City, she was instantly recognized wherever she went in town. By early 1932, her presence was requested at more and more social events, including a popular bridge club. These social gatherings became regular events, reported in detail by the Boulder City and Las Vegas newspapers.[24]

Early in 1932, Frank Crowe and Six Companies had been confronted with charges from the local Colored Citizens Labor and Protective Association (CCLPA) of Las Vegas. A local newspaper article reported that Blacks claimed "...construction work was under progress with no Negro labor whatsoever." Black job seekers further noted, "...on some of these jobs there were foreigners working while Negro American citizens were denied employment." On previous dams, there had always been an occasional Black working on Reclamation projects, but never before had Frank Crowe felt political pressure to ensure Black job opportunities. He was aware of a Six Companies decision to restrict "Mongolians." This prohibition, had for years, appeared as a standard clause in government contracts. Sensing this could be a political hot potato, Crowe notified W. A. Bechtel who responded by claiming that:

> "He had never heard of any refusal to employ colored people and that he would take the matter up immediately on his return to Boulder City, and see that provision was made for their employment on the work when and if they had the necessary experience."[25]

Bechtel, on his next visit to the site, let Frank Crowe know that the National Association for the Advancement of Colored People (NAACP), the CCLPA, and the Department of the Interior would be watching to see if Blacks would be offered jobs on the dam. Checking into the hiring preferences he saw that Nevada residents who had served in the military received top priority, then men from Arizona and California. On the issue of hiring Blacks, Leonard Blood, Deputy Director of the Nevada Office of Labor feared that the resulting tension caused by hiring Blacks would affect job performance and progress. He also worried about "housing and feeding 'colored labor' and the cost of providing separate facilities for them."[26] Crowe, determined not to be distracted from his engineering concerns, took no action, preferring to allow Bechtel and the politicians settle the discrimination problem.

Six Companies finally decided to break the color line and hire Blacks in July of 1932. That first week, ten Blacks secured jobs on Hoover Dam. By this time the entire work force numbered over 4,000, the Black contingent thus equaled only .25%, disproportionately small according to the 1930 Las Vegas census figures. However, by July 1932 there were no accurate census figures, as thousands of hungry desperate job seekers had invaded Las Vegas, Boulder City—indeed the whole area around the building site. Notwithstanding the *Las Vegas Age* reported on July 8, 1932, that newly hired Blacks had made great progress in their employment status:

> When the matter finally came to the attention of the Secretary of the Interior through the National Bar Association measures were taken to assure the Colored people of their just proportion of the work on this project. It is gratifying, not alone to the people of African descent, but to all lovers of fairplay that this question of Negro labor on Hoover Dam has been settled with justice and fairness.[27]

The Six Companies officers made a decision, early in the hiring process, to restrict Blacks to certain jobs, most of these men labored clearing and repairing roads throughout the dam site. Few secured the more high paying jobs in the tunnels, high scaling chipping and demolition, or equipment operators. A notable exception included a Black masonry crew that constructed beautiful rock barriers along the main road into the dam site. It is not clear whether Crowe was in on the decision to limit Black hiring. On several previous jobs, he had both worked alongside and hired Black men. Workers who had been with Crowe from the Jackson Lake Dam job recalled "Frank was always fair in hiring. He didn't care what your color was or where you came from. He just wanted good workers."[28]

Through much of the early summer of 1932 Frank Crowe worked long hours in perfecting the design requirements for the massive cableway system. Even though completed preliminary drawings looked good, Crowe realized that these cables would be responsible for carrying unprecedented heavy weights of freshly mixed concrete and other materials over unusually long distances. The key to the concrete stage, and thereby the early completion of the dam, lay in the efficient placing of concrete. Crowe, a pioneer in the use of the cableway system, had been its biggest proponent, having used it successfully at the Arrowrock, Guernsey, Van Giesen, Tieton and Deadwood Dam sites. Now he proposed a network of five cableways able to carry 20 tons. This network would "raise excavated material from the dam foundation and other points in the canyon, place concrete in the dam and appurtenant works, and handle equipment and other materials."[29] Crowe, alert to the fact that the cableway must be manufactured to exacting specifications and quality, to ensure smooth reliable service over many months, constantly kept Shea and Six Companies officials informed about any changes in his requirements. Shea was nervous too, the cableway system would be the single largest subcontract yet—requiring a 3-inch locked-coil smooth-surfaced track cable and supporting foundation.

In designing this system, Frank Crowe was at his best. The layout, specifications, and materials were all his initial idea. In the end, the final bid requirements and designs were his as well. The five cables, labeled D5 to D9 and anchored to movable supporting headtowers and tail towers, could stretch daringly out over the Black Canyon, providing access for men and materials to all construction sites. The spillways, both the Nevada and Arizona sides, would be served by cable D5 and D6. These cables needed to span almost a half-mile, some 2580 feet each. Cables D7 and D8, spanning 1385 feet maximum, covered the dam foundation area. Cable D9, stretching 1365 feet, would have the responsibility of providing access to the lower portals, and the penstock tunnels.

Crowe was pleased to hear on July 15 that Columbia Steel Company of San Francisco had won the bid to supply the all-important 3-inch main cables. He had worked with this company before and knew their history of supplying quality material on schedule. He also knew that Columbia had plans to have American Steel & Wire Company actually manufacture the Herculean-sized cable. The cable, comprised of dozens of intricately woven smaller steel cables, must not have any breaks or flaws. The outer casing of steel sheathing, likewise, needed a smooth strong facing. Crowe planned to use these cables in an around-the-clock effort to complete the dam well ahead of schedule, and any delays in replacing these major cables could prove catastrophic. In planning for every contingency, Crowe worked with Columbia executives and with Walker Young to begin erection of the D7 cable—the cable needed to bring concrete to the dam foundation—on or before September 15. Then, Crowe explained that he wanted to commence use of the cableway system in the following sequential time frame: D7—October 15; D9—October 21; D5—October 30; D8—November 7; D6—November 14.[30]

In March, the *Union Pacific Magazine* honored Frank Crowe with a special article entitled "Paul Bunyan of the Black Canyon." Likening Crowe to a major general in the army the author credits Crowe for being the "central figure in this struggle." "Nothing in this decade has captured the public imagination as has this daring attempt of man to tame a mighty river that has long defied him," the article asserted. Crowe is given tremendous accolades as a person who "loves this business of harnessing wild and turbulent streams." Stating that many fine engineers had done the planning and drawing of specifications to arrive at the construction point, the article boldly exclaimed, "it also required someone to actually do the job, it required a man who would be there day and night through the blistering heat and the searching winds of winter, a man who had not only the vision and genius of a builder but who had the stamina and driving force to carry the job through six years of 'high pressure' to completion." Among the successful accomplishments of Crowe mentioned in the article are, the driving of the four 56-foot diameter diversion-tunnels and his successful organization of men and machinery. The article stated, "it is characteristic of the man that he did not wait for the contract to be signed, but a few days after the bid was awarded he was on the

One of the most dangerous and exciting jobs involved chipping
loose rocks. High scalers dangled, by securely attached lifelines,
hundreds of feet down the canyon slope. (USBR)

job, with a crew, and personally starting the wheels in motion. The men who have
worked for him on his various jobs 'swear by him.' A few of these hearty construction stiffs started with Crowe as far back as Jackson Lake Dam." On a personal note, the reporter described Crowe as looking only forty instead of a "gentle-
man" approaching fifty. As requested, Crowe gave some information on his prior
background including his experiences on the Lower Yellowstone Dam and a list of
some of the other dams that he had worked on since then.[31]

Some interesting stories to come out of the 1931-32 era include many
human dramas and several involving animals. One such story involved the so-

called mascot of Hoover Dam. This shorthaired Labrador-type dog was born in Boulder City in 1932. As the dog grew up through that year and the next he started to strike out on his own and eventually found his way to the big transports loading men to go down to the dam site. No one thought that the dog would become so attached to the men, to the transports, and to the job. Interestingly, he eventually found his way to the railroad station heading down to the dam site. At least a few days a month he would catch the freight train of empty railroad cars at the Hemix concrete plant. While there were 5000 men on the job at one point and most of them at one time or another saw and interacted with the black Labrador, none claimed him as their own. The fun loving puppy freely roamed the work site riding trucks, dashing in and out of the tunnels, and running about the workers. When lunch came, the four-legged visitor eagerly made his rounds of the lunching workers. Later as the dog became a regular visitor to the dam site, lunch was actually prepared for him at the Anderson Brothers Mess Hall. According to one source, he would "carry his own paper sack lunch in his mouth aboard the transports, right along with the workmen." Amazingly the mascot developed an unusual ability to sense the end of a particular work shift, for when the shift whistle screeched signaling time to quit the Labrador would already be waiting at the elevators so as not to miss his ride back to Boulder City. On several occasions, the lucky canine rode around the construction site as Frank Crowe's companion in the boss's big Buick.

Crowe understood the importance of using air-compressed tools on a job the size of Hoover Dam. During consultation with his foremen and the executives of Six Companies it was decided that it would be in their best interest to buy all of the equipment from one recognized manufacturer. This would reduce negotiations with different companies; make installation, exchange, and maintenance of the equipment easier; and make it easier to keep the necessary spare parts available. There really was not much competition; he remembered as far back as Arrowrock Dam the leading role that Ingersoll-Rand had played in becoming the nation's leading manufacturer of air-compressor machines and tools. A job the size of Hoover Dam would provide a unique opportunity to use a wide variety of tools in many different applications. While the exact number of air tools or machines is uncertain, one source claims that there were over 500 such devices. The high scalers in chipping away loose rock from the canyon walls used "Jack hammers." Two-person jackhammers and drills were operated almost continuously in 1931 and 32, both in the riverbed and in the tunnels. There were at least 10 air-operated hoists at work. Crowe insisted that a complete blacksmith shop be erected in which Ingersoll-Rand drill sharpeners were installed. At top performance in 1932, 3,500 pieces of steel were reconditioned every 24 hours. To provide the air for all these tools, three separate and distinct compressor plants were constructed. Crowe, looking at the overall specifications and plot map of the dam site, spread the three compressors out geographically, with the number one plant located up-

President Herbert Hoover and official party are seen here inspecting Tunnel No. 2 during his 1932 tour. Left to right: Mr. Richey, secretary to the president; R. F. Walter, chief Bureau engineer; Mrs. Hoover; President Hoover; Mrs. Wilbur; R. L. Wilbur, Secretary of the Interior; E. O. Wattis, Six Companies; Frank Crowe. (USBR)

stream from the entrance to the diversion tunnels. Plant number two was located at the dam foundation site, and plant number three sat downstream just past the exit portholes of the diversion tunnels. Dozens of mechanics, electricians and air-compressor mechanics were hired to maintain the air-compressor tools and machines so that his full speed 24-hour operation could continue. As one source reported, "compressed air is in the forefront of the indispensable agencies at Hoover Dam."[32]

One of the more interesting issues that Crowe faced in preparing for the upcoming huge concreting operation was development of sizable and appropriate aggregate supplies. In 1932 he estimated that for the main dam itself, the power-house, and other works around the dam they would be mixing and placing 4,400,000 cubic yards of concrete. Original investigations uncovered a sizable gravel deposit, a thirty-foot deep bed of alluvial material several miles upstream from the dam site. Engineers estimated that the 100-acre gravel bed would just satisfy the needs of the Hoover Dam project. The site was owned by the government and turned over to Six Companies for use. Crowe, in long discussions with Shea and Felix Kahn argued for spending nearly one half million dollars of the bid money to provide what would become the world's largest screening and washing plant, consisting of some 350 tons of structural steel. Adjacent to the screening and washing plant would be the gravel plant station on the railroad leading to the dam site. While strict government specifications declared that aggregate in excess of 9 inches in diameter could not be used in any concrete mix, arrangements had to be made to provide for a variety of assorted sizes of aggregate. Six Companies carted gravel to the screening and sorting plant where several sizes were separated and delivered via conveyor belts to huge stockpiles. From there, plant engineers at the concrete mixing plant near the dam site could obtain the desired-size aggregate, everything from the minute all the way up to 9 inches. The highly mechanized system for digging up the deposits, transporting them to the screening, transporting them to the railroad, and then eventually bringing them to the dam site utilized less than 100 men.[33]

So much action surrounded the activities at the dam site during 1932 that it would be quite easy to overlook the progress made in setting up and expanding the town of Boulder City. While not directly involved in the running of the government-sponsored community, Crowe could exert tremendous influence on issues that might impact construction. When Walker Young announced that a town manager had been selected and that the choice was Sims Ely, a sixty-nine year old Federal Land Bank director from San Francisco, Boulder City residents—Crowe included, gasped. How could a man, who should be contemplating retirement, find the energy to administer an isolated wind-swept, vitality-sapping desert community? Crowe himself had remarked, "It's a young man's job" and "The old can't stand it."[34] The crabby-faced, stern-speaking Ely, who appeared to have been weaned on a pickle, quickly revealed that he was all business and no fun. Young gave him virtually unlimited power for day-to-day operation and management of the government-sponsored town. Ely's kingdom, consisting of over 500 buildings, rose impressively out of the desert sagebrush. Included in this were eight single men dormitories, each capable of housing 172 workers, 416 residences of mostly three and four bedrooms, a mess hall capable of serving 1300 patrons, a large fully-equipped laundry, and a well-stocked commissary. Crowe's carpentry crews had constructed all of these buildings, for use by Six Companies employees. In addition, Ely ruled over two spacious government office buildings, a thirty-man dormitory and seventy residences that housed U. S. Bureau of Reclamation inspectors and office personnel.[35]

Ely, seen by residents of the new town as cranky, soon established a tight hegemony over town activities. An able administrator, he despised waste and inefficiency. In this way, he resembled tight-fisted Frank Crowe. Crowe and

Tunnel lining operations. (USBR)

Young had received dozens of requests by individuals and groups desiring to open commercial establishments, in what they hoped would become, a thriving boomtown-type community. It became Ely's responsibility to decide how many permits would be given to eager entrepreneurs and who would get them. Under regulations approved by the Secretary of the Interior, leases for commercial and residential purposes could be granted at the discretion of the government and held until June 30, 1943, when it was determined construction was fully completed and a "necessary adjustment period" had elapsed. The adjustment period referred to the government's desire to have Boulder City become a full-incorporated community within the jurisdiction of the state of Nevada. By mid-1932 over 25 permits had been approved by Ely, with scores of others denied. He allowed two "wholesale gasoline and oil stations, a restaurant and short order stand, a tourist camp [trailer court], man's clothing and dry cleaning shop, building supplies yard, garage and filling station and lodging house." Additionally, he allowed a "bus terminal station, Western Union Telegraph office, barber shop, lunch room, laundry, electrical appliance store and several other stores."[36]

The rules for obtaining permits had been set out by Louis C. Crampton, an appointee of Secretary of the Interior Wilbur, back in March of 1931. He compiled his regulations in a small pamphlet designed to answer questions about Boulder City and setting up a business on the government reservation. Swamped with a deluge of requests from profit-minded would-be entrepreneurs, Crampton decided that only formal requests, made with an application and a $10 registration fee would be seriously considered. While over 4,000 informal inquires came through the Boulder City and Las Vegas offices of the Bureau, only 320 followed-up and sent in the requisite fee. Ely, careful to follow Crampton's rules, conservatively approved permits, allowing for selected competition in a variety of specialties such as markets, banks, doctors, lawyers, and dentists.

Interestingly, the Bureau allowed religious groups of several denominations to erect churches in Boulder City. The first, Grace Community Church, rose humbly amid the sweltering shelters of Ragtown in the summer of 1931. An interdenominational organization asked for and received permission to provide religious services from the River Camp Commissary near Cape Horn. Early parishioners recalled sitting on empty "bootleg hooch" kegs confiscated by federal authorities in a nearby raid. Popular Presbyterian Pastor Tom Stevenson, from Southern California joined the church in October that first year and he immediately led revivals from a tent in Ragtown. Pastor "Tom" and Frank Crowe became friends and the superintendent gave permission for Stevenson to use the Six Companies Mess Hall for services while Grace Community Church was being built. In 1932, other churches were established including St. Andrew's Catholic Church, St. Christopher's Episcopal Church, and a Mormon church. Crowe, raised as an Episcopalian, rarely attended church either here at Hoover Dam or at other locations. He insisted that his daughters attend Sunday school, while telling them, "I have gone to church so much when I was young that it will last for several generations."[37]

Rarely did a day go by when the "Old Man" did not visit the tunnel lining operations. Roughed out, the four diversion tunnels measured 56 feet in diameter, when lined with three feet of reinforced concrete; the finished subterranean conduits were calculated to divert the full current of the Colorado River. Crowe had ordered the lining operations to begin early in the year as workers completed the excavation of each tunnel. Tunnels Nos. 3 and 4 were the first to be lined. While the construction technique used to line the tunnels was not new, the sheer size of the undertaking confronted the veteran dam builder with more challenges. Workers used numerous special-purpose machines and huge interlocking concrete lining forms to imbed over 2,000 tons of reinforced steel into the setting concrete. Crowe realized that he would be setting another industry first. Experience proved that lining the lower portion first, or invert, which comprised 74 degrees of arc, allowed for trucks and heavy equipment to operate subsequently. Next, the two sidewalls comprising an arc span of 88 degrees each were lined followed by the roof, or arch section. Each section, some 40 feet in length, abutted with interlocking key ways to provide structural integrity. Concrete for the invert was either poured directly from flatbed trucks holding a total of four cubic yards of concrete or from a specially designed moving gantry that moved along on a rail system. Engineers designed a curved steel template that served to screed the freshly placed concrete into the desired curvature. Once placed and set, the elaborate forms and gantry were moved on to the next position farther along in the tunnel. When dried the invert was made flat, for truck passage, by bringing in three feet of sand. The sidewalls and arch sections required custom reinforced forms, as nothing this size had yet been attempted. Six Companies engineers worked with technicians at Consolidated Steel Corporation of Los Angeles to develop the desired specifications and structural requirements.[38]

Placing concrete in the sidewalls involved hoisting the concrete buckets from the truck beds upward to awaiting chutes that directed the fresh mix down the side of the inner form. Both sidewalls were worked simultaneously, with trucks coming and going around the clock. The usual procedure linked two 50-foot forms and a stop to makeup a "sectional pour" and this required on the average 50 hours of non-stop labor to do both sides of the tunnel. The arch, of course, required a special use of pneumatically placed concrete. Again, this technique was not new; as Crowe had supervised the same basic procedure on dams all the way back to Arrowrock. Screw jacks moved the arch form into place while workers setup the giant air-compressed concrete spraying gun and hopper. A headtower-type framework supported the two air receivers that supplied the "surge of compressed air necessary for discharging each batch of concrete." Crowe impressed visitors with the technology utilized at Hoover Dam. He would bring them into the tunnels when workers engaged in concreting the arches. There, the almost unbelievable sight of four cubic yards of freshly mixed concrete shooting upward into the form awed most everyone. As soon as the forms were removed, jet sprays sprinkled cool water over the drying surfaces. Then an asphalt-type coating air sprayed throughout, sealed the surface, making it watertight. The concrete used in the tunnel lining needed to adhere to strict quality and mixture specifications. Walker Young and assistant engineers constantly checked the mixture vats for correct proportion and consistency. The Bureau employed the latest in technology with a "machine that records essential facts concerning every batch of concrete as it is mixed." Young and Crowe, never fully trusting the devise, regularly sight-checked concrete batches, as the pair of engineers made their way through the tunnel lining operation.[39]

Employing 900 men, 300 per shift, Crowe was serious about completing the lining as quickly as possible. For, as it was completed he could fully divert the waters of the Colorado River. He encouraged each shift of workers to challenge each other to ever-greater production in concrete placements. Much pride and enthusiasm went into these challenges and foremen constantly looked for ways to streamline steps without shortcutting quality or safety. A typical daily placement averaged just over 2,000 cubic yards, with the record holding at 2,750 cubic yards on June 14, 1932. With a lot on the line, Crowe spent considerable time in the tunnels during the lining operation. Marion Allen, working as a finisher in one of the tunnels, recalled Crowe appearing, out of nowhere it seemed, during the wee hours of his graveyard shift. As he debated with another worker about a particular concern, Crowe standing unseen several feet behind them barked out, "Who is holding up this pour?" Both workers, and anyone within shouting distance, were immediately startled and "turned to see the tall, stooped figure of the superintendent of construction stalking off down the tunnel."[40]

On October 12 of 1932, Frank Crowe could not understand, all during the morning, why few of his friends said happy birthday to him. He did not know that Linnie had planned a special celebration for his fiftieth birthday. Led up to the impressive guest house, later that day, he was completely surprised by the awaiting throng of well-wishers including family members, Six Companies officials, Bureau of Reclamation personnel, and longtime "construction stiff" friends. His daughter Bettee remembered the happy occasion. "We ate a great big cake that had all fifty candles on it," she said. The modest engineer was slightly embarrassed by all the attention, yet excited when presented by Six Companies with a "special watch" and a "gold medal," recognizing his outstanding work on Hoover Dam. Steve Bechtel, Henry Kaiser and others who could not be there sent telegrams. "Happy Birthday Frank fifty good wishes for another fifty years of happiness," wrote Bechtel. Kaiser, already over fifty years old, chided Crowe, "Thank God you have joined my class. I congratulate you and accept you on your fiftieth birthday in the fifty-year class. Happy Birthday." After a few short speeches and congratulatory comments, a smiling Frank Crowe posed for photographs by a richly decorated cake.[41]

Much of the conversation for the next few days centered on the next big step, diverting the powerful Colorado River. The plan, implemented in mid-October, called for splitting the river up the middle by using a perpendicular dirt dike. Once sealed at the upper and lower ends, the Nevada portion of the bank could be dewatered allowing construction of the all-important upper cofferdam. Meanwhile, preparations continued to make Tunnel No. 4 ready to accept water from the awaiting river. On into November the excitement built even with the upcoming national election.

The outcome of the election stunned Crowe, a staunch Republican, and many of the dam workers, who saw Hoover as their "engineer President." They were even more stunned to learn that the dethroned chief executive announced that he wanted to visit the Boulder (Hoover) Dam construction site. Arriving late on November 12 the serious-looking Hoover was led down to Tunnel No.2 by Frank Crowe. Although the tunnels were well lit, the president, his wife, and the official welcoming committee made up of Secretary of the Interior Wilbur, Chief

Engineer Ray Walter of the Bureau of Reclamation, Six Companies executive E.
O. Wattis and others, could see little of the overall progress in Black Canyon. A
small crowd gathered to hear Hoover emphasize, in a short unemotional talk, the
impact that Hoover Dam would have on development in the Southwest. Dressed
in his best suit and wrapped in a long drab brown overcoat, a sullen-looking Crowe
posed with the equally sullen Hoover and his party, appearing quite stiff and uncomfortable. Hoover thanked Crowe and Walker Young, wished them a successful conclusion to the project, and abruptly left the federal reservation headed for
Las Vegas and his awaiting train.[42]

Before leaving the dam site, Crowe checked the swing shift's efforts to
prepare for the river diversion, scheduled for the next day. If true to form, Crowe
disposed of his tightly fitted necktie as he inspected Tunnel No. 4 and discussed,
with foremen, their progress. Rushing home to Boulder City to grab a few hours
rest, Frank debriefed with Linnie, telling her all about Hoover's tour, then he tried,
unsuccessfully to sleep. Tomorrow would be another big day, the first day in
human history that the uncompromising power of one of America's most powerful
and important water sources would be diverted and contained. Linnie understood,
probably better than Frank did, that this was an important moment in history—not
just in engineering history, but also in American history. The eyes of the nation
would be watching as her husband gave the word to begin the diversion. She
knew that reporters, by the dozens—from all over the nation, were gathered to
record the turning of the Colorado River and that the results would be wired immediately coast-to-coast to a nation eagerly grasping for good news. She also
knew that her husband had now become America's best-known engineer; for many
he was becoming a symbol of hope, a leader in America's economic revitalization
effort. It must have been difficult for both of them to sleep.[43]

Up early the next day, Frank Crowe gulped down his breakfast, jumped
into his Buick sedan and sped down the gently winding paved road to the dam site.
When he arrived, you could already sense the high expectations from everyone on
duty. Hundreds of men scheduled to work the swing and graveyard shifts had
asked special permission to watch the dike-breaking diversion operation. Photographers jockeyed for, what they thought, would be good vantage points from which
to capture the historic moment. Crowe immediately drove down to Tunnel No. 4
and was greeted by Woody Williams and Floyd Hunnington, tunnel superintendents, who happily announced that everything looked good for an 11:30 am dike
blasting. Number 4 tunnel now fully concreted and sealed lay still, a giant 50-foot
orifice, waiting to swallow the Colorado River. With great anticipation, Crowe
allowed Williams to give the order to blast the temporary cofferdam, the fragile
dirt wall separating the frothing river from the tunnel. Then in a carefully orches-
trated automotive ballet, tough well-beaten dump trucks, driven by equally tough
weather-beaten drivers, carefully moved their loads of rock out across the temporary bridge located just below the tunnel portals. One by one, for hours these

heavy-laden vehicles moved in a continuous parade, dumping more and more fill across the length of the river. As the fill reached the top surface of the muddy Colorado, a white froth grew larger and larger, as if the river itself was becoming more and more angry in Man's attempt to harness nature. However, Man would win out and the Colorado finally turned, first into the No. 4 tunnel then later into tunnel No. 3. Tunnel worker Marion Allen recalled the event, "I watched with a great deal of interest. They started dumping rock all the way across the river and gradually raising the water level above the coffer dam." Gradually was right, for the mighty river would not surrender so easily. All through the evening and the early morning hours of the next day the dumping proceeded. Finally, around 7:00 am, the newly formed rock barriers proudly appeared above the defeated Colorado. In an attempt to flank the dike, river water moved quickly to the right where, within minutes, "Big Red" consumed the sidebar and fell unexpectedly into Tunnel No. 4's open jaws. First, reluctantly, then playfully, the conquered river accepted its fate, gliding down the smooth sleek concrete surface. Some people heard cheers, most were silent, as if they had just witnessed a great battle, and out of respect, quietly observed the vanquished foe die. Yet, if the river were dead, it would, within minutes be reborn, stronger than ever at the outlet portal downstream. Without any prompting hundreds of workers, Crowe and close associates included, moved quickly to observation sites downstream. Nobody seemed to notice, save for a lone cameramen continuing to film the entrance portal, two daredevil cofferdam workers, standing poles in hand, furiously flailing these "extended arms" at bits and pieces of debris, in an effort to keep the portal open.

If the moment of inrushing water into the giant tunnel was not enough, eyewitnesses claimed that seeing, for the first time, thousands of gallons of raw, semi-tamed river water explode from the mouth of the exit portal, was a never to be forgotten memory. From vantage points looking straight down on the Arizona side of the river, it was amazing. First, nothing, then a rumble, then a small leakage of water and finally a shotgun-like explosion of dark white water, spraying outward and rushing onward as if suddenly released from captivity. Seconds passed as the river expended its energy and the water settled down, returning to its ancient riverbed, eagerly consuming every inch of river bottom it could reach, triumphantly announcing that, at best, Man could only temporarily corral its irresistible power. As the minutes passed, spectators watched as the leading edge of water hurried southward to join the receding Colorado River and form its thousand mile unbroken link once again. Lee Cairns, a longtime Crowe associate was there that day and later he told Allen that all the planning paid off. Crowe was worried that the tunnels might not accept the always deceptive and ever dangerous full-flow of the Colorado River. Cairns who had worked with Crowe on diverting the Jackson Lake reservoir flow and many others, realized that here in Black Canyon, you could not afford to create a large channel "in the center [of the river] which was difficult to control."[44] All of the water needed to go through the diversion tunnels so that the narrow canyon could quickly and adequately be dewatered. Soon tunnel No. 3 was accepting water; the diversion was a success. Crowe had done it again.

Newspapers across the nation, including the *New York Times*, reported the event as the successful completion of the first phase of work; and so it was. However, Crowe knew that this was no time to relax. While he clearly had beaten the odds so far, the famous "Crowe luck" would need to hold, for challenges that were more formidable lay directly in his path. Fortunately, he continued to get the full backing of Walker Young and Charlie Shea. He needed to satisfy Young, for Young represented the Bureau of Reclamation and held the power to delay or even worse, stop work should serious violations of the plans, specifications or described procedures be breached. Shea represented Six Companies and the incessant inquests of its nosy executives. However, Crowe was in a commanding position. The work was moving ahead nicely, almost a year ahead of schedule. The one serious strike of August 1931 became a faded memory and any other organized labor opposition appeared remote. Even though dozens of fatalities had occurred in and around the dam site, Crowe had dodged serious government or public reprimand and Six Companies lawyers were successfully arguing away most class action suits brought against the fledgling profit-hungry conglomerate. 1932 was about to become history and for Frank Crowe it was a triumphant year to remember.

Chapter 11

"You know that what you build will stand for centuries."
Hoover Dam, 1933-1935

Not only did the nation celebrate the turning of the Colorado River as a historical landmark, but also engineers from all over the world acclaimed this feat as the opening of a new era in the construction of very large concrete dams. With Crowe about ready to begin the arduous task of placing 3,220,000 cubic yards of concrete, curious foreign engineers besieged the State Department with pleas to be allowed extended visits. It seemed that every part of the world sent visitors in 1933 and they wanted to see one man, Frank Crowe. Large, very large concrete dams, meant economic success for developing countries. Irrigation provided reliable crop yields, or at least obviated dependence on natural rainfall, and thus satisfied food demands of ever growing populations. Stored water in huge reservoirs provided people and industries with all their non-food needs such as drinking, washing, and cooling. Most importantly, the huge dams could produce cheap clean hydroelectric power, one key that helped unlock a country's bid for successful industrialization. And so they came; in 1933 Crowe met with engineers and statesmen from: Scotland, Japan, Canada, England, Switzerland, China, Mexico, India, Austria, Germany, Congo, South Africa, Italy and other countries. The Italians, Swiss, and Germans, of course would look to harness waters streaming out of the massive Alps mountain range, while the Canadians knew that their portion of the Rocky Mountains represented a vast untapped source of water and power.

Interestingly, the Japanese and Mexicans came the most often and stayed the longest. Mexico City, already besieged by a growing population and existing on diminishing water reserves sent Jose Favola, Director of Water for the Federal District of Mexico. Just before his arrival another Mexican engineer Dr. Chavez Drosco, head engineer of the Rodriguez Dam near Tijuana visited and was most interested in diversion techniques. Japanese engineers, like their Mexican counterparts understood that their country, which was mostly quite mountainous, offered irrigation and industrial potential. In fact, one of their top government engineers, Sadao Kasai, arrived from Tokyo on January 6 and remained a week. No sooner had he left, and then his associate T. Kago showed up wanting to see as

much as possible.[1]   The popularity of Crowe and Hoover Dam realized political
payoffs for those seeking election to public office. It seemed that every elected
official in the entire Southwest wanted to have his or her name tied to the dam.
Many persons accomplished this by visiting the dam and talking with Crowe, Young
and other Reclamation officials. In April a party of no less than sixty representatives from the Los Angeles Farm Bureau received permission to tour the dam site
and discuss the irrigation consequences for the Los Angeles basin. Fred Cox,
Chief Hydrographer for the Imperial Valley Irrigation District was terribly curious
and wanted assurances that the dam could handle anything that the dangerous
Colorado could offer up. Along the same lines, Los Angeles County flood control
expert, F. C. Eaton was on the scene in April asking the same kind of questions.
Frank Crowe's daughter, Patricia, recalled that as the job progressed into 1933 and
34 her father was called to talk with visiting engineers, politicians, and foreign
engineers and guests at an ever-increasing pace. Frank Crowe disliked all the
attention that a national spotlight requires. He was much more comfortable being
"down in the canyon with the stiffs."[2]

Artists, ex-governors, actors, golf and sports personalities were among
those official visitors logged in the records as touring Hoover Dam in 1933. J. B.
Van Nuys, from southern California came looking to see what the big dam could
do for Los Angeles. From the same location came water board members, architects, and many, many industrialists. Interestingly, W. M. Wright, an astronomer
from Lick Observatory near San Jose, California, was listed among those touring
the site in June. The industrialists, looked to see how their machines or products
were, or could be used in large-scale dam construction and operation. Of particular note were representatives from compressed air companies such as Ingersol-
Rand, cable and hoist firms, like Lidgerwood, and dozens of heavy duty truck,
machinery, electrical motor companies. It really did seem that this was the place
to be—the "cutting edge" of America's use of new industrial technology and techniques.

Elwood Mead, as Commissioner of the Bureau of Reclamation, and therefore, the man everyone looked to for official government answers about the construction of the mighty dam, became besieged with letters and telegrams requesting information. He knew too that the public, heretofore not accustomed to engineering and technical terms such as "muck," "cofferdam," and "drilling jumbo" in
their vocabulary, decided to put out an informative pamphlet describing the construction and eventual benefits of Hoover Dam. He quickly concluded that a simple
question and answer format would satisfy and cover most inquiries. The little
pamphlet, when finished, did a noteworthy job in summarizing the project. From
simple questions such as "What are the purposes of this project?" to more involved topics including "What will be the principal machinery installations?" Mead
answered in a straightforward, easy-to-follow narrative. In an effort to promote
the government's investment and commitment to Boulder City, he raised the ques-

One of Frank Crowe's 8-cubic yard buckets is shown here delivering concrete to the foundation. (USBR)

tion, "Will the town be permanent?" His answer confidently stated, "It will no doubt be permanent, because the 730-foot dam and 115-mile lake will be a great attraction for tourists." He went on to say, "There are also many scenic wonders close by to attract visitors, including three national parks—Grand Canyon, Zion, and Bryce Canyon." Almost as an afterthought, he added a note about future employment possibilities in the area, "A sizable force will also be required for operation of the reservoir and power plant."[3]

Ray Walter, Chief Engineer of the Bureau, conferred with Crowe and Young in an effort to update the engineering world on what had been accomplished in 1932 and what could be expected for 1933. Walter, almost as tall as Crowe and equally shy when it came to dealing with news reporters, penned an extensive work summary for the January issue of the *Western Construction News and Highway Builder*. His plans called for building the upper and lower cofferdams, excavation of the main dam and spillway areas, and preparation to erect Crowe's carefully planned aerial cableway system. He announced that veteran cable and hoist contractors, Lidgerwood Manufacturing Company, was now busy fabricating the intricate three-inch cables. To reveal the unprecedented size of the government's commitment to Hoover Dam, Walter revealed that 27 million dollars had been expended through 1932 and that another 21 million had been dedicated for the period January 1, 1933 through June 30, 1934. Declaring that this would not prove sufficient, he noted that Mead was recommending that outgoing Interior Secretary Wilbur ask Congress for an additional 8 million dollars.[4]

Six Companies executives and the entire Bureau of Reclamation waited through January to see whom President-elect Roosevelt would name as his new Interior Secretary. Knowing FDR's penchant for progressive reforms and willingness to spend government dollars in order to fight the Depression, most everybody figured that it would be a Western democrat with reform credentials. Word spread that two Western senators, Hiram Johnson of California and Bronson Cutting of New Mexico, considered the job then quickly said no. Roosevelt was pointed to an enthusiastic ex-Bull Moose Party progressive, Harold Ickes. A member of the bar practicing in Chicago, Ickes had the "New Deal" fervor necessary to be a part of Roosevelt's new "brain trust" but lacked Western irrigation experience. Neither Roosevelt nor Ickes appeared to let this hinder the appointment and Ickes, a quick learner, jumped into the position with a passion for extending government influence.[5]

Frank Crowe tried hard to not get embroiled in the politics of the situation. His job was to build the dam and as long as Ickes supported the project and kept the money flowing, he refrained from criticism. Besides, it was beginning to appear that Roosevelt's promise of massive government spending to relieve the nation's economic woes would be kept. This meant a new round of irrigation projects and dams to be built, and Crowe with his success so far at Hoover would be in a commanding position to head the most prestigious and challenging engineering jobs offered.

This was no time to slough or lay back on his laurels, quite the opposite Crowe, pushing his men harder, concentrated on erecting the upper and lower cofferdams. The unpredictable Colorado, now flowing through diversion tunnels Nos. 3 and 4, could at any time send a tidal wave of new water against the puny temporary dike protecting the drying dam site. The two cofferdams, in themselves large dams, required their own foundations. The upper cofferdam, with primary responsibility for handling anything that the Colorado River threw at it, needed to stand nearly 100 feet in height, an unbelievable 600 feet in width at its base, with a crest width of 60 feet. Never had a "temporary dam" of this size been attempted. The engineering of the cofferdam was not a difficult task, however, it was unusually large. Crowe, wanting no opportunities for flood damage, from an unexpected storm, spent day after day down in the riverbed looking for inefficiency and searching for ways to speed up the operation. Interestingly, Crowe decided to use 3,300 cubic yards of concrete to reinforce the upstream face of the upper cofferdam. This impermeable surface would guarantee little or no erosion of the earth and rock fill lying just inches underneath. All through February the frenzy continued, Crowe not content until the last yard of concrete on the cofferdam had been placed.[6]

In March and April, the focus shifted to the lower cofferdam. Sitting just upstream from the lower diversion tunnel portals, it would have to keep river water, once it exited the portals, from reentering the work area. Similar to its upstream counterpart, the lower dam did not have a concrete surface nor was it as large. With a base thickness of about 200 feet and the height just over 50 feet, this lower river obstruction stood completed in April. Crowe himself was impressed with the filling in procedure of the cofferdams. Using scores of trucks and an around-the-clock schedule it was amazing to watch the daily rise in these structures. Truckers picked up their earth-fill mixture some four miles upstream at a large pit, while rock came from muck blasted and picked, by high-scalers, high up on the canyon's steep sides.

Crowe and Young had planned the cofferdam construction carefully. They wanted both temporary dams completed before any possibility of an early spring flood, and true to form, Crowe's luck held. In fact, tunnels Nos. 3 and 4, now accepting the full flow of the low-water level of the Colorado, never "flowed more than one-quarter full at any time since diversion of the river." At the same time, tunnels Nos. 1 and 2 were completed and Crowe gave orders to remove the temporary upstream dikes protecting them. With this done, Crowe had all four tunnels to handle flash floods and the expected late spring and summer high river levels. Now, he could finally focus on the big dam itself.

The forward-looking engineer had moved ahead with excavation of the Arizona and Nevada spillways, themselves no small project. Averaging 650 feet in length, 150 feet in width and 120 feet in depth the spillways received their first concrete from the Hi-Mix plant in early March. They were designed to accept floodwaters from the Colorado River, laterally on both sides of the river and to prevent any water from going over the top of the proposed dam. Design engineers did not want uncontrollable water to fall such a great distance and so near the powerhouse. To this end, work progressed on holing out inclined tunnels from each spillway downward into the diversion tunnels and out into the Colorado River. At the same time, four cuts were made into the canyon walls 100 to 300 feet upstream from the dam for the intake towers. The towers looked quite impressive on design drawings and served the dual purpose of routing water to the diversion tunnels and guiding water into the awaiting powerhouse turbines. Stacked one behind the other, the intake towers would average 75 feet in diameter and stand an impressive 384 feet high, some 50 feet above the crest of the dam itself. A series of concrete bridges, large enough to drive utility trucks on, eventually would connect the towers to each other and the dam.[7]

      With the news of work on Hoover Dam appearing regularly in most major newspapers it was inevitable that a flood of curious sightseers would descend on the dam site. On March 24-25 alone, 5,463 visitors passed through the reservation gate. Stories had spread about the size and complexity of the project. Ex-President Herbert Hoover returned on May 2 to see the progress on the dam. He arrived with his wife and son, was greeted by Young and Crowe and given a daytime tour of the construction. Within days of his departure from the dam site, Interior Secretary Ickes, in an obvious political move, shamed the ex-chief executive by proclaiming that the project would henceforth be called Boulder Dam. July weekends saw over 1100 visitors to Lookout Point, a vista view parking lot where a panoramic scene spread out before visitors, who came from every state "in the Southwest, as well as many eastern states." Tourists arriving on the July 4th weekend were astonished to hear the news of a ten-year old recovered drilling bit from the Black Canyon river bottom. The bit, designed for cutting through rock strata, contained eight diamonds estimated to be worth $2,500. The four and one half inch long and two inch diameter drill bit was in remarkable condition despite the blast that uncovered the find. The piece, "at the time the bit was lost it was worth about $175 a carat, and there were 21.15 carats in all." Taken to Denver, under guard, the cutting diamonds were found to be "undamaged and will be usable" in other construction capacities.[8]

      Throughout Crowe's busy unrelenting tenure at Black Canyon, he continued to find time to write family members particularly his sister Catherine and his mother. In one letter, dated January 10 to Catherine, Crowe described a recent weekend trip to Death Valley stating that he wanted to "see the country 310 feet below the sea." When he discovered that Catherine's daughter, Marion, was sick in the hospital, he sent one hundred dollars to help cover the fees, then he added that he "wanted you to send me the doctors bills when you get them." In another letter to Catherine, her brother recapped his trips to Los Angeles to watch the University of Southern California football team play St. Mary's and Stanford. On several occasions, Crowe brought his daughters with him to these games. He commented that, "Stanford, at Palo Alto, Calif. is the greatest school in U. S."[9] Jokingly, the engineer hinted at a possible teaching position at Stanford. "I have arranged with Hoover, who is a trustee and Wilbur its president to give me a job teaching pile driving when I get to [sic] old to work." He went on to tell Catherine that, all joking aside, he thought the Palo Alto school was located in a "lovely spot." "Am enclosing a little Xmas check," he wrote at the conclusion of this December 8 letter. All during the job at Hoover Dam, Frank sent photos of the work site and construction progress to Catherine, as he did to many family members.

In an interesting letter to his mother, Emma, Frank wrote extensively about driving across the desert to Los Angeles where he witnessed his first earthquake. There to inspect a small dam near the growing megalopolis, Crowe described the quake, "It was a 'pip'. The old hotel shook most of the night and the big pillars are pretty well cracked up, but still standing." Having heard that the devastation was extensive in the Long Beach area, the curious engineer detoured to see the damage. "Long Beach is a wreck," he exclaimed. The March 10, 1933 earthquake, centered in Long Beach, resulted in 115 deaths. In the same letter, he told his mother that the "kiddies" were "doing fine" and that Linnie had played her first game of golf. In describing the experience he said, "Boulder City course is in pure sand, so not to [sic] good."[10]

In July of 1933 Crowe's transportation superintendent, C. P. Bedford, published an article reviewing the necessity and success of trucks in the Hoover Dam operation. With Boulder City miles from the dam site, Crowe and Bedford knew that a reliable transportation system needed to be in place twenty-four hours a day. They selected International Harvester A-6 trucks with 210-inch wheelbases. "These transports make three trips a day, carrying crews back and forth between Boulder City and Black Canyon, an average of 75,000 passenger round-trips per month," Bedford wrote. Crowe, wanting more efficiency, agreed to allow the transportation superintendent to experiment building a 150-man double-decker bus.

To show no favoritism between major auto builders, Crowe and Bedford selected Ford to supply its light duty trucks and pickups. Four Chevrolet sedans were purchased for use by the hospital and general office staff. Crowe reserved his personal car and three others for assistant superintendents from Buick.[11] The *Los Angeles Times* published two photographs of Crowe on October 22, 1933, standing alongside his new 1933 Buick. One of the photographs, sponsored by Howard Automobile Company, boasted the headlines, "Buick is the choice of Frank T. Crowe: General Superintendent, Six Companies, Inc., Builders of Boulder Dam." The following advertisement attempted to link Buick's traditional reputation for elegance and efficiency with Crowe's reputation:

> For 20 years Crowe has driven Buicks. His record for
> the Six Companies, Inc., in the Boulder Dam construction proves
> he is a master of efficiency. He demands that which will do the
> job best. That is why Buick is his steadfast motorcar choice.[12]

The above-mentioned advertisement tied with a full-length story authored by Lynn Rogers of the *Los Angeles Times*. "Wonders of Hoover Dam Work Luring Autoists, splendid highways aid motorists to make trip to gigantic project with ease," read the opening headlines. The impressive full-page article included awe-inspiring sketches by newspaper artist Charles C. Owens. A Crowe 8-cubic yard concrete bucket majestically dipping down into the blackened depths of the busy dam site was featured in the foreground and appeared to dwarf men and machines. One of the supplemental drawings revealed, "From the observation point high on the Nevada wall visitors have a sweeping view of the dam under construction nearly a thousand feet below." In a powerful tempting invitation the article suggested, "And it's yours for the drive over inviting highways leading straight from Los Angeles to a balcony seat with sweeping view directly above the gigantic performance. Never before on a major construction project have such considerable provisions been made for the motorist sight-seer," Rogers claimed. One trip to the dam site was not enough, as Rogers explained that the "spectacle changes hourly in an advance that has smashed all precedents in conception and execution." "Catch the spirit of this on-rushing triumph and you will go there again and again as thousands of others have," the article cajoled. With a typical flair for the dramatic the talented newspaper writer went on, "To have seen narrow Black Canyon before this titanic work began was to be stunned with m [M]an's presumptuous challenge. Nothing there then but the whirling, murky waters of the Colorado river rushing between towering walls without even a foothold for man. Today! The river has been throttled and pushed aside through long tunnels; double-track railroads, truck ways and huge equipment are in busy operation on the canyon walls while from the bed of the world's most defiant river is rising the largest construction ever undertaken by m [M]an," Rogers declared.

From a front row seat at the observation point, Rogers noted motorists visiting the dam could see that "Working in swarms in the giant forms the men appear like ants, so immense is the whole scale." In a reference to Frank Crowe, Rogers saw that "all is so efficiently carried on that it seems like one great machine with myriads of little cogs geared in." "With General Superintendent Frank T. Crowe's typical thoroughness, everything was in place with complete exactness," observed Rogers. The newspaper reporter quoted new record-breaking figures for placing concrete on a daily, weekly and monthly schedule. The cableway system obviously impressed Rogers as he devoted much of the extensive article to the cableway delivery system. In observing some of the first bucketfuls of concrete he said, "The first bucket swing [swung] out from the Nevada walls suspended from carriers that traveled on three-inch cables. It was lowered with a science and signal system that seemingly gives each bucket human eyes and intelligence."[13]

After the disastrously hot summers of 1931 and 1932 Crowe and transportation chief Bedford met with Ford Motor Co. officials and looked into the over-heating problems of the work trucks. Automotive engineers understood that the cooling requirements in Black Canyon required a super efficient radiator. They built a 4-blade fan and heavy-duty radiator for its pickups and cars used by Crowe. Early results proved to Ford officials that it would be worth their time and effort to market the new cooling system on vehicles sold "throughout the hotter portions of

The placement of concrete moved ahead quickly in 1933-34, as Crowe's cableway
delivery system worked effectively. (USBR)

the United States." All of the heavy machinery brought to the dam site was hauled
around on specially adapted flatbed trucks. Built by International Harvester and
Moreland these "dirt grinders" carried powder, steel, lumber, pipe, and monstrous
sections of the tunnel concrete forms. All of these trucks boasted a 4-wheel drive
capacity and "Continental 16-H motors." Later, in an effort to have them carry
more loads, the truck beds were deepened and reinforced. Bedford added heavy-
duty springs, allowing them to carry net payloads up to 50 tons. All truck drivers
needed to prove their merit before being offered a job. Once on board, each driver
developed a special attachment to his vehicle, not unlike pilots of military aircraft.
Not relying on auto mechanics for upkeep, truck drivers constantly checked the
maintenance status of tires, engine and transmission themselves. Some drivers
personalized their machines to the extent of christening them with romantic, optimistic names. Truck accidents occurred regularly around the dam site despite
strict precautions. The most dramatic truck crashes involved runaway vehicles or
machines that plunged from the ramparts of Black Canyon in a spectacular 1000-

foot dive. One such event occurred early in 1933 when the driver of a muck truck left his vehicle idling near the edge of the cliff. Within seconds, the "heavy machine" slid over the precipice near the Arizona spillway: "catapulting three times in mid-air." Shocked observers looked up at that heart-stopping moment and were "presented a grotesque and awesome spectacle to those who saw its wild descent." Crowe immediately fired the embarrassed driver.[14]

As Crowe prepared to begin concreting operations of the dam itself, The *Los Angeles Times* assigned more and more reporters to cover the preparations. Chapin Hall, one such reporter, upon arriving at the dam site, took note of the small-engraved monument erected honoring Herbert Hoover that said, "Here m [M] an builds his vision into rock that future generations may be blessed." Hall criticized Interior Secretary Harold Ickes's decision to rename the project from Hoover Dam to Boulder Dam explaining that the name Hoover Dam still remained popular. Upon meeting Frank Crowe, Chapin was immediately impressed and he decided to probe Crowe's feelings about the enormity of the job. "I asked him how he would prefer to have this gargantuan brain child presented," explained Chapin, "and he replied, 'as an enduring benefit to mankind.'" "This man Crowe is worth considering for a moment," remarked the inquiring reporter. "He has the physique of an Olympic gladiator, temperament of an artist, hand of a musician, judgment of a Solomon, patience of a Job, poise of a Chief Justice, and the sociability of an elk," observed Chapin. In the article he was, once again, compared to Goethals and the building of the Panama Canal. Asking Crowe to describe his engineering experience, the veteran dam builder modestly stated, "I've spent my life in a hole, but I love it." Chapin was given a complete tour of the dam site by Crowe's assistants and when one of them was asked by Chapin as to the reason for the success of the project so far, he replied, "It's Frank Crowe. He's one great guy, and there isn't a man on the job who wouldn't go to hell for him."[15]

With articles such as this Crowe hit his peak for national public and engineering attention. As the year closed out, even his alumni college, the University of Maine wanted to publicize the efforts and accomplishments of their former engineering student. Alumni Secretary, Charles Crossland, began trying to put together a comprehensive article on Crowe's past achievements and present challenges beginning in February of 1933. Interestingly, Crossland guessed correctly when he surmised that Crowe himself would not be interested in supplying biographical information saying, "I am frank to say I have not written Mr. Crowe concerning this, judging him to be one who would prefer not to be concerned with material of this kind." Writing to J. F. Reis, Crowe's executive assistant in 1933, Crossland explained, "You doubtless know that Mr. Crowe is an alumnus of the University. For some time it has been my desire to have a real story about him, for unquestionably in the field of engineering, he ranks as one of, if not our foremost alumnus" Then Crossland remembered Crowe's mentor, "Certainly together with F. E. Weymouth, in charge of construction of the Metropolitan Aqueduct, they

The cableway system was used to move more than just concrete. Here we see the cableway lowering a train car down to the powerhouse. (USBR)

would rank at the top."[16]

Warren "Dad" Bechtel, President of Six Companies, in July died suddenly while on a trip to the U.S.S.R. Shea, Morrison and other executives were shocked. Bechtel, an international figure in his own right, was "beloved and respected by thousands" and the man responsible for holding the business combination together. Friends, including Crowe, recalled his unfailing loyalty and his respect for everyone on the job—no matter their position. From the earliest days of his humble pick-and-shovel start in construction to his prominent railroad executive position, Bechtel was remembered by many: "No engineer ever had to go after Bechtel to do a good job." Crowe had personally come to love "Dad's" great sense of humor and enthusiasm for taking risks. With his passing, the hurriedly

gathered group of Six Companies executives selected E. O. Wattis as their new
president.[17]

On June 6, 1933, the first concrete for the dam lifted from the loading
cars via Crowe's impressive aerial delivery system, arched out over the abyss of
Black Canyon and gently lowered into an awaiting form. Not content with the
original exposed bedrock, Crowe had insisted that excavation continue another 60
feet. This additional cutting formed a u-shaped slot in the river bottom; it would
be from here that the majestic dam would grow. Now with everything in place,
full-scale concrete placing operations could begin. The Lomix concrete plant,
already in operation for other parts of the dam, geared up for full output. Ingeniously, a railroad flatbed car was customized with a back wall and five lateral
partitions. This created four 10-foot compartments, where each could hold a concrete bucket. The open edge of the flatbed car facing the canyon allowed for the
quick and easy hook up to a cable. The partition walls, thick enough for a man to
walk on, allowed workers to hook and unhook buckets quickly. With buckets in
place, the flatbed car moved through the concrete mixers where two of the four
alternate buckets were filled with freshly mixed concrete. From the mixing plant,
the train, consisting of one engine and one flatbed car, moved close to the dam.
Now workers spotted waiting empty buckets dangling from cableways into the
two empty compartments. They quickly disengaged the cable connectors and signaled the engine personnel to move the train until a loaded bucket of concrete was
immediately underneath the awaiting cableway connector. Once both buckets
were hoisted and away, engineers steered the train back to the Lomix plant where
the two empty buckets were now filled. This procedure, repeated like clockwork
24-hours a day became routine and predictable, yet would be the key to Crowe's
phenomenal success in completing the dam well ahead of schedule. Through the
summer of 1933, cableway crews perfected the handling, loading, and spotting of
the specially designed 8-cubic yard buckets. The "Old Man" had designed to
dump the full eight yards as quickly as possible or as workers remembered later,
"like crap from a goose." When full, the heavy buckets weighed in at 20 tons and
when it is considered that they traveled along the cableway at speeds of several
hundred feet per minute and dropped vertically hundreds of feet, it can be imagined that great care and precision was needed.

Each cableway called for a signalman at the loading and dumping point.
Connected by telephone, the cableway guiders learned to work closely in giving
commands and listening for directions. When nearing either destination, cooperation proved essential in order to avoid hitting men, machines or the canyon
wall. Few accidents occurred and their record is one that is still talked about today
by ex-dam workers of that period. Once lowered into position above the correct
form, two workers reached up and unhooked safety latches, and then they guided
the bucket into the exact position required. Next, a signal was sent to the cable
operator approving for a "drop." Within seconds, the cable operator responded,

releasing a tidal wave of concrete that literally splattered downward. Without hesitating, the operators jerked the buckets skyward and toward the rail side of the canyon, watching carefully to gauge the right amount of speed so as to pendulum swing the bucket to a spot directly over the awaiting flatbed car.[18]

By the close of 1933, Crowe and his hardy band of dam builders looked back over an unprecedented construction achievement. Excavations were finished in the spillway channels, intake towers, dam foundation, abutments, Arizona canyon-wall outlet works, and the tunnels in the penstock and outlet systems and the adits to the tunnel plugs. All four diversion tunnels stood concreted. Both the upstream and downstream cofferdams provided full protection from nasty surprise floods. Thousands of cubic yards of concrete had been placed in the dam proper and it began to rise quickly. Men put the finishing touches on the Himix concrete mixing plant. This plant would come into use once the dam reached a certain height, forcing closure of the Lomix plant. All five 25-ton cableways, operated around-the-clock to set a new concrete placing record. The system assured instant delivery and pickup access to every portion of the dam, powerhouse, and towers. Also completed in record time were the spillway channels on the Nevada and Arizona sides, and work was underway on the incline tunnels to link each spillway with a diversion tunnel. Total count revealed that over 900,000 cubic yards of concrete had been placed in the dam, and the average top elevation at the end of the year was 720 feet or 214 feet above the low point at elevation 506 feet. A recap of weather conditions helped to explain some of the tremendous success that Crowe had in accomplishing these goals. No river floods of importance occurred in 1933. The most water came through on June 7, when an estimated 79,000 cubic feet per second of Colorado River water poured through the diversion tunnels. The lowest amount, a minuscule 2,900 c.f.s, was measured on January 7. Temperatures too, posed little trouble. While the hottest day, August 12, registered a blistering 125 degrees, daily fluctuations moderated well below that figure.[19]

As 1934 opened with low temperatures, excitement ran high among Six Companies officials. The leadership team, Crowe and his foremen, and the thousands of laborers, had moved construction well ahead of schedule. By now, the entire operation moved in a synchronous motion of well-understood and perfected job sequences. While every possible contingency had been considered, no one, Crowe included, could foresee the actual difficulties of construction without first getting into the work. Crowe incorrectly believed that he could keep a constant pulse on all aspects of the work. Yet, unlike all other jobs he commanded, Hoover Dam was too big for any one man. More and more he relied on his workers to carry out the orders of his foremen, and he relied on his foreman to follow the directions given them by the assistant superintendents, like "Woody" Williams. Crowe's long-standing policy was to keep his job superintendents and assistant superintendents informed about concerns and upcoming changes. In addition to calling regular weekly meetings, he constantly visited each job location and discussed progress. He let it be known to all assistant superintendents that he would check with foremen and workers whenever he wanted, not as a check on the level of competency of his team leaders, but because he wanted to get their opinion of day-to-day challenges. In this way, Crowe sought out alternative methods to get the work done more efficiently. However, there was more to it. He enjoyed nothing more than talking with the "construction stiffs," finding out where they had come from, how long they had worked in dam building and where those dams were. As he did earlier in the work, Crowe refused to be put on a schedule. He rarely announced exactly when and where he would be on the job site each day, save for scheduled meetings.

Charlie Shea, like Crowe, could not stay away from the canyon, the men, or the work. The noxious smell of burning rubber on over laden, muck-filled trucks along with the incessant clattering of jackhammers and air-compressed drills drew Shea to the job-site like ants to a picnic. Crowe and Shea often met at various times during the week, some scheduled, other times they were just drawn by a second sense to the same site location. Workers would look up form their work and see Crowe and Shea pointing and discussing some aspect of the work. When not convinced they had enough information about their discussion, it was not uncommon for Crowe and Shea to wade into the work area and start a conversation with the workers. Neither Crowe nor Shea in any way, forgot their humble construction beginnings, and through their reputations as tough taskmasters, they showed respect for all men under their leadership.

While not on the job site as Frank Crowe and Charlie Shea were, Henry Kaiser played an important role in the successful completion of Hoover Dam. Kaiser knew the rock aggregate business well. He conceived a plan for effectively handling the aggregates that worked so efficiently that Crowe remarked, "We never lost one hour on account of not having materials." With the start of concrete placement, Kaiser kept a close watch on the aggregate supply and his diligence helped Frank Crowe keep up the 24-hour everyday concrete placing schedule.[20]

On February 3, 1934, E. O. Wattis, President of Six Companies, suffered a heart attack in his home in Ogden, Utah and died. A hastily called meeting on February 13 elected Crowe's benefactor, Harry Morrison as the new president. Morrison had been serving as first vice-president. The executive change did not affect work on Hoover Dam, as Crowe concentrated on keeping the fast-paced concrete placing moving. Morrison, already completely confident of Crowe's ability, involved himself little in the day-to-day construction concerns, relying on Shea to keep him informed. Just a few days after the Wattis announcement, Crowe was informed that a worker had died in one of the concrete forms. Kenneth Walden was crushed while tripping the safety catch on the 8-yard concrete bucket. He had performed this task, uncountable times, but on this occasion, he did not attempt to move back after engaging the release lever on the bucket. Pushed hard against the solid reinforced concrete form by the bucket, Walden died within minutes. The young man had come out from Branson, Missouri, late in 1933 to earn a stake.[21]

Crowe barely had time to recover from losses mentioned above when news came from Los Angeles that his mother-in-law, Fanny Korts had passed away. Linnie and Frank knew that Fanny's medical condition had not been good in recent years, and for the past six weeks she had been in and out of hospitals, but there was no indication that anything serious was going on until only a few days before her death. Linnie spent the last days comforting her mother and was with her when she died.[22]

January and February, traditionally low production periods in heavy construction, set new high concrete placing records at Hoover Dam. Between the dam and powerhouse footings, Crowe's hard-working stiffs moved 186, 598 cubic yards of concrete. When calculating all concrete in and around the dam site, they hit 205,612 cubic yards. Crowe watched the process closely, looking for the slightest bit of inefficiency. After spending time at the gravel plant in early January, the plant ended the month with an exceptionally high total of 248, 547 cubic yards of excavated and sifted gravel. Wanting plenty of reserve supplies, to keep concrete mixing moving ahead, Crowe finally was satisfied when the aggregate plant cranked out 416,580 cubic yards of finished aggregate. Frank Crowe, never one to rest on his laurels, worked even more diligently in February to increase concrete output and placement. He spent long hours this month, in bitter cold, talking to and working with swing and graveyard shifts, to encourage higher efficiency. The plan worked, and at the end of the month, another new record was recorded. Dam and powerhouse concrete placement increased by 8,000 cubic yards, as did the overall total for other concrete jobs. Crowe did not hold back from hiring additional men, if he needed them. In February, government records reported 4,398 persons on payroll accounts and while this figure represented the highest ever, it would soon be overshot within a few months.

Approximately 500 men of the total working were not under Crowe's direct command. These workers labored for Babcock & Wilcox, contractors for the production and installation of the water diversion headers and penstocks. Under the able leadership of R. S. Campbell, project manager, the company worked closely with Crowe and government supervising engineer, Walker Young, in planning and constructing the huge steel regulatory devices. At the base of Crowe's dramatically placed intake towers, Campbell located two 30-foot diameter conduit connectors. From here, the huge cylindrical pre-fabricated tubing extended over a thousand feet, along the way 13-foot diameter penstocks branched off and ran downhill to the power plant generators. Then the conduit narrowed to 25 feet and ran downstream to the canyon wall outlets or to tunnel plug outlets. This complete water-regulating system comprised over 14,500 feet of headers and penstocks, of course, another mark for the record books.

During normal river levels, water would flow through the intake towers,

256 America's Master Dam Builder

careen down the 30-foot headers and be diverted through the lateral penstocks to the power turbines. Excess water could be sent on down the system and released dramatically through the canyon wall outlets where the squirting jet stream of turbulence would fall helplessly back into the river, or water would be channeled, less dramatically to the tunnel plug outlets. During floods, water cascading down both spillways would be safely funneled through the 50-foot spillway tunnels (used as diversion tunnels during construction) already concreted and in place. To first-time visitors, the whole water regulatory system appeared complex, a web of connecting tubes, penstocks, and conduits. Each of the main 30-foot headers was designed to accommodate a maximum of 33,500 cubic feet per second of rushing water that reached speeds close to 175 feet per second. The steel-fabricated penstocks required that the highest production standards be met and exceeded.[23]

The Babcock & Wilcox combine had successfully won the bid to build the penstocks, with a $10,908,000 commitment. Under the government contract, they had 1975 days in which to fabricate and install the 4700 feet of 30-foot headers, 1900 feet of 25-foot headers, 5600 feet of 13-foot penstocks, and 2300 feet of 8.5-foot outlet conduits. Realizing from the get-go that constructing the giant headers at their home plant in Gary, Indiana, and shipping them out to Nevada was impossible, the company set up a fabrication plant near the dam site. This location, named Bechtel, in honor of the Six Companies executive who pioneered new methods in steel production, was only a short distance from Boulder City and the dam site. Here a gigantic steel fabrication shop sprang up. Measuring 500 feet long and 85 feet wide the plant housed a variety of massive, especially designed tools and machines, to handle and form the thousands of varying thickness sheet metal plates arriving from the Gary, Indiana plant. One of the most impressive devices, a 40-foot long planer used pneumatically-operated plunger clamps to hold the sheet plate firmly while the edges of the plate are beveled to exacting specifications. Large vertical rollers, powered by a 150 horsepower motor imposed 1750 tons of pressure on the feeding plate, curving the metal quickly to the desired radius. Again, another record was set, as these rollers were the most powerful yet built. In addition, two powerful presses and a horizontal boring machine helped finish the production of each conduit. An assembly line procedure was used with impressive overhead cranes, each able to lift over 75 tons, and place the load down gently and precisely.

The critical area of concern in the production of the headers and penstocks was the ability of the finished tubing to resist water pressure. To this end, Babcock & Wilcox utilized new technology in the fusion-welding process to assure a quality product. They reported that their new technique could produce welded seams and joints that could withstand 1250 pounds per square inch, providing a wide margin of safety. For quality control, engineers used the latest in x-ray technology to inspect every inch of completed seams and joints. The two x-ray machines operated at a capacity of 300,000 volts. As exposures were taken, the film was immediately developed and checked. If defects were located repair crews cut out the section and re-welded the piece. The joint was then annealed to help relieve metallic stress[24]

Well before construction began on Hoover Dam, J. L. Savage, Chief Designing Engineer, at the Bureau of Reclamation, and his team of planners understood that unique problems needed to be solved on a dam of this size. The sheer mass of concrete required a consideration for the stresses placed on it when drying. Portland cement, at that time, composed of a variety of chemicals including carbonates, silicates, and oxides, underwent a severe chemical change when water was added. Hydration caused a crystallizing effect linking the cement mixture to the aggregates, but in so doing, released a tremendous amount of heat. The heat, if not dissipated quickly, raises the temperature of the drying concrete to dangerous levels. Small masses of concrete emit the heat, through radiation directly into the air, causing little or no internal structural stress. Reinforcing steel can be added throughout a concrete structure, which then serves to absorb much of the heat. This is called internal absorption and works well for small to medium sized concrete pours. The Reclamation Service, early in its history, learned to use reinforcing steel and to grout surface cracks. The problem is that one could never be sure if the developing cracks posed a danger to the structural integrity of the dam. If you grouted before the structure had cooled sufficiently, the grouting itself would crack, further weakening the dam. In the case of Hoover Dam, concrete engineers estimated a drying period of 125 years before post-concrete grouting could take place. On top of this, engineers were nervous that a dam of this size might produce heat effects that jeopardized the safety of the structure, and for this reason plans were put forward to artificially cool the setting concrete.

After looking at several possible solutions, Bureau engineers decided to adopt a two-pronged approach to cooling. First, the dam would be poured as a series of independent blocks set in tiers rising alternately so as to afford each block a maximum amount of exposure to air before another block was placed alongside. Second, a unique system of pre-cooling and refrigerated cooling pipes would be installed to immediately dissipate accumulating heat. If cooled properly, finished grouting could take place within a relatively short time after the placing of the concrete. Bureau of Reclamation engineers spent hundreds of hours calculating mathematically and testing concrete samples. It was found that a 40-degree temperature rise could be expected and that the quantity of heat to be taken out equaled "965 Btu's (British Thermal Units) per cubic yard of concrete for each degree that it was to be cooled." Thus, to lower the temperature the required 40-degrees, a total of 38,600 Btu's needed to be extracted per cubic yard.[25]

Frank Crowe must have gasped when he saw the plans for the miles of cooling pipe that needed to be installed in Hoover Dam. Never before had such an immense network of interlaced tubing been attempted. Never before was the contractor required to build a massive refrigeration plant to cool the circulated water.

Working with A. J. Ayers, chief engineer, and pipe foreman, A. L. Reed, Crowe implemented a procedure to lay the pipe as each concrete block was placed. Changing the original plan of using two inch piping at ten-foot intervals, the Bureau switched to one-inch pipe at five-foot intervals, spaced hexagonally. Calculations revealed a staggering 3,500,000 feet, or 662 miles of cooling pipe would be needed.

The refrigeration plant, built downstream a few hundred yards on the Nevada side of the canyon, sat near the same elevation as the railroad tracks hugging the Nevada side at elevation 720 feet. Bureau specifications originally calling for a water delivery rate of 2,100 gallons per minute (g.p.m.) were changed to demand an additional 900 gallons g.p.m. The idea was to send pre-cooled Colorado River water through the dam first to slowly bring the temperature down. Then refrigerated water would be delivered to bring the temperature down to a desired low level. Interestingly, the Bureau asked Crowe to cool the concrete through a range that extended from 45 degrees on the upstream face to 65 degrees on the downstream face. Engineers devised a plan to use an ammonia compression system, similar to the one used, at that time, to make ice. Pressurizing the ammonia can cause the ammonia to boil or evaporate at a desired temperature and "to obtain any cooling effect wanted within the limits of its thermal characteristics." By changing the vaporous state, large amounts of residual heat is absorbed. Water could then be circulated through this system at a reduced speed, allowing the water to cool to the required 40 degrees. Interestingly, Crowe, always looking to get the most out of his equipment, cleverly planned to use the four heavy Ingersol-Rand air-compression machines, used for operating the rock drills in the early stages of excavation, in the cooling plant. As it turned out, the gigantic air-compressors worked as expected, affording a high reliability rating. Crowe needed to worry about this phase of the operation, for any mechanical problems in the cooling plant would force costly delays in placing more concrete.

In all, more than ten large Cameron pumps worked around the clock to pump pre-cooled and refrigerated water through the freshly laid concrete blocks. A series of main lines and header pipes ran from the cooling plant to access corridors throughout the dam, branching out from there to the myriad of staggered one inch delivery tubes. Simple, yet intricate is the best way to describe the cooling system and for all its complexity of layout, the Bureau found that it more than did the job it was designed to do. Young's Bureau engineers placed measuring thermocouples at strategic locations as the concreting continued and they spent much time in checking the readings to assure proper cooling parameters. Should cooling progress too quickly in any section of the dam; the refrigerated water could be cutoff in a particular tubing loop until the temperature moderated. Bureau engineers worked feverishly with the first layers of concrete to gauge how the cooling process would work in actual practice on a concrete mass of such size and they quickly determined that an average flow rate of four g.p.m. provided the requisite cooling results. When temperatures hit normal in a particular level of the dam, the water was shut off to that loop. As one observer noted, "This operation of grouting and cooling makes the mass of the dam in each grouting lift a unified body of concrete with all temperature strains positively accounted for."[26]

Crowe spent many hours in and around the concrete blocks as the routine of setting up forms, installing and welding cooling pipes, concrete placing and tamping, and implanting of measuring devices moved inexorably forward. He was nervous that cooling pipe might be crushed, thus cutting off circulation to an entire loop, or he worried about a faulty welding job—just one small mistake and a major job delay could result. Crowe also wanted Hoover Dam to be the best built, and most stable structure in the history of American dam building. A lot was at stake besides his rising reputation. Should another disaster, such as the highly publicized collapse of St. Francis Dam in 1928 occur, the very future of dam building by state water groups and the Bureau would be called into question.

In March of 1934 Ayers had completed a short biographical article for the University of Maine, as per Charles Crossland's request. Entitled, "Francis T. Crowe, '05 Master Builder of Dams," the article reminisced about Crowe's Maine roots. Reminding everyone of Crowe's association with the university the article began "The 1904 'Gossip Editor' of the Maine 'Campus' [university newspaper] is now writing engineering history with master strokes across the deep abyss that is Black Canyon, in the Colorado River. There, as Superintendent for Six Companies, Inc., he is building a dam which far overshadows all similar previous engineering feats and which taxes the imagination of both engineer and spinner of yarns," Ayers wrote. Ayers, after consulting his boss, explained to the Maine readers that Crowe owed a great debt to Harold Boardman for he taught Crowe to enthusiastically embrace civil engineering as a interesting and creative field of study. Ayers quoted Crowe as saying, "Whatever I've been able to accomplish since I was handed my diploma, I attribute more than any other factor, to the inspiration supplied by my contacts with Professor Boardman." Crowe went on to claim, that it was Boardman, who allowed him to take advantage of Weymouth's early employment offer at the Lower Yellowstone Project.

In reviewing the phenomenal success in starting the Boulder project in the middle of a desert, Ayers commented, "A barren sand-blown rock-strewn desert, no water within twenty miles except the muddy river, a new railroad not entirely finished, and a make-shift highway for contact with town and the 'main line' were no assets for a fast start." Ayers added, "that it was a worth while venture at the award of contract, he had a fifty-man camp up in one day, a four-hundred-man camp going in two weeks, and had spent two hundred thousand dollars and gained two months' time before the ink was hardly dry on the signed contract." The article reviewed how Crowe had in eight months "licked the job," by overcoming the engineering obstacles and averting a long strike. On a more personal level, Ayers revealed that Frank Crowe "always believed in boys and young men, given them jobs and responsibility, found deep satisfaction in their development, occa-

sional disappointment in a failure, and built up an organization ranging from men
of twenty-five years' experience behind his driving lead to school boys getting
their first taste of hitting the ball." In a statement that clearly showed the loyalty
of the vast majority of workers to Crowe, Ayers proudly announced that each
member of Crowe's construction army "one and all of whom follow him because
they know he believes in them and would bank his last dollar on their coming
through." "In his business associates Crowe inspires confidence, because he believes he can do a thing, and then proceeds to do it," Ayers explained.

Crossland, who prepared the article for publication, was a bit disappointed
with Ayers for not giving more personal and professional background on the now
famous alumni. However, Crossland surmised that Frank Crowe did not want to
"toot his own horn," and so Crossland pulled selected quotes from the extensive
Los Angeles Times article of October 22, 1933. The article ended with Ayers stating that you could always "have his ear" [Crowe] when any of his crew were in
trouble. "Hard boiled in nearly everything, the only things which really get under
his [Crowe's] skin are the loss or serious injury of one of his men, or a failure of
one in whom he has placed confidence." Ayers admitted.[27]

Meanwhile, Frank Crowe, remained fixed on setting new records for concrete placing. March would be the month to do it. He worked closely with Shea,
and "Woody Williams," now reassigned from the tunnels, to help oversee the concrete placement. On March 17, with only 455 men employed in the actual work,
crews placed 9,264 cubic yards of concrete. The feat was surpassed three days
later when 458 men registered an incredible 10,401 cubic yards of concrete placed
in and around the dam. The three shifts were in a high-spirited mood of professional competition. Even though the work levels rose to new standards there were
no reported increases in injuries, as word spread that safety rules were still in
effect. Walker Young's Bureau inspectors worked double time to keep up with the
renewed quickened pace. With the weather about as comfortable as it gets, Crowe
felt that now was the time to "let the men go." Photographs caught a happy Crowe
standing, arms folded and smiling, while a shabbily dressed Shea stood alongside,
puffing heavily on a cigar and nodding approvingly.[28]

Both Crowe and Shea reeled when told of the news on April 20 that a
major accident involving a dozen men almost ended in a complete tragedy. Standing casually on the cableway-lifting skip (platform) George Tinker and the others
felt a sudden jerk, the skip fell instantly. The safety catch quickly engaged, abruptly
jerking the men upward after a fall of forty feet. Hurriedly, the skip was brought
down and workers rushed in to retrieve the shaken men. Six were seriously injured with spinal and neck problems, broken bones, and multiple bruises. Miraculously, three of the skip riders walked away with no apparent side effects. Later, it
was determined that the lifting clutch "started jerking and slipping, dropping several feet at a time." Had the safety catch not engaged, none would have survived.
Crowe was furious over this incident. He remembered the well-publicized skip

accident from January 1, 1933, and how it had provided more fodder for those accusing Six Companies, and therefore him, with negligence and carelessness. In this earlier accident, a high-rise fast moving skip loaded with 45 men "crashed into the cliffs on the Arizona side, piling the men in a heap." Twenty-five workers were injured, and amazingly there were no deaths. Later it was determined that "all the men [controlling the skip] were experienced and fully competent, but it is admitted that something went awry." A local newspaper reported that five of the victims of the January accident decided to quit their jobs due to the dangerous method of crossing the canyon and that "the morale of all [is] severely shaken."[29]

Work continued at high production rates throughout the spring and into the summer. Crowe's driving demands placed a burden on the Babcock & Wilcox project manager and his staff, as they needed to complete the installation of conduits, headers, and penstocks along with Crowe's construction. In May, the pipe fabricating and installing crews finished the 8.5-foot diameter pipes in the Arizona outlet tunnels and made good progress elsewhere. Meanwhile, Crowe hired more men and continued to place concrete blocks at a fast pace. Visitors coming every couple of weeks would see a noticeable change in the level of the dam and spillways. On May 26, Bureau engineers announced that it was safe to begin grouting the dam contraction joints. This was a major relief for Crowe, for now it was proven that the cooling pipes were doing their job. Over at the intake towers, Crowe ordered the upper and lower gates for the intake towers installed on both the Arizona and Nevada sides. The spillways too were given their gates in June and on the 6th of that month, Crowe watched as the second millionth cubic yard of concrete was placed. Records were being smashed everywhere. On June 10, Crowe worried when he was told that the project's electrical power had been cut. Frantically, calling Young he wanted to know what was going on. Later it was determined that a group of hunters near Victorville, California, using high powered rifles, shot out a number of high voltage insulators on the California to Nevada transmission line causing the interruption. Crowe kept track nervously as four hours and twenty-two minutes elapsed before power was restored.

Up and running again and with good progress assured Crowe, with Six Companies approval, granted a two-day Independence Day holiday. This allowed workers and their families to travel to southern California and other locations for the brief sojourn. Bureau Commissioner Mead arrived during this time to inspect the dam site and to confer with Young and Crowe. Work resumed on July 6. On July 20, 1934, with good weather and all phases of the operation in full swing, the employment peak of 5,251 persons was reached. This included government and contractor's payrolls. Never before in the annals of American irrigation construction had a single project within the United States involved so many workers. The mass of humanity and machines called for a strict vigilance on the part of Crowe's management team. Frequent performance and safety meetings occurred, and often, Crowe led the discussions in all three-shift meetings, requiring him to be alert and attentive for long hours. Temperatures climbed ominously during July and once again Crowe and staff worried about the safety of their men and impacts the heat would have on production. On July 27, the thermometer hit 125 degrees in Black Canyon, but work continued. Equipped with plenty of cool drinking water and other precautions the disaster of 1931 was not repeated.[30]

If handling the Hoover Dam job was not enough, Crowe and Six Companies, looking into the future, began bidding on a new round of Bureau dams. From the earliest planning, irrigation engineers at the Bureau of Reclamation understood the fact that an after bay, formed by a smaller dam, would be needed downstream from powerful Hoover Dam. This new structure, named Parker Dam for a nearby town in Arizona, would be 155 miles downstream and closer to Los Angeles and San Diego. From here, with fully regulated water released from Hoover Dam, an enormous aqueduct could be built to send a reliable water supply to southern California. The Metropolitan Water District, centered in Los Angeles, raised the necessary funds to build Parker Dam in conjunction with the Bureau of Reclamation. News of the thirteen million dollar project became public in the middle of 1934. Frank Crowe and Six Companies planned to bid for Parker Dam as soon as it came up for consideration. They correctly reasoned that they would have the requisite men and machines already in the area and thus have an advantage over bidding competitors.

Despite the relatively small size of Parker, Crowe was enthralled with the Bureau's design feature, calling for an unprecedented deep foundation. Planners at the Bureau, concerned about possible flooding from the Bill Williams River placed the dam at a point just below the confluence of the Colorado River and the Bill Williams River. They discovered that the V-shape of the Colorado's channel here contained unusually deep deposits of silt and sand, thereby requiring a 200-foot plus excavation operation. Usually, the foundation depth of excavations is 100 feet or less. Even the excavation for Hoover Dam involved digging down less than 200 feet. Looking at the specifications, the observant Crowe realized that here would be another project for the record books, another dam that would require diversion tunnels, upper and lower cofferdams, and cableways. The dam, on paper, was designed to be a constant-arch radius of 315 feet, rise to a maximum of 320 feet from lowest foundation to crest top and run 800 feet from the California riverbank to the Arizona side. Parker would have an overflow spillway with five 50 x 50-foot control gates.

All through June of 1934, Crowe and Shea spent long hours going over the Bureau's specifications for construction. Crowe wanted this dam almost as much as Hoover Dam and he convinced the Six Companies executives to go along with his extremely low bid of $4,239, 834. The Bureau opened four bids on July 26, 1934, and it was found that Crowe had "left a million dollars on the table," for the next nearest competitor, Southwestern Construction Group, Inc. of Los Angeles offered to do the job for $5,496,073. Of course, the Bureau of Reclamation was elated over the low bid, but Crowe needed to do some fast-talking to cool the Six Companies' chiefs, who saw profits flying out the window. The question became, "Can we trust Crowe's figures and calculations?" Talk spread about forfeiting the posting bond and abandoning the project, and rumors spread among the workers at Hoover Dam that "The Old Man had really slipped."[31]

Crowe could not worry about the off-again, on-again attitude of his superiors toward tackling Parker Dam, for he had plenty of concerns on Hoover to deal with. One major ongoing problem was his cement. Someone unaccustomed to concrete work might not realize the importance that bulk cement, and its handling, would play in the success of constructing a major dam. For Hoover Dam, Crowe expected to use five million barrels of cement, with daily usage hitting over 10,000 barrels. The Bureau of Reclamation had the responsibility of purchasing and delivering the required amount of cement and they purchased the large quantities from four manufacturers in southern California and from one mill in Utah. After months of testing and debates, Bureau engineers decided to order a combination of low-heat and moderate-heat type cements. Six Companies, Inc., had the responsibility of building and operating the cement plant. Here the bulk cement arriving from the different manufacturers could be mixed in desired proportion to achieve "a product of uniform workability, color, strength, and heat-generating properties." Crowe decided to locate the important cement plant near the Himix concrete mixing plant, where through a system of "pumping" workers could move the cement directly into the mixing plant operation. This would eliminate "all possible re-handling of cement." Through another pumping system, the precious powder could be sent to the Lomix concrete mixing plant. From the beginning of concreting in February of 1932 through to the end of the job, the cement plant operated without flaw.[32]

Crowe's legendary luck continued to hold through the summer of 1934. Even the Colorado River helped, passing a pitiful 1,700 cubic feet of water per second through the No. 1 diversion tunnel. This was an all-time record low. The timing was perfect for with the dam rising substantially, he ordered the gradual destruction of the lower cofferdam. He and Six Companies officials agreed to grant a two-day Labor Day holiday in early September. On September 17, a film crew from RKO Studios in Hollywood arrived to make "photographic sequences on the project for the film 'The Silver Streak.'"[33] Crowe worked hard to avoid being caught on camera. On occasions like this, he did not complain to Walker Young about such distractions, probably because he knew that Interior Secretary Ickes wanted all the positive publicity he could get from the project and because public support was still needed to guarantee funding to finish the project.

As the warm weather moderated in the fall of 1934, and word spread that the big dam was raising quickly, visitors continued to pour into the area. Sometimes Lookout Point was jammed with so many people and cars that Reservation police had to regulate traffic flow. Special requests for dam site meetings by various fraternal and professional organizations continued to be approved. On October 20, about 3,000 Shriners held a "ceremonial" at the site of the upper cofferdam. On November 10, an unusually large number of people came to see the dam. Deputies counted 5,794 persons driving in 1,489 cars admitted to the Black Canyon site. Diverse groups wanted tours of the site. Politicians and educators had already established a track record of attending on a regular basis, but in 1934 large numbers of others wrote letters to Young and Crowe, asking for official guest passes and accompanied tours. One group, not well noticed before at the dam, included military personnel. The Navy, oddly enough, appeared quite interested in this rising desert miracle. Listed on the government roll sheets were Admiral David Sellers, in command of the Pacific Fleet and Captain A. Staton, in command of the soon to be ill-fated battleship *Nevada*, among other admirals, and officers. A flight of scout planes from the *U.S.S Saratoga* flew into the Boulder City airport and Lieutenant R. S. Taylor, officer in charge was given a tour along with the other fliers. On another occasion, seven planes from the U. S. Navy Reserves flew in and remained for a couple of days. Foreign visitors also increased, with many top government engineers appearing from France, India, England, Hungary, Japan, Turkey, Canada, China, Syria, Mexico, Holland, Belgium, Italy, and New Zealand.[34]

One Japanese engineer Tokuhei Kuga, considered to be one of his country's top authorities on irrigation methods, returned to Japan after spending "considerable time" at Hoover Dam talking to Frank Crowe. Fresh from his American study tour, Kuga immediately became chief engineer, for construction of Otomari Dam, located near Hiroshima. As construction progressed on Otomari Dam, Kuga proudly sent pictures to the engineers at Hoover Dam. The 220-foot dam was designed as a curved arch dam that looked similar in design to Hoover Dam. The Japanese wrote that the concrete was "being poured from each side of the canyon...instead of from 'up above,' the method used in the building of Boulder Dam." With little wood in Japan, Kuga reported that he constructed the concrete forms from bamboo.[35]

November realized the first Bureau of Reclamation fatality when a swinging 8-cubic yard bucket crushed Kenneth Rankin, a concrete inspector. The details of the incident, as reported in the Las Vegas newspaper, left the reader wondering how such as accident could have happened. After all, the procedure for lifting and delivering the concrete buckets was well known to everyone operating in the area and Rankin had been on the job since the earliest days in March of 1931. The 33-year old government worker, an eight year veteran of dam work, did not have a record of careless behavior, on the contrary, Walker Young, his boss, had nothing but respect for the young inspector. Rankin's brother, also working on the dam, personally accompanied the body back to Kenneth Rankin's hometown, Ellensburg, Washington.[36]

The contractor's mess hall filled to capacity for each meal during this

Crowe (second from left) watches as the final concrete is placed in 1935. (USBR)

year as a harried cooking staff scurried about in an attempt to feed 1,120 hungry workers at a sitting. One observer visiting the mess hall in 1934 noted, "Wholesome and substantial meals are served, and I have been told that frequently at breakfast 7,500 eggs and 12,000 pancakes are prepared in eighteen minutes. The contractors' men are a hardy and fine looking lot, who work hard and have good appetites," he added. The visitor, while touring Boulder City wrote, "the town was laid out for a population of 4,000 or 5,000 people and is well occupied at this time." New buildings were continuing to go up in a boomtown-building spree. By this time, the town boasted churches, department stores, a theater and a variety of small businesses.[37]

With the end of the year approaching and the dam rising, Crowe shut down the Lomix concrete plant permanently as the three-millionth cubic yard of concrete was placed into the dam. A disastrous fire in late December shut down the office building of the Babcock & Wilcox Company, while at the same time Crowe, well ahead of schedule, suspended most construction activity for a two-day observance of the Christmas holiday. He was delighted to receive a visit from Weymouth and another former boss, D. C. Paul. Both engineers had worked with Crowe during the Lower Yellowstone and Minidoka Projects. Paul, despite his increasing age, remained active as a construction engineer. Closing out the year in style, Crowe's ever-vigilant and competitive crews, working on the coldest day of the year, set a record in cableway transportation when No. 7 cableway carried 277 buckets, each containing 8-cubic yards of concrete to the dam in one eight hour shift.[38]

1935 ushered in the final year of construction on mighty Hoover Dam. On February 1, the final diversion tunnel was closed off with the shutting of the bulkhead gate and the Colorado River began to back up in earnest against the strong thick concrete walls in Black Canyon. Engineers estimated that just one year of expected Colorado River flood water would be enough to fill more than half the capacity of the new reservoir, rising to several hundred feet against the face of the waiting dam. Crowe now focused his attention on the U-shaped power plant taking shape just below the downstream face of the dam. Running some 650 feet along the Nevada and Arizona sides of the canyon and traversing 350 feet at the base of the dam, the power plant made for a bold architectural design. Engineers had determined that the imposing building would fit nicely 150 feet above the normal downstream water level, once the dam was completed. With the structure snuggled against the natural sides of Black Canyon and with the possibility of falling rocks and other debris, the Bureau of Reclamation designed an extra strong roof. The final roof arrangement called for a 4.5-foot thick covering, more than enough to deflect the largest of falling rocks. Elevators on either side of the dam allowed for quick access to the power generators.[39]

The giant turbines, eventually fourteen in all, dwarfed previous hydroelectricity generators and workers handled the precious cargo with great care. During the year enough turbines were placed to handle accounts from the Bureau of Power & Light for the City of Los Angeles, Southern Sierra Power Company, and the Metropolitan Water District of Southern California. Bureau engineers coordinated the connection of Babcock & Wilcox's penstocks to the power plant, thus completing the route through which water would soon travel. Colorado River water would enter one of the gates of the four intake towers and fall quickly into the very large 30-foot header. From here, the water dropped slowly to four 13-foot diameter penstocks and then into the power plant squirrel cage where the fast running water would mechanically turn the power turbine, thus creating electrical energy.

Visitors in 1935 looking down into Black Canyon were not as visibly impressed with the power plant structure as they were with the dam and canyon. While the power plant reached nineteen stories high, it remained dwarfed by the 700-foot plus dam, now nearing completion. Crammed into this relatively small space were machines that would ultimately produce enough power to light every household in the United States in 1935 or "supply all the domestic light and power needed for 8,500,000 inhabitants of the Colorado River Basin states." More noticeable to visitors were the four monolithic concrete intake towers. Standing majestically tall, the 390-foot structures were linked with wide access bridges.[40]

The reservoir behind Hoover Dam is shown here beginning to fill in 1936. (USBR)

Even though the dam was nearing completion, Frank Crowe was not finished with labor problems. On March 1, the *Las Vegas Age* reported that federal authorities had seized Six Companies' labor records. Government lawyers acting on a tip from an ex-employee of Six Companies, John F. Wagner, charged Crowe and payroll office staff with maintaining two payroll accounts and that "the government has not been paid proper penalties for over-time violations in accordance with their contract." Wagner, who had worked as an assistant auditor, insisted that one of the payroll accounts had been held back from the government and that it contained numerous overtime violations. The government, in writing the Hoover Dam contract, had stated flatly that laborers would work only eight-hour shifts, but Six Companies understood that since the project was operating under unusually harsh and demanding circumstances a special understanding was in order. Interior Secretary Ickes investigated and within days, newspapers reported the impending case. Headlines, mostly negative, made Crowe and Six Companies look bad. Henry Kaiser, representing the conglomerate fumed at the accusations and immediately fought back. In letters to Ickes, he explained that the entire payroll operation remained under close government supervision throughout the construction period and how Six Companies had cooperated fully in working with government auditors and inspectors. He hired a publicity man to whip up a booklet entitled "So Boulder Dam was Built," a dramatic record of never-ending construction crises and how Six Companies successfully dealt with each obstacle; thousands of copies were air-mailed to Congressmen and high government officials. Kaiser himself went on the air to describe the immense human, physical and construction problems that had been overcome. Secretary Ickes, reluctant to pursue the matter enthusiastically and wanting a successful and quick closure to the project agreed to slap Six Companies with a reduced fine.[41]

On April 4, the first official car crossed the road crest of newly completed Hoover Dam. Walker Young, Frank Crowe, and others completed the ceremonial drive. As May came, Crowe still hovered over the tasks at-hand. These included finishing the power plant and placing the trashracks in the intake towers. The trashracks, would do exactly what their name indicated, keep floating debris from entering the intake towers and flowing into the extremely valuable power generating turbines. Grouting continued in all remaining joints and cracks that needed attention, and crews worked to finish both spillway connections. On May 30, Crowe appeared for the ceremony commemorating the one hundred plus men who died building Hoover Dam. Nevada senator Pat McCarran unveiled the memorial plague that read: "They Labored That Millions Might See a Brighter Day—In Memory of Our Fellowmen Who Lost Their Lives on the Construction of This Dam."

In May, humorist Will Rogers visited the dam, lunching with Crowe in the mess hall. Rogers, always curious about details, asked the seemingly shy engineer about the concrete placing operation and the cooling method used. After Crowe gave a brief answer to these initial inquiries, Rogers probed, "How many men do you have [working] on the job." Crowe, with a perfectly straight face answered without hesitating, "About half of them." Rogers laughed and returned, "I thought I was supposed to be the comedian."[42] Rogers upon finishing his meal stood on the wide wooden porch outside the mess hall where a good-sized crowd stood staring at him. Practical joker that he was, he first looked at Crowe then raised his head and started sniffing as if something peculiar was in the air. "I smell somebody from Oklahoma." After a rousing laugh from the crowd, several dam workers hailed Rogers acknowledging their home state. Crowe drove the comedian around Boulder City, finally ending up at Crowe's hilltop home. There the always easy-going, ready-to-please entertainer asked Frank Crowe for a rope. With Frank, Linnie and the kids watching Will Rogers demonstrated how to make and use a lasso—something Frank Crowe remembered well from his Yellowstone days. To the delight of young Patricia and Elizabeth, the agile westerner jumped easily between loops of the lasso.[43]

Shortly after this, Frank Crowe received an invitation to return to his alma mater, the University of Maine, to receive an honorary Doctor of Engineer-

Completed Hoover Dam. (USBR)

ing degree. Crowe eagerly accepted, for it would give him an opportunity to see the campus and talk with other alumni, students, and former faculty. It is not known whether Harold Boardman, Crowe's engineering instructor and Dean, who was still active in university affairs attended either the June 10th 64th graduation ceremonies, alumni banquet or had an opportunity to meet his now famous former student. After 269 seniors were awarded their degrees, University of Maine President Arthur A. Hauck spoke briefly of Frank Crowe's accomplishments and Trustee President Harmon G. Allen presented Crowe to the large commencement audience. "Frank Crowe is an engineer of great skill and exceptional administrative capacity," said Hauck. "Your achievements have gained for you an honored place among constructors of all times." Later at the banquet, Crowe gave what one observer called a "splendid address" on the challenges of building Hoover Dam.[44]

Finishing work on monolithic Hoover Dam progressed well until late June when a brewing labor protest erupted once again. For Crowe, this was the last thing he wanted to see. Construction difficulties could always be approached logically and scientifically, and usually solutions came quickly. Not so with human problems, particularly when the decision-making was not his. Crowe was not present when on July 12 approximately 300 carpenters, the entire contingent, refused to start work on their day shift. Someone in the Six Companies, referred to as "one official" ordered a change in working hours, demanding the day-shift carpenters to begin work one half hour earlier, 7:00 a.m. and forcing them to continue to work until 3:30 p.m.[45] Word spread to the concrete finishers, steel workers and others, and to labor union leaders that the strike "is 100% complete and it is possible that all construction work on the project will be halted if other labor unions follow the lead made by the carpenters." Walker Young, remembering the confrontations of the 1931 strike acted swiftly ordering project police and security forces to "take steps to prevent disorder where ever possible."[46]

Crowe hurriedly returned to Boulder City and was furious over the strike developments. He immediately reinstated the former daytime schedule. After discussing the issue with assistant superintendents, Crowe informally talked with some of the workers. "You know we're about through here. We'll be through here in a short time. No use of you losing all this work now," Crowe said.[47] Events, however, had moved inexorably out of his control and the unions saw this as an opportunity to ask for additional concessions. Crowe, on July 16, met with E. H. Fitzgerald, a federal intermediary and agreed to meet with union leaders to hear their demands. Morrison and Shea, knowing that the workers trusted and respected their boss, asked Crowe to represent Six Companies. L. A. Parker, member of the Operating Engineers, represented the various labor unions. Governor Kirman of Nevada named Reverend Sloan, pastor of the Baptist church in Las Vegas as the third member of the committee. Negotiations went on for days with Crowe conceding several demands such as a return to the eight-hour work shift, one half hour lunch on company time and instituting a six-day workweek. On another issue, that of a worker's blacklist, Crowe announced that Six Companies has not and never had any such list. The one critical demand asked that hourly wages be moved up from. $.75 to $1.00 and Crowe refused to budge on this stating he did not have the authority to move on this item. He asked for an adjournment of the negotiations in order to confer with Morrison, Kaiser, and lawyers of Six Companies in San Francisco.

Upon his return to Boulder City, Crowe announced that Six Companies agreed to all of the concessions that he had made including a statement that "after returning to work no discrimination be made against Union Strikers." On the wage issue, Six Companies refused to budge stating that the wages now paid "are fair and just and consistent with wages paid for like work in the Southwest." Parker pleased that he received major concessions, still pressed for the wage hike rationalizing that the wage increase is "a reasonable request." He revealed evidence to show that the "State of Arizona and the Public Works Administration wage funding groups have adopted wage scales equal to and better for skilled labor." Cognizant that they needed to apply more pressure on Crowe, Parker and Sloan predicted that unless Six Companies granted the pay hike "there is fast approaching a time when peaceful conditions of this strike will no longer exist." While throwing down the gauntlet to Six Companies, Parker and Sloan did not want to offend Crowe and his efforts. "We also want to say that Mr. Crowe has shown constant consideration in all his dealings with this Arbitration Board for the men on strike, and constantly thought of their welfare." The strike wore on for days, but with workers running out of money and realizing that they had actually won the argument to return working conditions to what they had been, resistance faded. One by one, carpenters and steelworkers returned to the job.[48]

President Franklin Roosevelt came west to dedicate the completion of Hoover Dam along with numerous Western Congressional members, scores of Bureau of Reclamation officials, local politicians, and thousands of curious and excited observers. On September 30, 1935, the controversial president delivered a high-powered speech before an estimated crowd of over 10,000. "Ten years ago the place where we are gathered was an unpeopled, forbidding desert," Roosevelt reminded everyone. The president described the Black Canyon dramatically when he said, "In the bottom of a gloomy canyon, whose precipitous walls rose to a height of more than 1,000 feet, flowed a turbulent, dangerous river. The mountains on either side were difficult of access, with neither road nor rail, and their rocks were protected neither by trees nor grass from the blazing heat of the sun," Roosevelt added. Frank Crowe, seated with the other Six Companies and Bureau dignitaries, waited for the president to talk about the engineering accomplishments and the human drama of building the world's biggest dam, and Roosevelt did not disappoint him, "The transformation wrought here is a twentieth-century marvel," the president declared. In an effort to recognize Crowe and Six Companies, Inc., President Roosevelt dramatically announced, "We recognize also the energy, resourcefulness, and zeal of the builders." The president's remarks pointed to the outstanding design characteristics of Hoover Dam and to the thousands of "construction stiffs" who worked relentlessly to conquer Black Canyon. "This is an engineering victory of the first order—another great achievement of American resourcefulness, skill, and determination," declared President Roosevelt.[49]

The president or Harold Ickes did not mention Crowe and Walker Young in their statement to the gathered thousands and the millions who listened on radio. Just days before Roosevelt's arrival Crowe and Young were noted as "two [engineers] who stand out above all the rest." "Facing work of a magnitude and

difficulty never before encountered, the two men mentioned were naturally placed
in their positions of unprecedented responsibility because they had, by experience
and untiring effort, fitted themselves for the work." According to one observer at
the dam dedication people were, "amazed that while various California politicians who, after all, had but little influence on the consummation of the project,
were lauded" neither Roosevelt or Ickes talked about "the two men of outstanding
ability and genius who were responsible for the proper placing of every bucket of
cement and every pound of concrete in the great structure were completely ignored." The newspaper columnist concluded by stating, "I have been asked many
times why they [Crowe & Young] were ignored, but have no answer."[50]

Frank Crowe's last official act as superintendent came on February 29,
1936. Ralph Lowry, who had replaced Walker Young as project engineer, walked
across one side of the dam crest roadway and met Crowe, who walked across from
the other side. "Take it. It's yours now," a relived Crowe said. After a brief conversation Crowe concluded, "It's a great dam, Ralph." Immediately Lowry re-
spectfully replied, "Well, you ought to know, Frank." With that brief exchange,
the nation's largest single contract ever executed concluded. The *New York Times*
reported "The dam is the highest in the world. It backs up water in a natural
reservoir, forming the greatest lake man ever made." The article pointed out that
the awarded original bid of $48,890,995.50 had been moved up to $54,000, 000
due to "changes made during the construction period." For all that money the
paper reminded readers that the completed 726-foot high dam was projected to
produce two million horsepower of electrical energy as well as permitting "reclamation of sufficient acreage to care for 5,000,000 persons." "It will supply domestic water for future millions in Southern California," the paper claimed. Speaking from his offices in Washington D. C., Secretary Ickes recognized the completion of Hoover Dam as "another milestone" in the history of the West. "Man has
asserted his mastery over a great and dangerous river, one which endangered tens
of thousands while it was unregulated, but which will be an active benefit to millions now that it is harnessed," Ickes proclaimed, mentioning the fact that the job
was brought in nearly two years ahead of schedule. In a final statement, Ickes
proudly announced, "The people of Southern California, Arizona, and Nevada are
to be congratulated today, for the security of their futures has been vastly increased."
For his part, Crowe understood all too well, the importance of what he had accomplished both in establishing new engineering standards, methods, and techniques
and in the human realm. Now as Ickes declared, "Water supplies have been guaranteed for their farms and cities. A source of a tremendous amount of cheap power
has been provided for use in increasing their comforts and developing their industries."[51]

Looking out over the smooth bold lines of Hoover Dam's downstream
concrete face, Frank Crowe must have felt great satisfaction. Here he supervised
a national project of massive proportions, one that would have a major impact on

the development of the entire Southwest. It was truly his conquest. Writing years later, *Fortune* magazine noted, "To the extent it can be said to belong to any single man, Boulder was Frank Crowe's triumph. For five long years the heat, the mud, the remorseless current, the swift floods, the jangling telephones were his responsibility," the article noted. Not only did he gain national and international recognition but also, it made Crowe wealthy. Profits for Six Companies amounted to $10,400,000, and Crowe's share, 2.5 percent registered a staggering $300,000. This was on top of his $18,000-a-year salary. Overnight, it seemed Frank Crowe had become famous and rich. "When you work for that crowd," Crowe remembered with satisfaction, "your work is appreciated."[52]

Crowe now reigned supreme as America's top engineer, his fame at first challenging, then surpassing, Panama Canal engineer George Goethals. Few engineers since Goethals found themselves on the front page of America's top newspapers. On an international scale, Crowe's outstanding performance at Hoover Dam proved to countries around the world, that large-scale dam building was now possible, that existing technology used wisely and imaginatively, could serve Man. When asked years later about his accomplishments at Hoover Dam he simply said, "There's something peculiarly satisfying about building a great dam. You know that what you build will stand for centuries."[53]

Chapter 12

"We are plugging along here, digging a hole in the riverbed 250
feet deep to find a foundation for our dam."
Parker Dam, 1936-1938

Frank Crowe's optimistic low bid on Parker Dam brought an early final approval from the Bureau of Reclamation on August 25, 1934, and between that date and September 11, a heated debate occurred about whether or not to proceed. Crowe and his proponent Charlie Shea argued that the unusual tunnel diversion and extra deep excavation posed a challenge, but nothing that could not be overcome using existing men and machines from Hoover Dam. Reluctantly, Six Companies' bosses approved the venture with the understanding that Shea would subcontract the job, and therefore be financially responsible, and that Crowe would transfer to the site as soon as his Hoover Dam responsibilities ended. In an unprecedented move to show confidence in his bid and his ability to finish the job with a profit, Crowe informed Shea that he would not take a salary for the duration of the construction, opting to gamble on a handsome share of the profits. Charlie Shea accepted this offer. Shea hired Perry Yates as superintendent of construction and work was progressing on the diversion tunnels, building the gravel screening plant and the concrete mixing plant, and preparing the upstream cofferdam when Crowe transferred to the job in March of 1936.[1]

Crowe learned that he would be working again with his old mentor Frank Weymouth, who was now serving as general manager for the Metropolitan Water District. Interestingly, one would think that Weymouth would be in the forefront of promoting the construction of Parker Dam, as it was a critical component of his overall aqueduct plan. Chief Engineer Ray Walter, Weymouth's replacement as the top engineer in the Bureau, wrote a letter to Bureau Commissioner Elwood Mead accusing Weymouth of refusing to cooperate with preparatory work on the dam claiming, "Mr. Weymouth has consistently declined to aid in securing an investigation of the lower Parker dam site." Walter hit hard when he claimed, "Ostensibly this attitude is based on a conviction on his part that a concrete dam cannot be built there and the site is not feasible." In disagreement with Weymouth, Walter wanted to move forward urging, "I see no reason to condemn the site without an investigation, since this matter is very vital to the State of Arizona. We should not leave the way open for just criticism on the charge that we abandoned the Parker site without proper investigation," Walter concluded. In a final shot at Weymouth, Walter surmised, "We have attempted to conjecture as to the real reason for Mr. Weymouth's attitude. It may be due to the power angle." His reference here was to alert Meade that the United States should have complete control of outflows of the dam and electrical power use.[2]

Weymouth and Walter exchanged letters again in March of 1934 when Weymouth suggested that the Bureau should give "careful and thorough consideration" to protecting the contractors from "delays beyond the control of the contractor." He was referring to possible legal delays that might result from a perceived complaint from the state of Arizona. Weymouth wanted the Bureau to consider injecting protecting language in the government specifications that "the District [Metropolitan Water] and the Reclamation Bureau can be properly protected and their interests safe-guarded." As if stating it in stronger language, Weymouth concluded, "These things will need to be kept in mind in writing the specifications." The patronizing tone of this last remark must have struck a sour note with Walter. Weymouth no longer was Chief Engineer of the Bureau, Walter was and he was not about to have his predecessor tell him what to do. In a response to Weymouth, Walter declared, "Under the standard practice by which we are now governed preparing specifications and entering into contracts for construction work, no mention is made in the specifications as to delays." Within days, Weymouth shot another letter to Walter showing how he had written special contingencies into the tunnel specifications for Parker granting delay allowances on the part of the contractor. He even enclosed a copy of the paper asking Walter, again, to consider including protecting language. It appeared that a serious problem was developing.[3]

The Parker Dam job had not gone well before Crowe reported for duty that spring. From the start, political controversy engulfed the project. The Bureau had made a special arrangement with California's Metropolitan Water District of Southern California, who was concurrently laying out the huge California River Aqueduct.[4] The idea was to link the aqueduct with the water stored by Parker Dam; in fact, the initial pumping lift plant was only two miles upstream from the proposed dam site. Naturally, Arizona, looking at its thirsty giant to the west, grew nervous about receiving its fair share of the water. It was understood that Arizona's Colorado River Indian Reservation and the Gila Valley lands would acquire future federal irrigation funds to develop irrigation. Yet, on the surface, it appeared that California, once hooked up to Colorado's water, would suck the river dry. Concern mounted in Arizona once Six Companies Inc. had officially acknowledged the Bureau's project approval.

Governor B. B. Moeur, known as a "fire-eater" would not stand by and allow the Metropolitan Water District to move ahead, ordering Arizona National Guard troops to the dam site.[5] He knew that the Bureau commissioner was pushing the project. Mead had developed a list of benefits for constructing Parker Dam. Mead concluded that the new dam was needed to: "(1) Re-regulate the flow of the Colorado River, thereby enabling the Government to develop more power, without injury to irrigation, than would otherwise be possible; (2) Protect Federal land of the Colorado River Indian Reservation from flood damage by temporarily impounding flood waters from the tributary streams of the main river below Boulder Dam, particularly the Bill Williams River; (3) Provide a source of power for use in the Gila and Parker Reclamation Projects in Arizona; (4) Improve navigation by regulating the River; (5) Stabilize the gradient of the river and prevent the scouring and undue lowering of the riverbed, which would otherwise result from releases of clear water at Boulder Dam." Almost as a side note, Mead added, "The Dam will also be of value to California agencies seeking to divert water from the river under contract with the Federal Government, but regardless of this function the Dam will be a valuable adjunct to the Boulder Project, and should, in any event, be built within the next fifteen years."

Mead admitted, in a letter to Secretary Ickes, that legal problems were festering, "The Arizona abutment is on land believed to be reserved to the United States and the legal right of the United States to construct the dam across the river at the proposed site seems secure." The commissioner continued, "Arizona has threatened, however, to use physical force to prevent construction of the dam and has sent armed men, members of the State Militia, to the dam site." Mead suggested the obvious next step when he said, "Of course, the questions involved cannot be settled by force of arms, and the rights of the parties should be determined by orderly processes of the courts." In fact, Mead urged Ickes not to stand by and wait for Arizona to start legal proceedings, stating that long delays in starting construction would result. In a final statement to urge action, Mead requested that Ickes notify the Attorney General's office and "if advised that suit to restrain Arizona from interfering with the construction of the dam is an appropriate means to this end, to institute such suit in the proper court, which, I assume, would be the Supreme Court of the United States."[6]

Mead assumed correctly and the case went to the Supreme Court, which promptly ruled that Arizona had a legitimate complaint and thus ordered the Bureau of Reclamation to halt construction. The Bureau then notified Shea and Six Companies that work was suspended until a political solution could be worked out. Not to be outdone, California legislators introduced a bill to Congress on May 12, 1935 that would "fully" authorize Parker Dam as a federal government project, thus restricting Arizona rights. Once enacted the measure would "grant blanket authority for flood control, navigation improvement and water conservation and land reclamation projects."[7] The rest of the year, federal and state negotiators worked to find a solution that would satisfy Arizona, California and the Bureau of Reclamation.

By January of 1936, the dispute of water rights having been settled, work on Parker Dam renewed. Mort Boss, superintendent of construction for Shea devised a three-level Hoover-type of drilling jumbo to drill the massive 29-foot river diversion tunnels. Shea cleverly used electrically operated industrial shovels from Hoover to efficiently, and quickly, remove blasted muck. Crowe kept in constant communication, either by wire or phone with the hard-working Shea. Crowe, known as the "Old Man" made the several-hour car drive from Hoover to Parker numerous times. After much discussion, Crowe and Shea decided to take on Parker Dam completely and on March 14 so notified the government. When Crowe reported to the site permanently in April, Shea was ready to hole through both diversion tunnels. In a flurry of action, reminiscent of his younger days, Crowe organized the shifts to prepare for the concrete lining of the cavernous tunnels. From May 10 to August 15, his crews slaved in oppressive heat, a re- minder of the Hoover Dam experience, to line 3,200 feet of tunnels. With tem- peratures unbelievably high, Crowe and Shea agreed to shut down work tempo- rarily as soon as the crews completed concreting. The thermometer read over 130 degrees for several consecutive days and what is most hard to comprehend is that random temperature readings revealed that nighttime conditions hardly improved— remaining at 110 degrees. In the tunnels, with cooler conditions, work crews performed well, but once outside the sun beat mercilessly down on everything and everyone. Whereas, in Black Canyon the one saving attribute had been the steep canyons, keeping direct sun off both workers and machines for extended hours of the day. At Parker, there was no hope, save in the tunnels, to escape.[8]

Back to work on September 16 Crowe's desert warriors, refreshed and excited about resuming work, completed tunnel portal concreting and prepared to divert the still dangerous Colorado River. On October 23, this task went smoothly, the Colorado turning as if ordered into the diversion tunnels. For the second time in history the mighty river's course slid from its ancient bed into the round smooth concrete cylinders prepared by Man. While not as widely reported in the newspa- pers, nor talked about in cities across the United States, the event thrilled Crowe and his workers. If Hoover Dam had handcuffed the Colorado River, Parker Dam shackled America's wildest stream.

Frank Crowe and Linnie realized that the primitive living conditions of the contractor's camp at Parker Dam was no place for children. The concerned couple sent their daughters, with a nanny, to a private school in Azusa, California, The LaRew School for Girls.[9] In a letter to his sister, Frank disclosed that Pat and Bettee were "doing fine. But, we hate to have them away," Crowe admitted. As if to rationalize the decision he explained, "But we are miles from anywhere out here. 300 miles to Los Angeles and 200 to Phoenix." Content with his modest Parker Dam home, Crowe revealed to his sister that the fall and winter weather is "grand." He explained how it helped "to makeup for the heat treatment we get in the summer." In a reference to his current work on Parker he said, "We are plug- ging along here, digging a hole in the riverbed 250 feet deep to find a foundation for our dam." As usual, the loving brother included a check for Catherine to "get yourself some kind of a present."[10] Within a short time, Frank and Linnie decided to buy a house in Southern California to get Linnie out of the oppressive heat and closer to the girls in school. Their spacious San Marino home became Frank's destination many weekends as he drove the one hundred miles plus over desert highways to see his family. Rare home movies show Frank relaxing with Linnie and the kids playing croquet on their back lawn. One amusing scene has Frank, Patricia, and Elizabeth standing in a semi-circle alternately pounding a croquet stake to a perfect rhythm. Their San Marino home, a sprawling Spanish hacienda, boasted a large well-manicured front yard and a wide second-story balcony. Another scene has the well-dressed girls, followed by Linnie wearing a full-length fur coat, getting into the family late model Buick sedan.[11]

Most of the workers, including Frank Crowe's nephew, John enjoyed working the cool crisp February days in the desert. It was 1937 and the air was clean and clear, and everyone looked forward to an early end to the monotonous excavation and the beginning of the concrete placing. Upstream, along the Bill Williams River and the Colorado River, nomad families fished, rested, and pondered their next move in the never-ending search for permanent employment. The day shift had started like any other with a quick breakfast at the company mess hall and a short ride out to the "hole" to begin digging. It started to rain and it continued. The river, rising noticeably by 10:00 am, concerned Crowe who watched as the diversion tunnel entrances disappeared. Dam worker, Marion Allen wrote later of several life threatening situations that day in his book on Parker Dam. According to an eyewitness, "There was one truck driver there with a white truck his company was trying to sell to the Shea Company. When seeing it was in a bad spot, he started across the bridge to Parker Dam to move it. When he got to the California side, the approach went out—he started to back up and the Arizona side went out, but the water was still rising." Saul "Red" Wixson, a dam worker and a good friend of Frank Crowe, attempted to rescue the trapped man. One of Wixson's crew "tried to throw a line across to the remaining section of bridge but the 3/4" rope was too heavy and after three or four tries he gave up." Thinking quickly, Wixson "hollered to them to unravel the rope, then tie a crescent wrench on the end of it. They finally got the rope across, hooked a cable to the line, and the driver pulled it across and hooked the cable to the truck bed." With the cable just skimming the ever-rising turbulent river, Wixson tied off his end of the line to the bridge, and once again hollered at the driver to raise the bed of his truck; the strong steel cable cleared the water. For several torturous minutes, Wixson and his men watched helplessly as the unknown truck driver attempted to "shimmy" across the rampaging river. As if choreographed in a blockbuster action film, the battered bridge began to give way and crumble under the pounding force of the Colorado River. The frightened truck driver jumped ashore to safety when the bridge broke apart. "The truck, cable, and bridge disappeared in the Colorado, never to be seen again, as far as anyone knows," mused Allen.[12]

Crowe's seasoned veterans, usually cool, calm, and collected during normal working situations, scrambled about trying to save equipment and themselves. John Crowe, given the job of operating the company rowboat, decided to launch his tiny craft and search for people in need of rescue. Not long after starting out, and with his arms already weary from straining against the ever-increasing power of the river's current, "Admiral" John found a local trapper clinging to the branches of a bending tree. John pleaded with the reluctant loner to jump into the relative safety of the rowboat. The trapper shouted back that he preferred to stay right where he was, and if the tree snapped the trapper said he planned to grab the bridge as he went under it. John quickly informed the man that there was no bridge left to grasp. With this news, the old man changed his mind. John also rowed an official of the Metropolitan Water District up river, "as they were afraid of bad publicity about flooding out the squatters along the Colorado." Fighting the strongest of currents the brave pair discovered one family "about three miles above the dam, and John said when they rowed up there the family—two boys about 25 or 30 and their mother—had moved their stove out of the cabin which was now about 10 feet under water." The stove sat safely high up on the ridge and the "mother was busy cooking dinner and the men were sitting there smoking their pipes." After struggling to make the riverbank, John's passenger hollered over to them asking if they needed any supplies. The answer came quickly, the isolated family wanted tobacco. John Crowe recalled later "he was sent back to their camp with a load of groceries and plenty of tobacco. They thanked him and were very appreciative, but couldn't understand why anyone was sending all those groceries."[13]

It was learned later that rain swelled the usually calm Bill Williams River sending, at one point, more that 100,000 cubic feet per second of water rushing into the Colorado River. Officials noted that the river, for a short while, at the dam site rose two feet in only five minutes. Frank Crowe and his chief assistant, Frank Bryant, consolidated the men into one work force and sent them to the lower cofferdam, where the water was back flushing dangerously close to the top of the earthen retainer. Should it spill over, or worse yet, break through the barrier, untold delays would ensue, entailing dewatering and cleanup. Crowe stood down in the middle of the desperate action, knowing that everyone had told him that Parker Dam would be his downfall, that he would lose money for sure on the problems inherent in trying to deal with a foundation so deep. The lower cofferdam was not his only problem. Nervously, the unperturbed dam builder eyed the upper cofferdam, now taking the full brunt of the liquid onslaught. However, as day turned into night, Crowe could see that the reinforcing of the lower cofferdam was holding and the diversion tunnels were deflecting just enough of the rampaging river to save the upper cofferdam from being swamped. The utility road on the California side of the river caved-in, dumping stranded vehicles and creating a

The Parker Dam flood swamping the construction site and backing up the
Colorado River for miles. (John & Mary Crowe)

depression. Here the water, forced like a gigantic venturi, blasted the California
riverbank. One observer who watched the churning mass where river water de-
molished earth noted that it was "just like hydraulic mining." More of the embankment disintegrated and after a while shocked workers saw the action "wash a
boat out of the bank." According to Marion Allen, "It was about 20 or 25 feet long
and had been buried for years."[14]

Crowe and company drew a huge sigh of relief when early the next morning the floodwaters receded noticeably. Miraculously, no one lost their life, although there were several serious injuries and many cuts and bruises. Damage
reports totaled a high, but acceptable loss, mostly from smashed or missing machinery. Crowe's luck had held again, and like a modern-day George Armstrong
Custer, he pondered how long he could keep playing the odds and win. As usual,
he wanted a quick cleanup and full resumption of excavation work. For the next
few weeks, everyone swapped flood stories and somehow the acts of individual
bravery during the rescue attempts and the amount of damage wrought by the
"Billy Williams" grew with every retelling.[15]

Back down in "the hole," Crowe measured the foundation depth at approximately 100 feet. After replacing lost or damaged equipment, Crowe counted
five large industrial cranes, each equipped with dragline buckets. These monstrous mechanical hands, had worked so well for him on countless occasions be-

fore, he saw them as his best hope to finish the excavation within the year. Additionally, he employed four large tractors to push the muck around and form piles for easy lifting, twenty (rented) Mack trucks for hauling, five smaller Ford trucks that had proven their worth in grueling Black Canyon, and hundreds of powerful drills, pumps, jackhammers, and air-compressed tools. It was the usual Crowe army using the usual Crowe tools of the trade, and day after day, the men dug deeper and deeper. Foundation depth records began falling and even Crowe himself could not believe the amount of ancient river silt that had been building up for eons.

Crowe had hoped that he would not be faced with labor problems, particularly since the total work force was small and many were devoted veterans of his construction army. However, the actions of the American Federation of Labor (AF L) and the Congress of Industrial Organizations (CIO) forced a strike. Both labor organizations wanted Shea and Crowe to have the right to represent the Parker Dam workers and thus negotiate salary and benefits with them. Shea hesitated. He preferred the freedom of hiring men from either organization or even men who had no union affiliation. On April 23, 1937, at noon, a strike was called and Crowe responded by shutting down the entire operation pending a settlement. Only a small number of workers remained to operate the pumps in the excavation pit and to wet the freshly laid concrete in the trash rack structure. Under an agreement made by the contractor with the AFL group, work was resumed at 8:00 a. m. April 30, but a picket line was maintained on the highway camp and near the dam site. On May 3rd, Shea and Crowe undertook policing of the campsite, ordered the pickets to leave, and established a check-in "Crossroads," eight miles away where it remained for several weeks. On June 19th, Crowe's guards were removed from the check-in station, but several were kept on duty around the work site until August 30. Marion Allen, working at Parker Dam later wrote about an incident during this time that involved Frank Crowe. A recent arrival to the dam site, John Trisdale, tried to be hired, but was refused repeatedly. He had experience working concrete, yet they were not hiring for that job at that time. He desperately needed a job. Soon a rope was strung up at the employment office with one side marked AFL, the other side CIO. Trisdale tried switching sides on different days, but still could not be hired. One day as he stood in the CIO line, Frank Crowe strolled by on his way to his office. He noticed Trisdale standing there dejectedly, stepped over to him and whispered, "Wrong side." Crowe moved off and Trisdale quickly leaped over the rope to the AFL area. "Two or three of the men asked what he had said, but Trisdale assured them that the 'Old Man' had said nothing," Allen wrote. Within an hour the shift supervisor came out to the hiring shack and hung a sign "Only American Federation hired." Trisdale was then hired and within days, most of the CIO men left the area.[16]

April, May and June saw Crowe and Shea, through their assistants push the excavation to a maximum effort. The master dam builder brought in cable-

This photo reveals the extreme depth of excavation necessary before placing the concrete foundation, July 27, 1937. (USBR)

ways Nos. 7 and 8 from the Hoover Dam job with the idea of using them in the final excavation stages. This would cut down on the number of truck trips required to carry out the muck. With truck grades running 10 degrees around hairpin turns, Crowe knew he was pushing the endurance of man and machine. The cableway set was vintage Crowe and sported a single tail tower anchored on the California side and two moveable headtowers set out on a 500-foot runway track. The arc shape provided angles of access to all excavation and concreting sites. Each cableway possessed the strength to lift a maximum of 25 tons, more than enough for the Parker Dam specifications. The extended length of the cable was 1,500 feet.[17]

Water seeped continually as the excavation deepened and Crowe realized that a permanent solution needed to be found. Shea and Bryant recommended that a battery of pumps be placed on a pontoon raft. Crowe quickly adopted the idea and asked master mechanic Si Bous, longtime Crowe co-worker, to set up four pumps, two 12-inch and two 8-inch heavy-duty machines. J. V. Allen, who had first met Crowe back on the Jackson Lake job, operated the pumps. Two 22-inch lines pushed the unwanted murky seepage up and out of the depression. Measuring the volume of water pumped revealed that an average of 17 to 18 feet passed through the meters every second. As the excavation went on, Crowe hoped that the amount of water moving into "the hole" would not increase dramatically. His luck held again, at least for a while, and the excavation moved ahead. The unprecedented excavation continued, and Crowe and Bryant noticed that the steep exposed slopes (8:1 ratio) began to now leak. Once the line of percolation intersected the excavation slope, the seeping water spilled out and ran downward. This phenomenon began to occur around the entire perimeter of the digging. Crowe knew from basic engineering facts that loose material, when wet, "would not stand on slopes steeper than 4:1 or 5:1." Quickly calling a brainstorming meeting, Crowe's ingenious team of engineers came up with a scheme to sink wells in the newly excavated slopes with the idea of sucking up as much below ground water as possible. This technique, along with the sump pumps still operating at the bottom of the dig, might keep the surface slopes intact and allow the job to continue safely.[18]

Crews scrambled to install a test well to see if the idea would work. A 26-inch diameter well was struck on the downstream slope. Then using a 200 horsepower deep well pump, workers began sucking large amounts of water. After a few days of trial, Crowe could see that this innovative method was going to work and so another well was installed on the upstream slope, attaining similar successful results. Eventually, a third well was sunk, as excavation crews approached bedrock. "Even with the two wells in operation, the slopes were so hazardous that, during the drilling of the third well, a slide occurred which left the drill rig perched on three wheels on the hauling road up the slope, and endangered a portion of the well already completed," wrote engineer L. P. Sowles. Eventually, a fourth well was required to handle the now increasing percolation.

Crowe now needed to worry constantly about slides that might, at any minute, bring down tons of water-laden muck. To make matters worse, "the hole" was forming into a huge funnel-like depression, focusing the gravity pull into a shrinking area covered with men and machines. A major water-mud slide would hamper, at best, and trap, at worse, any unfortunate men at the bottom. Crowe knew this was a critical period in the excavation, every bit as dangerous—maybe even more so, than the high scalers of Hoover Dam. He refused to allow the problem to go unsolved and he hated the idea that he did not have complete control over this phase of the work. Working with Bureau engineers and his own aides, Crowe calculated that by the time they hit bedrock they could expect a 37-second feet of percolation inflow. This increasing amount, when diagrammed out as a mathematical curve, allowed the wily engineer to plan successfully. More

Crowe and his men worked against the clock to reach the exposed bedrock. Here workers are setting the forms for the first concrete placement on the foundation. (USBR)

pumps came online as needed and when they finally struck bedrock on July 21, 1937, readings affirmed Crowe's calculations; exactly 37-second feet of water flowed.

With the safety of his workers uppermost, Crowe's men next erected two steel, sheet pile bulkheads into the downstream, most dangerous, slope. The arched manmade dams were well ribbed for added strength and anchored solidly at midway up the slope. Finally, to ensure no disastrous, last minute problems with water invading the now exposed riverbed, cautious Frank Crowe ordered two concrete arch walls installed, a 12-foot high barricade for the downstream side and a 15-foot wall for the upstream face. Now the final actions of preparing for concreting could begin, cleanup and the drilling of grout holes. Writing Bureau engineer E. A. Moritz, Crowe revealed how nervous he was about getting on with the concreting. "This is the most hazardous hole that I have ever seen. It is of interest to all concerned to get out of it as fast as possible," Crowe warned.[19]

Walking the bottom of the Parker Dam excavation proved to be nearly as awe-inspiring as the depths of Black Canyon. The eerie feeling that a huge powerful river flowed ominously high above you through massive fabricated diversion tunnels, put fear and excitement into all those who experienced the thrill. The world's deepest dam foundation, 250 feet below the flowing Colorado River, stood exposed. A relieved Frank Crowe wired Bureau Commissioner John C. Page declaring, "Happy to advise you have just reached bottom of the deepest hole ever dug by fool man."[20]

There was no time to admire the view or sense the fear for long, as Crowe moved to have all the usual components for placing concrete ready to go. Busily, he scurried about checking accessibility of cement, supplies of aggregate, and setting up the concrete mixing and delivery operation. Nothing unusual appeared to be on the horizon. He knew the steps well; he had worked through them so many times before. Yet, a sense of urgency began to set in. The wells and sump pumps were doing their jobs well, but Crowe did not like the idea that so much loose water was so close to the job, still a potential disaster. He wanted to get the concrete footings in and get on with the routine of concreting blocks of the main dam. He urged the men on even more. With two days to go before the first scheduled concrete placement, Crowe's famous luck faded. A massive power outage hit knocking out of action all of the essential sump pumps and well motors. Crowe, Bryant and others stood by helplessly as the percolating water, restrained now for weeks, poured from the slopes, carrying rocks and boulders downward in a huge muck slide. In ten minutes, the collapsed debris had reached the concrete arch barricades protecting the lowest excavation and Crowe desperately rushed to the scene trying to think of a plan of action. If the pumps remained off for more than a few minutes, all would be lost. The entire central depression would be filled with water, mud, and rocks, requiring a long delay. Crowe ordered Si Bous to set the pump switches to the off position to avoid motor blowout should a power surge happen. The pipe, light and flexible, carrying the muck out of the excavation collapsed when the pumps stopped and the material fell back into "the hole." Crowe, now shocked at the possibility that structural damage might occur to the pipe once the pumps came back on line and the pipes filled, could do nothing. For one of the few times in his prestigious building career, the "Old Man" was helpless. No one agrees how long the power was off, Bob Sass (son of Robert Sass) said the power outage lasted an hour; most agree that it seemed like a lifetime, for everything was at stake. Engineer Larry Soules, reported that the power remained off for only 15 minutes. When the power returned, everyone crossed their fingers as the pumps were turned on once again. Then all eyes shifted to the flattened sump pipe. It quickly filled, and held. The dangerous episode ended; a disaster was averted.[21]

On July 29, 1937, the entire construction team was thrilled, despite the repressive heat, when Frank Crowe gave the order to place the first bucket of concrete. The cableway operator moved the powerful device over to an awaiting flatbed railroad car, as they had done at Hoover, and there an awaiting 8-cubic yard bucket sat filled with precious specially mixed concrete. Ever so slowly, the load lifted skyward and proceeded to travel out over the huge deep hole. On command from the signalman below the load lowered to the center of the deepest excavation, elevation 150 feet. Workers rushed in to steady the swinging bucket, centering it over the projected dumpsite. Releasing the safety catches, both workers jumped back and the cableway operator released the sand, gravel, water and cement mix. Then without ceremony or hesitation, the bucket was pulled up and over to the train car and left to be refilled. Then operators picked up another full bucket. The concrete process was beginning and it would continue nonstop until the dam was built. Interestingly, Crowe was authorized to place the first layer of concrete directly into the area between the two concrete barrier walls. These walls had held off the sliding muck during the electrical outage; now they would hold back the concrete from within. With the placement of this unusual first layer, the placing process took on a much more familiar look, the block stepping-stone approach. Each block was similar in size to Hoover measuring 50 feet wide at the upstream face. The blocks were set alternately high and low between the radial contraction joints, which were fully keyed to link one block to another. Before a new block could be placed on an existing lower block, "a thorough cleanup of the block, inspection of all accessories and forms for the pour are followed by the placing of a layer of grout over the area to be immediately covered by concrete."[22]

The concrete block forms, constructed of shiplap and faced with 22-gauge metal, looked like huge wooden panels. Heavily reinforced by 2x10-inch studs and she-bolts every three feet, the massive panels were lifted by the cableway or by framing crews using "A" frames and large capacity hydraulic jacks. Ernest Banker, form boss for Crowe, worked closely with Frank Bryant to coordinate the checkerboard building block pattern in setting up forms and placing concrete. As they had done at Hoover, the form and concrete placing crews practiced their timing and movements repeatedly before concreting actually began. In no time at all, the crews grooved, with each man knowing exactly what to expect from every other man on the shift. This machine-like precision is what gave Crowe the edge over so many of the other talented superintendents building dams. His men knew each other so well and had worked with each other so long that the breaking-in time to coordinate effective construction actions was minimal. With the concrete placing routine well oiled, the heavily reinforced water-cooled dam rose quickly in the desert depression. E. A. Moritz, Bureau field engineer working with Crowe, wrote his superior Chief Engineer Walter happily announcing the commencing of concrete operations, "Although no concreting records will be broken during August we expect to get a substantial start. The job looks infinitely safer than it did a month or two ago and it is a great relief to know that the deepest dam in the world is on its way up."[23]

Crowe always looking for ways to move the work quicker, save money for the contractor and help his men, wrote a letter in August requesting "that the rate of placing concrete above elevation 200 be changed from a 72 hour interval between 5 ft. layer[s] to a 40 hour interval." He listed the following problems that would be solved if the request were granted: "Cut down our terrific pumping expenses as soon as possible. Next, enable us to use the cold water in the river during the winter season for cooling the dam. Third, permit us to build the very intricate concrete work on top of the dam before the summer heat of 1938." It was this kind of advance thinking (Crowe wrote the letter shortly after starting the concrete operation) that allowed him to finish the job ahead of schedule.[24] He was also in constant contact with his old mentor Weymouth and the latter sent a number of letters to Chief Engineer Walter and Moritz urging action on Crowe's requests to speed up the concreting. In May of 1937, Weymouth wrote Walter boosting Crowe's idea of using refrigerated water to hasten the concrete cooling instead of relying on Colorado River water. Weymouth declared that Crowe had not been "properly informed" as to the Bureau's intention and he recommended that a decision be made quickly.[25]

Living conditions loomed as a problem not only for Crowe, who made the decision to not have his children with him, but also for all workers. The Bureau of Reclamation did not want to build another full-blown community as it had at Boulder City, only a small-scale government support camp. The same was true of Charlie Shea. Already, financed to the hilt in the responsibility of building the dam, he agreed to erect only the necessary buildings, such as a mess hall, bunkhouses and offices. The company housing had electricity, water, and sewer, but it was inadequate to house the hundreds of men employed. Many workers, both married and single, chose to live near the dam site on the Colorado River. The land on either side of the road heading south from the dam site to the town of Parker, Arizona, was filled with temporary homesteads. Crowe allowed workers to buy lumber from the company. He even threw in the nails free and all the scrap lumber that could be hauled away. For a water supply, many families set up hundred gallon drums or tanks on platforms. Hosing or piping ran into the house, usually to a single portable steel sink. Families would carry their sinks with them from job to job. The problem for some was to acquire the pipe and necessary fittings. Both items were quite expensive. Marion Allen recalled a story told to him that workers began helping themselves to scrap pipe, hoses, and fittings. Foremen complained to Crowe who immediately put out a notice that all items were to be returned or he threatened to send "Moose" Mosebar, company security guard searching for them. Workers caught with stolen items, would be prosecuted. "The next day there was a pile of hose two or three feet high in front of the office—all colors, all kinds," wrote Allen. Crowe, looking at the pitiful pile of scrap, could see that these pieces were too short to be used anywhere on the job so he sent out another order for "everyone to come and get their hose." Crowe added that if anyone was caught taking more they would be fired immediately. For days, no one was brave enough to come and get his hose. Allen joked that finally after a week, the piled disappeared.[26]

Frank Crowe's office, modest compared to the large facilities of Hoover Dam, measured 12x14 feet with one desk and one other chair. Ex-Hoover worker, Marion Allen, now selling insurance in the area stopped by frequently to say hello to Crowe and Allen was shocked to see such a modest office. He remembered Crowe commenting on the lack of furniture, "People think better on their feet." On one occasion when Frank Crowe had called a meeting, the "Old Man" sat behind his desk leaning back in his chair while Bryant occupied the other chair. This left the overturned wastebasket for millionaire contractor boss Charlie Shea, and the rest of the group: design engineer John Crowe, engineer Larry Sowles, master mechanic Si Bous, foremen Floyd Bous and Red Wixson stood.[27]

For entertainment, most families listened to the radio, played cards, visited with other families or drove to nearby Parker, Arizona for a little shopping or possibly a movie. At the camp, dances were popular, as they had been as far back as the Saturday night bashes at Jackson Lake. The company allowed the dances to go on in a large hall and many guests brought their own refreshments, remembering these social gatherings as "always a fun time."[28] The Bureau and Shea agreed to construct a small school and hire teachers. The several buildings, each having to hold classes that extended over several grade levels, were "somewhat temporary and did not have the school atmosphere we had been accustomed," wrote former Parker Dam student Dave Bous. "Miss Watson was our school principal and was well liked by the students and their families," Bous remembered. With such a wide range of ages in each class, Watson encouraged her teachers to "create a family atmosphere, students helping each other wherever and whenever possible." Young Dave Bous remembered Frank Crowe when his father, Floyd introduced him. "My father often spoke of him and held him in great respect," said Dave Bous in reference to Crowe. He recalled, "Often Mr. Crowe would take me to the gravel plant for a swim and a short visit with my father, returning later to pick me up. I always looked forward to these times because Mr. Crowe would take time to tell me about the Parker project and sometimes tell me a story about working with my father on earlier jobs." Bous, in a letter to Allen describes that at age 14 he had school and job responsibilities. Working at "Bill's Place," a privately owned small store near the dam, he earned $.10 an hour washing dishes. He moved up to washing cars at $.25 an automobile, then finally to stocking shelves at the Anderson Brothers Company Store. Delighted to receive $.50 an hour, only $.20 less than some adults working on the dam, young Bous enjoyed the experience. He remembered Mrs. Frank Bryant tipping him regularly $.10 to $.25 for carrying home her groceries. Prices at the company store ran from $.15 for a quart of milk to $.25 for ten pounds of potatoes.[29]

George Bous, another son of longtime Crowe colleague Floyd Bous, drove a truck at Parker Dam and recalled working conditions there. "We all worked the relief shift witch [which] was 10 days on days, 10 days on swing, 10 days on graveyard," he recalled. Employees paid one dollar a day to live in the company dorm. Bous and friends, when the summer heat baked the area, "had to wet the bed sheets in order to get any sleep during the day." Tired of the dorm situation, Bous and some of his friends erected a small "tent house." It must have been rough living for they had no running water or electricity. The five occupants shared four beds; at least one of them was always working. He remembered his father was able to rent one of the two bedroom company homes until his unfortunate fatal accident at the gravel plant in September of 1937.[30]

Frank Crowe developed a special father-son relationship with his nephew John Crowe, and when John graduated with his engineering degree, Uncle Frank invited him to work as a design engineer at Parker Dam. Having worked previously with his uncle at Deadwood, John knew that the work would be demanding and that, being a family member cut no special slack or attention. John married his Idaho sweetheart in September of 1937 and brought her back to Parker. Mary Crowe recalled her first sight of their new home, "When we came back to Parker late in the evening Uncle Frank flagged us down and brought us in his house. He warned us our house was hardly the place to go just then." To the newlyweds surprise, John's dorm friends had added "little touches" like nailing the small picket fence to the roof, boarding up all the windows and painting graffiti greetings all over the exterior. Some of the salutations said, "The house that John built with no jack," "Crowe Palace," or "Crowe Love Nest." Everyone had a good laugh as John and Mary roamed the house discovering more "little touches." Frank insisted that the happy couple spend the next few days with him while they restored the house to a livable condition. Mary remembered that despite the isolation of their new home at Parker, they made the best of their surroundings and she added, "We enjoyed every minute we spent in that little house. It was a carefree and enjoyable time and on John's days off we spent many happy hours exploring the country, for it had its unique beauty and many old mines and back roads," she said. One of the most satisfying experiences she had was rafting down the Colorado River "on truck inner tubes." "The 'Silver Colorado' was full of silt and the only way it could be called silver was to see the silt reflected in the moonlight," Mary Crowe noted.

Mary Crowe could see the excitement on her husband's and on Frank Crowe's faces when the news came of the building of Shasta Dam. John who was trained as a designing engineer "spent many hours working on a bid Frank would put in for a group primarily the old 'Six Companies' of Hoover Dam." Mary worked with John "at the shop in the evenings making a contoured scale model of the future Shasta Dam and how concrete should be placed for it." The most exciting part of the planning, involved searching for an innovative cableway system to serve the anticipated large area. Eventually, John and Frank's plan would be adopted by Pacific Constructor's Inc., and the headtower, the main feature of the entire system, would be built "within 11 feet of where it had been placed on the contour

Parker Dam completed, 1938 (USBR)

mock-up made at Parker Dam."[31]

Crowe not only looked at the upcoming Shasta job, but also planned to help bid on gigantic Grand Coulee Dam in eastern Washington. While not as tall as Hoover Dam, nor as deep as ParkerDam, Grand Coulee would be the world's widest dam, 4,173 feet in length.[32] Crowe's old Six Companies had reformed to prepare a bid for the lucrative contract; Morrison and Kaiser wanted Crowe to come up, look over the job and help put the bid together. Immediately, Crowe was not impressed with the suggested concrete placing proposal. Grand Coulee, a straight-gravity concrete dam, already had its foundation in place from a previous contract. The new job would entail building a railroad track across the river, loading concrete buckets in hopper cars, driving the cars out to a form, and hoisting the buckets with cranes out over a form. Cableways would not be used here and Crowe never expected to be hired on as superintendent. Nevertheless, Crowe spent the first two weeks of December 1937 in Spokane, Washington, and at the proposed job site estimating each and every facet of the government specifications. While his bid for the Interior Construction Company (later Consolidated Builders Inc.) proved to be the lowest, Crowe explained to his sister, "I don't expect to be on the job. I will be here until July then I don't know what next."[33]

He knew that Shea needed him to finish Parker Dam and build two new dams going in close to Parker. Actually, he already had made up his mind that he wanted to go after Shasta Dam, where his cableway system could be used to maximum benefit.

Shea notified Crowe that Weymouth and the Metropolitan Water District planned to put two auxiliary dams in line with the Colorado River Aqueduct and that he, Shea, wanted to bid on them. After all they were, once again, in a position to bid lower than anyone else, as their equipment and men were already close. The dams, Gene Wash and Copper Basin, were located a few miles west of the Parker site. Weymouth knew that it would be good to have a reserve water supply coming from the Colorado and he planned to pump water up from above Parker Dam, pass it into the Gene Wash Reservoir and pump it a few more miles into the Copper Basin Reservoir. From here, the water would move directly to the Los Angeles area. Crowe noticed that both dams would be interesting concrete curved arch structures to build, though quite small. Crowe had final authority on both dams and he did visit the sites occasionally in late 1937 and early 1938. He selected John Sawyer as job superintendent. Crowe planned, with Sawyer, an interesting sequence to the excavation. On the 156-foot tall Gene Wash project he suggested "drilling, shooting," and mucking with a bulldozer, while on the 210-foot Copper Basin job he resorted to "high scalers" as he had done on Hoover to chip, blast, and scrape the canyon walls clean. Power shovels and trucks sat at the bottom on the narrow canyon to carry away the muck. True to Crowe tradition, it was decided to use a cableway system to place the concrete. The radial layout of the line looked quite similar to others he pioneered years before. Both dams required less than 20,000 cubic yards of concrete, so once the cableways were in position and the mixing plant set up, the dams rose swiftly. The main problems encountered on these jobs were enduring the irrepressible heat, particularly in steep Copper Basin where jutting canyon walls stifled air movement. Bob Sass Jr. recalled one difficult day, "Copper Basin was an especially sun baked spot, and I spent a really tough day there in the summer of 1938." An unexpected squall resulted in a downpour that quickly moved tons of muck up against the nearly completed dam. Sass was given the job of pushing the material, with a tractor, away from the dam. He recalled, "the temperature [was] about 120 degrees in the shade, and no shade. I think I drank 4 gallons of water that day."[34]

1938 saw a rapid end to the Parker Dam job with Crowe spending much time away from the job, bidding on new jobs or checking progress on the Gene Wash and Copper Basin projects. On February 19th, Crowe wrote Catherine, "Just a line to say we are all well. Am leaving this afternoon for Possum Kingdom, Texas, to bid on another dam. Our dam here is nearing completion."[35] Moreover, when he was not traveling to new construction locations, he was in his office reviewing specifications for Shea and others, acting as a consulting engineer for irrigation bids; and why not, he had never been beaten yet and was now regarded as America's preeminent dam builder. The very next month, the highly acclaimed and academically respected engineering journal, *Western Construction News*, declared, "In a hot, humid hole at the Parker Dam foundation, Frank Crowe has set another world record and reinforced the right to the title 'Master Dam Builder.'" He also spent much time writing letters to and responding to memoranda from Moritz, Walter, and Shea. Much of this correspondence had to do with the cleanup procedures and the expected date of completion.[36] In late January, crews at Parker started erecting the spillway regulating gates and by February, the entire cooling process for the concrete in the dam had been completed. A short flood on March 3rd and 4th from the Bill Williams River was easily contained and by the end of that month the powerhouse substructure was finished. A slight problem developed on April 7, when workers discovered a crack in the downstream face of the dam along the California abutment. On closer inspection, Crowe decided that it needed repair, even though this represented some difficulty, as concrete operations had shifted to the diversion tunnel plugs. However, Crowe reorganized the operation and the crack was repaired by June. With the tunnel plugs in place on July 1st, the Colorado River began flowing over the dam spillway. Parker Dam was done.[37]

While the public did not hear much about the construction of Parker Dam, the engineering field recognized, once again, another magnificent accomplishment. Hoover Dam had announced to the world that dams of previously unheard of heights could now be built, while Parker Dam showed engineers that deep foundation dams could be conquered. From the world's tallest to the world's deepest dam in eight years, Frank Crowe had seemingly set himself above and apart from all the old engineering standards and set America and the world on a new bold path for irrigation and dam building. Referring to Crowe's transition from Hoover Dam to his success at Parker Dam an engineering journal noted, "This accomplishment [Hoover Dam] would have been enough to last some construction men for several years. Not so Frank Crowe; he moved at once to take in his stride an even more difficult job." The article reminded readers that, "The engineer's assignment required that the Parker Dam foundation be sunk 250 ft. to bedrock and sloughing, water-soaked embankment of river silt be held back until rock was reached and concrete started up." In a direct reference to Crowe's contribution on the job, the article noted, "Courage, skill and judgment, born of long years of experience in conquering rivers, were his weapons in winning this right. The record is proof that his 'Get Results' motto is as much his own as it is for his subordinates." The magazine that ran this article, *Western Construction News*, realized that in Crowe, here was an excellent example and model of engineering success in the West and it prominently declared, "In a region noted for its immense dams and difficult construction undertakings, the West is justly proud of its own Master Dam Builder—Frank T. Crowe."[38]

Chapter 13

The "Old Man"
Shasta Dam, 1938-1940

Ever since European colonization of California began under the Spanish in the 1700s, it became obvious that water conservation and supply ranked as the most difficult problem to overcome. Early settlement, even under the Americans, concentrated along riverbanks and lakes. The problem centered around the fact that California's Mediterranean climate brought rain in the winter, followed by an extensive summer dry period. To make matters worse, most of the rain and snow fell in the distant northern portions of the state and in the Sierra Nevada Mountains; the water was largely inaccessible to population centers in the south and along the coast. Debate and discussion focused on how to capture, store, and deliver the water sources, and to what degree the government should become involved.

California statehood coincided with a severe drought, and the first lawmakers provided for a Surveyor General. Principal among the duties of this new office was a summation of California's water potential and a plan for implementing water delivery equitably. Droughts continued, with an especially long one in the 1863-64 water year. Grain crops throughout the state wilted, and state officials worried about feeding the increasing waves of newcomers. Everyone knew that irrigation could ease the problem, but tricky land-use and water-use rights stood in the way. Lawmakers in 1864 set the stage for state involvement by authorizing the incorporation of canal companies and irrigation districts. In addition, state water planners began drawing up water source maps and diagrams to assist local and regional water districts.

In 1873, President Ulysses S. Grant ordered a team of hydrologists in the Army Engineers to survey water sources in California's Central Valley. The team worked at identifying potential water concentrations, proposing future dam sites, and projecting canal links. Numerous farmers and cattle ranchers contributed their advice. Grant reported to Congress that the Central Valley was a great untapped agricultural resource that only needed irrigation to be one of America's most productive farming regions. The next year a Californian, B. S. Alexander, proposed an idea that was to become the basic water plan of the Central Valley Project.[1] Alexander argued that surplus water in the north state should be dammed and transported south using canals and aqueducts. The dams would curtail chronic flooding, generate electricity, and provide irrigation of the dry San Joaquin Valley. While his ideas appeared noteworthy, most Californians, including the legal system, dismissed the practicality of implementing a statewide water plan. Dozens of water rights' litigation cases had already proven that any provocative comprehensive water plan would face substantial opposition in the California courts.

The next forty years realized little movement by California to incorporate a statewide water system. The Army Engineers along with the Reclamation Service conducted more surveys of potential water sources and analyzed canal routes, yet organized political action did not materialize. A geographer for the United States Geological Survey, Colonel Robert B. Marshall, saw the need to have the California state legislature take the lead in preparing and funding a water plan. Marshall produced his informative *Irrigation of Twelve Million Acres in the Valley of California* in 1921, and immediately it gained statewide and national attention. He pointed to the need for a concentration of local irrigation districts/ projects to be regulated by a state water commission. Marshall also proposed that a huge dam be constructed near the headwaters of the Sacramento River, taking advantage of the river's traditional heavy winter flow.[2] From here, the stored water would be pumped south and parceled out by state water officials. The canals Marshall planned included several wide prototypes, capable of barge navigation, located on both the east and west sides of the Central Valley. Publicity from Marshall's book helped gain the attention of the state legislature. A state scientific investigation of Marshall's ideas followed, but a subsequent implementation plan, the Water and Power Bill, went down to defeat as the legislature could not find the means to finance a project of that extent. All through the 1920s, progressive planners put the Marshall bill on the ballot as a peoples' initiative measure. A well-planned and financed opposition led by Pacific Gas & Electric put out literature helping to defeat the proposal year after year.

By 1933 conditions in California, and the nation, had changed. Gripped in a disastrous Depression, liberals and conservatives alike understood that a comprehensive water plan would be necessary for California to recover. With much of the Midwest torn asunder by the driving "dust bowl," federal "New Deal" planners also knew that California played a vital role in helping to relieve the pressure of long-term unemployment. If only water could be delivered to the Central Valley, farmers would have a chance at a productive recovery. State officials also realized the opportunity they had in securing federal dollars to fund the water project. To this end, the state legislature passed the Central Valley Project Act in 1933, authorizing a bond promise totaling $170 million. Private power companies forced the state to place the initiative on the ballot again. This time, the people supported the proposal, passing it by a narrow margin of 30,000 votes.[3]

The Shasta Dam site before construction began. (USBR)

Proposal proponents such as Judge Francis Carr and State Senator John McColl, both northern California residents, traveled to Washington D.C. to convince the federal government to fund the state proposal. They knew that the government had already authorized funds for the construction of Hoover Dam, and construction was already moving ahead on that project. Carr and McColl also knew that any statewide plan needed to include a huge dam somewhere in northern California. The project would generate a permanent income for the area; an area that had been in economic depression ever since the end of World War I and the closing of the profitable copper mines and smelters. They lobbied hard and long, along with many other California water progressives, both Democratic and Republican.

Success came in 1935 when Congress passed the Rivers and Harbors Act. Over $12 million were allocated to the Central Valley Project. Subsequent legislation provided additional funding, as the project's full scope became known. The work was to begin on two new dams, one in northern California (Shasta) to harness the Sacramento River, and one in central California (Friant) to hold back the rapid waters of the San Joaquin River. Canals, aqueducts, pumping stations, smaller dams, and electrical transmission lines would all be added later. Ambitious in design and gigantic in nature, the Central Valley Project would provide America's fastest growing state with water and energy.[4]

As excitement grew with the federal governments' decision to fund the project, questions remained as to who would actually build the major component—Shasta Dam. Using the Hoover Dam experience as a model, Congress gave the United States Bureau of Reclamation authority to oversee dam construction. The Bureau quickly placed the Shasta Dam project under the New Deal funding agency of the Public Works Administration (PWA) thereby assuring an ongoing funding commitment from Congress. Bid specifications flowed from the Denver office of the Bureau to interested private construction companies, as had been done on Hoover and Parker Dams. Word spread quickly through construction circles and the scramble was on to consider the attractive federal contract. With Parker Dam nearing completion and Grand Coulee Dam already under construction from a previous contract, Henry Kaiser, Frank Crowe, and Six Companies looked forward to securing the Shasta Dam contract. Crowe, while poring over topographic maps of the proposed work site in Shasta County, realized that a unique large-scale cableway operation would be called for. He immediately called on his nephew, John Crowe, a respected engineer in his own right and others to consider the problem. At the same time, Kaiser worked at organizing a Six Companies California-based construction company to bid Shasta Dam. The result was the short-lived Shasta Construction Company. Through the spring of 1938 Crowe, Kaiser, and Shea went through the familiar steps of surveying onsite, calling possible subcontractors, reviewing work sequences and job rates, and discussing profit margins. Rumors floated about that an aggressive new construction conglomerate, Pacific Constructors Incorporated, was interested, and determined to get a piece of the federal dam building pie.[5]

Pacific Constructors, Incorporated (PCI), came into existence in 1937 when William A. Johnson, a leading southern California industrialist, successfully convinced other construction owners to form a joint venture and bid on the federal dam projects. Johnson brought in Steve Griffith, L. E. Dixon, Clyde Wood, Floyd Shofner, and D. W. Thurston, all experienced in completing heavy construction jobs. Their first bid on Grand Coulee Dam in Washington showed their inexperience at bidding for a large dam project. They overbid by $8 million, an embarrassingly high amount. Yet, this miscalculation worked in their favor, to the delight of investors, in the subsequent bid on Shasta Dam.

In preparing to bid on the Shasta job, the leadership team of Pacific Constructors decided to bring in additional construction companies, the best in the nation. To this end, the Arundel Corporation, W.E. Callahan Construction Co., the Gunther & Shirley Company, and the Foley Brothers, Inc. all accepted the invitation to join the bid on Shasta Dam. Most of the newcomers were anxious to acquire the job, but announced that they wanted to bid a "good safe figure," in which to assure a profit.[6] It was understood that trying to calculate all of the unseen expenses on a job the size of Shasta was most difficult, and extended delays could provoke financial reprisals from the federal government and destroy profits.

The U. S. Bureau of Reclamation beginning April 1 of 1938 called for bids for construction of Shasta Dam. With the bonds secured and realizing that they would be bidding against the veterans Crowe, Kaiser and Shea, Johnson ordered dozens of engineers from most of the associated companies of Pacific Constructors to the expected dam site, some ten miles north of Redding on the Sacramento River to check out all possible contingencies. Among these engineers, Ray Whinnery, Harvey Slocum, and L. E. Dixon took the lead. Ironically, they collaborated on engineering techniques and cost estimates used by Crowe during the Hoover Dam experience. All figures were checked and rechecked with the understanding that only a calculated low bid would wrest the job bid away from their overly confident competitor, Shasta Construction.

Like Crowe, PCI engineers knew that the most significant factor to be considered in estimating the Shasta Dam job focused on the method of concrete delivery. What would be the most cost effective manner in which to place the freshly mixed concrete in the correct form? Traditionally, concrete placing on large construction jobs had seen a variety of techniques used, including moveable troughs, trolley car dumpsters, and even animal pull-carts. By 1930, most engineers, following Crowe's lead, utilized an arrangement of cables that were anchored to one or more trestle mastheads. The buckets of concrete moved along the cableway and were dumped in the appropriate form. However, the proposed width of Shasta Dam, some 3,500 feet, appeared to be too great a distance to string and support a cable system. For weeks, Johnson listened as nervous engineers debated various cableway systems.

Other parameters needed to be considered also. Even though the New Deal legislation cranked out federal funds at a never-before seen pace and optimism ran high—at least among most Democrats, the economic future remained uncertain. A serious recession threatened. PCI and Shasta Construction officials worried as the bidding deadline neared. How do you calculate for inflation on a construction job that is planned to hire thousands of workers and extend six years in duration? Will Japanese aggression in China lead to war with the U. S., and will we be dragged into the deepening European crisis? Wages set by the federal government could be changed at any time. Would Congress raise the minimum wage in response to popular demand? PCI officials also worried about the numerous subcontractors. Could they be counted on to go the duration of the project, supplying materials and labor as needed and at the efficiency level expected?

Meeting in the Biltmore Hotel in Los Angeles, PCI partners conferred and negotiated a bid that all could live with. Ironically, most of the late joiners, representatives from Eastern companies like the Arundel Corporation argued for a

low bid of $34 million, while most of the original core PCI companies stated that
it would take $36 or $37 million to complete the dam. J. C. Maguire, Secretary for
PCI, remembered how the final bid was arrived at.

> The final bid price was arrived at in an amusing way. Carl Swenson
> [Foley Brothers, Inc.] was on the low side and was one of the lead-
> ers of that faction, arguing their cause forcefully. His wise old fa-
> ther, O. W. Swenson, had attended all the meetings and made a study
> of the estimates in his own quiet way. When price discussions got
> under way (and before anyone got down to naming a figure), he did
> a little figuring on the back of an envelope and on a card, he wrote
> his idea of a price for the job. He handed the card to Bill [William]
> Johnson and left the meeting. Bill proved to be among the highs
> and as usual took a leading part in the discussion. After the highs
> and lows had argued back and forth for a couple of hours the highs
> agreed among themselves to come down to $36,000,000.00. Bill,
> knowing that the figure on the card was about $35,990,000.00, said
> to Carl, "We will compromise with your father's figure," and pulled
> out the card. Carl was reluctant to give in, but stated very graciously
> that he would defer to his father's judgment and the others then fell
> in line, and the old gentleman's figure was agreed upon. When Joe
> Hogan accepted, he remarked that he would accept any price the
> group agreed on but if we bid over $34,000,000.00 we were just
> wasting our time. As it turned out, after the months of toil and effort
> estimating and figuring, it was the more or less psychic bid of a
> contractor of the old school that finally set the price for Shasta Dam.
> By such incidents are kingdoms won and lost.[7]

In contrast to the anxious and unsure PCI officials, Crowe was confident
yet cautious, and he spent the last days in May studying the Bureau specifications
on Shasta Dam, paying particular attention to the proposed unusually long diversion tunnel. He also worried about securing a labor force, as always the "Old
Man" could count on his faithful army of "construction stiffs," but a job the size of
Shasta would require thousands of men. Additionally, there was no readily available cement source; such as there had been at Deadwood. Knowing that Shasta
could well be America's last big dam, and his last job, Crowe wanted to be bold in
his bidding suggestions. On May 31, 1938, Crowe met Kaiser, Shea, and Bonneville
Dam veteran, Jack McKachern in Sacramento. They were confused about PCI's
participation in the bidding process. Reportedly, they were sending few, if any,
engineers or consultants to the Sacramento River dam site. Kaiser's contacts in
the construction industry were unable to help him discover how serious PCI was,
or, if they would even bid. It was on this note that Crowe edged toward finalizing

a conservative bid. Amazingly, with the number of parameters needing to be considered, Crowe and company considered a $36.2 million bid, very close to the bid that PCI had just arrived at. The figure provided a safe margin for contingencies and profit. Now a critical turning point occurred when McEachern ventured that the bid should be reduced to under $36 million.[8] Unbelievably, it was Frank Crowe, possibly worried about the cost of the cableway system he was proposing, who urged his backers not to lower the bid.[9] All his life he had taken the unknown risk, no matter what the construction challenge, to secure bids.

At 10:00 am on June 1, 1938, Dick Dixon, representing PCI arrived at the auditorium of the Bureau of Reclamation office and modestly presented his company's bid. Kaiser passed the envelope holding Shasta Construction's bid as Bureau officials, engineers, news writers, along with the usual crowd of salesmen of contractors' equipment, and supplies looked on. J. C. Maguire, secretary for PCI, recalled the exiting moment. "Finally they got down to opening the bids. The first one opened was that of Pacific Constructors. The total was read first and with that the bottom fell out of everything for Shasta Construction Company, as they knew they were beaten, barring an error or irregularity in the bid."[10] The opposing bids proved to be amazingly close, PCI offered to do the job for $35,939,450.00 while Shasta Construction followed with $36,202,357.00. PCI had won. Finally, they had succeeded in acquiring a major federal dam contract and denying Shasta Construction (Six Companies) continued dominance in bidding large dams. Quietly, a somber Crowe, a highly agitated Kaiser, and the rest of the Shasta Construction team retreated from the scene, returning to their hotel where, according to Maguire a "stormy session" followed in which "each blamed the other for not cutting their bid lower."

Not one to give up easily, the formidable Henry Kaiser stayed on in Sacramento, asking to review the PCI bid. Permission was given and he, searching in vain, discovered what he thought was an "irregularity" in PCI's bid statement. The Bureau's bidding notice contained the following statement: "The right is reserved as the interests of the Government may require to reject any and all bids, to waive any informality in bids received and accept or reject any item of any bid unless such bid is qualified by specific limitation." Kaiser found the PCI document contained the following statement, "Bid submitted is based on the award to us of all of the items bid upon." Thinking quickly, Kaiser reasoned that the phrase "all of the items bid upon" forced the Bureau of Reclamation to "do 100% of each quantity of each [bid] item" with PCI and he complained that this was contrary to the government's bidding statement. Grabbing at straws to save Shasta Construction's hopes, Kaiser also declared that he found the PCI bid to be "unbalanced," and that this would eventually cause higher costs for the government. Not wanting to get involved in this affair and the political brawl that was about to take place, a dejected Crowe returned to Parker Dam to await the outcome.

PCI president Johnson and Maguire prepared for the legal battle of their life as the contest for awarding the huge contract moved to the Denver office of the Bureau. There, Johnson and Maguire were successful in defending against Kaiser's accusations that the bid was unbalanced. Chief Engineer Walter backed PCI's bid and decided to pass on the other complaint of the "irregularity" to officials in Washington D.C.[11] John C. Page, Commissioner of the Reclamation, notified Johnson and Maguire that the Bureau's legal department would need time to decide the appropriateness of Kaiser's objection. After two difficult weeks in which the PCI officers lobbied members of Congress and secured additional legal counsel, Secretary of the Interior Harold Ickes announced that the PCI bid was good and the Shasta Dam contract would be awarded to them.[12]

Excited and reenergized, Johnson and Maguire reorganized PCI, adding new member companies, forming committees to handle different phases of the job, and ironically, searching for a General Superintendent of Construction. They needed an experienced dam construction engineer, someone who could handle the intricate, and oftentimes frustrating operational relationship between the U. S. Bureau of Reclamation inspectors, contracting construction company managers and supervisors, and the thousands of newly hired laborers. Through the construction grapevine, Crowe heard of the opening and immediately pondered the opportunity. It would mean ending his direct working relationship with Kaiser, Shea and the others associated with the old Six Companies. Hesitating for only a few days the revived Crowe sent word to Johnson that his services were available. Well known to all of the PCI officials and well respected, Crowe was enthusiastically hired. Already nationally recognized for his masterful handling of the tough Hoover Dam project he could be counted on to bring Shasta Dam in on time and under cost. The "Old Man's" reputation as a tough, yet fair, and rewarding supervisor had earned him the loyalty of hundreds of "construction stiffs" who looked to Crowe for future job opportunities. By hiring Crowe, PCI realized they were also hiring an already tested and proven dam construction crew—the best in the nation, and arguably, in the world. Within days of the hiring the aging, yet tireless engineer began sending the word out, nationwide, to his loyal band of dam builders. There was one big dam still to build.[13]

A full-scale migration to Shasta County escalated as the summer of 1938 progressed. The national press carried reports of preliminary Bureau of Reclamation work in the area and that some job hiring would begin immediately. With a pronounced downturn in the economy and the announcement that the dam would take five years to build, Crowe's "stiffs" saw this as a long-term employment opportunity. Men like Lloyd Hill and Art Corella; both Parker Dam builders followed the "Old Man" to Shasta. Pete Forte, whose father had worked on Hoover Dam, decided to follow his father in dam building. He was hired at Shasta and ended up working on his father's crew.[14] Along with these veteran dam builders, came hundreds of other men and their families, hoping to join the Crowe team.

Frank Crowe arrived on the Shasta Dam job in late June and quickly

The contractor's camp, known as Shasta Dam Village, is partially shown here with the dormitory (left) and mess hall (right) under construction. (USBR)

consulted with the designated Bureau engineer, Ralph Lowry. Lowry, who had been with Crowe at the conclusion of Hoover Dam, respected the "Old Man" and the engineering methods used by Crowe. The opposite also held true, and Crowe enjoyed Lowry's friendship as well as his reputation for flexibility in dealing with onsite construction problems. To round out the Bureau team that Crowe would be working with, Secretary of the Interior Harold Ickes named Walker Young as Chief Engineer for the California's Central Valley Project, of which Shasta Dam was the keystone. Raymond Walter remained in Denver directing both Lowry and Young. Ickes also named Roy Snell to be Lowry's assistant. Snell would work closely with Crowe's superintendents and foremen checking and verifying contract specifications.[15]

Ralph Lowry, Missouri born in 1889, graduated Washington State College with a B.S. and a M.S. degree in Civil Engineering. He worked on the Yakima Project after graduation but left three years before Crowe arrived in the area. He spent time in Denver as a design engineer, and then worked on the McKay Dam in Oregon and Gibson Dam in Montana before assignment to the Boulder project in

1930. On December 1, 1935, the Bureau named him Construction Engineer at Hoover Dam replacing Walker Young. He remained in this position until his transfer to the Shasta Dam project. The six foot, athletically inclined engineer matched Crowe's physical stamina for enduring long work hours while at the same time mentally juggling mathematical calculations, without the use of a slide rule, to estimate specifications for upcoming job requirements. Both men felt comfortable calling on the other any time during the day or night, and both men understood the importance of working as a team to maximize the work effort.[16]

By the time both Crowe and Lowry arrived in Shasta County, the survey crews had already laid out Kennett Camp (later renamed Toyon); what would become headquarters and home to scores of Bureau inspectors, engineers, and other government personnel. Not wanting to get involved again in community building, on a large scale, as they had done with Boulder City, the Bureau decided that they would only build quarters for their employees. The contractor would be required to construct a separate camp. By late July of 1938, construction of Toyon was well under way, and the main administrative building, dormitories, warehouses, a testing laboratory, a garage and fire station, and dozens of small homes neared completion later that month. The Bureau, made the construction in Toyon live up to exacting building standards. When completed later in 1938, Toyon shined as another "New Deal" model community. Full services, including running water, sewer, and electricity were available from the start. Home design and construction gave the appearance of a well-ordered and maintained living environment. Toyon residents such as George Van Eaton remarked that "everyone" wanted to live there, "it was probably the best housing in the area."[17]

Crowe realizing the limited housing at the government camp of Toyon, quickly called on his old carpenter superintendent Charlie Williams one more time. Shasta Dam Village, located a few hundred yards downstream from the dam site rose swiftly in the summer heat as Williams' men worked twelve and fourteen-hour shifts. Almost self-contained, Shasta Dam Village, or Contractor's Camp, boasted a huge dormitory, mess hall, recreation room, dry-goods store, and dozens of single-family homes.

Notwithstanding the rapid rise of Toyon and Shasta Dam Village, housing demands in the area reached critical levels by August as over two thousand unemployed men and their families converged on the dam site, located twelve miles to the north of the town of Redding. Quick-thinking and profit-minded entrepreneurs from Redding, Sacramento, and the Bay Area purchased land around the newly cut-in access road from nearby state Highway 99. The road, first named Grand Coulee Boulevard, was renamed Shasta Dam Boulevard; it soon became dotted with small businesses and homes. Two of the first establishments to open their doors to thirsty clients were The Silver Dollar and The Mint Pool Hall. By August, Shasta Dam Boulevard's dusty dirt surface carried considerable traffic to and from the dam site, and to the new nearby communities. From out of nowhere three community centers rose: Summit City, at the intersection of Shasta Dam Boulevard and the Kennett/Buckeye Road; Project City, at the intersection of Highway 99 and Shasta Dam Boulevard; and Central Valley, strung out for two miles on Shasta Dam Boulevard between Summit City and Project City. Collectively, they became known as the "Boomtown."[18]

All through the summer of 1938 Crowe's national construction team streamed into the area. Many of them dropped existing jobs to have one more opportunity to work with the "Old Man." Frank Crowe, who at fifty-five years old, could have retired on a secure financial basis, knowing that his engineering accomplishments would be long remembered. But, he did not look or feel fifty-five years old. Shasta Dam would be America's second tallest and second widest dam, and it offered him the unique challenge of planning and implementing the largest cableway system ever considered. With Linnie and the children in southern California, he threw all of his attention to attacking Shasta Dam.

As on every big dam construction project, Crowe needed to simultaneously start several key phases of the work, and he conferred with Lowry on the rerouting of the Southern Pacific railroad tracks. The tracks, where they now ran, if nothing was done, would be covered later, with the rising waters from Shasta Lake. Down at the dam site, Crowe started his men drilling a railroad by-pass tunnel that would later double as a Sacramento River diversion tunnel. Working in thin short-sleeved shirts and sporting protective steel hard hats, "tunnel hogs" sweated to excavate 1,820 feet into the hillside. Summer temperatures increased weekly, and then cleared 100 degrees. Boulder and Parker Dam veterans, surprised that this kind of heat could develop in such a northern location, recalled bitter memories of the searing heat and constant thirst of the Nevada desert. Nevertheless, work progressed on schedule. Throughout August, tunnel men, under the supervision of Woody Williams, placed heavy timbers as supports in the ever-deepening 28-foot high tunnel. Meanwhile, men in bulldozers struggled to clear out a road to the east abutment. Steep slopes made work dangerous as well as difficult. By September, crews cleared the future sites of the hospital and administrative offices. Also, a temporary truck bridge was built downstream from the dam site. This would afford access to the west abutment. On September 21, excited men began using power shovels and trucks to excavate for the foundation of the dam on the east abutment. Though the rocky clay soil proved difficult to penetrate, work progressed at a good pace. The combination of heavy equipment and body-hardened "construction stiffs," working alongside each other was amazing. Huge digging shovels scooped up material chipped and broken by men wrestling one and two-man hydraulic jackhammers.[19]

Almost daily through September, anxious new families arrived in the Boomtown area. Men looking for quick employment descended on the hiring offices in Redding and at the dam site. Newly arrived residents settled in numerous squatter camps along the Sacramento River (downstream, clear to Redding), and near Shasta Dam Boulevard. Official Bureau photographer B. D. Glaha, visited these families and recorded visually their plight. Some had only simple tent and tarp affairs for shelter. Others lived in trailers, or crude lean-tos built from scrap lumber. Many single men lived in their automobiles. While the number of men hired in the summer of 1938 only numbered in the hundreds, the unemployed counted on Crowe to begin mass hiring once the main excavation and concrete work began.

Education officials in Shasta County grew alarmed at the reported hundreds of migrant children moving into the squatter camps of the boomtowns. In consultation with Crowe and Lowry, the county school board proposed a new school for the area. Money however, was a problem and in a true spirit of cooperation, Lowry persuaded the Bureau of Reclamation to donate several acres at the key intersection of Shasta Dam Boulevard and the Kennett Road for a school site. Crowe, with permission from PCI officials provided much of the materials. Off-duty dam workers and quite a number of not-yet-hired job hopefuls pitched in with their labor to get the new school at Toyon up and running.

Matt Rumboltz, Toyon's first principal, and three teachers planned to open the school on October 3. Advanced sign-ups totaled 125 prospective students. When the school doors opened on October 10, more than 150 students stormed the not-yet-finished schoolhouse. Eleven days later the student population climbed to 213 and by the end of the month 256 students had enrolled. With the word out that a new school had opened, the student population steadily climbed to over 350 by the end of the year, and peaked at 400 in January of 1939, making it one of the largest rural schools in the nation. By this time, Rumboltz had been forced to expand his staff to ten full-time teachers, and two new rooms were hastily built. Students literally began coming "out of the windows." Individual class sizes ranged from a low of 36 to an unbelievable 73 students in one first grade class! Even Rumboltz's office was converted into classroom space. The principal had to conduct his administrative business in the hallway or outside under a tree.[20]

Crowe wanted to move Linnie and his children to Shasta Dam as soon as adequate housing could be obtained. He quickly decided against living at Shasta Dam Village as the area was remote and services would be quite limited. For the interim period, Crowe took up residence at the Redding Hotel. On one of his few days off, the veteran engineer previewed property in Redding. He became quite taken with a building lot located on the western boundary of the city limits. The land, perched on a ridge overlooking Redding, also commanded panoramic views of the entire Mt. Lassen volcanic mountain range and awe-inspiring Mt. Shasta. Crowe commenced building immediately, hiring off-duty dam workers to erect an impressive two-story structure. Writing his sister in October he commented that, "We are building a shack in Redding. Will start plastering tomorrow." Crowe moved into the stately home in early spring of 1939 with his family. He went on to tell Catherine about the work beginning at Shasta Dam and the labor situation, stating "We are getting this job started. Have 700 on the payroll. 100% A.F. of L.—closed shop. Is that American?? Well! we are trying to get along."[21]

With construction activity in full-swing Secretary of the Interior, Harold L. Ickes and others visited the Shasta site to speak about the importance of Shasta Dam for the people and economy of California. The ceremony was broadcast, by radio, to most of California and it helped set-off another influx of job-seeking men. Ickes was given a tour of the dam site and Toyon. He saw young Civilian Conservation Corps (CCC) employees grading driveways and landscaping the dorms.[22] Lowry and Crowe assured Ickes that everything was moving along on schedule, and that sufficient manpower would be available.

Late October through December saw a rapid increase in hiring as operations expanded. Finishing work continued on Shasta Dam Village, as warehouses, electrical and mechanical shops, single-family homes, were all completed. Excavation began on the west abutment and continued on the east side. Groups of wagon-mounted drilling rigs operated continuously on the river diversion channel and the lower abutments on both sides of the river. Designed to be operated by two men the wagon drills proved effective, if properly handled. One had to be watchful and careful of the powerful pulsating steel drill. The drills could be rotated to operate in the horizontal position thereby drilling horizontal blasting holes. Initial power for the hydraulic drills came from a large eight-unit compressor house. The plant could put out 11,000 cubic feet of air per minute. They also brought down the heavy duty power shovels to the rivers' edge to remove the drilled debris.

Beginning as early as 1936, U. S. Bureau of Reclamation engineers began an extensive investigation of sand and gravel deposits for concrete mixing. A large open-air warehouse was built to house the gravel samples obtained from around the area. By 1938, the list of acceptable sites had been shortened to two locations, Kutras Tract in Redding and the Hatch Tract—some twenty miles further downstream. Following this, the Bureau of Reclamation opened the bidding to private contractors.[23] Columbia Construction Company successfully bid the lowest, basing their figures for the Kutras site. The regular railroad was being rerouted from the dam site to an easterly location. The only other idea initially on the table for consideration was a massive trucking effort with three shifts of men driving back and forth along Highway 99. After further analysis it was decided to erect a unique industrial-capacity conveyor belt. Conceived as the most efficient way to transport the millions of tons of gravel, the belt system would extend nearly ten miles, making it the world's longest moving conveyance.[24]

At the dam site, construction crews installed drainage culverts, erected a railroad bridge, and installed a huge water tank on the east abutment; it would supply water to the contractor's camp. Most of the heavy equipment remained engaged in digging out the hillsides of the east and west slopes. The Bucyrus 48-B and the 120-B power shovels proved to be the workhorses of these early stages of abutment excavation. A fleet of 25 cubic yard capacity dump trucks hauled the excavated debris material to dump sites upstream.[25] Crowe initiated the three-shift schedule and day and night, the crews worked, through increasingly cooler weather.

The excavation and terracing of the abutments focused the attention of most visitors to the site. Every day the scene changed. From the top of the east slope, crowds could watch the dramatic blasting of each abutment. Then the big shovels and dump trucks moved in removing blasted material. Some of the fill was used to terrace each slope to the exact specifications necessary. The fill needed to be tamped effectively, and this was done with heavy tractors and a "sheep's foot" tamper. Back and forth the tractors went, compacting the debris while engineers measured the levels and monitored the quality of the fill. As Christmas 1938 drew near, work continued. The weather remained clear, yet cold. A "sea wall" for the river diversion rose swiftly on the east abutment. This concrete structure would confine the redirected Sacramento River water once dewatering of the main river channel became necessary. At this time, workers laid out a gigantic warehouse near the railroad tracks. It would be here that immense steel girders, railings, tubing, and other metal construction parts would be stored.

The Bureau of Reclamation used young Civilian Conservation Corps (CCC) workers in landscaping operations in and around the dam site. On December 22, 1938, Byron H. Eich, CCC official and Lowry inspected the reservoir clearing progress. Eich watched as his 18 to 25-year old cadets struggled to chop down pines and oaks, and rip out manzanita brush and poison oak. Run like a paramilitary outfit, the CCC paid $30 a month to the young uniformed men. Each volunteer sent a portion of their pay home to grateful parents. Living in barracks-like quarters, the CCC enrollees started the day at sunrise, worked hard until noon, ate a hearty lunch, and then continued their labors until 5:00 p.m. The youthful workers proved capable, as the brush clearing operation moved ahead of schedule and with few accidents. Shasta County had, at its peak in 1939, eleven CCC camps working on Bureau projects—a national record.[26]

As 1938 ended, much had been accomplished. No less than five new communities had sprung up where previously nothing had existed. An estimated population of 3,000 to 5,000 inhabited the area. The rerouting of the Southern Pacific Railroad proceeded, the river diversion sea wall stood nearly ready to divert the Sacramento River, incredible amounts of earth had been removed from the east and west slopes and the foundation channels deepened, bridges connected the work on both sides of the river, and roads connected the dam site with the outside world. The eyes of the nation were focusing on the area as continuing news of construction progress spread rapidly, and more and more job-hungry men migrated to the area.

As 1939 opened, workers returned from New Year's Day celebrations feeling fortunate to have a job and eager to continue excavating the east and west abutments, completing the diversion channel along the Sacramento River, and tunneling the railroad by-pass. Every day unemployed men gathered anxiously around the hiring shack at the dam site looking for posted openings and hoping that their skill specialty would be needed. On one occasion, a desperate job seeker told a PCI supervisor that he had a friend who had welding experience on Parker Dam. The foreman asked for the name of the friend, and the job-hopeful replied, "I am that man!"[27] He was hired on the spot. The easiest way to be hired on the dam project was to let a friend who already was employed help you. Friends would talk to supervisors and managers and by informal talk, a job offer would be made. Everyone understood that you had to prove yourself every day. No wimps allowed. All men reported to their work shift on time, worked hard, obeyed their supervisors, and followed the safety rules—to the letter. Superintendent Crowe insisted on strict safety compliance; he did not want negative publicity about pushing work ahead at the expense of his men's safety. Crowe suffered through large numbers of injuries and over a hundred fatalities on the dangerous Hoover Dam project and he (and the Bureau) did not want a repeat at Shasta.

Many phases of the work on Shasta Dam proved dangerous. However, in these initial stages of massive excavation, the danger factor increased with the use of high explosives employed to blast out the east and west abutment. The railroad by-pass tunnel also loomed as a potential hazard; weak structural zones and subsequent cave-ins in the cutout could be encountered at any time. Nonetheless, work pressed on. During January of 1939, workers dug deeper and deeper into the east abutment cutting an opening for the corewall—the side foundation of the dam itself. Powerful high-wattage night-lights installed on both abutments kept work going throughout dark hours. The huge five-yard capacity buckets of the Bucyrus-Erie electric shovels scooped blasted debris and poured the material into awaiting dump trucks, to be deposited where needed around the dam site. Day after day this routine continued.

Down in the railroad by-pass tunnel, crews struggled, working from both the north and south ends. In the dark, damp reaches of the tunnel head men labored to drill the tunnel facing, power shovel the debris onto awaiting "muck carts" and transport the "muck" via a rail track to larger dump trucks outside the tunnel. At a proposed length of 1820 feet, an excavated height of 28 feet, and a width of 26 feet, tunnel diggers realized the immensity of their part of the project.[28] The tunneling process involved raw excavation, initial timbering support followed with steel ribbing, placement of a reusable concrete lining form, interior cross-bracing, concrete pumping into the form, and final concrete tamping and finishing. The horseshoe-shaped form would then be moved on down to the next section of braced tunnel and the concrete process repeated. The distance from the form, to the excavated edge of rock, averaged two feet, and this area was filled with an extensive network of reinforcing rods before concrete was pumped in. In a situation similar to America's first transcontinental railroad building race between the Union Pacific and the Central Pacific Railroads, tunneling crews raced from both ends to excavate the furthest. Off-duty diggers discussed their progress and wagered on the breakthrough date.[29]

In late January Crowe wrote to his sister Catherine, responding to a request from her for some advice on purchasing real estate. The letter reveals an interesting side to Crowe's personal feelings. He describes his difficulty in trying to sell his houses in Boulder City, Parker Dam, and Pasadena. At the same time, he was trying to maintain his "getaway ranch" in Montana, which he bought ten years previously. He admitted to his sister that "it is just impossible for me to give you 'long distance' advice." Crowe ended by telling Catherine that government appropriations for Shasta Dam were being reviewed and that he was preparing to "layoff half my crew" if funds were halted. He admitted that even though his men know that the government was responsible for the threatened work slowdown, he felt that "they [his men] are crying for my neck."[30]

In February, scores of CCC youth continued their landscaping duties at the government camp of Toyon. Of primary importance was the administrative center. Just off Shasta Dam Boulevard, dam workers, local residents, and visiting dignitaries saw the government office first; and Bureau officials, mostly New Deal appointees, wanted to create a positive environment. Soon manicured lawns bordered by decorative boulders adorned the administrative center and many of the homes. To keep the appearance beautiful and orderly, individual home sites were carefully monitored. Residents were prohibited from altering the structure or radically changing the landscaping without permission from Bureau officials. Few complained about this lack of individual rights, in fact, most thought it was necessary and good; they felt fortunate to be living there. In the single men's dormitory, workers had a raucous good time. After finishing the daytime work shift, Toyon men ate dinner in the mess hall at Shasta Dam Village or in one of the eateries in the nearby boomtowns; there were no dining facilities at Toyon.[31] Since Toyon was a government installation, liquor could not be served; again, workers would pile into friends' cars and off they would go to Boomtown. There they could relax drinking beer, playing pool or cards, and "shoot the bull." And "shoot the bull" they did. One story led to another, as the hours passed by. Most stories centered around a worker's previous experiences working on other dam projects. Hoover Dam veterans loved to talk about the terrific danger involved in their work on Black Canyon. Ft. Peck dam builders spoke about the unique problems of building an earth-filled dam. All this drinking and bravado sometimes led to impromptu physical outbursts regarding the accuracy of someone's statement. More often, social mixing such as this, produced a strong bond of friendship and camaraderie that lasted on the job as well as off.[32]

On March 4, drillers from the southern side of the railroad diversion tunnel broke though to the drillers coming the other way. Quickly, the small hole was enlarged big enough to fit a man, and after laying down a 2x12-inch board for support, a grimy, dirt-covered driller crawled through the orifice and greeted his companions on the north side. Preparations followed to cut open the last section and prepare for the final concrete lining. Crowe was overheard to say, "One job down!" Soon to be reassigned tunnel workers, proud of their achievement of holing through ahead of schedule, celebrated for at least two days.[33] Southern Pacific Railroad workers now descended into the tunnel and began laying temporary tracks. On June 27, 1939 the first train, a westbound freight, cautiously eased through the tunnel.[34]

Members of the American Society of Civil Engineers visited the dam site in March. Crowe had invited them to see the progress on the dam and to give them a close-up view of the innovative engineering techniques that he was utilizing. The recently completed diversion tunnel impressed the engineers, and eyebrows rose when they stood at the tunnel entrance. Crowe's excellent planning and job sequencing was evident everywhere the visiting men looked. The engineers saw well coordinated batteries of wagon drills moving ahead with abutment excavation—drilling blasting holes at night and chipping away at critical rock fracture points in the daytime. The visitors knew that on a job the size of Shasta every aspect of the engineering must be well managed. Each phase complements, and is dependent on, the other phases. Crew foremen reported to Bureau team inspectors who in turn checked in with PCI shift foremen. The shift foremen consulted with Lowry and Crowe constantly, looking back to review progress, correct mistakes, and anticipate upcoming problems. After the tour, Crowe invited all 150 engineers to have dinner with him at the company mess hall.[35]

April of 1939 saw attention return to the main excavation on the slope abutments. Large-scale blasting rocked the west abutment on April 12. More and more newly hired men joined the wagon drill teams as they carved deeper into the hillside. Now agile workers scaling the steep walls of the uppermost portion of the west abutment hand dug blasting holes. Others, dangling dangerously from security ropes fastened to anchor posts chipped, dug, and shoveled rock debris. At an elevation of over 900 feet, the view was spectacular, yet frightening.

Amid all this activity hundreds of new visitors converged on the dam site, many to see the blasting. Politicians from the California State Legislature and officials from the Central Valley Project Association checked in regularly during this time. On May 13, 1939, more than 275 visitors appeared. Officials of Pacific Constructors Inc. including Frank Crowe, Clyde Woods, S. M. Griffith, and W. A. Johnson entertained most of this party with a special luncheon at the company mess hall.[36] These visitors were able to see new work beginning on the spillway section. They watched as tons of dirt and rock were cleared away. Some of the earth was taken to a newly constructed materials laboratory where tests provided information on where best to use the debris. The control laboratory boasted an elaborate chemistry bench, an automatic screening hopper and special storage racks. Here concrete samples were dried, stressed and tested. Sampling of concrete mixing, placing and hardening occurred in the laboratory in miniature scale. These same visitors watched as excavation began for the footings of the headtower. Huge 18-B cranes assisted in this task. In preparation for all the concrete placing, a new search began for supplemental sources of aggregate, should the need arise. To this end a special mobile aggregate testing unit, a converted woody station wagon, roamed the area in search of aggregate samples.[37]

On another occasion, June 3, over 100 CCC enrollees from camp BR-78, Orland Project, accompanied by project officials toured the Shasta site. Sporting brown army-like uniforms, boots, ties and African safari hats, these young men observed the advance stages of excavation. They also were able to see the now completed building and landscaping at the Government Camp (Toyon). With lawns in, curtains in the windows, cars parked on the street, and patio furniture in the back yard, the visitors saw a clean park-like, well-maintained environment.[38]

By June 7, blasting activity increased as PCI planners moved forward with the excavation of the spillway channel. Tons of dynamite exploded all during the following week and thousands of tons of debris were hauled away as dump trucks worked day and night. Now, Crowe realized that coordination of all the blasting, hauling, drilling, and concrete placing became paramount. In a relatively compact area, the safety of hundreds of workers' lives depended on knowing what each work crew was doing. For example, during blasting activity, rock chippers and muckers cleared the area, trucks stopped, and drill crews took a break. Some of the crews moved from the immediate dam site canyon to the east abutment roadway. Here they began grading and paving operations. The roadway would be particularly helpful once the winter rains began in October. Already several truck accidents had occurred due to loose dirt roadway sections. With the blasting complete, trucks and men were quickly brought back to the abutment slopes to drill and clear away loose debris. Then the blasting crews would come back in and the process would begin again.[39]

Through the long hot summer months of June, July, and August, off-duty dam workers, and teenagers formed summer softball leagues. The Bureau fielded a team of 16 players. They competed with local leagues from Shasta Dam Village and the Boomtowns. For added competition, teams from nearby Redding and Anderson played on a regular basis. By August of 1939, the competition was so keen that numerous wagers occurred and a championship tournament completed the competition in August. Despite the repressive summer heat the competition was surprisingly high and enthusiasm helped to keep their off-duty hours fulfilled. Makeshift ballparks sprang up on both abutments, across from Toyon, and several locations in the Boomtown area.[40]

Meanwhile, massive amounts of fill were dumped on the west abutment lower section to form the base for the penstock slide slope. The penstocks, once installed, would carry the water to the hydroelectric turbines. At the same time the area was excavated for the powerhouse, located several hundred feet downstream.

Crowe's headtower dominates the construction site at Shasta Dam. (USBR)

All through the month of September, activity increased away from the dam site. The aggregate plant at Kutras Tract (Redding) needed to be constructed. It would be from here that excavated aggregate, of varying size and quality, would be delivered to Coram (about a mile below the dam site), where the sand and

Preparations are being made to begin excavating the Sacramento Riverbed while
a cofferdam diverts the river. (USBR)

gravel was sorted and stockpiled. From Coram PCI built its own conveyor belt
that brought the material to the mixing plant.[41] The foundation for the aggregate
plant began at a point on the Kutras Tract where the Sacramento River takes a
sharp turn south. Working at the other end of the line, near the dam site, crews
began laying the foundation for the concrete mixing plant and for the aggregate
handling and storage area. Both of these facilities, located on the west side of the
river and downstream from the site, would take weeks to complete. While construction of the aggregate site at Kutras moved ahead rapidly, the Bureau of Reclamation concluded a contract with Henry Kaiser's Permanente Cement Co. to
supply the tons of cement that would be needed. All through the summer, Kaiser
worked at his San Jose Permanente facilities, expanding his operation in order to
fulfill Crowe's projected cement needs. Kaiser added storage silos, blending silos, laboratory, cement crusher, a new kiln, and an extensive conveyor belt loading
operation.[42]

    October saw some of the initial foundation construction and the initial
stages of erecting the steel girders for the giant cableway headtower. It would be
from the headtower that a series of cables would deliver precisely mixed concrete
to specific points on the dam. For months to come, October 1939 to June of 1940,

Shasta Dam conveyor belt ran almost ten miles from Redding to the construction site. (USBR)

the headtower would grow like a giant erector set—one girder at a time. Planned to be over 465 feet tall, the foundation girders extended an additional 102 feet below the surface. As the headtower grew daily so did the tail towers, the anchor supports for the other end of the cable system. These tail towers erected at strategic points on the downstream side of the dam would be moveable, sliding back and forth on tracks allowing for the exact placement of concrete buckets.[43]

As 1939 came to a close, work on the lower portions of the dam site halted when unexpected flooding from the Sacramento River occurred. Crews working on the powerhouse excavation and diversion channel could not continue with safety, and Crowe ordered the men to abandon the site. They were assigned other jobs at higher elevations. The flooding quickly subsided, but Crowe felt like he had been caught off guard and he realized that proper planning for future flooding would be critical.[44] Yet, the veteran engineer was soon tested again.

On January 2, 1940, construction "stiffs" busied themselves in Redding as they prepared the aggregate storage units, sorting rooms, and readied the conveyor belt. That same morning, down at the dam site, a long freight train puffed and chugged its way through the work area. By now, many trains had come through the temporary railroad tunnel by-pass. Many of these trains carried passengers, and train engineers always slowed the trains down so that they and their passengers could see, first-hand and down close, progress on building Shasta Dam. From the train, it would have appeared that the Sacramento River had swelled with re-

Ralph Lowry (left), Bureau engineer with Frank Crowe and the first
bucket of concrete on Shasta Dam, July 8, 1940. (USBR)

cent rains, as the swiftly running and rising water roared uncontested only 20 feet
below. Over at the Kutras Tract, concern mounted as rapidly moving waters threatened the aggregate plant. With a watchful eye, Crowe stood on the riverbank at
the dam site and pondered precautionary options. Within days, upstream creeks
such as Little Cow Creek, Cedar Creek, and the Pit River crested. Off and on
again rain kept Crowe guessing as to when an unexpected downstream deluge
might occur. Between rains, Crowe marveled at nearby snowcapped Mount Shasta,
knowing that the heavy snow pack would mean possible spring flooding.

By mid-January, the rain had stopped and the ground began to dry out.

Crowe drove his crews to make up lost time, and work proceeded on erecting ten large cement silos near the main aggregate storage unit at the dam site. Attention remained focused on continuing to build the main headtower. Plans called for installing the giant headtower girders in layers, or panels. The bottom panel, the longest, stood 75 feet in height. Each subsequent panel decreased in length as the steel girded pyramid rose. On January 29, the headtower stood over 260 feet tall as agile "steel monkey men" bolted panel girders in place. Each girder weighed an enormous 40 to 50 tons. A powerful crane, working from the center of the headtower raised the huge girders slowly and held them in place until they were securely bolted. From afar, it appeared as if the giant erect headtower was alive and working feverishly to build itself. From below skilled observers used hand signals and radios to direct the crane operators.[45]

At the same time, the aggregate plant in Redding moved into operational status. Piles of different sized aggregate and sand accumulated, and the workers readied the blending tunnel conveyor. It would be here that inspectors would mix the appropriate ratio of different sized aggregate before placing the mix on the main conveyor belt heading to the dam site. Once the operation started at the Kutras aggregate plant, consultants arrived and checked the progress. In addition to Lowry's almost daily visits, Walter R. Young, Supervising Engineer for the Central Valley Project reviewed operations. He met with a visiting team of consulting engineers from Stanford University, the University of California, and Columbia University. Lowry called for a special meeting of consulting engineers and Bureau inspectors on January 31. Three high-ranking officials from the Bureau office in Denver joined the above-mentioned group of academic engineers. After touring the facilities at the Kutras site, the talented group of engineers pored over technical plans for operating the conveyor belt.[46]

Good weather allowed newly hired work crews to begin installing the aggregate conveyor belt receiving station at the dam site. The belt, 36 inches wide, consisted of a special six-ply fabrication. Goodyear Rubber Company, already providing truck tires for the Shasta Dam job, hoped to gain worldwide recognition by having produced the world's longest conveyor belt. Giant rolls of belts were hauled by trucks out along the ten-mile proposed run and readied for installation. Workers began the arduous process of placing thousands of steel rollers on the conveyor belt wooden frame, and one by one, the conveyor flights neared completion.

All over the Shasta Dam work site, crews worked so fast that hardly anyone noticed the changing weather. By mid-February the rain began to fall, almost daily. Starting on February 26 and lasting for three days, it poured. On the 27th alone, six inches fell in just over four hours! The streams rose, dumping more and more water into the rapidly rising Sacramento River. Crowe quietly hoped for the deluge to stop. His worry centered not so much on the rising river, but on the loose muddy ground. Heavy construction work is difficult even under dry conditions. With the knee-deep mud, workers could not be expected to produce quality work, and safety became an issue. However, Crowe had more than mud to worry about. By the morning of the 27th PCI, officials measured the now-raging Sacramento River at 135,000 cubic feet per second at the dam site. The downpour continued. News came from upstream that the Pit River and Bully Hill Bridges were threatened, and Crowe realized that his operations were also vulnerable. The low-lying Kutras aggregate site in Redding quickly flooded; the operation shut down by noon.[47]

Nearby Redding residents, particularly farmers with scores of cattle grazing along the river channel nervously herded their stock to higher ground. Hundreds of curiosity seekers hurried down to the eroding riverbanks. Sporting umbrellas and raincoats these people braved the absolute drenching rain to watch the flood. Everyone knew it was a big one. First, branches of trees floated by, then timber from someone's home or barn drifted downstream. Others spotted cattle and chickens, most dead, some still struggling to survive. The initial excitement of observing a flood first-hand gave way to terror. The rain continued.[48]

The rain stopped briefly on the morning of the 28th, yet the accumulated flow past the dam site ballooned to over 185,000 c.f.s. (a record). Damage reports slowly came in. At the dam site fully one-third of the truck bridge had been ripped from its foundation and carried downstream. The diversion channel no longer existed, and the preliminary excavation of the powerhouse foundation sat submerged more than ten feet. The aggregate conveyor belt bridge at Coram disappeared, only the foundation piers remained. Redding was a disaster. The Kutras aggregate plant looked more like a giant lake. Damage proved extensive for miles downstream. Little could be done until the water receded.

The weather cleared on March 2 allowing officials an opportunity to gage the full extent of the wreckage. A fifty-yard wide gap had been ripped through the conveyor belt bridge at the Kutras site. Giant cranes, used to dragline gravel, listed and sank in the mucky river bottom. The primary gravel crusher itself had been crushed and destroyed. The remains of 24 tourist cabins and other privately owned buildings lay scattered around the Kutras tract aimlessly floating about. The main highway bridge into Redding also sustained significant damage. Entire concrete foundations, ripped out of the bedrock by the raging river, littered the rivers' edge along with twisted and mangled steel girders. Workers used the clearing skies to begin the arduous task of cleaning up the debris throughout a two-mile stretch of the Sacramento River. Workers engaged in repair operations noticed at least twenty dead cattle carcasses in the Kutras area.[49]

Crowe ordered two special work crews to immediately repair the torn-away truck bridge at the dam site. The bridge was critical to continued progress; it allowed for the transportation back and forth between the east and west abutments. Temporary scaffolding allowed for foot traffic to cross the bridge. Within two weeks, replacement girders arrived from Ohio and full-scale repairs moved ahead. By the end of March, the Kutras aggregate plant resumed preparation for sending gravel to the dam site and the various bridges stood repaired.

By April, the conveyor belt resumed full deliveries of aggregate to the Coram receiving site. Later that month the ground dried and with warming temperatures, an anxious and excited Crowe stood ready to begin concrete placing on the dam itself. He worked closely with his longtime friend "Red" Wixson to plan and rig the headtower cable system, the heart of Crowe's concrete placing scheme. Men worked through May to construct tail towers on the east slope, while Wixson's riggers prepared to string the 3-inch thick cables over two thousand feet across the canyon. Crowe had planned for seven cables, enough to cover every angle over the dam site, and by mid-June, four of the seven cables were fully rigged and ready to operate.[50]

On July 8, 1940, Crowe posed for a photograph with Lowry and PCI executives as the first bucket of concrete was placed in an east abutment form. Now, progress could proceed at a quick pace. Crowe watched as his men began excavating for the powerhouse, which was located on the west side of the river. Crowe called for the hiring of more men, as he wanted to move full swing into constructing the 50-foot square concrete forms. The five-foot high forms sprang up like building blocks in a checkerboard pattern, waiting to be filled with concrete by Crowe's improved 8-cubic yard buckets. By December, both the east and west portions of the dam had been concreted. 1940 ended, as it had started, with unusually high rainfall and a subsequent flood. Between December 15 and December 26, a single storm dropped 30.7 inches at the dam site. Crowe, once again, reluctantly ordered his men and machines out of the riverbed area where they were preparing to place concrete for the central foundation. A temporary cofferdam, designed to hold back floodwaters, succumbed to massive surges of onrushing waves. Crowe and his men angrily stood by as the overwhelmed cofferdam gave way, flooding the entire foundation area. Once the onslaught subsided, workers began the laborious job of dewatering the flooded site with sump pumps and specially designed gravity flumes. As the new year approached, Crowe, and his men, understood all too well the power of an unrestrained river.[51]

Chapter 14

"Dams have been good to me."
Shasta Dam, 1941-1945

All through early January, waters of the Sacramento River remained high, curtailing work in the riverbed and on lower portions of the powerhouse. Work focused on beginning to place concrete on the foundation of the east and west abutments. During this month, Goodyear Tire and Rubber Co. sent H.H. Brownell to Shasta Dam. The talented filmmaker visited every component of the Shasta Dam construction filming a motion picture to be released for educational purposes. Brownell saw drainage pumps working desperately to vacate the water around the flooded powerhouse foundation works. He filmed all stages of concrete placing and he caught glimpses of daring "rigger men" dangling high above the work site, inspecting cables.[1]

Meanwhile, at the Redding Kutras aggregate plant repairmen worked hard to replace flood damaged and completely wrecked machinery. Men laboring in this low lying area of the Sacramento River, continually had to deal with quickly rising waters that gushed forward without warning. Working in one spot for more than a few hours during the whole month of January proved difficult as the rains continued to come down. Flood damage to the south Kutras tract widened the riverbed more than one hundred feet, unprecedented in recorded history. Many of the dragline shovel-cranes, responsible for dredging gravel from the Sacramento Riverbed, had to be withdrawn to higher locations. This proved annoying, as the best pre-selected gravel size and sand deposits remained under water. Luckily, Crowe had planned for such a calamity; gravel and sand reserves already sat deposited in huge piles at the dam site.

One of the most interesting aspects of the early stages of concrete placing involved the intricate placement of the iron reinforcement bars. Several hundred feet of heavy-gauge rebar lined every new block. PCI foremen inspected the placement of the grid-like rebar system constantly, checking for proper connections and shifting seams. Even more difficult was the manner in which the workers had to move about. The rebar proved heavy enough for workers to climb on thus forming a ladder-like web throughout the concrete forming areas. Each block presented peculiar problems. Some of the blocks had extra lengths of cooling tubing, while others had gallery forms. The galleries seven feet in height and five feet in width provided access to inspect the interior portions of the dam; the schedule called for these inspections at regular intervals. Huge cranes placed the gallery sections, already pre-poured concrete forms, with great precision. Workers then ribbed the galleries with two-inch thick industrial rebar providing a solid joint connection once the main concrete placing began over the top of the gallery form.

Like a conductor of a great orchestra the headtower supervisors coordinated the placement of each bucket of concrete. The timing was critical. While one bucket was being withdrawn back to the headtower and lowered to receive a new 8-yard load of freshly mixed concrete, another bucket moved out from the headtower. By February, with the river still high and gushing between the east and west abutments, concrete pouring increased on the west abutment. A large contractor's layout board detailing the sequence of concrete placement stood down at the foremen's' headquarters. Here Crowe, Lowry, Bureau Inspectors, and PCI foremen checked the progress at each numbered foundation block.[2]

Now Crowe, the tireless engineer, ordered the operation at Shasta Dam to swing into full gear. As March appeared, even though waters remained high around the powerhouse, he set crews to work erecting forms and preparing for concrete placing. Scores of newly hired men went to work on the west-abutment foundation blocks. Crowe increased the size of concrete form crews and he organized new ones, expanding so that operations could continue at full speed during the swing shift and into the night. Well-placed floodlights allowed crews to inspect the day's concrete placing, construct new concrete forms, and to continue the placing. Hundreds of men worked on each shift. Around the middle of March Crowe hired additional men to construct a huge shop building at the Coram site. Here the giant 15-foot diameter penstocks would be fabricated.

April of 1941 stands out as a banner month, not only was dam construction in full swing but also the neighboring communities blossomed. More and more job hopefuls came to the area. With employment opportunities on the rise, the dam area communities celebrated the spring weather and their regular paychecks. The Shasta-Cascade Wonderland Association sponsored a program of luncheons, activities, and contests. One of the highlights of the celebration, the Miss Alice of Wonderland contest drew large crowds to the Toyon Community Center.[3] At the same time the Mutual Broadcasting Co. arrived at the dam site. Their plans called for a coast-to-coast radio broadcast. Nationally known commentator John B. Hughes interviewed Crowe as to the progress on the dam. He asked the superintendent if the dam would be completed within the designated time and if hiring would continue. Also interviewed on the broadcast were cableway operator Bill Ross and his wife. Other announcers such as Mel Venter and A.W. Scott toured the site interviewing workers and foremen.[4]

With concrete placing over one hundred feet high in the foundation, it

Initial diversion of the Sacramento River by the use of a "sea wall." Note the
dewatered riverbed to the left. (USBR)

became necessary to regularly check the condition of the setting concrete. Information needed to be gathered on the seals and joints observable from the numerous galleries. Specially trained Bureau inspectors moved through the galleries,
block by block, checking critical joints for movement, water leakage, and cracks.[5]
Every day, inspectors also moved across the exterior face and finish of the dam
foundation. Likewise, after every load of concrete dropped into the block forms,
workers checked the condition of the drying mix, immediately following the tamping procedure. After the inspection of the exterior surface, special concrete finishers moved over the block face and cemented a smooth finish to the rough puck-
marked surface. This procedure of final finishing, known as "sack-rubbed finishing," provided a protective seal coat. By April 7th of 1941 more than 800,000
yards of concrete had already been placed and finished.

On May 3rd of that year at 2:27 p.m. the first millionth cubic yard of
concrete was placed.[6] Crowe and officials from the Bureau and PCI were on hand
that afternoon on block 29-E and they were excited about the concrete placing
progress. Early problems coordinating the cableway system had, by now, been

worked out. Workers and observers, including the "Old Man," noted an efficient coordination of all phases of dam building by this time. Power plant construction soared as the weather dried in May. More and more men joined in the building. Both the oil storage tanks and power plant service bays were installed. With the increase of so many new men on the job it became difficult to maintain a clean safety record. While the fatalities, injuries, and accidents were well documented on the Hoover Dam job, Crowe and Lowry were determined to not have a repeat at Shasta Dam. But, accidents do happen and happen they did at Shasta Dam. Numerous cases of individual and group bravery in rescuing and assisting the injured had already occurred. On May 10th of 1941 Ralph Lowry presented the National Safety Council President's Medal to three men who assisted in saving B.S. Hodges on October 20, 1940. Hodges, working at the Coram tract hopper, lie buried in a small discharge gate after a cave in. George Base, Columbia Construction Co. employee, and Mark Whitaker, a Pacific Constructors workman, extricated Hodges. Standing nearby, N.A. Takala of the Bureau of Reclamation, rushed to the side of Hodges and successfully revived him through the use of artificial respiration.[7] Scores of newly hired men, to help promote proper safety measures, worked alongside veteran dam builders. All were required to wear hard hats, gloves, pants and long sleeved shirts made of heavy material. As the weather warmed this proved uncomfortable. Many men preferred to wear a heavy-duty brand of overalls. All wore heavy-duty boots.[8]

Safety became such an issue that Crowe, in consultation with Lowry and PCI management, decided to start a monthly newsletter devoted to updating workers. The publication known as *The Headtower* was introduced in June with a message from the "Old Man":

> If the publication "Headtower" will be successful in preventing just one serious accident, it will have served its purpose. I hope all our men will read it carefully, because none of us are too old to learn. I want you all to know that our accident prevention activities have always had my wholehearted approval, and I look to all of you to continue to do your part in carrying out our safety program.
>
> F. T. Crowe, General Superintendent[9]

The Mutual Broadcasting Company program, numerous newspaper accounts, and continuing news releases by the Bureau of Reclamation, all helped to bring many new visitors to the dam site. In June hundreds of visitors came daily. An expanded parking lot held dozens of cars and busses. Special groups, particularly educational classes, came to see the giant dam. All the way from Montana, where giant Fort Peck (an earth fill dam) was being built, came the senior class of the Montana School (College) of Mines. Crowe, whenever his schedule allowed, made time to stop and talk with visiting guests. He particularly enjoyed explaining the engineering aspects of the cableway to excited youngsters.[10]

The Kutras Gravel pit continued to provide a seemingly inexhaustible supply of aggregate. A giant powerful "grizzly and jaw crusher," installed earlier, smashed raw deposits of riverbed material. Sorting screens then separated the material into .75-inch and 1.50-inch size limits. The resulting gravel, moved onto the ten-mile long conveyor belt, headed north to the Coram transfer site. The belt crossed the Sacramento River twice and Highway 99 once. Special splashguards prevented rock from falling down onto passing automobiles. The highway crossing boasted a sign advertising to the passing public that this was the world's longest conveyor belt.[11]

July witnessed the arrival of the first 15-foot diameter penstock sections at the Coram fabrication plant. A monstrous 80-ton press held the plate steel sections as experienced welders, sweating from July temperatures and heat emitted from the arc-welders, seared the joints closed. Other workers, using heavy-duty grinders, smoothed end sections and prepared for the joining of another section. The penstocks, once installed, would bring rushing water from midway down the dam to the power turbines. Due to increased pressure of the funneled water at the lower end of the penstocks, engineers designed the lower sections to be stronger. They accomplished this by increasing the penstock thickness from .75-inch thick plate steel at the upper end to 2.38 inches in the lower sections.[12]

Finally, hot July and August weather dried the lower old Sacramento Riverbed. Underground water from both sides of the abutments had been draining into this lower area. Now crews safely moved into the area, setting forms for the dam foundation. Since this would be the lowest point, excavation needed to go deep; the width of the dam here would be its greatest. Cableway cranes hoisted 50-foot concrete forms into place as men scrambled to set each section. With so much loading, unloading, and handling of heavy equipment, it was only a matter of time before an accident would occur. Crowe knew this and he constantly reviewed safety procedures with his safety committee and each foreman. Despite these precautions a dam worker died, crushed at the headtower loading dock. The August 7 fatality forced Crowe and Lowry to call another special safety meeting. It was decided that any worker found not following proper safety procedures would lose his job immediately. Part of the ruling demanded that hardhat, gloves, and safety goggles must be worn (where designated) even though brutal summer temperatures climbed past the century mark. Disaster almost struck again on August 13 when a rockslide swept away two conveyor-belt foundation piers near the headtower. Crews working below the slide scurried to the side, abandoning trucks and equipment.[13]

Just four days later a radio team of Columbia Broadcasting System (CBS) personnel arrived to air a national program on work progress. The team included:

Will Thompson, Robert LeMond, and Tro Harper, announcers; Jim French, engineer; Fox Case, producer; and a young Chet Huntley, program director. On the afternoon of August 17, Huntley went on the air with a coast-to-coast live update. Throughout the rest of the day and into the evening, Huntley and his announcers roamed the work site interviewing Crowe and other PCI personnel, Bureau inspectors, and regular construction "stiffs." Lowry, dressed for the occasion, read from a prepared script. He reviewed the progress and talked about meeting the completion schedule. No references were made of the recent accidents, although he assured the radio audience that all precautions were being taken. LeMond, wearing a hard hat and overalls, went into the "pits," where he reported on the concrete placing routine during an actual dump. Meanwhile, colleague Tro Harper interviewed a hoist operator who was eager to talk about his job.[14]

Publicity for Crowe and Shasta Dam seemed everywhere. Frank Taylor interviewed him for the September issue of *This Week Magazine*. The title of the article, "He Puts Rivers to Work" summarized Crowe's career. The subtitle read, "Meet Frank T. Crowe, who can make rivers stand still—or run backwards—to play a vital part in America's defense program." Taylor had learned from other engineers that Crowe was already "a legendary figure," yet unknown to most Americans. Crowe explained that he had "lived in river bottoms" most of his adult life and that he did not care for publicity or recognition. As for doing some other kind of work Crowe, standing amid the noise and bustle of construction activity, clearly retorted, "I can't see why anybody would work in an office when he can be in a place like this." He continued, "Dams have been good to me." Realizing that he had the good fortune to have been in the right place at the right time, he acknowledged, "While I was learning to build them [dams], the American nation got started on the biggest dam building spree of all time. If I'd been born sooner, or later, I'd have missed the boat."[15]

1941 proved to be a popular year for visitors. In October, Secretary of the Interior Harold Ickes, his wife, and other government officials, arrived at the dam site for several days. Ickes, sporting a heavy overcoat, checked on the operations at several sites around the dam. He approved of the work progress, congratulating Crowe, Lowry, and Bureau Commissioner John C. Page. Of particular interest to Ickes was the Visitor's Center and Vista House. The working model of Shasta Dam and the panoramic Central Valley Project model appeared to serve as positive publicity for the New Deal program. Ickes also saw the first welded penstock tubing sections being placed on the dam. He worried about the narrow diversion channel. Ickes had been told of the great 1940 floods and he queried Crowe on his contingency plans should the quickly approaching winter season bring another deluge. Crowe pointed out that work was progressing well on the lowest portion of the old Sacramento Riverbed spillway and that water could be diverted through this area and the railroad by-pass tunnel shortly. On November 13, buckets of concrete began arriving at forms in the spillway foundation area.

While the concrete crews worked around the clock to begin the spillway foundation, heavy rains arrived. By December 3, the Sacramento River crested at 30,000 cubic feet per second. All work in the spillway foundation area had to be curtailed; Crowe ordered the evacuation of men and machines. Luckily, at the powerhouse, the foundation and the first two block levels had been completed. Here, Crowe pressed his men to continue work while the rising water swirled just a few feet below.

On Sunday, December 7, Crowe and everyone else working on the dam was shocked to discover the news of the Japanese bombing of Pearl Harbor. The next day, Bureau photographer T.B. Gibson busied himself taking pictures of the hastily placed guards. Worried that Japanese living in California might attempt to sabotage work on Shasta Dam, military officials, working with Bureau officials, ordered soldiers to protect strategic and vital operations at the dam. Crowe and Lowry did not object. They agreed that it would not take more than a handful of armed guards to protect key areas. Guards were added to all entry points, at the gravel plant, and at the railroad by-pass tunnel. Other soldiers cruised the 10-mile dirt road that paralleled the aggregate conveyor belt.[16]

Gibson hurried on to the hospital where his schedule called for a complete photo layout of the Shasta Dam Hospital. Ironically, just previous to his visit several injured dam workers had been released and when Gibson shot the hospital ward, few beds were occupied. The hospital, claimed to be the best equipped and staffed north of Sacramento, contained its own kitchen, a convalescing ward, a clinical laboratory, minor and major surgery rooms, administrative offices, and a nursing station. Under John C. Kirkpatrick, the dedicated and talented staff handled all worker injuries. On occasion, dependents of dam workers, admitted under a special participation plan, used the facilities.

War news spread quickly through the boomtown communities, Toyon, and Shasta Dam Village. Rumors persisted that a Japanese invasion was imminent and that the dam would be bombed as soon as Japanese planes came within range. Scattered newspaper reports helped to fuel the hysteria; within days of Pearl Harbor, several articles claimed that Japanese scout planes were cruising the California coast, from Los Angeles to Eureka.[17] Men discussed the possibility of enlisting, wondering how long the war would take, and if their job on the dam would still be available when they returned. And even though minor floodwater repeatedly swept through the dam area, Crowe and his foremen pushed their men to work harder in an attempt to get them to stay focused on their task. Crowe told his men that the government needed the water-generated electricity for America's war effort and that Shasta Dam would be receiving a defense-related project status. This meant that priority would be given to providing money and materials to finish the big dam. As Christmas approached dam workers and their families gave thanks for their relative prosperity and prayed for a quick end to the war. With the uncertainty of the year ahead, Crowe wrote a special Christmas message in the

December issue of *The Headtower*:

> Another year rolls around and the first thing we know, it is Christmas. There is a hustle and bustle of Christmas shopping, toys, and Christmas trees for the children, something for the house for mother and the usual ties and pairs of sox for dad........Then comes the festive Christmas dinner. Before you know it the year of 1941 is gone and 1942 has begun. Let us all try to make it a better and happier year than the last. I wish each one of you, your wives and children the most happy Christmas you have ever had.[18]

1942 started off on a nervous and apprehensive note. Everyone was concerned about the war. What would happen next? Would they pull us all off the Shasta job and ask us to fight? What would become of our families? If we did leave, could we get our jobs back after the war? These and other tough questions were being asked by hundreds of workers as they reported to jobs in January. Crowe and Lowry did not have all the answers. Their only concern remained, to complete the dam—on schedule and for cost. As January progressed the men had a difficult time keeping their minds on their work. Every day, war news drifted through the work area. Rumors of imminent Japanese invasion pervaded most of the conversation. Others seemed concerned that the war would be over before they had an opportunity to fight.[19]

As the men worried about the future of their jobs and their families, they worked in increasingly colder weather. Record low temperatures hit in January and three-foot icicles hung from wooden platforms and from concrete forms. Sporting thick shirts, overalls, gloves, and heavy work coats, they tried their best to complete tasks. Injuries occurred with men slipping and stumbling on glassy concrete surfaces. Crowe had a notion to curtail work, but he knew time lost is difficult to regain. The word was sent out by the safety committee that all men were to slow their work, taking extra precautions.

Down at Coram, the fabrication of the penstock sections moved ahead briskly. Additional welding crews started to join the 15-foot sections together and ready them for placement in the dam. Welders enjoyed the extra heat, and they happily chided their friends who had to work outside in the ice and snow. Two special X-Ray machines arrived. Technicians used these devices to check the quality of the welded joints, both on the inside and outside. The outside X-Ray machine was quite large and could examine a three-foot linear zone. The penstock sat on large rollers and was rotated with each new photograph. In this manner the entire circumference could be checked. Meanwhile, on the inside of the penstock, men used a smaller X-Ray device to check interior welds. The process involved highly trained technicians who examined the X-Rays immediately following film

Frank Crowe takes time out for this photograph as he supervises the concrete placement. (USBR)

development. They then reported to the fabrication foremen on the acceptability of the weld.[20]

If the welding inspection went well, approved penstock sections were loaded onto flatbed trailers and driven to the dam. Here riggers fastened cables from the headtower and signaled the ground level operator who then called up to the headtower operator. The giant tubing was lifted and placed onto temporary wooden cradles.

In March, Lowry was informed that local Indians were upset about the possibility of flooding nearby Curl Cemetery. The cemetery had been a traditional burial site and was still held in high regard by the local Wintu tribe. Not wanting to create a situation and in complete compliance, Lowry offered to send a work crew out to the cemetery and reinterr the bodies to other locations. This decision and the offer of help satisfied Indian leaders, and the work was carried out without incident.

At the same time, an unexpected March snowfall covered the dam area. Kids in the boomtowns built snowmen and engaged in snowball fights, while their fathers drearily reported to work. Actually, the snow did not accumulate and within days work production returned to normal levels. By the end of March, with the action in full swing, the three-millionth cubic yard of concrete was ceremoniously placed. This event signaled the halfway point in concrete pouring; yet, the "Old Man" knew much work lay ahead and he was being pressed to get the turbines online to generate electricity.[21]

Much of the work at Shasta Dam relied on the constant use of cables. Cables lifted just about everything over one hundred pounds. They varied in size from .5-inch truck and small machinery cables, to the massive three-inch main headtower cables. Cableway "monkeys" risked life and limb in a constant survey of cable conditions. Worn or deteriorating cables needed repair immediately. On more than one occasion the main headtower cables broke under the strain of carrying tons of concrete. Lashing down like a giant whip, the dangerous cable-ends sent nearby workers scurrying for cover. At least once, severe injuries occurred when a broken cable hit a cement finisher, flicking him from the supporting scaffolding like an enormous horsetail lashing a fly.[22] The machine shop busied itself repairing cables and returning them to active service.

Visitors to the site during the month of April praised Crowe for a rapidly rising concrete dam. Both the east and west concrete abutments were impressively high. All five penstocks rested in their foundations awaiting final hook-up to the power generation plant. Across the river, the power transmission yard began to take shape as large capacity transformers sat ready for installation. Yet, much work remained, and alarmingly, a manpower shortage appeared. Crowe and Lowry now became concerned that if more men left then progress on the dam would slow. Some of the most highly skilled workers, in a patriotic response to a national military call-up, resigned to join the service. In an attempt to help deal with the manpower shortage, Master Mechanic Red Malan designed a one-man pneumatic concrete vibrator. He wanted a device that would be as effective as the old two-man model. By the end of April, several of Malan's vibrators began operating on the east abutment. The machine worked well, and soon others were brought into use.

Still worried about manpower shortages, Crowe authorized a search for additional workers. Most able-bodied men in the immediate area, both in the boomtowns and in Redding, had already enlisted for military service or moved to the Bay Area for higher paying defense related jobs. There thousands found lucrative employment in Kaiser's new shipyards at Richmond and Alameda. Others went to Los Angeles or San Diego and worked in aircraft plants. Empty boomtown homes increased in number and Crowe decided to extend his search to the Sacramento area. There, "recruiters" convinced unemployed men, from a variety of backgrounds, to try a job at Shasta Dam. Few actually could be convinced, and those that did arrive, soon left the area once they saw the danger involved in much of the labor.[23]

Crowe had other concerns that kept him occupied for most of May. He

Shasta Dam rising quickly with the powerhouse (left) under construction. (USBR)

knew the importance of keeping the correct temperature for the massive concrete monolith he was building. The plans had originally called for one-inch copper cooling pipe to be installed five feet apart for every five-foot layer of concrete. Cool 50° F. Sacramento River water, pumped through the pipes, helped in the curing process. However, Bureau inspectors noticed that the initial blocks revealed uneven curing and considerable stress. Engineers recommended that the pumped water needed to be colder. Thinking quickly Crowe located and ordered construction of a warehouse-size refrigeration plant. Located at the base of the east abutment, the plant helped super cool water to a temperature of 35° F. then pass the chilly liquid through the cooling pipes. The downstream face of the quickly rising dam became dotted with cooling system headers, risers, and coil connections. The lines needed to be checked constantly for leaks. In the refrigeration plant, controllers monitored operating temperatures on the main condenser and closely watched the condition of the cooling pumps. Since concrete takes a long time to cure, the special cooling arrangements prevented structural stress and cracking.

While inspecting the cooling line system on May 21, Crowe received word of a tragic accident on the reservoir clearing operation. L. J. Guinn, a tractor and bulldozer operator, was crushed to death by his own machine. Working 3 1/2 miles upstream near the old Kennett copper mine site, Guinn and his partner, D. L. Foster, struggled to clear brush on rugged steep slopes. Foster's tractor stalled and after repeated attempts to restart the huge machine, he immediately hailed Guinn for assistance. Guinn stopped his bulldozer, set the brake and walked down to talk with Foster. Standing by Foster's tractor, both men looked up in horror to see Guinn's bulldozer coming down on them. The brake had failed and the twenty-ton machine thundered downhill smashing over brush and small trees. In an instant the runaway bulldozer collided with Foster's tractor, careened sideways and caught Guinn as he leaped. An uninjured Foster staggered over to help his partner and was sickened to find Guinn's head and chest crushed. The funeral, held several days later, was well attended by dam workers. Crowe and Lowry sent notes of condolences to family members.[24]

On the upstream face of the dam new energy and effort began on the construction of the "trashracks." Long cylindrical concrete protuberances, the five trashracks were designed to screen debris from entering each of the penstocks. With the warm dry weather of June, extra crews went to work setting concrete forms and installing reinforcement bars. Working the upstream face of the dam proved to be a completely different experience from that of the sloped downstream side. Looking straight down the vertical side unnerved some workers as they struggled with heavy equipment and unwieldy hand tools. The men adjusted within days, displaying their agility on narrow catwalks, vertical ladders, and temporary platforms.

From their vantage point hundreds of feet above the upstream slope, workers on the trashracks watched as dump truck after dump truck carted in land fill in an attempt to create a cofferdam in the river channel. This would funnel the Sacramento River along the western abutment, and give workers the opportunity to begin placing concrete in block forms located down in the riverbed. Digging deep into the old channel, excavators carved out rectangular depressions that would become the foundation of the most central portion of the dam and the spillway. Viewed from the top of the 460-foot headtower, workers in the river channel appeared as so many ants scurrying about, while giant bulldozers looked like tinker toys. From the vantage point of the channel, men looked upward and nervously eyed the concrete wall that held back the rapidly flowing Sacramento River. The proportions and scale of the entire scene humbled the proudest of men. Yet, here was Man, once again changing the course of a mighty river at will, and erecting a 600-foot high concrete structure that would last for thousands of years.[25]

To measure the amount of stress and strain on the newly placed concrete, a series of strain meters were installed at strategic locations. The extremely sensitive devices measured lateral and vertical pressure. Minute movements could then be correlated over time to give structural engineers an idea of what the mass of surrounding concrete was doing. In addition, a number of joint meters recorded expansion and contraction of each blocked concrete section. At regular intervals inspectors checked the meters, recorded computations, and discussed overall concrete behavior. Depending on the readings, officials could adjust the flow and temperature of cooling pipes in the problem area.

With little or no ceremony, Crowe and his "construction stiffs" dumped the 4-millionth yard of concrete into a form on August 31, 1942. Down in the riverbed diversion the "Old Man" and a group of foremen consulted with Bureau inspectors as they calculated the river diversion schedule. Timing was important. Constantly changing river levels had compounded his calculations on other jobs. Crowe remembered well; the Colorado River experience reminded him that you needed the cooperation of the weather and consistent water levels. However, his fears were unfounded. The Sacramento River is not nearly as long as the Colorado River and summer fluctuations in the northstate river levels are rare. There is simply no new rain in the summer months and the water level decreases proportionally as the summer progresses. With this in mind, Crowe instructed his block foremen to use the newly installed block row gates to alternately divert the Sacramento River, first along the east abutment, then the west. Then workers scrambled to place concrete on the drying row. This system of alternating river flow and concrete placing appeared to work well throughout September, and the blocks rose higher and higher in the riverbed channel. Now the idea was to allow the water to flow through a single row, block channel #44. Concerns had earlier been raised about the migrating salmon returning to spawn. In response, Bureau engineers cleverly constructed a series of 5-foot steps or jumps, forming a makeshift fish ladder in the channel and allowing salmon to pass upstream. With this done, the rest of the lower channel bed was prepared for concrete. Eventually, the plan called for raising the water level 70 feet and then diverting the river through the railroad by-pass tunnel.

Headtower editor Eugene Green, with Crowe's approval, expanded coverage of the war effort as the year progressed publishing letters from ex-dam workers now serving overseas and informing the men of America's war effort. Ads urged the dam workers to invest ten percent of their wages in war bonds and to recycle critical resources. Safety tips and warnings abounded in each issue of the newsletter, and on occasion, unusual accidents were highlighted; these could prove embarrassing to the worker, as was the case with newly hired helper Ben Dubos. The article read:

> It seems that one Ben Dubos, a helper, was removing some brick from atop a building and in so doing, had put out a deadfall and a sheave over which he passed a line on which was tied a barrel. Ben pulled the barrel to the top of the building and tied the line off on a post. He then went onto the roof and filled the barrel with bricks, then returned to the ground to lower the

load—and that's where the excitement started.

As Ben untied the line, the superior weight of the load of bricks pulled him heavenward and he was struck on the head and shoulders as the barrel came down past him. When Ben reached the top, the barrel had reached the bottom with a bump, which broke the bottom out of the barrel, unloaded the bricks, changed the weight balance again and Ben came down and the barrel went up. Ben was struck on the legs and hips as he and the barrel passed in flight. When Ben hit the ground, he let go of the rope and the barrel, a free agent by this time, came down and hit him again.

What made Ben mad about the whole thing was that he was only paid $25 compensation for the accident. He reasoned that since he had been struck three times, he should have had $75.[26]

1942 ended with work crews preparing to reinforce and concrete the south portal of the railroad by-pass tunnel, preparing it to receive the diverted Sacramento River. The spillway section rose over 100 feet, the powerhouse structure neared completion, the line of penstocks approached the powerhouse, the east abutment climbed passed the 500-foot mark in elevation, and the west abutment rose over 400 feet. Crowe could see that construction progress had been impressive, despite the pressures incurred and changes necessary during the troubling early war period.

War news in the early months of 1943 remained bleak with the Germans pushing closer to Moscow and Leningrad. Out in the Pacific, American forces had apparently stopped the tide of Japanese aggression, however, we did not have the ability to take the offensive. Concern over the war pervaded every aspect of work on the dam. Men talked constantly about war progress, wondering if any of their former dam working colleagues were seeing any action. Women in the boomtowns formed wartime sewing clubs, getting together weekly to sew a wide variety of garments that could be used by soldiers. Children formed collection clubs, scouring the dam area for tin, rubber, glass, and other useful scraps. Toyon School, built nearby to serve the children of the dam workers, focused much of the daily curriculum on global geography. Students mapped the war fronts, keeping track of where American forces were engaged.

Crowe, briefed regularly by Bureau officials on the need to generate power as soon as possible, moved to speed up the installation of power generating equipment. In January, scroll cases S-1 and S-2 were installed into their service bays in the powerhouse. The scroll case is the unit that accepts the inflowing lake waters. Vanes in the scroll case direct the water against the blades of the water wheel in the turbine and then discharge the water into the river. Built in sections and assembled with seals and gaskets, these units underwent pressure and leak testing before being lowered into the powerhouse.

Already in place and operating in the powerhouse was a 250-ton power crane. The large lift moved laterally across the entire main floor, providing unlimited access. Later, the crane would place all the necessary components to bring the powerhouse online, including the generators, main shafts, and electrical control panels. Electricians watched as over 20 power-switching terminals were eased into place. The seven-foot high panels capable of handling over 2300 volts of water-generated power were connected to miles of heavy gage electrical wire.[27]

Work moved along quickly on the installation of the scroll cases and other power generating equipment throughout January and February. During this time the five millionth cubic yard of concrete was set down into a form. Unusually cold winter weather forced men to wear heavier clothing; Crowe supplied thick gloves in an attempt to warm the worker's numbing hands. Concrete crews concentrated their efforts on building up the center blocks of the spillway. Progress by March revealed that the four spillway blocks had been built up over 300 feet. Block row #44 remained as the funnel way for the Sacramento River. One other block was kept low, in case flooding winter waters forced the use of additional diversion routes.

The low rainfall totals for the spring of 1943 kept the Sacramento River manageable. Crews working on makeshift platforms on the upstream side of the spillway constantly looked at the river levels before commencing to complete the concrete trashracks. By April it was clear to a greatly relieved Crowe that the river would not flood and contingency flood plans were scrapped. On the west abutment the river diversion tunnel stood ready to accept the Sacramento River. Men prepared the north and south portal openings, laying concrete funnel channels.

Beginning in May, temporary bulkhead gates placed into Block #44 diverted river water to another block. Inside Block #44 several work crews assembled concrete forms in preparation of intensive concrete placing to raise this level. In great anticipation, Crowe spent hours supervising this operation. Working in a canyon-like setting with the west abutment rising more than 500 feet and the 100-foot spillway section enclosing them, the men labored in an effort to quickly raise this critical block. Crowe's intricate cableway system worked well in this confined space. Radio operators signaled to headtower operators constantly giving them instructions to lift or lower, and move to the right or left. From the headtower little, if any, of the work in Block #44 could be seen. Incredibly, no accidents occurred and the "Old Man" was pleased to see, once again, that his cableway system ran without a flaw.

On June 23, 1943 bulldozers broke open the upstream dirt cofferdam located near the upstream portal opening the diversion tunnel. Sacramento River water gushed through the portal, slicing its way through the long tunnel shaft, emerging on the downstream side minutes later. Men all over the dam paused to watch the cascading water run down the south portal channel and crash into the river. The water level on the upstream side immediately went down, leaving the upstream face of the dam dry. An elated Crowe watched as workers installed a temporary floodgate in one of the lower blocks should the diversion tunnel fail to channel surges in water levels.

Additional work crews swarmed into the lower blocks intending to raise the lower blocks as soon as possible. In perfect coordination, cableway operators lowered concrete, gallery forms, elevator forms, and river outlet conduits. The conduits, 8.5 feet in diameter, would control most of the post-construction water releases from Shasta Dam. Engineered to exacting specifications, the tubing contained special contraction joints designed to "bend" with the curing of the concrete.[28]

Down in the powerhouse, installation of the penstocks resumed. Cranes placed the powerhouse penstock connectors on their foundations. Inside the powerhouse workers assembled and installed portions of the Unit #4 turbine, even though rumors abounded that the power generating equipment would not be fully installed. It appeared that a priority was given to Grand Coulee Dam. The powerhouse there had already been completed and government officials reasoned that the generators placed online at Grand Coulee could help supply electrical energy to the defense plants in and around Seattle as well as the Hanford Nuclear Plant.[29]

From August through the rest of the year new work crews prepared the downstream spillway apron area for concrete finishing. Men operating digging shovels loaded material from high areas onto dump trucks that redistributed the debris in low areas around the dam site. Concrete blocks in the apron, smaller than in the main dam, averaged 10-15 inches in height. During this entire procedure, no water could enter the downstream area. The diversion tunnel continued to reroute several thousand cubic feet per second, while overflow began to collect on the upstream face of the dam. A reservoir began to form.

For Frank Crowe a routine was soon established which included coming home to his large two-story house in Redding. He liked to relax by taking off his shoes, putting his feet up and reading the newspaper. Linnie, who worked hard at keeping a victory garden (she had enjoyed gardening ever since first meeting Frank) tried to help him unwind. After dinner, Frank listened to radio programs and, at times, played bridge, a favorite social activity of Linnie Crowe.[30]

Security at the dam site remained tight during 1943. Passes were required for all workers, and visitors could only observe from the Vista House. Soldiers were replaced by a Bureau police force that roamed the entire dam site checking limit fences for breaks. Wearing hard hats and sporting official enforcement badges, most of these older gentlemen never encountered trouble. They spent most of their time approving work passes at the different checkpoints.

During September the Bureau lowered a powerboat onto the quickly rising reservoir. Mainline crane #1 gently set the boat down near the center of the spillway amid floating boards and other debris. This marked the first occasion of a powerboat on the reservoir. Bureau photographer W. F. Richards used the boat to take pictures of the upstream face of the dam and of the inundated, now abandoned old mining town, of Kennett. Curious onlookers spotted the boat cruising the fledgling lake throughout the rest of that autumn[31].

Visitors noticed a concentration of men and machines near the center of the dam. Crowe, anxious to raise the central blocks to the already established level on each abutment, pushed his men to complete the job. There was some concern that approaching winter rains could overwhelm the capacity of the diversion tunnel causing the reservoir level to rise too quickly, endangering work crews in the center blocks. Activity abounded also on the extreme end of each abutment where experienced "stiffs" dug out and prepared for the final foundation concrete placing. Here the "cut" penetrated 40 to 50 feet into the side of each mountain slope. Extra rebar reinforcing would be placed here to anchor any lateral shifts caused by water pressure. Elsewhere, veteran dam workers had a difficult time reinforcing the penstock pedestals and framing supporting concrete forms. The problem resulted from the nature of the unique shape of the pedestal and the steep sloping ground. Concrete forms needed to be well fastened and anchored in order to provide an unmovable concrete form. Substituting heavier timber forms satisfied part of the problem.

Interior partitions and additional electrical panels, wiring, and generator frames all were installed in November and December. Across the river men worked hard to erect the basic steel frame complex that would support the large capacity electrical transmission lines. Work also continued on the main switchyard. Much of the electrical components including the internal wiring came from Westinghouse Electric Company. Men dwarfed by the multi-ton generators carefully and systematically assembled the generator rotors to exacting specifications.

At the November 1 Board of Directors meeting of the American Society of Civil Engineers (ASCE) Frank Crowe was recognized for his tremendous contribution to the engineering field when he was named for special honorary membership. Originally joining the ASCE in 1910 as an associate member, he became a full member in 1915. The Board's nomination referred to Crowe's "remarkable talent for leadership" and noting that "he had become the ranking officer on construction procedure for all projects and had acquired an enviable reputation for management of construction work and for developing new and improved construction methods and equipment."[32]

The year ended with the placing of the six-millionth cubic yard of concrete. Another special sign was made to advertise the event, but no official ceremonies occurred. Everyone knew that, by now, the dam was nearing completion. As the six-millionth cubic yard slopped into place in the rising central block area, Crowe and his veteran foremen estimated that the job would only take one more year.

Final river diversion through the by-pass tunnel. (USBR)

The final year of dam construction started amid a swirling snowstorm. Nearby residents in Redding, not accustomed to heavy snowfalls, struggled to keep their automobiles on the icy roads. Out at the dam site, most work crews ignored the falling flakes, pressing on with construction. Crowe was determined to keep his men on schedule and he ordered special shed roofs erected where dry working conditions were necessary. The blizzard knocked down several newly installed transmission line poles and wires. Emergency repair parties left the dam site in chained trucks and located the fallen structures; temporary repairs held the lines intact until the snow melted days later.

Lowry also worried at this time. A loose bolt was discovered on one of the guy rods used to anchor a newly arrived transformer. On top of this a tie rod, framing the main laminations of the generator core, bent out more than an inch causing lamination displacement. The entire transformer had to be "untanked," that is, lifted out of its supporting concrete bay holder and sent back for repair or replacement. This was another disappointing blow to the Bureau's plan of having one or two generators online by the completion of the concrete placing.

Due to the additional water pressure found in the spillway apron area, engineers needed to constantly test the strength of the concrete being placed there. In the testing laboratory, technicians spent hours crushing apron samples. These samples averaged six inches in diameter by twelve inches high and were cylindrical in shape. The samples were given 20 to 30 days to dry before testing in the "crusher." Testers used 90,000 to 105,000 pounds of pressure on the concrete samples, with strength readings averaging 3300 to 3650 P.S.I. These tests proved to be more than adequate for the stress factors encountered in the spillway apron.[33]

Early in 1944 Crowe was featured in the *Em Kayan* magazine, a monthly publication of the Morrison-Knudsen Company. In the article, Crowe was described as "six feet-three inches or more" with broad-shoulders. The interviewer commented that Crowe, "In his big, genial, easy-going good nature, freely admits his pride and vanity in building the big ones." The reference was to the fact that the plans for Shasta Dam originally called for a maximum height of 600 feet. Crowe convinced the Bureau to add two feet. He admitted, "Some son-of-a-gun will come along later and build another dam 600 feet high, and I want to push this one up above that round figure." Crowe went on to give much of the credit for the success of Shasta Dam to his office associates William V. "Bill" Greeley, Chief Engineer of the dam project and David C. May, Office Engineer.[34]

With the shortage of men during World War II, both the Bureau of Reclamation and Crowe hired women to fill vacant clerical and food service positions. At Bureau headquarters, in Toyon, women served as secretaries and assistants. At the dam site, women worked in the PCI headquarters, again engaging in office work.[35] One woman Opal Foxx worked in the mess hall. She arrived from Kansas wanting to see her sister and brother-in-law; he was already hired at the dam. She decided to stay and soon was hired to help in the large company mess hall. Since the dining room was open all night, she was given the 6 p.m. to 2 a.m. shift, working the eight hours for $3.20. Her main duties included preparing meals for 2000 men per shift. Determined to obtain housing close to her job, the confident Foxx obtained a company house in Shasta Dam Village; she shared the small cottage with several other women workers.[36]

Concrete placing increased in the spillway apron during January and February. While finishers floated the main spillway pad, others poured the arch deflectors--concrete channel bars designed to soften the impact of falling water from the dam. The arch deflectors, approximately 15 feet long, stood near the end of the spillway apron and were constructed using an extra strong concrete mix. The spillway sidewalls, also made of fortified concrete, rose at this same time. Built to accept the full force of the crashing Sacramento River, the channel sidewalls contained added layers of steel reinforcement. Above the sidewalls, the canyon rock protruded adding a dimension of natural strength.

Every day during good weather the Bureau powerboat cruised the small reservoir corralling debris jamming up near the diversion tunnel or gathering at the base of the dam. Word came down from Bureau headquarters that the crew of the powerboat was to tow a newly constructed service barge up the rising reservoir to Kennett. Once there, they were ordered to burn any standing wood structures. First to go was the still standing Gold Nugget Cafe, a popular eatery during the heyday of the copper mining boom before World War I. The barge served so well as a base of operations for crews assigned to patrol the new lake that Lowry ordered another barge constructed. By now everyone had abandoned Kennett, that is, all except Lawrence Bannon. He stubbornly held out. Securing a houseboat to reside in, Bannon commuted about Shasta reservoir in a small skiff. Government barge operators checked on Bannon every few days and he became a regular visitor to the dam.[37]

February saw a temporary dirt cofferdam piled just below the powerhouse. This became necessary when winter water from the diversion tunnel began to back up into the spillway apron. With the cofferdam in place extra work crews confidently labored at a feverish pace to finish the entire spillway area. On February 4, with reservoir levels rising, the decision was made to open river outlet tubes #2 and #3. Each of the 8.5 feet in diameter tubes worked well, with no major reported leaks from within the dam. On the spillway side, thousands of gallons of white water cascaded down crashing into the apron. Plowing into the dirt cofferdam, the newly released reservoir water quickly overwhelmed the 20-foot high barrier, smashing through and linking up the Sacramento River. For many workmen and visiting family members this sight was moving and memorable.[38]

Now came an important moment, the shutting of the service gates to the diversion tunnel. This procedure would effectively cutoff the diversion of the Sacramento River and place the full control of the reservoir on the dam and its outlet tubes. Utilizing a custom designed hoist, the gates were lifted into place, never to be opened again. As the diversion tunnel emptied, an elite crew was organized to move into the tunnel to construct a massive concrete plug, sealing off the reservoir water forever. Crowe and PCI engineer Bill Greeley designed a fabricated form of strong timbers that was erected at the plug site. This custom form shaped the concrete as it was pumped in over 1200 feet from the south portal. This became the world's longest concrete pumping operation.

The last bucket of concrete is being placed on Shasta Dam. Frank Crowe is standing just to the left of the sign. (USBR)

In the powerhouse, the process of completing #4 generator moved along. Precise connections and measurements preceded any electrical generator installation, and this job was no exception. Placing the rotor for #4 generator proved time consuming. The huge workshop crane loomed overhead as the operator lowered the two-foot hook and men fastened it to the rotor connector. On command, the crane operator lifted the gigantic rotor, slowly swinging it into position over the generator cage assembly. Using both voice and hand commands foremen on the assembly foundation motioned to gently lower the rotor. As it approached the assembly cage the powerful crane stopped. Workers scurried around the full circumference of the rotor placing sensitive levels along the top edge. Coordinating the readings, foremen determined the proper levels and motioned for the crane operator to continue to lower the rotor slowly. Once the rotor rested squarely and evenly on the generator supports, the crane let loose, moving to bring the rotor cap, or upper bearing truss, in its position. From here, the cap was bolted down, sealed and secured.[39]

Across the river, the switching yard transmission lines stretched south toward their first major destination, Oroville. The task of clearing a 30-foot path through the suggested southern route strained men and machines. Between huge majestic oaks and countless thickets of manzanita brush, lay clusters of annoying poison oak. Crews cut down the oaks; caravans of veteran bulldozer crews who swept away the small low-lying vegetation followed them. Now hole diggers went to work drilling through the tough hardpan of Shasta and Tehama Counties. Next, long flatbed trucks conveyed the transmission poles to their respective holes. There, portable heavy-duty cranes picked the long wooden supports and dropped them into place. Cross poles were erected in areas known to sustain high wind conditions. Through March electricians also strung the transmission lines, uncoiling the precious wires from 8-foot spools. In some cases where they could be used, horses successfully pulled the reels of transmission lines. Attached to 'come alongs,' the horses proved more than adequate in stringing operations. One by one, linemen systematically moved from one pole group to another securing transmission lines with the specified tension and installing insulators.

The rapidly rising water of the Shasta reservoir overwhelmed the base of the headtower in early March. Crowe ordered the concrete mixing plant to be relocated on higher ground along with all the accompanying equipment. The plan now called for a temporary catwalk to be strung from the old aggregate belt towers to the mid-level of the headtower. Reminiscent of a jungle canyon bridge, the catwalk swung laterally and vertically whenever men walked on it. Headtower cableway operators crossed over on this bridge, walking carefully, and reported to work. The headtower continued in its role of delivering concrete, only now, the cableway cranes picked up the concrete at a new concrete mixing location.

Thousands of pieces of floating debris made their way down to the dam, there to be trapped and removed by Bureau men working on government barges. Everything conceivable ended up thumping against the dam. House timbers and dead tree branches were the most common. In at least three cases complete homes would meander down the waterway, with roofs fully intact. Curious spectators began showing up regularly at the left abutment edge of the dam looking for debris of any value. Government personnel finally had to restrict this area as the amount of debris piled up.[40]

Shasta Dam completed, 1945 (USBR)

The powerhouse passed its first major hallmark on March 29, 1944, when Bureau electrical engineer, Irving C. Harris, placed service station generator #1 online. The generated power was used on location at the dam site, as the transmission lines were not yet completed. The excitement of generating power, quickly gave way to disappointment, when on April 13 the upper guide bearing failed forcing a complete shutdown of generator #1. Powerhouse technicians were amazed to see the deep scoring in the guide bearing. Repairing the scored surface proved unacceptable and a new guide bearing needed to be installed.

Problems began to appear for Crowe on the finished surface of the dam. Surface cracks, not unusual on a job as big as Shasta, needed to be cosmetically patched. Interestingly, cracks formed in rectangular areas ranging in size from a few inches to several feet in length. The effected area usually represented the depth of a particular concrete pour and resulted from premature curing. A special dry-patch cement mix was applied and reapplied as necessary. One of those engaged in this dangerous work was Marion Allen, a Hoover and Parker Dam veteran. Dangling from wooden scaffolding secured with ropes, the indomitable Allen methodically plastered cracks and checked leaks in block joints.[41]

In June, with Shasta Dam beginning to look completed, *Time* magazine honored Crowe with a two-page article. When asked about critical turning points on the Shasta job Crowe referred to the opening of the outlet valves, which could now handle flows from the Sacramento River. He retorted, "That meant we had the river licked." To press home his point the "Old Man" added, "Pinned down, shoulders right on the mat. Hell, that's what we came up here for." Crowe stated, as he had done in an earlier interview with *This Week Magazine*, that he had been lucky to have completed his engineering education just when the government was starting to build dams on a large-scale. He once again admitted, "If I'd been born sooner or later, I'd have missed the boat." Describing Crowe as "lean, tough and bull-voiced," the article claimed that his reputation included being able to read blueprints "at a glance" (or ignore them when necessary) and as "the man who could build dams faster than anyone else." Recalling a story from the Shasta job about how firm he stood on safety adherence the article said, "Frank Crowe hates carelessness. As a result Shasta has killed only twelve men. Once he bellowed at a worker: 'Watch what the hell you're doing or you'll fall and break your neck.' Retorted the worker: 'Well, it's my neck.' 'Yes, it's your neck now,' Crowe shot back, 'but as soon as you break it, it's mine.'" Giving him credit for building more dams than anyone in history, *Time* disclosed Crowe's financial windfall from Hoover Dam which included an $18,000 a year salary plus 2 1/2% of the calculated profits, estimated to be about $300,000.

With his career winding down the *Time* accolades boosted Crowe's reputation across the nation. Known as a "master builder," people were learning that his use of multiple cableways and his genius for organization proved decisive in the building of Hoover and Shasta Dams. Asked about his spending of $600,000 on the headtower and cableway system for Shasta, Crowe countered, "It was a half-million dollars cheaper than any scheme anybody else thought of." In a rare glimpse of his political views, the article offered that "Frank Crowe is rabidly against the Administration, which gave him so many dams to build, is scornful of the 'socialistic' cheap power they will produce." The use of the word "rabidly" is probably pushing the point too far, for Crowe, a loyal Republican from before the Hoover days, seldom allowed himself to become emotional about political issues or involvement—save the Six Companies sponsored interference in Boulder City during the 1932 presidential race.[42]

On through the summer months work moved ahead on installing electrical components in the powerhouse and switching yard, and placing concrete in the upper spillway blocks. Working in the searing July and August heat, men in bulldozers spent weeks backfilling the east and west abutments. Once backfilled, road-paving crews would come in and complete a permanent road connection to the top of the dam. The only major section left to complete was the three main drum-gate foundation chambers. The work here needed to be precise in order to accommodate the precision-engineered drum gates.

In October, the 102-foot spillway bridge beam arrived from the manufacturer on flat trailer-bed trucks. The huge steel cross girders were lifted by one of the main cableways cranes to temporary wooden piers on top of the dam. These mammoth monoliths would bear the full weight of the roadbed above and supply enclosure for the drum gates. Men hurried about like ants checking the placement of the heavy beam; its resting place was unusual in that the support pier actually extended out over the dam, with the counterbalancing pier located directly above the centerline. Moving in cat-like fashion sure-footed veterans ventured out onto the beam in order to disconnect the hoist lines. With four years of experience behind them, this kind of high-wire act seemed an everyday ordinary task.

November and December saw the last of the concrete placing and the completion of the switchyard. Most of the action centered on the drum gates, roadbed, and the two-service elevator shaft towers. Wanting to finish the concrete placing before Christmas, Crowe's hardworking crews struggled in the last part of December. As luck would have it, a powerful cloudburst dumped inches of rain on the dam site. Undaunted, Crowe agreed to let foremen contrive a makeshift protective cover to shield the drying concrete; the men continued to work in the rain. Workers waited patiently for breaks in the downpour to reset forms and call the headtower for another bucket of concrete. Then after quickly placing the load, another section of the canvas tent protective shield was hung over the newly poured section. This did not help those men attempting to pour their loads into forms on the two elevator towers. Work in this area slowed.

Finally, in a somewhat subdued formal ceremony conducted on December 22, 1944, the last bucket of concrete was placed on the dam proper.[43] Actually, the concrete continued to be placed after the New Year; it took one additional day until January 2, 1945 to complete the parapet walls of the elevator towers and to finish the Vista House. Everyone snapped pictures of the great event, knowing that for most of them, it would be their last big dam job. No other major dam construction projects were on the drawing boards, or even being talked about. Attention remained focused on America's all-out war effort.

PCI workers still on the payroll spent their time in early and mid-1945 dismantling the headtower, rounding-up and salvaging hundreds of tons of leftover materials, and hauling off the entire conveyor belt system. A local real estate/ construction company bought most of the small single-family structures that had been home to PCI workers and trucked the houses down to Chico, a prosperous valley community. A few of the homes were set up in Redding. Most of these structures, being well built, remain in use today. Ironically, two of them were situated just down the hill from Frank Crowe's beautiful home in Redding. Dam workers in the boomtowns either moved to the Bay Area or some other Bureau job in the West. Some workers remained in the area, hoping to put down permanent roots. Still others entered military service expecting to see duty in the Pacific.[44]

With the word out that Shasta Dam had been completed, hundreds of visitors and some foreign government engineers came to see the mighty dam in operation. From China came Tsin-Yu Lin, Director of the Kunming Lakeside Electrical Works and Hui Huang, Director of the Bureau of Hydroelectric Survey; they were given a top priority tour of the entire dam site. They wanted to see every phase of the operation in hopes of using this information for several major dam projects planned on the Yellow River. Faced with their own water problems, Iranian engineers also visited at this time. Much of the worldwide recognition came from the dozens of foreign correspondents that visited. Mervyn Weston, Staff and War Correspondent of *The Argus* (Melbourne, Australia), smiled as he saw, from the visitor's center, the breathtaking scene of Shasta Dam, Shasta Lake, and Mt. Shasta. Bureau of Reclamation visitors were constant. From Washington D. C. and regional offices came inspectors, managers, and curious engineers. Shasta Dam was big, and it was powerful, and everyone wanted to see it. In fact the crowds became so large and continuous that the Bureau converted an old International panel truck into a crowd control car, complete with loudspeakers. The Bureau tour guide moved along the dam roadway controlling crowd movement and giving impromptu lectures on dam construction and operation.[45]

From 1946 until 1950 much finishing work went on at and around the dam. One of the big jobs included installing the three gigantic drum gates and connecting the remaining penstock tubes to the powerhouse. PCI employees left and were replaced by men hired directly by the Bureau. The upper and lower visitors center needed interior finishing. Bolting down the permanent guide rails, running the full length of the dam crest roadway, kept men at work for weeks. Crews finished small electrical and plumbing jobs in and around the powerhouse. Workers, Bureau engineers, and everyone who had known the "Old Man" wondered if Shasta Dam was really the end for Frank Crowe and his army of construction stiffs, or would there be one more dam.

Epilogue

"Builder"
1945-46

In February of 1945 Frank Crowe journeyed to New York to attend a University of Maine special New York alumni meeting and to receive one of engineering's highest awards. During his remarks as featured speaker of the alumni meeting on the 6th, Crowe reviewed, for the audience, his remembrances of the University of Maine. He recalled how as an undergraduate he trained himself, by continual practice, to be a transit man. To improve his efficiency, he clocked himself so that he could "be the best damned transit man in the east." Guests were reminded how he met Frank Weymouth, who had come back to Maine to fetch his bride and agreed to give a series of lectures to the engineering students. Crowe revealed that as president of the undergraduate civil engineering society he had the opportunity to talk with Weymouth frequently and it was through this contact that he was able to go west. Crowe next talked about the loyalty of his men, some of whom had been with him since the earliest days of the old Reclamation Service. He noted that he was particularly proud of the fact that many sons of the Crowe construction army have joined his organization. Crowe remarked that he loved his men and their dedication to hard, honest work.[1] Crowe enjoyed having an opportunity to see and talk with alumni from Maine despite his reluctance to give a speech. With the night over he retired to his hotel suite to consider his speech for the annual meeting of America's exclusive engineering society.

"The Moles," an organization "composed of men now or formerly engaged in the construction of tunnel, subway, sewer, foundation, marine, sub-aqueous or other heavy construction" annually selected two men from across the nation for outstanding achievement in construction. "The Moles" organization helped to allow engineers from around the country to gather and initiate, and continue friendships that otherwise might not occur. The yearly dinner and celebration was also a time to exchange the latest in engineering advances and recognize noteworthy leadership. Their ultimate goal centered on raising construction standards and improving business ethics. The dinner was by invitation and only 500 tickets were distributed. The well-publicized event started with a seven-course meal in which Crowe sat in a special Dais area with engineering leaders, both civilian and military. Among the guests that night were Major Generals Eugene Reybold and T. M. Robins. Representing the Navy was Rear Admiral J. J. Manning. Interestingly, Major General Leslie R. Groves, the military commander of the Manhattan Project, which built the atomic bomb, was there as well as his superior Lt. General Brehon B. Somervell, head of the Army Corps of Engineers.[2]

The sumptuous meal, which included Green Turtle Au Sherry, Golden Straws, Breast of Chicken—Mascotte, and Potatoes Olivette, concluded at nine o'clock and the presentation of awards began. Noted construction engineer Carl L. Swenson presented the "Moles' Award" to Crowe citing "his skill, ingenuity, and engineering ability in the construction of vast public works, notably in the field of the world's highest and deepest dams." Swenson was, of course, speaking of Hoover and Shasta Dams as the "highest" and Parker Dam as the "deepest." Crowe's acceptance speech was not recorded but one observer that evening later wrote that Crowe's speech was "entirely appropriate to the occasion, meeting with hearty and frequent applause."[3] After the speech, a relieved Frank Crowe sat down and glanced at his award plaque. It read, "The Moles' Award to Frank T. Crowe for Outstanding Achievement in Construction With the Admiration and Esteem of Men Engaged in Construction." The tireless, selfless "Old Man" had reached the highest pinnacle of achievement and recognition of any engineer in American history. As Frank Crowe boarded the train to return to his home in Redding, California, the high-ranking military engineers headed south for Washington D. C., impressed with Crowe's straightforward, results-driven style.

On the evening of May 22, 1945 Frank Crowe received an important phone call at his beautiful two-story home overlooking Redding. The caller, a high ranking general in the War Department wanted to know if Crowe would be interested in a civilian position as engineer-in-charge of rebuilding the American occupied zone of defeated Germany. Crowe, well read as to the degree of physical destruction wrought on Germany, realized that this would be a big, multi-year operation. The offer included job security for as long as America remained in control of the area. On the face of it, the offer sounded great. Crowe would be given the opportunity to command an army of engineers and workers in an effort to rebuild factories, rail lines, public buildings, airports, and dams. During the war the British successfully knocked out the Ruhr River dams that powered much of Hitler's manufacturing potential. These dams and others needed immediate repair if power were to be restored and adequate irrigation water supplies become available.

Crowe seriously discussed the matter with Linnie, then with his close friends. No decision was made, until he discussed the matter with his doctor the next day. Though it was not generally known that Crowe had suffered a mild heart attack the year before, his doctor and his family were worried that the stress of this new international assignment might prove disastrous. That afternoon word spread quickly around the city about the government's interest in Crowe. At first, Crowe did not want to confirm the offer, but when pressed by reporters he announced his decision. "If I were 40 instead of 62" began Crowe, "I'd have taken a plane last night." Frank Crowe would not go to Germany.[4]

Another reason Crowe turned down the War Department's offer was that he had plenty of other lucrative engineering opportunities. Foremost on his list of commitments was chief consulting engineer to the Morrison-Knudsen Company. He had only recently returned from a trip to New York where he bid a job for the company and he was planning to go to Boise shortly to confer on another project. On estimating men and material for heavy construction jobs there was no one better than Frank Crowe. He knew the competition and he knew how to beat them. Ignoring his irregular bouts of chest pain, the peerless engineer worked long hours calculating the bid estimate for Davis Dam in Nevada.[5] When the bids were opened, Crowe's bid proved once again to be the lowest and Morrison-Knudsen had another job. Engineers from foreign countries constantly communicated their desire to employ him in a consulting capacity. Through 1945 he struck deals with the governments of India, China, and a couple of South American countries. Professionally, this was plenty for Frank Crowe and with his daughter, Patricia, married and living in San Francisco and his other daughter, Elizabeth, attending Stanford University, he figured that the time was right to relax and enjoy the beautiful northern California countryside, fish and raise cattle.

From the first moment Frank Crowe saw Shasta County, from the rolling oak-studded foothills east to the steep pine tree-covered mountains of the Cascade Mountain Range, he realized that this was a cattleman's paradise and probably a great place to retire. As early as 1938 and continuing through the building of Shasta Dam, Frank Crowe purchased Shasta County property, mostly cattle ranches. By 1945 he had amassed over 13,000 acres of land and ranches, the largest of which was a 6.004 acre parcel in the low-lying Bella Vista area. In Millville, he owned a 4,000-acre cattle ranch and several other parcels. One of his favorite purchases, and the one he spent a lot of time relaxing at was the 438-acre cattle ranch at Hat Creek. Cool open pastures framed by a mix of conifers and deciduous trees set an inviting scene for this 3-4,000 foot in elevation property. Located east of Redding approximately sixty miles, Crowe soon adopted this ranch setting as a Shangri-la, isolated far from the pressures of the dam and his recognizable presence in town.[6]

On the morning of February 26, 1946, John and Mary Crowe drove into Redding from their home east of town. Deciding to have lunch at the Lorenz Hotel, they happened upon "Uncle Frank" eating lunch with his chief engineer William V. "Bill" Greeley. Frank invited his nephew and wife to join them for lunch. Mary Crowe could tell from the moment she saw him that "Uncle Frank looked gray and tired." Despite this, Frank perked up at the sight of his engineer nephew and his expecting wife. "He seemed to have [a] fine time—ate his meal—

poked fun with M. F. [Mary Fran Crowe, John and Mary's five year old daughter] and kidded me," wrote Mary in her diary. Always thinking and worrying about his extended family, Frank called John over after lunch and insisted that he bring Mary into town until the baby was born. That was the last time they saw Frank Crowe alive. Later in the early evening, Crowe and Greeley were returning from an afternoon visit to Keswick Dam, the after bay structure for Shasta Dam, when Frank was "stricken." Greeley stopped the car and tried to revive Crowe by attempting artificial respiration. When this failed, Greeley promptly sped to Mercy Hospital in Redding, but Frank Crowe never regained consciousness and he was pronounced dead, of a heart attack, shortly after this by Coroner Claude Whiteman. John and Mary had returned home and decided to take Frank's advice and move into town. As they were packing, the phone rang. It was "Red" Wixson, longtime Crowe colleague, who disclosed the bad news. "I hope I never see John look so gray and shocked," Mary wrote, "He just walked out of the house to the car."[7]

Everyone, but the immediate family and close personal friends, had no idea that Crowe had suffered an earlier heart attack and was not in perfect health. "The news was shocking indeed," wrote University of Maine's Charles Crossland, "for not a soul on campus had any misgiving that Frank was not in excellent health." Newspapers around the country, from New York and Maine, on the east coast, to Los Angeles and San Francisco, on the west coast, reported Crowe's death, while Linnie personally wired close friends and family. Crowe's community of Redding was "shocked by the news and many people couldn't believe it was true" wrote one local reporter. Word spread rapidly throughout the construction world and hundreds of telegrams and messages arrived, many of them from construction presidents to "construction stiffs" promising to come to the funeral.

On March 1, 1946, Francis Trenholm Crowe was laid to rest. A simple Masonic service at the Veterans Memorial Hall in Redding was performed by M. P. Howard and Judge Albert F. Ross, in which Crowe's favorite song, "Home on the Range" played quietly in the background and was sung by Phil Storm. Crowe had first joined the Masons in St. Ignatius, Montana, where he was a member of the Flathead Lodge. As Crowe was also a Shriner, a special color guard attended. According to one reporter, "hundreds of local friends and his associates in engineering and construction from many parts of the west attended the rites." Pallbearers that day included Crowe's longtime dam building associates: Frank Bryant, Anthony "Si" Bous, Earl McAdams, Charles Silva, Robert Sass, George Bogvitch and Ben Rementeria. Taken to nearby McDonald's Chapel and Cemetery, the body was quickly interred.[8]

Within days of the funeral a flood of newspaper columns and magazine and journal articles began to appear eulogizing Frank Crowe and his accomplishments. Morrison-Knudsen featured a memorial article in which they called Crowe "A man of broad vision and tremendous, driving energy." He died "with his boots on" the article claimed, referring to a statement made by Crowe that "he'd never be content where he couldn't hear the sound of the shovels." The article made note of his recent success on getting the bid for Davis Dam and added, "While the Kortes Dam contract has not been awarded as this is written, bids were opened— and M-K's was lowest—on Tuesday, March 12, just two weeks after Frank Crowe passed away—a winner to the last."[9]

The *San Francisco Chronicle* called him "master builder of the West's great dams," giving him credit for inventing a "unique method of pouring concrete from seven cables radiating from a 465-foot headtower." The article recalled Crowe's dislike for office engineering work when it quoted Crowe as saying that he "never bellied up to a desk in my life." *Civil Engineering* in its April issue paid special honor to Crowe recognizing that he had achieved "World-wide fame as an engineer." The memorial tribute told readers that Crowe's drive and ambition became evident as soon as he entered the engineering field, "where he was not long in reaching positions of responsibility and leadership."[10]

One of the longest and most heartfelt tributes to Frank Crowe came from one of his Hoover Dam colleagues, A. E. Cahlan. "Perhaps the greatest builder of dams in the world, he was one of the humblest of humans," the eulogy began, "In forty years of construction work, he had gained recognition among the great, love and respect among the toilers who carried out his plans and executed his orders." Cahlan recalled how Crowe arrived at the Hoover Dam job as a stranger, but left after the completion of the dam as one of the best known and well loved residents. "You won't find Crowe's name on any of the plaques placed on the project.," Cahlan reminded readers. "He used to laugh about that, saying 'I was just a construction stiff.'" To Cahlan, who knew well, the term "construction stiff" was an endearing one, used to show respect and honor to those men committed to staying with the "Old Man" until the job was through. The term had to be earned, never given easily.

In an interesting look at Crowe's dealings with labor problems and strike situations Cahlan wrote, "I have never known a man with such a breadth of understanding. It extended from people to intricate problems and back to people again." "I have seen him," Cahlan continued, "in the midst of labor disputes when he felt he was getting a raw deal from persons he knew were professional agitators and troublemakers. They knew he knew it and it seemed they beset him because they loved to do battle with him." In an odd twist of interpretation Cahlan remarked, "They always lost but somehow seemed glad they did." In a revealing attempt to show Crowe's genuine concern for his worker's well-being Cahlan remembered, "He never could understand how his men would be taken in by these agitators, yet he never blamed them. He was indulgent and sympathetic. He'd razz them vigorously for being so foolish as to believe the interlopers, then lend them enough to tide their families over for the days they were off work protesting."

There is no doubt that Crowe became a paternalistic figure to so many of his men. They were part of his construction family and Cahlan wrote of an interesting episode at Hoover Dam that supports this claim. "I'll never forget the one big dispute during the Boulder Dam construction" Cahlan recalled. "He went through another battle with familiar adversaries, playing the game carefully and astutely as he would a poker hand. When he knew he had set the stage for final victory, he invited his workers back to the job and then took up a position atop a hill near the turn in the Las Vegas-Boulder City highway to await results. He knew they'd come back, and yet he thrilled way down deep when the first carload rolled by." Continuing the story, which has been verified by a number of dam workers returning to work after the 1931 strike ended, Cahlan observed, "They waved to him and he to them. All was forgiven. They were just part of his big family of 'construction stiffs' who had strayed from the fold temporarily and couldn't stay away. He never bawled them out or attempted any of the reprisals that many a less understanding boss would do in those days."[11]

Almost everyone who knew Crowe referred to him at one time or another as the "Old Master." During construction crises, he would be everywhere at once giving orders and checking every possible contingency. Yet, he never once appeared indecisive or emotionally involved. If he did, he kept it all inside. Workers remember seeing him, like a modern-day George Washington observing a battle unfold, walking briskly among the work and men encouraging them and never showing the least bit of hesitancy in giving orders. He thoroughly enjoyed pitting men and machines against nature and the greater the physical struggle, the more satisfaction he gained. At times Crowe realized that he was asking his men to give more than is usually expected of heavy construction workers, but he felt his men were the best at what they did. He understood, correctly, that these men placed great pride in being a member of Crowe's elite construction army.

Critics have accused him of living up to one of his nicknames "Hurry-up Crowe" too well, that he did quicken the pace without providing an adequate safe working environment and that he did this in the name of notoriety and greater profits. Yet, the preponderance of evidence points in exactly the opposite direction, that Crowe always placed the safety of his men first. Cahlan, who was quite close to Crowe, without reservation stated that whenever one of his men was injured "it stabbed him [Crowe] deeply." "He knew what it meant to men and families for accidents to happen and he worked unceasingly to eliminate all hazards." Dozens of ex-dam workers interviewed by this author unanimously confirmed the strong safety effort put forth by Crowe on all of his jobs. Some of those who had been with him as far back as Jackson Lake remembered that "safety was first." To them accidents were exactly what the word meant, an accident, and more often than not, involved a worker not adhering to standard work procedures.

It is amazing to consider how involved Frank Crowe became in the lives of his men. "He liked to get big jobs so he could take care of his 'boys,'" Cahlan recollected. "He knew them all by their first names, thousands upon thousands of them. And he gave them all, every opportunity for a better job." Crowe took particular pleasure in watching a son of one his men become excited about construction work and be hired on. Bernard "Woody" Williams was one such young man whom made the decision to go into dam building as his career. Williams quickly gained Crowe's attention with his dedicated hard-working qualities and the "Old Man" worked with him personally so that when Hoover Dam began, Williams was ready to become Crowe's "right-hand man." Williams went on to superintend his own construction projects.

It might prove difficult for readers to understand the close-knit bond of construction brotherhood that developed between Crowe and his men. Through the massive domestic changes caused by World War I, the uncertainty of the reactionary 1920s, the economic nightmare of the Great Depression and the global upheaval of World War II, Crowe represented stability in a very unstable world. Some workers saw this as an economic stability, where Crowe was, there was work. Others saw Crowe as a pseudo-father figure able to make sense out of the quagmire of social chaos. To them he offered a sense of belonging to something that was worth living for. A purpose, a powerful purpose, to build dams and irrigation works that would long outlive them and that would, in a dramatic way, contribute to the successful economic development of their country. One observer trying to deal with the loss of Frank Crowe tried to summarize the engineer's qualities and contributions. "Above and beyond all the great works he wrought, stands the man himself. To me, that's the REAL story. I can tell it no better than with the instances of his association with the men who comprised his crews. As word spread through the community [Boulder City] of his death, I had many calls to confirm the news. One, a husky, gnarled, unshaven man, had a look almost of terror in his eyes as he asked me the question. When I answered, his eyes filled with tears, and he said, 'I worked for him on Boulder Dam,' then turned and walked slowly away, weeping unashamedly. I could give you no finer tribute to my beloved friend."[12]

Much of the uncompromising loyalty that Crowe commanded sprung from his genuine belief that they were more important to him than a "high powered salesman or executive." A. H. Ayers, another high ranking Crowe confidant when asked to summarize his feeling about Crowe said that the "Old Man" is "hard-boiled in nearly everything, the only things which really get under his skin are the loss or serious injury of one of his men, or a failure of one in whom he has placed confidence." Ayers and numerous others alluded to the fact that Frank Crowe never asked anything from his men that he himself would not do. Through example "Crowe inspires confidence, because he believes he can do a thing, and then proceeds to do it."[13]

Rarely does history honor the engineers who, through the creation of innovative machines and effective coordination of workers, change the physical and economic face of a region or nation. Frank Crowe realized that he was in the right place at the right time, a period that he referred to as "the greatest dam-building spree of all times." By the time of America's massive war preparations geared up in the late 1930s Hoover Dam's fifteen high-powered water turbines were pumping out a tremendous volume of electrical energy fed directly into the burgeoning war production plants sprouting up all over Southern California. These factories played an essential role in producing America's war material, eventually overwhelming the production capability of all of our adversaries. The agricultural benefits derived from all of Crowe's dams also stand out as a major achievement. With the successful completion of Hoover, Parker, and Shasta Dams, California exploded in an unprecedented expansion of crop variety and productivity, literally becoming the most successful agricultural region in the world.

As Shasta Dam neared completion reporter Frank Taylor paid a visit to Crowe and spent several days following the " Old Man" in his work routine. Taylor marveled how Crowe continued to look for better and faster ways to move earth or concrete. He talked with one veteran foreman who said "He'd come down in the canyon by the river and look up this side and look up that side," pausing the dam worker looked at Taylor and added, "Then he'd scratch his head and go away. Pretty soon there'd be some machine we'd never seen before, and it would work, too."[14] Most of the time these "machines" were cableway configurations of one design or another. He loved the design challenges of customizing a system that fit particular canyon topography. And it would the colossal cableways that proved to be Crowe's greatest engineering contribution, for now dams of unprecedented size were technologically and economically feasible.

Frank Crowe, as Taylor stated, has "changed the map of America," both the cities and the farms. For better or worse, with assured huge reservoir water supplies delivered via the Los Angeles Aqueduct, Southern California's population and economy mushroomed. And what Hoover and Parker Dam did for Southern California, Shasta Dam did for Northern California. Indeed, the irrigation and dam building programs of the United States Reclamation Service, later the Bureau of Reclamation, powerfully transformed the entire American West and while one can argue the pros and cons of dam building today, particularly from an environmental standpoint, one must pause and appreciate the thousands of dam building laborers. Their efforts helped create a new American West.

In 1981 Boulder City officials celebrating their 50th anniversary, dedicated the Frank T. Crowe Park. Upon the small grass-covered triangular area were erected a monument to Crowe and the men who helped him build Hoover Dam. Nevada governor Robert List and other dignitaries joined Crowe's surviving family members and friends in praising his achievements. S. L. "Red" Wixson, a good friend of Frank Crowe, had raised money to buy the land which he then donated to the city.

On Frank Crowe's insistence, there was to be no elaborate funeral or monumental tombstone. His dams proved to be his monument and as he stated, "they will stand for centuries." The master dam builder's small rectangular grave

marker simply reads, "Frank T. Crowe, 1882-1946, Builder." With the work on
Shasta Dam progressing nicely Frank Crowe paused, looked up at the rising monolith and mused, "Look at that Shasta Dam. That will stand there forever, holding
back the river. And the powerhouse will keep right on turning out juice until
somebody discovers how to make power out of sunlight." How true his words are
still today, as scientists continue to pour millions of research dollars into developing cheap reliable photoelectric systems, Hoover, Parker, Shasta, Guernsey, Tieton,
Deadwood, Jackson Lake and all the other dams that Frank Crowe built continue
to provide a substantial portion of the American West's energy.

There is a special debt that history needs to pay, that we need to pay, to
honor those American traits we hold most dear. Traits that, though may appear
removed and remote in today's politically correct world, are nonetheless at the
very core of what America hoped to represent in the tumultuous years of the first
five decades of the twentieth century. Honest hard work and humility never go out
of fashion and it is to these traits that Frank Crowe is best measured. A well-
quoted phrase that he used after completing the monumental challenges of Hoover
and Parker Dams fully explains Frank Crowe, the engineer and Frank Crowe, the
man; "If you gentlemen want to see the fellow who really built this dam, go over to
the mess hall. He wears a tin hat, his average age is thirty-one and he can do
things."

Notes

Chapter 1

[1]Information taken from the Crowe family tree and from Patricia Crowe-Lee, interview with author, 10 Sept. 1996.
[2]"Memoirs of Francis Trenholm Crowe, Hon. M. ASCE," *Transactions*, (1946) American Society of Civil Engineers.
[3]"Construction: By a Damsite," *Time*, 19 June 1944.
[4]"Memoir 1818, Francis Trenholm Crowe, Hon. M. ASCE"
[5]John W. Ragle, *Governor Dummer Academy History*, 84. Numerous other alumni had distinguished careers in our early republic. Two others included Edward Preble and Tobias Lear. Preble held the rank on Commodore with the American naval forces in 1803, where aboard his famous flagship the *Constitution* he conducted the successful campaign against the Mediterranean pirates at Tripoli. Lear, who had been George Washington's private secretary for many years, served the Jeffersonian administration by negotiating a peaceful settlement with the Tripoli pirates.
[6]Ibid., 84.
[7]Elizabeth Crowe-Parry, interview by author, San Clemente, CA., 27 Jan. 1996.
[8]David C. Smith, *The First Century: A History of the University of Maine, 1865-1965*, (Orono, Maine: University of Maine Press, 1979).
[9]Military drill was a compulsory and a tradition at the University of Maine. All male students were required to join the local drill group, the Coburn Cadets, wear uniforms, drill, and go through several encampment and war game exercises. By the time Frank Crowe arrived in 1901, drill had lost its previous important role and many students considered it to be a burden, looking for excuses to absent themselves from duties and requirements.
[10]Elizabeth Crowe-Parry, interview by author, San Clemente, CA., 27 Jan. 1996.
[11]Transcripts of Frank Crowe from the University of Maine at Orono.
[12]Michael Robinson, *Water for the West: The Bureau of Reclamation, 1902-1977*, (Chicago: Public Works Historical Society), 17.
[13]Donald C. Jackson, "Engineering in the Progressive Era: A New Look at Frederick Haynes Newell and the U. S. Reclamation Service," *Technology and Culture 34*, No. 3, July, 1993, 539-545.
[14]Marion Allen, interview by author, Redding, CA., 10 July 1991.
[15]*The Prism*, Yearbook of the University of Maine, 1904.
[16]"Memoirs of Francis Trenholm Crowe."
[17]Department of the Interior, Bureau of Reclamation, *Lower Yellowstone Project—Annual Project History*, Through 1909—Vol. 1, National Archives of the USGS, Denver, Colorado. 35-36
[18]Elizabeth Crowe-Parry, telephone interview by author, 2 Aug. 1998.
[19]Allen, interview by author, Redding, CA., 10 July 1991.
[20]"Memoirs of Francis Trenholm Crowe."
[21]On April 19th of that year, John received a handsome offer to become Superintendent of

the Pulp and Paper Makers Felt Department for The Penman Manufacturing Co, Limited in St. Hyacinthe, Quebec, Canada. The mill was located some 30 miles from Montreal. John's salary consisted of a base wage of $3.00 per day; traveling expenses "when on the road" and an incentive commission of "one percent of the Nett [sic] Sales of Pulp and Paper Makers Felts." Letter from The Penman Manufacturing Co. to John Crowe, donated by John Hollstein, P.O. Box 69, Morrison, CO.

[22]Ibid., 2.

[23]According to his memoirs, Frank drove horses. This meant that when the train paused at watering stops he would drive them off the car, water and feed them, and then drive them back into the train car. John Crowe, Frank's nephew recalled that he heard Frank state that the stock was cattle—interview by author, 10 May. 1996.

[24]*The Maine*, a publication of the University of Maine Alumni Association, Fall 1991.

[25]University of Maine transcripts.

[26]*Maine Magazine*, a University of Maine Alumni Association Publication, Fall 1991. Boardman spent more than 40 years actively engaged or associated with the University of Maine. He started his teaching career in 1901, when Frank arrived. Boardman taught a variety of engineering courses. Opportunity called in 1903; he was made an associate professor and Dean of Engineering. A year later he was again promoted, this time to full professor. From a position as the Dean of the Civil Engineering Department and the first Dean of the College of Technology, he went on as an alumnus to serve as President of the university. In addition to Frank Crowe, Boardman had the privilege to work with Frank Banks (1906 graduate), the builder of Grand Coulee Dam, and Raymond E. Davis (1911) and George L. Freeman (1903), the design engineers and builders of the Oakland Bay Bridge.

[27]"Memoirs of Francis Trenholm Crowe."

Chapter 2

[1]Edrie Vinson, "Lower Yellowstone Project: United States Reclamation Service, 1907-08," Paper prepared for the Montana Department of Highways, 1988. p.3.

[2]Ibid, p.4.

[3]Ibid. p.4. The prediction according to Vinson had fallen considerably short of the twenty million mark, as of 1982 only two million acres had been irrigated.

[4]Department of the Interior, Bureau of Reclamation, *Lower Yellowstone Project—Annual Project History*, Through 1909—Vol. 1, National Archives of the USGS, Denver, Col.

[5]"Lower Yellowstone Irrigation Project,"*Our Jubilee, 1911-1961*, Mon-Dak Historical & Art Society, p.18.

[6]The final package bid revealed Weymouth's estimates to be very good. Some of the project components included: Diversion Dam $70,000, five million cubic yards of excavation $750,000, various aqueducts and siphons, to reach a grand total of $1,700,000 with engineering fees and a 20% contingency. These figures are rounded off and are part of the Annual Project History noted in #4 above. See "birdseye" view map of the Lower Yellowstone Project in *Focus on Our Roots*, Mon-Dak Historical Society, Sidney, Montana. p. 26.

[7]The U.S. Reclamation Service had agreed to build the office as a permanent housing facility for personnel, such as the Gate Keeper and Canal Rider, maintaining the dam and

canal. This camp was given the name Intake to signify the place where water from the river first entered the canal.

[8]*Lower Yellowstone Project—Annual Project History.*

[9]Crowe held this title throughout his time at the Lower Yellowstone Project and he transferred to the Minidoka Project with the same title. He was noted, in the July, 1910 issue of the *Reclamation Record* as an Instrumentman for the Snake River Storage Project.

[10]Marion Allen, Interview, Redding, CA 14 Mar. 1993.

[11]Elliot Paul, *Desperate Scenery*, New York: Random House, 1954. p. 46. During Crowe's residence at the University of Maine the "Two-Step" was one of the most requested at school sponsored and music club dances.

[12]Calderwood, p. 3.

[13]"The Yellowstone Valley," E. G. Greenup, in *Focus on Our Roots*, p. 5.

[14]"What I Know of the Lower Yellowstone," W. B. Overson, in *Focus on Our Roots*, p. 10.

[15]Elliot Paul, *A Ghost Town on the Yellowstone*, (New York: Random House, 1948), 137.

[16]Ibid. 138.

[17]"Likes the Yellowstone Better than Nebraska," W. M. Post, in *Focus on Our Roots*, p. 12.

[18]"The Yellowstone Valley Compared with Central States," W. J. Sweenley, in *Focus on Our Roots*, p. 12. On page 26 of the same book note the photograph of ice breaking apart on the Yellowstone River. This picture taken on March 4, 1910 attests to the icy conditions found in this area.

[19]Department of the Interior, Bureau of Reclamation, *Lower Yellowstone Project—Annual Project History, Through 1909—Vol. 1*, National Archives of the USGS, Denver, Col. p. 40. For detailed specifications for the Lower Yellowstone Diversion Dam including surveying elevations see United States Department of the Interior, Bureau of Reclamation. (1961). *Reclamation Project Data*. Washington, DC: U.S. Government Printing Office. p. 319.

[20]Elliot Paul, *A Ghost Town on the Yellowstone*, (New York: Random House, 1948), 129.

[21]Edrie Vinson, "Lower Yellowstone Project, United States Reclamation Service, 1907-1908." Montana Department of Highways, April 1988. Vinson, a noted architectural historian, provides and excellent summary of the first construction work. She also notes that the financial crisis of 1906-07 inflated the cost of the project to a much greater expense than the Reclamation Service ever conceived. See also "South Dakota State Historical Society/Office of History" on-line page entitled "South Dakota History Chronology" http://www.state.sd.us/state/executive/deca/cultural/soc_hist.htm

[22]Department of the Interior, Bureau of Reclamation, *Lower Yellowstone Project—Annual Project History, Through 1909—Vol. 1*, National Archives of the USGS, Denver, Col. p. 34. Elliot Paul, *A Ghost Town on the Yellowstone*, (New York: Random House, 1948), 177-179. The IWW had formed in the summer of 1905 in Chicago under the leadership of Eugene Debs, Daniel DeLeon and William Haywood. It is interesting to note that the largest contingent of new members during the first couple of years was from the Western Federation of Miners.

[23]"Another Champ...Alive at the Top is this M-K Old Timer" *The Em Kayan,* May, 1943. p.8. Later, Munn would rise to important positions in the Morrison-Knudsen Company: by 1943, he ran the company, holding the dual positions of President and Chairman of the Board.

[24]Letter from Crowe to Weymouth dated 4 Oct. 1919. Crowe was Project Manager of the Flathead Project in St. Ignatius, Montana.

[25]The photograph is taken from *Focus on Our Roots*, MonDak Historical & Art Society, p. 26. To see the boundaries of each division in the Lower Yellowstone Project see *General Map of the Lower Yellowstone Project, Specifications No. 136*, March 1907, U. S. Reclamation Service.

[26]See Frank Crowe "James Munn: Builder of Men and a Foster Parent of M-K," *The Em Kayan*, May 1943, p. 6 and also W. V. Greeley, S. O. Harper, and W. R. Young, "Memoirs of Deceased Members: Francis Trenholm Crowe, Hon. M. ASCE, *Transactions of the ASCE*, Vol. 113, Memoir No., p. 2.

[27]Ibid. p. 36. Frank A. Banks, a University of Maine engineering student one year behind Crowe and an acquaintance of his, arrived at this time to replace C. J. Woody as drafting engineer. J. L. Savage, an outstanding design engineer who would influence Crowe later in the following decades, also resigned around this time. He left the Service in June of 1908 to accept a private contracting offer. *The Monthly Bulletin*, United States Reclamation Service, July, 1908, p. 55. R. J. Newell, assistant engineer at Minidoka resigned the next month and a search through government records shows much movement of personnel within the Service. Newell accepted a position with the Great Shoshone and Twin Falls Water Power Company. August, 1908, p.71.

[28]*New York Times*, May 23, P. 2, col. 4. The article claims that Garfield possessed "a veritable second sight in picking for discharge the idle, trifling, and incompetent." Washington sources point to the fact that the Interior department had gained 1/3 again more employees for doing the same amount of work and something needed to be done. Garfield would pay the price for his high flung attempt to cutout government waste; vengeful congressional members would pressure new incoming President Taft to ax Garfield.

[29]William Warne, *The Bureau of Reclamation*, New York: Praeger Publishers, 1973, p. 26.

[30]See "Another Champ...alive and at the top is this M-K old timer," *The Em Kayan*, May 1943, p. 8.; Frank Crowe "James Munn: Builder of Men and a Foster Parent of M-K," *The Em Kayan*, May 1943, p. 7; and Department of the Interior, Bureau of Reclamation, *A History of the Minidoka Project, Idaho, to 1912 inclusive*. National Archives of the USGS, Denver, Colorado, August 1915. p. 20. The project histories detail the current wages given to carpenters, drillers, engineers, and even foremen.

[31]W. V. Greeley, S. O. Harper, and W. R. Young, "Memoirs of Deceased Members: Francis Trenholm Crowe, Hon. M. ASCE," *Transactions of the ASCE*, Vol. 113, Memoir No. 1818, p. 2.

[32]Frank Crowe "James Munn: Builder of Men and a Foster Parent of M-K," *The Em Kayan*, May 1943, pp. 6-7.

[33]*Reclamation Project Data*. Washington, DC: U.S. Government Printing Office. pp. 33-36.

[34]Ibid. 38-39.

[35]Department of the Interior, Bureau of Reclamation, *Lower Yellowstone Project—Annual Project History, Through 1909—Vol. 1*, National Archives of the USGS, Denver, Col. p. 34. It is difficult to follow the exact sequence of jobs for Crowe at this point in his career, due to the fact that as an employee of Munn and a contract-laborer for the Service, individual records have not been retained. His personal employment record with the Reclamation Service begins in 1916, well after his career had begun.

[36]Letter from Frank Crowe to his mother, Emma. Donated by John Hollstein, a great nephew of Frank Crowe. It is assumed that the money sent to Emma was either saved from his Service salary or it was profit made during work with Munn, or both.

[37]Weymouth's reassignment was officially effective on October 19, 1908 in the project history and announced nationwide in the *The Monthly Bulletin*, U.S. Reclamation Service, Washington D.C., November 1908. p. 103.

[38]*The Monthly Bulletin*, U.S. Reclamation Service, Washington D.C., August 1908. pp. 89-91.

[39]Department of the Interior, Bureau of Reclamation, *Lower Yellowstone Project—Annual Project History, Through 1909—Vol. 1*, National Archives of the USGS, Denver, Col. p. 36.

[40]*Courage Enough*, 1975. MonDak Heritage Center, Sidney, Montana. p. 6. By 1912, the main canal had been extended 8 miles with the addition of over 100 miles of laterals. Total cost for the project reached almost five million dollars. The project's success is described in the above mentioned publication referring to a statement by former project manager Axel Persson, where he notes that the newly irrigated area has become "a lush oasis, green with alfalfa, sugar beets, feed grains and other forage crops." Presson claims in "Lower Yellowstone Irrigation Project" that 7,000 acres of Montana were irrigated in the 1909-10 season. *Our Jubilee*, MonDak Heritage Center, Sidney Montana, p. 18.

[41]Department of the Interior, Bureau of Reclamation, *A History of the Minidoka Project, Idaho, to 1912 inclusive*. National Archives of the USGS, Denver, Colorado, August 1915. p. 3.

[42]United States Department of the Interior, Bureau of Reclamation. (1961). *Reclamation Project Data*. Washington, DC: U.S. Government Printing Office. p. 353. See also, Allen, M. (1981). *Early Jackson Hole*. Self published. Redding, CA. p. 79. Hitchcock was moved to action by Ross's report that contained impressive projections worked up by consulting engineer A. J. Wiley and his assistant J. L. Savage. Ross had already submitted the report to district headquarters in Boise where A. P. Davis, Assistant Chief Engineer and others had approved the engineering plans and cost estimates. See *Project History of the Minidoka Project*, pp-3-5.

[43]United States Department of the Interior, Bureau of Reclamation. (1961). *Reclamation Project Data*. Washington, DC: U.S. Government Printing Office. pp. 354-355. See also *Minidoka Water Resource Project*, a pamphlet of the U. S. Department of the Interior, Bureau of Reclamation.

[44]Department of the Interior, Bureau of Reclamation, *A History of the Minidoka Project, Idaho, to 1912 inclusive*. National Archives of the USGS, Denver, Colorado, August 1915. p. 5.

[45]United States Department of the Interior, Bureau of Reclamation. (1961). *Reclamation Project Data*. Washington, DC: U.S. Government Printing Office. pp. 354-351.

[46]See *Reclamation Record*, U.S. Reclamation Service, Washington D.C. for December, 1908, p. 106; January, 1909, p. 4, and February, 1909, p. 16. By December the Reclamation Service had named its newsletter the *Reclamation Record* replacing the former *Monthly Bulletin*.

[47]Ibid. April 1909, p. 39; July 1909, p. 68.

[48]Allen, p. 80.

[49] Unless otherwise noted, all temperature degrees are in the Fahrenheit scale.

[50]Bernfeld, B. "The Jackson Lake Dam: No Small Task," *Wyoming Horizons*, August 1985, 14.

[51]Ibid. Dam worker turned author, Marion Allen in his book entitled *Early Jackson Hole*, 1981, Redding, California: Press Room, covers the arduous Ashton-Moran freight road in

anecdotal detail—much of it based on his own recollections of the numerous trips he made. See chapter three of that book for a map, photographs, and accounts of the journeys.

[52]Letter from Marie Sass to Emma Crowe, June 23, 1909. Donated by John Hollstein.

[53]John Markham, "Building of Jackson Lake Brings Colorful Recollections," *The Post-Register*, April 4, 1972. A-10. Markam's recollections appear in numerous other locations including Allen's *Early Jackson Hole*. Markam notes that Crowe and Sass returned from their trip and reported to Helena, Montana. However, the Boise Project headquarters was located in Boise, Idaho and it is more likely that Sass wanted to visit his family, who lived in Helena. This would also provide the young enamored Crowe an opportunity to see his sweetheart, Marie Sass.

[54] Letter from Frank Crowe to his mother Emma, August 25, 1909. Donated by John Hollstein.

[55]Letter from Frank Crowe to his mother, Emma. August 27, 1909. Donated by John Hollstein.

[56]Letter from Frank Crowe to his mother, Emma. September 4, 1909. Donated by John Hollstein.

[57]Ibid. See Allen, p. 45. Notified of the dam break, Reclamation officials manipulated the water level in the Minidoka Diversion Dam, located downstream to minimize flood damage from that point on. See Department of the Interior, Bureau of Reclamation, *A History of the Minidoka Project, Idaho, to 1912 inclusive*. National Archives of the USGS, Denver, Colorado, August 1915. p. 42.

[58]John Markham, "Building of Jackson Lake Brings Colorful Recollections," *The Post-Register,* April 4, 1972. A-10.

[59]See U. S. Department of the Interior, *Reclamation Record Vol. 2*; July 1910, p. 64; September, p. 82; and November, p. 97.

[60]Allen, p. 87.

[61]See Elliot Paul, *Desperate Scenery*, pp. 88-89.

[62]See *Reclamation Record*. Vol II No. 12, December 1910, p. 106; Allen, *Early Jackson Hole*, pp. 88-89; Markham, "Building of Jackson Lake Brings Colorful Recollections," *The Post-Register*, April 4, 1972. A-10. There appears to be some disagreement as to who was the chief clerk on this operation. Official government records list Moore, but Markham explicitly claims that Joseph J. McEnroe started in that position from the very beginning. More likely is that Crowe employed several clerks, as his operation grew quite large. Rumors of Sass marrying had been officially announced in the first issue of the camp newspaper the "Dam Weekly," November 12, 1910: 4.

[63]Betsy Bernfeld, "The Jackson Lake Dam: no small task," *Wyoming Horizons*, August 4, 1985, p.14; *Casper Star Tribune*, August, 1985. See also Allen, *Early Jackson Hole*, p. 89.

[64]Ibid; see also Allen, pp. 90-91 and Elliot Paul, *Desperate Scenery*, p. 179.

[65]Paul, pp. 198-199. While the publishers of this book state that Paul's writings are "bizarre but always true tales." The author has refrained from interjecting the plethora of stories noted in Paul's books. At least three persons, in a position to know about Frank Crowe and Marie Sass from personal experience or family contact, have noted serious discrepancies, such as the name "Barbara" for Marie Sass. John Crowe, nephew, and later engineer with Crowe on a number of jobs, Elizabeth Mudron, Val Allen's daughter and Jackson Hole resident, and Pat Crowe, Frank's daughter have all noted accuracy problems in Paul's account. Each were interviewed on several separate occasions between 1995-1998.

[66]*The Dam Weekly*, November, 12, 1910: 2. Few copies of this informal newsletter exist, but read closely it gives an interesting insight into the social life of dam workers at Jackson Lake Dam.

[67]Betsy Bernfeld, "The Jackson Lake Dam: no small task," *Wyoming Horizons*, August 4, 1985, p.14

[68]Allen, *Early Jackson Hole*, p. 93.

[69]Elizabeth Mudron, interview in Redding, California, May 25, 1998. Pregnant women are particularly prone to kidney infection, as they are more likely to develop bladder infections. *The New Illustrated Medical Encyclopedia*, New York: Abradale Press, 1970. p. 803. Marie Sass' death is recorded as File Number 17, 1911, Bureau of Vital Statistics, State of Wyoming.

Chapter 3

[1]U. S. Department of the Interior, Reclamation Service, *Boise Project-Storage Unit, Feature Report, Testing and Preliminary Investigation, Vol. 1 Description*, 1912. Crowe's team looked at a total of seven or eight sites on the Boise River. Some of the places had colorful names such as, Rossi's, Joy's Creek, Alexander Flats, and Hellgate.

[2]Ibid., no page numbers. See subheading *Location*.

[3]*Reclamation Record*. Vol III No. 5, May 1911, p. 171 and No. 6. June 1911, p. 185.

[4]Ibid, October 1911, p. 250. See also the November issue.

[5]*Compressed Air Magazine*, 11 (Oct. 1906): 4233. See also *Compressed Air Magazine*, 12 (August, 1907): 4525.

[6]Charles Paul, U. S. Department of the Interior, Reclamation Service, *Boise Project-Storage Unit, Feature Report, Diversion Works*, (20 Jan. 1913): 3-6.

[7]James Munn, U. S. Department of the Interior, Reclamation Service, *Boise Project-Storage Unit, Feature Report, Construction Plant*, (27 Sep. 1915): 17-19.

[8]Ibid; The skips, made of solid steel, were 8 feet square and 2 feet deep. Once located over the designated dumpsite, workers pulled a release line and the bottom opened up. It is not certain if Crowe designed these conveyors, but they were certainly unique, due to their large size, to Reclamation projects.

[9]United State Department of the Interior, Reclamation Service, *Minidoka Project, Annual O & M Report*, 1910-15: 8-15.

[10]*Reclamation Record*. Vol IV, 1912; March: 42; April:58; May 75. These issues of the Reclamation Service provide an excellent monthly summary of the work progress at all of their major projects.

[11]Ibid; July 1912: 126. [I made an inquiry to the American Heart Association on June 1, 1998 to find out about the two methods of respiration mentioned.]

[12]Ibid; Vol. IV, 1913: January, 3; March, 50; April, 68; May, 87. In the February issue Crowe is listed in the Boise Project - Arrowrock Division personnel roster as "Engineer."

[13]Ibid; June, 110; July, 123; August, 153. Crowe was so anxious to get started on concreting the main, or second section of the dam that he pushed he crews to see if they could place record amounts. In a period of 12 days, his men placed 11,500 yards of concrete.

[14]Ibid; 1913: September, 176; October, 195. Large-scale construction projects usually encountered much higher levels of construction related fatalities. Much of the success at Arrowrock can be attributed to Crowe and Munn's constant concern for safety. Men who worked on numerous jobs for Crowe recalled vividly how strongly he enforced the safety

regulations and how he would fire any man not following the guidelines.
[15]Crowe's official transfer to the Pioneer Drainage Works is recorded in the November issue of the *Reclamation Record*. John Crowe, Frank Crowe's nephew recalled his uncle revisiting the drainage site years later and describing his unhappiness with his work on the Pioneer Drainage Project. Telephone interview with John Crowe, 2 June 1998.
[16]*The Idaho Statesman*, 14 Dec. 1913; John Crowe, interview with author, 1 Apr. 1995.
[17]*Reclamation Record*, 1914: June, 237; July-August, 285; see also Department of the Interior, Bureau of Reclamation, *A History of the Minidoka Project, Idaho, 1913-1916, The Jackson Lake Enlargement*. National Archives of the USGS, Denver, Colorado: 48.
[18]F. T. Crowe, "Draining the Pioneer Irrigation District," *Reclamation Record*, (October, 1914): 373-374.
[19]Department of the Interior, Bureau of Reclamation, *Annual Project History, No. 2, Jackson Lake Enlargement Project, Wyoming, 1914*. National Archives of the USGS, Denver, Colorado: 2, 5.
[20]Elizabeth Crowe-Parry, interview by author, Palo Alto, CA., 2 Aug. 1998.
[21]*Jackson's Hole Courier*, 24 Oct. 1914.
[22]*Reclamation Record*, 1915: June, 259. Weymouth's career had started when he graduated from the University of Maine in 1896. He began work on various projects in Massachusetts. Weymouth's early career is fascinating, as it includes several years on the Isthmian Canal Commission on surveys and estimates for a proposed oceanic canal through Nicaragua and railroad work in the Andes Mountains. Weymouth joined the Reclamation Service in July of 1902 and he was placed on the Lower Yellowstone Project, where he inspired Frank Crowe to come West. Bureau records reveal that Crowe was released from Jackson Hole on November 30, 1914, see Department of the Interior, Bureau of Reclamation, *Annual Project History, No. 2, Jackson Lake Enlargement Project, Wyoming, 1914*. National Archives of the USGS, Denver, Colorado: 44.
[23]*Jackson's Hole Courier*, 16 Sep. 1915. On numerous occasions, Crowe revealed to close friends and family members that one of the greatest appeals of dam building was inventing new tools and techniques for attacking the unique challenges of each new dam.
[24]William Balderson, "Dam building days: a narrative of 1914-1915." *Jackson Hole News*, 22 Nov. 1972, 13-14.
[25]Marion Allen, *Early Jackson Hole*, 100-101; Elizabeth Mudron, interview by author, Redding, CA., 20 July 1998.
[26]*Jackson's Hole Courier*, September 23; November 18; December 23, 1915. Before leaving Crowe informed the local population of area Jackson Lake area that he expected to complete the enlargement by September 1 of the next year.
[27]Ibid, 13 April 1916; *Reclamation Record*, 1916: May, 289; July, 385; August, 435-436; September, 481.
[28]Letters comprise part of the personnel record of Frank Crowe and are obtainable from the United States Office of Personnel Management, OPF/EMF Access Unit, P. O. Box 18673, St. Louis, Missouri 63118. Dates for letters in this citing extend from August 10 through August 25, 1916; *Reclamation Record*, October 1916, 473.
[29]Letter from Frank Crowe to the Farmers' Society of Equity, 19 Nov. 1916.
[30]*Reclamation Record*, October 1916, 473. Tabor's career with the Reclamation Service started in 1902 when the organization first began. He hired on as an assistant engineer. Crowe must have felt the pressure of replacing someone held in such high regard.
[31]Memoirs of Ernest Frederick Tabor, *Transactions* of the American Society of Civil Engi-

neers, 1916: 2218-19.

[32]*Reclamation Record*, Nov. 1916, 512. The conference ended with a short memorial speech summarizing the work of Tabor.

[33]Field memoranda dated; January 19, 23, 30 and March 12. These are all addressed to the division supervisors.

[34]Ibid; March 15 and April 28, 1917. A major part of his monthly responsibilities involved writing a project summary to appear in the Service's official journal, the *Reclamation Record*. In these monthly recaps, he needed to be as authoritative and concise as possible. A check of his listings in the journal reveal that as the years went on at Flathead, Crowe wrote less and less.

[35]Ibid. May 1917, 254.

[36]Ibid; June 15 and 22. Part of the problem for Crowe was that the messages coming from Weymouth and his Washington bosses directly ordered him to address the wartime concerns and much of it required long forms or detailed instructions.

[37]Personal memorandum from Crowe to all of his employees, March 4, 1918. These notes and memoranda are located in the Department of the Interior, United States Reclamation Service, *Annual Project History, Flathead Project, Montana, 1918*.

[38]Montana Department of Public Health & Human Services, Vital Statistics Bureau.

[39]Department of the Interior, United States Reclamation Service, *Annual Project History, Flathead Project, Montana, 1918*, "Introduction and General"

[40]Official Deferment Request and letter, Department of the Interior, United States Reclamation Service, 21 Sep. 1918. The papers and accompanying letter were sent from Weymouth's new office in Denver to Crowe at St. Ignatius, Montana. This information can be obtained by requesting his personnel file from the United States Office of Personnel Management, OPF/EMF Access Unit, P. O. Box 18673, St. Louis, Missouri 63118.

[41]*Reclamation Record*, Nov. 1917, 541.

[42]Department of the Interior, United States Reclamation Service, *Annual Project History, Flathead Project, Montana, 1918*, "Introduction and General"

[43]Official Notice of Government Leave, March 29 and April 26, 1919. These leave notices are available from the United States Office of Personnel Management, OPF/EMF Access Unit, P. O. Box 18673, St. Louis, Missouri 63118.

[44]Letter from Weymouth to Crowe dated 13 Aug. 1919. OPF/EMF.

[45]Letters dated 17 Sep. 1919; OPF/EMF.

[46]Letter from Crowe to Weymouth, 4 Oct. 1919; OPF/EMF.

[47]*The Daily Missoulian*, 3 Jan. 1920. Other committee members vented their frustration, with one man exclaiming, "We are up against a stonewall." A sense of defeat and general confusion permeated the meeting break-up, leaving everyone dissatisfied. Senator Dixon, in an attempt to find the source of the problem stated that private land companies and others had exploited the situation "which brought settlers to the land before it was ready for them, the region being opened in 1910." "The reservation never should have been opened, I believe, until the water was on the land."

[48]*The Daily Missoulian*, 4 Jan. 1920. Letters dated January 22, February 12 and June 1, 1920; OPF/EMF. On January 23, Crowe took Linnie to Bozeman, Montana where, for a week, he attended a meeting of the irrigation committee. This gave him time to be away from the day-to-day responsibilities of the Flathead Project and to ponder with Linnie the decision to resign. See *The Daily Missoulian*, 23 Jan. 1920.

[49]Ibid., 14 Jan. 1920.

[50]*Eureka Journal*, 26 Feb. 1920.

Chapter 4

[1]*Yakima Morning Herald*, 11 Jan. 1921. Congress had appropriated $750,000 for the construction of Tieton Dam, a large project for the times. It was estimated that the work could take as long as four years to build. Rimrock camp had initially been setup in 1917, but with America's entry into World War I, the camp was shut down and machinery dismantled. Tools and other equipment were stored—the Bureau even hired a caretaker to watch over the material. For a historical summary of the Yakima Project see *Yakima Water Resource Project*, pamphlet published by the United States Department of the Interior.
[2]*Yakima Morning Herald*, 13 Mar. 1921, p. 1. Weymouth had written to the newspaper in response to an inquiry made after the President had signed the appropriations bill on March 4, 1921.
[3]Ibid.
[4]The Yakima Project, one of the earliest to be funded by the Reclamation Act of 1902, was designed to irrigate an area of eastern Washington that received slight amounts of precipitation. Private irrigation companies had attempted to satisfy the demands of farmers, but additional land was needed for development and a large dam was called for. See *Yakima Water Resource Project*, pamphlet published by the United States Department of the Interior; *Yakima Morning Herald*, 13 Mar. 1921. E.F. Blaine of Seattle, representative of the Northwest Reclamation league and ex-Governor William Spry of Utah representative of the Western States Irrigation association, were credited for working hard to have "Mr. Fall come to the west."
[5]*Yakima Morning Herald*, 20 Mar. 1921. The paper included data on the current number of dams in that area as well. "There are 105 diversion dams and 10 storage dams on the Yakima River and its tributaries, as compared with 579 diversion dams and 115 storage dams in the state. The water is carried in 439 main canals having a total length of 1070 miles and a capacity for 7386-second feet of water. There are 477 laterals with a total length of 1156 miles. The 10 reservoirs have a storage capacity of 423,810-second feet.

[6]Ibid., 23 Mar. 1921; *Reclamation Record*, May 1921, 243.
[7]Ibid.
[8]Frank Crowe, "Tieton Dam, Yakima Project, Wash." *Reclamation Record*, Oct. 1921, 475.
[9]Ibid.
[10]Ibid.
[11]Frank Crowe, "Tieton Dam, Yakima Project, Wash." *Reclamation Record*, Oct. 1921, 475. Crowe described the Rimrock camp as fairly complete with a temporary power plant having a capacity of 270 kilowatts.
[12]Ibid., 24 Mar. 1921.
[13]Ibid., 25 Mar. 1921.
[14]Ibid.
[15]Ibid.
[16]Michael Robinson, *Water for the West: The Bureau of Reclamation, 1902-1977*, (Chicago: Public Works Historical Society, 1979), 43. *Yakima Morning Herald*, 26 Mar. 1921.
[17]*Reclamation Project Data*, United States Department of the Interior,(Washington DC: US Government Printing Office, 1961), 824; *Yakima Morning Herald*, 31 Mar. 1921.

[18] *Yakima Morning Herald*, 4 Mar. 1921; Frank Crowe, "Tieton Dam, Yakima Project, Wash." *Reclamation Record*, Oct. 1921, 475. Crowe explained that 1,400 feet of the diversion tunnel had already been dug from the proposed 2,200-foot tunnel when in the spring of 1918, "owing to shortage of labor and the extreme war conditions which faced the country, the work was closed down."

[19] Ibid.

[20] Paul Kleinsorge, *The Boulder Canyon Project*, (Stanford University Press, 1941), 58-59. Kleinsorge describes how a committee of commissioners from the seven Western states containing portions of the Colorado River came together during this time. *Yakima Morning Herald*, 9 Apr. 1921. The article stated that the projected extent of government participation on the "big dam" was not known. Local and state irrigation lobbyists were expected to go before Congress in the coming year to explore the extent of Reclamation Service involvement.

[21] *Yakima Morning Herald*, 20 Apr. 1921.

[22] Ibid.

[23] Ibid., 27 Apr. 1921.

[24] Ibid., 1 May 1921.

[25] Ibid.

[26] Ibid.

[27] Ibid.

[28] Ibid.

[29] *Reclamation Project Data*, United States Department of the Interior, (Washington DC: US Government Printing Office, 1961), 824. *Yakima Morning Herald*, 1 May 1921.

[30] Frank Crowe, "Tieton Dam, Yakima Project, Wash." *Reclamation Record*, Oct. 1921, 476. Crowe expected the core wall to be five feet thick below the riverbed and contain no reinforcing. Above the ground the core wall would taper, gently, to a one-foot thickness and be heavily reinforced.

[31] *Yakima Morning Herald*, 1 May 1921.

[32] According to Swing's plan, the federal government's financial commitment would be to pay for improvements to public and Indian lands on a pro-rata basis. Swing believed all of Davis's figures and projections that the mighty dam would impound a volume of water practically equal to two years' normal flow of the Colorado River. It was promised that "canals would divert it [the water] where needed." Swing explained how the disastrous flooding would be stopped and that a "maximum of 1,000,000 horse power hydro-electric energy which could be radiated throughout a 500-mile circle, reaching as far as San Diego in the south and Salt Lake [City] in the north" could be achieved. It was claimed that oil supplies would be saved and that the entire Southwest would be transformed, making industrial development possible.

[33] Soots wanted to press the point that if the federal government was not forth coming with canal funds that he would seek aid from the state reclamation service and his own Yakima irrigation sources. Soots wanted the exact water plan explained and Crownover revealed that the capacity of Tieton Dam storages would be near 202,000 acre feet and that this amount would supply about 100,000 acres with agricultural water. With a supply of 31,000 acres awarded to the Tieton area and 35,000 acres to the Yakima Irrigation District. Crownover explained that the surplus water would flow into the Tieton River, down the Naches and Yakima Rivers and into the Kennewick Irrigation District. This would help farmers in that area when the Yakima River ran low.

[34] *Yakima Morning Herald*, 21 May 1921.
[35] Ibid., 11 June 1921.
[36] Ibid., 16 June 1921.
[37] Ibid., 24 June 1921.
[38] "Memoir of David Christian Henny," *Transactions*, American Society of Civil Engineers, Vol. 101, 1936, 1577-1580.
[39] Ibid., 7 July 1921.
[40] Kenneth Jackson, *The Ku Klux Klan in the City, 1915-1930*. (New York: Oxford University Press, 1967), 193-195; *Yakima Morning Herald*, 17 July 1921.
[41] *Yakima Morning Herald*, 23 Aug. 1921.
[42] Ibid., 18 Sept. 1921. Crowe was impressed to see the extent of tunnel building that also went into this project. One tunnel punctured the divide between the Naches and Wenas Valleys and ran just under one mile in length—a Frank Crowe sized job. The other tunnel ran through East Selah and the Moxee. This tunnel was also about a mile in length.
[43] Ibid., 23 Sept. 1921; Frank Crowe, "Tieton Dam, Yakima Project, Wash." *Reclamation Record*, Oct. 1921, 476. Crowe, in his article, describes how he planned to hole out the 21-foot diameter diversion tunnel using a Class 45 Bucyrus shovel "remodeled with a short boom and A-frame and equipped with 1-yd bucket."
[44] Interviews with the Crowe's daughters Patricia and Elizabeth confirmed the point that Frank Crowe, had for a long time harbored the desire to raise prized cattle. *Yakima Morning Herald*, 25 Sep. 1921.
[45] Ibid., 27 Sept. 1921.
[46] Ibid., 29 Sept. 1921.
[47] Ibid., 7 Jan. 1922.

Chapter 5

[1] Expected repayments for 1921 had been half of the amount anticipated and an angry Congress was reluctant to authorize more spending. Michael Robinson, *Water for the West: The Bureau of Reclamation, 1902-1977*, (Chicago: Public Works Historical Society, 1979), 43. *Yakima Morning Herald*, 22 Feb. 1922.
[2] Ibid., 27 Apr. 1922.
[3] Ibid., 19 Mar. 1922.
[4] Ibid., 6 Apr. 1922.
[5] Frank Crowe, "Tieton Dam, Yakima Project, Wash.," *Reclamation Record*, Oct. 1921, 477.
[6] Ibid., April 1922, 89.
[7] Patricia Crowe-Lee interview, 10 Sept. 1996.
[8] *Yakima Morning Herald*, 27 Apr. 1922.
[9] This issue of retaining the Denver office was just one additional concern ominously threatening to disrupt the Reclamation Service. See Michael Robinson, *Water for the West: The Bureau of Reclamation, 1902-1977*, (Chicago: Public Works Historical Society, 1979), 42-48 for a more detailed treatment. *Yakima Morning Herald*, 27 Apr. 1922.
[10] *Yakima Morning Herald*, 5 May 1922.
[11] Ibid., 18 May 1922. Crownover liked the area so well that he asked Reclamation Service chiefs to keep him in the area. He served as assistant engineer under E. H. Baldwin at Lake Keechelus project, not far from Yakima. In fact, when Baldwin was reassigned Crownover

assumed primary responsibility for completing the job even though the Service assigned C. H. Swigart as the new superintendent of construction. This may have been a sore point with him, as he could naturally expect to be name superintendent of the Tieton Dam construction. Learning that he would once again be only an assistant, this time to Frank Crowe—an engineer known to demand loyalty from his workers, no doubt struck a sour note with Crownover from the beginning.

¹²Ibid., 2 Jun. 1922.

¹³Ibid., 16 Jun. 1922.

¹⁴Marion Allen, interview. Longtime dam worker and Crowe associate Marion Allen was not at Tieton Dam but he had known Crowe at the Jackson Lake Dam project and on the big jobs at Hoover, Parker, and Shasta Dams. Allen stated that this behavior was not unusual for the construction business at that time.

¹⁵*Yakima Morning Herald*, 5 July 1922.

¹⁶Ibid., 26 July 1922. County Auditor Edmund Riley, representing the interests of the dam workers tried to persuade Livesey that if a change was made to allow the workers to register and vote in Naches, you could expect a much greater turnout. Driving to Cowiche involved another 12 miles off the main road and away from Yakima.

¹⁷Ibid., 30 July 1922.

¹⁸Ibid., 16 Aug. 1922.

¹⁹Ibid., 18 Aug. 1922.

²⁰Davis knew that Congress was in no mood to commit additional funds to the project until Tieton Dam was completed. See Michael Robinson, *Water for the West: The Bureau of Reclamation, 1902-1977*, (Chicago: Public Works Historical Society, 1979), 42-48 and William Warne, The Bureau of Reclamation, (New York: Praeger Publishers, 1973) for more details on the relationship between Congress and the Reclamation Service at this time. *Yakima Morning Herald*, 18 Aug. 1922.

²¹*Yakima Morning Herald*, 24 Aug. 1922.

²²Ibid., 11 Oct. 1922. One of Rementeria old Spanish shipmates, Simon Jayo, also worked on Tieton Dam. On the job he was easy to spot, wearing a worn fedora, popular with Andalusian peoples.

²³Crowe remained close to Rementeria after the Tieton job finished. Rementeria later served as a pallbearer at Crowe's funeral.

²⁴Ibid.

²⁵Once again, Crowe's hurry-up schedule reflected his desire to finish the work before Congress cut back funding and to afford him another opportunity to look around for starting another dam. He always told friends and relatives that starting a dam was "twice as good as finishing one." Pat Crowe, Interview, 31 Jan. 1997. *Yakima Morning Herald*, 1 Nov. 1922.

²⁶*Yakima Morning Herald*, 14 Feb. 1923.

²⁷Ibid., 6 Mar. 1923.

²⁸Ibid., 13 Mar. 1923.

²⁹Ibid., 29 Apr. 1923.

³⁰Michael Robinson, *Water for the West: The Bureau of Reclamation, 1902-1977*, (Chicago: Public Works Historical Society, 1979), 43. *Yakima Morning Herald*, 10 June 1923.

³¹*Yakima Morning Herald*, 19 June 1923. Arthur P. Davis, who had been with the Reclamation Service since its inception in June of 1902, believed that the development of the West depended on irrigation. And, he hardly remained totally retired from the service. He could see that new men and new engineering techniques, such as Frank Crowe and his

cableway system, would be needed to construct the huge dams already on the drawing boards in Denver. It would be Davis who would give testimony and support for the building of Boulder Dam, based partly, at least, on the knowledge that the technology and enthusiasm for constructing the huge monoliths was now being tested on smaller dams such as Tieton.
[32]Ibid., 26 June 1923. Charlie Williams would go on to become one of Crowe's top assistants achieving fame as the superintendent in charge of carpentry work at Boulder Dam. In reporting the tragic event the Yakima Morning Herald summarized, "The death is the third to have occurred on the government job at Rimrock since 1921, but this number is considered low for construction work of that type."
[33]Michael Robinson, *Water for the West: The Bureau of Reclamation, 1902-1977*, (Chicago: Public Works Historical Society, 1979), 44; *Yakima Morning Herald*, 29 June 1923. Secretary of the Interior Work was on his way to Alaska on an inspection trip, so lawyers for the engineers presented their written statements to Acting Secretary Finney. Finney could do little but reiterate what Work had said earlier on the subject of changes in the Reclamation Service that focused on putting "an experienced business man in charge."
[34]Robinson in his book *Water for the West* flatly states that A. P. Davis was dismissed due to the fact the 1920s was a time when business was "revered" and that Work, in concert with this belief would bring "bureau chiefs into departments from the business world," and that this practice "is the safeguard of civil service efficiency." See page 44 for a further discussion. *Yakima Morning Herald*, 30 June 1923. A detailed rationale and procedure for the reorganization can be found in the November-December issue of the *Reclamation Record* for 1923. The reorganization was scheduled to take effect on December 1, 1923.
[35]*Yakima Morning Herald*, 6 July 1923. The editorial appeared in the Engineering New-Record, an engineering publication sent to all members. The scathing response was picked up and used by many newspapers, including the *Yakima Morning Herald*.
[36]Ibid.
[37]Ibid., 16 Aug. 1923.
[38]Ibid., 11 Sept. 1923.
[39]Ibid., 5 Oct. 1923. Shirakihara enjoyed talking with local reporters throughout his stay in the Yakima area. He revealed that he had been educated at the University of Tokyo and that his government was very interested in learning the latest engineering techniques for industrialization. He freely admitted that he was also a commissioned officer in the Japanese navy, which had this been in California, might have raised a few suspecting eyebrows. Already Californians, mostly white farmers and their local political representatives, accused the Japanese of sending over spies and informants as part of some evil master plan to subvert the economy and political balance in California.
[40]*Reclamation Record*, Nov.-Dec. 1923, 311-313. Named to the advisory board were: James R. Garfield, former Sec. of the Interior to T. Roosevelt; Thomas E. Campbell, former Governor of Arizona and chairman of the Colorado River Basin Project, 1921; Elwood Mead, noted irrigation engineer and future Bureau Commissioner; Oscar E. Bradfute, president of the American Farm Bureau; Julius H. Barnes, president of United States Chamber of Commerce; Dr. John A. Widtoe, former president of Agricultural College of Utah; and Clyde C. Dawson, irrigation lawyer.
[41]*Yakima Morning Herald*, 15 Dec. 1923.
[42]Ibid., 12 Mar. 1924. Crowe was continually interviewed in these early months of 1924 as to the predicted completion date of Tieton Dam. Local water users were, of course, most

anxious to realize the irrigation benefits and Yakima townspeople wanted additional water as well. He estimated on several occasions that the earthwork and concreting would be finished in August, while the spillway and accompanying machinery would be completed shortly thereafter.
[43]For more information on the importance of grouting see the several articles in *The Story of the Hoover Dam*, (Las Vegas: Nevada Publications), these are reprinted technical articles from *Compressed Air Magazine*, 1931-1935. *Yakima Morning Herald*, 22 Mar. 1924.

Chapter 6

[1]Wolf, *Big Dams*, 14. The eastern states remained under the jurisdiction of the U. S. Army Corps of Engineers.
[2]*Memoirs of Frank T. Crowe*, American Society of Civil Engineers, Memoir Number 1818.
[3]Telephone Interview, Patricia Crowe-Lee. Elizabeth, nicknamed Bettee, was born on 5 Jan. 1925 in Denver, Colorado.
[4]United States Bureau of Reclamation (USBR), *Annual Project History, North Platte Project, 1924-25*. Vol. 18. p. 2.
[5]Records of the United States Bureau of Reclamation, *Engineering & Research Center Project Reports, 1910-1955*, Box Number 661.
[6]Letter to A.J. Wiley, 29 Jan. 1925, (USBR). While he tried to keep his correspondence short, he was forced to provide long detailed accounts on numerous occasions. On January 25, he sent a multi-page explanation to Fort Laramie Division superintendent "commending and congratulating" him and his associates on the "showing made and the comprehensive yet concise manner in which the report is made."
[7]Wolf, *Big Dams*, 15. Wolf states that Secretary Work believed that private construction companies would be more efficient at building irrigation related projects and that Western-based companies had been lobbying, for some time, to be allowed to bid Reclamation jobs. Brit Storey, Senior Historian for the Bureau of Reclamation contends that the Reclamation Service tried to contract out jobs early in its existence but, bids often proved too high. This statement was made in a correspondence to the author on April 5, 2000.
[8]Letter from Superintendent of the North Platte Project in Mitchell, Nebraska, 10 Mar. 1925, (USBR).
[9]Western Union telegram from Frank Crowe to Reclamation Office in Washington, 20 Mar. 1925, (USBR).
[10]Western Union telegram from Dent to Crowe, 21 Mar. 1925, (USBR).
[11]Letter from Ray Walter to Commissioner Meade, 26 Mar. 1925, (USBR).
[12]Letter from W.H. Wattis to Ray Walter in Denver, 7 Apr. 1925, (USBR).
[13]More information on the Weymouth resignation and the appointment of Walter can be found in *New Reclamation Era*, Nov. 1924.
[14]*Memoirs of Frank T. Crowe*, Memoir Number 1818, 1946. Like Crowe, Weymouth would now go into private contracting business. He linked up with friend to form Brock & Weymouth in Philadelphia. After a brief period he joined the J. C. White Engineering Corporation in Mexico as their chief engineer. He worked closely with the National Irrigation Commission of Mexico building Calles Dam and a variety of smaller dams and canals. In 1929 Weymouth came back to the U. S. and was immediately engaged by the City of Los Angeles to study plans for the Colorado River Aqueduct. Later he was appointed as chief engineer of the Metropolitan Water District of Southern California, which now assumed

responsibility of overseeing the aqueduct project. He was in constant touch with Crowe, particularly after the latter's appointment as Superintendent of Construction at Boulder Dam, where they planned together to bring the Colorado's water to the Los Angeles area. Construction on the important aqueduct start in 1932, the same year Crowe was going full swing on Boulder Dam. The aqueduct was completed in June of 1941, just one month before Weymouth's death. *Memoirs of Frank Elwin Weymouth*, ASCE pp. 1712-1716.
[15]Wolf, *Big Dams*, 29-30.
[16]*Guernsey Gazette*, 15 May 1925.
[17]*Guernsey Gazette*, 22 May 1925. Detailed information on the bidding for Guernsey Dam can be found in *New Reclamation Era*, June 1925, 95.
[18]*Guernsey Gazette*, 5 June 1925. Charlie Williams was so well respected that when it came to carpentry, he was the last word. Crowe soon learned firsthand that when Williams said he would finish a building, he kept his word. It was a construction tradition, at least according to those who knew Williams that the carpentry crews first build homes and dormitories for themselves before starting other structures; and Guernsey was no exception. Charlie Williams completed a small comfortable house for his family before Crowe's quarters were completed.
[19]Ibid.
[20]*Guernsey Gazette*, 12 June 1925.
[21]Ibid.
[22]"Profile on Guernsey, Wyoming." Platte County Chamber of Commerce. Information is available on Guernsey and Lake Guernsey State Park.
[23]*Guernsey Gazette*, 26 June 1925.
[24]Ibid.
[25]*Guernsey Gazette*, 3 July 1925. It is assumed that Crowe received permission from Utah Construction officials, such as Wattis, to allow a private money making enterprise in the company town. As the Bureau of Reclamation was undergoing significant policy changes at the time, their policy for such undertakings was also not clear.
[26]*Guernsey Gazette*, 10 July 1925. No mention is made that a hospital or clinic had yet been completed at the time of the accident. It was however, common practice to have some medical facilities in place at the time that construction begins. While the town of Guernsey was close, two miles, it is not known whether a fully equipped medical facility was available there.
[27]*Guernsey Gazette*, 24 July 1925.
[28]Ibid. Sherman went on to name some of the committee members and key personnel in the Bureau of Reclamation that were helping to change Reclamation policy. He named Elwood Mead, Francis M. Goodwin, Assistant Secretary of the Interior, Thomas E. Campbell, former governor of Arizona, and John A. Widtson, agriculturist, educator and author. According to Sherman, Mead already had acquired a national reputation as an engineer and reclamationist, with additional expertise in economics and sociology.
[29]Ibid.
[30]Ibid.
[31]*Guernsey Gazette*, 31 July 1925. Crowe upon wanting to know more about the young worker killed in the accident investigated and found that his name was A. S. Petch. The man had come from Nevada with little experience in mining. However, the foreman hired Petch, as he appeared to be in good physical health and was quite strong. The record shows that he was well liked by his fellow miners. They guessed his age at 23. No one knew

where his next of kin were, but Crowe thought they might still be in England. Crowe released the body to J. McCallum, county coroner, who had the responsibility of notifying next of kin.

[32]Ibid.

[33]Ibid.

[34]United States Bureau of Reclamation (USBR), *Annual Project History, North Platte Project, 1926-27*. Vol. 18. pp. 1-2 of Chapter 2.

[35]U.S. Department of the Interior, Bureau of Reclamation, *Reclamation Project Data*. Washington: Government Printing Office, 1961. pp. 548-549; *Annual Project History, North Platte Project, 1924-25*.

[36]*Guernsey Gazette*, 7 Aug. 1925.

[37]*Guernsey Gazette*, 28 Aug. 1925.

[38]*Guernsey Gazette*, October 9, 1925; *New Reclamation Era*, Oct. 1925, 145.

[39]U.S. Department of the Interior, Bureau of Reclamation, *Reclamation Project Data*. Washington: Government Printing Office, 1961. pp. 555; *Guernsey Gazette*, 2 Oct. 1925. For an excellent explanation of the types of dam spillways and their construction see "Spillways" C. J. Hoffman, Chapter 8 of *Design of Small Dams* U.S. Bureau of Reclamation, Government Printing Office, Washington D. C., 1960.

[40]*Guernsey Gazette*, 6 Nov. 1925. Crowe estimated that the tunnel "came together 720 feet from the west portal and 361 feet from the east portal." A small 5 foot x 5 foot 123 foot long "pioneer" tunnel cross across the west end of the diversion tunnel providing ventilation for the main shaft.

[41]Ibid. The Burlington railroad entourage included: Hale Holden, President; E. P. Bracken, Vice President; A. W. Newton, Chief Engineer; F. G. Flynn, General Superintendent; F. F. Darrow, Assistant Chief Engineer and others.

[42]*Guernsey Gazette*, 4 Dec. 1925.

[43]*Guernsey Gazette*, 11 Dec. 1925.

[44]*Guernsey Gazette*, 25 Dec. 1925.

[45]*Guernsey Gazette*, 8 Jan. 1926. Local residents reminded Crowe that while February flow rates had remained low, the North Platte River was highly unpredictable. They pointed to the June 1917 debacle, where a flow rate of 21,000 feet per second followed a period of regular low flow. This avalanche of water washed out bridges and roads, and the town's water supply was hopelessly polluted.

[46]*Guernsey Gazette*, 22 Feb. 1926.

[47]*Guernsey Gazette*, 5 Feb. 1926.

[48]*Guernsey Gazette*, 12 Feb. 1926.

[49]*Guernsey Gazette*, 26 Feb. 1926.

[50]John Crowe and Patricia Crowe-Lee recalled Frank Crowe's long-standing friendship with Si Bous. Patricia Crowe-Lee, 10 Sep. 1996, San Clemente, CA; John Crowe, February 7, 1997, Whitmore, CA.

[51]*Guernsey Gazette*, 19 Mar. 1926.

[52]*Guernsey Gazette*, 26 Mar. 1926. The Guernsey Gazette made note that local residents who had been hired recently were handling the new trestle train operation. One was driving a train, another working one of the large steam shovels, and several others assisting in fill operations.

[53]U.S. Department of the Interior, Bureau of Reclamation, *Reclamation Project Data*. Washington: Government Printing Office, 1961. pp. 555; *Guernsey Gazette*, June 4, 1926. Word

would spread as to when Crowe expected to use blasting charges and crowds swelled on these days. While non-workers were kept well back from the blasting areas, they still had excellent viewing vantage points to observe the detonations. In the middle of May shocked visitors witnessed a blasting accident, in which a worker, John Lawler, was seriously injured when a flying rock from a distant blast struck his eye. Foremen notified Crowe immediately who then called for the ambulance. Events such as this plagued Crowe throughout his career, as crowds, in subsequent retellings of the events would exaggerate the injuries and conjecture haphazardly as to the causes. In this case, Lawler's injuries proved slight. He spent a few weeks at home before resuming work.

[54]Interview with John Crowe, 7 Feb. 1997, Whitmore, CA; *Guernsey Gazette*, June 25, 1926. Not more than a week after bringing home the new car, Linnie fell sick. Although no account was made as to what the problem was, it was noted that she remained "sick" for a week. *Guernsey Gazette*, 2 July 1926.

[55]*Guernsey Gazette*, 23 July 1926.

[56]Author interviews with numerous ex-dam workers brought out the point that Crowe was a master at planning job sequences so that men could move from one job to another. This encouraged the workers to hone a variety of skills; Telephone interview with John Crowe, 1 Feb. 1998; *Guernsey Gazette*, 23 Aug. 1926.

[57]U.S. Department of the Interior, Bureau of Reclamation, *Reclamation Project Data*. Washington: Government Printing Office, 1961. pp. 555.

[58]*Guernsey Gazette*, 26 Sep. 1926.

[59]*Guernsey Gazette*, 6 Nov. 1926.

[60]*Guernsey Gazette*, 12 Nov. 1926.

[61]John Crowe and other ex-dam workers remembered that Crowe was fascinated with cableways and their uses in dam construction. Later John Crowe would help Frank Crowe design the cableway system for Shasta Dam. Interview with John Crowe, 7 Feb. 1997, Whitmore, CA; *Guernsey Gazette*, 26 Nov. 1926.

[62]*Guernsey Gazette*, 26 Dec. 1926. Upon hearing the news of the fire, Bureau engineer Smith rushed to the scene in a vain effort to help. Within 30 minutes his car, which had just filled with water, was frozen solid, bursting the head and block of the engine and the radiator.

[63]U.S. Department of the Interior, Bureau of Reclamation, *Reclamation Project Data*. Washington: Government Printing Office, 1961. pp. 555; *Guernsey Gazette*, 4 Mar. 1927.

[64]*Guernsey Gazette*, 25 Mar. 1927. It was noted recorded as to the nature of the illness, only that she had been taken to the hospital. By the end of March, she was reported to be home and recuperating "nicely from her recent illness."

[65]*Guernsey Gazette*, 29 Apr. 1927.

[66]Ex-dam workers such as Marion Allen stated that once you had become part of Crowe's "construction stiff" army you could always count on another job. These workers would continually stay in touch with Frank Crowe to learn when the next project started. Interview with Marion Allen, 28 May 1993, Redding, CA; *Guernsey Gazette*, 8 July 1927.

[67]*Guernsey Gazette*, 15 July 1927.

[68]*Guernsey Gazette*, 5 Aug. 1927. The newspaper continued to praise the dam for boosting the population from 743 before the dam construction to over 1,000 after the completion of all work and the departure of all the dam workers.

Chapter 7

[1] *The Placer Herald,* 2 Apr. 1927.

[2] Refers to *The Placer Herald* on the "Bear River Dam" in the 23 July 1927 issue.

[3] Elizabeth Crowe-Parry, Interview, 15 July 1996.

[4] *Auburn Journal,* 29 Sep. 1927

[5] Ibid.

[6] *Western Construction News,* August, 1928, p. 394.

[7] *Auburn Journal,* 13 Oct. 1927. Crowe was under pressure to finish the dam by May, as the Nevada Irrigation District had promised the people of Placer County that the new dam and its impounded water would allow for the inexpensive sale of irrigation water. Estimates revealed that fruit farmers would only be paying "$18 an inch water for the fruit season next year."

[8] *Auburn Journal,* 20 Oct. 1927. According to many dam workers interviewed in preparation of this work, it became clear that standard operating procedure in locating to a new dam job site was to stay in the closest established town until carpenters finished construction camp housing.

[9] *Western Construction News,* April, 1928, 394. Usually in cases where gravel is hard-packed in rushing river streambeds, some form of sheet pilings must be used to prevent leakage. However, since the gravel in the Bear River graded to fine sand no additional precautions were needed. Crowe did employ a 6-inch centrifugal pump to suck out water seepage.

[10] Ibid., p. 395.

[11] Ibid., p. 395.

[12] Ibid., p. 397.

[13] Ibid.,p. 396. M. L. Dickinson, assistant engineer, under the supervision of E. E. Blackie, drew the final drawings and plans for Van Giesen Dam.

[14] *Cascade News,* 16 Mar. 1928. Late in April as Crowe was finishing Van Giesen Dam news came from Idaho that another dam, Crane Creek Dam, located in the Weiser River Valley, had ruptured. Hundreds of families below the dam were evacuated while a determined work crew of sixty men labored day and night to repair the gravel and rock filled dam. It was discovered later that the hole was caused by water seeping into the rock around the dam then leaking into the earth fill behind the concrete core.

[15] *Auburn Journal,* 17 May 1928. The St. Francis Dam, located on the Santa Clara River some 40 miles north of Los Angeles, collapsed on March 13 due to structural failure. News of the catastrophe had been the talk of the camp for weeks and anxious residents living downstream from Van Giesen besieged Crowe with questions and concerns about the safety of their dam.

[16] Telephone interview, John Crowe, 17 Oct. 1996.

[17] *USBR Project History, 1929,* Vol. 7, p.42.

[18] *Cascade News,* 15 Feb. 1929. 81. Even though this dam would stand only 160 feet high, it would still be considered a large construction project. The Bureau estimated $1.2 million for construction plus materials. Engineers calculated that Deadwood Dam would hold 160,000 acre-feet of water.

[19] *Cascade News,* 3 May 1929.

[20] *Cascade News,* 7 June 1929. Meade had consulted with members of the Idaho congressional delegation before agreeing on the settlement.

[21] *Cascade News,* 14 June 1929.

[22]*Cascade News*, 12 July 1929. Crowe, in compiling the bid discovered that Idaho's first Portland cement plant, which had just opened, would provide a close reliable source of this important concrete ingredient. Officials at the plant reported an inexhaustible supply of "raw materials, which are uniform in character, and cover an area of over 200 acres." The new plant, situated adjacent to the Union Pacific railroad line, was expected to deliver a daily output of 1500 barrels of cement.

[23]*USBR Project History, 1929*, p. 45. John Crowe, interview with author, 1 Apr. 1995. John Crowe recalled a fatal accident on the newly graded road into Deadwood Dam.

[24]*USBR Project History, 1929*, pp. 45-46.

[25]Ibid.

[26]*USBR Project History, 1929*, p. 49. Subcontracting became more and more a part of the bidding process for Morrison & Knudsen, Utah Construction and other Western construction companies. In this case, Knowles Brothers agreed to haul cement in their Coleman trucks for a rate of $8.50 a ton and other freight for $9.50. Cascade Investment Company settled on a fee of $.20 per yard-mile of gravel and sand with a guaranteed quota of 500 cubic yards per day.

[27]*USBR Project History, 1929*, p. 53.

[28]*Cascade News*, 13 July 1929.

[29]*USBR Project History, 1929*, p. 54.

[30]Patricia Crowe-Lee, interview with author, 10 Sept. 1996.

[31]Cascade News, July 12, 1929. More information on the bidding for Deadwood Dam can be found in the *New Reclamation Era,* Sept. 1929.

[32]Letter from Frank Crowe to his sister Catherine, December 26, 1929. The letter was donated by John Holstein, Catherine's grandson. While Crowe was at Deadwood after the first summer, Linnie and children lived in a comfortable house in Boise. Interview with Patricia Crowe-Lee, 10 Sept. 1996. Also John Crowe, interview with author, 1 Apr. 1995.

[33]John Crowe, Telephone interview, 30 Jan. 1998.

[34]*Cascade News*, 21 March 1930. This is not the first time Crowe used bobsleds to move equipment and workers. Ever since his first engineering experience on the Lower Yellowstone project, he had noted their efficiency and employed them in winter months.

[35]Cascade News, 18 Apr. 1930. The plane, an Eaglerock make, carried a pilot and two passengers.

[36]Cascade News, 6 June 1930.

[37]*Cascade News*, 27 June 1930.

[38]*Bureau of Reclamation: Project History, 1930* pp. 8-9. The Russian entourage included Gorge G. Laprometov, Alexander A. Gimsky, Akop W. Akopian, and Tatiana A. Kolpakova.

[39]*Cascade News*, 24 Oct. 1930.

[40]*USBR Project History, 1930*. The government report did not disclose how it planned to supply Keyes and his family during the long bitter cold winter ahead. Although not noted, it was assumed that Keyes was a Bureau engineer, not a Morrison & Knudsen or Utah Construction employee, as construction of the dam was completed and the contract satisfied.

[41]*Cascade News*, 28 Nov. 1930.

Chapter 8

[1]R. G. Skerrett, "America's Wonder River—The Colorado: How nature formed this amaz-

ing watercourse and how man had to face many hazards in it and in completing its exploration," *Compressed Air Magazine*, 36 Nov. 1931, 3628-33. For an excellent background to the Imperial Valley flooding from an engineer's point of view, see A. P. Davis, "Development of the Colorado River: The Justification of Hoover Dam," *Atlantic Monthly*, Feb. 1929, 254-263. The latter article by Davis was based on his previous studies accumulated over years as director of the Reclamation Service.

[2]Davis, *Atlantic Monthly*, 255-56. Davis goes on to defend his plan to build a high concrete dam versus several small dams, which some were advocating. One of his more potent arguments pointed to the fact that high dams produce hydroelectric power in greater quantities and for less money.

[3]Stevens, *Hoover Dam,* 18; see also R. G. Skerret "America's Wonder River—The Colorado" in *The Story of the Hoover Dam*. (Las Vegas: Nevada Publications), 19.

[4]Ibid., 25.

[5]Interview of Marion Allen by Dennis McBride, Video Collection, Boulder City Library. Transcript at the University of Nevada, Las Vegas Special Collections.

[6]C. H. Vivian, "Construction of the Hoover Dam: Some General Facts Regarding the Undertaking and the men who are directing it." *The Story of the Hoover Dam*, 29.

[7]"The Earth Movers I," *Fortune*, 28 August 1943, 103.

[8]"Damn Big Dam," *Time*, 23 March 1931, 14.

[9]"The Earth Movers I," 102.

[10]Ibid., 102-103.

[11]W. H. Wattis not only believed Crowe's promises of profit making, but he also based his decision on his previously successful Hetch Hetchy Dam Project experience. This public works structure impounding San Francisco's water was a seven million dollar job; Ibid., 103.

[12]Ibid., 104.

[13]Ibid.

[14]Ibid.

[15]Ibid., 105.

[16]Ibid., 106.

[17]"Henry J. Kaiser", *Fortune*, 28 October 1943, 47-48.

[18]Kaiser became interested in designing health care programs for the dam projects. "He has already tried and tested what he thinks could be a nationwide plan for medical care. The idea, which is ecstatically presented in a little book *Kaiser Wakes the Doctors* by Paul de Druiff, is simply one of putting medical care, like hospitalization, on an insurance basis. Back in 1936, when the Six Companies was building Parker Dam, the chief medical officer, Dr. Sidney Garfield, had tried the plan and made it work handsomely. At Grand Coulee and other projects, Kaiser set up a prepaid health plan costing 50 cents a week per man. He amortized the investment out of income." See Ibid., 261.

[19]*Project History, Hoover Dam, 1930-31*, U.S. Department of the Interior, Bureau of Reclamation, 67.

[20]"The Earth Movers I," 106.

[21]Ibid., 107.

[22]Ibid.

[23]Joseph Stevens, *Hoover Dam*, 45.

[24]Ibid., 46.

[25]Marion Allen, *Hoover Dam & Boulder City*, 40-42.

[26]"Earth Movers I," 107.

[27]"Damn Big Dam," *Time*, 14. In this same article Frank Crowe is mentioned as the "hard-rock engineer" who is in charge of construction . The article goes on to mention a list of preliminary tasks, such as completing rail and road transportation routes and constructing Boulder City. The article also notes that a new experimental concrete cooling process will be tried utilizing "a special ammonia refrigerator plant."

[28]Patricia Crowe-Lee, interview by author, 14 Dec. 1996.

[29]*Los Angeles Examiner*, 9 March 1931.

[30]*Project History, Hoover Dam 1930-31*, 66.

[31]Dennis McBride, *In the Beginning: A History of Boulder City, Nevada*, 14.

[32]Ibid., The three Spanish explorers were Francisco Coronado, Friar Francisco Escalante, and Don Garcia de Cardenas.

[33]McBride, *In the Beginning*, 14-15.

[34]*Western Construction News* ran a series of technical engineering articles beginning in March of 1931. Readers can find construction details such as the equipment Lewis Construction used to build the Boulder City to Canyon Spur. "Principal equipment includes three Thew-Lorain 1 1/2-yard shovels, one Northwest 1 1/2-yard dragline, five Ingersol-Rand 310-c.f.m. portable compressors, one Gardner-Denver sharpener and furnace, one Gardner-Denver stationary compressor with McCormich-Deering engine, four Kohler and one Delco 1500-watt Light plants, Le Tourneau and Ateco bulldozers, Le Tourneau scrapers and scarfifier, fifteen sterling and other trucks." S. J. Sanders "Construction Review-Hoover Dam, Nevada-Arizona," *Western Construction News*, 10 July 1931, 357.

[35]McBride, *In the Beginning*, 16.

[36]C.H. Vivian "Construction of the Hoover Dam: How the Contractors Handled the Huge and Costly Program of Preliminary Work," *The Story of Hoover Dam*, 33.

[37]Sanders, *Western Construction News*, 357.

[38]Marion Allen, interview by author, 28 May 1993; Elizabeth Mudron, interview by author, 20 Sep. 1993.

[39]Andrew J. Dunar and Dennis McBride, *Building Hoover Dam: An Oral History of the Great Depression*, (New York: MacMillian, 1993), 31.

[40]Ibid., 28-29.

[41]Ibid., 27-28.

[42]Ibid., 26-27.

[43]Interview with Elizabeth Mudron by author, Redding, Calif., 20 July 1998. Elizabeth Mudron is the daughter of Marion Allen, whose family had also come to Hoover Dam looking for work. Elizabeth obtained a job at a department store in Boulder City where she met Milton Mudron; later they married.

[44]"The Earth Movers, I" *Fortune*, 28 August 1943, 210.

[45]Ibid.

[46]Ibid.

[47]Ibid., 212.

[48]Ibid.

[49]Stevens, *Hoover Dam*, 57-58.

[50]Dunar & McBride, *Building Hoover Dam*, 43-44.

[51]Ibid., 44.

[52]Victor Castle, "Well, I Quit my Job at the Dam," *The Nation*, 133, No. 3451(1931), 207-08.

[53]Ibid., 45.
[54]Stevens, *Hoover Dam*, 60. The River Camp was finally abandoned toward the end of July with all single workers being relocated to the newly completed dormitories at Boulder City.

Chapter 9

[1]The No. 1 Tunnel length equaled 4,300 feet; No. 2 - 3879 feet; No. 3 - 3,560 feet; and No. 4 - 4,170 feet for a total of 15,909 feet. This does not count the two bisecting 10 x 8-foot adits cut prior to the main tunnel work.
[2]Huntington worked on the Big Creek Hydroelectric project in Southern California Edison Co., eventually becoming the tunnel superintendent. Fraser & Brace, Ltd., of Montreal recognized the unique talent for organizing men and machines for subterranean excavation hired him to dig a railroad tunnel in Columbia, South America. With this to his credit, construction machinery specialists, Ingersoll-Rand employed him as a special sales representative.
Philip Schuyler "Hoover Dam Constructionists" *Western Construction News*, pp. 637-38.
[3]Dunar & McBride, *Building Hoover Dam*, 85.
[4]Emery grew up along the Colorado River, his parents had homesteaded at Cottonwood Island. He ran a ferry across the river since age 14. With his own constructed houseboats and barges Emery earned a living transporting trappers, settlers, and sightseers. Beginning in the 1920s he escorted politicians and engineers to various proposed building sites for the dam. He recalls "He [Herbert Hoover] was no bother and easy to handle. By the same token, he was not the kind of a guy you could start up a conversation with."
Ibid. 7, 10.
[5]Norman S. Gallison, "Construction of the Hoover Dam: Details of the Driving of the Four Huge Tunnels Which will Divert the Colorado River Around the Dam Site." in *The Story of the Hoover Dam*, Las Vegas: Nevada Pub., p. 49.
[6]Dunbar & McBride, *Building Hoover Dam*, 87.
[7]John Crowe, interview with author, Whitmore, CA., 1 Apr. 1996.
[8]The rock known as "dead" breaks true if charges were set accurately. Geologists also reported that the volcanic andesite tuff beccia carried little internal water and held its shape and bearing well. Gallison, "Details of the Driving...", p. 52.
[9]John Crowe, interview with author, 1 Apr. 1996.
[10]Dunar & McBride, *Building Hoover Dam*, 32, 34.
[11]Ibid., 34.
[12]Stevens, *Hoover Dam*, 53-54.
[13]Stevens, *Hoover Dam*, 67-68.
[14]Guy Louis Rocha, "The IWW and the Boulder Canyon Project: The Final Death Throes of American Syndicalism," *Nevada Historical Society Quarterly*, 21, (Spring, 1978), 5. The issue of good food and drinkable water is a confusing one, as ex-dam workers interviewed by the author have mixed emotions about the issue. Actually, most of these men agreed that the food was very good, compared to what they had been eating, and that drinkable water was obtainable on the work site. Rocha agrees (see page 12) that the food accusation was "a questionable issue."
[15]York Peterson, "Hoover Dam" *Western Construction News*, 10 Sep. 1931, 474.
[16]Stevens, *Hoover Dam*, 70-71.

[17] *Las Vegas Evening Review-Journal,* August 8, 1931.
[18]Ibid., 72.
[19]Ibid., 73-74.
[20]Dunar & McBride, *Building Hoover Dam,* 51.
[21]Victor Castle, *The Nation,* 207-08.
[22]Frank Crowe letter dated August 22, 1931 to his mother Emma Crowe. Letter donated by John Hollstein. Hollstein is in possession of several letters that proved quite helpful in understanding Frank Crowe's family relationships.
[23]Castle, *The Nation,* 208.
[24]McBride, *In the Beginning,* 41.
[25]Dunar & McBride, *Building Hoover Dam,* 60-61.
[26]Ibid., 62.
[27]Ibid., 65-67.
[28]Ibid., 66-67.
[29]Ibid., 68. See also McBride, *In the Beginning,* 31-32.
[30]Ibid., 69.
[31]Marion Allen, *Hoover Dam,* 29-31.
[32]"Earth Movers I" *Fortune,* Vol. 28, August, 1943, 214.
[33]Patricia Crowe-Lee, interview by author, 14 Dec. 1996.

Chapter 10

[1]*Las Vegas Age,* 2 Jan. 1932.
[2]Ibid., 10 Jan. 1932. Mashburn must have been furious over Six Companies assertions that pumped air provided a healthy breathing environment in the depths of the tunnels. Having heard stories from various dam workers, he would seek to complete these into personal accounts abuses by Crowe and company. However, the key to the substantiation of workers' stories rested on resulting medical records liking respiratory ailments directly to job related tunnel experience.
[3]Norman S. Gallison, "Details of the Driving of the Four Huge Tunnels Which Will Divert the Colorado River Around the Dam Site," *Compressed Air Magazine,* 37 (May, 1932): 3804-10.
[4] Andrew Dunar and Dennis McBride. *Building Hoover Dam: An Oral History of the Great Depression,* (New York: Twayne Pub., 1993), 97-98.
[5] Ibid. 98.
[6] The smoker actually occurred on April 15, 1932, as reported in the *Las Vegas Age.* Moran's boxing concession authority had been granted before the smoker announcement, back on December 17, 1931, as reported in the *Las Vegas Age* on Dec. 18, 1931.
[7]Crowe had experienced the devastating affects of high winds before in Guernsey, Yakima, Montana and Idaho, but here in Nevada the searing blast of sand was a threat to his workers and his machinery. Kahn and Shea's harrowing landing was recorded in the *Las Vegas Age,* 15 Jan. 1932.
[8]Interview with Patricia Crowe-Lee by author, San Clemente, Calif., 14 Dec. 1996. The author was given permission to tour the home in July of 1996 and it is amazingly restored, close to its original condition. The home was indeed, comfortable, despite the outside summer heat.
[9]Andrew Dunar, and Dennis McBride. *Building Hoover Dam: An Oral History of the*

Great Depression, (New York: Twayne Pub., 1993), 91.

[10]*Las Vegas Age*, 27 Jan. 1932.

[11]Ibid.

[12]Ibid., 4 Feb. 1932. *The Las Vegas Age* ran an article reminding everyone that while much publicity had been given to the holing through of one of the main diversion tunnels, little credit was given to the fact that forty-eight tunnels, ranging from small ventilation adits to fourteen foot inspection tunnels had also been driven.

[13]Letter from Walker Young to Frank Crowe dated June 8, 1932; letter from Young to Ray Walter dated June 10, 1932, General Correspondence File: Boulder Dam, United States Department of the Interior, Bureau of Reclamation.

[14]Dunar and McBride, *Building Hoover Dam: An Oral History of the Great Depression*, 86.

[15]Ibid., 86-87.

[16]*Las Vegas Age*, 2 Feb. 1932.

[17]Elizabeth Crowe-Parry, interview with author, 2 Aug. 1998.

[18]*Las Vegas Age*, 10 Feb. 1932.

[19]Ibid., 11 Feb. 1932. Shortly after this time the Bureau delivered eleven train carloads of trees and shrubs. Five varieties of trees were planted: Arizona ash, black locust, Carolina poplar, Chinese elm, and sycamore. Wilbur told the press that the main government buildings, permanent residences, and local parks would all receive tree plantings. He urged that homeowners take special care in providing plenty of water for new plantings. As the government plantings began, Wilbur announced the winners of the local homeowner planting contest. To Wilbur and Young's delight, many Boulder City residents had entered the contest, landscaping their homes quite successfully. Competition was tough and several winners were selected.

[20]Ibid., 17 Feb. 1932.

[21]Interview with Patricia Crowe-Lee by author, San Clemente, Calif., 14 Dec. 1996; *Las Vegas Age*, 16 March 1932.

[22]John Page and Ralph Lowry would join Frank Crowe in the building of Shasta Dam in 1938. Page became Commissioner of the Bureau, while Lowry worked closely with Crowe as Bureau Construction Engineer.

[23]Interview with Patricia Crowe-Lee by author, San Clemente, Calif., 14 Dec. 1996.

[24]*Las Vegas Age*, 16 April 1932.

[25]Roosevelt Fitzgerald, "Blacks and the Boulder Dam Project," Nevada Historical Society, 24 (1981), 258. The term "Mongolians" at that time apparently was used to describe persons from East Asia, especially Japanese, Chinese and Koreans.

[26]Ibid., 259.

[27]*Las Vegas Age*, 8 July 1932.

[28]Interview with Marion Allen by author, Redding, Calif., Sept. 30, 1989. Other dam workers such as Ray Rogers, Dale Bryant, Harold Fortier and L. T. Thorton agreed with Allen's interpretation. Crowe listed a detailed summary of workers as: tunnels, 1300; miscellaneous river operations, 272; lower level mixing plant, 78; spillways, 162, mechanical department, 309; electrical department, 49; railroad inclined track, 124; gravel plant and pit, 79 [several Blacks worked here]; Boulder City construction, 144; and general office force, hospital, wholesale, etc., 116. The total for March 10, 1932 was 2,633. This does not include hundreds of subcontractor workers. *Las Vegas Age*, 10 March 1932.

[29]*Western Construction News*, 10 August 1932, 456.

[30]Ibid.

[31]Joel L. Priest, Jr., "'Paul Bunyan' of the Black Canyon", *The Union Pacific Magazine*, March 1932, 4-5.

[32]Copeland Lake, "Construction of the Hoover Dam: Compressed Air Plays a Vital Importance in This Huge Undertaking", *The Story of Hoover Dam*, (Las Vegas Nevada: Nevada Publications): 51-60. This article is one in a series produced by *Compressed Air Magazine* and later compiled in this publication.

[33]Allen S. Park, "A Description of the Methods of Obtaining and Preparing Aggregates", *Compressed Air Magazine*, 37 (Oct., 1932): 3937-42.

[34]Joseph Stevens, *Hoover Dam: An American Adventure*, (Norman, Oklahoma: University of Oklahoma Press, 1988), 44. Original source, Theodore White, "Building the Big Dam," *Harper's Magazine*, 171 (June, 1935): 113-20.

[35]Sims Ely, "Administration of Boulder City," *Annual Project History, Boulder Canyon Project, 1928-1931*, United States Department of the Interior, Bureau of Reclamation, 145.

[36]Ibid. 146.

[37]Dennis McBride, *In The Beginning: A History of Boulder City, Nevada*, (Boulder City/ Hoover Dam Museum, 1992), 57-61; Elizabeth Crowe-Parry, interview with author, 2 Aug. 1998.

[38]C. H. Vivian, "Construction of the Hoover Dam: Lining of the Diversion Tunnels with Concrete," *The Story of Hoover Dam*, (Las Vegas: Nevada Publications): 77-79.

[39]Ibid., 76, 81.

[40]Ibid., 84; Stevens, *Hoover Dam: An American Adventure*, 112.

[41]Interview with Elizabeth Crowe-Parry by author, Telephone, May 25, 1998. The telegrams, both sent by Western Union on October 12, 1932, were donated by John Holstein.

[42]*Las Vegas Evening-Journal*, Nov. 12, 1932; caption on Bureau of Reclamation Washington D. C. photo # 01439.

[43] Interview with Pat Crowe, 14, Dec. 1996.

[44]Marion Allen, *Hoover Dam & Boulder City*, (Redding, California: Self-Published, 1983): 85. See also "Construction of the Hoover Dam: A Resume of Current Activities and an Account of the Building of the Cofferdams," *The Story of Hoover Dam*, (Las Vegas: Nevada Publications): 86. An excellent exciting account of the diversion can be found in Stevens' *Hoover Dam*, pages 114-15.

Chapter 11

[1]*Engineering & Research Center Project Histoies, 1933-36*, Records of the Bureau of Reclamation, Book No. 260, United States Department of the Interior, Denver Archives.

[2]Interview with Patricia Crowe-Lee, 14 Dec. 1996.

[3]Elwood Mead, *Boulder Canyon Project—Questions and Answers*, United States Department of the Interior, Bureau of Reclamation, Washington D.C., January 3, 1933,

[4]Ray F. Walter, "U. S. Bureau of Reclamation Projects—Hoover Dam," *Western Construction News and Highway Builder*, 10 Jan. 1933: 23-24.

[5]Ickes spent much of his early career as a political leader in Chicago. He fled the Republican Party in 1912 along with other liberal thinking reformers and for a time he led the Illinois Progressive Party contingent. Flirting with the Republican Party once again in 1916, he failed to help Charles Evans Hughes get elected. Frustrated with Republican domination of the presidency and their apparent sellout to big business interests, Ickes

joined the Democratic Party and worked hard for Roosevelt in the 1932 election.

[6]Wesley R. Nelson, "Construction Progress on Hoover Dam," *Western Construction News and Highway Builder*, 10 May 1933: 219-220. Nelson was the assistant engineer for the Bureau working under Walker Young. See also *Reclamation Era*, Jan. 1933, 12.

[7]Ibid., 221; *Hoover Dam*, United States Department of the Interior, Bureau of Reclamation, (Washington, D. C.: U. S. Government Printing Office, 1985).

[8]*Las Vegas Evening -Journal*, 3 July 1933; *Boulder Canyon Annual Project History, 1933*, United States Department of the Interior, Bureau of Reclamation.

[9]Elizabeth Crowe-Parry, interview with author, 2 Aug. 1998.

[10]Letters donated by John Holstein. The series of letters range from August of 1932 to March of 1934. The letter to his mother was dated March 12, 1933.

[11]C. P. Bedford, "Hoover Dam Motor Transportation," *Western Construction New and Highway Builder,* (July, 1933), 303. More information on transportation on the Hoover Dam job can be found in Wesley Nelson, "Boulder Canyon Transportation," *Reclamation Era*, May 1935, 100.

[12]*Los Angeles Times*, 22 Oct. 1933. This ad was part of a special story written encouraging southern Californians to visit Boulder Dam.

[13]Ibid.

[14]C. P. Bedford, "Hoover Dam Motor Transportation," *Western Construction New and Highway Builder*, (July, 1933), 304-305; *Las Vegas Age*, 4 Jan. 1935.

[15]*Los Angeles Times*, 18 June 1933.

[16]Letter from Charles Crossland to J. F. Reis, December 1, 1933.

[17]*Western Construction New and Highway Builder*, (September, 1933).

[18]Lawrence Sowles, "Construction of the Boulder Dam: Description of the Methods of Pouring the Concrete," *The Story of Hoover Dam*, (Las Vegas: Nevada Publications), 112-116. This article originally appeared in *Compressed Air Magazine*, 39 (1934). Six Companies would complete much of the supporting foundation work for the cableway supporting system and the track laying. Other components of the cableway system were subcontracted as follows: The triple-tandem-drum hoist mechanism on towers, including traveling carriages with six cable track wheels—Lidgerwood Mfg. Company of Elizabeth, New Jersey; Operating ropes from 7/8 to 11/2-inch—Pacific Wire Rope Company of Los Angeles; Cable towers and fittings, including structural steel towers 60 to 120 feet high—Consolidated Steel Corporation of Los Angeles; electrical and control equipment, including 125-horsepower travel motors for moving towers and 500-horsepower hoist motors for operating winches—Westinghouse Electric & Mfg. Company of San Francisco; and pneumatic equipment in conjunction with cableways—Ingersoll-Rand Company of San Francisco. "Cableway Contracts Awarded for Hoover Dam" *Western Construction News*, 10 Aug. 1932, 456.

[19]*Boulder Canyon Annual Project History, 1933,* United States Department of the Interior, Bureau of Reclamation.

[20]"Earth Movers I," *Fortune* 28 (August, 1943): 214.

[21]*Boulder Canyon Annual Project History, 1934*, United States Department of the Interior, Bureau of Reclamation; *Las Vegas Evening Review Journal*, 20 Feb. 1934; *Las Vegas Evening Review Journal*, 6 Feb. 1934.

[22]*Las Vegas Evening Review Journal*, 26 Feb. 1934.

[23]Robert G. Skerrett, "Steel Headers and Penstocks for Hoover Dam Mark Notable Advance in Engineering Construction," *Western Construction News and Highways Builder* (March, 1934), 79. If the outlet values or turbines should be suddenly shut down a "water-

hammer" effect could occur, immediately raising the water pressure to 300 pounds per square inch.

[24]Ibid. 80-81; Robert Ridgeway, "Boulder Dam," *Harvard Alumni Bulletin*, (1934), 871.

[25]Lawrence P. Sowles, "How the Concrete is Being Cooled as It is Poured," *Compressed Air Magazine 38*, (Nov. 1933), 104-107.

[26]Ibid, 109-110.

[27]A. H. Ayers, "Frank T. Crowe, '05 Master Builder of Dams," *The Maine Alumnus 1934*, University of Maine at Orono. 93-94.

[28]"Hoover Dam Workers Pour 10,401 CU. YD. of Concrete in Three Shifts March 20," *Western Construction News*, (April, 1934), 132.

[29]*Las Vegas Evening Review Journal*, 20 April 1934; *Las Vegas Age*, 1 Jan. 1935.

[30]*Boulder Canyon Annual Project History, 1934*, United States Department of the Interior, Bureau of Reclamation.

[31]*Parker Dam Annual Project History, 1934-36 Vol.1*, United States Department of the Interior, Bureau of Reclamation; Marion Allen, *Rio Colorado & Parker Dam*, (Redding, California: self-published, 1987), 44-45. The Southwestern Construction Group, Inc., was made up of the Bent Bros., of Los Angeles; Winston Bros., of Los Angeles; L. E. Dixon Co., William C. Crowell and W. A. Johnson companies. Johnson would later help form Pacific Constructors Inc,. and win the bid for Shasta Dam; *Las Vegas Evening Review Journal*, 26 July 1934.

[32]J. P. Yates, "Bulk Cement Handling at Boulder Dam," *Western Construction News*, (August, 1934), 249-251.

[33]*Las Vegas Age*, 13 July 1933; *Las Vegas Evening Review Journal*, 25 July 1934. Warner Brothers was already preparing to shoot "The Cinch" using Las Vegas and Hoover Dam as a background.

[34]*Boulder Canyon Annual Project History, 1934*, United States Department of the Interior, Bureau of Reclamation.

[35]*Las Vegas Evening Review Journal*, 6 Aug. 1934.

[36]*Las Vegas Age*, 16 Nov. 1934.

[37]Robert Ridgeway, "Boulder Dam," *Harvard Alumni Bulletin*, (1934), 871.

[38]*Boulder Canyon Annual Project History, 1934*, United States Department of the Interior, Bureau of Reclamation.

[39]Paul Kleinsorge, *The Boulder Canyon Project: Historical and Economic Aspects*, (Stanford University Press, 1941), 214-215; *Las Vegas Age*, 1 Feb. 1935. Several articles in and around this date talk about the ability of Hoover Dam to corral the expected floodwaters coming down the Colorado River.

[40]Wesley R. Nelson, "Construction of the Boulder Dam: How the $35,000,000 Power Plant will Appear when Completely Equipped," *The Story of the Hoover Dam*, (Las Vegas: Nevada Publications), 138-143.

[41]*Las Vegas Age*, 1 Mar. 1935. See Stevens' book *Hoover Dam* pages 232-234 for a detailed account of this incident.

[42]Allen, *Hoover Dam*, 29.

[43]Patricia Crowe-Lee, interview with author, 10 Sept. 1996. Frank Crowe had been trying to teach a few lassoing tricks to his children and so he jumped at the opportunity to have Rogers demonstrate.

[44]*Maine*, June 10, 1935; e-mail note from Pam Oakes, University of Maine, 12 Feb. 1996.

[45] It was later learned that Shell Modglin, the powerhouse superintendent, sent a memo

dated the day before ordering the change in working hours.

[46]*Las Vegas Age*, 12 July 1935.

[47]Statement by Marion Allen in *Building Hoover Dam*, 272. Allen refers to a "company man out of San Francisco" named Malden as the one who ordered the change in hours.

[48]*Las Vegas Age*, 26 July 1935.

[49]"President Roosevelt Dedicates Boulder Dam, September 30, 1935," *Reclamation Era*, 25 (October, 1935): 193-94, 196; *Construction of Hoover Dam*, United States Department of the Interior, Bureau of Reclamation, (published jointly by the Bureau of Reclamation and KC Publications, 1976), 49-50. According to Elizabeth Crowe-Parry, Frank Crowe's daughter, Frank Crowe was part of the official presidential greeting committee and he drove Eleanor Roosevelt to the ceremony. However, photos of the event appear to contradict this statement.

[50]*Las Vegas Age*, 4 Oct. 1935.

[51]*New York Times*, 1 Mar. 1936. See also Michael Robinson *Water for the West*, 53-54.

[52]"Earth Movers I," *Fortune* 28 (Aug. 1943), 211, 214.

[53]Ibid., 214.

Chapter 12

[1]Marion Allen, *Rio Colorado & Parker Dam*, (Redding, California: self-published, 1987), 46. Allen also indicates that Six Companies allowed Shea to use heavy equipment from the Hoover Dam job as part of the deal for Shea to subcontract Parker Dam.

[2]Letter from Ray Walter to Elwood Mead, March 22, 1932, *General Correspondence File: Parker Dam*, United States Department of the Interior, Bureau of Reclamation.

[3]Ibid., Letter for Frank Weymouth to Ray Walter dated March 17, 1934; Letter from Ray Walter to Weymouth dated March 27, 1934; response letter from Weymouth to Walter dated March 31, 1934. In an almost too obvious slip of the language, Weymouth uses the term "Reclamation Bureau," a recollection back to his days with the Reclamation Service, instead of the formal Bureau of Reclamation.

[4]A readable and authoritative source for the background on Los Angeles's desperate quest for more water can be found in *The Story of Hoover Dam*, United States Department of the Interior, Bureau of Reclamation, (Washington D. C.: U. S. Government Printing Office, 1971), 44-47.

[5]*Las Vegas Evening Review Journal*, 14 Mar. 1934. According to the newspaper account the "army" of guardsmen had to fight off hordes of mosquitoes, but there was never any danger of violence as the dam workers kept completely away from the Arizona riverbank. Although they carried weapons, the soldiers were given strict orders not to fire on workers "under any circumstances."

[6]Draft letter from Elwood Mead to Harold Ickes, March 27, 1934, *General Correspondence File: Parker Dam*, United States Department of the Interior, Bureau of Reclamation.

[7]"Authorization sought in Congress for Parker Dam Construction", *Western Construction News*, (June, 1935), 153.

[8]*Parker Dam Project, Annual Project History, 1936*, United States Department of the Interior, Bureau of Reclamation; "Parker Dam Operations Centered on Diversion Tunnel Driving and Plant," *Western Construction News*, (January, 1936); also see the March issue of *Western Construction News*. Interestingly, A. H. Ayers, chief engineer for Six Companies, told reporters in Las Vegas back in July of 1934 that "this new project being located in what

382 America's Master Dam Builder

is described as being the hottest spot in the United States." *Las Vegas Evening Review Journal*, 26 July 1934.

[9]Patricia Crowe-Lee, interview with author, 31 Jan. 1997. Frank Crowe, had movies taken of his girls while at The La Rew School. The scenes show a matron-at-arms ringing an assembly bell early in the morning, followed by dozens of young girls dashing out of their rooms and lining up for morning exercises. After a quick breakfast, Patricia and Elizabeth go through a morning routine of painting, swimming and tennis lessons.

[10]Letter from Frank Crowe to his sister, Catherine, December 13, 1936. Donated by John Holstein.

[11]Crowe family movies taped to video by the author in 1997; Elizabeth Mudron, interview by author, 20 July 1998.

[12]Allen, *Rio Colorado & Parker Dam*, 71-73.

[13]Ibid. 74. In a later interview, October 4, 1998, John Crowe recalled that squatter "boys" could have been older than he first indicated.

[14]Ibid. Some of the workers hypothesized that the boat might have been used by Western irrigation pioneer Arthur Powell Davis on one of his survey trips down the Colorado River.

[15]The Bill Williams River flooded again on February 14 and a third time on March 17. The later deluge, "carrying many considerable stretches of the road to the gravel plant and suspending concrete operations for a period of 8 days." *Parker Dam Project, Annual Project History, 1937*, United States Department of the Interior, Bureau of Reclamation.

[16]Ibid.; Allen, *Rio Colorado & Parker Dam*, 69. Allen notes that shortly after the Trisdale incident the C.I.O. representatives drove out to their pickets on the line and pulled them.

[17]*Western Construction News*, (February, 1937)

[18]Ibid., (March, 1938), 96-97.

[19]Letter from Frank Crowe to E. A. Moritz, June 1, 1937, *General Correspondence File: Parker Dam*, United States Department of the Interior, Bureau of Reclamation.

[20]Frank Taylor, "He Puts Rivers to Work," *This Week Magazine*, 12 Jan. 1941, 12.

[21]Allen, *Rio Colorado & Parker Dam*, 79; *Western Construction News*, (March, 1938), 98.

[22]Patricia Crowe-Lee recalled her father was elated about the first concrete but, how much he hated "to go down into the hole in such heat." Interview with author, 10 Sept. 1996.

[23]Letter from E. A. Moritz to Ray Walter dated July 31, 1937, *General Correspondence File: Parker Dam*, United States Department of the Interior, Bureau of Reclamation.

[24]Ibid., Letter from Frank Crowe to E. A. Moritz dated August 26, 1937.

[25]Ibid., Letter from Frank Weymouth to Ray Walter dated May, 4, 1937. The Bureau memoranda for March 1937 displayed daily above average air and water temperatures. Early March suffered several days over 90 degrees, while water temperatures moved into the 60s.

[26]Ibid., 96.

[27]Ibid., 94. Crowe enjoyed his short visits with Allen, for once again he could relive his Jackson Lake adventures, sharing stories.

[28]Letter from Frances Sass to Marion Allen, October 28, 1986 as shown in Allen's *Rio Colorado & Parker Dam*, 98.

[29]Letter from Dave Bous to Marion Allen, November 19, 1986 as shown in Allen's *Rio Colorado & Parker Dam*, 102-03.

[30]Letter from George Bous to Marion Allen, November 12, 1986 as shown in Allen's *Rio Colorado & Parker Dam*, 101.

[31]Undated letter from Mary Crowe to Marion Allen as shown in Allen's *Rio Colorado &*

Parker Dam, 106.
[32]*The Grand Coulee Dam and the Columbia Basin Reclamation Project*, United States Department of the Interior, Bureau of Reclamation.
[33]Letter from Frank Crowe to his sister Catherine, 13 Dec. 1937. Both John and Mary Crowe recalled that Frank was not excited about the Grand Coulee job. Interview of Mary Crowe by author, 1 Apr. 1995.
[34]L. P. Sowles, "Contractor Uses Cableway for Building Small Concrete Arch Dams on Aqueduct," *Western Construction News*, (August, 1938); undated letter from Bob Sass Jr. to Marion Allen as shown in Allen's *Rio Colorado & Parker Dam*, 126.
[35]Letter from Frank Crowe to his sister Catherine, 19 Feb. 1938. Donated by John Holstein.
[36]A variety of letters can be studied using the *General Correspondence File: Parker Dam*, United States Department of the Interior, Bureau of Reclamation. Some of Crowe's correspondence is quite extensive, up to three pages type written and single spaced, including detailed engineering data. Such is the case of the June 1, 1937, where Crowe writes Moritz describing the impact of Hoover Dam's predicted releases and the temperature of the water.
[37]*Parker Dam Project, Annual Project History, 1938*, United States Department of the Interior, Bureau of Reclamation.
[38]"A Master Dam Builder," *Western Construction News*, (March, 1938).

Chapter 13

[1]Kelley, *Battling the Inland Sea*, 127.
[2]Bean, *California: An Interpretive History*, 303.
[3]Pacific Constructors Incorporated (PCI), *Shasta Dam and Its Builders* (original version), 6.
[4]*Reclamation Project Data*, 98.
[5]Wolf, *Big Dams*, 57.
[6]Allen, *Shasta Dam and Its Builders* (republished version), 30-31.
[7]Ibid., 36-37.
[8]Wolf, *Big Dams*, 58.
[9]Even though Crowe had carefully considered the Shasta cableway system, even to the extent of building, with his nephew John Crowe, a detailed model, the veteran dam builder had been told by numerous engineers in the field of heavy construction that his system could encounter serious technical problems, in terms of load stress and durability. John Crowe, interview, February 1, 1998.
[10]Allen, *Shasta Dam and Its Builders*. 38.
[11]Maguire believed that Bureau officials in Denver sided against Kaiser and his group because they had "'hogged' the big dam building business for several years...and these officials wanted to see some new faces in the picture and welcomed our competition." Allen, *Shasta Dam and Its Builders*, 40.
[12]Kaiser was hoping that the Bureau would, at least, call for new bids, thus allowing Crowe and Shasta Construction officials to recalculate and lower their bid. Such practice was not uncommon in the early days of the Bureau bidding process, but by the late 1930s, rebidding declarations were rare.
[13]John Crowe recalled Frank Crowe telling him that a phone call came through checking to see if Frank would be interested in being PCI's superintendent of construction. Interview

with author, 1 Apr. 1995.
[14]Lloyd Hill, Art Corella, and Pete Forte. Interview with author, 18 Sep. 1993.
[15]*The Searchlight*, 1 May 1938.
[16]Ted Lowry, personal interview, March 3, 1992. Ralph Lowry, known as "Tedd" to close friends, had played basketball, track, football, and baseball in college. He served both as president of the athletic association and associated student body.
[17]George Van Eaton, audio tape II-A7, Redding Museum of Art & History; Lloyd Hill, interview with author, 18 Sep. 1993.
[18]Rocca, *Shasta Dam Boomtowns:* Community Building in the New Deal Era, 85.
[19]Rocca, *America's Shasta Dam: A History of Construction, 1936-1945*, 16.
[20]Rocca, *Shasta Dam Boomtowns*, 91.
[21]Letter from Frank Crowe to his sister Catherine, October 2, 1938. Donated by John Holstein.
[22]Shasta County led the nation for a time with the most CCC camps, 11. These young men, dressed in military style uniforms throughout the area, help clear the reservoir site.
[23]*Western Construction News*, December, 1938, p. 448; *Shasta Dam and its Builders,* 1987, p. 147.
[24] The conveyor belt consisted of twenty-six flights, or sections. 200-horsepower motors powered the belt uphill; as the load shifted to the downhill slope, the motors worked as generators supplying electricity to the power line. The three foot wide belt moved at a speed of over 500 feet per minute and delivered over 1,000 tons of aggregate per hour. Once started the belt ran for over four years. *Shasta Dam and its Builders,* 1987, p. 147-48.
[25]Rocca, *America's Shasta Dam*, p. 17.
[26] Most of the actual clearing of the reservoir site was completed by John Crowe and "Red" Wixson, who beginning in July of 1940, won a series of bids for the work. The partners, driving huge powerful tractors, plowed through tough thickets of manzanita brush and ripped-out tall Digger Pine and other trees. They burned much of the timber. The mountainous terrain and unpredictable weather conditions hampered, but did not deter Crowe and Wixson.
[27]Marion Allen, interview by author, Redding, CA., 28 May 1993.
[28]C. S. Downing, *First Information Book for Shasta Dam Guides*, 1952, unpublished, p. 38.
[29]Marion Allen, interview by author, Redding, CA., 28 May 1993.
[30]Letter from Frank Crowe to his sister Catherine, 26 Jan. 1939.
[31]Lyn Parker, interview by author, Redding, CA., 28 Mar. 1990. Parker, the youngest Bureau inspector at Boulder Dam, arrived on the Shasta Dam early and was one of the first to be housed in Toyon.
[32]Ray Rogers and Harold Fortier, interviews by author, Central Valley [now Shasta Lake City], CA., 30 Sep. 1989. Both Rogers and Fortier worked on the dam and lived in the boomtowns.
[33]Marion Allen, interview by author, Redding, CA., 28 May 1993.
[34]C. S. Downing, *First Information Book for Shasta Dam Guides*, 1952, unpublished, p. 39. For months, the tunnel carried all rail north-south connections, until the railroad bypass project was completed.
[35]*Western Construction News*, April, 1939. p.150.
[36]*Shasta Dam Archive Photographs & Captions, 1939*, Shasta Dam, CA., This photograph and caption is part of the extensive archival collection taken by official Bureau of Reclamation photographers.

[37]Ibid.
[38]Ibid.
[39]L. T. Thorton, interview by author, Redding, CA., 30 Sep. 1989. Thorton was a dam worker and resident of the boomtowns.
[40]Ray Rogers, Pete Forte, and Walter Kuenhe, interviews by author, Redding, CA., 30 Sep. 1989.
[41]C. S. Downing, First Information Book for Shasta Dam Guides, 1952, unpublished, p. 9.
[42]*Shasta Dam Archive Photographs & Captions, 1939*, Shasta Dam, CA., The photos and captions in this section of the archives show Kaiser's San Jose plant.
[43]Allen, *Shasta Dam and Its Builders*, p. 94.
[44]Allen, Interview, 28 May 1993.
[45]PCI official architectural blueprints, *Cableway Data*, drawn by John Crowe, nephew of Frank Crowe. 10 Apr. 1940.
[46]Rocca, *America's Shasta Dam*, pp.54-55.
[47]Allen, *Shasta Dam and Its Builders*, pp. 104-105.
[48]The accounts of the 1940 flood were recalled by several of the dam workers and local residents including Marion Allen, Opal Foxx, Lyn Parker and others. The author interviewed these dam workers in Central Valley, CA on 30 Sep. 1989.
[49]*Redding Record-Searchlight*, 4 Mar. 1940.
[50]Allen, *Shasta Dam and Its Builders*, pp. 96-97. The cableways carried all of the concrete placed at Shasta Dam, but the system also hauled forms, steel girders, other material, and men. Cables 1-3 extended the furthest, over 2,600 feet—a record for the time. These first three cables handled nearly four million tons of cargo each before the dam was completed.
[51]Ibid, p. 108.

Chapter 14

[1]*Shasta Dam Archive Photographs & Captions, 1940*, Shasta Dam, CA., One of the photographs in this section shows Brownell, high above the work site, filming all phases of the operation.
[2]*Shasta Dam Archive Photographs & Captions, 1941*, Shasta Dam, CA., The photograph clearly shows the left abutment sequence of concrete placing. The form blocks were numbered from one to thirty-eight, with one being the far eastern block. Various colored circles, representing stages of completion, were pinned to reveal overall progress.
[3]Matt Rumboltz, interview with author, 13 Sept. 1989.
[4]Al M. Rocca, *America's Shasta Dam*, 85.
[5]*Shasta Dam Archive Photographs & Captions, #2681, 1941*, Shasta Dam, CA.
[6]*Shasta Dam Archive Photographs & Captions, #2756, 1941*, Shasta Dam, CA.
[7]Rocca, *America's Shasta Dam*, 99.
[8]Allen, Interview, 28 May 1993.
[9]*The Headtower*, June, 1941. Interesting non-construction articles and personal short stories pervade issues of this newsletter. It is an excellent source of information on the actions of Crowe's foremen, on and off-duty. This document is unpublished. The author obtained a copy from ex-dam worker Marion Allen.
[10]Pat Crowe, Interview, 10 Sep. 1996.
[11]Rocca, *America's Shasta Dam*, p. 78.
[12]George Kirov, *Shasta Dam*, San Francisco: Balakshin Printing Company, 1941, p. 33.

[13]*Redding Record-Searchlight*, 8 Aug. 1941. Jesse Day, a rigger, was killed in the August 7 accident when he was struck by a loaded concrete dinky near the headtower. He was rushed to the PCI hospital where doctors could do nothing for his massive spinal injuries. He was 31 years old.

[14]Rocca, *America's Shasta Dam*, pp. 85-87.

[15]"He Puts Rivers to Work", *This Week Magazine*, 13 Sep. 1941. pp. 4, 12.

[16]*Redding Record-Searchlight*, 8 Dec. 1941. City of Redding residents gathered on this day and organized a home guard, volunteering to stand vigilance at the P G & E plant, other utility centers, and key roadways.

[17]See newspaper accounts [Redding Record-Searchlight and most west coast newspapers] from December 7 to December 20, 1941. One report said that planes were only 23 miles offshore, while another reported that enemy aircraft had already penetrated the Coast Ranges.

[18]*The Headtower*, December, 1941.

[19]Several ex-dam workers discussed the hardships and anguish of the days and weeks following the Pearl Harbor attack including: Lloyd Hill, Art Corella, Pete Forte, and Opal Foxx. Interviews, 24 Sep. 1994, Central Valley, California at the annual Shasta Dam Worker's Reunion.

[20]See Rocca, *America's Shasta Dam*, pp. 109-111 and Allen, *Shasta Dam and Its Builders*, p. 142.

[21]John Crowe, interview, 7 Feb. 1997, Whitmore, California.

[22]F. K. Taylor, interview, 24 Sep. 1994.

[23]Many of the ex-dam workers recalled the movement of men in and out of the Shasta Dam area. Interviews with Bob Sass, Loral Butcher, Walter Kuehne, and Grant Magnusson confirmed the large outflow in early 1942. These interviews were conducted 30 Sept. 1989. Several men, including Lloyd Hill, worked off-again and on-again at Shasta Dam and jobs in the defense industry. Interview with author, 18 Sept. 1993.

[24]*Redding Record-Searchlight*, 22 May 1942.

[25]Allen, Interview, 28 May 1993.

[26]*The Headtower*, October, 1942.

[27]George Kirov, *Shasta Dam*, 1941, unpublished, pp. 33-34.

[28]Rocca, *America's Shasta Dam*, pp. 138-139.

[29]Allen, *Shasta Dam and Its Builders*, p. 142.

[30]Elizabeth Crowe-Parry, Interview with author, 2 Aug. 1998.

[31]Rocca, *America's Shasta Dam*, pp. 140-141.

[32]*Southwest Builder & Contractor*, December 3, 1943; *Engineering News Record*, 4 Nov. 1943, p. 77.

[33]Ibid. p. 149.

[34]"Big is the Word for Shasta Dam" *The Em Kayan*, January, 1944, pp. 18-19.

[35]Estelle Hedstrom, interview, 30 Sept. 1989, Central Valley, CA.

[36]Opal Foxx, interview, 24 Sept. 1994, Central Valley, CA. The author filmed an excellent video tape of the Foxx interview in which the woman dam worker provided numerous anecdotal stories describing her experiences living in the company town and work in the mess hall.

[37]Rocca, *America's Shasta Dam*, p. 150.

[38]Allen and other dam workers interviewed remembered this event.

[39]See Rocca, *America's Shasta Dam*, p. 150. See also C. S. Downing, *First Information*

Book for Shasta Dam Guides, 1952, unpublished, pp. 80-85 for technical information on the generators, draft tubes, governers, and exciters.

[40]Rocca, *America's Shasta Dam,* p. 146.

[41]Allen, Interview, 28 May 1993. Allen remained in the Redding area and became involved in writing and publishing numerous books on dam building and history. Among his most popular and important works are *Hoover Dam & Boulder City, Early Jackson Hole, Rio Colorado & Parker Dam,* and a republishing of PCI's *Shasta Dam and Its Builders.* The author is greatly indebted for the many phone and personal interviews that provided me with a deeper understanding of dam building in western America.

[42]*Time,* 19 June 1940.

[43]Allen, *Shasta Dam and Its Builders,* p. 107.

[44]Various interviews with ex-dam workers such as Wilbur Smith, Ray Rogers, and LeRoy Hull attested to the great fluidity following the closing months at Shasta Dam. The Bureau needed hundreds of men to complete Keswick Dam, the after bay for Shasta Dam and to do finishing work all around the dam site. Interview with LeRoy Hull, and Wilbur Smith on 17 July 1990, Ray Rogers on 30 Sep. 1989.

[45]Rocca, *America's Shasta Dam,* p. 147.

Epilogue

[1]Notes of remarks by Frank T. Crowe of the New York Alumni Meeting, 6 Feb. 1945. Courtesy of the University of Maine Engineering Department.

[2]Program and seating list of the 1945 Moles Award Dinner, Roosevelt Hotel, New York City, 7 Feb. 1945.

[3]Letter from W. E. Belcher to Charles Crossland, 9 Feb. 1945. Courtesy of the University of Maine.

[4]*Redding-Record Searchlight,* 23 May 1945.

[5]"Frank T. Crowe: A Peerless Builder," *The Em Kayan,* April 1946, 11.

[6]Property parcel information was obtained from the Shasta County Recorders' Office; see also *Redding-Record Searchlight,* 10 Sept. 1947.

[7]Excerpt from the personal diary of Mary Crowe, 26 Feb. 1946. Mary Crowe learned that Frank Crowe had died around 6:00 p.m.

[8]*Redding Record-Searchlight,* 28 Feb. 1946; Ibid., 1 Mar. 1946.

[9]"Frank T. Crowe: A Peerless Builder," *The Em Kayan,* April 1946, 11.

[10]"Frank Crowe Builder of Dams, Dies," *San Francisco Chronicle,* 28 Feb. 1946; "Honorary Member Francis T. Crowe Dies," *Civil Engineering,* April 1946, 181.

[11]A. E. Cahlan, "From Where I Sit," *Las Vegas Evening Review-Journal,* 28 Feb. 1946.

[12]A. E. Cahlan, "From Where I Sit," *Las Vegas Evening Review-Journal,* 28 Feb. 1946.

[13]A. H. Ayers, "Francis T. Crowe, '05 Master Builder of Dams," *The Maine Alumnus,* March 1934, 93-94.

[14]Frank J. Taylor, "He Puts Rivers to Work," *This Week Magazine,* 13 Dec. 1941, 5.

Selected Bibliography

Allen, Marion. *Early Jackson Hole*. Redding, Calif: Self-published, 1981.

_____. *Hoover Dam & Boulder City*. Redding, Calif.: Self-published, 1983.

_____. *Rio Colorado & Parker Dam*. Redding, Calif.: Self-published, 1987.

_____. *Shasta Dam and Its Builders* (republished version), Redding, Calif.: Self-published, 1987.

Ayers, A. H. "Frank T. Crowe, '05 Master Builder of Dams," *The Maine Alumnus 1934*, University of Maine at Orono. 93-94.

Balderson, William. "Dam Building Days: A Narrative of 1914-1915," *Jackson Hole News*, Nov. 1972.

Bean, Walton and James Rawls. *California: An Interpretative History*, New York: McGraw Hill, 1988.

Bedford, C. P. "Hoover Dam Motor Transportation," *Western Construction New and Highway Builder*, July 1933.

Bernfeld, Betsy. "The Jackson Lake Dam: No Small Task," *Wyoming Horizons*, Aug. 1985.

Calderwood, R.M. "Irrigation in the Lower Yellowstone Valley," *Focus on Our Roots*, MonDak Historical & Art Society.

Castle, Victor. "Well, I Quit my Job at the Dam," *The Nation*, 133, No. 3451, 1931.

Crowe, Frank. "James Munn: Builder of Men and a Foster Parent of M-K," *The Em Kayan*, May 1943.

_____. "Tieton Dam, Yakima Project, Wash." *Reclamation Record*, Oct. 1921.

Davis, Arthur P. "Memoir of Ernest Frederick Tabor, M. Am. Soc. C. E." *Transactions of the ASCE*, 1916.

. "Development of the Colorado River: The Justification of Hoover Dam," *Atlantic Monthly*, 143 Feb. 1929.

Downing, C. S. *First Information Book for Shasta Dam Guides*, unpublished, 1952.

Dunar, Andrew J., and Dennis McBride. *Building Hoover Dam: An Oral History of the Great Depression*. New York: Twayne Pub., 1993.

Ely, Sims. "Administration of Boulder City," *Annual Project History, Boulder Canyon Project, 1928-1931*, United States Department of the Interior, Bureau of Reclamation, 145.

Fitzgerald, Roosevelt. "Blacks and the Boulder Dam Project," *Nevada Historical Society*, 24, 1981.

Gallison, Norman S. "Details of the Driving of the Four Huge Tunnels Which Will Divert the Colorado River Around the Dam Site," *Compressed Air Magazine*, May 1932.

_____. "Construction of the Hoover Dam: Details of the Driving of the Four Huge Tunnels Which will Divert the Colorado River Around the Dam Site." *The Story of the Hoover Dam*. Las Vegas: Nevada Pub.

Greeley, W. V., S. O. Harper, and W. R. Young, "Memoirs of Deceased Members: Francis Trenholm Crowe, Hon. M. ASCE," *Transactions of the ASCE*, 1946.

Hinds, Julian, "Memoirs of Frank Elwin Weymouth," *Transactions*, The American Society of Civil Engineers, 1941.

Jackson, Kenneth. *The Ku Klux Klan in the City, 1915-1930*. New York: Oxford University Press, 1967.

Kirov, George. *Shasta Dam*, San Francisco: Balakshin Printing Company, 1941.

Kleinsorge, Paul. *The Boulder Canyon Project: Historical and Economic Aspects*. Stanford University Press, 1941.

Lake, Copeland. "Construction of the Hoover Dam: Compressed Air Plays a Vital Importance in This Huge Undertaking," *The Story of Hoover Dam*, Las Vegas Nevada: Nevada Publications.

Markham, John. "Building of Jackson Lake Brings Colorful Recollections," *The Post-Register*, Apr. 1972.

McBride, Dennis. *In the Beginning: A History of Boulder City, Nevada*. Boulder City/ Hoover Dam Museum. 1992.

Mead, Elwood. *Boulder Canyon Project—Questions and Answers*, United States Department of the Interior, Bureau of Reclamation, Washington, D.C., Jan. 1933.

Munn, James. U. S. Department of the Interior, Reclamation Service, *Boise Project-Storage Unit, Feature Report, Construction Plant*, 1915.

Nelson, Wesley. "Construction Progress on Hoover Dam," *Western Construction News and Highway Builder*, May 1933.

_____. "Boulder Canyon Transportation," R*eclamation Era*, May 1935.
_____. "Construction of the Boulder Dam: How the $35,000,000 Power Plant will Appear when Completely Equipped," *The Story of the Hoover Dam*, Las Vegas: Nevada Publications.

Park, Allen S. "A Description of the Methods of Obtaining and Preparing Aggregates," *Compressed Air Magazine*, Oct. 1932.

Paul, Charles. U. S. Department of the Interior, Reclamation Service, *Boise Project-Storage Unit, Feature Report, Diversion Works*, 1913.

Paul, Elliot. *A Ghost Town on the Yellowstone*. New York: Random House, 1948.

_____. *Desperate Scenery*. New York: Random House, 1954.

Peterson, York. "Hoover Dam" Western Construction News, Sep. 1931.

Priest, Joel L., Jr. "'Paul Bunyan' of the Black Canyon," *The Union Pacific Magazine*, March 1932.

Ragle, John W. *Governor Dummer Academy History, 1763-1963*. South Byfield, Massachusetts: Governor Dummer Academy, 1963.

Ridgeway, Robert. "Boulder Dam," *Harvard Alumni Bulletin*, 1934.

Robinson, Michael. *Water for the West: The Bureau of Reclamation, 1902-1977*, Chicago: Public Works Historical Society, 1978.

Rocca, Al M. *The Shasta Dam Boomtowns: Community Building in the New Deal Era*, Redding: Redding Museum of Art & History, 1993.

Rocca, Al M. *America's Shasta Dam: A History of Construction, 1936-1945*. Redding: Redding Museum of Art & History, 1995.

Rocha, Guy Louis. "The IWW and the Boulder Canyon Project: The Final Death Throes of American Syndicalism," *Nevada Historical Society Quarterly*, Spring, 1978.

Sanders, S. J. "Construction Review-Hoover Dam, Nevada-Arizona," *Western Construction News*, July 1931.

Savage, J. L. and J. C. Stevens. "Memoirs of David Christiaan Henny, M. Am. Soc. C.E."

Transactions of the ASCE, 1936.

Schuyler, Philip. "Hoover Dam Constructionists" *Western Construction News*, Dec. 1931.

Skerrett, Robert G. "America's Wonder River—The Colorado: How Nature Formed this Amazing Watercourse and How Man had to Face Many Hazards in it and in Completing its Exploration," *Compressed Air Magazine*, Nov. 1931.

_____. "Steel Headers and Penstocks for Hoover Dam Mark Notable Advance in Engineering Construction," *Western Construction News and Highways Builder*, March 1934.

Smith, David C. *The First Century: A History of the University of Maine, 1865-1965*, Orono, Maine: University of Maine Press, 1979.

Sowles, Lawrence P. "How the Concrete is Being Cooled as It is Poured," *Compressed Air Magazine 38*, Nov. 1933.

_____. "Contractor Uses Cableway for Building Small Concrete Arch Dams on Aqueduct," *Western Construction News*, Aug. 1938.

Stevens, Joseph. *Hoover Dam: An American Adventure*. Norman: University of Oklahoma Press, 1988.

Sweenley, W. J. "The Yellowstone Valley Compared with Central States," *Focus on Our Roots*. Sidney, Montana: Mon-Dak Historical Society.

Vinson, Edrie. "Lower Yellowstone Project: United States Reclamation Service, 1907-08," Paper prepared for the Montana Department of Highways, 1988.

Vivian, C.H. "Construction of the Hoover Dam: How the Contractors Handled the Huge and Costly Program of Preliminary Work," *The Story of Hoover Dam*.

_____. "Construction of the Hoover Dam: Some General Facts Regarding the Undertaking and the Men Who are Directing it." *The Story of the Hoover Dam*. Las Vegas, Nevada: Nevada Publications.

_____. "Construction of the Hoover Dam: Lining of the Diversion Tunnels with Concrete," *The Story of Hoover Dam*. Las Vegas, Nevada: Nevada Publications.

Walter, Ray F. "U. S. Bureau of Reclamation Projects—Hoover Dam," *Western Construction News and Highway Builder*, Jan. 1933.

Warne, William. *The Bureau of Reclamation*, New York: Praeger Publishers, 1973.

Wolf, Donald. *Big Dams*, Norman: University of Oklahoma Press, 1996.

Yates, J. P. "Bulk Cement Handling at Boulder Dam," *Western Construction News*, Aug. 1934.

Index

Made in the USA
Monee, IL
27 March 2024

55934439R00246